Northeast India

Joe Bindloss

Mark Elliott, Patrick Horton, Kate James

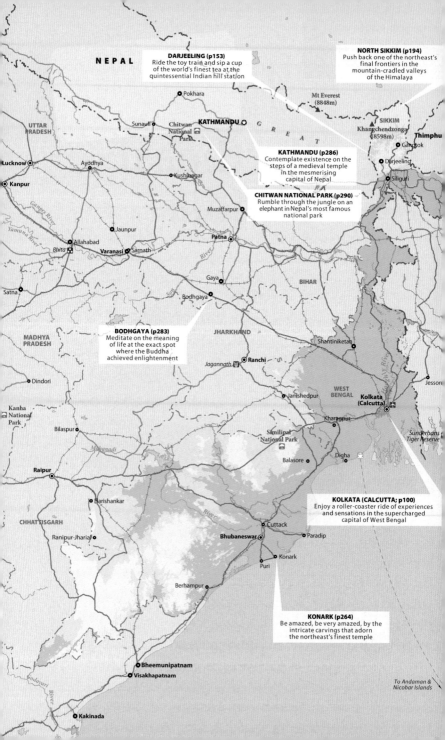

NEPAL

DARJEELING (p153)
Ride the toy train and sip a cup of the world's finest tea at the quintessential Indian hill station

NORTH SIKKIM (p194)
Push back one of the northeast's final frontiers in the mountain-cradled valleys of the Himalaya

Pokhara

Mt Everest (8848m)

Sunauli

Chitwan National Park

KATHMANDU

G R E A T

SIKKIM

Khangchendzonga (8598m)

Thimphu

Gangtok

Darjeeling

Siliguri

KATHMANDU (p286)
Contemplate existence on the steps of a medieval temple in the mesmerising capital of Nepal

UTTAR PRADESH

Lucknow

Ayodhya

Kushinagar

CHITWAN NATIONAL PARK (p290)
Rumble through the jungle on an elephant in Nepal's most famous national park

Kanpur

Muzaffarpur

Ganga River

Jaunpur

Yamuna River

Allahabad

Bhita

Varanasi Sarnath

Patna

River

Gaya

BIHAR

Satna

Bodhgaya

MADHYA PRADESH

Son

JHARKHAND

Shantiniketan

BODHGAYA (p283)
Meditate on the meaning of life at the exact spot where the Buddha achieved enlightenment

Jagannath **Ranchi**

Dindori

River

Jessore

WEST BENGAL

Jamshedpur

Kolkata (Calcutta)

Kanha National Park

Bilaspur

Kharagpur

Mahanadi

Similipal National Park

Sunderbans Tiger Reserve

Raipur

Balasore

Digha

Harishankar

River

CHHATTISGARH

Ranipur-Jharial

KOLKATA (CALCUTTA; p100)
Enjoy a roller-coaster ride of experiences and sensations in the supercharged capital of West Bengal

Cuttack

Bhubaneswar Paradip

Puri Konark

Berhampur

KONARK (p264)
Be amazed, be very amazed, by the intricate carvings that adorn the northeast's finest temple

Bheemunipatnam

Visakhapatnam

Godavari River

To Andaman & Nicobar Islands

Kakinada

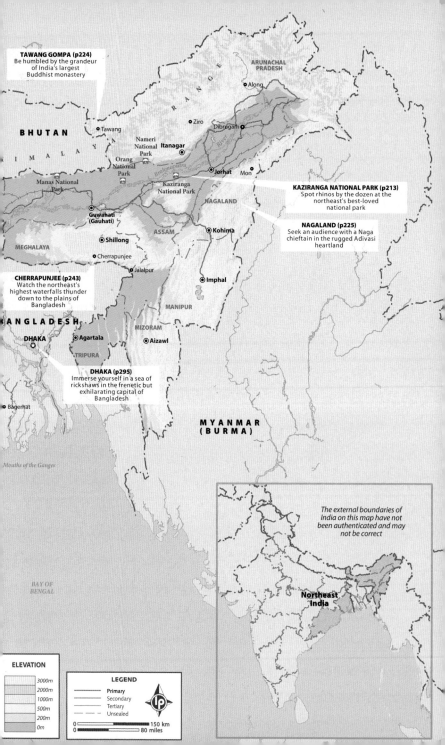

TAWANG GOMPA (p224)
Be humbled by the grandeur of India's largest Buddhist monastery

ARUNACHAL PRADESH

● Along

● Ziro

Dibrugarh ◉

BHUTAN

● Tawang

Nameri National Park

Itanagar ◉

Orang National Park

Brahmaputra River

Manas National Park

Jorhat ◉

Mon ●

Kaziranga National Park

NAGALAND

KAZIRANGA NATIONAL PARK (p213)
Spot rhinos by the dozen at the northeast's best-loved national park

Guwahati (Gauhati) ◉

ASSAM

◉ Kohima

NAGALAND (p225)
Seek an audience with a Naga chieftain in the rugged Adivasi heartland

MEGHALAYA

◉ Shillong

● Cherrapunjee

● Jalalpur

◉ Imphal

CHERRAPUNJEE (p243)
Watch the northeast's highest waterfalls thunder down to the plains of Bangladesh

MANIPUR

BANGLADESH

DHAKA ✪

MIZORAM

◉ Agartala

◉ Aizawl

TRIPURA

DHAKA (p295)
Immerse yourself in a sea of rickshaws in the frenetic but exhilarating capital of Bangladesh

● Bagerhat

MYANMAR (BURMA)

Mouths of the Ganges

The external boundaries of India on this map have not been authenticated and may not be correct

BAY OF BENGAL

Northeast India

ELEVATION

	3000m
	2000m
	1000m
	500m
	200m
	0m

LEGEND

Primary
Secondary
Tertiary
Unsealed

0 ————— 150 km
0 ————— 80 miles

Northeast India Highlights

Himalayan trekking, Tantric temples, hill stations, thundering waterfalls and villages of bamboo houses in dense jungle – travellers who love to connect with isolated peoples in glorious landscapes love the northeast of India. Sound like you? It sounds like our adventurous writers, staff and readers, who have picked their highlights of the region.

RICHARD I'ANS

① SENSATIONAL SIKKIM

This is one place (p173) which is sure to remain in my memory forever. Surrounded by the mighty Himalaya, in the early morning one can see Khangchendzonga, the third highest peak. The sun rays fall on the snow-capped mountain making it golden. A place where nature lives at its best.

sharadab, traveller

THE STREETS OF KOLKATA (CALCUTTA)

Children playing, men bathing, women washing; lives ebb and flow. Eating rice, selling bananas, sweeping dust; vivid colours glow. Taxis honking, autos beeping, cycle-wallahs running; harmony and chaos juxtapose (p100).

raviashish, traveller

TOM COCKREM

TAWANG GOMPA

Absorb the spiritual atmosphere of Tawang Gompa (p224), with an interior decorated in a full paint-box set of colours.

Patrick Horton, Lonely Planet author

JOE BINDLOSS

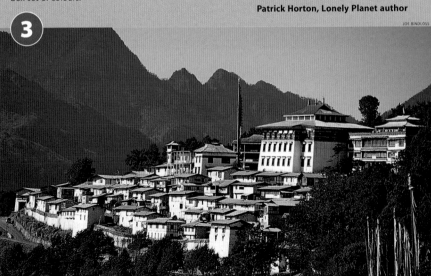

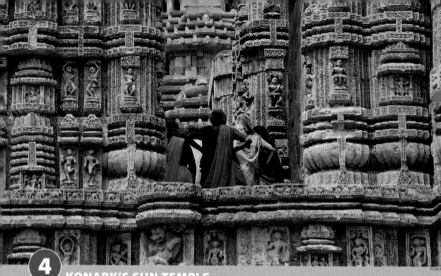

KEREN

4 KONARK'S SUN TEMPLE

You can spend all day admiring the carved religious, erotic and everyday scenes at this World Heritage Site (p265).

Kate James, Lonely Planet author

LINDSAY BROW

5 SILIGURI TO DARJEELING

This journey was along narrow, twisting mountain roads and took us from extreme heat into wintry cold. The (vast, flat) whole of India was laid out alongside and below us as we climbed the foothills of the Himalaya (p145).

taj2, traveller

THE MONASTERY LOOP

There's a small monastery high above Khecheopalri Lake (p190). The evening ceremony, led by a novice under the watchful eyes of the lama, is a cacophony of gongs, bells, drums, cymbals, horns and conch shells interspersed with ritual chanting. As with the locals, oil was poured into our left hands, splashed onto our faces, then finally poured over our heads. As incense sticks were passed around, a beautiful murmur, half song, half chant, rose from the gloom and an overwhelming feeling of serenity descended upon the temple. Later, we slid back down the rain-soaked hill totally at peace with the world.

Steve Waters, Lonely Planet staff

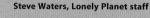
RICHARD I'ANSON

6

MEGHALAYA

When clouds sail into your room. Columns of vapour. Monsoon-induced insomnia. The hammer-hammer- hammering of raindrops on a tin roof. Little yellow flowers. Trees that circle a lake (p239).

soulcurry, traveller

JOHNNY HAGLUND

7

PATRICK HOR

8 BOATING IN BHITARKANIKA WILDLIFE SANCTUARY

Kingfishers darted past, spotted deer drank by the bank and huge crocodiles suddenly surfaced right next to us. And no other boats on our stretch of the mangroves (p275).

Kate James, Lonely Planet author

RICHARD I'ANS

9 GOECHA LA

Get up close and personal to Khangchendzonga from Goecha La (p192), a 4940m pass that's the climax of an eight-day Khangchendzonga trek from Yuksom.

Patrick Horton, Lonely Planet author

Contents

Regional Map Contents

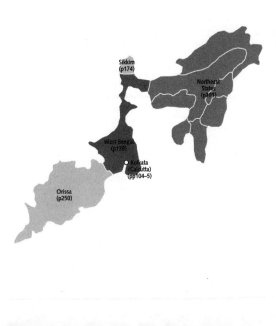

Destination Northeast India

People often describe the northeast of India as a backwater – we prefer to think of it as the gateway to a wild frontier. Only tenuously connected to the rest of India, Sikkim and the 'Seven Sisters' – the states of Assam, Meghalaya, Tripura, Arunachal Pradesh, Nagaland, Manipur and Mizoram – are a world apart from the Indian plains. This is the 'Wild East' of India, where a string of Adivasi (tribal) societies have had their way of life protected by impregnable jungles, densely forested hills and the curtain wall of the Himalaya.

In language, culture and attitude, the people of the far northeast take their cues as much from Tibet and Southeast Asia as from the rest of India. Even the Mughals and the British Empire failed to bring this remote corner of the subcontinent into the Indian mainstream. The maps of the Northeast States created at Independence bear little relation to the cultural boundaries of the northeast, which cross state and international borders, marking the homelands of hundreds of different Adivasi communities.

A little of the frontier feel has rubbed off on the states abutting the northeast. Orissa to the south is a sleepy sprawl of rice fields and fishing villages that washes out into the Bay of Bengal, with its own Adivasi heartland in the hills of the Eastern Ghats. To the west, West Bengal shares borders with three neighbouring countries – Nepal, Bhutan and Bangladesh – opening up some exciting opportunities for old-fashioned overland travel.

The doorway to this fascinating and little-explored region is Kolkata, India's fourth largest city after Delhi, Mumbai and Bengaluru (Bangalore). From this fast and furious metropolis, you can escape to a different India, where adventures (and the possibility of a one-horned Indian rhinoceros) lurk at the end of every dirt road, and where foreign travellers are still a novelty. However, a lack of tourists also means a lack of infrastructure. You'll have to be much more independent and tolerant of discomfort and inconvenience if you want to explore this untamed corner of the country.

Travellers should note that political tensions run high in the northeast. The seven Northeast States have almost as many separatist movements as there are peoples, and dozens of armed insurgent groups are fighting the Indian government for an independent homeland. Security in the region improves and deteriorates with the changing political climate, but the wave of devastating bombings that hit Assam in 2008 would seem to indicate that the political situation is at a low ebb.

Conversely, it has never been easier to visit the northeast. Access to the states that border China is controlled by a complicated series of permits, but each year the restrictions become slightly less onerous, making it possible to travel deeper into the northeast. That said, you still need an easy-to-obtain permit for Sikkim, and foreigners are required to travel as part of a group to visit Arunachal Pradesh, Nagaland, Mizoram and Manipur. If you plan to visit any of these four states, apply through a local tour agency well ahead of time.

For travellers, the northeast offers a mix of famous sights and unexpected delights. Kolkata is a must-visit on any travel itinerary, and Konark in Orissa is arguably the most famous Hindu temple in India. West Bengal has the legendary Sunderbans Tiger Reserve and the quintessential Indian hill station at Darjeeling, and Sikkim has excellent trekking and more Himalayan viewpoints that you can shake a spyglass at.

FAST FACTS

Population: West Bengal 80,221,171, Orissa 36,706,920, Sikkim 540,493, Northeast States 38,495,089 (2001 census)

GDP growth rate: West Bengal 8.5%, Assam 4.5% (2006)

Rural unemployment rate: West Bengal 11.1%, Arunachal Pradesh 0.8% (2001)

Female participation in labour: Orissa 24.7%, Sikkim 53%

National inflation: 11%

National population growth rate: 1.58%

National literacy rate: 54% (women) and 76% (men)

National life expectancy: 66 years (women) and 63 years (men)

Share of India's tea harvest: 70%

In the far northeast, Assam is the most accessible of the Northeast States, with tranquil tea gardens, Tantric temples and national parks full of rumbling rhinos, while Meghalaya boasts thundering waterfalls and dramatic views, and Tripura offers a window onto pre-Partition Bengal. The four permit states – Arunachal Pradesh, Nagaland, Mizoram and Manipur – are something else again, an edgy frontier where villages of bamboo houses melt seamlessly into the jungle.

Nevertheless, in recent years, the northeast has made the news for all the wrong reasons. Assam barely had time to celebrate a peaceful resolution to the conflict with Bodo separatists before a new wave of violence hit the state in 2008. Bomb attacks on trains and markets continued through 2009, linked to Bodo hardliners and organizations fighting for a separate homeland for Adivasi tea workers, for the Dimasa and Karbi people and for the ethnic Assamese. A weak government response to the devastating floods on the Brahmaputra in 2008 may well be a contributing factor.

The imposition of central rule in Nagaland in 2008 also caused resentment, but no significant increase in violence, though scuffles were reported between the National Socialist Council of Nagaland and other rebel Naga groups. Probably the most risky areas are Manipur and northern Tripura, where Adivasi insurgents continue to stage attacks against Hindi- and Urdu-speaking migrant workers.

Before you cancel your plane ticket, be aware that these hotspots represent only a tiny part of the northeast. Sikkim, Orissa and West Bengal are no more risky than Goa or Rajasthan, and Mizoram managed to stay peaceful and addicted to guitar-based rock throughout 2008, despite a plague of rats linked to the blooming of its bamboo forests (last time the forests bloomed in 1959, it caused a state-wide famine).

Few travellers encounter problems of any kind in Arunachal Pradesh or Meghalaya, and even Assam and Nagaland can be negotiated safely if you pay attention to local news reports and avoid travel during times of political tension. If things look hairy, head to safe havens like Kolkata, Sikkim and the West Bengal hills, and roam northeast when the situation calms.

For our money, the rewards of travelling in this region still vastly outweigh the risks. With a little advance preparation, it's easy to stay safe and travel far off the beaten track, and even risk-averse travellers can unleash the inner pioneer in the peaceful backwoods of Sikkim, Orissa and West Bengal. Above all else, the northeast is a place where the maps have gaps and trails can be blazed – pack your pith helmet and see what you can discover…

Getting Started

Compared to more established destinations like Kerala and Rajasthan, the northeast of India is a wild frontier. The tribes, temples, mountains and monasteries of this blissfully untouched corner of the country are only just being discovered by travellers, though the gateway cities of Kolkata (Calcutta) and Darjeeling are established stops on the traveller circuit. From these hubs, you can escape to a different India, where foreign visitors are still a novelty and where the landscape throbs to the beat of drums and the chattering of birds in the jungle.

This is India at its most undiluted – an evocative, energising infusion of sights, sounds, smells and sensations. Infrastructure is limited once you leave the tourist hubs, and a certain degree of self-sufficiency is essential, not least because you can travel for weeks here without encountering another traveller. Because of the low visitor numbers, there are refreshingly few scams waiting for new arrivals, but you still need to prepare yourself for the challenges that India can deliver.

India is the second-most populous nation on earth and the crowds and congestion can turn even a short bus journey into a long, draining ordeal. You will have to get used to being stared at, photographed, prodded and engaged in deep conversation by complete strangers on a regular basis. Then there's the infamous Indian bureaucracy – at times it can seem like nothing gets done without a complicated form, countersigned and filled out in triplicate. But this all adds to the intensity of travel on the subcontinent – after visiting India, other countries can feel like they have the sound turned down.

If this is your first trip to India, take a few days to acclimatise before you head off into the unknown. Read up about the region before you travel and pay particular attention to the cultural and religious framework. India makes a lot more sense when you understand some of the complex religious and social rules that govern the way people behave. Luck favours the prepared – start planning your trip at least a month in advance to make time for immunisations and applying for visas and permits.

Two essential virtues for travel in India are patience and flexibility, particularly when using public transport. Delays and cancellations are par for the course and you'll have a much more relaxing time if you accept that in India, you get there when you get there. Always build some flexibility into your plans and be prepared to change your itinerary if anything off the route catches your attention.

HOW MUCH?

A sweet *paan* Rs5

A thali (plate meal) Rs40 to Rs80

Three-hour bus ride Rs50 to Rs100

Budget hotel Rs100 to Rs500

Jeep tour per day US$20 to US$50

THE INDIA EXPERIENCE

India is not a country you just see, it is a country you experience. As well as sightseeing make some time for the following:

- Food, fireworks and fun at India's fantastic festivals (see p18)
- Advanced retail therapy at the northeast's shops, markets and state emporiums (see p315)
- Giving something back, by volunteering on a local development project (see p323)
- A bit of adventure, like an elephant safari in Assam or a rafting trip in Sikkim (see p92)
- Getting educated – learn a language, pick up some recipes or improve your yoga on a course in the northeast (see p306)

Above all else, give yourself some time to relax. Every now and then, find a quiet spot to sit back and smell the wafts of incense – then when you're ready, throw yourself back into the wonderful, energetic maelstrom that is India.

WHEN TO GO

As with any trip to the tropics, it pays to heed the climate when planning a trip to northeast India. Different areas are affected by different climatic patterns at different times of year, and the local topography can also affect the weather. Generally speaking, the climate is defined by three seasons – the hot, the wet (also known as the monsoon) and the cool. Most visitors come during the 'cool' months from November to mid-February.

See Climate Charts (p305) for more information.

See the 'Fast Facts' box at the start of each regional chapter for the best times to visit specific regions. Apart from the weather, you may also want to time your visit to coincide with the best festivals and special events – see p18.

The Hot

After the cool winter, temperatures start to climb in March and April, peaking just before the breaking of the monsoon rains in May or June. This can be an unbelievably sticky and uncomfortable time to visit the lowlands and many people retreat to the hill stations in West Bengal and the Northeast States. The plains of Assam, southern West Bengal and Orissa in particular bake like a bread oven – take advantage of AC where you can find it. Late in May the first signs of the monsoon appear – high humidity, electrical storms, sudden rain showers and dust storms that turn day into night. Carry an umbrella or raincoat or get soaked.

DON'T LEAVE HOME WITHOUT...

- Getting a visa (p322) and travel insurance (p310) and investigating the permit situation for the Northeast States (p199)
- Seeking medical advice about vaccinations (p343) and anti-malarial drugs (p346)
- Clothes that cover your shoulders and legs – modesty is the default dress code (see p44)
- Lots of film or memory cards for your camera, particularly at festival time
- A permanent marker – for scrawling addresses on cloth-wrapped parcels at the post office.
- An mp3 player or personal music player – for instant privacy on buses and trains
- Good-quality earplugs, for noisy hotels, trains and buses
- A well-concealed money belt, with a stash of emergency cash (p308)
- Sunscreen lotion, lip balm and good, UV-resistant sunglasses, particularly in the mountains
- A small LED torch for poorly lit streets, power cuts and finding the toilet at night in mountain lodges
- A small pocket knife – for cutting open mangoes and a thousand other Boy Scout tasks
- A universal sink plug – few hotels have them
- Tampons – sanitary napkins are widely available but tampons are rare outside of big cities
- Mosquito repellent and a mozzie net or plug-in mosquito killer
- The eye mask from your flight – light pollution is a major problem in budget hotels
- Your sense of humour!

The Wet

Most of the rain in the northeast comes from the heavy southwest monsoon. Showers become more frequent and heavier in June and temperatures fall a few degrees, but the cooling effect doesn't last long – the period from July to September is marked by persistent high temperatures and massive humidity.

Although it doesn't rain solidly all day, it rains virtually every day. National parks turn into quagmires and roads through the hills are frequently blocked by landslides. On the flip side, many interesting festivals take place at this time of year – see the itinerary on p25 for more on monsoon travel.

The Cool

From October to February, the rains slow to a trickle and temperatures become more bearable. This is the peak season for tourism and there is heavy competition for rooms and tourist quota seats on trains. November and December are the best times to visit national parks in the plains. To enjoy the best of the mountain views, visit Sikkim, the West Bengal Hills and Arunachal Pradesh in October or November, before the icy fingers of winter grip the Himalaya.

COSTS & MONEY

Travelling around the northeast can cost as much or as little as you like, depending on where you go and the level of luxury you crave. Once you leave the mainstream tourist circuit, budget options may be limited, or undesirable. If you visit any of the permit-only states, you may be required to travel on an expensive chartered jeep tour, which will also dramatically ratchet up your costs.

Meals, hotel rooms and tickets for buses and trains can cost just a few pennies or as much as you would pay for the same services in the West. The best way to assess the costs for your trip is to read the relevant regional chapters of this book. Expect to spend considerably more in large cities such as Kolkata, if only because there are more things to spend money on.

How does this all translate to a daily budget? As a rough indication, shoestring travellers can get by on Rs500 to Rs800 per day, staying in dorms or rooms with shared bathrooms, travelling on cheaper classes of bus and train, and eating at local restaurants. Add in an evening beer and you'll need closer to Rs1000.

It's worth spending a little more for hotel rooms with hot water and private bathrooms, the occasional slap-up curry dinner, more comfortable seats on buses and trains, and local transport by autorickshaw and taxi. Midrange travellers can get by on Rs1000 to Rs2000 per day, or less in smaller, not-so-touristy towns.

At the top end, the sky is the limit. A budget of $US200 per day will open up the most luxurious accommodation and the fastest and most comfortable classes of long-distance travel – including internal flights – allowing you to see the sights on your own time scale.

In all classes, accommodation prices fluctuate with demand. During the peak tourist season and major festivals, many hotels charge at least double the normal rate. You'll also pay extra for AC, a private bathroom with a tub or a Himalayan view. Most hotels in the northeast fall somewhere within the following ranges:

Budget: Single rooms Rs100 to Rs400; doubles Rs200 to Rs500
Midrange: Single rooms Rs300 to Rs1500; doubles Rs500 to Rs1800
Top end: Single and double rooms Rs1800 upwards

TOP 10

FABULOUS FESTIVALS

The northeast is always colourful. At festival time, it goes into overdrive. Here are some of the best:

1 Gangasagar Mela – January; Sagar Island

2 Losar – February/March; Sikkim, West Bengal and Arunachal Pradesh

3 Holi/Dol Yatra – February/March; India-wide

4 Ambubachi Mela – June; Guwahati

5 Rath Yatra – June/July; Puri and Kolkata

6 Durga Puja/Dussehra – September/October; Bengal-wide but especially in Kolkata

7 Diwali – October/November; India-wide

8 Kolkata Film Festival – November; Kolkata

9 Hornbill Festival – December; Kohima, Nagaland

10 Losoong – December/January; Sikkim

ROUSING READS

India has inspired some seminal literary works – bookworms should hunt down the following:

1 *Midnight's Children* – a mystical novel set at the precise moment of Indian Independence, by Salman Rushdie

2 *A Suitable Boy* – a tale of politics and marriage partly set in Kolkata, by Vikram Seth

3 *A Fine Balance* – a unique perspective on the legacy of Independence, by Rohinton Mistry

4 *The Inheritance of Loss* – Man Booker–prize-winning novel set in 1980s Kalimpong, by Kiran Desai

5 *White Mughals* – stories of British colonials who 'went native', by William Dalrymple

6 *Hullabaloo in the Guava Orchard* – a modern tale of white-collar rebellion, by Kiran Desai

7 *City of Joy* – the book that created the Western image of Kolkata, by Dominique Lapierre

8 *Shesher Kobita* – Shillong-based romance from Rabindranath Tagore

9 *The Raj Quartet* – four tomes detailing the fall of the Raj, by Paul Scott

10 *The Calcutta Chromosome* – a time-travelling thriller, by Amitav Ghosh

FANTASTIC FLICKS

Mumbai may have Bollywood, but Kolkata is the capital of Indian arthouse cinema – check out the following classic Indian films:

1 *Pather Panchali* – a tragic tale of 1920s Bengal from the great Satyajit Ray

2 *Pyaasa* – a 1950s classic, starring, produced and directed by Bengal-raised Guru Dutt

3 *The Cloud-Capped Star* – a dark but beautifully filmed Kolkata melodrama by Ritwik Ghatak

4 *Ek Din Pratidin* – a ground-breaking exploration of the status of Bengali women, by Mrinal Sen

5 *Gandhi* – a cast of thousands and some epic locations in Richard Attenborough's Oscar-winning biopic

6 *Mother India* – a rousing fable of family conflict through the generations, by Mehboob Khan

7 *Lagaan* – villagers defeat the British in cricket and in life in this hit by Ashutosh Gowariker

8 *Sholay* – the highest-grossing Bollywood film of all time, by Ramesh Sippy

9 *Bose: The Forgotten Hero* – controversial tale of the Bengal freedom fighter, by Shyam Benegal

10 *Devdas* – A lavish, big-budget romance set in period Bengal, from Sanjay Leela Bhansali

Travel costs will depend on the class and speed of travel. Domestic flights cost much more than buses or trains, but look out for bargain promotional fares on budget airlines. Shoestring travellers can cover huge distances incredible cheaply in slow 'ordinary' buses and fan-cooled sleeper carriages on trains. Travelling long distances in unreserved 2nd-class train carriages is cheap as chapatis, and as uncomfortable as sitting on a cactus. AC will boost up the price of all tickets.

Most towns have inexpensive suburban trains or buses; it costs more to travel by rickshaw, autorickshaw and taxi. Renting a car with a driver can seem expensive, but costs plummet if you split the fare with other travellers. For more information, see the Transport chapter (p332).

TRAVEL LITERATURE

Kolkata has spawned a dozen travelogues all by itself. The essential reading list should include *Calcutta* by Geoffrey Moorhouse, Simon Winchester's *Calcutta*, and *The Weekenders: Adventures in Calcutta*, featuring the musings of Monica Ali, Irvine Welsh, Tony Hawks and others.

In *The Sorcerer's Apprentice*, Tahir Shah tells of his travels through India to learn the art of illusion under the guidance of a mysterious master magician from Kolkata. Every traveller to India should read *No Full Stops in India* and *India in Slow Motion* by Mark Tully, the BBC's correspondent for India for 25 years.

The backpacker scene in India is entertainingly sent up in William Sutcliffe's *Are You Experienced?*. Misadventures of a darker sort are explored in Anita Desai's *Journey to Ithaca*, the tale of a young European couple who lose their way on a quest for spiritual enlightenment.

Gita Mehta's *Karma Cola* amusingly and cynically describes the collision between India looking to the West for technology and modern methods, and the West descending upon India in search of wisdom and enlightenment.

The Northeast States fall off the radar of all but the most intrepid travel writers. Mark Shand describes an epic voyage along the Brahmaputra River in *River Dog*. In Alexander Frater's *Chasing the Monsoon*, the author races after the monsoon from Kovalam (Kerala) to Meghalaya (Northeast States).

INTERNET RESOURCES

Rediff (www.rediff.com) An extensive India portal, good for news on the northeast.
Incredible India (www.incredibleindia.org) The official government tourism site.
Northeast India (www.northeast-india.com) Tourism site covering highlights of the northeast.
123 India (www.123india.com) India-wide portal for news, sport and culture.
Sify (www.sify.com) Extensive India links from one of India's biggest ISPs.
Lonely Planet (www.lonelyplanet.com) Online travel information, hotel bookings and reader comments on the Thorn Tree.

Events Calendar

India officially follows the European Gregorian calendar but most holidays and festivals follow the Indian or Tibetan lunar calendars, tied to the cycle of the moon, or the Islamic calendar, which shifts forward 11 days each year (12 days in leap years). As a result, the exact dates of festivals change from year to year. The region-wide holidays and festivals listed here are arranged according to the Indian lunar calendar – also see the 'Festivals in…' boxed texts in the regional chapters. Contact local tourist offices for exact dates or check the web – see http://festivals .iloveindia.com and www.festivalsofindia.in.

MAGHA (JANUARY–FEBRUARY)

REPUBLIC DAY   26 January
This public holiday celebrates the founding of the Republic of India in 1950.

BHOGALI BIHU (MAKAR SANKRANTI IN BENGAL)
Farmers celebrate the winter rice harvest with buffalo fights and fires lit in honour of Agni, the Hindu god of fire.

VASANT PANCHAMI
Hindus honour Saraswati, the goddess of learning, by wearing yellow and placing educational objects in front of idols of the goddess for her blessing.

PHALGUNA (FEBRUARY–MARCH)

HOLI
Hindus celebrate the beginning of spring by throwing coloured water and *gulal* (powder; also called *abeer*) at anyone in range. Bengalis celebrate the festival as Dol Yatra – when idols of Krishna and Radha are rocked on ritual swings.

EID-MILAD-UN-NABI
This Islamic festival celebrates the birth of the Prophet Mohammed; it falls on 27 February in 2010 and 16 February in 2011.

SHIVARATRI
This day of Hindu fasting recalls the *tandava* (cosmic dance) of Shiva, ending in the anointing of linga (phallic symbols) in Shaivite areas.

CHAITRA (MARCH–APRIL)

MAHAVIR JAYANTI
This is a Jain festival, commemorating the birth of Mahavir, the founder of Jainism.

RAMANAVAMI
Hindus celebrate the birth of Rama with processions, music and feasting, and enactments of scenes from the Ramayana, particularly in Vaishnavite areas.

EASTER
A Christian holiday marking the Crucifixion and Resurrection of Jesus Christ, Easter is widely celebrated in the Northeast States.

VAISAKHA (APRIL–MAY)

BUDDHA JAYANTI
In Sikkim, West Bengal and western Arunachal Pradesh, Buddhists celebrate the birth of the historical Buddha.

JYAISTHA (MAY–JUNE)

Only regional festivals fall in this period – see the regional chapters for details.

ASADHA (JUNE–JULY)

RATH YATRA (CAR FESTIVAL)
Effigies of Jagannath (Vishnu) are hauled through cities on man-powered chariots; the biggest celebrations are at Puri in Orissa (p261) and Mahesh in West Bengal.

SRAVANA (JULY–AUGUST)

NAAG PANCHAMI
This Hindu festival is dedicated to Ananta, the god of serpents. Snakes are venerated as totems against monsoon flooding and other evils (see the boxed text, p84).

RAKSHA BANDHAN (NARIAL PURNIMA)
On the full moon, girls fix amulets known as *rakhis* to the wrists of brothers and male friends to protect them in the coming year.

BHADRA (AUGUST–SEPTEMBER)

INDEPENDENCE DAY 15 August
This exuberant public holiday marks the anniversary of India's Independence in 1947.

DRUKPA TESHI
This Buddhist festival celebrates the first teaching given by Siddhartha Gautama.

GANESH CHATURTHI
Hindus celebrate the birth of Ganesh by parading clay idols through the streets, then ceremonially immersing the effigies in rivers, water tanks or the sea.

JANMASTAMI
The anniversary of Krishna's birth is celebrated with gleeful abandon by followers of Vishnu.

SHRAVAN PURNIMA
On this day of fasting, high-caste Hindus replace the sacred thread looped over their left shoulder and bathe in temple tanks and sacred lakes.

PATETI
The minority Parsi community celebrates the Zoroastrian new year at this time.

RAMADAN
Thirty days of fasting mark the ninth month of the Islamic calendar, when the Koran was revealed to the Prophet Mohammed; the fast starts on 11 August in 2010 and 1 August in 2011.

ASVINA (SEPTEMBER–OCTOBER)

NAVRATRI (FESTIVAL OF NINE NIGHTS)
This Hindu festival celebrates the goddess Durga in all her incarnations. Special dances are held and the goddesses Lakshmi and Saraswati also get special praise.

DURGA PUJA
Symbolising the triumph of good over evil, Durga Puja commemorates the victory of the goddess Durga over buffalo-headed demon Mahishasura. This is the biggest annual festival in Kolkata, West Bengal and Assam, where thousands of images of the goddess are displayed then ritually immersed in rivers, tanks and the sea. See the boxed text, p102.

DUSSEHRA
Vaishnavites celebrate the victory of the Hindu god Rama over the demon-king Ravana on the same dates as Durga Puja.

GANDHI JAYANTI 2 October
This national holiday is a solemn celebration of Mohandas (Mahatma) Gandhi's birth.

EID AL-FITR
Muslims celebrate the end of Ramadan with three days of festivities, starting 30 days after the start of the fast.

KARTIKA (OCTOBER–NOVEMBER)

DIWALI (DEEPAVAALI)
Hindus celebrate the 'festival of lights' for five days, giving gifts, lighting fireworks and burning butter and oil lamps to guide Rama home from exile.

GOVARDHANA PUJA
A Vaishnavite Hindu festival celebrating the lifting of Govardhan Hill by Krishna.

EID AL-ADHA
Muslims commemorate Ibrahim's readiness to sacrifice his son to God; the festival falls on 27 November in 2009, 16 November in 2010 and 6 November in 2011.

AGRAHAYANA (NOVEMBER–DECEMBER)

NANAK JAYANTI
The birthday of Guru Nanak, the founder of Sikhism, is celebrated with prayer readings and processions.

PAUSA (DECEMBER–JANUARY)

CHRISTMAS DAY 25 December
Christians celebrate the birth of Jesus Christ.

LOSAR
Tibetan New Year is celebrated by Tibetan Buddhists in Sikkim, Arunachal Pradesh and West Bengal. Exact dates vary from region to region.

LOSOONG
New Year for the people of Sikkim, with processions and monastery dances, is celebrated by Sikkimese across the northeast.

MUHARRAM
Shia Muslims commemorate the martyrdom of the Prophet Mohammed's grandson, Imam; the festival starts on 18 December in 2009, 7 December in 2010 and 26 November in 2011.

Itineraries
CLASSIC ROUTES

A SHORT HOP THROUGH THE HILLS   One Week

A week is a tight schedule, but the following itinerary will tick off some memorable experiences. To save time, book flights in advance (see p332).

Devote day one to exploring **Kolkata** (Calcutta, p100), making time for the glorious **Victoria Memorial** (p107) and **Indian Museum** (p110). On day two, fly north to Bagdogra near **Siliguri** (p145) and take a jeep to the green hills of **Darjeeling** (p153).

On day three, catch the sunrise over Khangchendzonga Falls from **Tiger Hill** (p157), then arrange your permit for Sikkim. Next day, travel by jeep to **Gangtok** (p176) for a taste of Buddhist culture, and more mountain views on a 'three-point tour' (p179).

You'll only have a day or so for the Northeast States, so zip back downhill to Siliguri on day five, and take the overnight train to **Guwahati** (p204) in Assam. On day six, charter a jeep for an overnight rhino-spotting trip to **Kaziranga National Park** (p213). Returning to Guwahati on day seven, you should have just enough time to visit the eerie **Kamakhya Mandir temple** (p204) before catching an afternoon flight back to Kolkata.

A whistle-stop tour of the northeast, with stops in steamy Kolkata, tea-tastic Darjeeling, gompa-ringed Gangtok and Assam's Kaziranga National Park.

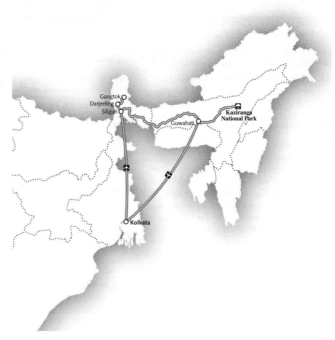

ONCE AROUND THE BRAHMAPUTRA   One Month

This grand tour starts and ends in bustling **Kolkata** (p100), taking in most of the famous sights of the northeast as it criss-crosses the mighty Brahmaputra River. To maximise your time, arrange train travel in advance at the Foreign Tourist Bureau (p133) in Kolkata.

Devote the first few days to the sights of Kolkata, including the cultural centres founded by **Ramakrishna** (p118) and **Rabindranath Tagore** (p117). Fly on to **Agartala** (p235), the sleepy capital of Tripura, and visit the **Tripura Sundari Mandir** (p239) and **Neermahal Palace** (p239).

Providing things are secure, take the overnight bus to **Shillong** (p240), the pleasant capital of Meghalaya. Haggle for tribal artefacts at the **Iew Duh market** (p241) and head east to **Cherrapunjee** (p243) to see the thundering waterfalls.

For week two, connect through **Guwahati** (p204) – the Assamese capital – to **Kaziranga National Park** (p213) for an intimate meeting with a rhino, or **Manas National Park** (p210) for a chance at spotting a tiger. Continue west to the temples and Ahom relics of **Sivasagar** (p216), then retrace your steps to Guwahati to visit atmospheric **Kamakhya Mandir** (p204).

Start week three with an overnight train ride to **Siliguri** (p145) and visit **Kalimpong** (p167) on your way north to **Gangtok** (p176). Explore the surrounding countryside (p182), then head west to **Pelling** (p187) for jaw-dropping mountain views and butter tea at the gompas of the Monastery Loop (p190).

For the last week head south to **Darjeeling** (p153), taking time for a ride on the famous **toy train** (p158), and then roll south again by jeep and train to Kolkata, for a well-deserved slap-up meal. Spend your last few days exploring the lowlands of West Bengal, with trips to the swampy jungles of **Sunderbans Tiger Reserve** (p139) or the terracotta temple town of **Bishnupur** (p142).

A loop around the northeast, starting and ending in Kolkata and taking in snippets of Tripura and Meghalaya, rhinos and temples in Assam, mountains and monasteries in Sikkim, and high and low elevations in West Bengal.

ROADS LESS TRAVELLED

NORTH & SOUTH   Three Months

This itinerary offers a broad sweep across the northeast. First, take your time in **Kolkata** (p100) and detour southeast for a boat cruise through **Sunderbans Tiger Reserve** (p139). Returning to Kolkata, ride the rails south to **Bhubaneswar** (p250) and take a day trip to the Jain caves at **Udayagiri** and **Khandagiri** (p254). Swing through **Puri** (p258), then head south to the birdwatching paradise of **Chilika Lake** (p266) and **Gopalpur-on-Sea** (p268) for a taste of the Orissan seaside.

Head inland to **Similipal National Park** (p274) to spot tigers, deer and wild elephants, then cross back into West Bengal. Visit the temples of **Bishnupur** (p142), then make for **Malda** (p144) to explore the ruins of **Gaur** and **Pandua** (p145).

The Siliguri–Darjeeling–Sikkim loop is well trodden, so prioritise backwaters of the Bengal hills like **Mirik** (p150) and **Kurseong** (p151), or take a trek from busy **Darjeeling** (p153) to the peaceful **Singalila Ridge** (p166). Cutting northeast to **Gangtok** (p176), escape the crowds in the remote mountain villages of **Thanggu** and **Tsopta** (p197).

Return to Siliguri, for a train to **Guwahati** (p204). With the appropriate permit, you can head north to Arunachal Pradesh. Highlights include the spectacular **Tawang Gompa** (p224) and the tribal loop through **Ziro** (p220).

There should be time to catch the highlights of Assam before you return to Guwahati for the flight back to Kolkata. Finally, sneak out for one more excursion through the atmospheric delta towns of **Serampore** (p141), **Chandarnagar** (p142) and **Hooghly** (p142).

A chance to explore the northeast in depth, away from the maddening crowds; highlights include sleepy corners of Orissa, little-visited towns in the Hooghly Delta and hidden tribal valleys in Arunachal Pradesh.

ALL THE NORTHEAST AND MORE...   Six Months

The Indian six-month multiple-entry tourist visa gives you time to get deep into the northeast. Starting in **Kolkata** (p100), arrange a visa for overland travel through Bangladesh, then head on by bus to **Dhaka** (p295), with a side-trip through **Jessore** (p298) to fascinating **Bagerhat** (p299). From the frenetic Bangladeshi capital, continue east to **Agartala** (p235) in Tripura, to explore Meghalaya from the capital, **Shillong** (p240).

Continuing to Assam, take in well-known stops such as **Guwahati** (p204) and **Kaziranga National Park** (p213) and get off the beaten track at the peaceful ecocamp at **Potasali** (p213) or a tea-plantation retreat at **Jorhat** (p215).

You should have time for several tribal tours in the Northeast States (p24). Continuing west from Guwahati, visit **Manas National Park** (p210) and **Jaldhapara Wildlife Sanctuary** (p149) for more unspoiled nature.

Slingshot through **Siliguri** (p145) to Sikkim, to be wowed by Buddhist monasteries and Himalayan viewpoints in **Pelling** (p187). Steel yourself for the testing **Goecha La trek** (p192), or take a tour to rugged **North Sikkim** (p195), then duck south to the hill stations of **Mirik** (p150), **Kurseong** (p151), **Darjeeling** (p153) and **Kalimpong** (p167).

From the Nepali border post at **Kakarbhitta** (p290), take the long bus ride to **Kathmandu** (p286). Roam around the Nepali capital, then head south through **Chitwan National Park** (p290) to the birthplace of the Buddha at **Lumbini** (p292).

Cross back to India at **Sunauli** (p292) and head through **Patna** (p278) to walk in the footsteps of Buddha at **Bodhgaya** (p283). Finish the trip in Orissa, with detours to temple-crammed **Bhubaneswar** (p250), famous **Konark** (p264) and **Puri** (p258), tribal tours near **Jeypore** (p270) and wildlife-spotting at **Bhitarkanika Wildlife Sanctuary** (p275), before returning to Kolkata – what a circuit!

A northeastern odyssey, snaking from Kolkata across water-logged Bangladesh to the backwaters of the Northeast States, pinballing through the hills of Sikkim and West Bengal, then looping back through Nepal, Bihar and Orissa.

TAILORED TRIPS

A NORTHEAST SAFARI

The northeast is the least-developed corner of India and untamed nature lurks around every corner. Signature species include tigers, leopards, elephants, crocodiles, rare birds, like the great Indian hornbill, and the endangered one-horned Indian rhino, found only in the northeast and remote parts of Nepal.

Starting from **Kolkata** (p100), head southeast to seek tigers in the rain-drenched creeks of **Sunderbans Tiger Reserve** (p139), then southwest to hunt for crocodiles in **Bhitarkanika Wildlife Sanctuary** (p275). Continue south to the birdwatchers' paradise of **Chilika Lake** (p266) and explore the little-seen wildlife sanctuaries of **Debrigarh** and **Badrama** (p274) near Sambalpur.

Next, go north to see wild elephants at **Similipal National Park** (p274), and connect through Kolkata to **Darjeeling** (p153) to organise a trek through **Singalila National Park** (p166). Further north in Sikkim, elusive red pandas

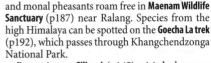

and monal pheasants roam free in **Maenam Wildlife Sanctuary** (p187) near Ralang. Species from the high Himalaya can be spotted on the **Goecha La trek** (p192), which passes through Khangchendzonga National Park.

Returning to **Siliguri** (p145), visit lush, green **Jaldhapara Wildlife Sanctuary** (p149) and take a wildlife-spotting river-boat ride through Assam's **Manas National Park** (p210), then take time to commune with one-horned Indian rhinos at **Kaziranga National Park** (p213) or **Pobitora National Park** (p210).

Enthusiasts can squeeze in **Nameri National Park** (p213) near Tezpur or a gibbon-spotting trek through Meghalaya's **Nokrek Biosphere Reserve** (p246), before flying back from **Guwahati** (p204) to Kolkata.

THE TRIBAL CIRCUIT

With enough time, you can push deep into tribal heartlands, but be sure to make permit arrangements (p199) and check the security situation first (p307). Start in **Kolkata** (p100) and fly to **Agartala** (p235), then ramble north to see ancient Hindu rock art at **Kailasahar** (p239). Head southeast to **Aizawl** (p233), and explore the surrounding Mizo villages.

Roll north to **Shillong** (p240) and visit **Smit** (p243) and **Cherrapunjee** (p243) for some Khasi culture, then drop in on Garo tribal villages in the **Garo Hills** (p246). Connect through **Guwahati** (p204) to **Upper Assam** (p214) to glimpse rural Assamese life.

Next, tour the Naga villages around **Mon** (p229). Continuing to Arunachal Pradesh, explore Adi and Apatani villages near **Ziro** (p220) and Monpa villages near **Tawang Gompa** (p224). To continue the tribal theme, visit Assam's **Manas National Park** (p210) with a local Bodo guide. More tribal encounters are possible in **North Sikkim** (p195) and on tours to Adivasi areas near **Jeypore** (p270) in Orissa – best arranged in **Bhubaneswar** (p250) or **Puri** (p258).

THE NORTHEAST IN STYLE

Travelling through the northeast doesn't have to mean slumming it. There are plenty of ways to add a little class as you explore this fascinating back-water of India.

Start in **Kolkata** (p100) with a colonial-style sojourn at the **Tollygunge Club** (p124) and a day at the races at the **Royal Calcutta Turf Club** (p130), followed by a slap-up dinner at **Peter Cat** (p127).

Heading south from Kolkata, travel 1st class on the *Howrah-Puri Express* to **Puri** (p258) and arrange a tour to **Similipal National Park** (p274) to comb the jungle for tigers or **Bhitarkanika Wildlife Sanctuary** (p275) to scan the swamps for saltwater crocodiles.

Returning to Kolkata, ride the rails north to Siliguri and change to the famous **toy train** (p149) to **Darjeeling** (p153). Book into the luxurious **Elgin** (p162) and have a long, refined high tea on the lawn.

Returning to **Siliguri** (p145), arrange a helicopter transfer to **Gangtok** in Sikkim (p182) and dig deep for a **scenic flight** (p179) around mighty Khangchendzonga.

Retrace your steps to Siliguri and fly on to **Guwahati** (p204), the lively capital of Assam. See the rhinos of **Kaziranga National Park** in style by staying at the elegant Wild Grass Resort (p214), then take a luxury cruise along the Brahmaputra with **Jungle Travels India** (p206) and enjoy a peaceful tea-plantation retreat near **Jorhat** (p215), before whistling back to Kolkata by air.

WHAT TO DO WHEN IT'S WET

The monsoon lashes India with incredible amounts of precipitation from June to September. Most tourists stay away, but this is peak festival season and you'll get to see the northeast in a completely different light.

Start off your travels in **Kolkata** (p100), which changes character dramati-cally during the monsoon. The Hooghly frequently breaches its banks, and hand-pulled rickshaws are the only vehicles that can make it through the waterlogged streets.

Although the mountain views vanish behind swirling clouds, the **Yumthang Valley** (p196) in Sikkim becomes a carpet of flowers in the run-up to the monsoon. The gathering rain-clouds in May/June do nothing to dampen the celebrations for the Drupchen festival at **Rumtek** (p183), or the Saga Dawa festival, marked by parades of Buddhist scriptures in **Gangtok** (p176) and other monastery towns.

The June–July period can be hot and soggy, but this is the time to catch one of India's great spectacles, the Rath Yatra chariot festival at **Puri** (p258) in Orissa. There are similar celebrations in **Kolkata** (p101) and **Mahesh** in West Bengal (p137). In Agartala in Tripura, the **Chaturdasha Devata Mandir** (p237) hosts the week-long Kharchi Puja festival in July.

In August, snake charmers flock to **Bishnupur** (p142) in West Bengal for the slithering Jhapan Festival. The tail end of the monsoon is also the time to see the waterfalls of **Cherrapunjee** (p243) in Meghalaya at their gushing best.

History

India had already lived through five thousand years of history by the time the first European set foot on its shores. Visitors often struggle to cope with the vast scale of Indian history, overwhelmed by the myriad characters in this epic play of human endeavour. The history of India has been a constant process of reinvention and accumulation, with each successive culture leaving its own indelible mark on the subcontinent. India today is a patchwork of cultures and customs that form a living map of the invasions, resistance movements and philosophical leaps that shaped the subcontinent.

IN THE BEGINNING WAS THE WORD, AND THE WORD WAS OM…

There are certain threads woven through Indian history that provide a tantalising glimpse of the beliefs and customs of the original inhabitants of the Indus Valley, the cradle of Indian civilisation. The concept of om – the oneness of the divine – and the Trimurti – the three divine forces of creation, preservation and destruction – were borrowed from pre-Vedic (predating the writing of the Vedas, the Hindu holy texts) religions, in the same way that Christianity borrowed from European and Middle Eastern paganism.

Harappa (www.harappa.com) provides an illustrated yet scholarly coverage of everything you need to know about the ancient Indus Valley civilisations.

The first inhabitants of India were nomadic tribes, who settled into cities in the Indus Valley (in what is today the Pakistan Punjab) by about 3500 BC. The next 1000 years were dominated by Harappan culture, the first ancient civilisation in India. Many elements of Harappan culture would later become assimilated into Hinduism: clay figurines found at these sites suggest worship of a mother goddess (the basis for *shakti*-worship – see p52), and black stone pillars and images of bulls hint at a tribal origin for the cult of Shiva.

HISTORY IN BLACK AND WHITE

Harappan civilisation fell into decline from the beginning of the 2nd millennium BC, which saw the rise of Aryan Vedic culture and the appearance of the first distinct culture in the northeast. The exact circumstances of this changeover of power have been hotly debated ever since.

The Hindu cult of phallus worship – identified with Shiva and the lingam symbol – has its origins in ancient Harappan culture.

Many Indians associate the arrival of the Aryans (from a Sanskrit word meaning noble) with the start of the divide between light-skinned and dark-skinned Indians, which remains a powerful undercurrent in Indian society today.

According to this black and white version of history, pale-skinned Aryans from central Asia swept into dark-skinned India. However, this

TIMELINE

3500–2000 BC	2000 BC	1500–1200 BC
Harappan culture flourishes in the Indus Valley, the cradle of Indian civilisation. Archaeological evidence hints at the worship of Devi (the mother goddess) and Shiva lingams (phallic symbols).	Aryan tribes enter northern India from central Asia, bringing with them the Sanskrit language. Indians trace the divide between dark-skinned Dravidians from South India and lighter-skinned people from North India to this time.	During the Vedic-Aryan period, the Hindu sacred scriptures are written in Sanskrit and the caste system formalised. India emerges as a Hindu nation during this period.

idea is being challenged by a new generation of historians who claim that the Aryan invasion was an influx of ideas rather than men with swords.

What is certain is that northern India came to be dominated by Aryan culture and languages – including Sanskrit – from the second millennium BC. The Hindu sacred scriptures, the Vedas (p50), were written during this period of transition (1500–1200 BC) and the caste system was formalised as Hinduism came to dominate the subcontinent.

The Assamese kingdom of Pragjyotisha (Land of Eastern Light) is first recorded in the Mahabharata – composed between 800 BC and 400 BC.

THE LIGHT OF THE EAST

While Aryans and Dravidians were forging kingdoms in the central plains, a new civilisation was emerging in the northeast. By the first millennium BC, a kingdom known as Pragjyotisha (Land of Eastern Light) had risen in modern-day Assam, with its capital in Pragjyotishpura (now Guwahati). Known later as Kamarupa, this early kingdom may have stretched as far west as modern-day Nepal.

By the 7th century BC, four large states had taken shape on the subcontinent. In Bengal, the powerful kingdom of Magadha rose to prominence, covering much of West Bengal, Bangladesh and Bihar. However, it was philosophy rather than military might that came to define the east of India, which saw the birth of two of the world's great religions.

In around 563 BC, Prince Siddhartha Gautama was born in the neighbouring province of Kapilavastu in modern-day Nepal. After abandoning a life of luxury, the prince went on to meditate under the Bodhi tree at Bodhgaya in Bihar where he achieved enlightenment, giving birth to Buddhism (see p54). Thousands of people abandoned Hinduism to pursue a life where social status was not defined by the circumstances of their birth.

A short distance away in Bihar, a Hindu ascetic called Mahavir founded a rival faith to Buddhism – Jainism – based on similar concepts of liberation from the earthly plane and a rejection of the caste system (see p56). For many low-caste Indians, the light of the east was the light of liberation.

The Wonder That Was India by AL Basham offers detailed descriptions of the Indian civilisations, major religions, origins of the caste system and social customs.

THE FATHER OF INDIA?

The first pan-Indian empire rose at Patna under king Chandragupta Maurya, but it was under the emperor Ashoka (r 273–232 BC) that the Maurya dynasty reached its greatest heights. In a series of bloody campaigns, Ashoka extended the Maurya empire to include most of Pakistan, Bangladesh, Nepal and almost all of northern India.

Then, after a particularly brutal battle with the kingdom of Kalinga in Orissa, he had a change of heart. Ashoka converted to Buddhism in 262 BC, making it the state religion and cutting a radical swath through the caste traditions put in place by Hinduism.

Ashoka's rule was characterised by flourishing art and sculpture, and the emperor left a record of his moral teachings engraved in stone columns and

Emperor Ashoka's ability to rule over his empire was assisted by a standing army consisting of 9000 elephants, 30,000 cavalry and 600,000 infantry.

800–400 BC	599–527 BC	528 BC
The kingdom of Pragjyotisha is mentioned in the verses of the newly composed Mahabharata, the epic poem telling the story of the Kaurava and Pandava princes.	The life of Mahavir, founder of Jainism, one of the four great religions to rise on the Indian subcontinent. Like the Buddha, Mahavir was born a prince and abandoned his wealth to pursue a life of contemplation.	Siddhartha Gautama attains enlightenment under the Bodhi tree at Bodhgaya, marking the foundation of Buddhism. After 80 years on earth, the Buddha died and was cremated at Vaishali in Bihar.

hewn into the sides of mountains. Ashoka also sent Buddhist missionaries across the empire – including his daughter, Sanghamitta, who introduced Buddhism to Sri Lanka.

The long shadow that Ashoka casts over India is evident from the fact that Ashoka's standard, the lion-topped column, is now the Indian seal and national emblem: four lions sitting back-to-back atop an abacus decorated with a frieze of animals and the inscription 'truth alone triumphs'.

Ashoka was a hard act to follow – his successors were weak and the Mauryan empire collapsed altogether in 184 BC. In Orissa, Buddhism was slowly displaced by Jainism, and Hinduism regained ground elsewhere.

Visit the website www .cs.colostate.edu /~malaiya/ashoka .html for a translation of Ashoka's famous rock-carved edicts.

A PATCHWORK OF KINGDOMS

The medieval period was marked by the rise and fall of a dozen kingdoms and empires, each of which bloomed briefly but brightly, creating some of the most definitive styles of religious art and temple architecture in the subcontinent's history. This period was also marked by a 500-year power struggle between followers of Hinduism, Buddhism and Jainism, with each successive kingdom pushing the pendulum in one direction or the other.

The fall of the Mauryas provided space for another great power to rise, the Gupta empire, founded in AD 319 by King Chandragupta I. The Guptas developed a lavish and distinctive style of religious art, and Chinese pilgrim Fahsien, visiting India at the time, described a people 'rich and contented', ruled over by enlightened and just kings. Towards the end of the Gupta period, Hinduism saw a massive revival and Jainism and Buddhism went into slow decline.

The end of the Gupta era came in AD 510, when the massed Gupta armies were defeated by the Hunnish leader Toramana, whose son Mihirakula was a fierce advocate of Shaivite Hinduism. The relative enlightenment of the Buddhist era was rapidly eclipsed by a return to the rigid dogma of *jati* (social communities often linked to specific occupations) and caste.

With the passing of the Guptas, India again dissolved into a sprawl of separate kingdoms. In around AD 606, the first recorded independent king of Bengal came to power. The Bengali king Shashanka unified the tribes and kingdoms around the Brahmaputra River delta, but his death sparked the beginning of more than a century of anarchy and unrest.

During these dark days, the political theory of *matsyanyaya* (law of the fishes, where big fish eats little fish) was formed, based on the notion that people turn on one another when there is no strong leader – ie the big fish eat the little fish. This realisation led to India's first-ever democratic election. The gathered chieftains of Bengal appointed Gopala I as the first Pala king in AD 750, ushering in a much-needed period of calm and stability. The Pala empire ruled over parts of Bengal, Bihar and Assam for 400 years, with Hindus and Buddhists granted equal rights and status.

Perhaps the most famous of Ashoka's edicts was this:

'All men are my children. I am like a father to them. As every father desires the good and the happiness of his children, I wish that all men should be happy always.'

AD 262	AD 319	AD 510
The Mauryan empire spreads Buddhism across ancient India after the Emperor Ashoka converts in AD 262. Ashoka leaves engraved pillars as evidence of his pilgrimages to Buddhist sites around the subcontinent, including at Lumbini in Nepal.	King Chandragupta I establishes the harmonious Gupta empire, which goes on to create some of the most distinctive styles of religious painting and carving in Indian history.	The Guptas are defeated by the Hunnish leader Toramana, marking the rise of Shaivite Hinduism and the end of royal patronage for Jainism and Buddhism.

THE ROAMING RELIGION

Founded on the India–Nepal border in around 528 BC by Siddhartha Gautama, Buddhism became the dominant religion in the subcontinent before losing ground to a resurgent form of Hinduism from the 5th century. At one time, the religion was found as far afield as Sri Lanka, Bangladesh and Afghanistan, and merchant sailors transported the faith southwards through the seafaring kingdoms of Southeast Asia.

As Shaivite and Vaishnavite sects of Hinduism took hold of the eastern heartlands of India, the only place left for Buddhism to go was north. Born in the 8th century in the Swat Valley in what is now Pakistan, the Indian monk Padmasambhava (Guru Rinpoche) roamed across the Himalaya, spreading a form of Buddhism that soon became infused with elements of Tantric Hinduism and Bon, the ancient indigenous religion of Tibet.

Defined by complex symbolism and a love of idolatry that might have dismayed its founder, this new form of Buddhism was adopted as the state religion of Tibet by King Trisong Detse (AD 755–797). As Buddhism waned on the plains, it grew ever stronger in the Himalaya. Followers of Tibetan Buddhism transported the religion back across the mountains to Nepal, Sikkim, Bhutan and Arunachal Pradesh.

Most of the Buddhists practising in India today follow this mystical Tibetan form of Buddhism as opposed to the simple and austere version preached by Siddhartha Gautama.

Meanwhile, Orissa was shaken by the arrival of King Yayati Kesari in the 7th century. An enthusiastic supporter of Vaishnavite Hinduism, Kesari shifted his capital to Bhubaneswar (p250), and encouraged his people to switch from Jainism to Hinduism. Orissan temple-building reached its zenith under the succeeding Ganga dynasty, who created the remarkable sun temple at Konark (p265).

Over in Bengal, the Palas faced a growing threat from the neighbouring Gaur kingdom, and were later defeated by the Buddhist Chandra dynasty from southern Bengal in the 11th century. A century later, the Sena dynasty from Karnataka reintroduced orthodox Hinduism and spread their language (the prototype for modern Bengali) deep into Bengal, Orissa and Assam.

India: A History by John Keay is an astute and readable account of subcontinental history spanning from the Harappan civilisation to Indian Independence.

FIVE HUNDRED YEARS OF CONQUEST

From the 11th century, the established religions of India faced a new threat from Islam, which was transported south and east by waves of invaders from Central Asia, including Mahmud of Ghazni (971–1030), who launched devastating raids on Hindu cities across North India.

Islam was fundamentally different from the indigenous religions that had grown up around the subcontinent. It followed a single god. It respected no central religious authority. And in the hands of warlords such as Mohammed of Ghur (1175–1206) it came with a simple message – convert or be conquered.

AD 750	1095	1175–1206
The Pala kingdom is founded in Bengal after India's first public election. The Pala empire rules over parts of Bengal, Bihar and Assam for 400 years.	The Sena dynasty is founded by King Hemanta Sen, restoring the cultural dominance of Hinduism in the northeast. The dynasty ended with the death of Keshab Sen in 1230.	The reign of Mohammed of Ghur, who captured Delhi and appointed the first Muslim governor of India, Qutb-ud-din Aybak, who later expanded the borders of the Mamluke empire across the region.

In 1192, the Ghurid leader seized Delhi, appointing his general, Qutb-ud-din Aybak, as governor and, later, sultan. The forces of Qutb-ud-din pushed out across northern India in a devastating wave. Bihar fell in 1193, and the Sena king of Bengal, Laxman Sen, was defeated in around 1204, bringing most of Bengal into the Sultanate of Bangala.

Qutb-ud-din died in 1210 after falling off his horse in a polo match, but the dynasty that he established continued his campaign of conquest and conversion. Over the next 150 years, a succession of minor Muslim dynasties ruled over kingdoms that contracted and expanded in line with the military exploits of their leaders.

The last of the great sultans, Firoz Shah, was killed in 1388 and the fate of the sultanate was sealed when the Mongol leader Tamerlane (Timur) made a devastating raid from Samarkand (in Central Asia) into India in 1398. Delhi's non-Muslim inhabitants suffered the worst of the carnage – some accounts claim that Tamerlane's soldiers slaughtered every Hindu in the city.

> The Ahom dynasty of Assam was one of the longest-lived empires in Indian history – the descendents of Sukaphaa ruled for 589 years.

THE MUGHALS

After the barbarity of the preceding centuries, the Mughals ushered in an era of artistic refinement and relative calm. The founder of the Mughal line, Babur (r 1526–30), was a descendant of both Genghis Khan and Tamerlane. In 1525, he marched into Punjab from Kabul and defeated the sultan of Delhi at the Battle of Panipat in 1526.

Thus was founded the Mughal line, which ruled over much of India until the arrival of the British. Babur was succeeded by Humayun (r 1530–56), and then Akbar (r 1556–1605), who extended the empire until he ruled over a mammoth area. Bengal was seized in 1576 and placed under the rule of appointed governors, before passing to the nawabs of Murshidabad – local Muslim rulers who accepted the authority of the Mughals.

True to his name, Akbar (which means 'great' in Arabic) was probably the greatest of the Mughals. As well as being a man of culture, the Great Mughal also had a reputation for fairness in an age characterised by brutality. He saw that the number of Hindus in India was too great to defeat, and sought instead to incorporate the Hindu people as subjects of Mughal India.

> The Emperor Akbar formulated a new religion, Deen Ilahi, which combined the best parts of all the faiths he encountered in India.

Nevertheless, the tolerance of Akbar was relative. The king continued to wage war against kingdoms that refused to bend to his will. Non-Muslims were granted certain rights but were compelled to live under foreign laws – even today, many Hindus, Buddhists and Jains regard the Mughal era as a time when their culture was under siege.

Conversely, Indians who converted to Islam were granted widespread freedoms and favours. For many impoverished, low-caste Indians, conver-

1204	1228	1526
Bengal formally comes under Islamic rule with the defeat of Laxman Sen, ruler of the Sena Kingdom, by the Turkic general Muhammed Bakhtiyar Khilji of Delhi. Many Hindu and Buddhist sites in the northeast are looted and destroyed.	Chaolung Sukaphaa founds the Ahom dynasty in Assam, vanquishing the Naga people and establishing a new capital at Charaideo near present-day Sivasagar in Upper Assam.	Descended from Tamerlane and Genghis Khan, Babur becomes the first Mughal emperor, founding India's most famous dynasty, which rules over India for almost three centuries.

sion offered an escape from the restrictions of the caste system. For others, conversion was a route to political favour.

The artistic style of the Mughals was formalised at this time, with the construction of hundreds of forts, mosques and palaces, incorporating onion domes, the pointed Mughal arch and the use of pietra dura – a mosaic of semi-precious stones inlaid into marble. The enlightened period of Mughal rule ended with Aurangzeb (r 1658–1707), a religious zealot who sent his armies to every boundary of the empire and imposed strict Islamic law across the subcontinent.

Resistance to the Mughals was spearheaded by the Marathas, a warlike Hindu dynasty founded by the charismatic Chhatrapati Shivaji. From 1646 to 1680 Shivaji confronted the Mughals across most of central India, killing a fifth of Aurangzeb's armies and reclaiming the majority of the Indian plains for Hindu India.

With Aurangzeb's death in 1707, the Mughal empire's fortunes rapidly declined. The Mughals lost Delhi in 1739 to Persia's Nadir Shah, and successive Mughals presided over smaller and smaller kingdoms. The Maratha expansion westwards was halted in 1761 by Ahmad Shah Durani from Afghanistan, but by then a new power had arrived on the scene – the British empire.

Maratha leader Chhatrapati Shivaji is said to have defeated the Mughal general Afzal Khan in hand-to-hand combat using a set of metal spikes bent to resemble tiger claws.

THE GREAT LORDS OF AHOM

While Muslim rulers were forging empires in western India and Bengal, in Assam, the conquerors were coming from the other direction. In 1228, Chaolung (Great Lord) Sukaphaa, a Shan prince from Burma (Myanmar), defeated the Naga people and asserted his control over the Brahmaputra Valley. There, he made allegiances with local chieftains and founded a new capital at Charaideo near present-day Sivasagar (p216) in 1253. Thus began the Ahom dynasty, one of the longest-lived kingdoms in Indian history.

A Tibeto-Burman people, the Ahom followed a religion based on animism, rather than the strict orthodoxy of Hinduism, Buddhism or Islam, and they spoke the Tai language, part of a family of languages found across southern China and Southeast Asia. Intermarriage and clan allegiances created a distinct Assamese ethnic identity that persists to this day in parts of Assam.

Over the following centuries, the Ahom pushed west, defeating a series of smaller kingdoms, including the Chutiya and Kacharis of central Assam. This westwards expansion was checked by the kingdom of Koch, which controlled the western part of Kamarupa. The push back began in earnest in the 16th century, when the Mughals attempted to expand their domain into northeastern India.

However, the Great Lords put up a fierce resistance. The Mughals finally gave up their campaign during the reign of Aurangzeb (r 1658–1707), after the Ahom defeated the Mughal army in an epic naval battle on the Brahmaputra near Guwahati (see p204). It took another century for the Ahom kingdom to fall after a devastating left–right manoeuvre from the Burmese in 1817 and the British in 1826.

1556–1605	**1600**	**1646–1680**
Reign of Akbar, the greatest of the Mughals. During this period, many of India's most enduring schools of art and architecture are established, and unpopular taxes on non-Muslims are repealed.	Britain's Queen Elizabeth I grants a trading charter to the East India Company, which negotiates the right to establish trading posts at locations around India.	The Hindu armies of Chhatrapati Shivaji drive back the Muslim forces of Aurangzeb, marking the resurgence of a Hindu national identity in India. He is still regarded as a folk hero by Hindu nationalists.

FOUR HUNDRED YEARS OF PLUNDER

From the 16th century onwards, the notion of *matsyanyaya* was given a new twist by the arrival of the European 'East India' companies. What started life as a trade movement soon developed into a full-scale invasion. Whereas previous invaders were motived by the glory of god, the Europeans saw the subcontinent as a vast depot of natural resources to be exported and sold for the glory of king (or queen) and country.

The first serious European interest in the northeast came in 1579, when Portuguese traders established a trading post at Hooghly in West Bengal, but the local nawab withdraw his support and a subsequent British depot also foundered. The great leap forward (for the British) and backwards (for the locals) came in 1690, when the nawab of Bengal granted permission for the East India Company to establish a formal trading post at Calcutta (Kolkata – see p101).

At first, the Muslim rulers of north India had mostly cordial relations with European trading companies. Trade bought in vast amounts of money and the fruits of Europe's technological revolution, including firearms, which were used to suppress local rebellions. However, it soon became clear that the new arrivals were more interested in taking out of India than putting in.

In 1717, the British were granted the freedom to trade in Bengal by the Mughal emperor Farrukhsiyar (r 1713–1719), but the local nawab seized Calcutta in 1756, imprisoning the British residents in a tiny cell – the notorious 'Black Hole of Calcutta' – where many died of suffocation. Predictably, the government in London demanded swift action.

When the two sides came together at the Battle of Plassey in 1757, the forces of Nawab Siraj-ud-daulah were roundly defeated by the private militia of the East India Company. Robert Clive – aka Clive of India – was appointed by the company as its first 'governor of Bengal' and the British trading mission began to take on a distinctly imperialist flavour.

A puppet nawab was placed on the throne of Bengal, and the company's agents engaged in a period of unbridled profiteering. Subsequent victories at the Battle of Baksar in 1764 and Dhaka in 1765 consolidated British control over eastern India. Signed on 16 August 1765 by the Mughal emperor Shah Alam II (r 1761–1805), the Treaty of Allahabad granted the British East India Company full administrative rights over Bengal. With the stroke of a pen, the province was annexed from the subcontinent and absorbed into the British empire.

Like the Mughals, the British exploited the Bengali system of *zamindars* (landowners) to ease the burden of administration and help with tax collection. While a handful of Bengali families grew fabulously wealthy, the impoverished and landless peasantry were pressed to work as indentured labour, living in vast shanty towns surrounding Calcutta.

White Mughals by William Dalrymple tells the true, tragic love story of an East India Company soldier who married an Indian Muslim princess, interwoven with harem politics, intrigue and espionage.

Plain Tales from the Raj by Charles Allen (ed) is a fascinating series of interviews with people who played a role in British India on both sides of the table.

1690	1765	1772
The British are granted permission to establish a formal depot at Calcutta (Kolkata) – the first East India Company trading post in the northeast – by the nawab of Bengal.	Mughal emperor Shah Alam II signs the Treaty of Allahabad, granting the British formal administrative rights over Bengal – a pivotal moment in the creation of British India.	Governor Warren Hastings transfers the offices of the colonial administration from Murshidabad to Calcutta (Kolkata), which becomes the official capital of British India.

The early years of British rule were not happy ones. While the wealth of the Indian subcontinent flowed out of its ports, the new subjects of the British empire faced starvation. Between 1769 and 1773, a major drought caused crops to fail across Bengal, leading to a massive famine that killed up to a third of the Bengali population. Predictably, the colonial garrisons did not go short of food.

Calcutta became the official capital of British India in 1772 and the British trade machine went into overdrive. Iron and coal mining were developed, tea plantations were established in the Bengal hills, and spices, coffee and cotton became key crops elsewhere in the country.

Although British territory in India was nominally administered by the East India Company until 1858, the British government became increasingly involved in political affairs. Taking advantage of the implosion of the Mughal empire, the British governor, Warren Hastings, spread the influence and interests of the company across the subcontinent, using a mixture of carrot (typically trade agreements and treaties that enshrined the power of the local gentry) and stick (generally the kind of stick that fires a musket-ball).

The only serious challengers to British expansion were the Marathas, the Hindu dynasty that drove the Mughals from the central plains. After three long and bloody Anglo–Maratha wars, the last of the Maratha territory fell to the British in 1818. Further campaigns wrested control of the Punjab from the Sikhs in 1849.

In the far northeast, the Ahom dynasty in Assam finally succumbed to a Burmese invasion from Mandalay in 1817. With help from Meitei forces from Manipur, the British drove the Burmese back across the border in 1826, claiming the province for the British empire in the process.

Back in Bengal, the first railway in the northeast started operating out of Calcutta in 1845. The British were also responsible for the postal service, irrigation schemes, drainage programs to combat malaria, and increased law and order, including the abolition of human sacrifice, which was widely practised by the members of the fanatical Thuggee cult in West Bengal. Nevertheless, these 'what did the Romans ever do for us?' arguments have to be balanced against the exploitation and abuse of the native population.

After the First Indian Uprising (p34) in 1857, India became a formal possession of the British government, and the colonial administration turned its attention to 'civilising' the natives. English was imposed as the language of administration – replacing Persian, the state language of the Mughals – and the Indian gentry were encouraged to adopt the lifestyle of the British aristocracy, complete with polo matches, silver service picnics, gin and tonics at sundown, and tea on the lawn.

This was the era of the Western Orientalised Gentleman – the children of wealthy Indians, educated at exclusive private schools in England and the colonies. Although the term was later abbreviated into a racist epithet, this

Railway buffs should visit the website of the Indian Railways Fan Club (www.irfca.org), which includes a video gallery on the world's largest rail network.

1817	1845	1857
The Ahom dynasty in Assam is defeated by Burmese invaders from Mandalay. British and Manipuri forces drive the Burmese back in 1826, and Assam becomes a province of the British empire.	The first train rolls out of Calcutta train station, marking the beginning of the Indian Railways company, which goes on to become the largest employer in the world, with 1.6 million workers.	British control over India is severely tested by the First War of Independence (Indian Uprising). Thousands of Indian troops mutiny against their British officers before the revolt is put down by military force.

THE FIRST WAR OF INDEPENDENCE: THE INDIAN UPRISING

The 1857 Indian Uprising – known at the time as the Indian Mutiny and later relabelled as the First War of Independence – started quite unexpectedly at an army barracks in Uttar Pradesh on 10 May 1857. A rumour leaked out that a new type of bullet was greased with cow fat or pork fat, taboo to Hindus and Muslims respectively. Since loading a rifle involved biting the end off the waxed cartridge, these rumours provoked considerable unrest. The British officers lined up the Indian troops and imprisoned anyone who refused to bite the ends off their bullets.

The following morning, the soldiers of the garrison rebelled, shot their officers and marched to Delhi. The soldiers and peasants rallied around the ageing Bahadur Shah Zafar – the last ruler of the Mughal dynasty – in Delhi, but the campaign was poorly coordinated and the mutineers were soon suppressed. Almost immediately the East India Company was wound up and direct control of the country was assumed by the British government, which announced its support for the existing rulers of the princely states, as long they promised their loyalty to the British empire.

---

privileged class was to give India most of its great reformers, thinkers and political leaders when the Raj (British rule) finally began to unravel.

Interestingly, a few Brits went the other way – going native and adopting local customs, costume and religions. India had its 'white Mughals' – men like General James Kirkpatrick, who converted to Islam and married a Muslim noblewoman, a decision which cost him his job and his fortune. Other Englishmen vanished into the foothills of the Himalaya in search of mystical truths and the gateway to the legendary kingdom of Shangri-La.

In some ways, India found it easier to adjust to being British than the British found it to adjust to being in India. Thousands of recruits signed up to the British Army for the chance to make a new life in the colonies. They arrived to find a land of sweltering heat, rebellious locals, soul-destroying monsoon rains and malaria. Some died of disease, some were killed in uprisings, some committed suicide and many more fled back to England.

Conversely, many nawabs and maharajas were able to operate with comparative freedom under the Raj. The caste system and the social hierarchy of the Mughals remained intact, and princely states that played ball with the colonial administration were largely left to their own devices. In many ways, the British simply added a new tier to the existing social structure and placed themselves at the top of the pile.

In 2003, Bengali landowners obtained a high-court ruling that the British trader Job Charnock should no longer be officially regarded as the founder of Kolkata.

THE ROAD TO FREEDOM

As the administrators of the Raj grew fat from Indian labour, the populace started to talk openly – among themselves at least – about rebellion. Founded by educated Indians from Calcutta University, with support from an enlightened British civil servant named Allan Octavian Hume, the Indian

1858	1885	1919
In response to the Indian Uprising, the British government assumes formal control over India, marking the beginning of the Raj. Mohandas (Mahatma) Gandhi is born a year later.	The Indian National Congress Party is founded in Bombay (Mumbai) by a team of Indian intellectuals and begins its campaign for Indian involvement in the administration of India.	British troops open fire on unarmed protesters at Jallianwala Bagh in Amritsar, killing more than 1000. The massacre marks a turning point in popular support for independence from British rule.

National Congress met for the first time in 1885 and began agitating for Indian participation in the government of India.

A highly unpopular attempt to partition Bengal by the British viceroy Lord Curzon in 1905 resulted in mass demonstrations, pitting Muslims who supported the move against Hindus who rejected the idea. The Muslim community formed its own political party, the Muslim League, in Dhaka in 1906.

With the outbreak of WWI, the political situation eased. India contributed hugely to the war (over one million Indian volunteers were enlisted and sent overseas, suffering more than 100,000 casualties), but the promised rewards of Indian autonomy failed to materialise, and disillusionment swelled.

Disturbances were particularly persistent in the Punjab and, in April 1919, following riots in Amritsar, a British army contingent was sent to quell the unrest, killing more than 1000 unarmed protesters. News of the massacre spread rapidly throughout India, turning huge numbers of otherwise apolitical Indians into Congress supporters.

At this time, the Congress movement found a new leader in Mohandas Gandhi (see the boxed text, p36), who led a brilliant campaign of nonviolent resistance to British rule. However, there were voices calling for more direct action – most notably former Congress leader Subhas Chandra Bose, who created a militaristic opposition party in Bengal, the All India Forward Bloc.

The mass movement led by Gandhi soon gained momentum, but once again communal tensions rose to the surface. As in other parts of the empire, the British stoked the flames of communal unrest as a pretext for remaining in India 'to keep the peace'. By the 1930s Muslims began to raise the possibility of a separate Islamic state and the independence movement became increasingly divided.

In Calcutta, Bose created the Bengal Volunteers, a revolutionary militia that staged a series of deadly attacks on colonial policemen, even killing the Inspector General of Prisons in his office in Dalhousie Square (the square was later renamed BBD Bagh in honour of the assassins – see p113). His rallying cry 'Jai Hind' – 'Victory to India' – can still be heard at political meetings across the country.

Political events were partially disrupted by WWII when large numbers of Congress supporters and independence activists were jailed to prevent disruption to the war effort. For Bose, the time had come to fight. Escaping from prison, Bose fled to Germany and sought backing from the Axis powers for a military strike against the British in the northeast.

In 1943, he led the Indian National Army (INA) against the British in Burma and later in Manipur and Kohima, but the campaign foundered. After the defeat of the Japanese at Imphal and Kohima – two of the bloodiest battles of WWII – Bose fled towards Japan. Official reports state that Bose died en route in a plane crash over Taiwan in 1945, though nationalists claim that Bose escaped to freedom in the Communist bloc.

> For an insight into the enduring popularity of Bengali nationalist leader Subhas Chandra Bose, visit www.subhaschandra bose.org.

> A wonderful collection of works and teachings by Mahatma Gandhi can be viewed on the websites www.mahatma.com and www.gandhiserve.org.

1943	15 August 1947	October 1947
Subhas Chandra Bose leads the Indian National Army against the British in Burma and the Northeast States. After losing heavily, he is allegedly killed in a plane crash en route to Taiwan.	India becomes independent from Great Britain and East and West Pakistan come into being as separate nations. Over the following year, nearly half a million people die in intercommunal violence.	The first India–Pakistan War breaks out after the Sikh Maharaja Hari Singh leads the Muslim-majority state of Kashmir into India. The controversial Line of Control between India and Pakistan is established.

MAHATMA GANDHI

One of the great human beings of the 20th century, Mohandas Karamchand Gandhi was born on 2 October 1869 in Porbandar, Gujarat. After studying in London (1888–91), he worked as a barrister in South Africa, before returning to India in 1915 to campaign for Indian self-determination. Unlike other Independence leaders, Gandhi's campaign was based on peaceful demonstrations and a doctrine of *ahimsa* (nonviolence), earning him the title 'Mahatma' (Great Soul) among his supporters.

By 1920 Gandhi was a key figure in the Indian National Congress, and he coordinated a national campaign of noncooperation or *satyagraha* (nonviolent protest) to British rule, famously defying the hated 'salt tax' by making his own salt. He was imprisoned but released in 1931 to represent the Indian National Congress at the second Round Table Conference in London.

Gandhi won the hearts of the British people with his impassioned rhetoric – when asked for his opinion of Western civilisation, he suggested that it would be 'a good idea' – but he was jailed again on his return to India and immediately began a hunger strike to pressure the government to bring in new laws to protect the Untouchables (the lowest caste).

Although the campaign was successful, Gandhi resigned his parliamentary seat in 1934, only to return in 1942 with the Quit India campaign, in which he urged the British to leave India immediately. His actions were deemed subversive and he and most of the Congress leadership were imprisoned.

In the bargaining that followed the end of WWII, Gandhi was largely excluded and watched helplessly as plans were made to partition the country. While the rest of the country was celebrating, Gandhi began a final fast in Calcutta to protest against growing intercommunal violence, which alienated many Hindu hardliners. On his way to a prayer meeting in Delhi on 30 January 1948, he was assassinated by a Hindu zealot.

Today, Gandhi is best remembered for his incredible bravery and steadfast adherence to the principles of nonviolence. One quote from Gandhi, conceived at the height of the struggle for independence, adroitly sums up the philosophy of *ahimsa:* 'There are many causes that I am prepared to die for but no causes that I am prepared to kill for'.

A GAME OF THREE HALVES

The Labour Party victory in the British elections in July 1945 transformed Indian independence from an idea into a political reality. By this stage, however, the independence movement was divided. Mohammed Ali Jinnah, the leader of the Muslim League, championed a separate Islamic state, while the Congress Party, led by Jawaharlal Nehru, campaigned for an independent, secular India.

In 1946, the seeds of mutual distrust between Hindus and Muslims produced their terrible harvest. A 'Direct Action Day', called by the Muslim League in August 1946, led to the mass slaughter of Hindus in Calcutta, which prompted reprisals against Muslims. Bloodshed erupted across the country.

The BBC radio series *This Sceptred Isle* provides a vivid description of the fall of British India. A CD of the series is available online from www.bbc shop.com – request Empire Volume 3.

30 January 1948	26 January 1950	1962
After coming off a hunger strike, Mahatma Gandhi is assassinated in Delhi by a Hindu extremist. The funeral service by the Yamuna River in Delhi attracts nearly one million mourners.	Drafted by Dr BR Ambedkar, the Indian Constitution comes into force, making India a formal democratic republic. Henceforth, the day is observed as Republic Day.	China goes to war with India over the North-East Frontier Area (Northeast States), as part of its claim to all territory formerly occupied by Tibet.

With their plans to 'divide and rule' coming apart at the seams, the British government acceded to the demands of the Muslim League for a two-state solution. Gandhi was the only staunch opponent, correctly prophesying the violence that would follow. As intercommunal riots raged around the subcontinent, the British viceroy Lord Mountbatten made the precipitous decision to grant India its independence on 15 August 1947.

The decision to divide the country into separate Hindu and Muslim territories was immensely tricky. Some areas were clearly Hindu or Muslim, but others had evenly mixed populations, and there were isolated 'islands' of communities in areas predominantly settled by other religions. Moreover, the two overwhelmingly Muslim regions were on opposite sides of the country and, therefore, Pakistan would inevitably have an eastern and a western half.

Predictably, Partition was a disaster. Calcutta, with its Hindu majority, port facilities and jute mills, was divided from East Bengal, which had a Muslim majority, large-scale jute production, and no mills or port facilities. One million Bengalis became refugees in the mass movement across the new border, but this was nothing compared to the carnage in the Punjab. By the time the chaos had run its course, more than 10 million people had changed sides and at least 500,000 had died in communal violence.

A NEW INDIAN DYNASTY

Independent India's first prime minister, Jawaharlal Nehru, founded a new political dynasty to rival anything produced by the Mughals. His wife, Karmala Nehru, was a pre-Independence leader of Congress; his daughter and grandson both served as prime minister; and his granddaughter-in-law, Sonia Gandhi, is still a pivotal figure in politics as the president of the Indian National Congress. Eight other members of the Nehru clan have served in local or national government.

As India adjusted to the realities of self-determination, Nehru tried to steer the nation towards a policy of nonalignment, balancing cordial relations with Britain and Commonwealth membership with overtures to the USSR – to counter the growing belligerence of communist China and US military support for Pakistan. Commonwealth status allowed thousands of Indians to travel to Britain to work, sending millions of pounds worth of remittances home to their families in India (a neat reversal of the situation in colonial times).

Three districts remained thorns in the side of the new administration. The majority-Muslim state of Kashmir was led into India by a Sikh maharaja, triggering the first of four India–Pakistan wars just weeks after the two countries came into existence. In the northeast, British Assam was chopped up into seven states, sowing the seeds for much of the Adivasi unrest that was to follow, while Punjab saw growing unrest among Sikhs, who were denied their own nation at Independence.

You've probably seen *Gandhi,* starring Ben Kingsley and 300,000 extras, but watch it again because few films trace the country's path to independence so evocatively.

India's Struggle for Independence by Bipan Chandra expertly chronicles the history of India from 1857 to 1947.

More than a dozen members of Jawaharlal Nehru's family have served in the Indian government.

1971	1984	1991
West Pakistan invades East Pakistan to prevent the division of Pakistan, leading to the third India–Pakistan War. Bangladesh gains its independence, at a cost of perhaps as many as three million lives.	Indira Gandhi is assassinated by her Sikh bodyguards after sending troops to flush out separatist militants from the Golden Temple, the most sacred site in the Sikh religion.	Prime minister Rajiv Gandhi is assassinated in Tamil Nadu by a Tamil militant after lending Indian support to a crackdown on Tamil separatist rebels in Sri Lanka.

lonelyplanet.com

In 1962, India and China went to war over the North-East Frontier Area (NEFA; now the Northeast States), desired by China as part of its dubious claim to all lands formerly occupied by Tibet. Although China eventually withdrew its forces, the Chinese government still refuses to acknowledge the Indian claim to Sikkim and Arunachal Pradesh.

A series of separatist movements emerged in the 'seven sister' states of the northeast. By the 1980s, there were more than 300 insurgent armies fighting for an independent homeland for different Adivasi communities. Wars with Pakistan in 1965 (over Kashmir) and 1971 (over Bangladesh) also contributed to a sense among many Indians of having enemies on all sides. In the midst of it all, the hugely popular Nehru died in 1964 and his daughter Indira Gandhi (no relation to Mahatma Gandhi) was elected as prime minister in 1966.

The tenure of Indira Gandhi produced its own problems. After a forced program of sterilisation for the poor caused widespread unrest, she declared a state of emergency in 1975 (which later became known as the Emergency), boosting the economy but causing even more unrest through slum clearances and the arrest of political opponents.

Indira was bundled out of office in the 1977 elections, but bounced back in 1980 with an even larger majority. Four years later, she was assassinated by her Sikh bodyguards, following an ill-considered decision to send in the Indian army to flush out Sikh separatists from Amritsar's Golden Temple. The following Hindu–Sikh riots left more than 3000 people dead (mostly Sikhs).

Indira Gandhi's son Rajiv, a former pilot, became the next prime minister in 1984, but he was dragged down by corruption scandals and his inability to quell communal unrest. In 1991, he was assassinated by a Sri Lankan gunman in Tamil Nadu – allegedly in response to Indian support for action against Tamil separatists in Sri Lanka.

Congress Party retained power in the 1991 elections, but the Hindu-revivalist Bharatiya Janata Party (BJP) emerged as the largest party in the 1996 elections, and were kept from power only by a hastily assembled coalition of secular parties. Campaigning on a platform of Hindu nationalism, the BJP won the elections in 1998 and again in 1999, becoming the first nonsecular party to hold national power in India.

The BJP era was marked by a massive upsurge in communal violence, with numerous attacks against civilians by Islamic radicals and similar attacks on Muslims by rioting Hindu mobs. India–Pakistan relations reached a new low in 1998 when the BJP government detonated five nuclear devices in the deserts of Rajasthan. Pakistan responded with its own nuclear tests, then launched an incursion into Kashmir at Kargil. The spectre of nuclear conflict loomed until the UN talked the two countries back from the brink.

The Nehrus and the Gandhis is Tariq Ali's astute portrait-history of these families and the India over which they cast their long shadow.

In 1997 KR Narayanan became India's president, the first member of the lowest Untouchable Hindu caste to hold the position.

In 2004 Sikh Prime Minister, Manmohan Singh, became the first member of any religious minority community to hold India's highest elected office.

1998	May 2004	24 May 2005
Bharatiya Janata Party (BJP) wins national elections and conducts nuclear tests. Tit-for-tat tests carried out by Pakistan bring the region to the brink of war.	Congress Party wins the national elections, but Sonia Gandhi steps aside in favour of former finance minister Manmohan Singh, who becomes India's 17th prime minister.	Indian government signs a ceasefire with Bodo separatists in Assam, ending 19 years of conflict. Former rebels find new work as guards at Manas National Park.

The Congress Party swept back to power in 2004 under the leadership of Sonia Gandhi, the Italian-born wife of the late Rajiv Gandhi; she surprisingly declined the job of prime minister, passing it on to former finance minister, Dr Manmohan Singh.

Long regarded as having a 'steady hand', Singh made a personal mission of easing relations with Pakistan and quelling the conflicts in Kashmir and the Northeast States. Massive investment was funnelled into industries in the northeast and ceasefires were signed with many insurgent groups, including the Bodo rebels in Assam and the main Naga rebel groups in Nagaland.

Talks with Pakistan initially produced positive results. However, relations crumbled after a string of deadly attacks by Pakistani and Kashmiri militants in Delhi, Mumbai and other Indian cities between 2006 and 2009. Back in the northeast, peace overtures took a massive step backwards with a string of deadly bomb attacks by Adivasi insurgents in Assam and Nagaland in early 2009.

On 16 April 2009, Indians went to the polls, returning the Congress party as the head of a stable coalition government. Manmohan Singh also returned as prime minister, immediately pledging to focus on bringing India out of the global economic crisis.

For the time being, economic concerns have replaced worries about terrorism and communal violence, but these issues are likely to return to the political agenda once India weathers the current financial storm. Rahul Gandhi, the son of Sonia Gandhi and an ardent campaigner against religious and caste-based violence, has already been put forward as a possible future prime minister.

Of the 545 seats in the Lok Sabha (Lower House of India's bicameral parliament), 120 are reserved for Scheduled Castes & Tribes.

In 2006, US President George Bush signed a deal granting India the right to produce 50 new nuclear warheads a year.

July 2006	11 July 2006	April 2009
Nathu La, a pass between Sikkim and China, reopens after 44 years, marking a thaw in India–China relations. Traders are allowed to cross the border for the first time since the rise of Chinese communism.	Deadly bomb attacks on commuter trains in Mumbai set back negotiations between India and Pakistan by decades. Over the next few years, Pakistani and Kashmiri militants launch attacks on cities across India.	Congress triumphs in the Indian national elections. Prime minister Manmohan Singh promises to lead India out of the global economic downturn.

The Culture

REGIONAL IDENTITY

Indians are famously proud of their country and their history and heritage, but travellers often comment that the northeast is the least 'Indian' part of India. In large cities such as Kolkata (Calcutta) and Bhubaneswar, a strong Indian identity prevails, but elsewhere people tend to define themselves primarily by their religion or their ethnic group.

The sense of being part of greater India decreases the further east you travel. Bengal was a distinct region before the British came to India and, despite the trauma of Partition, many people from West Bengal and Bangladesh still describe themselves as Bengali. People from Sikkim describe themselves as Sikkimese, and Adivasi (tribal) people from Nagaland see themselves as Nagas first and Indians second, if at all.

This fragmented cultural identity has its origins in the northeast's convoluted political history. Over the centuries, the region was carved up into arbitrary kingdoms by a series of invaders who showed scant respect for the culture, customs and Adivasi boundaries of the indigenous people. Many people in the northeast feel no more loyalty towards the modern Indian government than they did towards invading Mughal, Burmese and British armies in the past.

This sense of being somehow separate from the rest of India has fuelled strong separatist sentiments in the region. During the struggle for Indian independence, Bengalis were more inspired by the violent revolution preached by Subhas Chandra Bose than by the peaceful resistance preached by Mahatma Gandhi. Tensions between Assam (which then included all the Northeast States) and Bengal were increased in WWII when Adivasi people found themselves fighting alongside the British against the Japanese and the Indian National Army.

The Indian constitution recognises 573 Scheduled Tribes – there are 23 peoples just in Assam and 65 in Arunachal Pradesh.

Nevertheless, certain common traits unite people across the region. Perhaps the most obvious thing that travellers will notice is how tightly spirituality is woven into day-to-day life. India is officially secular, but religious ritual and rites are seamlessly woven into most aspects of life, from the morning *puja* (prayers) to the way shopkeepers thank the gods for the first transaction of the day.

Along with religion, the family forms the focal point of Indian society. Marriage and children are the most important goals in life for men and women and the family 'honour' (which can loosely be defined as the degree to which family members follow accepted social mores) is taken very seriously.

India remains a profoundly male-dominated society. Men – usually the breadwinners – are considered the head of the household, and members of the extended family (particularly the husband's in-laws) also play an important role in family decisions. The Western-style nuclear family, living independently of the previous generation, is rarely seen outside of Kolkata and other metropolitan areas.

As religion and family are considered sacrosanct, travellers can expect to be grilled constantly about these subjects, especially in rural areas. As well as being asked about your religion and marital status, you may be quizzed about your age, qualifications, education, profession and income, and often how much various items in your luggage cost in your home country. Most of this is natural curiosity and it is perfectly acceptable to decline to answer or to ask the same questions back.

National pride is another India-wide characteristic, though in Adivasi areas this is often replaced by regional or Adivasi pride. Indians place great stock in their history, their cultural and social achievements and their growing status as a world power. This can occasionally spill over into overt nationalism, particularly where relations between India and Pakistan are concerned.

India's nuclear arsenal is another source of national pride, though the relationship between Indians and nuclear weapons is less enthusiastic than on the Pakistan side of the border, where every town has a monument to the Pakistani nuclear project. Relations with Bangladesh tend to be more cordial, though economic migration into India has led to growing resentment in some parts of the northeast.

One thing that can be disconcerting is the enthusiasm Indians have for everything modern. Fads like American fast food and mobile phones are sweeping the country and many locals have a rather rose-tinted vision of what life is like in the West. Don't be surprised if you get drawn into some convoluted conversations about the relative merits of India and your home country – with you standing up for India!

Nevertheless, the speed of change in Indian society is quite breathtaking. The last decade has seen a seismic shift in the lifestyles of tens of millions of Indians, with growing wealth and disposable income. Thanks to the internet and mobile phone revolution, mass communication has come to the masses and people are throwing themselves into the 21st century with gusto.

Human sacrifice was common in the northeast until the colonial era, linked to the ancient cult of *shakti* (female spiritual power) worship.

LIFESTYLE
Traditional Culture
MARRIAGE, BIRTH & DEATH

Marriage is seen as the pinnacle of personal achievement in India and choosing the right partner is the most important decision in life. Although 'love marriages' are becoming common in larger cities, arranged marriage is still the norm. However, the process is rarely one-sided – although parents play the major role in selecting candidates for marriage, prospective brides and grooms usually have a say throughout the proceedings. As one young Kolkata groom explained: 'My marriage was arranged, but my parents love me, so why would they pick somebody unpleasant for me to marry?'

Typically, discreet inquiries are made within the local community. If a suitable match is not found, families turn to professional matchmakers, or place advertisements in newspapers or on the internet. Daily newspapers in India contain reams of matrimonial adverts, describing every facet of

In big cities, such as Kolkata, the average cost of a wedding is pegged at around US$12,000.

NOT ENOUGH BRIDES TO GO AROUND

Like neighbouring China, India is facing a shortage of women. In many states in the northeast, there are more boys than girls, causing severe problems when male suitors go looking for brides. In parts of Arunachal Pradesh the sex ratio is just three females to four males – ie 25% more boys than girls.

In more developed parts of India, this disparity in numbers has been put down to selective abortions of females, but the sex ratio has been skewed for centuries in Adivasi areas by the high death rate of women from disease and complications in childbirth. Several peoples have come up with a unique solution: polyandry – women marrying more than one husband.

Most common in Buddhist people such as the Lepchas of Sikkim and the Monpas, Khambas and Membas of Arunachal Pradesh, fraternal polyandry involves several brothers marrying the same wife. Among other advantages, polyandry keeps family agricultural estates intact from generation to generation and ensures that a man is always around to help the family while the other brothers are away herding yaks in remote parts of the countryside.

the potential groom or bride, from their caste, age and education to their complexion, habits and employment prospects. When a suitable candidate is found, horoscopes are checked and, if propitious, there's a meeting between the two families. If all goes well, the couple are allowed to meet to see if they get on before things proceed to marriage.

The legal marriage age in India is 18, though girls marry earlier in many rural areas. Dowries are still a key issue in many arranged marriages, despite being illegal. Many families plunge into debt to raise the required cash and there are tragic reports of brides being murdered over inadequate dowry payments – according to UN estimates, more than 5000 women die as a result of dowry-related disputes every year.

In Hindu weddings, the ceremony is officiated by a Brahmin priest and the marriage is formalised when the couple walk around a sacred fire seven times. The celebrations tend to be quite energetic – in traditional weddings the groom leads the wedding party through the streets on horseback, with musical accompaniment provided by a raucous marching band wearing lanterns on their hats to illuminate the procession.

Islamic weddings have their own special rules. On the eve of the wedding ceremony, henna patterns known as *mehndi* are drawn on the hands and neck of the bride by female relatives. For the actual *nikaah* (wedding ceremony) male and female guests are separated and passages are read from the Quran. The wedding is formalised when the bride and groom read aloud from the *nikaahnama* (wedding contracts).

Other religions have their own unique rites. Buddhist weddings are presided over by a senior lama (monk) from the local monastery; two candles are lit symbolising the union of the two families, and the couple read out their responsibilities to each other from a Buddhist text called the *Sigilovdda Sutta*.

The Adivasis of the Northeast States have their own rituals. In Tripura the groom must enter the house of his prospective bride and serve her family for up to a year to prove he has the skills to care for the daughter. Naga weddings are nominally Christian, but Adivasi customs persist, including the passing of livestock and other assets between families to seal the marriage contract. In all Indian communities, marriage is seen as a union between two families as much as a union between two individuals.

Divorce is permitted by Indian law but frowned on by society. Divorced men suffer few consequences, but women may be completely ostracised, even by their own families. Among the higher castes, widows are expected not to remarry and are admonished to wear white and lead pious, celibate lives – see p56 for more on the role of women in India. By contrast, many people in the northeast grant divorced women an automatic settlement of land and property.

As a rule, most Indian women live with their husband's family once married and assume the household duties outlined by their mother-in-law. Not surprisingly, the mother–daughter-in-law relationship can be a prickly one, as reflected in the many Indian TV soap operas and Bollywood movies that revolve around this theme.

The birth of a child is another momentous occasion, with its own set of special ceremonies, which take place at various auspicious times during the early years of childhood, including the casting of the first horoscope, name-giving, the eating of the first solid food and the first haircut.

Hindus cremate their dead on wooden pyres and funeral ceremonies are designed to purify and console both the living and the deceased. Funerals are often carried out at burning ghats (ceremonial steps) beside sacred rivers such as the Brahmaputra. Cremations are often carried out within 24 hours of death and there is no tradition of embalming the body.

Matchmaking has embraced the cyber age with websites such as www .shaadi.com and www .bharatmatrimony .com catering to tens of millions of Indians and Non-Resident Indians (NRIs).

Based on Rabindranath Tagore's novel, *Chokher Bali*, directed by Rituparno Ghosh, is a poignant film about a young widow living in early-20th-century Bengal who challenges the rules of widowhood – something unthinkable in that era.

ADIVASIS

India's Adivasis ('original inhabitants' in Sanskrit) are descended from the peoples who lived in India before the rise of the Vedic civilisation. Adivasis make up 8% of the total population but the northeast has the largest concentration of Adivasis in the country – around 90% of the population in Arunachal Pradesh, Meghalaya, Mizoram and Nagaland, and 20% to 30% of the population in Orissa, Assam, Manipur, Sikkim and Tripura.

Neglect and exploitation are serious problems for Adivasi people. Although the Scheduled Tribes have political representation thanks to the parliamentary quota system, the vast majority of Adivasis depend on subsistence agriculture and the literacy rate for Adivasis is just 29.6%, less than half the national average. Many Adivasis in the northeast have been displaced by state-sanctioned industrial projects such as the Subansiri hydroelectric scheme, and excluded from government compensation schemes because of their inability to prove they legally 'own' the land.

Adivasi culture is also increasingly giving way to the culture of the plains, with government-funded schools teaching Hindi and Assamese in place of tribal languages. Simultaneously, Western Christian missionaries are establishing charitable schools that encourage conversion and only teach in English. For more on the complex cultures of the northeast, see p46.

Although tours to Adivasi areas provide much-needed income for Adivasi communities, travellers are also playing a part in the erosion of traditional culture. To minimise your impact, look for tour companies that employ Adivasi people as guides and make a direct financial contribution to the communities they visit.

One important aspect of the Hindu death rituals is *sharadda* – paying respect to one's ancestors by offering water and rice cakes – repeated annually. After the cremation the ashes are collected and, 13 days after the death (when blood relatives are deemed ritually pure), a member of the family scatters them in a holy river or the ocean.

Indian Buddhists also cremate their dead, while Muslims bury the dead in marked graves with a formal service of Islamic verses.

All of the Adivasi peoples have their own funeral rites, linked to religion and Adivasi customs. Animist Nagas from the Angami group bury their dead beside their homes, or next to village paths, so the deceased can find the way to the narrow trail leading to paradise. In very remote areas, Nagas still perform 'platform burials', where the body of the deceased is placed on a bamboo platform to decay in the open air.

Indian newspapers are full of editorials blaming mobile phones and internet chat rooms for falling morality among young Indians – a bit like the West in that regard…

THE CASTE SYSTEM

Although the caste system is weakening, it still wields considerable power in India, especially in rural areas. The caste that Hindus are born into will largely determine their social standing, as well as their career and marriage prospects. Castes are further divided into thousands of *jati,* social communities that are often linked to specific occupations. Surnames often reflect the *jati* that a person belongs to. Conservative Hindus will only marry someone of the same *jati.*

Caste is the basic social structure of Hindu society. Living a righteous life and fulfilling your dharma (moral duty) raises your chances of being born into a higher caste and thus into better circumstances. Hindus are born into one of four varnas (castes): Brahmin (priests and teachers), Kshatriya (warriors), Vaishya (merchants) and Shudra (labourers).

Beneath these four castes are the Dalits (formerly known as Untouchables), who hold menial jobs such as sweeping and latrine cleaning. Officially referred to as the Scheduled Castes, the Dalits have also been known as the Depressed Classes and Other Backward Classes, which gives some indication of their status in society. Most of the Adivasis of the northeast also fall into the catch-all grouping of Scheduled Castes & Tribes under the Indian constitution.

Over the centuries many Dalits have sought to change their status by adopting another faith. The low status of many Indian Muslims today is largely a consequence of their historic origins as low-caste converts from Hinduism. Many Muslim communities in India are still bound by the same notions of *jati* that govern Hindu society.

One of the founding philosophies of Buddhism was the rejection of the caste system, and many low-caste Hindus still convert to Buddhism to escape the cycle of caste-dictated poverty. The author of India's constitution, Dr BR Ambedkar, was a life-long campaigner against the unfair treatment of Dalits and he famously converted to Buddhism along with 500,000 supporters in 1956.

To improve the position of Dalits, the government reserves a quota of public-sector jobs, parliamentary seats and university places exclusively for members of the Scheduled Castes & Tribes, accounting for almost 50% of sought-after government jobs.

At the bottom of the social heap are the Denotified Tribes, a diverse group of Adivasi people condemned as being 'addicted to the systematic commission of non-bailable offences' under a perverse British colonial law. These people were known as the Criminal Tribes right up until 1952, when they were reclassified as 'habitual offenders'.

High-caste Indians may refuse to shake hands with anyone who is not a Brahmin – this is a result of taboos about ritual purity and is not intended to be rude.

DOS & DON'TS

Like the rest of India, the northeast has many time-honoured traditions. You won't be expected to get everything right, but common sense and courtesy will take you a long way. If in doubt, watch what the locals do, or simply ask.

Dressing conservatively (both women and men) always wins a warm response from locals – women should also read the Women Travellers section (p325). Refrain from kissing and cuddling in public as this is frowned upon in Indian society. Nudity in public is definitely not on, and you should cover up (eg with shorts and a T-shirt) even when swimming.

Religious Etiquette

When visiting a sacred site, always dress and behave respectfully – don't wear shorts or sleeveless tops (this applies to men and women) and refrain from smoking. Loud and intrusive behaviour isn't appreciated, and neither are public displays of affection.

Before entering any holy place, remove your shoes (tip the shoe-minder a few rupees when retrieving them) and check if you are permitted to enter and if photography is allowed. Socks are usually OK. Religious etiquette advises against touching locals on the head, or directing the soles of your feet at a person, religious shrine or image of a deity. Touching any image of a deity is frowned upon if not done with the proper respect.

Women and sometimes men must cover their heads at some places of worship, especially at gurdwaras (Sikh temples), so carry a scarf along with you just to be prepared. There are some sites that do not admit women at all and some that will deny entry to nonadherents of their faith – inquire before you enter. Inside, women may be required to sit apart from men, and some shrines have dedicated entrances for women. Some Jain and Hindu temples request that leather items are left outside.

Greetings

The handshake is the most common greeting between men in India, but always shake with the right hand, as the left is used for personal ablutions. Generally, women bow with the hands brought together at the chest or head level instead of shaking hands.

Many members of the Denotified Tribes are nomadic or seminomadic Adivasi people, forced by the wider community to eke out a living on society's fringes, particularly in Bihar and Orissa. In 2007 the UN formally asked India to repeal the Habitual Offenders Act. Although the Indian government has yet to accede to this request, an official quota of jobs and college places was set aside for members of the Denotified Tribes in 2008.

For more information on the work of caste-reform campaigner Dr BR Ambedkar, visit www.ambedkar.org.

PILGRIMAGES

Devout Hindus are expected to go on *yatra* (pilgrimage) at least once a year to implore the gods or goddesses to grant a wish, to take the ashes of a cremated relative to a holy river, or to gain spiritual merit. The northeast has hundreds of pilgrimage sites linked to locations from Hindu legends, and pilgrims from the northeast make journeys across the country to such sites as Varanasi, Haridwar and the Char Dham temples of Uttaranchal.

Muslims also make pilgrimages to shrines around India, and also try to make the trip to Mecca in Saudi Arabia once in their lifetime. A special division of the Indian government arranges flights to Jeddah for around 170,000 pilgrims every year. You can recognise male *hajis* – pilgrims who have been to Mecca – by their henna-dyed beards.

Two insightful books about India's caste system are *Interrogating Caste* by Dipankar Gupta and *Translating Caste* edited by Tapan Basu.

Pilgrimages are less important to the northeast's Adivasis, but Buddhists often travel to monasteries, sacred lakes and sites associated with the Buddha and bodhisattvas (saints) such as Padmasambhava (Guru Rinpoche), including Bodhgaya (p283) and Lumbini (p292).

When Indians greet someone older they will often touch their feet as a sign of respect, but foreigners are not expected to follow this ritual. Before visiting Adivasi villages in the Northeast States, you may need to seek an audience with the local chieftain to ask for permission to enter.

Eating Etiquette

When visiting someone's home it's considered good manners to remove your shoes before entering the house and to wash your hands before the main meal. Wait to be served food or until you are invited to help yourself – if you're unsure about protocol, simply wait for your host to direct you.

It's customary to use your right hand for eating as the left hand is used for personal ablutions. In many Indian communities, food that has touched someone else's mouth is ritually impure – never offer someone anything you have put to your lips. When drinking from a shared water container, hold it slightly above your mouth (thus avoiding contact between your lips and the mouth of the container).

When eating in a restaurant, there is an etiquette to paying the bill. If you are invited by someone else, the assumption is that they will pick up the tab. Conversely, many hangers-on befriend foreigners specifically in the hope of a free drink or meal – you'll have to use your judgment depending on the situation.

Photography Etiquette

Exercise sensitivity when taking photos of people, especially women. Be sure to obtain permission in advance. Taking photos inside a shrine, at a funeral, at a religious ceremony or of people publicly bathing (including rivers) can be offensive – so ask first. Photography, particularly flash photography, is prohibited in many temples, monasteries and mosques – again, ask before you snap.

Other Traveller Tips

Because of the cultural gap, many locals may be unsure what kind of information you are after when you ask questions. Always try to phrase questions to encourage the exact response you are looking for. It's also worth noting that the commonly used sideways wobble of the head can mean anything from yes to no, maybe or I have no idea.

Most festivals are a magnet for pilgrims, and the resulting crowds can be unbelievable. Every year, hundreds of people are crushed to death in stampedes at religious gatherings – see p307 for information on visiting festivals safely.

Contemporary Issues
SEPARATISM

The seven Northeast States were originally part of the British administrative district of Assam, but new boundaries were drawn up at Independence with little thought for the territorial boundaries of the northeast Adivasis. These lines sketched on a map have been a source of conflict ever since.

Most of the Adivasi groups in the northeast claim to face discrimination from mainstream Indian society and neglect from central government, and separatist movements have sprung up across the northeast, with dozens of insurgent armies fighting for an independent Adivasi homeland.

The problems have been exacerbated by competition for resources from economic migrants from Bangladesh and money flowing to rebels from militant movements in Pakistan. Rebels claim that the Indian government has also fuelled the unrest through heavy-handed policing and by failing to represent the interests of Adivasi communities.

Some conflicts have been resolved as rebels have been integrated within the political framework – most notably in Mizoram, which was wracked by violence throughout the 1980s. The Bodo separatist movement in Assam and the Naga rebellion in Nagaland also seem to be moving towards a political solution.

However, dozens more conflicts remain unresolved. In 2008 Assam faced a spate of deadly attacks by rebels from a string of rival insurgent groups. Railway stations and trains travelling through Assam and Nagaland seem to be particularly popular targets.

Rebel attacks pose an ongoing risk to travellers – see p307 and p199 for information on safe travel in the Northeast States.

The government-run National AIDS Control Organisation has more information on India's AIDS crisis – see www.nacoonline.org.

HIV/AIDS

According to the World Health Organisation, there were 2.4 million people living with HIV and AIDS in India in 2008, a sharp decrease in the figures for 2005. Sadly, this was a result of a statistical error, not falling numbers of people carrying the disease. In fact, infection figures may be much higher than the official count as many people do not come forward for treatment.

Apart from sex workers and the truck drivers and migrant workers who use their services, intravenous drug users also fall into the high-risk category, particularly in the northeast, which is flooded with drugs from Myanmar's Golden Triangle. As in Africa, the problem is made worse by poverty, lack of education and the refusal of men to use condoms, a position reinforced by the teachings of foreign missionaries.

Sexually transmitted hepatitis infections are also soaring and India's discriminatory anti-gay laws (see opposite) hamper treatment and education. For more on health issues in India, see the Health chapter (p342).

According to the UN, around 20% of India's gross national product comes from child labour.

CHILD LABOUR

Although child labour is illegal, India is believed to have 60 million child labourers – the highest rate in the world. Poorly enforced laws and the lack of a social security system are cited as major causes of the problem. Child labour is driven as much by poverty as by exploitation; many families cannot afford to support their children and are forced to send them out to work to avoid starvation.

AN INSURGENT FOR EVERY SEASON

There are an estimated 300 insurgent groups operating in the Northeast States, most fighting for a separate homeland for minority groups. However, the idea of dividing seven states into 300 independent homelands is neither practical nor realistic. In recent years, Assam has been hit by a string of bomb attacks carried out by rebels fighting for a separate homeland for the Assamese, for members of the Karbi and Dimasa, for Islamist migrants from Bangladesh, and for Adivasi tea-plantation workers. Neighbouring Nagaland has groups fighting for a Naga homeland, for a socialist state and for homelands for individual Naga groups and religions. Ironically, though the insurgents share a common goal – independence from Indian rule – most of the violence results from factional disputes between rival insurgent armies.

Children work in agriculture, in hotels and restaurants, in factories picking rags and making cigarettes, fireworks and bricks, and particularly in the textile and carpet-weaving industries. In 2008, a number of Indian suppliers for the British fashion chain Primark were exposed to be using children as young as nine to embroider designs onto T-shirts.

Most attempts to target employers have failed through lack of enforcement, but children (aged below 14) were banned from working as labourers in households and the hospitality trade in 2006 – expanding on an existing ban on children in hazardous jobs. Employers can be punished with fines and the government has started a program of rehabilitation for displaced child labourers.

However, many are sceptical about this 'rehabilitation'. Without compulsory education and an economic alternative to child labour for the poor, these laws may just move children from one industry to another, or drive them onto the streets as beggars or criminals.

Be wary of large crowds at religious celebrations – festival stampedes cause around 500 deaths in India every year.

GAY & LESBIAN ISSUES

India is believed to have between 70 and 100 million gay, lesbian and transgender people, but homosexual relations are condemned by Indian society and forbidden under section 377 of the national legislation. There have been no convictions for committing 'carnal intercourse against the order of nature' (that is, anal intercourse) since the 1980s, but the law is widely used to harass and blackmail gay people.

Most gay people are forced to live a secret life by the threat of harassment and the expectations of Indian society. Male transsexuals have traditionally been forced to live on the periphery of society as *hijras* – see the boxed text, p48. However, more liberal sections of society in Kolkata and other large cities are becoming more tolerant of homosexuality.

There were gay pride marches in Delhi, Bengaluru (Bangalore) and Kolkata in 2008, and more and more high-profile personalities are joining the campaign to repeal section 377, including Nobel prize–winning economist Amartya Sen and writers Vikram Seth and Arundhati Roy. The latest legal challenge to the act is currently with the high court in Delhi.

For details about gay support groups and publications/websites, see p310.

POVERTY

Although the quality of life for most Indians has increased massively since Independence, India remains one of the most impoverished countries in the world. An estimated 42% of Indians live below the official poverty line, most in rural areas, and international aid organisations are divided over whether the problem is getting worse or better.

For an introduction to the diverse peoples of the northeast, read *The Seven Sisters of India* by Peter van Ham and Aglaja Stirm – it's widely available in India.

HIJRAS

The most visible nonheterosexuals in Indian society are the *hijras*, a caste of transvestites and eunuchs who adopt female clothing and characteristics. Some are gay, some are hermaphrodites and some were unfortunate enough to be kidnapped and castrated as children. In Indian society, *hijras* operate as a third sex, working as prostitutes and wandering entertainers; they are often invited to perform rituals for Hindu weddings and family celebrations. However, discrimination is widespread and *hijras* are one of the groups most at risk from HIV/AIDS. A number of Indian and international NGOs have recently taken up the cause of promoting understanding of *hijras* and combating AIDS in the *hijra* community.

Read more about *hijras* in *The Invisibles* by Zia Jaffrey, and *Ardhanarishvara the Androgyne* by Dr Alka Pande.

According to government figures, India's three worst-performing states (in economic terms) are Bihar, Orissa and Assam. The main causes of poverty are illiteracy, dependency on subsistence agriculture and overpopulation. Despite the massive fall in child mortality since Independence, the average family in India still has four children. At the current rate of increase, the Indian population may reach 1.4 billion – nearly four times the population at Independence – by 2010.

Despite a ballooning middle class, 35% to 40% of the Indian population survives on less than US$1.25 per day (about Rs60), and the 70% of the population who live in rural areas earn less than a quarter of the wages earned by city dwellers. Although state governments set a minimum wage for many occupations, the average daily wage in the northeast is less than Rs100, and many workers, particularly women, earn much less.

For foreign visitors, poverty is often the most confronting aspect of travelling on the subcontinent. Whether you give to beggars is a matter of personal choice; however, your money can often be put to better long-term use if donated to a reputable charity. Charities and development organisations always need assistance from volunteers – see p323 for some suggested organisations.

VIOLENCE AGAINST WOMEN

In common with other male-dominated societies, India has a high incidence of domestic violence, marital rape and other crimes against women, which are often carried out with the collusion of family members and local community leaders. Predictably, there is a strong religious element to many of these crimes.

Although the tradition of *sati*, where widows are burned to death on the funeral pyre of their husbands, is now rare, women can face dire consequences if they fail to live up to the expectations of their husband or his family – for example, failing to produce a son. Women who form a relationship with somebody of a different caste or religion, or a person whom male relatives do not approve of, may also be perceived to have brought dishonour on the family.

According to the All India Democratic Women's Association, as many as 10% of all murders of women are 'honour killings', carried out to restore the standing of the family in the local community. Fewer than one in 250 cases are reported to the police, and only 10% of reported cases are pursued through the legal system. A similarly depressing situation exists around rape and domestic violence.

Children contribute 33% of household income in tea-producing areas of West Bengal and Assam.

In October 2006 the Indian parliament passed a landmark bill (on top of existing legislation) giving increased protection and rights to women suffering domestic abuse. The new law covers any form of physical, sexual (including marital rape), emotional and economic abuse, particularly in relation to dowry demands. Perpetrators face imprisonment and fines, and women are legally permitted to remain in the marital house (in the past many were thrown out and made destitute).

Although the law is a step in the right direction, there are considerable obstacles to enforcement, particularly in rural communities. Few women outside the major cities are educated, so there is only limited awareness of the new laws, and many women are too frightened to speak out for fear of social stigma and persecution.

Another serious issue is female infanticide. The financial burden of providing a dowry for daughters leads many families to abort female foetuses. Although abotion is illegal, an estimated 2500 female children are aborted every day in India, adding to the growing gender imbalance in the country (see the boxed text, p41).

SMOKING

India has the world's second-largest number of smokers, after China, and an estimated 600,000 Indians die of tobacco-related diseases every year, including mouth and throat cancer caused by chewing tobacco in the form of *paan* (a mixture of betel nut and leaves; see the boxed text, p75). Following the example of many countries in Europe, India took the bold step of banning smoking in all public places on 2 October 2008, the anniversary of the birth of Gandhi.

However, local people have responded angrily to the stiff fines imposed on smokers, which can amount to as much as a day's wages. Many experts also regard the law as unenforceable – similar laws on spitting and urinating in public are almost universally flouted. Despite this, antismoking campaigners see many benefits to the ban – among other things, a number of deadly train fires and explosions at firework factories have been attributed to unextinguished cigarettes and bidis (Indian tendu-leaf roll-ups).

> Although around one-third of India's population subsists on less than US$1 per day, the country has more than 100,000 millionaires (in US$).

POPULATION

India is tipped to exceed China as the planet's most populous nation by 2035. At the time of the last population census in 2001, India was home to a staggering 1,028,737,436 people, but estimates for 2008 place the figure at closer to 1.15 billion.

The states of West Bengal, Orissa, Sikkim and the seven Northeast States have a combined population of around 143 million – around 14% of India's total population. Kolkata is India's second-largest city, with 13,205,697 people, but an estimated 75% of the population of the northeast lives in rural areas.

> India has one of the world's largest diasporas – over 25 million people in 130 countries – which pumped US$27 billion into India's economy in 2007 alone.

INDIA'S BOOMING ECONOMY

Despite the global economic downturn, the Indian economy is still on an upward curve. According to some studies, India's GDP could overtake France and Italy by 2020 – partly a result of the meteoric rise of information technology (IT) and outsourcing, with hundreds of Western businesses relocating to India to take advantage of low labour costs. The IT industry already employs one million Indians, with a further two million benefiting indirectly – outsourcing was valued at US$11 billion in 2008.

The new wealth from these industries is creating a revolution in a country that previously depended on agriculture and hand-woven textiles as its main industries. However, wealth has been concentrated in boom cities such as Bengaluru (Bangalore) and Hyderabad, nicknamed Cyberabad by locals. The main benefits to the northeast have been increased services on budget airlines – accompanied by increased freight – and massive investment in hydroelectricity to provide power for all the new computers.

For more statistics, see the **Census of India** (www.censusindia.gov.in) website. For regional populations, see the Fast Facts boxes at the start of each regional chapter.

RELIGION

Religion suffuses every aspect of life in India, from the ritual bathing carried out by Hindus at the local tank (ceremonial pond) to the evening call of the muezzin (prayer leader) from the local mosque. Every day, hundreds of Indians decide to devote their lives to spiritualism, abandoning their possessions to become Buddhist monks, wandering sadhus (spiritual men) or fakirs (Muslim ascetics who have taken a vow of poverty).

Hinduism is practised by approximately 82% of Indians, though the proportion is much lower in most of the Northeast States, where Christianity, Buddhism and Adivasi religions dominate. Today, Hindus form the majority in West Bengal, Orissa, Assam, Tripura and Sikkim, which is often incorrectly regarded as a Buddhist state.

Islam was introduced to northern India by waves of invading armies from the 11th to the 17th centuries, and immigration from Bangladesh has swelled the Muslim proportion of the West Bengal and Assam populations to around 25%. Many Indian Muslims have family links with neighbouring Bangladesh and Pakistan. In other states, Muslims make up less than 2% of the population.

The northeast also has significant numbers of Christians, a result of decades of conversions by Western missionaries. Around 85% of the population in Mizoram and Nagaland, 65% of the population in Meghalaya and 30% of the population in Manipur are Christian, compared to a national average of just 2.3%.

Buddhism is widely practised in Sikkim (by 30% of the population) and the mountainous west of Arunachal Pradesh (by 13% of the population). Many people in the Northeast States still follow traditional Adivasi religions – animists make up around 40% of the population in Arunachal Pradesh. The northeast also has small populations of Jains, Sikhs and other minority religions.

Communal Conflict

Religious conflict has been a long and bloody part of India's history. The media tends to focus solely on recent events, but most religious violence in India has its origins in the waves of foreign invasion that began in the 11th century,

To accommodate all possible aspects of the divine, the Hindu pantheon is said to contain a staggering 330 million deities.

The official but exiled government of Tibet, headed by the Dalai Lama, is based in Dharamsala in northern India.

HOLY BOOKS

Like all religions, Hinduism has its own sacred texts. Written in Sanskrit between 1500 BC and 1200 BC, the Vedas form the basis of orthodox Hinduism. These sacred texts are divided into four groups: Rig-Veda (hymns), Yajur-Veda (sacrificial prayers), Sama-Veda (chants) and Atharva-Veda (ceremonial knowledge). A second group of texts, the Puranas, tell the legends and parables of the Hindu deities. Further tales of the gods appear in two epic Sanskrit poems – the Ramayana and the Mahabharata – see p53.

Islam draws primarily on the Quran, believed to be the literal word of Allah, as revealed to the prophet Mohammed; and the Hadith, derived from conversations with the Prophet. The Sikhs follow the Guru Granth Sahib, the collected teachings of the Sikh gurus, which were first recorded in the 16th century. The core text of Buddhism is the Tripitaka, a collection of sutras (scriptures) containing the teachings of the Buddha. In Tibetan Buddhism, the sutras are divided into the Kanjur (the literal words of Buddha) and Tanjur (conversations with the Buddha). Jains have their own text, the Kalpa Sutra, telling the story of the 24 Jinas (Jain prophets).

when Hindus, Buddhists, Sikhs, Jains and Adivasi people faced persecution and enslavement at the hands of followers of monotheistic religions.

The main schism – between Hindus and Muslims – is further inflamed by memories of the intercommunal violence that followed Partition (p36). Since Partition, political and religious leaders from both communities have fanned the flames of intercommunal violence, with Muslims frequently coming out worse from the encounters.

Kashmir has been wracked by intercommunal violence ever since Independence, spawning two major wars between India and Pakistan. Most of the high-profile terrorist attacks on Indian cities in recent years have some link to Kashmir and Pakistan. Conversely, Hindu extremists and supporters of the Hindu-nationalist Bharatiya Janata Party (BJP) have been accused of a string of attacks on Muslims, Christians and Buddhists in recent years.

Hinduism

Hinduism has no founder, central authority or hierarchy and, unlike Judeo-Christian religions, there is no proselytising agenda. Essentially, Hindus believe in Brahman, who is eternal, uncreated and infinite. The multitude of gods and goddesses are merely manifestations – knowable aspects – of this formless, ageless phenomenon.

However, there are several distinct schools of Hinduism, linked to the three Trimurti deities, who represent creation, preservation and destruction. Shaivites regard Shiva as the prime deity, while Vaishnavites venerate the many incarnations of Vishnu. Worship of Brahma was eclipsed early in the foundation of Hinduism by the worship of Shiva and Vishnu. Today, there are just three Brahma temples in the whole of India.

Hindus believe that earthly life is cyclical, with human beings repeatedly reborn (a process known as samsara) and the quality of each rebirth is dependent upon your karma (conduct or action) in previous lives. It is believed that living a righteous life and fulfilling your dharma (social duty) will enhance your chances of being born into a higher caste and better circumstances. If bad karma has accumulated, rebirth may take animal form but, ultimately, only humans can gain sufficient self-knowledge to achieve moksha (liberation from the cycle of birth, death and rebirth).

Numerology and astrology play an important role in Hindu rituals. Horoscopes and sacred numbers are used to predict auspicious dates for weddings and religious rituals.

Shakunthala Jagannathan's *Hinduism – An Introduction* unravels the basic tenets of Hinduism – if you have no prior knowledge, this book is a terrific starting point.

GODS & GODDESSES

As the ultimate godhead, Brahman is formless, eternal and the source of all existence. Brahman is impossible for the human mind to fully conceive of, so the godhead is usually represented through the Trimurti.

Brahma

Brahma was the creator of the universe and the source of humanity. Brahma is generally depicted with four crowned and bearded heads, facing towards each point of the compass. His consort is Saraswati, the goddess of learning, and his vehicle is a swan. He is sometimes shown sitting on a lotus that rises from Vishnu's navel, symbolising the interdependence of the gods.

Vishnu

The preserver or sustainer, Vishnu protects and sustains all that is good in the world. He is usually depicted with four arms, holding a lotus, a chakra

SHAKTI WORSHIP

In the northeast, Hinduism has strong links to *shakti* worship, a Tantric cult based on the venera-tion of female spiritual power. All of the female incarnations of Hindu deities have their origins in the concept of Devi, the universal mother goddess, a tradition which predates Hinduism by thousands, perhaps tens of thousands, of years. In modern Hinduism, *shakti* is identified with Kali and Durga, the wrathful and violent incarnations of Shiva's consort, Parvati.

The cult of *shakti* worship is particularly strong in Assam, Tripura and West Bengal. Human sacrifices were carried out to honour Kali in Kolkata and other parts of the northeast right up until the British era. Today, the victims falling beneath the sacrificial knife are mainly goats, pigeons, chickens and buffaloes, but there are still occasional reports of human sacrifices in rural areas.

Shakti worship is also linked to the tradition of *sati,* where widows were burned alive on their husbands' funeral pyres, recalling the legend of Shiva's first wife, Sati, who immolated herself in protest at an insult to her husband. Today, incidents of *sati* are mainly confined to Rajasthan, but pilgrims still flock to the 52 *Shakti peeth* temples, where parts of the charred corpse of the goddess allegedly fell to earth. Kolkata's Kalighat temple (p115) is dedicated to the goddess's toes and Guwahati's Kamakhya Mandir (p204) is devoted to Sati's genitals.

An even more extreme version of Hinduism is followed by the Aghoris, an ancient cult that split from mainstream Shaivism in the 14th century. These extreme ascetics live around cremation grounds and are alleged to practise cannibalism and necrophilia. Interestingly, some practices of the Aghori – for example, using human skulls as bowls – can also be seen in depictions of Tibetan Buddhist deities.

(discus), a mace and a conch shell, which is to be blown like a trumpet, symbolising the cosmic vibration from which all existence emanates. His consort is Lakshmi, the goddess of wealth, and his vehicle is Garuda, half-bird, half-man. The Ganges is said to flow from his feet.

Vishnu has 22 incarnations – the most revered are Rama, the hero of the Ramayana, and Krishna, the blue-skinned hero of the Mahabharata. Krishna's dalliances with the *gopis* (milkmaids) and his love for Radha have inspired countless paintings and songs. Some Hindus also worship the Buddha and Jesus as incarnations of Vishnu.

Shiva

Shiva is the destroyer, but through the cosmic dance he facilitated creation – indeed, many worshippers credit Shiva rather than Brahma with creation of the universe. Shiva's creative role is symbolised by the lingam, a sym-bolic phallus, marked with three white stripes – the *tripundra,* symbolising knowledge, purity and penance.

Shaivite sadhus allow their hair to become matted and dreadlocked and wander from temple to temple performing religious rituals and begging for alms. Many smoke ganja (marijuana) in stone chillums (straight pipes), following the example of Shiva, who allegedly introduced the plant to the Indian plains from the Himalaya. You can distinguish Shaivite sadhus from Vaishnavite sadhus by the *tripundra* symbol marked on their foreheads.

Shiva takes many forms, including Pashupati, champion of the animals, and Nataraja, lord of the *tandava* (cosmic dance), who paces out the cos-mos's creation and destruction. The focal point of worship at Shiva temples is normally a lingam – often mounted on top of a yoni, the Hindu symbol for the female genitals.

Shiva is frequently depicted holding a trident (representative of the Trimurti) and riding Nandi, his loyal bull – a symbol of power, justice and moral order. Shiva's consort, Parvati, is revered as the source of *shakti* – divine female power (see the boxed text, above).

Shiva is often character-ised as the lord of yoga, a Himalaya-dwelling, ganja-smoking ascetic with matted hair, an ash-smeared body and a third eye symbolising wisdom. Sadhus base their lives on this characterisation of Shiva.

Other Prominent Deities

Loved across India, elephant-headed Ganesh is the god of good fortune, remover of obstacles and patron of scribes. His broken tusk was used to write sections of the Mahabharata and his animal mount is a mouse, shrew or rat. According to legend, Ganesh was born to Parvati while Shiva was travelling and grew up without knowing his father. When Shiva returned, the protective Ganesh blocked the doorway and Shiva lopped off his head in rage. When he discovered that he had slaughtered his own son, Shiva vowed to replace Ganesh's head with that of the first creature he came across, which happened to be an elephant.

Hanuman, the king of monkeys, is the hero of the Ramayana and loyal ally of Rama, but he is also regarded as an avatar (incarnation) of Shiva. He is seen as the embodiment of the concept of bhakti (faith).

HOLY TEXTS

The practices and beliefs of Hinduism are recorded in a series of Sanskrit texts – see the boxed text, p50 for an overview.

The Mahabharata

Thought to have been composed around the 1st millennium BC, this epic poem focuses on the exploits of Krishna, an incarnation of Vishnu in human form. The story follows the conflict between the heroic gods (Pandavas) and the demons (Kauravas), two rival dynasties fighting for control of the kingdom of Hastinapura. Both sides were evenly matched until Krishna acted as charioteer for the Pandava archer Arjuna, leading to triumph for the Pandavas.

The Ramayana

Composed around the 3rd or 2nd century BC, the Ramayana is believed to be mostly the work of the poet Valmiki. Like the Mahabharata, it deals with conflict between the gods and demons.

The story goes that the childless King of Ayodhya called upon the gods to provide him with a son. His wife gave birth to a boy named Rama, but the child was really an incarnation of Vishnu. Later, Rama won the hand of the princess Sita in a competition and was chosen by his father to inherit the kingdom, but his stepmother intervened and put her son in Rama's place.

Rama, Sita and Rama's brother, Lakshmana, were exiled to the forests, where Rama and Lakshmana battled demons and dark forces. During these adventures Rama spurned the advances of Surpnakha, sister of Ravana, the demon king of Lanka, said to be in modern Sri Lanka. In revenge, Ravana captured Sita and spirited her away to his palace. The rest of the poem describes Rama's quest to rescue Sita, assisted by the loyal monkey god Hanuman and his army of monkeys.

Rama is almost certainly a real historical king and the battle against Ravana may refer to a historic battle between the Aryan rulers of India and the Dravidian rulers of neighbouring Sri Lanka.

SACRED ANIMALS & PLANTS

Animals, particularly snakes and cows, have long been worshipped on the subcontinent. The cow represents fertility and nurturing, while snakes (especially cobras) are associated with fertility and welfare. Naga stones carved with images of snakes serve the dual purpose of protecting humans from snakes and propitiating the snake gods who control the monsoons. Monkeys are afforded special respect because of their connection with Hanuman.

The monkey god Hanuman was the basis for the Chinese Buddhist deity Sun Wukong, hero of *Journey to the West*, the basis for the TV series *Monkey* and the smash-hit Damon Albarn and Jamie Hewlet opera.

Two impressive publications containing English translations of holy Hindu texts are *The Bhagavad Gita* by S Radhakrishnan and *The Valmiki Ramayana* by Romesh Dutt.

Plants can also have sacred associations. The banyan tree symbolises the Trimurti, while mango trees are symbolic of love. Meanwhile, the lotus – India's national flower – is believed to have emerged from the primeval waters and is mystically connected to the mythical centre of the earth through its stem.

The rudraksha tree is said to have grown from the tears of Shiva, and its seeds are sold as amulets at religious markets across the subcontinent. Ayurveda (Indian herbal medicine) attributes all sorts of health benefits to wearing strings of rudraksha seeds.

Held every three years in one of four locations around India, the Kumbh Mela is the largest human gathering on earth, attracting up to 100 million Hindu devotees.

WORSHIP

Worship and ritual play a paramount role in Hinduism. In most Hindu homes, families start the day by offering prayers to the deities in the family shrine. Outside of the home, temples and sacred sites such as rivers, ponds and lakes are the focal point of Hindu worship.

The ritual of *puja* (literally, respect or adoration) ranges from silent prayer to elaborate ceremonies and animal sacrifices. Devotees leave the temple with a handful of *prasad* (temple-blessed food), which is humbly shared among friends and family. Other forms of worship include *aarti* (the auspicious lighting of lamps or candles) and the playing of soul-soothing bhajans (devotional songs).

Islam

Islam was founded in a region of what is now Saudi Arabia by the Prophet Mohammed in the 7th century AD. The Arabic term *islam* means to surrender, and believers (Muslims) undertake to surrender to the will of Allah (God). The will of Allah was revealed to Mohammed and recorded in the Quran, which forms a guide for all aspects of Muslim life. Islam is monotheistic and builds on the previous teachings of Christianity and Judaism. However, Islam recognises no religious hierarchy – divine authority comes directly from the Quran.

The portal website www .islam.com contains information on all aspects of Muslim worship, from Islamic festivals to recommended Muslim baby names.

Following Mohammed's death, a succession dispute split the movement. Most Muslims in India are Sunnis, who follow the dynasty of Abu Bakr, the first Muslim caliph of Arabia. Shi'ia Muslims reject Abu Bakr and follow the direct bloodline of Mohammed. Shi'ia Muslims believe that only imams (religious teachers) can reveal the true meaning of the Quran.

All Muslims share a belief in the Five Pillars of Islam:

- Shahadah – the declaration of faith: 'There is no God but Allah; Mohammed is his prophet'.
- Prayer – ideally five times a day; the muezzin (prayer leader) calls the faithful to prayer from the minarets of every mosque.
- Zakat – tax, usually taking the form of a charitable donation.
- Fasting – observing the fasting month of Ramadan; children, the sick, pregnant women, the elderly and travellers are usually exempt.
- Haj – the ritual pilgrimage to Mecca, which all Muslims aspire to do at least once in their lifetime.

For more insights into Tibetan Buddhism, read the teachings of the Dalai Lama – useful introductory texts include *Transforming the Mind* and *The Way to Freedom*, or visit www.dalailama .com.

Buddhism

A major religion in Sikkim, Arunachal Pradesh and parts of West Bengal, Buddhism is based on the teachings of Siddhartha Gautama, the historical Buddha, who is thought to have lived from about 563 to 483 BC in the kingdom of Kalipavastu, straddling the India–Nepal border. Born a prince, the Buddha encountered the suffering of ordinary people for the first time aged 29. He abandoned his luxurious life and embarked on a quest for emancipation from the world of suffering. The Buddha finally achieved nirvana (the state of full awareness) at Bodhgaya (p283) in Bihar aged 35.

After his death, the message of Buddhism was spread across Asia by his followers, including the Emperor Ashoka and Padmasambhava (Guru Rinpoche), the Indian monk who introduced Buddhism to Tibet. Most Buddhists in India today follow the Tibetan tradition, reintroduced by monks travelling south over the Himalaya in the 15th century and by modern refugees from Tibet.

For an excellent guide to all things Buddhist, browse the resources on www.dharmanet.org.

The Buddha taught that existence is based on Four Noble Truths – that life is rooted in suffering, that suffering is caused by craving worldly things, that one can find release from suffering by eliminating craving and that the way to eliminate craving is by following the Noble Eightfold Path. This path consists of right understanding, right intention, right speech, right action, right livelihood, right effort, right awareness and right concentration. By successfully complying with these one can attain nirvana.

Christianity

There are two large pockets of Christianity in India. South Indian Christians trace their conversion (possibly spuriously) to St Thomas the Apostle in AD 52, while the Christians of the northeast were converted by European missionaries in the 18th century. Christianity is now the main religion in Nagaland, Meghalaya and Mizoram, and Christians form a significant minority in Manipur and Arunachal Pradesh. The Christians of the northeast represent a broad sweep of Christian traditions – Catholics, Anglicans, Lutherans, Baptists, Presbyterians, Methodists and Pentecostals – reflecting the beliefs of the missionaries who came to India to spread the word.

Northeast India is one of the last places in the world where Christianity is actually gaining converts – aided by missionaries from 40 different Christian churches.

Animism

Although Christianity is the most popular religion in Adivasi areas, many Adivasis follow traditional animist religions, particularly in Arunachal Pradesh. Most Adivasi religions are based on Donyi-Polo (Sun–Moon) worship, which emphasises the oneness of all living things. The sun and moon are venerated as symbols of Bo Bomong, the omnipresent supreme force, and devotees believe all life can be traced back to Sedi Melo, a combination of male and female spiritual power.

The Donyi-Polo religion experienced a major revival in the 1990s under the leadership of chief minister Gegong Apang and Talom Rukbo, a community worker who campaigned against the conversion agenda of Christian missionaries. People in eastern Arunachal Pradesh worship deities known as Rangfrah and Rangsanhum, but followers of these religions are deliberately targeted by missionaries and Christian insurgent groups.

Traditional Naga costume is linked to vanished battle rituals. Many Nagas still wear a *yanra* necklace, which once symbolised how many heads the wearer had taken in battle.

Among the Nagas, particularly the Angami, Christianity is infused with elements of animist religions. Important *terhoma* (animist deities) include Kenopfu (the creator), Metsimo (the guardian of the path to paradise), Ukepenopfu (the sky god, whom the righteous join in paradise) and Ayepi (a spirit who dwells inside the home, similar to the Burmese *nat* or the Thai deity Phra Phum Chao Thi).

Other Religions

In the northeast, you may also encounter Sikhs, identifiable by the beards and turbans worn by male followers of the faith. Founded in the Punjab in the 15th century, Sikhism is a monotheistic religion that incorporates elements of Hinduism and Sufism (Islamic mysticism), including the belief in rebirth and karma.

Fundamental to Sikhism is the concept of Khalsa, a chosen race of soldier–saints who abide by strict moral codes (including abstinence from alcohol, tobacco and drugs) and fight for *dharmayudha* (righteousness). Members of the Khalsa can be recognised by the five Sikh emblems: *kesh* (uncut hair and unshaven beards), *kangha* (the comb), *kaccha* (loose shorts worn by men and women, symbolising the control of sexual desire), *kirpan* (the dagger or sword) and *karra* (the steel bangle, symbolising fearlessness).

Predominantly a west-coast religion, Zoroastrianism is followed by small numbers of traders in the northeast. This ancient religion was founded by Zoroaster (Zarathustra) in Persia and carried to India by refugees after the rise of Islam in the 10th century. Many elements of later Judaeo-Christian religions were derived from Zoroastrian traditions.

Another minority are the Jains, followers of an ancient dharmic philosophy that arose in the 6th century BC in Bihar. Founded by Mahavira, Jainism teaches that moksha can be attained by achieving complete purity of the soul. Nonviolence, strict vegetarianism and a rejection of the caste system are core philosophies. Jains follow the teachings of 24 enlightened teachers known as *tirthankars* (or Jinas).

WOMEN IN NORTHEAST INDIA

Women in the northeast face the same challenges as women in the rest of the country. Although mothers have a special role in Indian society and women are entitled to vote and own property, men wield most of the power – in the home as well as in business and the government. Only 22% of women are part of the official labour force, but women make a huge contribution to the family income through small-scale agriculture and cottage industries.

Although the percentage of women in politics has risen over the past decade, they are still underrepresented in the national parliament, accounting for around only 10% of seats. The Women's Reservation Bill, which proposes a 33% reservation of seats for women in parliament, is set to pass into law in 2009, following a decade-long campaign by women's rights campaigners.

Women in rural areas have fewer opportunities and are much more likely to have their lives controlled by male relatives. Many international NGOs are backing microfinance schemes allowing village women to start small businesses, increasing their power within the household. In low-income families, girls can be regarded as a liability because of the cost of the marriage dowry – the driving force behind India's high rates of female infanticide. For more on issues facing women in India, see p48.

Although the constitution allows for divorcees (and widows) to remarry, women who do are frequently considered outcasts from society. A woman who seeks divorce may even be rejected by her own family. Despite this, divorces are reportedly growing by 15% per annum, with most cases registered in large cities.

Women haven't always had such a low status in Indian society. Before the rise of modern Hinduism and Islam, women played an active role in the priesthood and had much more power in social affairs. Devi (mother goddess) worship is a legacy of this period in Indian history. Several groups in Arunachal Pradesh and Meghalaya still follow a matrilineal pattern of inheritance (from mother to daughter).

Women travellers should also read p324.

ARTS

India has a rich legacy in the arts. Indeed, some of the most remarkable examples of artisanship can be found in the most surprising of situations – on hand-painted movie billboards, in the magnificent paintings on trucks

---

Around 7200 people in Mizoram follow Judaism – the Bnei Menashe sect believe that Manmasi, the mythical ancestor of the Mizos, was the son of Joseph in the Old Testament.

Sati: A Study of Widow Burning in India by Sakuntala Narasimhan looks at the startling history of *sati* (a widow's suicide on her husband's funeral pyre; now banned) on the subcontinent.

Many Indian women decorate their hands and feet with intricate patterns known as *mehndi*, using a paste made from the leaves of the henna plant. The patterns normally fade after three to four weeks.

and cycle rickshaws, and in the delicate tracery of *mehndi* (henna) on the hands of Indian women. Then there are the fabulous classical arts of India – music, painting, metalwork, sculpture and the glorious architecture of India's temples.

Dance

Classical Indian dance has been practised at temples and religious ceremonies for millennia, making this a far more established art form than Western ballet. The themes for Indian dances are derived from Hindu mythology and classical literature – the study of dance often has profound religious overtones, incorporating elements of yoga and ayurveda (Indian herbal medicine).

Classical dance in the northeast got a major boost in 1901 when Rabindranath Tagore set up a dance school at Shantiniketan (p143). Aside from formal performances at cultural festivals in Kolkata and other major cities, traditional dances are performed at many festivals, particularly in Adivasi areas. Classical forms to watch out for include:

- Bharata Natyam (also spelled *bharatanatyam*) – a Tamil dance form now embraced throughout India. Dance movements recall the motion of fire, and the ritual dances of the *apsaras* (celestial handmaidens).
- Kathak – with Hindu and Islamic influences, *kathak* was particularly popular with the Mughals. *Kathak* suffered a period of notoriety for its risqué depictions of the Krishna and Radha love story.
- Manipuri – originally from Manipur, this delicate, lyrical dance came to mainstream attention in the 1920s under the influence of Bengali writer Rabindranath Tagore.
- Odissi – claimed to be India's oldest classical dance form, Odissi was performed in Orissa as early as 2200 BC.
- Satriya – classical Assamese dance, first practised in the *satras* (Hindu monasteries) of Majuli Island.

India's folk dances are widespread and varied, particularly in Adivasi areas. In Assam, young men and women come together in April for folk dances known as *bihu* to usher in the Assamese New Year. Tripuris carry out the *hajgiri* dance to honour Lakshmi and ensure plentiful harvests.

Naga Adivasis have similar dances celebrating festivals and the changing seasons, often performed in traditional costume: the *khamba lim* dance is said to mimic the mating ritual of the peacock. You can see a variety of Naga dances at the annual **Hornbill Festival** (www.hornbillfestival.com), held every December in Kohima (see p227).

Honouring the female-dominated royal family of Meghalaya, Khasi women perform the slow *nongkrem* dance in October in the village of Smit (p243), near Shillong, to pray for a good harvest. As well as classical dance, Manipuris are famous for their folk dances. Holi is marked by the energetic *dhol-cholom* (drum dance), incorporating dramatic leaps and twirls, while the *thang-ta* dance recalls the traditional Manipuri martial art of sword and shield fighting.

Orissan folk dances include *chhau*, a dance based on traditional martial arts that draws on themes from the Ramayana and Mahabharata. In Sikkim and Arunachal Pradesh, dances focus on Buddhist legends. Major Buddhist festivals are celebrated with *chaam* dances, which feature elaborate costumes and wild-eyed masks of Buddhist deities. During Losar (Tibetan New Year in February/March) you may also be able to see *lhamo*, traditional Tibetan opera, invented by the 14th-century yogi Drupthok Thangthong Gyalpo.

Many women wear anklets and toe rings as decoration, but these are always made of silver – wearing gold on the feet is taboo.

For more information on issues affecting women in modern India, visit www .indiatogether.org /women, www.sawnet .org and www.sewa.org.

Indian Classical Dance by Leela Venkataraman and Avinash Pasricha is a lavishly illustrated book with good descriptions about the various Indian dance forms, including Bharata Natyam, Odissi, Kuchipudi and Kathakali.

Music

If your only experience of Indian music has been trippy sitar solos from psychedelic '60s pop, prepare to be amazed. Indian classical music can trace its roots back to Vedic times, when religious poems chanted by priests were collated in the Rig-Veda (see the boxed text, p50). As it is performed today, Indian classical music can be broadly divided into Carnatic (South Indian, with a focus on singing) and Hindustani (North Indian) styles, but both are played all over the country.

Core features include the *raga* (the melodic framework) and *tala* (the rhythmic meter characterised by the number of beats). The most common *tala*, *tintal*, has 16 beats. The audience follows the *tala* by clapping at the appropriate beat, which in *tintal* is at beats one, five and 13. There's no clap at beat nine; that's the *khali* (empty section), which is indicated by a wave of the hand.

Significantly, there is no fixed speed for the *tala* – musicians speed up and slow down the cycle throughout the *raga* to add energy and drama. Musicians use the first beat of the *tala*, *sam*, as a reference point for improvisation and melodies. There is no fixed pitch in Indian music; *swaras* (notes) are defined relative to the drone note, *sa*.

Indian music is melodic rather than harmonic. A drone instrument – typically a *tanpura* (like a fretless sitar, with four strings tuned to the same tone) or a *surpeti* (a hand-pumped harmonium) – plays a single note repeatedly, setting the base tone for the *raga*. Other instruments then improvise the melody within the tonic framework set by the drone.

In India drums provide melody as well as rhythm. The tabla (treble drum, tuned to the appropriate tone) and doogri (bass drum) are played as a pair using the fingertips, and drummers improvise around the *tala*, rather than providing a constant metronome for other musicians.

One of the best-known melody instruments is the sitar, a stringed, fretted instrument with a soundbox made from a dried gourd and a series of 'sympathetic' strings that resonate in harmony with the plucked strings. By far the most famous sitarist is the Bengali musician Ravi Shankar (father of American singer Norah Jones).

Indian folk music is widespread and varied. Wandering musicians, magicians, snake charmers and storytellers often use song to entertain their audiences, drawing on events from the Hindu epics. At Hindu temples, listen out for bhajans – Hindu devotional songs. In Muslim areas, you may come across *ghazals* (Urdu songs derived from poetry) and *qawwali* (Islamic devotional singing), performed at mosques or at musical concerts.

The Buddhists of the northeast use ritual chanting from the sutras (sacred Buddhist texts) as part of the daily *puja* ceremony, accompanied by a ringing cacophony of cymbals, gongs and Tibetan horns. The Adivasis of the northeast have their own unique music, with a focus on singing and drumming. Western-style heavy rock has also taken off in a big way in Adivasi areas, particularly in Nagaland and Mizoram.

By far the most common music you will hear in India is filmi – the scores from Indian films. Most Indian films are actually musicals, and while actors sing the songs onscreen, a whole industry exists behind the scenes, composing and producing the film scores. These days, a lot of filmi music consists of rather cheesy pop-techno tunes, not the lyrically poetic and mellow melodies of old times. Big hit movies are invariably accompanied by a hit soundtrack CD.

Cinema

There is growing international interest in Indian cinema as a result of Bollywood spin-offs like *Bride & Prejudice* and *Slumdog Millionaire,* but

Delve into India's vibrant performing-arts scene – especially Indian classical dance – at www.artindia.net.

Fans of Indian music should look no further than www.musicindiaonline.com, a fantastic music portal with an archive of hundreds of downloadable songs and instrumentals.

India's film industry started life way back in 1897 when the first Indian-made motion picture, *Panorama of Calcutta,* was screened in Calcutta (Kolkata). India's first feature film, *Raja Harishchandra,* was released in Bombay (Mumbai) in 1913, and the first Bengali feature, *Billwamangal,* was produced in Calcutta in 1919.

Today, India's film industry is the biggest in the world. Studios in Bollywood (in Mumbai) produce a staggering 1000 movies per year, compared to the 600 films produced annually in Hollywood, and there are smaller studios in Chennai (Kollywood, named for the Kodambakkam district), Kolkata (nicknamed Tollywood, after the district of Tollygunge) and other cities, producing features in minority languages.

Characterised by big-name stars, exotic foreign locations and extravagant song-and-dance routines, the Hindi blockbusters produced by Bollywood attract a worldwide audience of around 3.7 billion people. However, film purists look to Bengal as the home of Indian art-house cinema. Bengali films have complex plot lines, dialogue in Bengali and a conspicuous absence of big-production song-and-dance numbers.

Mainstream films have plots that resonate with ordinary people – love, war, sport, family conflicts and the downtrodden overcoming oppression, corruption and poverty. Mid-plot, characters are suddenly transported to London or the Swiss Alps for sequin-covered song-and-dance routines, often featuring hundreds of extras. Kung-fu fight sequences crop up in most films as heroes battle love rivals, gangsters and corrupt cops to save the day and win the girl.

Reflecting local morality, sex scenes weave an elaborate dance of suggestion and innuendo. The lack of nudity is compensated for by heroines writhing to music in clinging wet saris. Even kissing is taboo, though smooches are slowly creeping onto the big screen, provoking outcry from community leaders. Quite a few films have fallen foul of moral and religious sensibilities, triggering violent protests and even attacks on cinemas.

Most of the hundreds of blockbusters released ever year flop, but those that succeed propel their stars, and the singers and musicians behind the scenes, to unimaginable fame and glory. Stars such as Shah Rukh Khan, Preity Zinta, Aishwarya Rai and Amitabh and Abishek Bachchan are some of the world's most recognised people.

Indian art-house cinema takes the day-to-day drama of human life as its base. Some of the finest films in Indian history have come from Bengali legends such as Guru Dutt, Ritwik Ghatak, Aparna Sen, Mrinal Sen and Satyajit Ray. If you see no other Indian art-house film, try to catch Ray's *Apu* trilogy for a heart-rending introduction to the trials of rural life in the northeast.

Bengal has also given India some of its great screen beauties, including Rituparna Sengupta and Rani Mukerji. *Dwando,* the first Bengali film to receive a global release, was filmed in Kolkata by award-winning director Suman Ghosh in 2009.

Perhaps the most famous film-maker to come out of the Northeast States was the poet Jyotiprasad Agarwala, who directed *Joymati,* the first Assamese film, in 1935. The only surviving print of the film languished in a storeroom until 1976, when undamaged portions of the reel were incorporated into the documentary *Rupkonwar Jyotiprasad aru Joymati.* Modern Assamese directors of note include Bhabendra Nath Saikia and Jahnu Barua.

For more film recommendations, see the boxed text, p16.

Literature

Classical Indian literature is still defined by the works of the great Sanskrit poets who penned the Ramayana and Mahabharata, but later works in

Indian film-score composer AR Rahman is one of the top 10 best-selling recording artists of all time, with an amazing 300 million cassettes, records and CDs sold since 1992.

Perhaps the most compelling film about the role of women in rural India is Mehboob Khan's *Mother India,* a moving tale of love, loss and the maternal bond.

Encyclopedia of Indian Cinema by Ashish Rajadhyaksha and Paul Willemen comprehensively chronicles India's cinema history from 1897 to the 21st century.

RABINDRANATH TAGORE

India's best-loved poet, writer, painter, patriot and patron of the arts, Rabindranath Tagore (or Rabi Babu as he's known to Bengalis) has had an unparalleled impact on Bengali culture. Born to a wealthy, prominent family in Calcutta (Kolkata) in 1861, he began writing as a young boy and never stopped, dictating his last poem only hours before his death in 1941.

As well as being a vocal figure in the Indian independence movement, Tagore is credited with introducing India's historical and cultural greatness to the Western world. He won the Nobel Prize for Literature in 1913 with his mystical collection of poems *Gitanjali* (Song Offering) and, in his later years, he toured around Asia, America and Europe, spreading a message of human unity and global understanding. The ground-breaking university founded by Tagore at Shantiniketan continues to nurture Indian art forms and present them to the world.

For all his internationalism, Tagore is best remembered as a Bengali patriot, writing the words and music for both the Indian and Bangladeshi national anthems. In 1915 Tagore was awarded a knighthood by the British, but he surrendered it in 1919 as a protest against the Amritsar massacre. Tagore's family home in Kolkata (see p117) is now a museum and pilgrimage site. For an introduction to Tagore's work, read his *Selected Short Stories*, available around the world.

Hindu, English, Bengali and other regional languages have also contributed to India's rich literary tapestry.

Many of the great Bengali authors have links to the Bengal Renaissance movement, which flourished from the 19th century onwards. Celebrated Renaissance writers include social reformer Ram Mohan Roy and nationalist hero Bankimchandra Chatterjee, whose poem *Bande Mataram* was used as an anthem by the Indian Independence movement. Bengalis also celebrate the incendiary political writings of Independence leader Subhas Chandra Bose. Assam's most famous literary son was the poet Jyotiprasad Agarwala, who also directed the first Assamese film, *Joymoti*.

For excellent information on Bengali literature, including online translations of work by Bengali authors, see www.parabaas.com.

The person most credited with propelling India's cultural richness to global acclaim is Bengali poet and cultural icon Rabindranath Tagore – see the boxed text, above. Another revered Bengali poet was Kazi Nazrul Islam, who became the national poet of Bangladesh after Partition.

Many modern Bengali authors write in Bengali, making their work a little inaccessible to nonspeakers, but several books by Ashutosh Mukherjee and Sharat Chandra Chatterjee are available in English translations – Sharat's legendary novella *Devdas* has been made into eight successive Indian films, most recently in 2002. UK-born Bengali writer Jhumpa Lahiri won the 2000 Pulitzer Prize for Fiction for *Interpreter of Maladies*, a tremendous collection of short stories, several set in Bengal.

For a comprehensive guide to the speeches, writings and life of Bengali hero Subhas Chandra Bose, visit www.subhaschandrabose.org.

India's latest shining literary star is India-born Kiran Desai, who won the 2006 Man Booker Prize for her superb novel *The Inheritance of Loss*, set in Kalimpong. The youngest woman to ever win the Booker Prize, Desai is the daughter of the Bengali-German novelist Anita Desai, who received three Booker Prize nominations herself.

Other Indian authors worth reading for their insights into Indian culture include Kerala-born Arundhati Roy, who won the Booker Prize for *The God of Small Things*, and Booker and Nobel Prize–winning author VS Naipaul (although born in Trinidad, his book *India: A Million Mutinies Now* has to be one of the most penetrating insights into Indian life). And you can't overlook Mumbai-born Salman Rushdie, who bagged the Booker Prize in 1981 for *Midnight's Children*, a fantastical metaphor for India's modern history, told through the eyes of children born at the exact moment of Indian Independence.

For details about English-language Indian literature, from historical to contemporary times, check out www.indianenglishliterature.com.

For further recommendations, see p16.

Architecture

India's architectural traditions are best expressed in its fabulous temples, mosques, monasteries and palaces. India's religious buildings come in an incredible variety of forms, with strict rules linked to specific regions and the worship of specific deities.

Although temple architects have free rein to decorate their temples with as many statues and carvings as they see fit, the layout and structure of the buildings themselves is dictated by rules laid down in sacred texts. Based on numerology, astrology, astronomy and religious law, these rules govern everything from the structure of the roof to the direction doors must face.

Essentially a Hindu temple is a map of the universe. Images of the temple deity reside in a plain central chamber, the *garbhagriha* (inner shrine or sanctum sanctorum), symbolising the womb-cave from which the universe emerged. In most temples the shrine is surmounted by a *sikhara,* a curvilinear tower, usually topped with an ribbed stone disk known as an *amlaka,* and a *khalasa,* shaped like a traditional water pot. Some temples have *mandapas* (pillared pavilion in front of a temple) covered by smaller *sikharas.*

Some of the most dramatic temple *sikharas* in the northeast are found in Orissa – the temples of Bhubaneswar (p250) feature ornate *sikharas* that drip with carvings, while the partially destroyed Sun Temple (p265) at Konark was built in the shape of a gigantic chariot, covered with bas-reliefs.

Perhaps the most distinctive style of temple architecture in the northeast is the Bengali hut style – a square shrine (the perfect shape in Hinduism) surmounted by a rounded dome or *sikhara*-like towers. Famous examples include Kolkata's Dakshineswar Kali Temple (p118) and the Tripura Sundari Mandir (p239) near Agartala. Migrant workers from the south have built temples in the Dravidian style, reached through soaring pyramidal gateway towers known as *gopurams,* often covered with hundreds of carvings of Hindu deities.

The Buddhist architecture of Sikkim, West Bengal and Arunachal Pradesh is defined by gompas (monasteries) and stupas – dome-like ceremonial towers used to enshrine sacred objects or the ashes of revered lamas (Buddhist monks). Like Hindu temples, stupas have a distinctive structure, with each layer of the structure representing a different aspect of Buddhist philosophy.

The interiors of monasteries are frequently decorated with vivid murals depicting characters from Tantric Buddhist mythology. Although some monasteries are centuries old, the murals are renewed regularly by local Buddhists as a sign of devotion and to accrue good karma for future incarnations. For more on Buddhist architecture, see the boxed text, p62.

India's Muslim invaders introduced new architectural conventions from Persia and Arabia, including arched cloisters and the famous onion dome. The architectural traditions of the Mughals live on in the mosques of Northeast India, with their ceremonial courtyards and fountains (for ritual washing) and towering minarets (prayer towers). All mosques are centred on a mihrab (niche) indicating the direction of Mecca.

Churches in India reflect the fashions and trends of European and American ecclesiastical architecture. Kolkata and the hill stations of West Bengal have a number of stately British-era churches, and the modernist churches of various Christian sects can be found all over the Northeast States.

Aside from religious architecture, Kolkata features some fabulously ostentatious colonial buildings from the British era, many slowly crumbling into ruin. Architectural highlights of the city include the Victoria Memorial (p107),

For more on the myriad forms and fascinating traditions of Indian temple architecture, visit www.indiantemples.com.

KNOW YOUR GOMPAS

The rugged hills of Sikkim, Arunachal Pradesh and West Bengal are dotted with atmospheric gompas (Buddhist monasteries). However, Buddhist mythology is incredibly complicated and you can spend hours exploring a gompa and still manage to understand only a fraction of what you are seeing. Fortunately, many Buddhist monks speak English and will gladly explain things if you ask.

The focal point of a gompa is the *dukhang* (prayer hall) where monks assemble for the morning *puja* (prayer or offering). The walls may be covered in vivid murals or *thangkas* (cloth paintings) of bodhisattvas (enlightened beings) and *dharmapalas* (protector deities) depicted in frightful poses to symbolise the eternal fight against ignorance.

The focal point of the *dukhang* is an altar, which is topped by statues of Buddha and various bodhisattvas – Sakyamuni (the historical Buddha), Avalokitesvara (the deity of compassion) and Guru Rinpoche (Padmasambhava) are three of the most popular deities. Butter lamps, butter sculptures (slightly psychedelic symbolic models made from coloured butter and dough) and seven bowls of water (which represent the seven elements of prayer) are placed on the altar as offerings.

By the entrance to the *dukhang* you'll find a mural depicting the wheel of life – a graphic representation of the core elements of Buddhist philosophy (see www.buddhanet.net/wheel1 .htm for an interactive description of the wheel of life). The doorway may be flanked by *mani dungkhor* – chambers containing enormous prayer wheels stuffed with thousands of copies of the Buddhist mantra 'Om mani padme hum' (Praise to the jewel in the lotus).

This mantra also appears on the smaller prayer wheels around the outer wall and the fluttering prayer flags outside. Each spin, or gust of wind, carries these prayers to heaven. On the monastery roof you'll see a statue of two deer on either side of the Wheel of Law, symbolising the Buddha's first sermon at the deer park in Sarnath.

The best time to visit any gompa is during the morning or afternoon *puja*, which take place at around 7am and 3pm – visitors are welcome to watch, but observe the following rules:

- Remove your shoes and hat before you enter a gompa.
- Ask before taking photos.
- Do not smoke.
- Do not step over or sit on the monks' cushions.
- During ceremonies, enter quietly and stand by the wall near the main entrance.
- Always walk around stupas and chortens in a clockwise direction.
- It is appropriate to make a donation before you leave.

the administrative buildings around BBD Bagh (p111) and the miniature Versailles-on-the-Hooghly that is the Marble Palace (p117). There are more fine colonial buildings in Darjeeling (p153), Shillong (p240) and on the tea estates of Assam (p215).

The Adivasis of the Northeast States have their own unique architecture, based on bamboo and rainforest timber. Each group has its own style of building, but most houses are raised on stilts to increase airflow and discourage rats and other pests. Animist villagers in Arunachal Pradesh decorate their homes with woven bamboo fetishes to propitiate the spirits. Many Naga villages feature a long communal dormitory known as a *morung*, where adolescent men live until they marry.

Architecture buffs will appreciate *Masterpieces of Traditional Indian Architecture* by Satish Grover and *The History of Architecture in India* by Christopher Tadgell, both of which include insights into temple architecture.

Painting

Indians have been putting pictures on the walls since prehistoric times, and the subcontinent has evolved a series of artistic movements that are as complex and varied as anything produced by Impressionism or the Renaissance. In ancient history, primitive artists painted scenes on the walls of caves, setting the foundations for the richly decorated temple caves of the early Hindu and Buddhist eras.

Much of this artistic legacy was destroyed by the Mughals as part of their purge of idolatry, but monasteries in inaccessible mountain areas such as Sikkim and Arunachal Pradesh have protected some fine examples of Buddhist monastery art. With help from Tibetan refugees, ancient styles of painting have been revived, with new monasteries providing opportunities for new generations of temple artists.

The Mughals replaced indigenous arts with their own painting styles, most famously in the form of Mughal miniatures. This delicate style of painting rose to prominence in the time of Akbar (1542–1605), and various styles developed around the country. Most large museums in the northeast display original Mughal paintings and you can find some impressive re-creations by modern artists.

Modern art was kick-started in the 20th century by the Bengal School – a reactionary movement led by students of the Calcutta School of Art – which sought to rekindle interest in traditional Indian art. This philosophy inspired many of the paintings of Rabindranath Tagore (see the boxed text, p60), as well as Jamini Roy and other prestigious Bengali artists. Other Indian artists to keep an eye out for include Francis Newton Souza, Tyeb Mehta, Syed Haider Raza, Akbar Padamsee, Ram Kumar and Maqbool Fida Husain.

Modern paintings are exhibited regularly in galleries in larger cities – Kolkata's Centre for International Modern Art (p116) is one of the best places to catch cutting-edge Bengali painting.

Indian Art by Roy Craven provides a sound overview of India's art history, tracing its early beginnings in the Indus Valley to the development of various forms of Hindu, Islamic and Buddhist art.

SPORT
Cricket
Cricket is more than just the national sport – it is the national obsession. Children play in every open space, using planks of wood and old tennis balls to honour their heroes in the national team – cricketers such as ace batsman Sachin Tendulkar (the Little Master), all-rounder Sourav Ganguly (the Bengal Tiger) and Sikh off-spin bowler Harbhajan Singh (fondly dubbed the Turbanator).

India's first recorded first-class cricket match was in 1864. The national cricket team won its first test series in 1952 at Chennai against England, and the team brought home the cricket World Cup in 1983 and the trophy for the first World Twenty20 in 2007.

Local matches are played across the northeast, and international matches are played at various stadiums, including Kolkata's Ranji (Eden Gardens) Stadium (p130), from October to April. Match tickets are usually advertised in the local press a few weeks in advance. Note that fixtures may be moved to locations outside of India as a result of the attacks in Lahore and Mumbai by Pakistani militants in 2008-9.

For the latest cricket news, point your browser towards http://cricket .timesofindia.indiatimes.com.

Hockey
India is one of just a handful of countries to play field hockey. Between 1928 and 1956, India won six consecutive Olympic gold medals but, with the fading influence of the sport, there have been no gold medals since 1980. Nevertheless, it's one of the sports you'll encounter on cable TV – and occasionally live. Two recommended hockey websites are www.indianhockey .com and www.bharatiyahockey.org.

A LEAGUE OF MILLIONAIRES

Indian cricket has recently been revolutionised by the creation of the Indian Premier League (www .iplt20.com), whose million-dollar match fees have attracted players from across the world. Led by Shane Warne, the Rajasthan Royals triumphed in 2008, while the Deccan Chargers conquered the field during the 2009 tournament, held in South Africa because of security fears over the Indian national elections. The **Kolkata Knight Riders** (www.kkr.in), partly owned by actor Shah Rukh Khan, are the northeast's finest.

Soccer

Through scintillating text and pictures, *The Illustrated History of Indian Cricket* by Boria Majumdar adeptly explores this popular sport, from its origins right up to modern times.

Many Indians know more about England's Manchester United than the teams playing in the National Football League, but the sport is much more popular in the northeast, with three Kolkata teams in the Premier Division: Mohun Bagan, East Bengal and the evocatively named Mohammedan Sporting. The president of FIFA (Fédération Internationale de Football Association) visited Kolkata in 2007 to raise the profile of Indian soccer. For more information on the sport, see www.indianfootball.com and www.the-aiff.com.

Polo

One of the oldest team sports on earth, polo was allegedly invented in Manipur (though Afghanistan and Iran also claim this honour). The sport flourished under the Mughals and later the British, who established a polo club in Kolkata in 1862, now one of the world's oldest. Interest in polo declined sharply after Independence, but you can still catch a few chukkas (polo sessions) in Kolkata and more widely in Manipur, where 35 teams compete in the state league. Check local newspapers for details.

Tennis

To follow the latest exploits of Sourav Ganguly, visit the fanzine site www.souravganguly.net.

Tennis is currently big news in India. As doubles partners, Leander Paes and Mahesh Bhupathi were the first Indians to win Wimbledon's prestigious title in 1999, and the two players have since won prestigious titles in Australia and the US. Sania Mirza thrashed US Open champion Svetlana Kuznetsova at the Dubai Open in 2005 and, while her singles performance has faltered slightly in recent years, she is still ranked highly in the doubles. Kolkata's Netaji Indoor Stadium is an important venue for national and international tournaments – for schedules, contact the **All India Tennis Association** (www.aitate nnis.com).

Other Sports

Keeping your finger on the pulse of Indian sporting news is just a click away on www.sify.com/sports.

Horse racing takes place throughout the cooler winter months at tracks across India, including Kolkata's Maidan racecourse (p130), with huge amounts of money changing hands through legal (and illegal) gambling. The website www.indiarace.com has more details of race meetings.

Another traditional sport that has survived is kabaddi, essentially an elaborate game of tag, where players must catch a member of the opposite team while holding a single breath of air and repeating the word 'kabaddi'. The first ever Asian Kabaddi Championship was held in Kolkata in 1980 – for details of upcoming tournaments, contact the **International Kabaddi Federation** (www.kabadd iikf.com).

MEDIA

The Indian media enjoys extensive freedom of expression, ensuring some fiery editorials in the **Hindu** (www.hinduonnet.com), the **Times of India** (http:// timesofindia.indiatimes.com) and other national newspapers. Kolkata's **Telegraph** (www.telegraphindia.com) is a respected national daily, and the northeast has numerous local papers, magazines and journals in a range of languages and dialects. Other useful publications are listed in the boxed text, p302. See www.onlinenewspapers.com/india.htm for a nationwide list of Indian magazines and newspapers.

Indian TV was originally dominated by the dreary government-controlled national broadcaster **Doordarshan** (www.ddindia.gov.in). However, recent years have seen an explosion in satellite TV channels, covering everything from news, culture and Bollywood films to bhajan. Most providers offer a handful of English-language movie and news channels among the Indian soap operas, gameshows and Hindi blockbusters.

Programs on the government-controlled **All India Radio** (AIR; www.allindiaradio .org) include news, interviews, music and sport. There are also mushrooming nationwide private channels that offer music (in an incredible array of forms), news, sport and chat – covering many subjects once considered taboo, such as sexual and marital problems.

Consult local newspapers for TV and radio listings.

For links to major Indian English-language newspapers, head straight to www.samachar.com.

Food & Drink

Indian food is rightly famous around the world, and the northeast has made some unique contributions to the national cuisine. Naga dog curry and fermented mushrooms from Meghalaya are probably acquired tastes, but most travellers will appreciate the fresh and saltwater fish dishes cooked up by Bengali chefs, or the tart and sour flavours of Assamese curries. Every corner of the northeast has its own distinctive delicacies – the states bordering the Himalaya dine on *momos* (Tibetan dumplings) and noodle soups, Oriya (Orissan) cooking features subtle spices and sweet desserts, and Adivasi (tribal) cooking is a whirl of exotic meats and jungle ingredients.

Indian pepper was so valued in medieval times that it was used in Europe in lieu of money – hence the phrase 'peppercorn rent'.

STAPLES & SPECIALITIES
Spices
The spices used in Indian cooking form a culinary map of medieval trade routes. Coriander has been grown in India for millennia and Christopher Columbus was actually searching for Indian black peppercorns when he stumbled across America. Curry leaves and green cardamoms are cash crops in the steamy south, while black cardamoms flourish in the foothills of the Himalaya. Cinnamon and ginger came to India through China, turmeric, nutmeg and cloves were shipped in from Southeast Asia and tamarind arrived from Africa. Saffron was introduced to Kashmir from the Mediterranean and cumin was imported from Egypt. Even the chilli that gives Indian food its famous punch arrived by sea, imported from South America by Portuguese traders in the 16th century.

India was only introduced to the chilli pepper in the 16th century. Prior to the colonial era, heat was added to food using black peppercorns.

There is no such thing as a 'curry' in India – the term comes from the Tamil word *kari*, meaning either 'black pepper' or 'spiced sauce'. Instead, most dishes are defined by their ingredients, cooking style and the masala (spice) mix used in their preparation. Perhaps the most famous spice mix is *garam* (hot) masala – built on a foundation of cinnamon, roasted cumin, cloves, nutmeg, chilli and green or black cardamoms.

Rice
What bread and potatoes are to Western cooking, rice is to Indian cuisine. Boiled rice is served as the starch accompaniment to a fascinating variety of thalis (plate meals) and 'wet' and 'dry' sauces. In rural areas, people may subsist almost entirely on a diet of rice and dhal (stewed lentils or pulses). The Assamese are fond of *chira* – unhusked rice, beaten flat and softened with yoghurt and jaggery (palm sugar) for breakfast. This is just one of dozens of *jolpan* (snacks) served as a morning meal in Assam.

India produces a staggering 96.43 million tonnes of rice a year, much of it grown in Orissa and West Bengal.

As well as fragrant basmati rice, farmers in the Northeast States cultivate Thai-style glutinous rice, which is baked into *pithas* (rice cakes) and ground down and fermented to make *lau-pani* (rice wine, similar to Nepali *chang*). In Adivasi areas, glutinous rice is mixed with meat or fish and roasted inside tubes of bamboo or in banana-leaf parcels.

Pulao (fried rice with vegetables) was bought to India by the Mughals; unlike in the West, it is served as a main course, not a side dish. Another rice dish to seek out is jeera rice, prepared with ghee (clarified butter) and cumin. Muslim areas serve rice fried with meat as biryanis, while Chinese and Tibetan restaurants prepare a less oily version of fried rice with chicken, egg, vegetables or meat – livened up with a variety of chilli-based condiments (some ferociously hot).

Bread & Noodles

A fascinating variety of unleavened breads are used to mop up sauces. The words roti and chapati are used interchangeably to describe unleavened round bread made with whole-wheat flour and cooked on a *tawa* (flat hotplate). In some areas, roti is more like naan – a light, puffy bread cooked in a tandoor (clay oven), often coated in butter or filled with garlic, fruit or mince.

Puri, or *poori,* is deep-fried dough puffed up like a soft, crispy balloon. It's often served with *channa* (chickpea curry) for breakfast. Flaky *paratha* – unleavened bread fried in ghee – is often filled with *aloo* (potato) or paneer (unfermented cheese). You'll also find Western-style white bread, served as a base for omelettes at street stalls.

In Tibetan-influenced areas, such as Sikkim and Arunachal Pradesh, *tsampa* (roasted barley flour) is served as a dense porridge, mixed with milk or butter tea. Various kinds of white flour are used to make noodles and the dough wrappers for *momos* – steamed or fried dumplings stuffed with vegetables, cheese or meat.

Fat *thanthuk* (pulled noodles) are used in Tibetan soups, while thin yellow noodles are used for chow mein (Chinese-style fried noodles), which is particularly delicious with buffalo meat. Many Tibetan restaurants serve *tingmo* (steamed Tibetan bread) and *kapse* (fried Tibetan bread) – often flavoured with garlic but eaten with butter and honey.

> Throwing *tsampa* (roasted barley flour) in the air at Buddhist festivals is believed to bring good luck.

Dhal

All of India is united in its love for dhal (lentils or pulses), which are served in stews such as dhal makhani (black lentils, slow-cooked with butter) or *tarka dhal* (yellow lentil soup) or fried with a tongue-tingling range of spices. Almost every thali comes with a bowl of dhal to help the rice go down. Dhal also forms the base for Indian *namkin* (savoury nibbles) and the mustard-flavoured *sambar* sauce served with dosas (lentil pancakes) and other south Indian dishes.

You may encounter up to 60 different pulses: the most common are *chana,* a slightly sweeter version of the yellow split pea; yellow or green *moong dhal* (mung beans); salmon-coloured *masoor* (red lentils); *tuvar dhal* (yellow lentils; also known as *arhar* and *toor*); *rajma* (kidney beans); *kabuli chana* (chickpeas); *urad* (black gram or lentils); and *lobhia* (black-eyed peas).

> Pat Chapman (www .patchapman.co.uk) organises specialist eating tours of India, including trips to Kolkata (Calcutta) and Darjeeling.

Meat

Meat is bound by all sorts of taboos in Indian culture. Chicken appears everywhere and in everything, but for religious reasons, Hindus will not eat beef, Muslims avoid pork, and Jains and many Buddhists will not eat any kind of meat. However, pork is a popular meat for many Adivasi peoples of the northeast, who draw their culinary cues from Southeast Asia. Dog meat also appears on Adivasi menus, along with a host of bush meats, including many endangered species – see p84.

The Buddhist peoples of Sikkim and Arunachal Pradesh enjoy buffalo meat, often fried with noodles or rolled into *momos.* Yaks are considered too useful to be wasted on something as transient as a meal, but their milk is used to make cheese and butter. Nine times out of ten, mutton is actually goat meat, and it is usually served as bony pieces – you normally get more meat for your money if you order chicken.

Fish & Seafood

Fish crop up in a bewildering variety of northeast dishes, both as a source of protein and as a flavouring. Northeastern cuisine makes extensive use of farmed fish, including carp varieties such as *katla* and *rui* (rohu), *magur*

> Fish is an integral part of the Bengali diet, but many diners are being put off by the high levels of mercury in fish caught in the Bay of Bengal.

(catfish) and *chingri* (river prawns). *Ilish hilsa,* a small bony fish that migrates into Indian rivers from the sea, is the favourite fish of Bengal. *Bhetki* (sea bass) is a popular white fish for grills and curries. Also look out for *shukti* – dried and salted sea fish, used as a pungent seasoning. However, be warned that many of the species of fish served in the northeast have lots of small bones.

Fruit & Vegetables

For recipes online, go to: www.mamtaskitchen .com, www.indiaexpress .com/cooking, http:// sutapa.com or www .recipesindian.com.

Sabzi (vegetables) come fried, roasted, curried, stuffed, baked, mashed into *koftas* (dumplings) or wrapped in batter to make deep-fried pakora or *bhajia,* both types of vegetable fritters. Pakora and *bhajia* are perfect snacks to munch on the bus or train – vendors flash-fry them in giant woks so they are almost always safe to eat.

Potatoes are cooked with various masalas, or mashed and fried for the street snack *aloo tikka* (mashed potato patties). Cauliflower is often cooked with potatoes to make *aloo gobi* (potato-and-cauliflower curry). Fresh green peas turn up stir-fried with other vegetables in *pulaos* and biryanis and as *mattar paneer* (peas and unfermented cheese in gravy).

Eggplant/aubergine, known locally as *baigan* or brinjal, can either be curried or sliced and deep-fried. Many curries make use of *saag,* a generic term for leafy greens such as mustard, spinach and fenugreek leaves. Bumpy-skinned *karela* (bitter gourd) and *bhindi* (okra) are usually fried dry with spices.

Apples, pears, bananas, grapes, coconuts, guavas, papayas and citrus fruits such as oranges (usually yellowy-green), tangerines, grapefruits, pineapples, kumquats and sweet limes are sold all over India. Locals enjoy fruit cut into slices and dusted with *chaat masala* (black rock salt, pepper, powdered mango and spices). In the hills, look out for wild strawberries along mountain trails.

India has more than 500 varieties of mangoes, and provides almost 60% of the world's mango supply.

The mango originated in northeast India, before it was cultivated and diversified by Indian farmers. Fat *fazli* mangoes are the speciality of West Bengal – to eat them with a minimum of mess, cut a large slice from either side of the seed and make criss-cross cuts to the flesh, then pop them inside out to make a 'hedgehog' of easy-to-bite-off cubes.

Pickles, Chutneys & Relishes

There are dozens of varieties of Indian *chatnis* (chutneys). Chopped onions and radish are served as a side dish with *pudina chatni* (mint, onion, garlic, chilli, ginger, lemon juice and spices). If you order a thali, you'll usually find a spoonful of *achar* (pickles) on the side. Fiery red lime pickle is made from juiced limes mashed with chilli, mustard oil and spices. Other ingredients used in *achar* include mango, lemons, ginger and various garden vegetables – every Indian family has its own recipe.

The banana is widely used as a vegetable in the northeast. Orissan cooks serve plantains (green bananas) with vegetables in the popular *dalma* stew, and Bengalis use banana pith *(thor)* and flowers *(mochar)* in all sorts of spicy sauces.

As well as *sambar* (soupy south Indian mustard and tamarind sauce), south Indian meals are served with coconut chutney, a red-hot mix of coconut, chilli, spices and curd. Another popular condiment is raita (spiced yoghurt, with shredded cucumber, carrot or diced pineapple). The typical Chinese or Tibetan sauce rack contains soy sauce, chopped chillies in vinegar, and a pungent red or green paste made from chillies, garlic and vinegar.

Dairy

Cows are not raised for meat in India, but their milk crops up everywhere, including in refreshing cups of chai (sweet milky tea). *Dahi* (curd/yoghurt) is served as a side dish to counter hot spices or stirred into curries, soups and marinades.

Yoghurt is also the main ingredient for lassi – a delicious sweet or savoury yoghurt shake. Ghee is used for frying and flavouring. In Tibetan-influenced areas, tea is prepared with salted butter in place of milk in a hand-pumped wooden churn.

Paneer is cooked in a similar way to meat – look out for delicious skewers of spiced paneer, cooked in the tandoor. Most Indian sweets are also built on a base of milk flavoured with dried fruit or nuts, and sweetened with flavoured syrup or jaggery (palm sugar).

Hard cheeses were bought to the mountains of West Bengal by Swiss missionaries in the 1950s, and cheese factories across the Himalaya still use the 'Emmenthal technique'. Small cubes of 'Kalimpong cheese', which can be hard as rubber, are sold throughout Sikkim and the West Bengal Hills.

> Eating a little *dahi* (curd) every day will populate your intestines with healthy lactobacteria, which can help prevent stomach upsets.

Sweets

Although Cadbury and Nestlé chocolate is made under license in India, most locals only have eyes for *mithai* – traditional Indian sweets. The main ingredients for *mithai* are milk, sugar (or jaggery) and fruit and nuts, and the finished sweets are often wrapped in edible silver foil. Popular types of *mithai* include *barfi* (a fudgelike sweet), halwa (an Arabic sweetmeat made with nuts and fruit), *ladoos* (gram flour and semolina sweetmeats), and *jalebis* (orange-coloured whorls of deep-fried batter that are dunked in sugar syrup).

Some sweets are more like desserts. Invented in Kolkata (Calcutta), *rasgulla* is a sweet treat made from balls of *chhana* (unpressed paneer) flavoured with rosewater. Another syrupy treat is *gulab jamun* – deep-fried balls of dough soaked in rose-flavoured syrup. The most popular pudding is *kheer,* a creamy rice pudding flavoured with cardamom, saffron, pistachios, flaked almonds, cashews and dried fruit. *Kulfi* is a firm-textured ice cream made with milk, nuts (often pistachio) and fruit. *Falooda* is an Arabic-inspired dessert drink of milk, tapioca and vermicelli noodles, flavoured with rose syrup.

> Each year, at least 13 tonnes of pure silver are converted into edible foil for wrapping Indian sweets.

INDIA-WIDE CUISINE

Some dishes are found all over India, transported across the subcontinent by migrant workers and invading armies. However, popular Indian dishes served in the West rarely appear on menus inside India, partly because most 'Indian restaurants' overseas are actually Bangladeshi or Pakistani restaurants.

North Indian Cuisine

The charcoal-fired tandoor is the workhorse of Punjabi cuisine. It is used to prepare naan and all sorts of kebabs: *sheekh* (spiced lamb or chicken mince on iron skewers), *tangri* (chicken drumsticks), *boti* (spicy bite-sized bits of boneless lamb), *tikka* (marinated chunks of chicken, fish or paneer) and, of course, the ubiquitous tandoori chicken, sold as a 'whole' or 'half' bird.

Menus across the northeast feature 'Mughlai dishes' that recall the lavish tastes of the Mughals. Popular Mughlai staples include *murg dopiaza* (chicken in a rich onion sauce), rogan josh (Kashmiri lamb and tomato curry), *dum aloo* (potatoes stuffed with nuts and paneer in a tomato-based sauce) and 'Mughlai chicken' (the default chicken curry of the north).

> At railways stations and markets, look for vendors selling *peitha* (sweet pumpkin crystallised with sugar syrup) – you can find their stands by following the buzzing honey bees attracted by the sweet smell.

South Indian Cuisine

No matter where you go in India, you will find south Indian cuisine. Food is typically vegetarian, and almost every dish is served with spicy coconut chutney and *sambar,* a peppery sauce flavoured with mustard seed, tamarind, ground lentils and chilli.

The most common dishes are *idlis,* spongy fermented rice cakes, cooked in a steamer, and dosas – savoury pancakes made from fermented rice and lentil flour. Common varieties include the *masala dosa* (stuffed with spiced potatoes), the *rava dosa* (with a semolina batter) and the Mysore dosa (a potato-filled dosa with extra garlic and chilli).

Other widely eaten snacks include *vadas* (doughnut-shaped deep-fried lentil savouries) and *appams* or *uttappams* (crisp-collared rice-flour and coconut-milk pancakes).

REGIONAL CUISINES

Kolkata & West Bengal

Recommended Bengali cookbooks include *The Calcutta Cookbook* by Minakshie Dasgupta and *Bengali Cooking: Seasons and Festivals* by Chitrita Banerji, which also explains the customs and significance of different Bengali dishes.

The Bengalis are some of the most inventive cooks in India. The key flavours of Bengali curries come from jaggery, *malaikari* (coconut milk), *shorsher tel* (mustard oil) and *posto* (poppy seed). Because of the proximity of the ocean and the Hooghly Delta, fish crops up everywhere in Bengali cooking; the definitive Bengali fish dish is *bhetki paturi* (*bhetki* fish steamed in banana leaf) served with *luchi* (small *puris*).

Bengal is also famous for its confectionary and local sweet shops stock dozens of varieties of *mithai*. Popular treats include *misthi dhoi* (curd sweetened with jaggery) and *rasgulla*. See the boxed text, p125, for more on Bengali cuisine.

Orissa

Oriya (Orissan) cooking is known for its subtle flavours and delicate spices. Many Orissans work as fishers so freshwater and saltwater fish are core ingredients. You can also find curries prepared with *kankada* (crab) and *chungudi* (prawns), often in a rich coconut sauces. As well as common garden vegetables, plantains (green bananas), jackfruit and papaya are cooked up in savoury sauces.

Tamarind adds a distinctive sour punch to Oriya cooking and many dishes are flavoured with *pancha-phutana,* a mix of cumin, mustard, fennel, fenugreek and *kala zeera* (black *nigella* seeds). Popular Oriya dishes to look out for include *dalma* (a spiced lentil sauce with vegetables, fruit and plantain), *alu palak saag* (spinach and potatoes) and *ambul* (fish cooked with mustard and tangy dried mangoes).

The website www.123orissa.com /cuisine has the low-down on Oriya (Orissan) cooking.

Puddings and sweets are as popular in Orissa as in Bengal. *Kheer* – creamy Indian rice pudding – was allegedly invented in Orissa 2000 years ago. It's still prepared daily in the famous Jagannath temple in Puri (p259).

Sikkim

As in Nepal and Bhutan, Sikkimese cooks take their inspiration from Tibet. Two dishes you'll find everywhere are chow mein and *momos*. Soups include *thukpa* (with Tibetan noodles) and hot-and-sour soup, a spicy, sinus-clearing blend of vegetables, chilli, eggs and vinegar. *Tsampa*, barley-flour dough, is the default starch.

Monisha Bharadwaj's *The Indian Kitchen* is a beautifully presented cookbook with more than 200 traditional recipes. It contains handy tips such as how to prepare fresh spice mixes.

In rural areas you may find condiments such as *mesu* (a pickle of sour fermented bamboo shoots) and *sidra ko achar* (pickled fish with tomato and chilli). The Sikkimese make extensive use of *chhurpi* (local cottage cheese) and black lentils, served stewed as *khalo dhal*. In the harsh winters, Sikkimese cooks turn to fermented ingredients such as *kinema* (preserved soybeans), *gundruk* (pickled greens) and *radish* (fermented radish).

You may also find Bhutanese-inspired dishes such as *ema datsi* (a fiery soup made from chilli and melted cheese) and *phagshapa* (fried pork fat with radishes and chillies).

Northeast States

The diverse people of the Northeast States have produced dozens of cuisines and signature dishes.

ARUNACHAL PRADESH

The food of northern Arunachal Pradesh is similar to Tibetan, Bhutanese and Sikkimese cooking. *Momos, tsampa* and *thukpa* crop up everywhere, along with soups and stews that show the influence of neighbouring Myanmar (Burma). People from the lowlands have a similar diet to the Nagas – see below. The local spirit is *apong* – made from fermented millet or rice.

ASSAM

Assamese cooking features strong flavours but few spices – turmeric, mustard and fenugreek are the main flavourings. Chilli is frequently absent from Assamese curries, which is ironic as the state produces the hottest chillies on earth (see the sidebar, below). One uniquely Assamese ingredient is *thekera* – a sour seasoning derived from a plant in the mangosteen family. Traditionally, meals begin with *khar* (an alkaline sauce, prepared using ash from burned plantain fibre) and end with *tenga* (a lime-flavoured fish stew, made from pieces of sweet-tasting *rohu* fish).

The Assamese enjoy duck meat and pork, but many Assamese Hindus avoid chicken. Rice is the standard accompaniment – many areas serve up Thai-style glutinous rice as well as basmati-like *joha* rice. Assamese breakfasts involve an assortment of *jolpan* (little snacks), including *pitha* (rice cakes), *bora saul* (glutinous rice with curd and jaggery), *chira* (beaten rice), *kath aloo* (yams) and *tilor laru* (sweet sesame seed balls).

MANIPUR & MIZORAM

Fish are farmed in bamboo cages in lakes and ponds all over Manipur and most local dishes are flavoured with *ngari* – fermented fish paste. It's a major ingredient in *iromba,* a pungent vegetable and bamboo-shoot stew. Other distinctive Manipur dishes include *kangsoi* (vegetables stewed with dried fish) and *kobok* (puffed or roasted rice sweetened with molasses).

The cuisine of Mizoram is based on pork, chicken, bamboo shoots and rice. Many dishes are boiled, and flavour is added using *rawt,* a paste of chillies, ginger and onion. Again, rice wine is a popular quaff – in Manipur and Mizoram, it's known as *zu.*

MEGHALAYA

The Khasi people, who make up the ethnic majority of central Meghalaya, make extensive use of pork – commonly served as *jadoh* (red rice cooked with pork) or *jastem* (rice with pork in turmeric gravy). Many dishes feature the pungent flavour of *tungrymbai* (fermented soybeans), similar to Sikkimese *kinema.* The influence of Assam is clear from rice-flour snacks such as *putharo* (rice-batter crepes), *pukhen* (sweet fried rice cakes) and *pusla* (steamed rice cakes wrapped in leaves).

The Garo from western Meghalaya make extensive use of *nakham* (dried fish), normally served in a spicy soup known as *nakham bitchi,* while the Jaintas of eastern Meghalaya have a taste for wild mushrooms, which are fermented so they can be eaten out of season.

NAGALAND

The culinary influences in Nagaland came west from Myanmar, rather than east from India. Nagas have a taste for all kinds of fish, as well as pork, and dog is widely consumed for special occasions. Meat is dried or smoked and

Balti cooking was invented as a marketing ploy by expat Indians in northern England. In India, 'balti' is just an alternative name for the common wok, also known as a *kadhai.*

The Assamese *bih-jolokia* (ghost-chilli) has been measured at 1.04 million Scoville units – four times the heat of Tabasco sauce. In April 2009, Anandita Dutta Tamuly consumed 51 in two minutes in front of British TV chef Gordon Ramsay, who failed to finish one.

The Naga love of fish may come from their seafaring origins – according to Adivasi legends, the Nagas came to the northeast from the sea in wooden canoes.

many dishes are flavoured with chilli and *akhuni* (fermented soybeans). Extensive use is made of glutinous rice, which is often steamed inside banana leaves or roasted in segments of bamboo stem. The Nagas are also fond of *zutho* – rice wine. The Nagas are great fans of bush meat, which tends to mean anything they can catch, driving many animal species towards extinction.

Madhur Jaffery is famous for introducing the British to Indian cooking. Now British-born TV chef Manju Malhi (www .manjumalhi.co.uk) is returning the favour by introducing India to the flavours of British-Indian cooking.

TRIPURA
Like Bengalis, Tripurans are passionately fond of fresh and dried fish. *Shidol* (a fermented preserve made of tiny freshwater fish) is a mainstay of every Tripuran kitchen. Popular fish dishes include *nona ilish paturi* (salted pieces of *hilsa* fish, wrapped in an edible leaf and fried) and *pithali* (dried fish stew). Pork and bamboo shoots are popular ingredients in Adivasi areas, and Adivasi cooking is similar to the cuisine of neighbouring Mizoram.

DRINKS
Nonalcoholic Drinks
Chai (tea), the national drink, is the perfect antidote to the rigours of the road – the vendor's chant of '*garam* chai, *garam* chai' ('hot tea, hot tea') will become one of the most welcome sounds of your trip. Traditionally, tea leaves are boiled with milk and sugar and poured through a sieve, creating a strong, sweet brew. Cardamom, ginger, cinnamon and cloves are often added to the pan to create *masala chai*.

More upmarket restaurants serve European-style tea: just leaves, water and milk or lemon. If you want tea made with water instead of milk, ask for 'milk separate'. In mountain areas and traveller towns, restaurants offer refreshing lemon tea, spruced up with ginger and honey.

In recent years the number of Indian coffee drinkers has skyrocketed, with swanky coffee chains such as Barista and Café Coffee Day appearing across the subcontinent. Most large cities in the northeast also have 'coffee houses' linked to southern coffee-growing cooperatives.

'Lime soda' is another Indian institution – just soda water, the juice of a small lime and salt or sugar. The drink is effectively isotonic and great when you're feeling dehydrated. If spices and sugar are added as well, it's known as *masala soda*. Another popular thirst quencher is *jal jeera*, made from lime juice, cumin, mint and rock salt.

Lassis (yoghurt shakes) can be sweet, salty or fruit flavoured, while *badam* milk (served hot or cold) is flavoured with almonds. *Gola*, fruit-flavoured syrup, served over crushed ice, is the local version of the slurpee. Fresh-juice vendors can be found everywhere, but juice is mixed with water, which may not be clean. If in doubt, stick to packaged juices, such as Maaza (mango juice), Appy (apple juice) and Frooti (mango again).

For information about drinking water see the boxed text, p348.

TEA – INDIA'S NATIONAL TREASURE
The tea plantations of West Bengal and Assam are famous for their fine black teas, which are normally served without milk. You can tour the tea estates around Darjeeling (p153) and Jorhat (p214) to see the leaves being harvested, fermented and dried. Grown in lowland areas, Assamese tea is blended and used to make chai all over the country. Highland teas from the hills around Darjeeling are more refined – dealers regularly pay more than US$100 per kilo for Darjeeling's Finest Tippy Golden Flowery Orange Pekoe, made from just the tips of the leaves. The official abbreviation for this superlative brew is FTGFOP – tea enthusiasts often claim that this stands for 'Far Too Good For Ordinary People'.

TIP FOR BEER DRINKERS

The glycerol used as a preservative in Indian beer can cause headaches. To avoid a thumping cranium, open the bottle and quickly tip it upside down, with the top immersed, into a full glass of water. An oily film (the glycerol) descends into the water – when this stops, pull the bottle out quickly and enjoy a glycerol-free beer.

Alcoholic Drinks

People in the northeast love 'country liquor' – spirits distilled both legally and illegally out of anything lying to hand. All the Northeast States have their own local 'rice wines' made from fermented rice, known variously as *lau-pani, zutho, zu* or *raksi.* Other local versions of hooch include toddy, distilled from fermented palm sugar, and *mahua,* distilled from the fermented flowers of the *mahua* tree. All these spirits are safe to drink when pure, but dodgy vendors have been known to spice them with methyl alcohol and other dangerous additives – talk to locals about safe places to sample these drinks.

Beer is guzzled across the northeast. Most of the domestic brands are straightforward pilsners of around 5% alcohol by volume; travellers champion Kingfisher, but every state has its own local beers. Drinkers in the northeast have a preference for 'strong beers' – syrupy, headache-causing concoctions around the 8% alcohol mark. In Sikkim, look out for tongba (see p181) – warm beer prepared from fermented millet and hot water. It's served in a metal-bound wooden pot and sipped through a bamboo straw.

Better restaurants in Kolkata serve very drinkable red and white wines from Chateau Indage, Grover Vineyards and Sula Vineyards, produced by the vineyards of Maharashtra and Karnataka. Indian-Made Foreign Liquors (IMFLs) are similar to the overseas versions but made locally with a base of rectified spirit. They're perfectly drinkable but rarely subtle. There are also plenty of local rums, whiskies, brandies and gins, though all seem to taste broadly the same.

Sikkim is famous for its novelty liquor bottles – Old Monk Rum comes in a monk-shaped bottle, the Old Gold Whisky bottle is shaped like a dagger and the Sikkim Fireball Brandy bottle is a bright red ball.

CELEBRATIONS

Food, particularly sweets, plays a major role in the festivals of the northeast. Northeast treats include *pithas* (sweet rice cakes), handed out at the Bhogali Bihu/Makar Sankranti festival in January/February, and boxes of *mithai* passed around at Diwali in October/November.

Ramadan is the Islamic month of fasting, when Muslims abstain from eating, drinking or smoking between sunrise and sunset. On the final day of Ramadan, the fast is broken with the Eid al-Fitr feast, marked by meaty biryanis and a huge proliferation of special sweets.

Some of the northeast's most exotic dishes are reserved for festivals – see p18 for listings.

WHERE TO EAT

In northeast India, restaurants are often known as 'hotels'. Signboards draw attention to the fact that a restaurant is 'veg' (vegetarian, plus dairy and eggs), 'pure veg' (vegetarian, no eggs) or 'nonveg' (anything goes). Many restaurants advertise themselves as 'multicuisine' – meaning that they serve north Indian standards, a few local dishes, and some token Chinese dishes such as fried rice and 'chicken chilli' (battered chicken in a spicy garlic sauce).

The best places to find regional food are small local canteens and *dhabas* – the ubiquitous roadside restaurants catering to travellers along India's highways, known in some areas as *bhojanalayas.* Indian sweets, cheap dosas and other south Indian vegetarian snacks are sold at 'fast food' restaurants, also known as *misthan bhandars.* Almost all hotels have restaurants and these are often the best places to eat in smaller towns.

EATING INDIAN STYLE

Most Indians eat with their right hand as the left is reserved for toilet duties. You can use your left hand for holding drinks and serving yourself from a communal bowl, but it shouldn't be used for bringing food to your mouth. Before and after a meal, it's good manners to wash your hands – most restaurants have a sink in the dining room expressly for this purpose. If you're worried about hygiene, carry a small bar of soap in your day pack.

Once your meal is served, mix the food with your fingertips. If you are having dhal and *sabzi* (vegetables) mix the dhal into your rice and have the *sabzi* in small scoops with each mouthful. If you are having fish or meat curry, mix the gravy into your rice and take the flesh off the bones from the side of your plate. Scoop up lumps of the mix with your fingertips and use your thumb to shovel the food into your mouth.

In backpacker-oriented areas, you'll also find menus designed to appeal to traveller palettes. Popular items include Western-style packet soups, spaghetti, pizzas, burritos and that old backpacker failsafe, the banana pancake. Sometimes, the pizzas are quite convincing; other times, you'll end up with a chapatti covered in tomato sauce and paneer.

Street Food

Street Foods of India by Vimla and Deb Kumar Mukerji gives recipes of some of the subcontinent's favourite munchies, from samosas, to kulfi (pistachio-flavoured sweets).

There is always something frying, boiling, roasting, peeling, juicing, simmering, mixing or baking on the streets of northeast India, and it's usually delicious. The golden rule is to eat where the locals eat – busy food stalls almost always serve fresh and hygienic food, and empty stalls tend to be empty for a reason.

Popular street snacks include *chaat* (Indian-style spiced salad) and vegetables fried up as *pakora* or *bhajia* (vegetable fritters) in spicy gram-flour batters. Fried samosas – pyramid-shaped pastries filled with spiced vegetables or (occasionally) meat – are a perfect snack food for long train and bus journeys.

Meat is more of a gamble, but you can find street stalls serving tasty lamb and chicken kebabs in Muslim areas. Again, following the golden rule should keep you safe. Street food needn't be unfamiliar – omelettes, slammed between two slices of white bread, are sold everywhere.

WHERE TO DRINK

Saunf (sonf) – the traditional Indian palate cleanser – is served as tiny coloured candies or loose green seeds with sugar crystals on the side. Pop a few seeds in your mouth after eating for cool, fresh breath.

Alcohol is sold in restaurants, bars and licensed liquor stores throughout West Bengal, Orissa and Sikkim but Mizoram, Manipur and Tripura are all difficult places to find a drink, except in Adivasi areas. Many states have regular dry days when the sale of alcohol from liquor shops is banned, usually coinciding with the full moon. Your best chance of finding an alcoholic drink in a 'dry' area is to visit the bar at a top-end hotel.

Bars and pubs are only found in larger cities, usually at hotels. Elsewhere, people drink at restaurants. Note that Indian bars are often seedy, male-dominated affairs – not really the kind of place thirsty female travellers would want to venture into alone.

VEGETARIANS & VEGANS

Around 70% of the world's vegetarians are Indian, so it should be no surprise that India produces some of the best vegetarian food on the planet. However, there's little understanding of veganism (the term 'pure vegetarian' means without eggs), and animal products such as milk, butter, ghee and curd are included in most Indian dishes. Chefs can prepare vegan food on demand if you can make yourself understood, or you can seek out restaurants owned by the Jain community, who avoid all animal products, as well as onions, garlic and potatoes. For tips for vegans travelling abroad, see www.vegansworldnetwork.org.

EATING WITH KIDS

Restaurants rarely have children's menus; however, Western fast food is widely available and finger food, such as pakora (deep-fried battered vegetables), dosas (thin lentil-flour pancakes) and finger chips (seasoned hot potato chips), goes down fairly easily. Mildly spiced dhal is only an inch away from being processed baby-food.

As long as it is peeled or washed in purified water, fruit can offset the unhealthiness of lots of fried food. Try 'hedgehogging' some mangoes (see p68) to keep the little ones entertained at breakfast. Bottled water, cartons of fruit juice and bottles of soft drink are usually safe to drink – Frooti and Maaza brands of mango juice always go down well.

> Indian Hindus have a special ceremony, known as *annaprashan* (*mukhe bhaat* in Bengal), for when a baby eats its first meal of rice.

HABITS & CUSTOMS

Three main meals a day is the norm in India. Breakfast favourites include roti/chapattis with curried pulses, *channa puri* (chickpea curry and fried bread), hot *parathas,* dhal and rice, and *idli sambar* – steamed south Indian rice-flour patties with a hot, sour dipping sauce. In areas frequented by backpackers, you can find Western staples such as cornflakes, muesli, toast, porridge and pancakes – including the ubiquitous banana pancake.

Lunches tend to consist of dishes that can be eaten quickly – thalis, rice with sauces and snack meals at street stands. Dinner is usually the main meal of the day – curried vegetables or meat are served with rice or Indian breads, various side condiments and dhal. Traditionally, Indian finish meals with a pinch of *saunf* – see the sidebar, opposite. Another popular digestive is *paan* – see the boxed text, below.

City restaurants stay open till 10pm or later, but in rural areas, everything can shut down for the night as soon as it gets dark.

> Legend says that Buddha, after falling asleep during meditation, decided to cut his eyelids off in an act of penance. The lids grew into the tea plant, which, when brewed, banished sleep.

Food & Religion

Eating in India can be influenced by all sorts of religious taboos. Hindus avoid foods that are thought to inhibit physical and spiritual development – the taboo on eating beef is the most rigid restriction, as the cow is the spiritual vehicle of Shiva and therefore a sacred animal.

Devout Hindus (and Jains) also avoid alcohol and foods such as garlic and onions, which are thought to heat the blood and arouse sexual desire. Ashrams may also ban stimulating foods and desire-inflaming drinks such as hot chocolate, tea, coffee and fizzy soft drinks.

FLASH PAAN

India's favourite digestive, *paan* is a mildly intoxicating mix of betel nut (the fruit of the areca palm) and betel leaves (from an unrelated plant) mixed with alkali paste and chewed until a sensation of numbness creeps across the mouth. Chewing *paan* turns your saliva – and eventually your teeth and gums – a deep blood-red. Prolonged chewing has been linked to gum disease and oral cancer, but government attempts to ban *paan* have met fierce resistance from the public.

Once the mix starts to lose its flavour, the dregs are ejected into a spittoon – or more commonly onto the pavement. Those gouts of 'blood' seen on walls all over India are more likely to be *paan* juice. Some *paan* contains bitter-tasting tobacco or dried coconut – 'sweet *paan*' is sweetened with syrup, sugar or dried fruit. However you take it, *paan* is definitely an acquired taste, but every visitor to India should try it at least once.

Pork is taboo for Muslims and most adherents of the faith also avoid alcohol. Coffee and tea are also avoided by the devout. Halal is the term for all permitted foods, and haram for those prohibited. Fasting is considered an opportunity to earn the approval of Allah, to wipe the sin slate clean and to understand the suffering of the poor.

Jainism's central tenet is to avoid causing harm to any living creature. For this reason, Jains are vegetarian and also abstain from consuming dairy products and vegetables that grow underground because of the potential to harm insects during cultivation. Buddhists are more pragmatic – vegetarianism is common, but not a requirement.

India's Sikh, Christian and Parsi communities have few restrictions on what they can eat, but Adivasi communities in the northeast have their own complicated eating taboos, with proscriptions on pork, beef, poultry and eggs in some areas.

> Hindus offer ritual food known as *prasad* to the gods whenever they visit temples – priests hand out a palm-full of *prasad* to all visitors, but you should be careful of stomach upsets from contaminated offerings.

COOKING COURSES

Cooking courses are cropping up all over the country, though so far there are only a few to be found in the northeast. Kali Travel Home (see p119) in Kolkata gets consistently good reviews for its Bengali cooking classes. You could always try asking at your hotel to see if it can arrange a private class.

EAT YOUR WORDS
Useful Phrases
BENGALI

What would you recommend?	*Aapni ki kete bohlen?*
I'm vegetarian.	*Aami vejiterian.*
I'd like the … , please.	*Aami…, chai pleez.*
Please bring a/the …	*… aanen pleez*
bill	*bilta*
fork	*akta kata*
glass	*akta glash*
a glass of wine	*ak glash wain*
knife	*akta churi*
menu	*menuta*
mineral water	*mineral watar*
plate	*plet*
spoon	*akta chamuch*
I don't eat …	*Aami … kai na*
Could you prepare a meal without …?	*Aapni ki… chara kabar tohiri kohrte paaren?*
beef	*gohrur mangshoh*
fish	*maach*
meat	*maangshoh*
meat stock	*mangsher stok*
pork	*shuohrer mangshoh*
poultry	*hash murgi*
I'm allergic to…	*Aamar… e alarji aache*
nuts	*baadam*
seafood	*maach*
shellfish	*chingri maach*
That was delicious.	*Kub moja chiloh.*

HINDI

What would you recommend?	*Aap ke kyaal meng kyaa achchaa hogaa?*
I'm (a) vegetarian.	*Main hoong shaakaahaaree.*
I'd like the ... , please.	*Muje ... chaahiye.*
Please bring a/the ...	*... laaiye*
bill	*bil*
fork	*kaangtaa*
glass	*glaas*
glass of wine	*sharaab kee kaa glaas*
knife	*chaakoo*
menu	*menyoo*
mineral water	*minral vaatar*
plate	*plet*
spoon	*chammach*
I don't eat ...	*Maing ... naheeng kaataa/kaatee (m/f).*
Could you prepare a meal without ...?	*Kyaa aap ... ke binaa kaanaa taiyaar kar sakte/saktee haing? (m/f).*
beef	*gaay ke gosht*
fish	*machlee*
meat stock	*gosht ke staak*
pork	*suar ke gosht*
poultry	*murgee*
red meat (goat)	*bakree ka gosht*
I'm allergic to ...	*Muje ... kee elarjee hai.*
nuts	*meve*
seafood	*machlee*
shellfish	*shelfish*
That was delicious.	*Kub moja chiloh.*

Food & Drink Glossary

achar – pickle
aloo – potato; also *alu*
aloo tikka – mashed potato patty
appam – south Indian rice pancake, also *uttapam*

badam – nuts, usually almond
baigan – eggplant/aubergine; also known as brinjal
barfi – fudgelike sweet made from milk
bhajia – vegetable fritter
bhindi – okra
bhujia – gram-flour noodles
biryani – fragrant spiced steamed rice with meat or vegetables

chaat – Indian-style spiced salad, often prepared with *namkin*
chai – tea
channa – spiced chickpeas
chapati – round unleavened Indian-style bread; also known as roti
chatni – chutney
chawal – rice

dahi – curd/yoghurt
dhal – curried lentil dish; a staple food of India
dhansak – Parsi sauce with curried lentils and rice
dopiaza – a rich curry sauce with double *(do)* onions *(piaza)*
dosa – south Indian lentil-flour pancake

falooda – rose-flavoured drink made with milk, cream, nuts and noodles
farsan – savoury nibbles

ghee – clarified butter
gobi – cauliflower
gosht – lamb or mutton, sometimes called 'josh'
gulab jamun – deep-fried balls of dough soaked in rose-flavoured syrup

halwa – soft sweetmeat made with nuts and fruit

idli – south Indian spongy, round, fermented rice cake

jaggery – hard, brown, sugarlike sweetener made from palm sap
jal jeera – a salted lemon juice drink with cumin
jalebi – orange-coloured whorls of deep-fried batter dunked in sugar syrup

karela – bitter gourd
keema – spiced minced meat
kheer – creamy rice pudding
kofta – balls of minced vegetables or meat
korma – a creamy sauce with curd and ground nuts
kulfi – flavoured (often with pistachio) firm-textured ice cream

ladoo – sweetmeat ball made with gram flour and semolina; also *ladu*
lassi – refreshing yoghurt-and-iced-water drink

maachli – fish
methi – fenugreek
misthi dhoi – Bengali sweet; curd sweetened with *jaggery*
mithai – Indian sweets
momo – Tibetan steamed or fried dumpling stuffed with vegetables or meat
Mughlai – used for any number of meat sauces from the central plains
murg – chicken; also *murgi*
murli – white radish

naan – tandoor-cooked flat bread
namak – salt
namkin – savoury nibbles

pakora – vegetables fried in lentil-flour batter, also spelt *pakoda*
paneer – soft, unfermented cheese made from milk curd
pani – water
pappadam – thin pulse-flour crisps; also *papad*
paratha – Indian-style flaky fried bread
pilaf – see *pulao*
pulao – rice cooked in stock and flavoured with spices; also *pulau* or *pilaf*
puri – flat savoury dough that puffs up when deep fried; also *poori*

raita – mildly spiced yoghurt with fruit or vegetables
rasam – *dhal*-based broth flavoured with tamarind
rasgulla – sweet little balls of cream cheese flavoured with rose water
rogan josh – rich, spicy lamb curry

saag – leafy greens
sabzi – vegetables
sambar – soupy south Indian mustard and tamarind sauce
samosa – deep-fried pastry triangles filled with spiced vegetables/meat
sev – crisp, vermicelli-like gram-flour noodles
saunf/sonf – fennel seeds, used as a digestive and mouth freshener after meals

tandoor – clay oven
tawa – flat hotplate/iron griddle
thali – all-you-can-eat plate meals, served on a compartmentalised plate
thukpa – Tibetan noodle soup
tiffin – snack; also refers to meal container often made of stainless steel
tikka – spiced, marinated chunks of chicken, *paneer* etc
toddy – alcoholic drink, tapped from palm trees
tsampa – Tibetan staple of roast barley flour

uttappam – south Indian rice pancake, also *appam*

vada – south Indian deep-fried lentil ring-doughnut

Environment

THE LAND

Few countries on earth offer such a breathtaking variety of landscapes as India. The terrain climbs from waterlogged marshlands and arid deserts, through steamy jungles and dense pine and rhododendron forests, to the snowy heights of the Himalaya. Most of these environments are represented in the northeast, with one important addition – the salty, estuarine rivulets and islands of the Sunderbans – the vast delta where the Hooghly, the Brahmaputra and the Ganges empty into the Bay of Bengal.

The Himalaya

Creating an impregnable boundary between India and its neighbours to the north, the ice-capped peaks of the Himalaya are the highest mountains on earth. Interestingly, the Himalaya is also one of the youngest mountain ranges in the world – this enormous ridge began to rise about 80 million years ago, when Laurasia, the main landmass in the northern hemisphere, tore away from Gondwanaland in the southern hemisphere.

The Indian landmass was pulled across the divide by plate tectonics and thrust against the soft sedimentary crust of Laurasia, buckling the plate upwards to form the Himalaya. The Indo-Australian plate is still sliding under the Eurasian plate at a rate of 67mm per year, adding 5mm to the height of the Himalaya every 12 months.

Fossils of 150 million-year-old sea creatures can still be found at 5000m in the Himalaya – proof that these rocks once lay at the bottom of the Tethys Sea.

The Northeast Hills

To the northeast, India is screened from the plains of Myanmar (Burma) by a range of densely folded hills, marking the point of impact between the Indian and Eurasian plates. Rising abruptly from the plains, the Naga, Manipur and Chin Hills are drained by dozens of rivers that empty into the Bay of Bengal. The entire region was once densely forested, but deforestation through logging and slash-and-burn agriculture is altering the landscape at an alarming rate.

Floating between Assam and Bangladesh is the soaring Meghalaya Plateau, a limestone massif thrust upwards by tectonic forces and eroded into wild shapes by the world's highest annual rainfall – a staggering 12,000mm per year.

There is a strong cultural divide between the Indian plains and the hills – an idea played up in Rudyard Kipling's culturally fascinating *Plain Tales from the Hills*, first published in Kolkata (Calcutta) in 1888.

The Bengal & Assamese Plains

Dotted with small villages, rice paddies and patches of jungle, the vast plains of central India wash out into the rain-drenched wetlands of Assam and West Bengal. Snaking west through Assam, the Brahmaputra River is the lifeblood of the northeast, rising as the Yaluzangbu in Tibet and merging with the Ganges before flowing into the Bay of Bengal in Bangladesh.

The people of the northeast have a love-hate relationship with the Brahmaputra. Every monsoon, the river swells and bursts its banks, destroying villages and roads but flooding the rice paddies with mineral-rich silt. Even in the dry season, the river can reach 10km wide. In recent years, the Indian government has harnessed many of the tributaries of the Brahmaputra to provide hydroelectric power for the northeast.

The Coast

Sprawling across the border between India and Bangladesh, the salt marshes of the Sunderbans (opposite) are covered by the largest mangrove forest in the world, sprawling over thousands of swampy islands in the delta of the

THE STAGGERING SUNDERBANS

Unsurveyed until 1911, the Sunderbans is the world's largest mangrove forest, covering 4143 sq km of islands and sandbars and 1874 sq km of rivers, creeks and inlets. Straddling the border between West Bengal and Bangladesh, this primordial forest used to be even bigger, but human expansion has reduced tree cover by 40% over the last century. The main threats to the Sunderbans are firewood gathering and shrimp farming, which also affects fish stocks in the Bay of Bengal by reducing the nursery grounds available to wild species.

The dominant tree in the Sunderbans is the *sundari* – a hardy, mangrove species whose wood is much sought-after for boat building and fuel. *Sundari* trees have evolved special techniques for dealing with the intense salinity of the water – including the ability to excrete salt through their leaves. Since 2001 the Sunderbans has been protected as a Unesco International Biosphere Reserve for its incredible biodiversity; at the last count, the mangroves were home to 334 plant species, 120 fish species, 35 types of reptiles, 270 bird species and 42 mammal species, including 30,000 spotted deer and 289 royal Bengal tigers.

The *baghs* (tigers) of the Sunderbans are the most notorious man-eaters in India, killing some 100 humans a year, most of them wood collectors, honey gatherers and fisherfolk. The tigers have such a fearsome reputation that local villagers wear masks of faces on the back of their heads whenever they enter the forest in order to trick tigers into thinking they are being watched. Officials from the Sunderbans Tiger Reserve go one step further, with spiked body armour and neck braces to offset the very real risk of attack.

Visitors can spot tigers from boat tours through the creeks. See p139 for information.

Hooghly and Brahmaputra rivers. Malaria, human-eating tigers and a lack of fresh water all serve to keep human habitation to a minimum.

Heading south from the Sunderbans, the coast becomes drier and the swamps give way to shallow sandy beaches. Most of Orissa is a flat alluvial plain, used for intense rice cultivation, but patches of forest remain on the Chota Nagpur Plateau in the north and west of the state.

WILDLIFE

With a staggering 89,451 recorded species of fauna, India has some of the richest biodiversity in the world. Wildlife-watching has become one of the country's prime tourist activities, but many of the creatures that inspired *The Jungle Book* can now only be seen in India's national parks – see p86 for a list of national parks and sanctuaries in the northeast and the best times to visit them.

For an evocative introduction to the Sunderbans, read Amitav Ghosh's The Hungry Tide, a thoughtful exploration of the conflict between man and nature.

Animals

Indian wildlife is fascinating and diverse, but all of India's wild animals are threatened by habitat loss, poaching, hunting for bush meat, and pollution – all consequences of the relentless growth of India's human population.

LOWLAND ANIMALS

The jungles of the northeast provide shelter for a menagerie of animals that define the subcontinent – elephants, monkeys, leopards, rhinos and, of course, the royal Bengal tiger. Unfortunately, almost all of these large mammals are threatened by hunting and human competition for land, water and other resources.

South of Kolkata (Calcutta), the vast Sunderbans delta provides a home to tigers (see p139), wild boars, deer and countless species of bird and snakes. Chitals (spotted deer – the main prey species for tigers) have evolved the ability to secrete salt from their glands to cope with the inhospitable, salt-laden environment.

The World Wide Fund for Nature (WWF; www .wwfindia.org) promotes environmental protection and wildlife conservation in India; see its website for offices around the country.

FAREWELL TIGER?

The star animal of the Indian subcontinent, the royal Bengal tiger faces a growing threat from the trade in animal parts for Chinese medicine and the smuggling of furs for traditional Tibetan costumes. Officially, tigers are protected by the Convention on International Trade in Endangered Species (Cites; www.cites.org), but a whole tiger carcass can fetch upwards of US$10,000 on the black market, providing a powerful incentive for poachers.

Although there is no evidence that tiger medicines are effective, spurious health benefits are linked to every part of the tiger, from the teeth to the penis, which is said to increase sexual vigour. China has recently suggested allowing tigers to be farmed on a commercial basis, a decision that would massively increase the demand for parts from wild tigers.

The last census of Indian tigers in 2008 used hidden cameras to record tiger numbers instead of the discredited pugmark-counting technique. Their conclusions were sobering. Nationwide statistics suggested a 50% drop in the number of tigers over five years to just 1400 animals. Conservationists have suggested that the current population of tigers in the Sunderbans (p139) may be as low as 50 individuals – less than a fifth of the 'official' count of 289.

The India-wide tiger population is now too low to maintain a viable gene pool. However, a recent study of the 15,000 tigers in captivity worldwide has suggested that there is still enough variety in the global tiger population to preserve the genetic integrity of the species. This would require a massive breeding program, and worldwide action to stop habitat loss through human overpopulation and the trade in tiger parts.

The waterways of the Sunderbans are home to saltwater crocodiles, sea turtles and deadly bull sharks, who swim upriver from the Bay of Bengal. Locals claim that for every 10 people killed in the Sunderbans, five are pounced on by tigers, three are dragged under by crocodiles and two end up in the bellies of sharks. In past centuries, Hindu zealots threw themselves into the shark-infested waters off Sagar Island (p141) to be consumed as human sacrifices.

The jungles of Orissa and the Northeast States provide shelter for tigers, leopards, panthers, clouded leopards, jungle cats, civet cats, sloth bears and numerous species of deer and antelope, including sambar and the tiny muntjac (barking deer), whose hoarse call rings through the forest at dusk.

Guar (an ancestor of the modern water buffalo) are found in forests across the northeast, and *mithun* – another wild buffalo domesticated by Adivasis (tribal people) – can be seen in Nagaland and Arunachal Pradesh. *Mithun* and buffalo horns are widely used as decoration on traditional Adivasi houses.

Wild elephants are found in several national parks in Orissa, Assam and West Bengal, and domesticated elephants are used for forestry in some parts of the northeast. The endangered one-horned Indian rhinoceros – *Rhinoceros unicornis* (literally 'nose horn one horn') in Latin – is the signature species of Assam's Kaziranga National Park (see p213). Smaller numbers of rhinos are also found in nearby Manas National Park (p210), Pobitora National Park (p210) and the Jaldhapara Wildlife Sanctuary in West Bengal (p149).

Gangetic dolphins – one of the rarest mammals of all – are still found in the Brahmputra. Around 200 are thought to range along the river, hunting by sonar through the turgid, silt-filled waters.

ANIMALS OF THE HIMALAYA

The Himalaya harbours its own range of hardy creatures. Yaks are a common beast of burden in northern Arunachal Pradesh and Sikkim. Officially, only males can be called yaks – the proper name for female yaks is *dri*. To make things more complicated, most 'yaks' are actually *dzo* (male) or *dzomo* (female) – a cross between yaks and domestic cattle.

For more on the fate of tigers in the Sunderbans, point your web browser towards www.sundarban tigerproject.info or http://projecttiger.nic.in /sundarbans.htm.

India's national animal is the tiger, its national bird is the peacock and its national flower is the lotus. The national emblem of India is a column topped by three Asiatic lions.

Wild herbivores of the Himalaya include urial (wild sheep) and bharal (blue sheep), kiang (Tibetan wild ass), Himalayan ibex (a graceful mountain antelope), Himalayan tahr (mountain goat) and the rare chiru (Tibetan antelope), which is threatened by hunting for its soft fur, which is used to made shahtoosh shawls.

Perhaps the most endangered herbivore of all is the diminutive musk-deer, hunted almost to extinction for the scent produced by glands in its abdomen. Another animal just clinging on in the bamboo thickets of the eastern Himalaya is the red panda, a member of the racoon family, which survives on a diet of young bamboo shoots.

Predators of the Himalaya include black and brown bears and the desperately rare snow leopard. Tiny populations cling on in Sikkim and Arunachal Pradesh but these perfectly adapted predators are almost never seen, even by the scientists who study them.

You may recognise the Indian names for animals such as the tiger (*bagh*, or *sher* from the Persian), elephant (*haathi*) and bear (*bahlu*) from Rudyard Kipling's *The Jungle Book*.

PRIMATES

Monkeys are probably the most common wild animal you will see in the northeast, particularly in the hills. Monkeys are tolerated by locals, if not exactly adored, because of their connection to the monkey-god Hanuman, loyal friend of Rama in the Ramayana.

Primates of the northeast range from the extremely rare hoolock gibbon and slow loris to species that are so common as to be a pest, most notably the stocky and aggressive rhesus macaque. These simian hoodlums wander around hill stations and temples in huge gangs, making daring raids to steal bananas and other snacks from humans who let down their guard.

Other monkeys to look out for include the elegant grey langur and the golden langur – a slender, graceful monkey with golden orange fur and a famously calm temperament. Tame golden langurs can be seen at the Umananda Mandir in Guwahati (p205).

REPTILES & AMPHIBIANS

India has 238 species of snake, and 50 of these slithering serpents are poisonous, including the legendary king cobra, the world's largest venomous snake. These monster snakes hunt in the rice paddies and jungles of the northeast, feeding mainly on other snakes. Snake charmers prefer to take their chances with the smaller Indian cobra, which has a distinctive flared hood. Other poisonous snakes include the krait, Russell's viper and the saw-scaled viper.

Constrictors include the reticulated python and the gigantic Indian python, which can reach 9m in length. In the wild, pythons feed on anything they can squeeze into their coils, including deer and wild pigs, domestic dogs, cats and livestock. The northeast is also home to the remarkable flying snake, which can flatten its body to glide between the treetops.

India has hundreds of species of toad, frog, tortoise and terrapin. In ponds and temple tanks, you may spot the huge and ponderous Indian softshell turtle, which is often deliberately introduced to keep the waters free from mosquito larvae and other pests.

The Indian cobra is also known as the spectacled cobra because of the distinctive 'eye-glasses' pattern on the back of its hood.

India boasts several species of crocodile – the English word 'mugger' is derived from the Hindi term for these stealthy predators. The brackish waterways of the Sunderbans (p81) and Bhitarkanika Wildlife Sanctuary (p275) are the hunting ground of the saltwater crocodile, which can grow to 5m in length. The curious-looking gharial, with its narrow snout evolved for eating fish, has been pulled back from extinction by conservation projects in central India – small numbers of animals are also thought to live in the Brahamputra.

SLIPPERY SPIRITS

In Indian folklore, snakes are revered as relatives of the *nagas* – half-human, half-snake deities who control the rains. Snake-worship is still common among the Adivasis (tribal people) of Orissa, and people across the subcontinent make offerings to snakes during the festival of Nag Panchami (p18), which coincides with the time of year when snakes and humans are driven together by the monsoon floods and snake bites are most common.

The snake crops up repeatedly in Indian mythology. Shiva is often depicted with a cobra around his neck, a symbol of fertility, and Vishnu reclines on the coils of Ananta-Shesha, the 1000-headed serpent, who carries the planets of the universe on his hoods. The Buddha is often depicted on a similar scaly bed. Christians in the northeast associate the snake with the serpent from the Garden of Eden, while animists regard snakes as deities who should be respected and propitiated to ensure a swift end to the monsoon.

BIRDS

The abode of hornbills, herons and hill mynas, the northeast is an ornithologists paradise. Exotic species can be spotted in the most mundane of situations – storks roost on the top of telegraph poles, and telephone wires are lit up like Christmas garlands by iridescent flycatchers and kingfishers. For the best birdwatching opportunities, visit the reserves listed in the boxed text, p92.

Each area of the northeast has its own signature species. The lakes of Orissa attract hundreds of species of migratory bird, including cranes, herons, ospreys and flamingos, while the hill forests of the Northeast States are home to the great Indian hornbill, the largest of all hornbills. Hornbill beaks are used as ornamentation by many Adivasis in Nagaland and Arunachal Pradesh.

In the foothills of the Himalaya, including in Arunachal Pradesh and Sikkim, look out for the striking monal pheasant. Female birds of this species are a dowdy brown, whereas males shimmer in purple, green and gold. Other notable birds include storks, parrots, rare francolins and floricans, and the Steppe eagle and griffon vulture, both of which are often spotted soaring over the foothills of the Himalaya.

> Must-have books for birdwatchers include the *Pocket Guide to Birds of the Indian Subcontinent* by Richard Grimmett, Carol Inskipp and Tim Inskipp; *A Birdwatchers' Guide to India* by Krys Kazmierczak and Raj Singh; and *The Book of Indian Birds* by Salim Ali.

ENDANGERED SPECIES

More than 120 species of Indian mammal appeared on the 2008 'Red List' of threatened animals produced by the **International Union for the Conservation of Nature** (IUCN; www.iucnredlist.org). Tigers, elephants and rhinos were all on the list, alongside the hundreds of species of plant, insect, bird, fish, reptile and amphibian that are also fighting for their very survival.

In 1972 the Wildlife Protection Act was introduced to stem the abuse of wildlife, followed by a string of similar pieces of legislation with bold ambitions but few teeth with which to enforce them. **Project Tiger** (http://projecttiger.nic.in), founded in 1973, was hailed as the big success story of Indian conservation. However, conservation groups have accused wardens of exaggerating tiger numbers and being complicit in poaching. Today, the main threats to wildlife continue to be habitat loss due to human encroachment and poaching by Adivasis, insurgents and squatter farmers.

> In the early 20th century there were believed to be at least 40,000 wild tigers in India. Current estimates suggest there are fewer than 1500.

Conservation in the northeast is complicated by the fact that many species – and many poachers – roam across international borders. Many Adivasis hunt rare species for bush meat and for horns, feathers and teeth used in Adivasi costumes, and pelts, bones, ivory and rhino horns are smuggled across the border to China and Tibet for use in Chinese medicine (see the boxed text, p82). Think twice before you support this trade by buying souvenirs made from animal parts.

In the water, the freshwater dolphins of the Brahmaputra are in dire straits from pollution and human competition, with gill-net fishing and hydroelectric dams being major threats. The sea turtle population on the Orissa coast also faces problems; see the boxed text, p269.

Plants

India's total forest cover is estimated to be around 20% of its total land area, although the Forestry Survey of India has set an optimistic target of 33% forest cover by 2012. The country boasts 49,219 plant species, of which around 5200 are endemic. Among these species are many plants used in ayurveda (traditional herbal medicine), which have the potential to open the door to new medical treatments.

Tropical forests occur in the hills of the Northeast States, and large areas of savannah and jungle are found in lowland areas of Assam, West Bengal, Tripura and Orissa. Distinctive trees of the lowlands include the hardwood sal, whose sturdy leaves are used as naturally biodegradable plates.

Religious sites are frequently marked by pipal or banyan trees, with their dangling aerial roots. Mangoes have been cultivated in India since at least 2000 BC and many believe that the original mango tree came from the northeast. All these species face a challenge from introduced species such as the eucalyptus, a water-hungry species introduced by the British to dry out malarial swamps.

The foothills of the Himalaya preserve classic alpine species, including blue pine and deodar (Himalayan cedars), and deciduous forests of apple, chestnut, birch, plum rhododendron and cinnamon. Hardy plants such as anemones, edelweiss and gentians grow above the tree-line, while rare orchids and other wildflowers appear every summer in high mountain meadows.

NATIONAL PARKS & WILDLIFE SANCTUARIES

Although the northeast is caught up in India's population explosion, this was always one of the least inhabited parts of the country. Away from large population centres in West Bengal, Assam and Orissa, there are still large areas of pristine, untouched wilderness, many of them preserved as national parks and wildlife sanctuaries.

India has more than 90 national parks, more than 500 animal sanctuaries (including the 28 tiger reserves established as part of Project Tiger; see opposite), and dozens of smaller reserves and protected forests preserving nearly 5% of the surface area of the country. An additional 19 areas in the northeast are under consideration as new national parks, including six reserves in Arunachal Pradesh.

In addition to the official parks and reserves, six areas have been designated as biosphere reserves – the Sunderbans in West Bengal, Khangchendzonga in Sikkim, Similipal in Orissa, Nokrek in Meghalaya, and Manas and Dibru-Saikhowa in Assam, which provide safe migration channels for wildlife across international borders.

For information on parks and reserves commonly visited by travellers in the northeast see the boxed text, p86 – but there are many more; see the list of parks on www.indianwildlifeportal.com/national-parks for some ideas. As well as providing a financial incentive for locals to preserve wildlife, visiting one of India's nature reserves will provide you with a healthy reminder that human beings are not always at the top of the evolutionary ladder.

Wildlife reserves tend to be off the beaten track and infrastructure can be limited – book transport and accommodation in advance, and check

The Wildlife Protection Society of India (www.wpsi-india.org) is a prominent wildlife conservation organisation that campaigns for animal welfare through education, lobbying and legal action against poachers.

See our Indian Safari itinerary (p24) for recommended national parks. Otherwise, pick up a copy of *Indian National Parks & Sanctuaries* by Anand Khati or *Handbook of National Parks, Wildlife Sanctuaries and Biosphere Reserves in India* by SS Negi.

As well as the protected reserves, be sure to check out Chilika Lake in Orissa (p266), one of India's premier spots for birdwatching.

MAJOR NATIONAL PARKS & WILDLIFE SANCTUARIES

Park/Sanctuary	Page	Location	Features	Best time to visit
Badrama Wildlife Sanctuary	p274	near Sambalpur, Orissa	hill forests around the Hirakud reservoir: deer, antelope, sloth bears, langur monkeys & migratory birds in winter	Oct-May
Balpakhram National Park	p247	near Baghmara, Meghalaya	elevated deciduous forests: elephants, tigers, hoolock gibbons, deer, hornbills & pitcher plants	Oct-May
Bhitarkanika Wildlife Sanctuary	p275	northeast Orissa	estuarine mangrove forests: saltwater crocodiles, water monitors, pythons, wild boars & chitals	Dec-Feb
Chandaka Wildlife Sanctuary	p258	eastern Orissa	upland forest: elephants, leopards, chitals, sambar & crocodiles	Oct-May
Debrigarh Wildlife Sanctuary	p274	near Sambalpur, Orissa	dry deciduous forest: tigers, leopards, deer, boars, sloth bears & bird life	Oct-May
Jaldhapara Wildlife Sanctuary	p149	northern West Bengal	forest & grasslands: Indian one-horned rhinos, deer & elephants	mid-Oct–May
Kaziranga National Park	p213	Assam, Northeast States	dense grasslands & swamp: rhinos, deer, buffalo, elephants, tigers & bird life	Feb-Mar
Maenam Wildlife Sanctuary	p187	near Ravangla, Sikkim	hill forests from 2300m to 3200m: red pandas, serow, deer & eye-catching pheasants	Mar-May, Sep-Nov
Manas National Park	p210	near Guwahati, Assam	lowland forest & rivers: tigers, deer, rare birds, langurs, hispid hare & pygmy hog	Feb-Mar
Nameri National Park	p213	near Tezpur, Assam	forests & riverside grasslands: deer, tigers, bear, leopards, birdwatching walks & rafting trips	Nov-Apr
Pobitora National Park	p210	near Guwahati, Assam	riverside forest & grassland: rhinos, viewed on elephant safaris	Feb-Mar
Sepahijala Wildlife Sanctuary	p238	near Agartala, Tripura	lakeside forests: spectacled monkeys & migratory birds in winter	Oct-Mar
Similipal National Park	p274	Balasore, Orissa	forest & waterfalls: tigers, leopards, elephants, crocodiles & bird life	Nov-Jun
Sunderbans Tiger Reserve	p139	southern West Bengal	mangrove forests: tigers, deer, monkeys & bird life	Oct-Mar

opening times, permit requirements and entry fees before you visit. Visits in the monsoon are complicated by rain-drenched trails. For more on wildlife safaris, see p92.

ENVIRONMENTAL ISSUES

With more than one billion people, expanding industrialisation and urbanisation, widespread poverty and corruption, and chemical-intensive agriculture, India faces more challenges than most countries when it comes to environmental protection. An estimated 65% of India's land is degraded in some way, and the government has fallen short on almost all of its targets for environmental protection.

The government has introduced dozens of environmental laws in recent years, but companies – including state-owned corporations – continue to flout the rules. In 2006, several plants operated by the Indian Oil Corporation (IOC) in Assam were threatened with closure after discharging polluted wastewater into the Brahmaputra, and in 2009, the Wildlife Society of Orissa accused the IOC of ignoring safety protocols after a major oil spill close to the turtle sanctuary at Gahirmatha Beach. Along with local wildlife, the people most affected are low-caste rural farmers and Adivasis who have limited political representation and few resources to fight the commercial ambitions of big business.

Get the low-down on Indian environmental issues at Down to Earth (www.downtoearth.org .in), an online magazine that delves into stories overlooked by the mainstream media.

Air pollution in many Indian cities has been measured at more than double the maximum safe level recommended by the World Health Organization.

RESPONSIBLE TRAVEL

The northeast is often described as the most unspoiled part of India, but overpopulation is bringing more and more people into conflict with nature and with each other, and government policy invariably prioritises development over environmental and cultural concerns.

As anywhere, tourists tread a fine line between providing an incentive for positive change and making the problem worse. Always consider your environmental and cultural impact as you travel, particularly around the northeast.

Environmental Considerations

Make a positive contribution to the environment by giving your money to businesses that operate according to sound environmental principles. Look for accommodation options and tour agencies that minimise their environmental impact through recycling and the use of sustainable resources. Safaris run by national parks are usually formulated with the best interests of the wildlife in mind.

If you go walking in wilderness areas, follow the recommendations for responsible trekking on p96. Sikkim and other mountain areas have banned plastic bags – help out by refusing plastic packaging wherever possible. Purifying your own water will always win you a gold star (see p348).

Cultural Considerations

When touring Adivasi (tribal) areas, be aware of your influence on local people. Your very presence in remote areas may be one of factors driving people to abandon traditional customs. Seek out tour companies that employ local villagers as guides and that reinvest profits from tours into sustainable development programs. One innovative scheme is the Manas Maozigendri (MMES; p211) project in Assam, which employs former Bodo insurgents to protect the forest from poachers.

Volunteering can be one way to make a positive contribution to the well-being of people in the northeast; see p323.

Useful Resources

For more tips on responsible travel, visit www.responsible-travel.org, or view the web-based Responsible Travel Guidebook at www.worldexpeditions.com.

India's environmental problems are depressingly familiar. Between 11% and 27% of India's agricultural output is lost due to soil degradation through over-farming and loss of tree cover – a particular problem in the Northeast States. Pollution from industry, human habitation and agricultural chemicals is further affecting the health and quality of life for India's rural poor.

The human cost is heart-rending – crushing levels of debt and poverty drive hundreds of farmers to suicide every year. Lurking behind all these problems is a basic Malthusian truth: there are simply too many people for India to support at its current level of development. While the Indian government could undoubtedly do more, some share of blame must also fall on Western farm subsidies that artificially reduce the cost of imported produce, undermining prices for Indian farmers.

Noise pollution in major cities has been measured at over 90 decibels – more than one and a half times the recognised 'safe' limit. Bring earplugs!

Pollution

Spend five minutes in Kolkata or any large Indian city and you will start to feel the effects of the choking air pollution caused by industry and vehicle emissions. Indian diesel reportedly contains around 50 to 200 times more sulphur than European diesel and the ageing engines of Indian vehicles would fail most emissions tests in Europe or the USA.

Delhi and Mumbai (Bombay) have switched their public transport systems to less-polluting Compressed Natural Gas (CNG), but plans to extend the scheme to Kolkata have been held up by wrangles over cost. In the meantime, some 70% of Kolkata residents continue to suffer from respiratory diseases triggered by atmospheric pollution.

Industry remains one of the biggest polluters in the northeast. Factories share space with residential housing in most large cities and government controls on emissions are almost nonexistent. Watercourses across the northeast are polluted by chemical run-off from factories and agricultural land, killing wildlife and causing toxic algal blooms.

In 2008, the worst floods in 50 years left more than three million people homeless in Assam, Bihar and southern Nepal.

Many of the problems seen today are a direct result of the Green Revolution of the 1960s, when a quantum leap in agricultural output was achieved using chemical fertilisers and pesticides (for which Western agrochemical companies must take a share of responsibility). Ironically, the use of genetically modified (GM) crops is reducing dependence on chemical pesticides, while increasing dependence on Western seed producers.

The massive growth of budget air travel is also pumping ever more greenhouse gas into the atmosphere – modern ideas such as carbon balancing hold little truck in a nation embracing the freedom of the skies for the first time. Domestic air travel in India is growing by 30% to 40% every year, despite the impact of global fuel prices and the economic downturn.

Climate Change

Changing global climate patterns, which many experts link to soaring carbon emissions, have been creating dangerous extremes of weather across the northeast. India stands behind most Western nations in the global league of per capita carbon emissions, but as a consequence of its massive population, the subcontinent is one the largest overall polluters, and one of the regions that is likely to suffer most from of the effects of climate change.

More than 70% of Indian-grown tea is consumed within India, and chai-wallahs (tea vendors) are being particularly hit by soaring tea prices, linked to changing weather patterns.

Elevated monsoon rainfall is already causing widespread flooding and destruction across the northeast, with Kolkata and the Assam plains being particularly affected. Kolkata's flood defences consist of earth embankments along the Hooghly, similar to the measures which failed to protect New Orleans during Hurricane Katrina.

The problem is not limited to the plains. Hill towns in West Bengal and Sikkim have experienced devastating landslides, while whole islands in the Sunderbans delta have been inundated by rising sea levels. In coastal areas, rising salinity has damaged farmland and killed off endangered species, a problem exacerbated in Orissa by a series of devastating cyclones in recent years.

Changing weather patterns and rising global temperatures are also increasing the rate of glaciers melting in the Himalaya, with severe effects downstream. In 2008, floods swept into Assam after hydroelectric dams overflowed in Bhutan and Arunachal Pradesh. In the same year, more than one million people were made homeless in Bihar by flooding on the Sapt Kosi River in Nepal. In mountain areas, glacial lakes are swelling to dangerous levels, increasing the risk of sudden, deadly flash floods triggered by earthquakes or landslides.

Conversely, other areas are experiencing reduced rainfall, causing drought and panic over access to water supplies. Drought has even reached the Khasi Hills of Meghalaya, formerly the wettest place on earth. Tea production in Assam – which produces 70% of India's tea – fell by 10% in the 2008–9 winter harvest as a result of reduced winter rainfall, pushing global tea prices to record levels. To make matters worse, Assam's economically important oil industry has been accused of dumping waste water into rivers, polluting tea gardens and rural farmland. Several of Assam's largest oil refineries were threatened with closure by the Assam Pollution Control Board in 2007 after releasing discharge with five times the permitted levels of pollutants into local rivers.

India's Ministry of Environment & Forests (http://envfor.nic.in) was originally established by the British to promote the rapid commercial exploitation of forest resources.

Changing weather patterns have affected other crops, pushing up the price of essential foodstuffs. In 2008, the Indian government took the radical step of banning the export of all forms of rice except basmati, to ensure affordable rice for Indian families.

Deforestation

Since the 1960s, a third of Bengal's mangrove forests have been cleared and the damming of rivers for irrigation and hydroelectric power has dramatically reduced the flow of fresh water into the Sunderbans Reserve. Rising levels of salinity are now threatening many rare species of plant and animal, and the loss of mangroves is reducing the nursery grounds for the fish that stock the Bay of Bengal.

India's first Five Year Plan in 1951 recognised the importance of forests for soil conservation, and various policies have been introduced over the following decades to increase forest cover. Almost all have been flouted by officials, criminals and by ordinary people clearing forests for firewood and allowing grazing in forest areas. Try to minimise the use of wood-burning stoves while you travel – particularly while trekking in the mountains of Sikkim.

By far the biggest threat to forestry in the northeast is firewood harvesting, particularly by illegal squatters. Since Partition in 1947, tens of thousands of landless peasants have flooded across the border from Nepal and Bangladesh, settling in wilderness areas across the northeast. Traditional slash-and-burn agriculture has also had a devastating effect on forestry, particularly in Nagaland, Mizoram, Manipur and Arunachal Pradesh.

The loss of forest cover has led to a marked increase in erosion and landslides during the monsoon, and rainfall quickly leeches the nutrients out of exposed soil, driving farmers to clear ever larger areas of forest. There are knock-on effects in the lowlands, such as increased drainage from the hills and deadly floods, which are becoming more common.

The Dalai Lama, the spiritual leader of Tibetan Buddhism, is an ardent campaigner on environmental issues – read some of his environmental teachings at www .dalailama.com.

The problems are particularly acute in Orissa, where marginalised Adivasi communities are forced to practise shifting agriculture (where land is cultivated and then abandoned) in order to survive. Clearing of woodland for cattle fodder and fuel has led to a massive increase in silt run-off into rivers and estuaries, choking important wetlands and reducing the volume of drinking water in many reservoirs.

Denotification, a process that allows states to relax the ban on the commercial exploitation of protected areas, is another factor. Officially, the states are supposed to earmark an equivalent area for afforestation, but many of these 'new forests' are used to grow oil palms for the production of biofuels, a form of forestry that dramatically increases the rate of carbon release from the soil. Following the example of Europe, India recently announced plans to source 20% of its diesel from biofuels by 2012, which is likely to dramatically increase the amount of old growth forest being cleared for oil palm plantations.

However, there are positive developments. Numerous charities are working with rural communities to encourage tree planting, and many religious and community leaders have joined the movement, including the Dalai Lama. Oxfam is currently funding a major scheme to plant 211,000 mango, papaya, guava, banana, drumstick, neem and *subadul* saplings in Bihar, Assam and West Bengal by 2011.

Plastic Waste

Although the average Indian uses 2kg of plastic per year; the average European gets through 60kg.

Ah, plastic! What a wonderful invention. Only a tiny proportion of plastic products can be reused or recycled and plastic rubbish can persist in the environment for 1000 years. Across the northeast, plastic bags and bottles litter streets, streams and beaches; animals choke on the waste and the plastic clogs water courses, increasing the risk of landslides and water-borne diseases. Campaigners estimate that about 75% of plastics used are discarded within a week and only 15% are recycled.

Travellers may feel that efforts to avoid plastic are futile when locals toss rubbish from every bus window, but Western companies are the driving

---

INDIA'S HYDROELECTRIC REVOLUTION

With an ever-increasing human population becoming ever hungrier for electric power, hydroelectricity has become big business, and nowhere more so than in Arunachal Pradesh. The state has the potential to supply a third of India's electricity needs and dozens of new hydroelectric plants have sprung up in locations along the tributaries of the Brahmaputra, turning falling water into tens of millions of rupees.

Unfortunately Indian hydroelectricity is not quite as green as it sounds. To create the new hydroelectric plants, whole valley systems are being flooded, displacing dozens of peoples from their ancestral homelands. Construction of the Subansiri Lower Project (SLP), India's largest dam, is set to displace 5000 people from the Apatani, Nishi and Hill Miri peoples. Ironically, only two villages are being destroyed by the dam itself; the rest will be displaced by a new forest reserve, designed to replace an existing forest reserve which is being submerged by the dam.

Unlike the Narmada Valley Development in central India, the SLP has no nationwide campaigns and no celebrities questioning the environmental impact of hydroelectric power. Few of the Adivasi (tribal) groups have the money to take on the combined forces of government and big business in the courts, and the land provided by the state government for relocation is frequently unsuitable for the traditional types of farming and forestry practised by Adivasi people.

However with the UN heavily promoting the projects as a tool for flood control, the construction of more dams in Arunachal Pradesh is almost a foregone conclusion. Plans are afoot for two more huge hydro-schemes on the upper Subansiri River – even though approval for the Subansiri Lower Project was only granted on the condition that no further dams would be built upstream.

force behind disposable plastic packaging. A massive proportion of the nonbiodegradable waste in the northeast is made up of disposable sachets of shampoo and other products, produced by Western companies for sale to developing nations whose inhabitants cannot afford large bottles.

However there are some welcome signs of change. Sikkim banned plastic bags in 1997 after several children died tragically in a landslide caused by a build up of discarded plastic bags, and Dhaka in Bangladesh followed suit in 2002. A similar ban in Darjeeling, Kalimpong and Kurseong finally came into force in March 2007. As well as reducing plastic waste, the ban has revived the fortunes of Bengal's ailing jute industry, which produced most of the bags used for packaging in India before the invention of the plastic bag.

You can do your bit to help by purifying your own water – see p348 – or carrying a canteen and obtaining refills of boiled or purified water from guest houses as you travel. Also set a good example by refusing plastic bags (and explaining why!) and, at train stations, insisting on soft drinks in recyclable glass bottles and tea in terracotta cups.

See http://bicn.com/acic for more information on Bengal's arsenic contamination crisis.

Water Resources

Arguably the biggest threat to public health in India is inadequate access to clean drinking water and proper sanitation. Sewage contamination of drinking water remains the main cause of communicable disease across the subcontinent. With India's population set to double by 2050, agricultural, industrial and domestic water usage are all expected to spiral, despite government policies designed to control water use.

The northeast is in the surprising position of suffering from both too much rainfall and droughts. Climate change is increasing levels of monsoon rainfall, causing flooding and landslides, but elevated areas have faced droughts because of increased drainage caused by deforestation.

The Subansiri Lower Project (SLP) has the capacity to produce 2000 megawatts of electricity – equivalent to three nuclear power stations.

In coastal areas, particularly in the Sunderbans, rising sea levels and damming of rivers for irrigation and hydroelectric power have led to a marked increase in water salinity. In Orissa the problem has been exacerbated by a series of tropical cyclones, bringing salt water far inland. Industry, farming and human habitation also contribute to the pollution of drinking water across the northeast.

In lowland areas of the northeast, including Tripura, Assam and West Bengal, villagers are being poisoned by water polluted with arsenic, which leeches out of the bedrock into wells and boreholes. Although the problem is much more widely reported in neighbouring Nepal and Bangladesh, arsenic poisoning is blamed for one in 10 deaths in areas with contaminated drinking water. As is the case elsewhere, the root of the problem is overpopulation, with more and more shallow wells being dug to provide water for squatter farmers.

Water distribution is another volatile issue. Since 1947 an estimated 35 million people in India have been displaced by major dams, mostly built for hydroelectricity projects to provide energy for this increasingly power-hungry nation. For more information, see the boxed text, opposite.

Activities

The northeast covers every imaginable terrain, from steamy swamps and jungles to the ice-gripped summits of the Himalaya. With all this to play with, the opportunities for adventurous activities are endless – take your pick from trekking, mountaineering, jungle safaris, elephant rides, white-water rafting…the list goes on and on. However, this is one of the frontiers of travel in south Asia and many activities must be arranged through tour agencies, which can increase the cost. Some of the most popular activities are covered in the following sections.

CHOOSING A TOUR OPERATOR

Regardless of what you decide to do, you need to exercise a little caution when choosing an operator. We receive regular reports of dodgy companies taking poorly equipped tourists into dangerous situations. Remember that travel agents are only middle-men and the final decisions about safety and equipment come down to the people actually operating the trip.

Check out all tour operators, trekking companies and activity providers carefully and make sure they have all the necessary safety equipment before you hand over your money. If anything is substandard, let the operator know. If they refuse to make the necessary changes, go with another company. For any activity, make sure that you have adequate insurance (see p310). Make sure that you know in advance what you are getting, then make sure that what you get matches what you paid for.

Where possible, stick to companies that provide activities themselves. If you go through an agency, look for an accredited operator – see the sidebar, left. Note that dodgy operators often change their names to sound like trusted companies, or display signs claiming to offer 'tourist information'. It's a good idea to consult the official state or national tourism offices for recommendations of approved operators, or talk to fellow travellers for first-hand advice.

> Better travel agencies are licensed by the Travel Agents Association of India (www.travelagents ofindia.com), the Indian Association of Tour Operators (www.iato.in) or the Adventure Tour Operators Association of India (www.atoai.org).

OUTDOOR ACTIVITIES

Having come to one of the great travel frontiers of Asia, it makes sense to get out into the great outdoors to see the signature wild beasts of the northeast, and explore the Adivasi (tribal) heartland of India. With the rapid pace of development in India, wild animals and traditional culture are vanishing fast, but tourism – if sensitively managed – has the potential to preserve both for future generations. Be sure to follow the rules of responsible travel – see the boxed texts, p87 and p96.

> The website www.birding .in is a one-stop shop for birdwatchers in India, with listings of birdwatching sites and all the species you are likely to see.

MEETING THE WILDLIFE

India has some of the most amazing flora and fauna on earth – from lumbering elephants and growling tigers to forests of rhododendrons and lakes that sing with exotic birdlife. Here are some excellent ways to get up close and personal with Indian wildlife.

Birdwatching

India has some of the world's major bird breeding and feeding grounds. To spot such high-profile species as pink flamingos and Indian hornbills, visit the following birdwatching sites in the northeast. Bring good binoculars from home, and carry one of the guidebooks recommended in the sidebar, p84.

Northeast States Birding tours by raft or on foot at Nameri National Park (p213), and other national parks in Assam — see p200.

Orissa This coastal state is inundated with migrating birds from November to January at Similipal National Park (p274), Bhitarkanika Wildlife Sanctuary (p275), Chandaka Wildlife Sanctuary (p258), the Badrama and Debrigarh Wildlife Sanctuaries (p274) and Chilika Lake (p266).

Sikkim Birding tours with Sikkim Tours & Travels (p179) in Gangtok, Dungmali Guest House in Namchi (p185) and Khecheopalri Trekkers Hut at Khecheopalri Lake (p190).

West Bengal Birdwatching tours through Gurudongma Tours & Travels (p168) and leisurely spotting at Orchid Retreat (p170) in Kalimpong.

Nepal Seek 450 species of bird at Chitwan National Park (p290).

> The Wildlife Protection Society of India (www.wpsi-india.org/tiger) is campaigning to save tigers in the wild — see the website for listings of tiger reserves.

Elephant Safaris

Elephant rides provide an amazing way to get close to Indian wildlife. Many of the northeast's national parks have their own working elephants, which can be hired for safaris into areas that are inaccessible to jeeps and walkers. You might even find yourself just metres from a rumbling rhino or a snarling Bengal tiger. As well as being a fairytale travel experience, elephant rides are much less disturbing to wildlife than noisy jeeps. To find out the best times to visit parks, see regional chapters and the boxed text, p86.

Northeast States Elephant safaris to spot one-horned Indian rhinos and other rare species at Kaziranga National Park (p213) and other national parks in Assam (see p200).

West Bengal Jumbo rides around Jaldhapara Wildlife Sanctuary (p149) to spot Indian rhinos.

Nepal Tramping by elephant into Chitwan National Park (p291).

Horse Riding

Several hill stations in West Bengal offer pony rides, from gentle ambles through town to more serious pony treks through the forest. Good places to saddle up include the following:

Northeast States Pony treks around Dibrugarh with Purvi Discovery (Assam; p217).

West Bengal Leisurely pony rides at Mirik (p151) and Darjeeling (p160).

> Before you leave home, pick up a copy of *Wild India* by Guy Mountfort and Gerald Cubitt to get you inspired about the animals you'll see on safari.

Jeep Safaris

If you can't find an elephant to ride, a jeep safari is a good second best. The northeast has numerous jeep safaris rattling through the jungles of national parks, or climbing dirt roads through the mountains to remote Adivasi villages, temples and monasteries. You can normally arrange a custom itinerary, either with travel agents or directly with jeep drivers. Popular options include the following:

Northeast States Jeeps to Adivasi villages in the Northeast States can be arranged in Guwahati (p206) and other towns. Jeeps also offer wildlife-spotting tours in many of Assam's national parks — see p200.

Orissa Animal-focused jeep safaris in Similipal National Park (p274) and Badrama and Debrigarh Wildlife Sanctuaries (p274).

Sikkim Agencies in Gangtok (p179) can arrange jeep tours to remote valleys in north Sikkim (p195).

Nepal Animal-spotting jeep trips around Chitwan National Park (p291).

> One you get past the curious layout, the website www.indianadventureportal.com has some excellent resources on adventure activities across India.

ADVENTURE ACTIVITIES

The northeast is paradise for adrenaline junkies. Trekking is possible across the region, including in the Adivasi hills of the Northeast States and the wind-scoured valleys of the Himalaya. Among other adrenaline-charged activities, it's possible to rock climb near Darjeeling, go caving in Meghalaya, raft mighty rivers in West Bengal and trek to remote Himalayan passes in Sikkim. See the following sections for some suggestions. Remember to take out adequate insurance cover for any adventure activities before you travel (see p310). If you continue through Nepal, there are even more options – pick up Lonely Planet's *Nepal* or *Trekking in the Nepal Himalaya* books for details.

For a perfect introduction to a boat ride along the Brahmaputra, read Mark Shand's drifting travelogue *River Dog*.

Boat Tours

After riding an elephant, the most evocative way to explore the jungles of the northeast is by boat. You could drift through national parks in West Bengal or Assam or take an epic multiday riverboat trip on the Brahmaputra (see the boxed text, p203). Here are some options:

Northeast States Riverboat cruises along the Brahmaputra River in Assam with Jungle Travels India (p206), boat trips to Majuli Island (p215), atmospheric Brahmaputra ferry rides from Dibrugarh (p218), boat trips to Tripura's Neermahal Palace (p239) and wildlife-spotting rafting trips at Manas National Park (p211) and Nameri National Park (p213).

Orissa Boat tours to hunt for crocodiles, freshwater dolphins and birds at Bhitarkanika Wildlife Sanctuary (p276) and Chilika Lake (p266).

West Bengal Track tigers by boat in the huge Sunderbans Tiger Reserve (p139).

Nepal Animal-watching canoe tours on the Rapti River in Chitwan National Park (p291).

Caving

Meghalaya has 750 recorded caves, but only 250 have ever been explored.

Millennia of torrential monsoon rains have hollowed out an amazing system of caves underneath the limestone plateau of Meghalaya, including the 22km-long Krem Um Im-Liat Prah/Krem Labbit system, India's longest cave. Caving trips can be arranged through tour agents such as Cultural Pursuits Adventures in Shillong (p240). However, this is serious caving and the area is vulnerable to sudden floods – it would be unwise to cave here without an experienced local guide, and it's best to bring equipment from home.

Cultural Tours

Tours to Adivasi areas are permitted in several parts of the northeast, providing a fascinating window onto the traditional customs of India's Adivasis (see the boxed texts, p43 and p271 for more on the Adivasis of the northeast). However, some tours have been criticised for exploiting local people and dramatically altering the culture of Adivasi communities. Seek out tour agencies that employ local villagers as guides and seek to minimise the effect of tourism on Adivasi people. Reputable Adivasi tours include the following:

The website www.india together.org/society /adivasis.htm has an archive of articles about the issues facing India's Adivasi people.

Northeast States For tours of Adivasi regions in the Northeast States, contact the travel agencies listed in Guwahati (p206), Dibrugarh (p217), Shillong (p240), Kohima (p227), Aizawl (p233), Itanagar (p219) and Bomdila (p223).

Orissa Tours to visit Adivasi communities and textile-producing villages can be arranged in Bhubaneswar (p254) and Puri (p261) or you could make your own arrangements in Jeypore (p272).

Cycling & Motorcycling

There are some sensational organised motorcycle tours that rumble through Sikkim as part of the popular West Bengal–Sikkim–Bhutan circuit, or you can rent a motorcycle and set your own itinerary. For recommended motorcycle tours, see p337, and for information on buying or renting a motorcycle in India, see p337.

Sikkim is particularly appealing for cyclists – there's hardly any traffic and the quiet mountain roads are surrounded by breathtaking scenery. One interesting option would be to start in Sikkim and continue west through Nepal via the border crossing at Kakarbhitta, crossing back into India at one of the crossings south of Kathmandu – see p286 for more information on this route.

It's best to bring your own bike if you intend to tackle the hills, though good-quality mountain bikes are available in Kolkata (Calcutta) – see p333 for general information on cycling in India.

Kayaking & White-Water Rafting

Across the northeast, mighty rivers charge down from the hills and mountains, offering some fantastic opportunities for white-water rafting. Several rafting companies operate wet and wild trips on the Rangeet and Teesta Rivers on the border between Sikkim and West Bengal – the main rafting season is from September to November and March to June and the level of rapids varies from modest Grade II to raging Grade IV. Few companies offer trips in the monsoon as the rivers swell to dangerous levels.

Rafting operators offer multiday rafting safaris as well short thrill rides, but be sure to check the safety procedures before joining any rafting trip and make sure that life jackets are in good working order. Most agencies are based in Darjeeling (p160) and Teesta Bazaar (p172) in West Bengal.

Although there are no commercial operators, Arunachal Pradesh is reputed to offer some of the world's most spectacular rafting – try contacting travel agents in the Northeast States or the rafting agencies in Darjeeling or Teesta Bazaar to see if they can arrange a bespoke trip.

Rock Climbing & Mountaineering

The mountains and cliffs of Sikkim, West Bengal, Arunachal Pradesh, Meghalaya and Assam offer some dramatic opportunities for mountaineering and rock climbing for climbers with their own gear. The northeast has everything from frozen waterfalls and alpine routes to big walls and escarpments, but you'll need to bring everything with you from home – including ropes, boots, harnesses, chalk and protection. If you are planning some exploration climbing – for example on the cliffs around Cherrapunjee in Meghalaya (p243) – carry a rack with plenty of nuts, hexacentrics, cams, quickdraws and slings, some industrial rigging karabiners as disposable anchors and spare rolls of climbing tape for jamming off-width cracks.

Darjeeling has a number of climbing centres that offer mountaineering and rock-climbing training courses – both indoors and outdoors – from March to December. Courses run on set dates and most of the equipment you need is provided, but bring your own warm-weather clothing. For more information, see p160.

For serious climbing expeditions to peaks above 6000m, you must arrange permits and permission from the **Indian Mountaineering Foundation** (www.indmount .org). Fees range from US$1500 to US$8000 per expedition, depending on the height of the peak. Many peaks lie in restricted areas near the China border and climbers must pay additional fees for Inner Line and Restricted Area Permits, plus any national park fees that apply.

Delhi-based **Peak Adventure Tours** (www.peakadventuretour.com) is one company arranging fully supported mountaineering trips in Sikkim, including ascents of Zemu Peak (7730m), Dome Khang (7442m) and Kabru North (7395m). Note that the Sikkimese regard Khangchendzonga as a guardian deity, and climbers are not permitted to summit the peak from the Indian side.

For information on the world-class climbing options in Nepal, pick up Lonely Planet's *Nepal* or *Trekking in the Nepal Himalaya* books.

Trekking

As you might suspect from a region hemmed in by the Himalaya, the northeast offers some amazing trekking, with remote temples, Buddhist monasteries, high-altitude lakes and mountain passes as possible desti-

For a great introduction to cycling around Sikkim, including photos and video clips, see the informative blog on the website www.cycling aroundtheworld.nl /Sikkim.

See www.thebmc.co.uk /Feature.aspx?id=2074 for an update on climbing peaks in Sikkim and how to get permission to climb them.

The last 10m of India's highest mountain, Khangchendzonga (8598m), is off-limits to climbers as a sign of respect to local Buddhists.

nations. Many peaks above 5000m can be climbed by trekkers as well as mountaineers, and it is possible to arrange some steamy low-altitude trekking through Adivasi areas of Nagaland, Mizoram, Meghalaya and Arunachal Pradesh through travel agents in the Northeast States – see p200 for some recommended companies.

However, be aware that the trekking industry is not as well developed as in neighbouring Nepal. Accommodation is only available on a handful of routes and trekkers must carry everything they need, including food, sleeping bags, emergency equipment and (on some routes) drinking water. Acute mountain sickness is also a risk on any routes over 3000m – see p349. Finally you need to consider permits, as many routes pass close to the disputed border between India and Tibet.

Because of the lack of infrastructure, independent trekking in northeast India can be risky. Most people opt for organised treks with local

RESPONSIBLE TREKKING

To help preserve India's natural beauty, consider the following tips when trekking. Try to choose trekking agencies and tour operators that focus on sustainable, low-impact tourism.

Rubbish

- Carry out all rubbish (including cigarette butts, sanitary napkins, tampons and condoms) and any rubbish you may find. Set a good example as well as reducing pollution.
- Never bury rubbish: digging encourages erosion and buried rubbish may be dug up and consumed by animals (this can be harmful to them).
- Take reusable containers or stuff sacks. Avoid plastic bags and plastic water bottles.
- Carry a canteen and a water filtration or purification system in remote areas. In villages, refill your canteen with boiled water or filtered water provided by local environmental organisations.

Human Waste Disposal

- To prevent the spread of disease, use toilets where provided. If there aren't any, bury your waste. Dig a small hole (15cm) at least 100m from any watercourse (bring a lightweight trowel) and adequately cover it with soil and a rock. Use minimal toilet paper (preferably none). In snow, dig down to the soil.
- If the area is inhabited, ask locals if they have any concerns about your chosen toilet site.
- Ensure that these guidelines are applied to portable toilet tents used by trekking groups. All members (including porters) should use them.

Washing

- Don't use detergents or toothpaste in or near watercourses, even if they are biodegradable.
- For personal washing, use biodegradable soap and a water container at least 50m away from the watercourse. Disperse the waste water widely so the soil can adequately filter it.
- Wash cooking utensils 50m away from watercourses using a scourer, sand or snow instead of detergent.

Clothing, Fires & Cooking

- Bring proper clothing for the extreme cold of the mountains – research weather conditions in advance and seek professional advice on clothes and equipment. This will reduce the need for fires for warmth.

trekking agencies, though it is sometimes possible to hire your own porters, packhorses and guides through local tourist offices. If you do make your own arrangements, ensure that your guide speaks English and make an emergency plan for evacuation from the route. Tell someone at the trailhead where you are going and when you intend to be back, and never trek alone. On any organised trek, make sure that you have all the equipment you need and ensure that you know exactly what is included in the fee you agree upon. See the boxed text, below, for advice on responsible trekking.

Sikkim is the premier trekking destination in the northeast, but special permits are required for the main treks. Travel agencies in Gangtok (p179) can arrange treks all over Sikkim, including the epic ascent to the 4940m Goecha La (p192). Many independent travellers trek stages of the leisurely 'Monastic Loop' around West Sikkim (no permit

If you don't feel up to climbing the mountains of Sikkim, you could always wear the fragrance – Sikkim by Lancôme was launched in 1971, and it still retails for US$100 per 50mL.

- Cutting wood causes deforestation – a major problem in India – so avoid open fires and stay in lodgings that don't use wood to cook or heat water where possible.
- Use a lightweight kerosene, alcohol or Shellite (white gas) stove and avoid stoves powered by disposable butane-gas canisters.
- If you must light an open fire, try to use existing fireplaces and only use dead, fallen wood. Be sure to fully extinguish a fire, for example by spreading the embers and flooding them with sand or water.

Cultural Sensitivity

- Respect local cultural practices when interacting with communities, including local attitudes to modesty.
- Observe official regulations in areas you visit. Many rules are there to protect the local way of life.
- Do not hand out pens, sweets or money to children; this promotes begging. If you want to give, donate to local schools and community centres.
- Always seek permission from landowners if you intend to enter private property.
- Where possible, trek with a local guide. This way, money from tourism will directly benefit the people it affects.

Flora & Fauna

- Always stick to existing tracks. Blazing new trails will create new watercourses, contributing to erosion. Walk through rather than around mud patches and puddles – walking around the edge increases the area being degraded.
- Don't pick flowers or other plants – covering vegetation plays a vital role in keeping the topsoil in place.
- Avoid disturbing wild or domesticated animals and shut any gates you open.
- Hunting is illegal in India and it adds to the pressure on species already endangered by loss of habitat – don't do it.
- Refrain from feeding wildlife (don't leave food scraps behind either). Wild animals can become dependent on handouts and random feeding can lead to attacks on humans, unbalanced animal populations and disease. Place foodstuffs out of reach while you camp (tie packs to rafters or trees).

required), which passes a series of monasteries and mountain viewpoints (see p190).

More treks are possible near Darjeeling in West Bengal, including the dramatic Singalila Ridge Trek (p166) along the Nepal border, which rivals the early stages of the Khanchendzonga ascent in neighbouring Nepal. In Meghalaya, Cherrapunjee Holiday Resort (p245) offers treks through deep jungle, crossing gorges on the surreal 'living bridges' woven from growing trees by Khasi people.

If you take an excursion through Nepal, you can enjoy some of the best – and best-supported – trekking in the world. Pick up Lonely Planet's *Nepal* or *Trekking in the Nepal Himalaya* books for details.

HOLISTIC & SPIRITUAL ACTIVITIES

Not all activities in northeast India have to involve hauling yourself up mountains. Travellers who have an interest in spirituality or alternative therapies will find courses and treatments that focus on healing body and mind. After all, this is the country that gave the world meditation, massage, mantras and ayurveda (traditional Indian herbal medicine). Many holistic and spiritual activities are also available in Nepal – Lonely Planet's *Nepal* or *Trekking in the Nepal Himalaya* books have all the details.

MEDITATION

Most Indian spa treatments are based on ayurveda (Indian herbal medicine) – read *The Handbook of Ayurveda* by Shantha Godagama for an introduction to the most popular techniques.

Buddhist pilgrims flock to Bodhgaya in Bihar – a global centre for the study of meditation and Tibetan Buddhism. Numerous monasteries and Buddhist retreats around the Mahabodhi Temple offer residential and drop-in courses – see p284. Meditation courses are also offered by Kolkata's Aurobindo Bhawan (p119).

SPA TREATMENTS

If you just want to enjoy the effects of India's healing arts, the northeast has several upmarket spas, and private practitioners of massage and other traditional therapies can be found in larger towns and cities. However, be cautious of one-on-one massages by private operators, particularly in tourist towns.

Recommended spots for indulgence:

Kolkata Exclusive Banyan Tree spa treatments at the Oberoi Grand (p122).

Orissa Plush resort spas in Bhubaneswar (p256).

YOGA

India is famous as the home of yoga – a system of mental and physical exercises designed to train the consciousness for perfect control of mind and body. The most common yoga forms are hatha (following the *shatkarma* system of postures and meditation), ashtanga (following the 'eight limbs' system), pranayama (controlled yogic breathing) and Iyengar (a variation of ashtanga using physical aids for advanced postures).

The portal site www .buddhanet.net has excellent links and resources on all aspects of Buddhism, including a directory of contacts covering every state in India.

Most of the opportunities for yoga practice in the northeast are found in ashrams – residential religious centres that follow the philosophy of a particular guru (spiritual guide). Some ashrams require a minimum time commitment; most require a donation, and residents may be required to follow strict rules on silence, diet and behaviour while staying there. As spiritual communities, most ashrams also have a proselytising agenda – make sure you are happy with the ashram ethos before you commit to a stay.

Alternatively, many upmarket hotels have spas that offer yoga and alternative therapies without the religious overtones (see opposite) and there are also several private yoga centres – readers have recommended the courses run by Art of Living (see p119) in Kolkata. Laughter yoga – which is based on the therapeutic effects of a group giggle – is also popular. Several clubs meet daily in Kolkata's Rabindra Sarovar park (p116).

The following ashrams in the northeast offer training in yoga:

Kolkata Belur Math (Kolkata; p118), the headquarters of the Ramakrishna Mission; branches are found countrywide.

West Bengal International Society for Krishna Consciousness (Iskcon; Mayapura; p144), headquarters of the Hare Krishna movement, with branches all over India.

Based on the healing power of laughter, laughter yoga is a growing phenomenon in the northeast. See www.laughteryoga.org for more on the movement.

Kolkata (Calcutta)

India's second-biggest city is a daily festival of human existence, simultaneously noble and squalid, cultured and desperate. And everything plays out before your very eyes on teeming streets where not an inch of space is wasted. By its old spelling, Calcutta conjures up images of human suffering to most Westerners. But Bengalis have long been infuriated by one-sided depictions of their vibrant capital. Kolkata is locally regarded as the intellectual and cultural capital of the nation. Several of India's great 19th- and 20th-century heroes were Kolkatans, including guru-philosopher Ramakrishna, Nobel Prize–winning poet Rabindranath Tagore and celebrated film director Satyajit Ray. Dozens of venues showcase Bengali dance, poetry, art, music, film and theatre. And while poverty is certainly in your face, the dapper Bengali gentry continue to frequent grand old gentlemen's clubs, back horses at the Calcutta Racetrack and play soothing rounds of golf at some of India's finest courses.

As the former capital of British India, Kolkata retains a feast of colonial architecture, with more than a few fine buildings in photogenic states of semicollapse. The city still has many slums but is developing dynamic new-town suburbs and a rash of AC shopping malls. Kolkata's also a fabulous place to sample the mild, fruity tang of Bengali cuisine.

Friendlier than India's other megacities, Kolkata is really a city you 'feel' more than just visit. But don't come between May and September unless you're prepared for a very serious drenching.

HIGHLIGHTS

- Watch goddesses coming to life in the curious lanes of **Kumartuli** (p118) or **Kalighat Rd** (p115).

- Ponder the contradictions of the magnificent **Victoria Memorial** (p107) which remains Kolkata's most splendid building 60 years after the end of the colonial era.

- Venture into **Bhojohari Manna** (p125) to sample the best of lipsmackingly authentic Bengali cuisine

- Discover the enlightened universalist idealism of Ramakrishna at **Belur Math** (p118) and of Rabindranath Tagore at **Tagore's House** (p117).

- **Volunteer** (p323) to help the destitute.

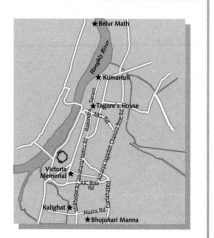

FESTIVALS IN KOLKATA

Dover Lane Music Conference (www.thedoverlanemusicconference.org/schedule.php; late Jan) Indian classical music at Rabindra Sarovar.

Kolkata Boi Mela (www.kolkatabookfaironline.com; late Jan/early Feb) Asia's biggest book fair.

Saraswati Puja (early Feb) Prayers for educational success, all dressed in yellow.

Rath Yatra (Jun/Jul) Major Krishna chariot festival similar to the Puri equivalent (p258).

Durga Puja (www.durga-puja.org; Oct) Kolkata's biggest festival, see p102.

Lakshmi Puja (Oct) on the full moon after Durga Puja and **Kali Puja** (Diwali, Nov) feature more idol dunking.

Kolkata Film Festival (www.kff.in; mid-Nov) Week-long festival of Bengali and international movies.

HISTORY

In the Hindu epics, the God Shiva was understandably dismayed to happen upon the charred corpse of Sati, his newly wed wife (an incarnation of Kali). However, his decision to destroy the world in retribution was considered somewhat of an over-reaction by fellow deities. Vishnu interceded to stop Shiva's 'dance of destruction', but in so doing dismembered Sati's cadaver into 51 pieces. These gory chunks landed at widely disbursed points across India. One of her toes fell at Kalikata (now Kalighat, p115), where the site became honoured by a much revered temple.

Famed as Kalikata/Kalighat might have been, the place was still a fairly typical rural backwater when British merchant Job Charnock showed up in 1686. Charnock reckoned the Hooghly River bend would make an ideal settlement, and by 1698 the villages of Sutanuti, Gobindapur and Kalikata had been formally signed over to the British East India Company. The British thereupon created a miniature version of London-on-Hooghly, with stately buildings, wide boulevards, English churches and grand formal gardens. The grand illusion vanished abruptly at Calcutta's frayed edges where Indians servicing the Raj lived in cramped, overcrowded bustis (slums).

The most notable hiccup in the city's meteoric rise came in 1756, when Siraj-ud-daula, the nawab of nearby Murshidabad, recaptured the city. Dozens of members of the colonial aristocracy were imprisoned in a cramped room beneath Fort William. By morning, around 40 of them were dead from suffocation. The British press exaggerated numbers, drumming up moral outrage back home: the legend of the 'Black Hole of Calcutta' was born.

The following year, Clive of India retook Calcutta for Britain. The nawab sought aid from the French but was soundly defeated at the Battle of Plassey (now Palashi), thanks mainly to the treachery of former allies. A stronger fort was built and the town became British India's official capital, though well into the late 18th century one could still hunt tigers in the bamboo forests around where Sudder St lies today.

The late 19th–century Bengal Renaissance movement saw a great cultural reawakening among middle-class Calcuttans. This was further galvanised by the massively unpopular 1905 division of Bengal, sowing the seeds of the Indian Independence movement. Bengal was reunited in 1911, but the British promptly transferred their colonial capital to less troublesome Delhi.

Initially loss of political power had little effect on Calcutta's economic status. However, the impact of partition was devastating. While West Pakistan and Punjab saw a fairly equal (if bloody) exchange of populations, migration in Bengal was almost entirely one way. Around four million Hindu refugees from East Bengal arrived, choking Calcutta's already overpopulated bustis. For a period, people really were dying of hunger in the streets, creating Calcutta's abiding image of abject poverty. No sooner had these refugees been absorbed than a second vast wave arrived during the 1971 India–Pakistan War.

After India's partition the port of Calcutta was hit very hard by the loss of its main natural hinterland, now behind closed Pakistan–Bangladesh borders. Labour unrest spiralled

---

FAST FACTS

Population 14.7 million

Area 185 sq km

Telephone code ☎ 033

Main language Bengali

When to go October to March

out of control, while the city's dominant party (Communist Party of India) spent most of its efforts attacking the feudal system of land ownership. Well-intentioned attempts to set strict rent controls have since backfired: where tenants still pay as little as Rs1 a month, landlords have no interest in maintaining or upgrading properties so many fine old buildings are crumbling before one's eyes.

Since 2001 Calcutta has officially adopted the more phonetic spelling, Kolkata. Around the same time the city administration implemented a new business-friendly attitude that has encouraged a noticeable economic resurgence.

ORIENTATION

Administrative Kolkata takes up several blocks of colonial-era buildings around BBD Bagh. North of here lanes are narrow and intriguingly vibrant. Well south in Alipore and around Rabindra Sarovar are wealthier suburbs. Budget travellers head for the Sudder St area where you'll find travel agencies, moneychangers and Kolkata's only sprinkling of backpacker cafes. Upmarket dining and boutiques are prevalent around Elgin, Camac and Park Sts. The central business district is around Shakespeare Sarani though corporate offices are increasingly relocating to Sector 5 of Salt Lake City, a large new-town area northeast of centre.

Maps

Various commercially sold city maps verge on fiction. The *Inside India Series: Kolkata* (Rs90 from Crossword, see right) is better than most,

if lacking detail. More comprehensive online maps based on Google Earth images include **Maplandia** (www.maplandia.com).

INFORMATION
Bookshops

Classic Books/Earthcare Books (Map p108; ☎ 22296551; www.earthcarebooks.com; 10 Middleton St; ☺ 11am-7pm Mon-Sat, 11-3pm Sun) Charming family publisher-bookshop with strengths in development, environmentalism, politics, spirituality and women's issues. Located behind Drive-Inn.

Crossword (Map p108; ☎ 22836502; www.crossword bookstores.com; 8 Elgin Rd; ☺ 10.30am-8.30pm) Spacious three-storey chain bookshop with cafe (coffee Rs18-44). Sells *Times Food Guide* (Rs100).

Oxford Bookstore (Map p108; ☎ 22297662; www .oxfordbookstore.com; 17 Park St; ☺ 10am-9pm Mon-Sat, 11am-8pm Sun; 🖳) Excellent full-range bookshop with browse-seating and cafe.

Seagull Bookstore (Map pp104-5; ☎ 24765869; www .seagullindia.com; 31A SP Mukherjee Rd; ☺ 10.30am-7.30pm) Academic bookshop with particular strengths in humanities, regional politics and social sciences. Enter from the lane leading to Indira cinema.

Huddled around the Sudder–Mirza Ghalib St junction (Map p108) are several small traveller-oriented bookstalls including **Bookland** 6/1 Sudder St; ☺ 8am-9pm) and **Cosmos Books** (14 Mirza Ghalib St; ☺ 9am-9pm).

Internet Access

Most internet centres will charge at least 30 minutes' minimum usage.

Cyber Indya (Map p108; 6 Ballygunge Circular Rd; per hr Rs15-20; ☺ 9am-10pm; 🖳)

DURGA PUJA

Much as Carnival transforms Rio or New Orleans, Durga Puja brings Kolkata to chaotically colourful life. For five days people venerate gaudily painted idols of 10-armed goddess Durga and her entourage (see p118). These are displayed in *pandals* (marquees) that dominate yards, block roads or fill little parks. In the last 30 years, design competitions and increasing corporate sponsorship have seen *pandals* growing ever more ornate and complex. Some have topical or political messages, such as the 2008 *pandal* shaped like a car factory (at the time West Bengal was still arguing with Tata over the controversial Nano car plant, see p137).

West Bengal Tourism takes tourists around a selection of the best *pandals* but getting anywhere close can take hours given their popularity. After five days the festival's climax comes when myriad Durga idols are thrown into the sacred Hooghly River amid singing, water throwing, fireworks and indescribable traffic congestion. If you just want pandal photos and not the festival aspect, consider visiting just after Durga Puja when the idol has gone but *pandals* have yet to be deconstructed.

Many diaspora Bengalis return to Kolkata for Durga Puja so hotels fill up. Then afterwards so many go away on holiday that getting rail or air tickets out can be virtually impossible for weeks.

Cyber Zoom (Map p108; 27B Park St; per hr Rs15; ☾ 9am-11pm; 🖳)

E-Merge (i-Way) (Map p108; 59B Park St; per hr Rs30; ☾ 10am-10pm Mon-Sat, 11.30am-10pm Sun; 🖳) Amusingly dated personal booths but good AC and fast connections.

Enternet (Map p108; Chowringhee Lane; per hr Rs20; ☾ 10am-9.30pm) Decent connection.

Hotline/Saree Palace (Map p108; 7 Sudder St; per hr Rs15; ☾ 8.30am-11.30) New flat-screens, pleasant owners and long hours. Fabrics for sale too.

Junction 96 (Map p116; Sarat Bose Rd; per hr Rs15; ☾ 9.30am-9pm Mon-Sat; 🖳)

Nav-Softyn (Map p112; 3 Khetra Das Rd; per half/full hr Rs20/30; ☾ 11am-8pm Mon-Sat; 🖳) Cramped but refreshingly air-conditioned down a narrow alley.

Sky@ber (Airport, International Terminal; per half-hr Rs60; ☾ 24hr)

Internet Resources

Useful websites for Kolkata include http://kolkata.clickindia.com, www.wbtourism.com /kolkata/index.htm and www.calcuttaweb .com.

Left Luggage

Many Sudder St hotels will store bags for a small fee. At the airport, a useful **baggage store** (small/large bag per 24hrs Rs5/10; ☾ 24hr) is diagonally across the car park from the international terminal. At Howrah and Sealdah train stations **cloakrooms** (bags Rs10-15 per day; ☾ 24hr) require users to show valid long-distance train tickets.

Libraries

Asiatic Society (Map p108; ☎ 22290779; www.asiatic societycal.com; 1 Park St; admission free; ☾ 10am-5.30pm Mon-Fri) Priceless collection of ancient books and illuminated manuscripts. A few of these are displayed in a mothballed one-room museum, including a letter signed by Shah Jahan and a 250 BC Ashokan inscription. Getting to see them involves a hilariously bureaucratic procedure and five separate sign-ins on four different floors. Bring your passport.

Sri Aurobindo Library (Map p108; Aurobindo Bhawan ☎ 24765865; 8 Shakespeare Sarani; ☾ 12.30pm-7pm Mon-Sat) Bring ID. Annual membership is Rs20.

National Library (Map pp104-5; ☎ 24791381; www.nl india.org; Alipore; ☾ 9am-8pm Mon-Fri, 9.30am-6pm Sat & Sun) The largest collection in India. Books are too numerous for open shelving so are accessed from vaults by request slip. Membership is free but requires two photos.

Seagull Arts Library (Map pp104-5; www.seagullindia .com; 31A SP Mukherjee Rd; day membership Rs50) Above

Seagull Bookstore. It also runs an arts/exhibition room at 36C SP Mukherjee Rd.

Medical Services

Apollo Gleneagles Clinic (Map pp104-5; ☎ 24618028; www.apollogleneagles.in; 48/1F Lila Roy Sarani, Gariahat Rd; ☾ 8am-8pm) Health checks and dental work; its sister **hospital** (Map pp104-5; ☎ 23203040; EM Bypass) offers 24-hour ambulance service.

Bellevue Clinic (Map p108; ☎ 22872321; www .bellevueclinic.com; 9 Loudon St) Upmarket central hospital with renowned eye-clinic.

Mission of Mercy Hospital (Map p108; ☎ 22296666; www.momhospital.org; 2/7 Sarat Bose Rd) Out-patients' department offers inexpensive doctors' consultations (Rs75).

SRL Ranbaxy Path Lab (Map p108; ☎ 22271315; Chowringhee Mansion; ☾ 7.30am-7.30pm Mon-Sat) Same-day tests for dengue fever (Rs900 to Rs2700).

Wockhardt Medical Centre (Map p108; ☎ 24754320; www.wockhardhospitals.net; 2/7 Sarat Bose Rd) Reliably modern for doctor's consultations (Rs300; ☾ 10.30am-noon).

For fuller listings see www.kolkatainformation .com/diagnostic.html or www.calcuttaweb .com/doctor.php.

Money

ATMs are widespread. Many private money-changers around Sudder St offer exchange rates several percent better than banks and some will exchange travellers cheques, but shop around and double-check their maths. Bangladesh takas are hard to change.

Camara Bank (Map p108; Kyd St) Handy ATM near Sudder St.

Globe Forex (Map p108; ☎ 22828780; 11 Ho Chi Minh Sarani; ☾ 9.30am-6.30pm Mon-Fri, 9.30am-2.30pm Sat) Good rates for cash and travellers cheques, Rs25 commission.

Hilson Hotel (Map p108; Sudder St; ☾ 9am-9pm) Great rates and long hours from this backpacker guesthouse foyer, Rs20 commission.

Permits

For any permit bring your passport, visa-style photographs and photocopies of both passport identity page and Indian visa.

FOREIGNERS' REGIONAL REGISTRATION OFFICE (FRRO)

From outside, the **Foreigners' Regional Registration Office** (FRRO; Map p108; ☎ 22837034; 237 AJC Bose Rd; ☾ 11am-5pm Mon-Fri) looks like a grand 1930s cinema building. It issues free permits for Sikkim

KOLKATA

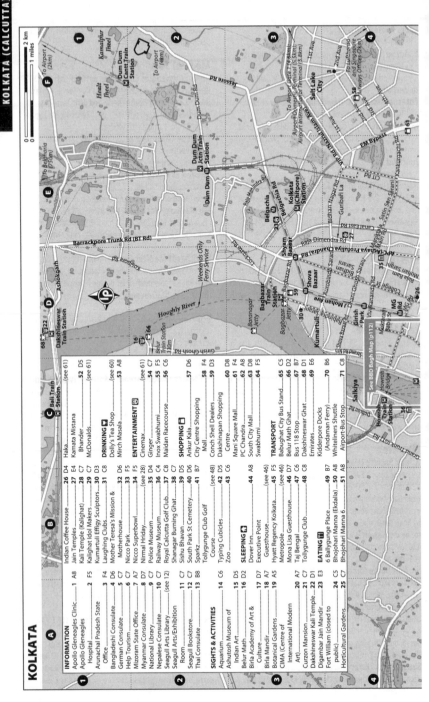

INFORMATION
Apollo Gleneagles Clinic......	1 A8
Apollo Gleneagles	
Hospital..............................	2 F5
Arunachal Pradesh State	
Office................................	3 F4
Bangladeshi Consulate........	4 D6
German Consulate...............	5 C7
Help Tourism......................	6 C7
Mizoram State Office..........	7 A7
Myanmar Consulate............	8 D7
National Library..................	9 C7
Nepalese Consulate.............	10 C7
Seagull Arts Library...........	(see 12)
Seagull Arts/Exhibition	
Room................................	11 C7
Seagull Bookstore...............	12 C7
Thai Consulate....................	13 B8

SIGHTS & ACTIVITIES
Aquarium...........................	14 C6
Ashutosh Museum of	
Indian Art.........................	15 D5
Belur Math.........................	16 D2
Biria Academy of Art &	
Culture.............................	17 D7
Biria Mandir.......................	18 A7
Botanical Gardens..............	19 A5
CIMA (Centre of	
International Modern	
Art)....................................	20 A7
Curzon Mansion.................	21 D7
Dakshineswar Kali Temple...	22 D1
Digambar Jain Mandir.........	23 E3
Fort William (closed to	
public)..............................	24 C5
Horticultural Gardens.........	25 A8

Indian Coffee House............	26 D4
Jain Temples......................	27 E4
Kali Temple (Kalighat).........	28 C7
Kalighat Idol Makers...........	29 C7
Kumartuli Effigy Sculptors...	30 D3
Laughing Clubs...................	31 C8
Mother Teresa's Mission &	
Motherhouse.....................	32 D6
Nicco Park.........................	33 F5
Nicco Superbowl................	34 F5
Nirmal Hriday....................	(see 28)
Police Museum...................	35 D4
Railway Museum.................	36 C4
Royal Calcutta Golf Club.....	37 C8
Shanagar Burning Ghat.......	38 C7
Sishu Bhavan.....................	39 D5
South Park St Cemetery......	40 D6
Sparkz..............................	41 B7
Tollygunge Club Golf	
Course..............................	42 D5
Typing Cubicles..................	43 C6
Zoo...................................	44 A8

SLEEPING
Dover Inn..........................	45 F5
Executive Point	
Guesthouse.......................	(see 46)
Hyatt Regency Kolkata........	46 F5
Metropole..........................	47 C6
Mona Lisa Guesthouse........	48 C8
Taj Bengal.........................	
Tollygunge Club.................	

EATING
6 Ballygunge Place..............	49 B7
Bhojohri Manna (Ekdalia)....	50 A8
Bhojohri Manna 6...............	51 A8

Haka.................................	52 D5
Kamata Mistana.................	(see 61)
Bhander............................	53 A8
McDonalds.........................	(see 61)

DRINKING
Dolly's Tea Shop.................	(see 60)
Mirch Masala......................	53 A8

ENTERTAINMENT
Cinemax............................	(see 61)
Ginger...............................	54 C7
Inox Swabhumi...................	55 F5
Maidan Racecourse.............	56 C6

SHOPPING
Ankur Kala.........................	57 D6
City Centre Shopping	
Mall..................................	58 F4
Conch Shell Dealers............	59 D3
Dakshinapan Shopping	
Centre..............................	60 D8
Mani Square Mall...............	61 F4
PC Chandra........................	62 A8
South City Mall..................	63 D8
Swabhumi..........................	64 F5

TRANSPORT
Babughat City Bus Stand.....	65 C5
Belur Math Ghat.................	66 D2
Bus 118 Stop......................	67 B7
Dakshineswar Ghat.............	68 D1
Emirates............................	69 E6
Kidderpore Docks	
(Andaman Ferry)...............	70 B6
Whiteliners Shuttle..............	
Airport-Bus Stop................	71 C8

To Airport (2km)
Kamaljhar Jheel
To Airport (2km)
Dum Dum Cantt Train Station
Jessore Rd
Heult Jheel
To Airport (4km)
Salt Lake City
To Airport Gate 1 (4.6km)
Airport Domestic Terminal (5.5km)
Airport International Terminal (5.8km)
Railways Offices (2km) 2nd Ave
EM Bypass
Barrackpore Trunk Rd (BT Rd)
Dum Dum Jctn Train Station
Dum Dum Station
Belgachia
Shyam Bazaar
Shova Bazaar
Hooghly River
Dakshineswar Train Station
Belur Train Station 3.0km
Bagbazar Train Station
Kumartuli
Girish Park
MG Rd
Salkiya
Howrah Train Station
Howrah Bridge

2 km
1 miles

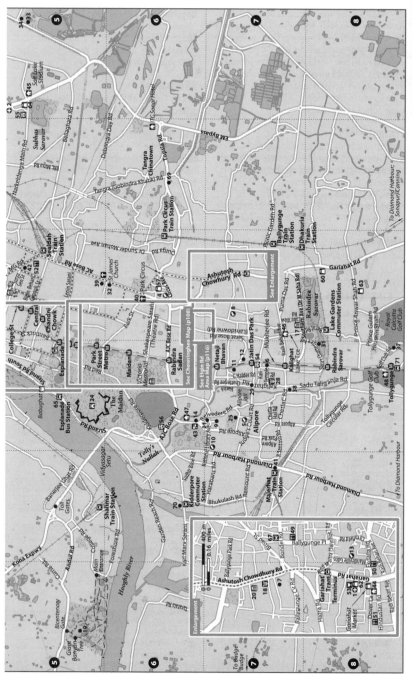

in one working day. Permits for Manipur, Arunachal Pradesh (but not Tawang) and Nagaland (Mon and Phek only) are available to groups of four applicants at Rs1350 per person per permit in one working day if you arrived in India via Kolkata airport, but will take much longer if you arrived elsewhere (they track down your entry papers). The FFRO won't issue Mizoram permits.

STATE OFFICES
Indian nationals can get state-specific Inner Line permits at the following state offices but, except for Sikkim, foreigners shouldn't expect any permit help whatsoever.
Arunachal Pradesh (Map pp104-5; ☎ 23341243; Arunachal Bhawan, Block CE 109, Sector 1, Salt Lake City)
Manipur (Map p108; ☎ 24758163; Manipur Bhawan, 26 Rowland Rd)
Mizoram (Map pp104-5; ☎ 24617887; Mizoram Bhawan, 24 Old Ballygunge Rd) Take the lane beside 23 AC.

Nagaland (Map p108; ☎ 22825247; Nagaland House, 11 Shakespeare Sarani)
Sikkim (Map p108; ☎ 22817905; Sikkim House, 4/1 Middleton St; ☷ 10.30am-4pm Mon-Fri, 10.30am-2pm Sat) Permits usually issued within 24hrs.

Photography
Electro Photo-Lab (Map p108; ☎ 22498743; 14 Sudder St; ☷ 10.30am-9.30pm Mon-Sat, noon-7pm Sun) Instant passport photos (eight mugshots Rs60), film developing, digiprints, camera to CD (Rs60 per disk).
Global Studio (Map p108; ☎ 22829156; 4 Ho Chi Minh Sarani; ☷ 8am-8pm Mon-Fri, 10am-6pm Sat) Hole-in-the-wall studio for passport photos (Rs50 for four).
Summer Photographic (Map p112; Moti Lal Market; ☷ 10am-9pm) Stocks Sensia 100 slide film (Rs180).

Post
Kolkata's imposing **General Post Office** (GPO; Map p112; BBD Bagh; ☷ 6am-8pm Mon-Sat, 10am-3.30pm Sun;

STREET NAMES

After Independence, the Indian government changed any street name that had Raj-era connotations. The Communists continued the process. Humorously they chose to rename Harrington St such that the US found its consulate on a road named for then arch-enemy Ho Chi Minh.

Today citizens and taxis mostly use the British-era names while, confusingly, most maps, street signs and business cards use the new names (or sometimes both). This text uses what we found, quite unscientifically, to be the most commonly employed variant, *italicised* in the list below:

Old name	New name
Ballygunge Rd	Ashutosh Chowdhury Ave *(AC Rd)*
Brabourne Rd	Biplabi Trailokya Maharaja Rd
Camac St	Abinindranath Tagore St
Central Ave	*Chittaranjan (CR) Ave*
Chitpore Rd	*Rabindra Sarani*
Chowringhee Rd	Jawaharlal Nehru Rd
Free School St	*Mirza Ghalib St*
Harrington St	*Ho Chi Minh Sarani*
Harrison Rd	Mahatma Gandhi *(MG)* Rd
Hungerford St	Picasso Bithi
Kyd St	Dr M Ishaque Rd
Lansdowne Rd	*Sarat Bose Rd*
Loudon St	Dr UM Bramhchari St
Lower Circular Rd	*AJC Bose Rd*
Old Courthouse St	Hemant Basu Sarani
Park St	Mother Teresa Sarani
Rowden St	Sarojini Naidu Sarani
Theatre Rd	*Shakespeare Sarani*
Victoria Terrace	*Gorky Terrace*
Waterloo St	Nawab Siraj-ud-Daula Sarani
Wellesley St	*RAK* (Rafi Ahmed Kidwai) *Rd*
Wood St	Dr Martin Luther King Sarani

parcel service from 10am) is an attraction in itself (see p114). Convenient branch post offices include Park St (Map p108), CR Ave (Map p112) and Mirza Ghalib St (Map p108).

Courier services include the following:

DHL (Map p108; ☎ 64538605; 28/2 Shakespeare Sarani; ⏱ 24hrs)

FedEx (☎ 22834325; Crescent Tower, 229 AJC Bose Rd; ⏱ 11am-8pm Mon-Sat)

Telephone

The **Central Telegraph Office** (Map p112; ⏱ 24hr) is under reconstruction but calls are cheap from ubiquitous PCO/STD/ISD booths throughout the city. Numerous stalls around Sudder St sell Vodafone SIM-cards (Rs200 including Rs10 credit) if you provide a visa-style photograph and passport photocopies. SIM procurement for foreigners seems much harder elsewhere in Kolkata.

Tourist Information

Cal Calling (Rs45) Very useful monthly info-booklet sold at Oxford Bookstore.

CityInfo (www.explocity.com) Advertisement-led listings pamphlet available free from better hotels.

India Tourism (Map p108; ☎ 22825813; 4 Shakespeare Sarani; ⏱ 10am-6pm Mon-Fri, 10am-1pm Sat) Helpful young staff, free Kolkata maps.

West Bengal Tourism (Map p112; ☎ 22437260; www.wbtourism.com; 3/2 BBD Bagh; ⏱ 10.30am-1.30pm & 2-5.30pm Mon-Fri, 10.30am-1pm Sat) Comfortable, recently redecorated office mostly set up to sell tours (last sales 4.30pm).

Travel Agencies

For city tour agents see p119.

Help Tourism (Map pp104-5; ☎ 24549682; www.help tourism.com; 67A Kali Temple Rd, Kalighat) Personalised ecotours.

STIC Travel (Map p108; ☎ 22265989; 3C Camac St; www.stictravel.com; ⏱ 9am-1pm & 2-5.30pm Mon-Fri, 9am-2pm Sat)

Super Travel (Map p108; Super Guesthouse) One of numerous agencies on Sudder St and Chowringhee Lane.

Thomas Cook (Map p108; ☎ 22830473; www.thomas cook.in; 19B Shakespeare Sarani; ⏱ 9.30am-6pm)

Visa Extension

In a dire medical emergency, the **Foreigners' Regional Registration Office** (FRRO; Map p108; ☎ 22837034; 237 AJC Bose Rd; ⏱ 11am-5pm Mon-Fri) just might extend your Indian tourist visa by a few days given a medical report and confirmed air-ticket out. Don't count on it.

DANGERS & ANNOYANCES

Kolkata feels remarkably unthreatening. Predictable beggar hassle around the Sudder St traveller ghetto is a minor irritant. Crossing the road is a more day-to-day worry: the mad traffic takes no prisoners. *Bandhs* (strikes) occur with monotonous regularity, closing shops and stopping all land transport (including taxis to the airport). Monsoon-season flooding is highly inconvenient but rickshaw-wallahs somehow manage to ferry passengers through knee-deep, waterlogged streets.

SIGHTS

Most attractions that don't charge for photography forbid it.

Chowringhee Area

Sites appear on Map p108, except where otherwise noted.

VICTORIA MEMORIAL

Set in an attractive, well-tended **park** (admission Rs4; ⏱ 5.30am-7pm), the incredible **Victoria Memorial** (VM; ☎ 22235142; admission Indian/foreigner Rs10/150; ⏱ 10am-5pm Tue-Sun, last tickets 4.30pm) is a vast, beautifully proportioned confection of white marble domes: think US Capitol meets Taj Mahal. Built to commemorate Queen Victoria's 1901 diamond jubilee, the structure was finally finished nearly 20 years after her death. Had it been built for a beautiful Indian princess rather than a dead colonial queen, it would surely rate as one of India's greatest buildings.

The VM is magnificently photogenic viewed across reflecting ponds from the northeast. Inside there's an impressive soaring central chamber but the ground floor galleries of prints and paintings are displayed on thoughtlessly insensitive whitewashed hardboard hoardings that clash with the original splendour. Nonetheless the Kolkata Gallery traces an impressively even-handed history of the city and there is an upstairs gallery of manuscripts and portraits that is better presented. Don't miss the statues in the main entrance hall: King George V faces his wife Mary but looks more a queen himself in his camp posing britches. No wonder interior photography is forbidden.

By day, entrance is from the park's north or south gates (though you can exit to the east). For the informative English-language **sound-and-light show** (Indian/foreigner Rs10/20; ⏱ 7.15pm Tue-Sun Nov-Feb, 7.45pm Tue-Sun Mar-Jun, no shows in summer) enter from the east gate.

CHOWRINGHEE

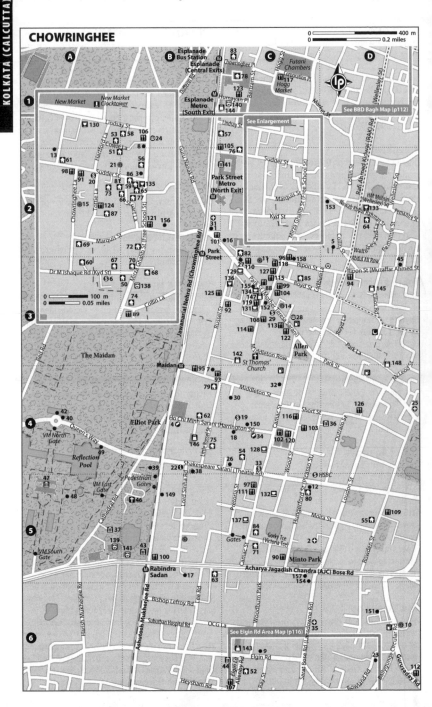

KOLKATA IN...

Two Days

First day, tour the **Indian Museum** (below), admire the grandiose **Victoria Memorial** (p107) and surrounding attractions then pick up a Marble Palace permit at India Tourism (p107, for tomorrow) before dining and dancing on Park or Camac Sts. Next day wander randomly from the **Maidan** (opposite) through the crumbling colonial wonderland of **BBD Bagh** (p113) then use tram 6 to chug up Rabindra Sarani to fascinating **Kumartuli** (p118). Return by metro to the bizarre **Marble Palace** (p117) or by ferry to Howrah then cross the famous bridge to colourful **Mullik Ghat flower market** (p114).

Two Weeks

Consider approaching the city thematically.

Traditional Kolkata Hand-drawn rickshaws (p135), effigy-makers in Kumartuli (p118), goats sacrifices at Kalighat (p115)

Colonial Kolkata The General Post Office (p113), golf at the Tollygunge Club (p119), a flutter at the Maidan racecourse (p130), garden beers at the Fairlawn Hotel (p129)

Modern Kolkata Dancing at Tantra nightclub (p129), coffee at Barista (p128), cocktails at Roxy (p129), browsing at Oxford Bookstore (p102)

Squalid Kolkata Street kids on Howrah train station (p114), Old Chinatown (p114), volunteering (p119) to help the destitute

Multicultural Kolkata Synagogues, mosques and churches of Barabazaar (p114), Belur Math (p118), meditation evenings (p119), reading Tagore (p117), laughing-yoga at Rabindra Sarovar (p116)

AROUND THE VM

In the evenings around the VM's north gate, local couples surreptitiously fondle (and more) in the surrounding gardens, ride in fancy **horse carriages** along Queens Way or watch the sweetly gaudy play of **musical fountains**.

Loosely styled on the Buddhist stupa at Sarnath, the **Birla Planetarium** (☎ 22231516; Chowringhee Rd) is one of the world's largest. Its exterior looks impressive when floodlit. Inside, its outer circle forms a small but well-presented, tomb-like gallery featuring astronomer busts and fading star-gazer pictures. The **star shows** (admission Rs30; ✆ 1.30pm & 6.30pm in English) are slow moving, thickly accented introductions to the night sky.

With its central crenellated tower, the 1847 **St Paul's Cathedral** (☎ 22230127; Cathedral Rd; ✆ 9am-noon & 3-6pm) would look quite at home in Cambridgeshire. Inside, its extraordinarily broad, unbuttressed nave twitters with birdsong and retains the original hardwood pews. Don't miss the stained-glass west window by pre-Raphaelite maestro Sir Edward Burne-Jones.

The bright, ground-floor gallery of the **Academy of Fine Arts** (☎ 22234302; 2 Cathedral Rd; admission free; ✆ 3-8pm) has changing exhibitions featuring local contemporary artists but the upstairs **museum** section is under reconstruction.

THE MAIDAN

After the 'Black Hole' fiasco, a moated 'second' **Fort William** (Map pp104–5; closed to public) was constructed in octagonal, Vaubanesque form (1758). The whole village of Gobindapur was flattened to give the new fort's cannons a clear line of fire. Though sad for then-residents, this created the **Maidan** (pronounced moi-dan), a vast 3km-long park that is today as fundamental to Kolkata as Central Park is to New York City. Fort William remains hidden within a walled military zone, but for an amusingly far-fetched tale of someone who managed to get in, read Simon Winchester's *Calcutta*.

INDIAN MUSEUM

Kolkata's old-fashioned main **museum** (☎ 22499979; Chowringhee Rd; Indian/foreigner/camera Rs10/150/50; ✆ 10am-4.30pm Tue-Sun, guided tours 10.30am, 12.30pm, 3.15pm, last entry 4pm) fills a glorious colonnaded palace around a central lawn. Extensive exhibits include fabulous 1000-year-old Hindu sculptures, lumpy minerals, a whole dangling whale skeleton and endless pinned insects. Gag at the pickled human embryos (gallery 19), notice the surreal Glyptodon dinosaur-armadillo (gallery 11) and don't miss the impressive life-size reproduction of the 2nd-century BC Barhut Gateway. No bags are allowed inside. Handbags can be checked in at the entrance but don't arrive with a backpack.

PARK STREET
Today Park St is one of Kolkata's top commercial avenues. But when it was constructed in the 1760s, it was a simple causeway across uninhabited marshlands built for mourners to access the then-new **South Park Street Cemetery** (Map pp104–5; cnr Park St & AJC Bose Rd; donation expected; ☒ 7.30am-4.30pm Mon-Fri, 7.30am-11am Sat). These days that cemetery remains a wonderful oasis of calm with mossy Raj-era graves – from rotundas to soaring pyramids – jostling for space in a lightly manicured jungle. To support the cemetery's maintenance, a Rs30 donation is appropriate, or buy the guidebook (Rs100) from the gatekeeper.

If strolling south from Park St, check out the latest modern art in the bright, calm **Aakriti Gallery** (Map p108; 1st fl, 12/3 Hungerford St; admission free; ☒ 11am-7pm Mon-Sat).

MOTHER TERESA'S MISSION
The Missionaries of Charity's **Motherhouse** (Map pp104–5; ☎ 22172277; www.motherteresa.org; 54a AJC Bose Rd; ☒ visits 8am-noon & 3-6pm Fri-Wed) is entered via the first alley north of Ripon St. Pilgrims arrive here regularly to pay homage at Mother

Teresa's large, sober **tomb**. Exhibits in a small adjacent **museum** include Teresa's worn sandals and battered enamel dinner-bowl. Upstairs, **'Mother's room'** where she worked and slept from 1953 to 1997, is preserved in all its simplicity with a crown-of-thorns above her modest camp bed.

The charity's numerous Kolkata sites welcome short-term volunteers, qualified or not. Start by attending a briefing two blocks north at **Sishu Bhavan** (Map pp104–5; 78 AJC Bose Rd; ☒ 3pm Mon, Wed & Fri).

BBD Bagh Area
Sites appear on Map p112, except where otherwise noted.

NORTH OF THE MAIDAN
Curiosities around New Market (see p130) include the fascinatingly crumbling **Futani Chambers**, the perfect '50s-style facade of **Elite Cinema**, the brilliant colonial-era **Metropolitan Building** and the fanciful **Tipu Sultan's Mosque**, hidden behind an almost impenetrable ring of market stalls.

Rising above Esplanade bus station, the 1828 **Sahid Minar** is a 48m-tall round-topped obelisk originally celebrating an 1814 British military victory over Nepal. Somewhat resembling the grand **Raj Bhavan** (http://rajbhavankolkata.nic.in/; closed to public) was designed in 1799 along the lines of Kedleston Hall, the Derbyshire home of the

---

MOTHER TERESA

For many people, Mother Teresa (1910–97) was the living image of human sacrifice. Born Agnes Gonxha Bojaxhiu to Albanian parents in then-Ottoman Üsküp (now Skopje in Macedonia), she joined the Irish Order of Loreto nuns and worked for over a decade teaching in Calcutta's **St Mary's High School** (Map p108; ☎ 22298451; 92 Ripon St). Horrified by the city's spiralling poverty she established a new order, the **Missionaries of Charity** (www.motherteresa.org) and, in 1952, opened Nirmal Hridy (Sacred Heart; see p115). This was the first of many refuges offering free shelter and a little human dignity to the destitute and dying. Although the order expanded into an international charity, Mother Teresa herself continued to live in absolute simplicity. She was awarded the Nobel Peace Prize in 1979 and beatified by the Vatican in October 2003, the first official step towards being made a saint.

But this 'Saint of the Gutters' is not universally beloved. For some Kolkatans it's slightly galling to find their cultured, predominantly Hindu city popularly linked in the world's mind with a Catholic heroine whose work underlined the city's least appealing facet. Meanwhile Germaine Greer has accused Mother Teresa of religious imperialism, while Christopher Hitchens' book, *The Missionary Position*, decries the donations from dictators and corrupt tycoons. Many have questioned the Missionaries of Charity's minimal medical background and Teresa's staunchly Catholic position against contraception, which seems particularly untenable given Kolkata's growing AIDS and hepatitis epidemic. Of course, the organisation was never primarily focused on saving lives, simply offering a little love to the dying. Before Mother Teresa, even that was an unknown luxury for the truly destitute.

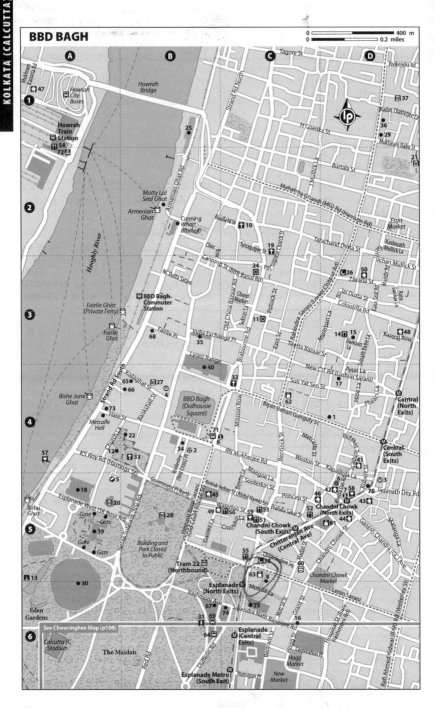

BBD BAGH

Curzon family. By strange coincidence, one of its most famous masters a century later would be none other than Lord Curzon. Today the building is the official residence of the West Bengal governor and visitors may only peep through the ornate giant gates.

The vast **Ranji Stadium** hosting Kolkata cricket matches is commonly nicknamed for the **Eden Gardens** (admission free; ⏰ 1pm-6pm) that lie behind. Those gardens feature a lake and picturesque **Burmese pagoda**. Entry is usually limited to the south gate, but a small, more convenient north portal near Gate 12 of Ranji Stadium is occasionally open. Bring ID.

The resplendent 1872 **High Court** building is a wonderful architectural confection reputedly modelled on the Cloth Hall in Ypres (Flanders). For the best view, approach from the south walking past the western end of the low-domed **West Bengal Assembly building**. Beside is the imposing colonnaded cube of the former **Town Hall building** (4 Esplanade West) where **Kolkata Panorama** (☎ 22483085; weekdays/weekends Rs10/15; ⏰ 11am-6pm Tue-Sun) introduces the city's heritage through

a lively collection of working models and interactive exhibits. It's well designed, though historically selective, and many foreigners will struggle to appreciate fully the detailed sections on Bengali popular culture. The accompanying guide makes it awkward to 'escape' quickly.

ST JOHN'S CHURCH

More colonnades buttress the stone-spired 1787 **St John's Church** (☎ 22436098; KS Roy Rd; ⏰ 8am-5pm). The small, portrait-draped room on the right as you enter was once used as an office by Warren Hastings, Bengal's first British Governor-General.

In the church's somewhat overgrown **graveyard** (admission Rs10) are two curious octagonal monuments. The **mausoleum of Job Charnock** celebrates Kolkata's disputed 'founder'. A 1902 **Black Hole Memorial** was hidden away here in 1940.

AROUND BBD BAGH

Arranged around BBD Bagh is much of Kolkata's finest colonial architecture. Originally called Tank Sq, its palm-lined central reservoir-lake ('tank') once supplied the young city's water. Some locals still use its later-colonial name **Dalhousie Sq**, commemorating British Lieutenant-Governor Lord Dalhousie. But with delicious irony, the square is now re-renamed after the nationalists who tried to assassinate him. In fact the BBD trio (Binoy, Badal and Dinesh) bungled their 1930 raid, killing instead an unlucky prisons inspector. Nonetheless the attack was a highly symbolic moment in the self-determination struggle. The assassination took place within the photogenic 1780 **Writers' Building**, whose glorious south facade looks something like a French provincial city hall. Originally built for clerks ('writers') of the East India Company, it's still a haven of pen-pushing bureaucracy.

There are many other imposing colonial edifices. The red-brick **Standard Buildings** (32 BBD Bagh) have carved nymphs and wonderful wrought-iron balconies at the rear. The former **Standard Chartered Building** (Netaji Subhash Rd) has a vaguely Moorish feel, while **St Andrews Church** has a fine Wren-style spire. The 1866 **General Post Office** (see p106) was built on the ruins of the original Fort William, site of the infamous 'Black Hole of Calcutta' (see p101). Beneath its vast central cupola occasional mini-exhibitions are held around a statue of a traditional Bengali mail-runner. In a nearby building there's a loveable little **philatelic museum** (☎ 22437331; Koilaghat St; admission free; ☽ 11am-4pm Mon-Sat).

BARABAZAAR
Scattered north and northeast of BBD Bagh lies a wide scattering of religious buildings. Alone none warrants a special trip, but weaving between them is a great excuse to explore some of Kolkata's most vibrantly chaotic alleys. Looking like a tall-spired church, **Moghan David Synagogue** (Canning St) is somewhat more impressive than **BethEl Synagogue** (Pollock St). The 1797 Portuguese-Catholic **Holy Rosary Cathedral** (Brabourne Rd; ☽ 6am-11am) has eye-catching crown-topped side towers. Hidden away amid the bustle of Old China Bazaar St, the 1707 **Armenian Church** (Armenian St; ☽ 9am-11am Sun) is claimed to be Kolkata's oldest place of Christian worship. It has a low, but finely proportioned, whitewashed spire that's best spied from Bonfield Lane. To the east the 1926 red-sandstone **Nakhoda Mosque** (1 Zakaria St) rises impressively above the bustling shop

fronts of ever-fascinating Rabindra Sarani. Its roof, bristling with domes and minarets, was loosely modelled on Akbar's Mausoleum at Sikandra.

OLD CHINATOWN
On ragged little Damzen Lane there's a former **Chinese Church** and an old **Chinese Temple** (now used as a local school) along with a bright turquoise home whose oversized **gateway** (10 Damzen Lane) was built to allow passage for the family's domestic elephants. For nearly two centuries this area was home to a predominantly Christianised Chinese community, many of whom fled or were interned during a fit of anti-Chinese fervour during the 1962 war. These days, Kolkata's unexotic newer Chinatown is in Tangra and the old Chinatown area is pretty run down. Beside the ruined but once-grand 1924 **Nangking Restaurant**, a rubbish heap (due for eventual removal) supports a community of destitute scavengers who scrape together a miserable existence living in tent-and-box shacks on neighbouring pavements. Very humbling to see.

Hooghly Riverbank
The Hooghly River's chocolate sludge might look unappealing, but it's holy to Hindu Kolkatans whose main festivals involve plunging divine images into its waters (see p101). Riverside **ghats** are interesting any dawn or dusk when die-hard devotees bathe and make offerings. A photogenic if distinctly seedy vantage point is **Babu Ghat** (Map pp104-5), hidden behind a grubby, pseudo-Greek gateway near Eden Gardens.

HOWRAH (HAORA)
Kolkata's 705m-long architectural icon, **Howrah bridge** (Rabindra Setu; Map p112) is a vibrating abstraction of steel cantilevers, traffic fumes and sweat. Although built back in WWII, it remains one of the world's busiest bridges. Beneath the east end, **Mullik Ghat flower market** is a sensory overload of sights and smells. It's very photogenic but beware that photography of the bridge itself is strictly prohibited. You might be able to sneak a discreet shot from one of the various river-ferries that ply across the Hooghly to the vast **Howrah train station**. That 1906 edifice has clusters of towers topped in terracotta tiles giving it a look reminiscent of a Spanish desert citadel. The station serves millions daily, emptying

trains picked clean by legions of destitute street children who are the subject of much charity work and plenty of moving prose.

Some 500m south, the open-air **Railway Museum** (admission Rs5; ☉ 1-8pm Fri-Wed) has a two-storey model of Howrah train station, several 19th-century steam locos and a **toy-train ride** (Rs10).

West Kolkata

BOTANICAL GARDENS

Founded in 1786, the 109-hectare **Botanical Gardens** (Map pp104-5; ☎ 26685357; Indian/foreigner Rs5/50; ☉ 5.30am-5pm Oct-Feb, 5am-5.30pm Mar-Sep) played an important role in cultivating tea long before it became a household commodity. Today there's a cactus house, palm collection, river-overlook and a boating lake with splendid Giant Amazon Lily pads, but the biggest draw is a 250-year-old **banyan tree**, 140m across. It's reputedly the world's largest but the central trunk rotted away in the 1920s leaving a curious 'forest' of cross-branches and linked aerial roots that have become virtual trees of their own.

The banyan is five minutes' walk from the park's Bicentenary Gate (Andul Rd) or 25 minutes' walk from the gardens' main gate where bus 55 and minibus 6 from Howrah/Esplanade (Rs7) terminate. Taxis from Shakespeare Sarani charge around Rs90 via the elegant **Vidyasagar Setu** (Hooghly Suspension Bridge).

South Kolkata

KALIGHAT

Kalighat's ancient **Kali Temple** (Map pp104-5; ☎ 22231516; ☉ 5am-2pm & 4-10pm winter, 4am-2pm & 3-10.30pm Apr-Oct) is Kolkata's holiest spot for Hindus and possibly the source of its name (p101). Today's version, a 1809 rebuild, has floral- and peacock-motif tiles that look more Victorian than Hindu. The double-stage roof is painted silver-grey with rainbow highlights. More interesting than the architecture are the jostling pilgrim queues that snake into the main hall to fling hibiscus flowers at a crowned, three-eyed Kali image. Priests loitering around the temple might whisk you to the front of the queue for an obligatory 'donation' (significant money). Behind the bell pavilion but still within the mandir complex, goats are ritually beheaded to honour the ever-demanding goddess, or, as a local guide described it, to buy 'God power'.

The temple is somewhat hidden within a maze of alleys jammed with **market stalls** selling votive flowers, brassware, religious artefacts and pictures of Kali. From Kalighat metro station (with its four-storey **Mother Teresa mosaic**) walk towards the putrid Tolisnala Stream where **Shanagar Burning Ghat** hosts an impressive gaggle of monuments celebrating those cremated here. Turn north up Tollygunge Rd which becomes vibrant Kalighat Rd after one block. The temple is situated to the right down the footpath immediately before **Nirmal Hriday** (251 Kalighat Rd). That's Mother Teresa's world famous, if surprisingly small, home for the dying (see p111), its roof corners pimpled with neo-Mughal minidomes.

Walking further north up lively Kalighat Rd, notice unsophisticated pot-painter artisans at work in the west-leading lane just before **Kalighat Market**. After curving across Hazra Rd upper Kalighat Rd hosts numerous image makers: less famous but almost as intriguing as those in Kumartuli (p118).

ALIPORE

Kolkata's 16-hectare **zoo** (Map pp104-5; ☎ 24791152; Alipore Rd; admission Rs10; ☉ 9am-5pm Fri-Wed) first opened in 1875. The spacious lawns and lakeside promenades are very popular with weekend picnickers (hence all the rubbish). Grass is so high in the moated Bengal Tiger enclosure that it's hard to spot the animals but it's better than several more confining cages and the aviaries whose thick rusty-black wire-mesh rather obscures viewing. Across the road an **aquarium** (Rs3; ☉ 10.30am-5pm Fri-Wed) displays a few sorry tankfuls of fish. Get here by bus 230 from Rabindra Sadan.

Directly south of the zoo's entrance, the (private) access road to the National Library (www.nlindia.org, India's biggest) loops around the very regal **Curzon Mansion**, once the colonial Viceroy's residence. It's not (yet) a museum.

Around 1km southeast, the lawn, tropical trees and flowering shrubs of the delightful **Horticultural Gardens** (Map pp104-5; admission Rs10; ☉ 6-10am & 2-7pm) offer some respite from the traffic rumble.

ELGIN ROAD & GARIAHAT

Netaji Bhawan (Map p108; ☎ 24756139; www.netaji .org; 38/2 Elgin Rd; adult/child Rs5/2; ☉ 11am-4.15pm

Tue-Sun), an interesting museum celebrating the life and vision of controversial independence radical Subhas Chandra Bose (opposite), maintains several rooms decorated in 1940s style. It was Bose's brother's residence from which Subhas made his famous 'Great Escape' from British-imposed house arrest in January 1941. The veteran getaway car is parked in the drive.

For cutting-edge contemporary Bengali art visit **CIMA** (Centre for International Modern Art; Map pp104-5; ☎ 24858509; Sunny Towers, 2nd fl, 43 Ashutosh Chowdhury Rd; admission free; ◷ 11am-7pm Tue-Sat, 3-7pm Mon) a well-lit, six-room gallery with an eclectic gift shop.

Nearby, the 20th-century **Birla Mandir** (Map pp104-5; Gariahat Rd; ◷ 6-11.30am & 4.30-9pm Nov-Mar,

5.30-11am & 4.30-9pm Apr-Oct) is a large Lakshmi Narayan temple complex in cream-coloured sandstone whose three corn-cob shaped towers are more impressive for their size than their carvings.

RABINDRA SAROVAR

Around dawn, middle-class Kolkatans arrive en masse to exercise in the parkland surrounding **Rabindra Sarovar** (Map pp104–5), a lake that prettily reflects the hazy sunrise. As well as jogging, rowing and meditation, some people form circles to do group-yoga routines culminating in ho-ho ha-ha-ha laugh-ins. These are the informal **Laughing Clubs** (◷ 6am-7am), engagingly described by Tony Hawks in *The Weekenders: Adventures*

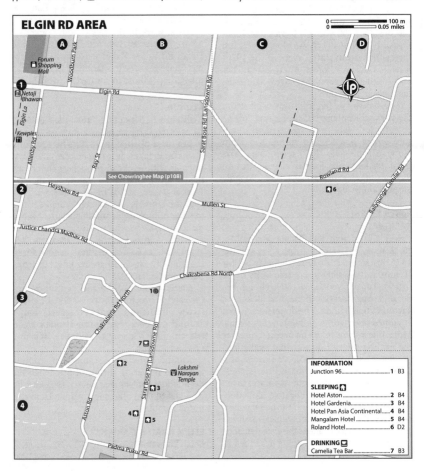

ELGIN RD AREA

0   100 m
0   0.05 miles

See Chowringhee Map (p108)

INFORMATION		
Junction 96..................................	1	B3

SLEEPING		
Hotel Aston...................................	2	B4
Hotel Gardenia.............................	3	B4
Hotel Pan Asia Continental......	4	B4
Mangalam Hotel	5	B4
Roland Hotel................................	6	D2

DRINKING		
Camelia Tea Bar..........................	7	B3

in Calcutta. Even if forced, a good giggle can be refreshingly therapeutic.

In the manicured lawns of the **Birla Academy of Art & Culture** (Map pp104-5; ☎ 24666802; 109 Southern Ave; admission Rs2; ☒ 4-7pm Tue-Sun) stands an androgynous three-storey **Krishna Statue**, a flute dangling from his stone cod-piece. Next-door, **Lake Kalibari** is a small but revered Kali shrine.

North Kolkata
The following sights are on Map pp104–5.

KOLKATA UNIVERSITY AREA
Tucked behind Kolkata University's Central Library, the **Ashutosh Museum of Indian Art** (☎ 22410071; www.caluniv.ac.in; Centenary Bldg, 87/1 College St; admission Rs10; ☒ 11.30am-4.30pm Mon-Fri) displays a priceless if slightly dry collection of fabulous antique Indian sculpture, brass-work and Bengali terracotta. It's down the first lane off College St as you walk north from Coloola Rd.

Nearby, the mythic **Indian Coffee House** (1st fl, 15 Bankim Chatterjee St; coffee Rs8, snack meals Rs20-35; ☒ 9am-9pm Mon-Sat, 9am-12.30pm & 5-9pm Sun) was once a meeting place of freedom fighters, bohemians and revolutionaries. Today its crusty high ceilings and grimy walls ring with deafening student conversation but despite the dishwater coffee, it's perversely fascinating. One block south of MG Rd, walk 20m east off College St and it's upstairs on the left.

The section of MG Rd between here and Sealdah Station is an inspiring chaos of mouldering generations-old box shops, potion sellers and card-makers beneath dishevelled occasionally grand old facades. Notice the little **typing-cubicles** on Surya Sen St.

MARBLE PALACE
This grand 1853 **mansion** (☎ 22393310; 46 Muktaram Babu St; ☒ 10am-4pm Tue-Wed & Fri-Sun) is indulgently overstuffed with statues, Victoriana, Belgian glassware and fine paintings – there's even a reputedly original Rubens. The music room is lavishly floored with marble inlay but much of the antique furniture remains haphazardly draped in torn old dustsheets. It's an odd place where admission is technically free, but guards, guides and even the toilet monitor all expect tips. Before visiting you need to get a permission note from either West Bengal Tourism or India Tourism (see p107).

From MG Rd metro, walk two blocks north and turn west at 171 Chittaranjan Ave. To continue to Tagore's House, continue west down Muktaram Babu St, turn right on Rabindra Sarani, and walk two blocks north passing the wonderful olde-worlde **Ram Prasad apothecary shop** (Map p112; 204 Rabindra Sarani; ☒ 8.30am-8.30pm Mon-Sat) and several **stone-carving workshops**.

TAGORE'S HOUSE
Within Rabindra Bharati University, the comfortable 1784 family mansion of Rabindranath Tagore (p60) has become an extensive, shrine-like **museum** (Rabindra Bharati Museum; Map p112 ☎ 22181744; 246D Rabindra Sarani; Indian/foreigner Rs10/50, student Rs5/25; ☒ 10.30am-4.30pm Tue-Sun) to India's greatest modern poet. Even if his personal effects don't inspire you, some of the well-chosen quotations might spark an interest in Tagore's deeply universalist philosophy. There's also a decent gallery of paintings by his family and contemporaries. The 1930 photo of Tagore taken with Einstein could win a 'World's Wildest Hair' competition.

Tram 6 connects to Kumartuli.

SUBHAS CHANDRA BOSE
During the early 1940s the two most prominent figures in the Indian anticolonial campaign were Gandhi (who favoured nonviolence) and Subhas Chandra Bose (who certainly didn't). Eminently intelligent, Cambridge-educated Bose managed to become Chief Executive of Calcutta despite periods in jail following accusations of assault and terrorism. During WWII he fled first to Germany, then to Japan. Along with Rash Behari Bose, he developed the Indian National Army (INA), mostly by recruiting Indian soldiers from Japanese POW camps and armed by Hitler. The INA then marched with Japan's invading force towards northeastern India, getting bogged down, and were eventually defeated in Manipur and Nagaland. Bose fled the scene but later perished in a mysterious plane crash.

Today his image is somewhat ambivalent in much of India, but in Bengal, Bose remains a hero nicknamed Netaji (revered leader). Patriotic songs are intoned before his many statues and Kolkata's airport is named for him.

KUMARTULI

This fascinating district is named for the *kumar* (sculptors) who fashion giant **puja effigies** of the gods that will eventually be ritually immersed in the holy Hooghly (p102). Different workshops specialise in creating clay straw frames, adding clay coatings or painting the divine features. Craftsmen are busiest from August till November for the Durga and Kali festivals (p102).

To explore Kumartuli, take the narrow lane west from 499 Rabindra Sorani and then turn north on Banamali Sakar St. A short walk west down Charan Banerjee St will lead you to a ghat where the clay-mud is brought in. A pleasant five-minute wander north up the riverbank past Kashi Mitra Burning Ghat leads to Bagbazar Jetty whence ferries (Rs4) cross to Howrah (four hourly) and Baranagar (twice hourly) or shared tuk-tuks run along Bagbazar Rd in the direction of Shova Bazaar metro.

POLICE MUSEUM

Worth a short stop if you're passing, this dinky, column-fronted 1814 house was once owned by Raja Rammohun Roy, the Bengal Renaissance intellectual credited with coining the English term 'Hindi'. Later used as a police station, it now hosts a well-presented little **museum** (Map pp104–5; ☎ 23607704; 113 APC Rd; admission free; ☽ 11am-5pm Mon-Fri) most interestingly displaying various historical weapons and giving the story of who they killed and how the crime was solved.

JAIN TEMPLES

Three eye-catching **Jain temples** (Badridas Temple St; donation appropriate; ☽ 6am-noon & 3-7pm) are grouped together two short blocks east of Raja Dinendra Rd (1.6km from Shyam Bazaar metro, two big blocks south of Aurobindo Sarani). The best known is 1867 **Sheetalnathji Jain Mandir**. Its dazzling if somewhat unrefined pastiche of colourful mosaics, spires, columns and slivered figurines looks like a work of Gaudi. Directly south, the quieter **Sri Sri Channa Probhuji Mandir** has a fine gateway arch and plenty of greenery. The sedate 1810 **Dadaji Jain Mandir** has a central marble tomb-temple patterned with silver studs.

In bird-filled gardens 250km west of Belgachia Metro is the **Digambar Jain Mandir** (☽ 6am-noon & 5-7pm) with a tall lighthouse-style tower encasing a meditating statuette.

DAKSHINESWAR KALI TEMPLE

The heart of this vibrant complex of 14 temples is a red-and-yellow 1847 **Kali Temple** (☎ 25645222; ☽ 6.30am-noon & 3-8.30pm) shaped like an Indian Sacré-Coeur. This was where Ramakrishna started his remarkable spiritual journey and his small room in the outer northwest corner of the temple precinct is now a place of special meditative reverence. On Sunday the extensive complex is thronged with devotees.

Bus DN9/1 from Dum Dum metro (Rs5) terminates at the start of the temple's 400m hawker-jammed access lane. To continue to Belur Math take one of the leave-when-full river boats (Rs7, 20 minutes). Bring a hat as they're uncovered.

BELUR MATH

This attractively landscaped riverside **religious centre** (☎ 26545892; www.sriramakrishna.org/belur.htm; Grand Trunk Rd; ☽ 6.30am-noon & 3.30-8.30pm) is the headquarters of the Ramakrishna Mission. Amid the palms and manicured lawns, its centrepiece is the unique 1938 **Ramakrishna Mandir** (☽ 6.30am-12.30 & 3.30-8pm), which somehow manages to look like a cathedral, Indian palace and Istanbul's Ayasofya all at the same time. This combination is deliberate and is perfectly in keeping with the message of the 19th-century Indian sage **Ramakrishna Paramahamsa** who preached the unity of all religions.

Behind the main mandir near the Hooghly riverbank, there are a number of smaller **shrines** (☽ 6.30-11.30am & 3.30-5.15pm), including the **Sri Sarada Devi Temple** entombing the guru's wife. Larger yet essentially rather similar in design, the 1924 **Swami Vivekananda Temple** marks the cremation spot of the mission's founder and Ramakrishna's most famous disciple. **Swami Vivekananda's room** is also preserved.

Accessed from the car park, the beautifully presented, dual-level **museum** (admission Rs3; ☽ 8.30-11.30am & 3.30-5.30pm Tue-Sun) charts Ramakrishna's life and travels, with mock-ups of buildings in which he stayed from Rajasthan to New York.

Take minibus 10 or bus 54/1 from Esplanade, or bus 56 from Howrah train station. Boats to Dakshineswar go against the current so it's better to arrive that way. Weekends only, boats run eight times daily to Bagbazar near Kumartuli (left).

ACTIVITIES

There are two modern six-lane tenpin bowling alleys:

Sparkz (Map pp104-5; ☎ 24481744; Diamond Harbour Rd, Alipore; ◷ noon-11pm) Beneath Majerhat Bridge, bus 77A from Esplanade.

Nicco Superbowl (Map pp104-5; ☎ 23576052; www .niccoparks.com/amusement-park/facilities.asp; Salt Lake City; ◷ noon-10pm)

Nicco Superbowl is beside **Nicco Park** (www .niccoparks.com; admission Rs50, rides Rs15-40; ◷ 11am-8pm) with its roller-coaster and fairground rides. Take bus 201 from Belgachia metro.

Cooking Courses

Several times weekly Kali Travel Home (right) arranges highly recommended three-hour Bengali **cooking courses** (www.traveleastindia .com/cooking_classes/cooking_classes.html; Rs500-700) led by local housewives in their homes. Costs include food.

Golf

The beautiful golf course at the **Tollygunge Club** (Map pp104-5; ☎ 24732316 ext 142; www.the tollygungeclub.com/home.htm; SP Mukherjee Rd) charges Rs1740 green fees for visitors but only Rs175 if you're staying here. Renting clubs costs around Rs300.

The magnificent **Royal Calcutta Golf Club** (Map pp104-5; ☎ 24731288; www.royalCalcuttagolf club.com/history.htm; 18 Golf Club Rd) was established in 1829, making it the oldest golf club in the world outside Britain. Foreign guests pay US$50 plus Rs300 for club rental and Rs125 caddy fees.

Meditation, Yoga & Dance

The **Aurobindo Bhawan** (Map p108; ☎ 22822162; 8 Shakespeare Sarani; ◷ 8am-8pm) has a city centre garden-oasis with open-air meditation space to sit as you wish or to join half-hour group **meditations** (◷ 7pm Thu & Sun). Ask about **meditation lessons** (free; ◷ 5pm Tue) and **classical Indian dance lessons** in various styles: **Odissi** (Rs100; ◷ 5pm Mon), **Bharata Natyam** (Rs100; 4.30pm Thu), **Kathak** (Rs150; 5pm Fri, Sat). Tailor-made yoga-exercise programS can be arranged.

Art of Living (www.artofliving.org; aolkol@vsnl .net) runs five-day yoga courses at varying locations.

Volunteering

Several organisations welcome foreign volunteers (see p323).

TOURS

West Bengal Tourism's full-day sightseeing **bus tour** (Rs200; ◷ 8.30am) is a relative bargain but gives only sweaty, drive-by glimpses of most sights and rushes round Belur Math and Dakshineswar in barely half an hour apiece. The office (BBD Bagh, p107) opens at 7am to sell last-minute tickets but trips are cancelled when there are less than 15 customers (cancellations least likely on Sunday).

Blue Sky Cafe (p124) organises five-hour **van tours** (Rs550 per person; ◷ 8.30am Thu, Sat & Sun) including Kalighat and the Marble Palace (minimum three guests).

Enthusiastic expats at **Kali Travel Home** (☎ /fax 25587980; www.traveleastindia.com) offer very personal accompanied city-walks and longer customised tours around Bengal, Darjeeling and Sikkim.

For excursions to the Sunderbans Tiger Reserve, see p139.

SLEEPING

In summer big off-season discounts are possible but AC will be virtually essential. In winter fan rooms are fine but demand is high, so you might have to take whatever's available. Things rot rapidly in this climate and renovations are cyclical so ideally look before you book.

Although there are numerous cheap hotels in other areas (notably around Sealdah station), the Sudder St area is the only one where most budget hotels accept foreigners. Standards vary considerably but even in many of the better cheapies, peeling paint and damp patches come as standard and putting a mat on the bed to guard against bed-bugs is generally wise. Be prepared for furniture scars even in upper midrange places. Many lock their gates by midnight so if you're planning to be late, forewarn the staff.

Top-end hotels are very pricey but internet discounters (eg www.yatra.com) can shave up to 50% off rack rates.

Most hotels add luxury tax (5%) but some tack on further service charges (up to 25%). For fairness we quote total prices.

Sudder & Park St Areas

Looks can be deceptive. Some eye-catchingly smart facades mask lacklustre, mustily disappointing rooms. Other very survivable places are hidden within buildings that look like crumbling wrecks. The following options appear on Map p108.

BUDGET

If you want to pay under Rs400 a room it can be done. But don't expect to enjoy the experience.

> The one-eyed manager limped awkwardly up the stairs to show us this miserable pit of a room. Over the bed someone had scribbled 'This is the worst night of my life'. Unable to keep up with us as we fled, the hobbling manager shouted out ever-lower prices. But zero rupees wouldn't have been cheap enough. We realised then that in Kolkata 'budget' accommodation represented a whole new league of nastiness.
>
> *Maud Hennessy, Sudder St backpacker*

One positive point for the ultracheap hotels Paragon, Maria and Modern Lodge is that each has a roof terrace with plastic seats (albeit utterly decrepit) where you can sit and hang out with fellow slummers. Don't assume that the cheapest rooms listed below will have power points or windows.

Hotel Maria (☎ 22520860, 22224444; 5/1 Stuart Lane; d/q Rs300/450, dm/s/d without bathroom Rs70/150/200; 🖳) Mouldering but peaceful old mansion whose dorm offers zero privacy but plenty of air. It's pleasantly set in a green courtyard and has on-site internet for Rs15 per hour.

Paragon Hotel (☎ 22522445; 2 Stuart Lane; dm Rs90, r without bathroom Rs150-330) Coffin-box rooms are as spirit-crushing as you'd expect for the price and the jam-packed dorms are windowless. Bring your own padlock.

Modern Lodge (☎ 22524960; 1 Stuart Lane; r Rs250, without bathroom r from Rs100) Although not really modern at all, Modern Lodge probably offers the best value of all the ultrabudget dives. High-ceilinged rooms are as ragged as ever but there's a somewhat atmospheric old 1st-floor sitting room and a peaceful roof terrace.

Centrepoint Guest House (☎ 22520953; ian_rashid @yahoo.com; 20 Mirza Ghalib St; dm Rs100, s/d without bathroom from Rs300/350, with AC s/d Rs500/600) Rooms are barebones boxes but repainted and with less damp than many. Three large 4th-floor bunk-dorms are nominally sex-segregated and have under-bed safe-boxes (bring a padlock). Their shared showers and toilets are on the open terrace.

Continental Guesthouse (☎ 22520663; Sudder St; s/d without bathroom from Rs150/200, d with toilet Rs350) Aesthetically rooms are much nicer than most other cheapies, but low ceilings mean a tendency to over-heat and there's only one shared toilet for over a dozen rooms.

Timestar Hotel (☎ 22528028; 2 Tottie Lane; s/d from Rs200/325) This chunky-walled colonial mansion house has tatty walls but newly tiled floors and high enough ceilings in the upstairs rooms that they don't overheat so badly.

Hotel Paramount (☎ 22290066; 33/4 Mirza Ghalib St; s/d with fan Rs275/375, with AC Rs650/700; 🖳) If everything on Sudder St is full, several basic places are tucked away down a dauntingly uninspiring side alley. Better than most of these, the Paramount is a warren of 60 mostly repainted rooms, but look first as many rooms lack natural light.

Hotel Gulistan (☎ 22260963; hotelgulistan@gmail .com; 30F Mirza Ghalib St; d fan/AC from Rs350/550; 🖳) The banana-yellow cheapies have caged-in mini-balconies and the best Rs750 rooms have newly tiled walls. All are a little claustrophobic but this is about the cheapest place to have AC and, being new, rooms are passably clean.

Hotel Pioneer International (☎ 22520557; 1st fl, 1 Marquis St; d without/with AC Rs450/650) Wobbly wooden stairs within an unpromisingly aged house lead to a hotel whose six rooms are neat with new tiled floors and multilingual TV. Friendly, helpful staff. Some readers found the mattresses rather itchy.

our pick Hotel Aafreen (☎ 22654146; afreen-cal @yahoo.co.in; Nawab Abdur Rahman St; d with fan/AC Rs450/700; 🖳) Offering midrange quality at budget prices, the Aafreen's paintwork is mostly intact, staff are obliging, the lift works and freshly tiled bathrooms have hot water.

Ashreen Guest House (☎ 22520889; ashreen_guest house@yahoo.com; 2 Cowie Lane; d Rs495, d/tr with AC Rs840/960; 🖳) Still one of Kolkata's best-value minihotels, the rooms are small but sparkling clean with geysers and playful interior touches. Service is caring and proactive but there's often a waiting list. If the Ashreen is full they may send you across the road to the co-managed Afridi International in which six rooms (so far) are fully upgraded but the rest are typical Sudder St cheapies.

Aafreen Tower (☎ 22293280; aafreen_tower@yahoo .co.in; 9A Kyd St; d with fan/AC Rs600/900; 🖳) A glass elevator and bright orange-and-gold corridors lead to decent-sized, well-ventilated rooms which remain an excellent deal, although some of the glossily ornate fittings show a little wear.

Super Guesthouse (☎ 22520995; super_guesthouse @hotmail.com; Sudder St 6; d 660-2500; 🕱) This all-AC guesthouse occupies three separate but very close-by buildings and runs a restaurant, bar and helpful travel agency. The Rs660 double rooms were suffering damp when we visited but the new Rs1100 ones were great value for money. Some lack natural light.

Chowringhee YMCA (☎ 22492192; 25 Chowringhee Rd; s/d Rs600/900 plus Rs50 'membership', with AC Rs250-300 extra; 🕱) Asia's oldest YMCA looks pretty run down as you climb the once-grand steps to the little reception box (open 8am to 8pm) but above the Corinthian-columned badminton court there is an open courtyard surrounded by very reasonably priced ensuite rooms with optional AC. Breakfast is included.

Hotel Pushpak (☎ 22265841; www.hotelpushpak international.com; 10 Kyd St; with fan s/d Rs700/900, with AC Rs1050/1260, deluxe s/d rs1400/1600; 🕱) Retro touches in the corridors don't quite create style but the paintings and statuary give a human touch and the pleasant beige-cream rooms have neat little geyser bathrooms. Two deluxe rooms come with king bed and fridge.

Sunflower Guest House (☎ 22299401; 5th fl, 7 Royd St; d/tr from Rs750/850, with AC Rs950/1000) In a venerable old apartment block, assiduously cleaned if largely unadorned, high-ceilinged rooms have freshly tiled bathrooms with geysers. Take the original 1940s lift (with 2006 workings) to the top of the 1865 Solomon Mansions building and seek out staff behind the little roof garden.

CKT Inn (☎ 22520130; cktinn_kolkata@yahoo.co.in; 3rd fl, 12/1 Lindsay St; s/d Rs825/1100; 🕱) CKT's furniture has some art deco touches, south-facing rooms are peaceful, central AC is effective but carpets are slightly rucked. Enter from the side of an unlikely office building and take the cramped cage lift.

MIDRANGE

Hotel VIP InterContinental (☎ 22520150; vipinter continental@rediffmail.com; 44 Mirza Ghalib St; s/d from Rs1150/1205, super-deluxe r Rs1790; 🕱) Behind the very narrow, one-desk reception hall, the friendly little VIP InterContinental has small but well air-conditioned rooms in varying styles all with stone floors and hot

water in presentable little bathrooms. The Super Deluxe rooms are unexpectedly hip. Don't confuse with the nearby Hotel VIP Continental whose dashing foyer hides sad corridors and seriously overpriced rooms.

Fairlawn Hotel (☎ 22521510; www.fairlawnhotel .com; 13A Sudder St; s/d Rs2215/2658; 🕱) Taking guests since 1936, the Fairlawn is a characterful 1783 Raj-era home fronted by tropical greenery. The stairs and the sitting room are smothered with photos, family mementos and articles celebrating the hotel's nonagenarian owner. While not luxurious, most of the rooms have been recently freshened up. Most sport kettles, fridges and a sitting area, though bathtubs are painted rather than enamelled. Breakfast and tea are included in the price.

Dee Empressa Hotel (☎ 40021888; www.deeempresa .com; 12/2A Kyd St; s/d/ste Rs3780/4410/4830; 🕱) The two-storey atrium, flat-screen TVs and silk bed sashes give this new 48-room tower a mild chic, though the elaborately uniformed doormen seem a touch too much and the lift is overworked. The marble-floored rooms are very clean but not large.

Housez 43 (☎ 22276020; www.housez43.com; 43 Mirza Ghalib St; s/d from Rs4000/4500; 🕱) Bright colours, funky lamps and odd-shaped mirrors bring character to this handily central boutique hotel. Some rooms are trendier than others.

Lytton Hotel (☎ 22491872/3; www.lyttonhotelindia .com; 14 Sudder St; s/d/ste Rs4350/5550/6825; 🕱) This slightly old-fashioned but well-maintained hotel has Tiffany-style panels in the stairwells, period touches in the bedrooms and arty sinks in the modest-sized bathrooms. Room sizes vary significantly.

TOP END

Peerless Inn (☎ 44003900; www.sarovarhotels.com; 12 Nehru Rd; s/d/ste Rs11,025/12,075/16,800; 🕱 💻) Straightforward business-style rooms have fine linens and elements of local embroidery that contrast with ill-chosen carpets and old-fashioned cup chairs. The modest 9th-floor weight-training gym has great views across the Maidan to Vidyasagar Setu.

Park Hotel (☎ 22499000; www.theparkhotels.com; 17 Park St; d Rs12,600-17,850; 🕱 💻 🕱) Perfectly central and hosting much of the city's nightlife, one of the Park's pricier floors uses stylish black-on-black decor, though some of the contemporary goldfish-bowl wash basins already look tired. Live music buffets the small, overworked lobby till 4am at weekends and on Wednesday with noise carrying through especially to the rather disappointing cheaper rooms.

our pick Oberoi Grand (☎ 22492323; www.oberoikolkata.com; 15 Chowringhee Rd; s/d/ste Rs19,950/21,525/36,750; ❄ 🖳 ☎) This marvellous oasis of genteel calm deserves every point of its five stars. A vast antique chandelier, gilt-capitalled columns, classical music and the scent of fresh lilies welcome you to the sumptuous lobby. Immaculate accommodation oozes atmosphere with a fresh rose on arrival and four-poster beds in upper-category rooms. The limpid swimming pool is ringed with palms, staff anticipate your needs and a Banyan Tree spa massages away any cares.

Southern Chowringhee

Most Southern Chowringhee hotels (Map p108) are comparatively upmarket catering for business clientele.

Hotel Victerrace (☎ 22800713; 1B Gorky Tce; d standard/deluxe Rs1125/1610; ❄) This 50-room maze of narrow, overheated passageways links cramped, slightly musty but recently repainted standard rooms and roomier if slightly dated deluxe ones.

Sikkim House (☎ 22815328; 4/1 Middleton St; d/ste Rs1200/1500; ⏰ reception 8am-10pm; ❄) Sikkimese guests get first call on these large, clean if fairly functional all-AC rooms but tourists may stay if there's a vacancy.

Pallavi International (Hathwa Regency; ☎ 22891340; pallaviint_kol@yahoo.co.in; 10E Hungerford St; d with/without AC Rs2100/1890; ❄) Sepia photos and a family tree are clues that this low-key apartment-block guesthouse is owned by a maharaja (of Hutwa, Bihar). However, while the reception area is smart, the rooms are more functional with lacklustre furniture.

Old Kenilworth Hotel (Purdey's Inn; ☎ 22825325; 7 Little Russell St; d without/with AC Rs2250/2940; ❄) Run by the Anglo-Armenian Purdey family since 1948, this is more of a spacious homestay than a hotel. Rooms are very large if sparse with items of '50s-style furniture and unique Heath Robinson–style rope-drag fans on some high ceilings. There's a private lawn, but no restaurant nor lift.

Allenby Inn (☎ 24869984; allenbyinn@vsnl.net; 1/2 Allenby Rd; s/d/ste Rs3150/3675/4200; ❄) Spread over several floors of an apartment block with fashionable trimmings and lashings of ab-

stract art, some of the 25 rooms are very large, though towels could be softer. Two 5th-floor 'suites' share a very spacious dining area and small kitchen.

Astor (☎ 22829950; http://astorkolkata.com; 15 Shakespeare Sarani; s/d/ste Rs5250/5775/8925; ❄) Artful floodlighting brings out the best of the Astor's solid 1905 architecture while some floors are quaintly uneven and stairways have original wrought-iron banisters. Rooms have some attractive three-colour woodwork though the floral bedspreads maintain that nursing-home feel. A few of the cheaper singles (Rs4725) are windowless.

Bigboss (☎ 22901111; www.bigbosspalace.com; 11/1A Rowden St; s/d/ste/deluxe Rs5775/6300/7140/7875; ❄) Above a 24-hour restaurant-coffee shop, most rooms are no-nonsense new business affairs though deluxe suites have unusual two-person jacuzzi baths.

Senator Hotel (☎ 22893000; www.thesenatorhotel.com; 15 Camac St; s/d from Rs6825/7925; ❄) Clashing coloured walls, green-marble floors and oriental vases fail at giving the foyer its desired high-fashion look, but the rooms play a straight bat: comfortable if neither large nor really luxurious. Sixth-floor 'diamond' rooms (Rs9000) are brighter, with flat-screen TVs.

Golden Park (☎ 228833939; www.thegoldenpark.com; 13 Ho Chi Minh Sarani; s/d/ste Rs8400/9450/11,650; ❄) The central, wood-panelled atrium has giant Chinese vases and a three-storey Shakespearean-style relief. Recently repainted rooms continue the classical theme with pictorial bed-boards but lack in-room safes and have somewhat faded bathrobes.

Kenilworth (☎ 22823939; www.kenilworthhotels.com/kolkata/index_g.htm; 1 Little Russell St; s/d Rs10,500/11,550; ❄) The deep lobby of cream marble, dark wood and chandeliers contrasts successfully with a more contemporary cafe that spills out onto a pleasant lawn dining area. Pleasing fully equipped rooms have sensitive lighting, restrained sunny colour schemes and large mirrors. Suites are in an old mansion opposite.

HHI (Hotel Hindusthan International; ☎ 40018000; www.hhihotels.com; 235/1 AJC Bose Rd; d walk-in/internet-rate from Rs11,550/6786; ❄ 🖳 ☎) This vast 1960s-style concrete tower has been elegantly remodelled inside, especially the exclusive Colony business floor (8th floor, d Rs18,900). Standard 3rd-floor rooms are also well renovated but some corridors have damp-patches, dated decor and low ceilings. North-facing rooms suffer some road noise.

South of Elgin Rd

The following options appear on Map p116.

Hotel Aston (☎ 24863145; hotelaston@gmail.com; 3 Aston Rd; s/d/ste Rs1380/1495/1955; 🗷 🖵) Attractive, modestly stylish little rooms with up-lit surround panels and neat little hot-water bathrooms in a blessedly quiet minor street behind the Samilton Hotel.

Hotel Gardenia (☎ 24863249; www.heritagegardenia.com; 42/1B Sarat Bose Rd; s/d Rs1610/1840; 🗷) Beside the colourful Lakshmi Narayan temple, the Gardenia's 'executive rooms' have a low-key sense of modernist style. A few 'deluxe singles' (Rs1380) are somewhat cramped.

Roland Hotel (☎ 30517600; info@rolandhotel.com; 28A Rowland Rd; s/d from Rs1805/2085; 🗷) This older 30-room hotel has been enlivened with some abstract art and padded bed-boards with fancy coloured mirrorwork adding character to the corridors.

Mangalam Hotel (☎ 24865083; mangalamhotel @yahoo.co.in; 44A Sarat Bose Rd; s/d from Rs2310/3045; 🗷) This brand new all-AC 28-bed hotel has fun parallelogram mirrors, two-colour bed-boards and small but geyser-equipped bathrooms. It has more style than the bigger Hotel Pan-Asia (www.hotelpanasiacontinental.com) opposite.

Gariahat & Rabindra Sarovar

A relatively small selection of accommodation is scattered widely about these middle-class districts on map pp104–5.

Mona Lisa Guesthouse (☎ 24632323; barinde @vsnl.net; 172A Sarat Bose Rd; s/d from Rs805/966; 🗷) Dangling rooftop bougainvillea and some rather strange wall murals give a little personality to this aging but clean-enough all-AC guesthouse.

Executive Point Guesthouse (☎ 24863249; www.hotelexecutivepoint.com; 8B Lake Terrace; s/d from Rs1255/1675; 🗷) This popular midrange guesthouse is often full midweek with regular business clients. Rates include breakfast.

Dover Inn (☎ 24619226; dover_inn@rediffmail.com; 1/7 Dover Lane; r Rs1260-2205; 🗷) Handy for Gariahat market, Dover Inn's 13 no-nonsense AC rooms are reasonable value if lacking character and natural light.

Metropole (☎ 40086969; www.metropole.co.in; 174 Sarat Bose Rd; s/d Rs4410/5040; 🗷) This small, stylishly modern boutique hotel has two-toned dark-wood furniture, soft leather bed-boards, flat-screen TVs and many useful amenities. It's so new that they still had newspaper covering the carpets when we visited.

BBD Bagh Area

Most options are handy for Chandni Chowk metro and appear on Map p112. There's no traveller scene here but hotels are fair value by Kolkata standards.

Bengal Buddhist Association (Bauddha Dharmankur Sabha; ☎ 22117138; bds1892@dataone.in; Buddhist Temple Rd; tw without/with AC Rs250/600; 🗷) Although intended for Buddhist students, anyone can rent these clean, simple rooms. Shared bathrooms have geysers and the three en-suite rooms have AC (but are otherwise just as spartan). The courtyard location is quiet but gates lock from 10.30pm to 5am.

Moon Guesthouse (☎ 22342403; moonguest@rediff mail.com; 1st fl, 17 Zakaria St; s Rs300-600, d Rs675-875; 🗷) In the bustling Islamic quarter, this old-fashioned 22-room hotel has an unexplained old gramophone in the tiny lobby. Rooms were upgraded a few years ago and while many now look rather battered, some, like decent AC room 108, have windows and geyser.

Kohinoor Guesthouse (☎ 22374758; 1 Kaviraj Row; d with/without bathroom Rs570/450, with AC Rs800) Tucked quietly away in a back alley, this place has clean rooms and bathrooms that are decent if tiny. Little English is spoken.

Broadway Hotel (☎ 22363930; http://business .vsnl.com/broadway; 27A Ganesh Chandra Ave; s/d/tr from Rs475/575/730) This excellent-value, well-maintained old hotel has a vaguely 1950s feel. Most rooms are generously large with high ceilings. Corner rooms offer plenty of light and the free newspaper under the door is a nice touch.

Esplanade Chambers (☎ 22127101; GC Ave; s/tw/d from Rs880/1210/1430; 🗷) Two floors up off a narrow alley, rooms here vary from unadorned narrow singles to sweet little mini-suites complete with ornaments and brassware on the bookshelves (once the apartment of the hotel's congenial owner). AC works well and showers run hot.

Club Inn (☎ 22345132; clubinn@cal2.vsnl.net.in; s Rs935-1565, d Rs1040-1670 🗷) The reception has low ceilings and stair carpets are worn but rooms are upliftingly clean and well-presented with fridge, AC, tiled floors and hot water. For the cheapest rooms, bathrooms are private but across the hall.

Hotel Embassy (☎ 22129702; ssspareworld@hotmail.com; 27 Princep St; s/d from Rs1000/1100; ☒) Most rooms are competently if unexotically renovated in Kolkata's answer to New York's Flatiron Building. The attached bar-restaurant is noisy at night.

Manthan (☎ 22489577; nnpl@cal2.vsnl.net.in; 3 Waterloo St; d Rs2310-2620; ☒) A fine old, stout-walled colonial house has been brought splendidly back to life with plenty of tasteful touches and well-selected dark woodwork. The four rooms are decked out in an elegant boutique-hotel style but as they range around a banquet room you won't get much sleep during weddings.

Howrah

Howrah Hotel (Map p112; ☎ 26413878; www.the howrahhotel.com; 1 Mukhram Kanoria Rd; s/d/tr without bathroom from Rs165/280/400 , s/d/tr/q from Rs250/355/445/585) Though pretty run-down, this characterful 1890 mansion retains elements of original tilework and Italian chequer-board marble flooring. The inner courtyard is an unexpected oasis of birdsong and the brilliantly antiquated reception has featured in three movies. The small, tatty rooms are as survivable as Sudder St equivalents. It's only two minutes' walk from Howrah train station's northern exit. Enter around the corner from the outwardly neater but actually less appealing Hotel Bhimsain. Reception stays open 24 hours.

Outer Kolkata

The following appear on Map pp104–5.

our pick **Tollygunge Club** (☎ 24732316; www.tolly gungeclub.org; d/ste Rs3090/3764; ☒) Set in idyllic calm amongst mature trees and golf greens, this otherwise-exclusive colonial-era club rents good, motel-standard guest rooms. Guests get temporary club membership allowing access to the wonderful Raj-era Wills Lounge bar (dress-code enforced) and, except Monday, use of many sporting facilities including especially reasonable rates for the wonderful golf course. Book ahead.

Hyatt Regency (☎ 23351235; http://kolkata.regency .hyatt.com; EM Bypass; weekend/weekday d from Rs11,025/12,075; ☒ ▯ ☒) Preening itself above a palm-slope entry drive, Kolkata's most impressive modern hotel uses vast windows to great effect in its inviting open-plan restaurants and has guest rooms with inspired marble-sweep bathrooms.

Taj Bengal (☎ 22233939; www.tajhotels.com/Luxury /taj%20bengal, Kolkata; 34B Belvedere Rd, Alipore; s/d from 18,961/20,597, Taj Club s/d Rs23,686/25,322; ☒ ▯ ☒) The vast, international-standard Taj Bengal hotel houses an eight-storey atrium in which cellists serenade and painters sketch. The 1990s architecture is softened by a great range of local antiques, carved panels and terracotta reliefs. The self-sufficient Taj Club level has 24-hour butler service, free laundry, private restaurant and exclusive bar with leather-padded sofas and free-drink happy hours.

Airport Area

An accommodation booth in the airport's domestic terminal suggests numerous 'airport area' hotels but most, like **Hotel Heritage** (www.heritagengardenia.com), are over 2km away down VIP Rd. The following suggestions are walkably close to the terminals, such that you're well placed should a strike paralyse city road transport.

Hotel Airways (☎ 25127280; www.hotelairways .com; Jessore Rd; s/d/tr/q from Rs300/450/550/650, with AC Rs650/750/900/1000; ☒ ▯) Fan rooms are sweltering claustrophobic boxes and road rumble can be annoying but the AC rooms are refreshingly cool and decor is gently pleasant. The small, covered rooftop restaurant (mains Rs40 to Rs70) overlooks the airport. It's 100m northeast of (pedestrian-only) Airport Gate 2 and easy to spot at night, festooned with fairy lights.

Sheela's Guesthouse (☎ 25129381; 1/1 Jessore Rd; s/d from Rs500/700, with AC Rs987/1523; ☒) The pink-and-turquoise colour-scheme lacks taste and carpets are ragged but AC rooms have decent wrought-iron furniture and hot water. It's located 200m northeast of Hotel Airways.

EATING
Traveller Cafes

Half a dozen cafes around Sudder St serve backpacker-favourites like banana pancakes, muesli and toasted sandwiches complimented by fresh fruit juices and a range of good-value Indian dishes. However, none has any special vibe.

Blue Sky Cafe (Map p108; Chowringhee Lane; mains Rs22-165; ☒ 6.30am-10.30pm; ☒) Reasonable AC, reliable food, witty waiters and almost stylish with high-backed zinc chairs at long glass tables.

BENGALI CUISINE

Fruity and mildly spiced, Bengali food favours the sweet, rich notes of jaggery (palm sugar), *daab* (young coconut), *malaikari* (coconut milk) and *posto* (poppy seed). Typical Bengali curry types include the light, coriander-scented *jhol*, drier spicier *jhal* and richer, ginger-based *kalia*. Mustard notes feature in *shorshe* curries and *paturi* dishes which come steamed in a banana leaf. *Chingri* (river prawns) and excellent fish (particularly *bhekti*, *ilish* and swordfish-like *aier*) are more characteristic than meat or chicken *(murgir)*. Excellent vegetarian choices include *mochar ghonto* (mashed banana-flower, potato and coconut) and *doi begun* (eggplant in creamy sauce). *Gobindobhog bhaat* (steamed rice) or *luchi* (small puris) are the usual accompaniment. A traditional soft drink is *aampora shorbat* made from cooked green mangoes with added lime zing.

Bengali desserts and sweets are legendary. Most characteristic is *mishti dhoi* (curd deliciously sweetened with jaggery).

For recipes and a great Bengali menu decoder visit http://sutapa.com.

Fresh & Juicy (Map p108; Chowringhee Lane; mains Rs25-60; 6.30am-10pm) Good inexpensive food and excellent banana lassis (Rs20) make up for a total lack of decor in this simple five-table cafe

Super Chicken (Map p108; Sudder St; mains Rs35-100; 8-11pm;) Succulent chicken tikka and a full menu of tempting alternatives in a small new, well–air conditioned room.

Restaurants

Most restaurants add 12.5% tax to bills. A few posher places add further 'service charges'. Tips are welcome at cheaper places and expected at most expensive restaurants. The *Times Food Guide* (Rs100) covers hundreds of restaurants, though reviews are suspiciously uncritical.

BENGALI

Bengali cuisine is a wonderful discovery, with a whole new vocabulary of names and flavours (see above). Portion sizes are often tapas-sized so in cheaper places order two or three dishes along with rice/*luchi* and sweet tomato-*khejur* (date) chutney.

Radhuni (Map p108; 17G Mirza Ghalib St; dishes Rs15-90, rice Rs10; 7.30am-11pm;) Unpretentious place for local breakfasts and surprisingly credit-able, pre-prepared Bengali food.

Flamez (Map p108; 22264251; Mirza Ghalib St; dishes Rs40-130, rice Rs45; noon-11pm;) Confuse your taste-buds with *sukto*, a vegetarian curry that blurs the sweet-savoury divide. Indian and non-Bengali 'coastal' cuisines are also available.

ourpick Bhojohari Manna (Ekdalia) (Map pp104-5; 24401933; www.bhojohorimanna.org; 9/18 Ekdalia Rd aka PC Sorcan Sarani; dishes Rs20-190; noon-9pm;) Serving sublime Bengali food, it was this tiny restaurant-cum-takeaway that launched the now-growing chain. Pick items ticked on the daily-changing whiteboard. There's no better place to splurge on coconut-tempered *chingri malaikari*, featuring prawns so big they speak lobster. Sketches on the walls are by the father of celebrated film-director Satyajit Ray.

Bhojohari Manna 6 (Map pp104-5; 24663941; www.bhojohorimanna.org; 18/1 Hindustan Rd; dishes Rs45-190, rice Rs30, thalis Rs145-170; noon-9pm;) Bhojohari Manna's latest and most spacious branch is less daunting for non-Bengali speakers, has gently stylish decor and serves complete thalis.

Kewpies (Map p108; 24861600; 2 Elgin Lane; dishes Rs58-125, prawn dishes Rs325, rice Rs30, thalis Rs195-415; 12.30-3pm & 7.30-11pm Tue-Sun;) Unless you're shunted into the less-appealing central overflow room, dining at Kewpies feels like being invited to a dinner party in the chef's eclectic, gently old-fashioned home. First-rate Bengali food comes in small but fairly priced portions. Minimum spend is Rs220 per person.

6 Ballygunge Place (Map pp104-5; 24603922; 6 Ballygunge Pl; dishes Rs95-245, prawn dishes Rs255-355, rice Rs65; 12.30-3.30pm & 7.30-10.30pm Tue-Sun;) This sturdy but not over-formal Raj-era mansion offers lunch-time buffets with six main courses plus deserts, chutneys and rice allowing a good all-round introduction to Bengali food. Minibus 118 from Jatin Das Park metro stops a block north on Bondel Rd.

Oh! Calcutta (Map p108; 22837161; 4th fl, Forum Mall, Elgin Rd; mains Rs180-625, rice Rs120, beer Rs216; 12.30-3pm & 7-11pm;) Shutter-edged mirror 'windows', B&W photography and

...sually upmarket ...ealing Bengali-fusion ...e feather-light and fresh ...he subtleties of *koraishatir* ...ea-cakes in ginger).

INDIAN REGIONAL

As well as the following listed options, there are many cheaper stalwarts around Hogg market (Map p108).

Anand (Map p112; ☎ 22129757; 19 CR Ave; dosas Rs30-73; ⏰ 9-9.30pm Thu-Tue; ❸) Prize-winning pure-veg dosas served in a well-kept if somewhat old-fashioned family restaurant with bamboo and mirror-tiled ceilings.

Dustarkhwan (Map p108; ☎ 22275596; 6 Ripon St; mains Rs35-110; ⏰ noon-11.30pm; ❸) Reliable curries, piled-high biriyanis (Rs100) and vampire-repelling garlic chicken-balls served inexpensively in a well air-conditioned if none-too-stylish local restaurant. Cheaper options next door.

Crystal Chimney (Map p108; CR Ave; ⏰ noon-10pm Tue-Sun) Located next door to Anand, this tiny place serves good *momos* and chilli chicken.

Jarokha (Map p108; www.guptabros.com; 1st fl, Gupta Brothers, Mirza Ghalib St; mains Rs75-110, rice Rs60, thalis Rs110; ⏰ 12.30pm-4pm & 7-10.30pm) The thali is a good deal in this cosy, attractively vegetarian dining room with Indian historical-fantasy decor, reached via a spiral stairway from within Gupta Brothers (p128).

our pick **Teej** (Map p108; ☎ 22170730; www.teej.in; 1st fl, 2 Russell St; mains Rs110-175, rice Rs120, thalis Rs265-350, beers Rs140; ⏰ noon-3.30pm & 7-10.30pm; ❸) Superbly painted with Mughal-style murals the wonderfully atmospheric interior feels like a Rajasthani *haveli* (traditional, ornately decorated residence). The excellent, 100% vegetarian food is predominantly Rajasthani, too.

Riviera (Map p108; ☎ 22274974; 1st fl, 24 Park St; mains Rs165-320, rice Rs60; ⏰ noon-3pm & 7-11.30pm) 'Coastal' cuisine picks the best from a variety of Indian regions: Puducherry stuffed prawns, Mangalore *bhekti* curry, coconut-flavoured Keralan dishes and Chettinad chicken. Vegetarians can order from the menu of attached Angaar Restaurant.

INDO-CHINESE

Locals rate the food in Tangra-Chinatown but prices there seem inflated, decor is rarely inspiring and chefs are non-Chinese so it's hardly worth the awkward trip.

Gypsy Restaurant (Map p112; GC Ave; mains Rs25-55, rice Rs15; ⏰ noon-10pm) Unusually bright, clean and well appointed for such an inexpensive, open-sided diner.

The Heritage (Map p108; ☎ 22900940; 9A Short St; mains Rs45-75, rice Rs30, breakfast snacks Rs30-60; ⏰ noon-11pm) The decor isn't memorable and party-wrapped chairs will prove hard to clean but staff are obliging and the very reasonable 100%-veg food is packed with marvellously complex flavours. A former gallery behind hosts a rare hookah parlour (water-pipe Rs160 to Rs230, mocktails Rs45 to Rs75) to have survived the October 2008 smoking ban.

Midway (Map p108; ☎ 22290487; 2C Middleton Row; mains Rs55-145, momos Rs20, rice Rs40; ⏰ noon-11pm; ❸) Incredibly good-value thalis (veg/non-veg Rs55/65) are served in this attractively designed new chrome and lime-green modernist restaurant.

Bar-B-Q (Map p108; ☎ 22299078; 1st fl, 43 Park St; mains Rs115-160, rice Rs70, beers Rs120; ⏰ noon-4pm & 7-10.45pm) Three interconnected dining rooms offer different but similar menus in this enduring family favourite. Decor is comfortably unpretentious.

On Track (Map p108; ☎ 22273955; Mirza Ghalib St; mains Rs120-190, rice Rs70; ⏰ 11am-3.30pm & 7-11pm) Dine in the curious, upmarket Pullman carriages of a mock steam train while your kids play video games in the locomotive. No alcohol.

EAST ASIAN

While many Indo-Chinese places serve a selection of both cuisines and some other 'China restaurants' are rowdy drinking dens, the listings below are specialist oriental restaurants. There are three 'real' Chinese restaurants on Mirza Ghalib St south of Sudder St (Map p108): cheap-if-bland Hong Kong, midrange Golden Dragon and swish Tung Fong which does a Rs250 lunch buffet. For Thai food, pricy alternatives include hotel restaurants at the Lytton and Oberoi hotels (both Map p108) or Haka (Map pp104–5) at Mani Square Mall.

Song Hay (Map p112; ☎ 22480974; 3 Waterloo St; lunch mains Rs21-75, dinner mains Rs44-160, rice Rs16; beer Rs75; ⏰ 11am-10.30pm; ❸) This modest but prize-winning restaurant cooks authentic Chinese food at prices that are especially reasonable before 5pm when half-priced, half-size portions are available.

Bayleaf (Map p112; ☎ 64542244; Waterloo St; mains Rs50-85, prawn mains Rs120-150, rice Rs30; 🕙 11.30am-11pm; ❄) Tibetan, Burmese and semi-Thai options bolster some imaginative Chinese cuisine like the delicious mushroom delights (half mushrooms stuffed with paneer, deep-fried and served in mild sauce). The decor is black seats at black-glass tables.

Mainland China (Map p108; ☎ 22837964; www .mainlandchinaindia.com/contact_kolkata.html; 3A Gurusaday Rd; mains Rs210-675, rice Rs120, beer Rs216; 🕙 12.30-3.30pm & 7-11.30pm) Consistent, upmarket Chinese food in sophisticated surroundings. Reservations advised.

Jong's (Map p108; ☎ 22490369; Sudder St; mains Rs290-590, rice Rs125, beer Rs160; 🕙 12.30-3pm & 7.30-11pm Wed-Mon) This double-character restaurant is magnificently wooden-panelled like a Raj-oriental gentleman's club with silver-plated cutlery, antique-style umbrellas and lazy wind chimes dangling overhead. Free nibbles precede the meal, but the Thai and Korean options lack kick and teppanyaki isn't done at the table.

MULTICUISINE

The following offer selections of European and Indian fare.

Food First (Map p108; 5 Camac St; mains Rs35-110; 🕙 11am-10.30pm; ❄) Looking like an upmarket fast-food place but waiter-served, widely varying cuisines are prepared at in-view cooking stations.

Drive Inn (Map p108; 10 Middleton St; mains Rs46-82, rice Rs31, juices Rs18-25; 🕙 11.15am-10pm) Sandwiches, *chaats* (snacks) and plate-lickingly good vegetarian food are served in a modest open-air 'garden' with simple fan-pavilion tables. Try the stuffed capsicum.

Mocambo (Map p108; ☎ 22290095; Mirza Ghalib St; mains Rs83-210, beer Rs108; 🕙 11am-11pm; ❄) Despite somewhat old-fashioned red leather scoop-seats and benches, Mocambo has a very loyal following for its mixed grills (Rs189), fish Wellington (Rs192), chicken Kiev (Rs181) and *bhekti* meunière (well they don't have trout).

Peter Cat (Map p108; ☎ 22298841; Middleton Row; mains Rs85-250, rice Rs89, beers/cocktails from Rs108/81; 🕙 11am-11pm; ❄) Opposite KFC, this phenomenally popular Kolkata institution offers fizzing sizzlers, great *chelo*-kebabs (barbecued fingers of spiced, ground-lamb) and beers quaffed from pewter tankards. Waiters wear Rajasthani costumes in an atmosphere redolent of a mood-lit 1970s steakhouse.

Amber/Essence (Map p112; ☎ 22483477; 2nd fl, 11 Waterloo St; mains Rs102-193, beer Rs110; 🕙 1.30pm-11pm; ❄) This pleasantly semi-trendy middle-class restaurant has back-lit panels and triangular lamp niches, though their signature brain curry isn't to everyone's taste.

Marco Polo (Map p108; ☎ 22273939; 24 Park St; mains Rs170-395, rice Rs125, beer Rs120, wine Rs1100; 🕙 1.30pm-11pm; ❄) This invitingly modern, spacious split-level restaurant takes diners on a tempting culinary world tour from Bengal to Italy via Goa, China and even Hungary.

ITALIAN & TEX-MEX

Jalapenos (Map p108; ☎ 22820204; 10 Wood St; mains Rs85-250; 🕙 11.30am-10.15pm; ❄) In a pleasant, high-ceilinged room with mock wooden beams and little alcoves decorated with spice bottles, the food is enjoyable as long as you don't expect much resemblance to the Tex-Mex and Mediterranean names on the menu.

Pizza Hut (Map p108; ☎ 22814343; 22 Camac St; pizzas Rs75-485; 🕙 11am-11pm) Popular with travellers seeking a taste of home.

Fire & Ice (Map p108; ☎ 22884073; www.fireand icepizzeria.com; Kanak Bldg, Middleton St; pizzas Rs210-320, pastas Rs240-300, beers Rs130; 🕙 11am-11.30pm; ❄) Self-consciously handsome wait-staff sporting black shirts and bandanas bring forth real Italian pastas and pizzas whose fresh-baked thin crusts are Kolkata's best, though the home-made mozzarella melts in a rather odd fashion.

Little Italy (Map p108; ☎ 22825152; 8th fl, Fort Knox Tower, Camac St; pizzas Rs230-465, pastas Rs315-435, small beers Rs145; 🕙 12.15-3.30pm & 7-10.45pm) À la mode but charmingly relaxed, Little Italy manages a remarkable range of great Italian food considering it's 100% vegetarian. Reservations recommended.

Quick Eats
FAST FOOD

Beef Hotel (Map p108; Tegiya Darbar Hotel; Collin Ln; mains Rs5-20; 🕙 7-11.45pm) If your stomach's stronger than your wallet you can fill up on rice and veg curry for just Rs8 at this entirely un-lovely, rubbish-strewn eatery. We didn't get sick.

Haldiram (Map p108; 58 Chowringhee Rd; Rs30-85; 🕙 7am-10pm) Excellent value pay-then-queue vegetarian thalis (Rs60 to Rs66), *dosas* (Rs30 to Rs42), burgers (Rs28 to Rs48) and Bengalis sweets.

Snack stalls (Map; p108; Humayan Pl; ☪ 10am-9pm) Pastry stalls, KFC, Dominos Pizza and Barista Coffee front the New Empire cinema while over the road a colourful series of local stall-shops serve cheap *dosas*, chow mein and great fresh juices. More stalls line Bertram St and nearby Madge Lane.

There's a more spacious **KFC** (Map; p108; Middleton Row; ☪ 11am-11pm) just off Park St. For a hamburger-free **McDonalds** head out to Mani Square Mall (Map pp104-5).

Shopping malls (p130) all have food courts.

ROLL HOUSES

Bengal's trademark fast food is the *kati roll.* No, that's nothing like a bread roll. Take a *paratha roti*, fry it with a one-sided coating of egg then fill with sliced onions, chilli and your choice of stuffing (curried chicken, grilled meat or paneer). Roll it up in a twist of paper and it's ready to eat, generally on the street. Typical hole-in-the-wall serveries include **Hot Kati Rolls** (Map p108; 1/1 Park St; rolls Rs12-50; ☪ 11am-10.30pm) and **Kuzums** (Map p108; 27 Park St; rolls Rs12-45; ☪ noon-11.30pm). **Nizams** (Map p112; 23/24 Hogg St; rolls Rs15-60, kebabs Rs55-80; ☪ noon-11pm) is unusual in having seating, albeit with blandly rebuilt new decor.

SWEETS, CAKES & PASTRIES

The following offer only takeaway unless otherwise noted.

KC Das (Map p112; Lenin Sarani; sweets Rs3-16; ☪ 7.30am-9.30pm) This historic, if not especially atmospheric, Bengali sweet shop invented *rasgulla* (syrupy sponge balls) in 1868. Seating available.

Gupta Brothers (Map p108; www.guptabros.com; Mirza Ghalib St; sweets Rs3-10; ☪ 7.30am-10.30pm; ✿) Classic sweet shop that's now a local snack chain. Their Rs6 veg cutlet balls burst with flavour.

Kamata Mistana Bhander (Map pp104-5; 4 MG Rd; sweets Rs3-10; ☪ 8.30am-9pm) Nostalgic olde-worlde Bengali sweet shop with marble-topped cashier's desk in the shadow of MG Rd where the market mayhem of Sisir Bazaar hides access pathways to Sealdah station.

Kathleen Confectioners (Map p108; 12 Mirza Ghalib St; snacks Rs9-30; ☪ 8am-8pm; ✿) The sickly sweet cakes aren't exactly the promised 'Taste of Hapinezz' but their savoury pastries are delicious. Stand-and-eat tables offer free filter water if you dare to use the shared metal cup.

There are many other branches, including one on AJC Bose Rd.

Tea Table 2 (Map p108; Tottie Ln; snacks Rs13-25; ☪ 10am-7pm Mon-Sat) This basic bakery sales window sells fresh pastries and cakes otherwise destined for the much more expensive (yet oddly decrepit) Tea Table café on Park St. Two simple seats.

Bisk Farm (Map p108; www.biskfarm.com; Hungerford St; pastries Rs15-20, sandwiches Rs22-25, coffee Rs7; ☪ 10am-8.30pm) Bulk biscuit maker Bisk Farm sells inexpensive fresh pastries along with its trademark mass-produced cookies.

Kookie Jar (Map p108; Rowden St; pastries Rs20-60; ☪ 8am-10pm; ✿) Kolkata's most heavenly takeaway cakes and fudge brownies (Rs32) along with multigrain bread (Rs50), Mexican chicken wraps (Rs55) and fluffy pastries.

Gangaur (Map p108; http://gangaur.org; 2 Russell St; sweets Rs9-25; ☪ 7.30am-8pm; ✿) Upper-market Bengali sweet shop.

ICE CREAM

New Zealand Natural (Map p108; Wood St 4A; small/large cone Rs55/75; ☪ 10am-11.30pm; ✿) Predominantly takeaway ice-cream parlour with delicious berry-fruit sorbets.

DRINKING
Cafes

Ashalayam (Map p108; www.ashalayam.org; 1st fl, 44 Mirza Ghalib St; coffee Rs6-15; ☪ 10.30am-7pm Mon-Fri, 10.30am-3.30pm Sat; ✿) Play chess at low wicker tables while sipping cheap machine-frothed Nescafe in this calm, bright charity craft-shop cafe (see p131).

Flury's (Map p108; Park St; coffees Rs60-145, sandwiches Rs40; ☪ 7.30am-9.45pm; ✿) Great espressos (Rs60) and iced tea (Rs60) layered like a tequila sunrise in an enticing art deco palace-cafe.

Cafe Coffee Day (Map p108; Wood St; coffees Rs40-75; ☪ 10.30am-11pm; ✿) is the most appealing branch of the Starbucks-style chain thanks to its garden terrace. Along with **Barista** (Map p108; Humayan Pl; coffees Rs24-50; ☪ 9am-10pm; ✿) there are numerous alternative branches (see maps), some cheaper, in which to linger in AC comfort.

Teashops

Camelia Tea Bar (Map p116; 1st fl, Samilton Hotel, 37 Sarat Bose Rd; teas Rs18-50; ☪ 7am-11pm) This little roof garden has some broken furniture and suffers from road noise but the multifarious cocktail-style teas are highly imaginative. Grappa tea uses blackcurrant, crushed grapes and lemon juice, spicy Thai-chai adds a well-gauged chilli hit to Indian masala chai.

Dolly's Tea Shop (Map pp104-5; ☎ 24237838, mobile 9830115787; Unit G62, Dakshinapan Shopping Centre, teas Rs15-100, snacks Rs20-70; ☒ 10.30am-7.30pm Mon-Sat) Teak-panels, rattan chairs, tea-crate tables and the regal presence of matriarch Dolly transform what would otherwise be just another unit in the dreary Dakshinapan shopping centre into a charming little oasis that attracts a wonderfully eclectic clientele. Toasted sandwiches or apple pie accompany over 50 choices of tea.

ChaBar (Map p108; Oxford Bookshop, Park St; teas Rs25-75, coffees Rs40-120; ☒ 6.30am-11.30pm) A full menu of teas to taste while you book-browse. Tangy thimbles of ginger-chai (Rs30) come hugged by pewter monkeys.

Tea Moods (Map p108; www.premiertea.net; 8 Camac St) Elegant sales outlet for fine packaged teas with tastings available. Not a cafe.

Bars

While most better bars are in hotels or restaurants, cheaper places are usually dingy and overwhelmingly male-dominated with a penchant for over-loud music.

Broadway Bar (Map p112; Broadway Hotel, beers Rs70; ☒ 11am-10.30pm) Back-street Paris? Chicago 1930s? Prague 1980s? This cavernous, unpretentious old-men's pub defies easy parallels but has a compulsive left-bank fascination with cheap booze, 20 ceiling fans, grimy walls, marble floors and, thankfully, no music.

Fairlawn Hotel (Map p108; 13A Sudder St; beers Rs90; ☒ 11.30-2pm & 2.30-9pm) Half rainforest, half Santa-grotto the small tropical garden in the historic Fairlawn is strung with fairy lights and plastic fruit creating a unique and rather loveable place for a cold brew (no spirits).

Mirch Masala (Map pp104-5; ☎ 24618900; Monoronjan Roy Sarani; mains Rs75-220, beers Rs95, cocktails Rs110; ☒ noon-3pm & 7am-10.30pm) Old clocks, fake trees, half a taxi chassis and a north-Indian menu presented like a gossip magazine combine to create an amusing ambience that feels like a Bollywood Tex-Mex joint. Take the lane beside Pantaloons department store. Lunchtime food discounts are available for all-female groups.

Rocks (Map p112; 9 Waterloo St; beers from Rs100; ☒ ground fl 11am-midnight, 2nd fl 7pm-midnight) Different floors offer different experiences of local drinking culture. The ground floor

is a musty old-boys' dive w[...] has proficient, if ear-splitti[...] Bengali music.

Blue & Beyond Restaurant (Map p108; ☎ 22[...] 9th fl, Lindsay Hotel, Lindsay St; beers Rs110, mains Rs95-1[...] ☒ 11am-11pm) The open-air rooftop terrace offers unusual views over New Market.

Floatel (Map p112; www.floatelhotel.com; Strand Rd; buffet lunch/dinner Rs399/499; beers Rs150; ☒ bar noon-midnight; ☒) Although primarily a restaurant, wide river views make the Floatel a fine place for a sunset drink.

Roxy (Map p108; Park Hotel; small beers Rs175; ☒ 6pm-midnight Sun-Tue, 6pm-4am Wed, Fri & Sat; ☒) With unusually mellow music and a *Clockwork Orange* retro-futuristic atmosphere, Roxy is the most poised of several fun pub-bars around and within the Park Hotel.

Wine Shops

Several '**wine shops**' (☒ typically 10am-10pm, beer Rs47) are marked on Map p108 including **National Stores** (☒ Tue-Sun), **Scotts** (Mon-Sat), **Shaw Brothers** (☒ Fri-Wed) beside Mocambo and **Extacy** (☒ Fri-Wed). **Republic Stores** (Map p112; 13B CR Ave; ☒ 10am-10pm) is beside Chandni Chowk metro.

ENTERTAINMENT

Events and cultural happenings are announced in the *Telegraph* newspaper's *Metro* section and the various listings brochures (p107).

Nightclubs

Kolkata's party nights are Wednesday, Friday and Saturday when clubs open till 4am. On other nights most are half empty and close at midnight. Note the difference between entry charge and cover charge: the latter can be recouped in drinks or food to the same value. Either is charged *per couple* and single men (known as *stags*) are generally excluded.

Tantra (Map p108; Park Hotel; entry Rs500-1000, small beers Rs225) Considered Kolkata's top club, contemporary sounds throb through the single dance floor and not-so-chilled chill-out zone around a central island bar with an overhead observation bridge.

Marrakech (Map p108; Cinnamon Restaurant, 1st fl, 24 Park St; cover Rs500, beers Rs135) This Moroccan-themed bar-club has octagonal tables and low, cushion-seated alcoves set around a small, pulsating dance floor.

Shisha (Map p108; 5th fl, Block D, 22 Camac St; cover variable, small beers Rs170) On Wednesday, Friday and Saturday nights this normally mellow

...d the party

6 Camac St; cover
...s of vertical red
...e dancing in a
...al styles vary.
...ement, HHI Hotel, 235/1
...0) Around 8pm this
cellar ... ...pty set from *Cheers*.
After 11pm... ...DJs thump out house
or trance music fo... ...late crowd who arrive
here after other places start closing.

Ginger (Map pp104-5; ☎ 24863052; 104 SP Mukherjee Rd; no cover, small beers Rs120; ☑ 9pm-late Wed, Fri, Sat) Kolkata's best hope for stags, Ginger can be fun with a group watching the majority-male clientele whoop to 1990s dance hits.

Cultural Programs

Kolkata's famous poetry, music, art, film and dance are regularly showcased at the **Nandan Complex** (Map p108; 1/1A AJC Bose Rd) comprising theatre halls **Rabindra Sadan** (☎ 22239936) and **Sisir Mancha** (☎ 22235317) plus art-house **Nandan Cinema** (☎ 22231210).

Cinemas

Cinemas are ubiquitous. Of at least nine around New Market, **New Empire Cinema** (Map p108; ☎ 22491299; 1-2 Humayan Pl; tickets Rs50-150) is the most comfortable. **Inox Elgin Rd** (Map p108; ☎ 23584499; www.inoxmovies.com; 4th fl, Forum Shopping Mall, 10/3 Elgin Rd; tickets Rs140-230) is a modern multiplex, bookable online.

Other modern cinemas include the following:

Imax (Map pp104-5; Mani Square Mall, EM Bypass) Large-screen, high-definition movie theatre due to open soon.

Inox Elgin Rd (Map p108; ☎ 23584499; www.inox movies.com; 4th fl, Forum Shopping Mall, 10/3 Elgin Rd; tickets Rs140-230) Modern multiplex, bookable online.

Inox Swabhumi (Map pp104-5; ☎ 23208900; www .inoxmovies.com; Maulana Abdul Kalam Azad Sarani; tickets Rs140-230) Modern four-screen complex with bar and restaurant. Bookable online.

Live Music

Bars like Rocks (p129) have local bands squealing high-volume Indian music. Those hidden within **Hotel Majestic** (Map p112; Madan St) and **Hotel VIP International** (Map p108; Mirza Ghalib St) feature all female singers for the delectation of drooling all-male drinkers. Western rock and heavy-rock cover bands play nightly at the Anglo-pub **Someplace Else**

(Map p108; Park Hotel; beers Rs200; ☑ from 9.30pm). No cover charges.

Spectator Sports

Dozens of sports clubs on the Maidan practise everything from cricket to kabaddi. Even if you don't know Ganguly from a googly, the electric atmosphere of a **cricket** match at Ranji Stadium (p111) is an unforgettable experience. Pre-book **ICL** (http://indiancricketleague.in/tickets .html) tickets online.

The Victoria Memorial provides a beautiful backdrop to the **Royal Calcutta Turf Club** (Maidan racecourse; ☎ 22291104; www.rctconline.com; Acharya Jagdish Rd; admission from Rs14) from whose 19th-century grandstands you can watch some of India's best horse racing at over 40 annual meets.

SHOPPING

New Market is a pestilential nest of handicraft touts. Come before 8am, while touts are sleeping, to admire the grand colonial clock tower and to calmly appreciate the nearby, atmospheric Hogg Market (selling fresh food and live chickens). Traditional, ultracrowded shopping alleys spread in confusing profusion north of BBD Bagh. Rabindra Sarani offers intriguing thematic groupings of trades at different points.

Gleaming new shopping malls include **South City Mall** (Map pp104-5; Prince Anwar Shah Rd), **Forum Mall** (Map p108; Elgin Rd), **Mani Square Mall** (Map pp104-5; EM Bypass) and **E-Mall** (Map p112; CR Ave). **Swabhumi** (Map pp104-5; www.swabhumi.com; admission Rs20; ☑ noon-10pm) is a shopping centre-cum-cultural park with stylised Bengali architecture and 6pm 'events'.

Crafts & Souvenirs

GOVERNMENTAL EMPORIA

State-government emporia sell good-quality souvenirs at decent fixed prices. A large number of them are gathered together at the **Dakshinapan Shopping Centre** (Map pp104-5; Gariahat Rd; ☑ 11am-7pm Mon-Fri, to 2pm Sat), whose soul-crushing 1970s architecture is slightly softened by the presence of Dolly's Tea Shop (p128). Fabrics here are good value and **Purbasha** (unit F4/5 upstairs) has great deals on bamboo- and cane-ware from Tripura.

Similar cane-ware along with pearls, fabrics and Assam tea is available more centrally at **Assam Craft Emporium** (Map p108; ☎ 22298331; Assam House, 8 Russell St; ☑ 10.30am-6pm Mon-Fri, 10.30am-

2.30pm Sat). **Nagaland Emporium** (Map p108; 11 Shakespeare Sarani; ⏰ 10am-6pm Mon-Fri, 10am-2pm Sat) sells Naga crafts, including traditional shawls and double-face bronze 'trophy' necklaces for wannabe headhunters.

The impressive, if comparatively pricey, **Central Cottage Industries Emporium** (Map p112; www .cottageemporiumindia.com; Metropolitan Bldg, 7 Chowringhee Rd; ⏰ 10am-7pm Mon-Fri, to 2pm Sat) showcases handicrafts from right across India.

CHARITY COOPERATIVES

You can support reputable endeavours by buying gifts at the following places:

Ankur Kala (Map pp104–5; ☎ 22878476; www.ankur kala.org; 3 Meher Ali Rd) This cooperative training centre empowers women from the slums. Their small showroom sells batik, stitch-work, attractive greetings cards and leatherware. From the junction of Park St and AJC Bose Rd, walk two blocks east, turn south passing Tiger Inn and crossing Shakespeare Sarani then look for a big '3' on the alley gate.

Ashalayam (Map p108; www.ashalayam.org; Mirza Ghalib St) Buying super greetings cards, handmade paper and fabrics funds the (ex)street kids who made them (see p128).

Women's Friendly Society (Map p108; ☎ 22295285; 29 Park Lane; ⏰ 8am-1pm & 2-5pm Mon-Fri, 8am-1pm Sat) This 120-year-old charity for destitute women sells somewhat twee hand-embroidered tableware, fabrics and children's clothes from a fine, if aging, Raj-era mansion.

Clothing

Kolkata is great value for tailored or off-the-rack clothing. Smart shirts cost just Rs100 from Chowringhee Rd **Hawkers Market** (Map p108). Choice around Newmarket is endless while **local tailors** (Map p108) on Elliot Rd are less tourist-oriented.

Musical Instruments

Shops and workshops along Rabindra Sarani sell a great range of musical instruments. For tablas and other percussion try numbers 248, 264 and 268B near Tagore's House (p117). For sitars (from Rs4000) or violins (from Rs2000) visit **Mondal & Sons** (Map p112; ☎ 22349658; 8 Rabindra Sarani; ⏰ 10am-6pm Mon-Fri, 10am-2.30pm Sat). Family run since the 1850s, the Mondals count Yehudi Menuhin among their satisfied customers.

Jewellery

Rash Behari Ave has numerous jewellers. A reputable if upmarket address for gold is **PC Chandra** (☎ 24618684; www.pcchandra.com;

10.30am-7pm Tue-Sat, 2pm-7pm Mon) whose aging guards sport unwieldy old rifles.

For traditional white-hoop bangles visit speciality **conch-shell dealers** on Bagbazar Rd (Map pp104–5).

Music

Peddlers sell Bengali pop CDs on street corners, but for a vast selection of genres visit the flashy, AC chain shop **Music World** (Map p108; Middleton Row; ⏰ 9am-9.30pm).

Umbrellas

Rajkumar Bros (Map p112; 5 Lenin Sarani; ⏰ 11am-10pm) is one of several outlets for KC Paul brollies (from Rs100), commonly considered the best brand available.

GETTING THERE & AWAY

Air

Kolkata's **Netaji Subhash Bose International Airport** (NSBIA; ☎ 25118787) offers direct connections to London and Frankfurt plus several Asian cities.

INTERNATIONAL

Air India (Map p108; ☎ 22822356/59; 50 Chowringhee Rd)

Air India Express (www.airindiaexpress.in) Budget flights to Bangkok, Dhaka and Singapore.

Biman Bangladesh Airlines (Map p108; ☎ 22491879; www.bimanair.com; Room 126, Lytton Hotel, Sudder St) Flies to Dhaka.

British Airways (☎ 98-31377470) Flies to London

China Eastern Airlines (Map p108; ☎ 40448887; c/o InterGlobe, Ground fl, Landmark Bldg, 228A AJC Bose Rd) Flies to Kunming (Yunnan).

Druk Air (Map p108; ☎ 22902429; 51 Tivoli Court, 1A Ballygunge Circular Rd) Flies to Bhutan and Bangkok.

Emirates (Map pp104–5; ☎ 40099555; Trinity Tower, 83 Topsia Rd) Flies to Dubai.

GMG Airlines (Map p108; ☎ 30283030; www.gmgair lines.com; 20H Park St) Flies to Chittagong (Rs5930) and Dhaka (Rs4580), Bangladesh.

Gulf Air (Map p108; ☎ 22901522; 3rd fl, Landmark Bldg, 228A AJC Bose Rd) Flies to Bahrain.

Indian Airlines (see p132) Flies to Kathmandu (Nepal) and Yangon (Burma).

JET Airways (p132) Flies to Bangkok and Dhaka.

Lufthansa (Off Map pp104–5; ☎ 22299365; 8th fl, IT Park Tower, DN62, Sector 5, Salt Lake City) Flies to Frankfurt.

Singapore Airlines (Off Map pp104–5; ☎ 23675422; 9th fl, IT Park Tower, DN62, Sector 5, Salt Lake City)

Thai Airways International (Map p108; ☎ 22838865; 8th fl, Crescent Towers, 229 AJC Bose Rd) Flies to Bangkok.

United Airways Bangladesh (Map p108; ☎ 93-39998587; www.uabdl.com; 55B Mirza Ghalib St) Flies to Dhaka, Chittagong and Barisal.

DOMESTIC

Indian Airlines (IC; Map p112; ☎ 22114433; 39 Chittaranjan Ave; ☯ 9am-8pm)

IndiGo (Map p108; 6E; http://book.goindigo.in)

Jet Airways (Map p108; 9W; ☎ 39840000; www.jetairways.com; 18D Park St; ☯ 8am-8pm Mon-Sat, 9am-5.30pm Sun)

JetLite (S2; www.jetlite.com)

Kingfisher (IT; www.flykingfisher.com)

spiceJet (SG; www.spicejet.com)

Boat

Sporadic ferries to Port Blair (Andaman Islands) depart from **Kidderpore Docks** (Map pp104-5; Karl Marx Sarani), entered from Gate 3 opposite Kidderpore commuter train station. Tickets (Rs1700 to Rs7640) go on sale 10 days before departure at the **Shipping Corporation of**

India (Map p112; ☎ 22484921; Hare St; ☯ 10am-1pm & 2.30-5pm Mon-Fri).

Bus
INTERNATIONAL
Several Marquis St agencies run Bangladesh-bound services involving a change of vehicle at the Benapol border. **Shohagh Paribahan** (Map p108; ☎ 22520757; 21A Marquis St; ☯ 5am-9.30pm) runs six daily buses to Dhaka (Rs660, 13 hours). **GreenLine** (Map p108; ☎ 22520757; 12B Marquis St; ☯ 4am-11pm) has 5am and 6am Dhaka buses (Rs700) and buses to Chittagong (Rs1080, 22 hours) at 10am and 1pm.

A **Bhutan Postbus** departs 7am to Phuentsholing from Esplanade bus station where there's a special **ticket booth** (☯ 9.30am-1pm & 2-6pm Mon-Sat).

DOMESTIC
From Esplanade
For Darjeeling or Sikkim take one of many night buses to Siliguri (Rs325 to 650, 12 hours), departing between 6pm and 8pm from

---

MAJOR TRAINS FROM KOLKATA

Departures daily unless otherwise stated

Useful for	Train no & name	Duration (hr)	Departures
Bhubaneswar	2073 *Shatabdi*	7	1.40pm Mon-Sat (HWH)
Chennai	2841 *Coromandal*	26½	2.50pm (HWH)
	2839 *Chennai Mail*	28	11.45pm (HWH)
via Bhubaneswar		6¾ hours	
Delhi	2381 *Poorva* via Gaya	23	8.05am/8.20am (HWH)
	0231	22½	11.45am Tue, Wed & Sat (HWH)
	2329 *Sam. Kranti*	23	1pm Mon, Fri (SDAH)
Gorakhpur	5047 *Purbanchal*	17¾	2.30pm Mon, Tue, Thu & Sat (CP)
Guwahati	2345 *Saraighat*	17½	4pm (HWH)
	5657 *Kanchenjunga*	22	6.45am (SDAH)
	via Malda	(7 hours)	
Jammu	3151 *Tawi Exp*	45½	11.45am (CP)
via Lucknow		23 hours	
Malda	3465 *Howrah-Malda*	5	3.15pm Mon-Sat (HWH)
Mumbai CST	2810 *Mumbai Mail*	33	8.15pm (HWH)
New Jalpaiguri	2343 *Darjeeling Mail*	10	10.05pm (SDAH)
	3147 *CoochBehar*	12	7.35pm Mon, Wed & Sat (SDAH)
Patna	3111 *Delhi Lal Quila*	10½	8.10pm (CP)
Puri	2837 *Howrah-Puri*	9¼	10.35pm (HWH)
	8409 *SriJagannath*	9½	7pm daily (HWH)
Siliguri Jctn	3149 *Kanchankaya*	12	7.35pm Tue, Thu, Fri & Sun (SDAH)
Varanasi	3005 *Amritsar Mail*	15	7.10pm (HWH)

2S=seat, CC=AC chair-car, 2AC=AC two-tier, 3AC=AC three-tier, SL=non-AC sleeper, HWH=ex-Howrah, SDAH=ex-Sealdah, CP=ex-Chitpur

Esplanade bus stand (Map p112). For Malda, CSTC buses leave at 7am, 8.30am, 9.30am and 10.45am with LNB overnighters at 9.45pm (Rs120, 9hrs).

From Babughat

Babughat bus stand (Map pp104–5) is beside Eden Gardens commuter train station. Numerous companies including Whiteliners (☎ 40195000; www.whiteliners.in) run overnight services to Ranchi (Rs210, 10 hours) and to Puri (Rs330, 12 hours) via Bhubaneswar (Rs295, 9½ hours). Arrive by 5pm if you have any baggage.

Car

Autoriders (☎ 22823561; 10A Ho Chi Minh Sarani; ☾ 7am-10pm) hires out chauffeur-driven cars from Rs1350 per eight-hour day (up to 80km, add Rs13 per extra kilometre). Ask for discounts.

Readers have recommended taxi driver Mr Singh (☎ 98-30151794) for city and West Bengal trips.

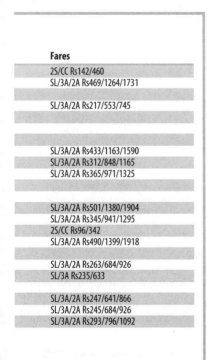

Fares

2S/CC Rs142/460
SL/3A/2A Rs469/1264/1731

SL/3A/2A Rs217/553/745

SL/3A/2A Rs433/1163/1590
SL/3A/2A Rs312/848/1165
SL/3A/2A Rs365/971/1325

SL/3A/2A Rs501/1380/1904
SL/3A/2A Rs345/941/1295
2S/CC Rs96/342
SL/3A/2A Rs490/1399/1918

SL/3A/2A Rs263/684/926
SL/3A Rs235/633

SL/3A/2A Rs247/641/866
SL/3A/2A Rs245/684/926
SL/3A/2A Rs293/796/1092

Train
INTERNATIONAL

For Dhaka, Bangladesh, the new Maitree Express (Rs368-920, 12 hours) runs Saturday and Sunday departing Kolkata (Chitpur) Station at 7.20am, returning from Dhaka Cantt at 8.30am. You must have Darsana marked on your Bangladesh visa. Purchase tickets at a special desk (☾ 10am-5pm Mon-Thu, 10am-3pm Fri & Sat, 10am-2pm Sun) within Eastern Railways' Foreign Tourist Bureau (below).

DOMESTIC

Check carefully whether your long-distance train departs from Howrah (Haora; HWH, Map pp104–5), Sealdah (SDAH, Map pp104–5) or 'Kolkata' (Chitpore) Station (CP, pp104–5).

BOOKINGS

Buying tickets is usually easiest by internet or through Sudder St agencies. Eastern Railways' Foreign Tourist Bureau (Map p112; ☎ 22224206; 6 Fairlie Pl; ☾ 10am-5pm Mon-Sat, 10am-2pm Sun) has a tourist quota for most trains ex-Kolkata, but you must show foreign-exchange receipts or pay in US dollars or euros. Computerised booking offices (Map p112; 14 Strand Rd South & Koilaghat St; ☾ 8am-8pm Mon-Sat, 8am-2pm Sun) offer tickets on the wider train network but have no tourist quota.

GETTING AROUND

Tickets on most public transport cost Rs4 to Rs8. Men shouldn't sit in assigned 'Ladies' seats'.

To/From the Airport

NSBIA Airport is 5km east of Dum Dum, itself 20 minutes by metro (Rs6) from central Kolkata.

SUBURBAN TRAIN

From Biman Bandar the airport train station, trains go to Sealdah at 10.45pm, to Majerhat (Map pp104–5) via BBD Bagh Commuter Station (Map p112) at 7.40am and 1.54pm, and to Majerhat via Ballygunge (Map pp104–5) at 10.40am and 6.45pm. These, plus a 6.30am train, stop at Dum Dum Junction metro interchange. Don't mistakenly alight at Dum Dum Cantt.

TAXI

Fixed-price taxis to Dum Dum metro/Sudder St/Howrah cost Rs140/230/255. Prepay in the terminal then cross over to the rank of yellow cabs ignoring touts in between.

DOMESTIC FLIGHTS FROM KOLKATA

Destination	Airlines (& days if less than daily)	Duration
Agartala	IC, IT, 6E, 9W	55min
Ahmedabad	6E daily, IC Thu & Sun	2¾hr
Aizawl	IC, IT	1½hr
Bagdogra (Siliguri)	IT, SG, 9W daily, IC Tue, Thu & Sat	55min
Bengaluru (Bangalore)	IC, IT, SG, S2, 9W	2hr
Bhubaneswar	IT, 9W	55min
Chennai	IC, IT, SG, 6E, 9W	2hr
Delhi	IC, IT, SG, S2, 6E, 9W	2hr
Dibrugarh	IC Tue-Thu, Sat & Sun, S2/9W Mon-Sat	1½hr
	IT Mon, Wed, Fri & Sun via Guwahati	3hr
Dimapur	IC, usually indirect	1-2hr
Gaya	IC Fri	1hr
Goa	6E via Bangalore	6hr
	IT via Mumbai	4½hr
Guwahati	IC, IT, SG, S2, 6E, 9W,	1¼hr
Hyderabad	IT, 6E, 9W daily, IC Tue-Thu, Sat & Sun	2hr
Imphal	IC, IT, 6E	1¼hr
	S2/9W Mon-Wed, Fri & Sat via Guwahati	2¾
Indore via Raipur	IT	4½
Jaipur	6E, IC	2½hr
Jammu via Delhi	IT	4hr
Jamshedpur (Jharkand)	IT	55min
Jorhat	9W Mon, Wed & Fri,	1½hr
	IC Tue, Thu & Sat via Shillong	3hr
	via Guwahati IT Tue, Thu & Sat, S2 Thu & Sun	2¾
Lilabari (North Lakhimpur)	IT Tue & Thu via Guwahati	3hr
Lucknow	S2	1½hr
Mumbai	IC, IT, SG, S2, 9W	2½hr
Nagpur	6E, S2	1¾
Patna	IT, S2	1hr
Port Blair	IC, IT, S2	2hr
Raipur	IT	2hr
Ranchi	IT, S2	1¼hr
Shillong	IC Tue, Thu & Sat	1¾hr
Silchar	IC, IT	1½hr
Visakhapatnam (Vizag)	IT, S2	1½hr

BUS

Crushed-full city buses run regularly but are hard with luggage. From **Airport Gate 1** (900m southwest of the terminals) minibus 151 runs to BBD Bagh, bus 46 to Esplanade via VIP Rd and Whiteliners Shuttle to Tollygunge Metro.

Buses DN9/1 and 30B (bound eventually for Babughat) pick up along Jessore Rd and run via Dum Dum metro (25 minutes), passing Kolkata's original 1848 ordinance factory, responsible for infamous hollow-tipped Dum-Dum bullets, banned in 1899. From the international terminal, Jessore Rd is just 400m northwest: walk straight out of the terminal keeping the Hindu temple to your direct left and exit the walled airport zone through the

pedestrian-only **Airport Gate 2½** (opposite a sweet shop just east of Ankur Travel).

Alternatively from the domestic terminal, walk 700m northwest; exit via pedestrian-only **Airport Gate 2** (opposite Ahaar Restaurant).

Bus

Passenger-crammed mechanical sweat-boxes hurtle along at frightening speeds wherever the chronic congestion abates. Most buses' route-numbers are written in Western-script even when signboards aren't. Pay aboard.

Ferry

The fastest way from central Kolkata to Howrah train station is generally by **river**

ferry (Rs4; ⊗ 8am-8pm Mon-Sat) departing every 15 minutes from Bagbazar, Armenian, Fairlie, Bishe June and Babu Ghats.

Metro

Kolkata's one-line **Metro** (Rs4-8; ⊗ 7am-9.45pm Mon-Sat, 2pm-9.45pm Sun) is the city's most stress-free form of public transport. For BBD Bagh use Central or Chandni Chowk stations, for Sudder St area use Esplanade or Park St. A new cross line between Salt Lake City and Howrah is planned.

Rickshaw

Kolkata is the last bastion of human-powered 'tana rickshaws', especially around New Market. During monsoon, high-wheeled rickshaws are the transport most able to cope in the worst-flooded streets. Although rickshaw pullers sometimes charge foreigners disproportionate fares, many are virtually destitute, sleeping on the pavements beneath their rented chariots at night so tips are heartily appreciated.

Autorickshaws squeeze aboard five passengers to operate as share-taxis on fixed routes(from Rs2.50 per short hop).

Taxi

Kolkata's ubiquitous yellow Ambassador cabs charge around Rs10 per kilometre (minimum Rs22). To calculate short-trip fares, double the taxi-meter reading and add two rupees. That will be a couple of rupees under for longer trips when you can consult the driver's conversion chart. Just make sure the meter's switched on. That's usually easier when flagging down a passing cab than if approaching a parked one.

Beware that around 1pm, the one-way system on many major roads reverses direction! Not surprisingly many taxis are reluctant to make journeys around this chaotic time.

There are prepaid taxi booths at Howrah Station, Sealdah Station and both airport terminals.

Tram

Routes 20 and 26 link Sealdah train station, Mother Teresa's Motherhouse and Park Circle, with the 26 continuing south to Gariahat terminus. Route 6 links Kumartuli and the sights of upper Rabindra Sarani. The website www.calcuttatramways.com has partly correct route information.

West Bengal

Stretching from the jagged northern hills down to the paddy fields of the Gangetic plains and into the sultry mangrove delta of the Bay of Bengal, few states offer such a rich range of destinations and experiences as West Bengal.

The 'toy train' of the Darjeeling Himalayan Railway chugs up the hills through British-era hill stations, looping its way to Darjeeling, still a summer retreat and a quintessential remnant of the Raj. Here, amid Himalayan giants and renowned tea estates, lies a network of mountain treks and gushing rivers ripe for white-water rafting. These mountain retreats offer a glimpse into the Himalayan peoples and cultures of Sikkim, Bhutan, Nepal and Tibet.

As you head to the plains, brilliant green fields of rice surround bustling trading towns, mud-and-thatch villages, and vestiges of Bengal's glorious history: ornate, terracotta-tiled Hindu temples and monumental ruins of the Muslim nawabs (ruling princes). Further south, the delta rivers of the Sunderbans run through the world's most extensive mangrove forest; inside are darting kingfishers, spotted deer and the elusive Royal Bengal tiger.

West Bengal was the cradle of the Indian Renaissance and national freedom movement, and has long been considered the country's cultural heartland, famous for its eminent writers, artists, spiritualists and revolutionaries. Overshadowed perhaps by the reputation of its capital Kolkata (Calcutta), the rest of West Bengal sees surprisingly few foreign tourists. Perhaps visitors should learn from the Bengalis themselves, enthusiastic travellers who never tire of exploring their own fascinating and diverse region.

HIGHLIGHTS

- Enjoy 360-degree views over Nepal, Sikkim and West Bengal from mountaintop ridges on the **Singalila Ridge Trek** (p166)

- Ride (or walk alongside) the **toy train** (p158) between the tea towns of Kurseong and Darjeeling

- Meander up the wide **Hooghly River** (p141) to uncover colonial and Mughal relics in Serampore, Chandarnagar and Hooghly

- Ride the rapids in a white-water rafting trip down the Teesta River from **Teesta Bazaar** (p172)

- Admire intricate scenes from the Hindu epics carved on the medieval terracotta temples of **Bishnupur** (p142)

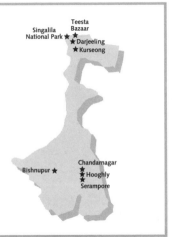

History

Referred to as Vanga in the Mahabharata, this region has a long history predating the Aryan invasions of India. It was part of the Mauryan empire in the 3rd century BC before being overrun by the Guptas. For three centuries from around the 9th century AD, the Pala dynasty controlled a large area based in Bengal and including parts of Orissa, Bihar and modern Bangladesh.

Bengal was brought under Muslim control by Qutb-ud-din, first of the sultans of Delhi, at the end of the 12th century. Following the death of Aurangzeb in 1707, Bengal became an independent Muslim state.

The British established a trading post in Kolkata in 1698, which quickly prospered. Sensing rich pickings, Siraj-ud-daula, the nawab of Bengal, came down from his capital at Murshidabad and easily took Kolkata in 1756. Robert Clive defeated him the following year at the Battle of Plassey, helped by the treachery of Siraj-ud-daula's uncle, Mir Jafar, who commanded the greater part of the nawab's army. He was rewarded by succeeding his nephew as nawab, but after the Battle of Buxar in 1764 the British took full control of Bengal.

In 1947 Indian independence from Britain and the subsequent partition of the country saw the state of Bengal divided on religious grounds, causing the upheaval of millions of Bengalis.

Climate

The monsoon deluges West Bengal from mid-June until late September and the resulting flooding wreaks havoc with the roads and railways from the plains to the hills.

Information

Useful websites include those of the **state government** (www.wbgov.com) and the **tourist department** (www.wbtourism.com).

Activities

TREKKING

While pleasant walks along pine-scented trails are possible in all West Bengal's hill stations, the best multiday treks are organised from Kalimpong (see p168) and Darjeeling (see p166).

RAFTING

Adrenalin-pumping white-water rafting trips are held on the mighty Teesta and Rangeet

FESTIVALS IN WEST BENGAL

Lepcha & Bhutia New Year (Jan; West Bengal Hills, p145) Colourful fairs and traditional dances in and around Darjeeling.

Gangasagar Mela (mid-Jan; Sagar Island, p141) The most intense West Bengal festival; hundreds of thousands of Hindu pilgrims converge where the Ganges meets the sea, to bathe en masse.

Magh Mela (6-8 Feb; Shantiniketan, p143) Crafts take centre stage at this festival.

Bengali New Year (Naba Barsha; mid-Apr; statewide) A statewide holiday celebrates the first day in the Bengali calendar.

Rath Yatra (Car Festival; Jun & Jul; Mahesh, p141) Celebrated by pulling Lord Jagannath's chariot in Mahesh, 3km from Serampore.

Jhapan Festival (mid-Aug; Bishnupur, p142) Draws snake charmers to honour the goddess Manasa, the central figure of snake worship.

Fulpati (Sep & Oct; Darjeeling, p153) Linked to Durga Puja, this predominantly Nepali festival is also celebrated by Lepchas and others with processions and dancing from Ghoom to Darjeeling.

Durga Puja (Oct; statewide) Across the state, especially in Kolkata (Calcutta), temporary *pandals* (castles) are raised and intense celebrations take place to worship Durga. After four colourful days, beautiful images of the 10-armed goddess are immersed in the rivers.

Darjeeling Carnival (7-16 Nov; Darjeeling, p153) Celebrating the region's unity with cultural shows, activities, children's festivals, jazz music and even a contest for *momo* (Tibetan dumpling) eating.

Jagaddhatri Puja (Nov; Chandarnagar, p142) Honours the goddess Jagaddhatri.

Rash Mela (Nov; Cooch Behar & the Sunderbans) Immortalises the union of Lord Krishna and Radha.

Teesta Tea & Tourism Festival (Nov; West Bengal Hills, p145) Features cultural events.

Paush Mela (Dec; Shantiniketan, p143) Folk music, dance, theatre and Baul songs radiate over town.

Bishnupur Festival (late Dec; Bishnupur, p142) Highlights handicrafts and local music.

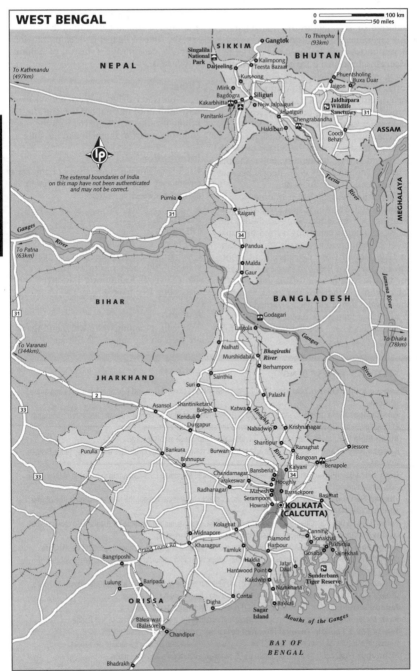

WEST BENGAL

| 0 | 100 km |
| 0 | 50 miles |

Rivers from the tiny riverside town of Teesta Bazaar (p172), and can be organised in Darjeeling (see p160).

Getting There & Around

The vast majority who enter West Bengal arrive in Kolkata. Siliguri's Bagdogra airport has services to Kolkata, Delhi and Guwahati, as well as daily helicopter flights to Gangtok.

Most land arrivals are by train: main lines run south to Bhubaneswar and Chennai (Madras), and west to Gaya, Varanasi and Delhi. Other lines connect the state to Assam in the northeast and Jharkhand in the southwest. Numerous long-distance buses also connect surrounding states.

Most cities and towns within West Bengal are connected by rail and bus, while overcrowded share jeeps ply the winding roads of the West Bengal Hills.

SOUTH OF KOLKATA

SUNDERBANS TIGER RESERVE

Home to one of the largest concentrations of tigers on the planet, this 2585-sq-km **reserve** (☎ 03218-55280; admission per day Rs15) is a network of channels and semisubmerged mangroves that is part of the world's largest river delta. Royal Bengal tigers (officially estimated to number 289) lurk in the impenetrable depths of the mangrove forests, and also swim the delta's innumerable channels. Although they do sometimes kill villagers working in the Sunderbans, tigers are typically shy, and sightings are the very rare exception. Nevertheless, cruising the broad waterways through the world's biggest mangrove forest and watching wildlife, whether it be a

FAST FACTS

Population 80.2 million
Area 87,853 sq km
Capital Kolkata (Calcutta)
Main language Bengali
When to go West Bengal Hills, October to December and March to May; Lower Plains, October to March

spotted deer, 2m-long water monitor or luminescent kingfisher, is a world away from Kolkata's chaos.

The best time to visit is between October and March. Visiting independently is difficult, with tricky transport connections (and possibly permits) to organise, and it's not cheap; you'll have to bear the cost of boat rentals alone. Organised tours (see below) are the easy and comfortable alternative.

At Sajnekhali, the official gateway into the reserve, you'll find the **Mangrove Interpretation Centre** (⏰ 8.30am-5pm) with a small turtle and crocodile hatchery, a collection of pickled wildlife and a blackboard with the date of the last tiger-spotting chalked up. **Boats** (3hr from Rs700, with guide per Indian/foreigner Rs150/200, permit Rs100) are available for hire.

Permits

The permit requirement for foreigners visiting the reserve has been dropped temporarily: for fresh information check with the West Bengal Tourism centre (p107) in Kolkata, or your tour operator.

Tours

Tours prices vary widely. They typically include return transport from Kolkata, as

WEST BENGAL

LIVING AMONG TIGERS

For those who live and work in the Sunderbans, tigers are an everyday part of life. Muslims and Hindus alike revere the tiger-god Dakshin Roy and the forest saviour Bonobibi, who protects them from the man-eaters. Wives of men working in the Sunderbans have even taken to living their days as widows; only when their husbands return do they don their marital ornamentation.

Since tigers are less likely to attack if they suspect they're being watched, honey collectors and woodcutters wear masks of human faces on the backs of their heads. The tigers' extraordinary swimming prowess mean fishermen are not immune; at night tigers have been known to climb aboard fishing boats, which are anchored midstream, and abscond with not-so-happy prey.

Thanks to strategic perimeter fencing near villages, the numbers of human deaths attributed to tigers has dropped from an estimated 200 a year to about 30, despite an (official) increasing tiger population.

WEST BENGAL

SURVIVING THE TIGER *Niranjan Raptan*

My village here in Sunderbans is Jamespur. Another village is called Annpur; they're named after the children of Daniel Hamilton [an English trader who developed the Sunderbans area in the late 19th century].

When I was 18, I was in the mangroves, collecting honey with my uncle. Suddenly a tiger jumped out at us. My uncle threw himself over me. The tiger ran away, but my uncle died from his wounds. That was 42 years ago, he died saving me.

Over the next years I kept going out and collecting honey and fishing, and I saw many more tigers. One day I met the forest field director Mr Sandal and he asked me about when I had seen tigers, and then he asked me 'Do you want to be a guide?' – and you know, I said 'What's a guide?'

I came from a poor family, I had no education, I didn't speak English, but now it's 28 years later and I know all the scientific names of the mangrove plants and animals, all the English and Bengali names, and tourists have been my teachers of English.

I'll tell you about the Sunderbans tiger. He's very clever, he will always attack from behind. The tiger isn't naturally a man-eater, but lack of adequate prey has caused him to take anything he can eat – wild pigs, even crabs, and man. Old tigers that are starving, they swim across the river and take the goat, or the man.

I've seen many tigers. You know, if you close your eyes you can picture your home in your country? I can close my eyes and see the tigers. I don't need a camera. When you see the mother with her cubs, they want to play, but they have no cricket ball, no doll! So the mother says 'Look behind me' and she moves her tail and the cubs chase it and play. Of course she's training them for hunting too.

Niranjan Raptan is a guide in the Sunderbans Tiger Reserve

---

well as all the fees, but do check what is and isn't included.

West Bengal Tourism (p107) organises weekly boat cruises during the months from September to January, costing from Rs2150 per person for one night and two half-days, including food and on-board accommodation. Trips with a worthwhile extra day start from Rs3000.

Sunderban Tiger Camp (☎ 033-32935749; www.sun derbantigercamp.com; ⌗) provides expert guides and quality accommodation (on dry land) with good food and even a bar. Tiger-spotting excursions are on-board comfortable river boats with ample shade. Traditional entertainment is arranged for the evenings. All-inclusive prices range from Rs2750/4440 per person for one-/two-night trips staying in comfortable tents to Rs3500/5650 for fan-cooled huts and Rs4050/7450 for the more luxurious AC cottages.

The following agencies run recommended Sunderbans tours for smaller groups, with an emphasis on environmental and cultural sensitivity. They include hotel transfers in Kolkata.

Help Tourism (p107; 1/2 nights for 2 people all-inclusive from Rs11,400/18,900) Longer trips also available.

Kali Travel Home (☎ /fax 033-25587980; www .traveleastindia.com; 1/2 nights for 2 people all-inclusive from Rs14,000/18,500)

Sleeping & Eating

Sajnekhali Tourist Lodge (☎ 03218-214960; dm/d incl half-board Rs250/700) This lodge is perfectly located in Sajnekhali, but its rooms are dark and dank. Some private tour operators use this accommodation option so bookings are essential. Dorms can't be booked in advance.

Getting There & Away

From Babu Ghat in Kolkata get a bus to Sonakhali (three hours, Rs40 hourly); aim for the first departure at 6.30am. Then go by boat to Gosaba (Rs11, 1½ hours, hourly), where there are shared cycle-rickshaws to Pakhirala (Rs8, 40 minutes). From there, take another boat across the river to Sajnekhali (Rs4, 10 minutes). The last Kolkata bus leaves Sonakhali at 4.30pm.

DIAMOND HARBOUR
☎ 03174 / pop 37,238

Diamond Harbour, once the main port of the East India Company, rests 51km south of Kolkata, where the Hooghly turns south and flows into open sea. It's a good staging area for points in the south.

While Diamond Harbour is a popular picnic spot, there isn't much to see. Across the water are the smoking chimneys of industrial Haldia Island.

Diamond Harbour Tourist Centre (Sagarika Tourist Lodge; ☎/fax 255246; dm Rs150, d from Rs300, with AC from Rs700; ❄️) is a rather dank but feasible overnight stop with a cavernous cafeteria-style restaurant. The better rooms back onto the ocean.

About 12km from Diamond Harbour is the very luxurious **Ffort Raichak** (☎ 033-22852385; www.ffort.com; s/d from Rd 7000/8000; ❄️ 💻 🏊), catering to film stars and petrochemical executives going to and from Haldia. It sits in beautiful, extensive gardens and has all the amenities you'd expect, including restaurants, a classy bar and a spa centre that offers the works.

Buses from Kolkata's Esplanade (Rs27, 1½ hours) come and go every 30 minutes.

SAGAR ISLAND

According to legend, after the sage Kapil reduced King Sagar's 60,000 sons to ashes, it was at Sagar Island that the Ganges revived their souls by flowing over their dusty remains. Each year the **Gangasagar Mela** (see boxed text, p137) is held here, near the Kapil Muni Temple, honouring the legend. Accommodation on the island is always booked out a long way ahead of the mela; a better way to see the festival is the two-day, one-night boat tour run from Kolkata by West Bengal Tourism (p107), with accommodation on board (per person in berth/cabin Rs6500/8000).

From Diamond Harbour, take a bus to Hardwood Point (Rs20, one hour), where a ferry (Rs8, 25 minutes) crosses the Hooghly to Sagar Island. Buses run the 30km from the ferry landing to the temple (Rs25, 45 minutes).

BAKKALI
☎ 03210

Bakkali is a beach town 132km south of Kolkata. The white-sand beach is rather desolate and exposed, but OK for a stroll. An hour north is the photogenic fishing village of **Namkhana**; your vehicle will have to cross the river by ferry here, which may involve a wait of up to two hours.

A few minutes' walk from Bakkali's beach is the government-run **Bakkali Tourist Lodge** (☎ 225260; dm/d/tr Rs126/499/790, d with AC Rs893; ❄️). It's rather neglected (an impression not helped by monsoon muds that engulfed the grounds when we were there), but comfortable and friendly enough. There's a decent restaurant here.

A more upmarket choice is **Hotel Dolphin** (☎ 9836543585; Chowrasta, 24 Parganas South; d Rs400, with AC Rs800-1500), set in a neat garden. The clean rooms have huge beds and cable TV. It's about 10 minutes' walk from the beach.

A couple of kilometres out of Bakkali is **Henry Island** (d Rs600-1200; ❄️), an aquaculture project with some clean rooms and cottages. Some rooms have balconies and there's a rooftop terrace with views of the mangroves and across to the Sunderbans. There's no restaurant but you can order food (and even beer) in advance. Booking is strictly in advance through the **fisheries department** (☎ 033-23376470; sfdcltd@yahoo.com) in Kolkata. An autorickshaw van will bring you here from Bakkali for Rs60.

A government bus departs from Kolkata's Esplanade for Bakkali daily at 7am (Rs75, 4½ hours).

DIGHA
☎ 03220

Digha, once known as the 'Brighton of the East' but probably closer in spirit to Blackpool these days, is located on the Bay of Bengal, 185km southwest of Kolkata. The beach isn't especially attractive, and it's often packed full of Bengali holidaymakers enjoying themselves noisily into the night. A less crowded seaside hideaway can be found 14km northeast at **Shankarpur**.

There are plenty of hotels here. The **Digha Tourist Lodge** (☎ 266255; fax 266256; dm Rs100, d with/without AC from Rs700/300; ❄️) has spacious rooms and offers good value, but look at a few rooms as they vary widely.

Several buses run daily from Kolkata's Esplanade (Rs75, five hours).

NORTH OF KOLKATA

UP THE HOOGHLY

On the Hooghly River, 25km north of Kolkata, **Serampore** was a Danish trading centre until Denmark's holdings in India were transferred to the East India Company in 1845. **Serampore College** was founded by the first Baptist mis-

WEST BENGAL

sionary to India, William Carey, and houses a library that was once one of the largest in the country. The college grounds contain impressive colonial buildings, a pleasant garden with labelled plants from around the world, and a remarkable cast-iron gate donated by the Danish king. The small **Carey Museum** (🕑 10am-5pm Mon-Fri) contains a few pictures and relics, and a bust of the man.

Further upriver is the former French outpost of **Chandarnagar**, where you can visit the **Eglise du Sacre Coeur** (Sacred Heart Church) and the nearby 18th-century mansion now housing the **Cultural Institut de Chandarnagar** (admission free; 🕑 11am-5.30pm, closed Thu & Sat), with collections documenting this colonial outpost. A few blocks north is the atmospheric, decaying **Sacred Heart Cemetery**.

In 1537 the Portuguese set up a factory in **Hooghly**, 41km north of Kolkata, which became an important trading port long before Kolkata rose to prominence. Climb the lofty clocktower of the romantically crumbling **Imambara** (admission Rs5; 🕑 8am-6pm Dec-Jul, to 5.30pm

Aug-Nov), where the view over the river (not to mention the climb) will take your breath away. The building was constructed in 1806 to host the Shiite procession of Muharram. Only 1km south of Hooghly, **Chinsura** was exchanged by the Dutch for the British possessions on the (Indonesian) island of Sumatra in 1825. There is a fort and a Dutch cemetery, 1km to the west.

About 6km north of Hooghly, **Bansberia** has two interesting temples. The 13 *sikharas* (spires) at **Hansewari** look like something you'd expect to see in St Petersburg, while the ornate terracotta tiles covering the **Vasudev Temple** resemble those seen in Bishnupur.

BISHNUPUR
☎ 03244 / pop 61,943

Known for its beautiful terracotta temples, Bishnupur flourished as the capital of the Malla kings from the 16th to the early 19th centuries. The architecture of these intriguing **temples** (Indian/foreigner Rs5/100; 🕑 dawn-dusk) is a bold mix of Bengali, Islamic and Orissan

---

UP ON THE FARM, DOWN ON THE FARM

If you want to get off the tourist track and enjoy views and solitude, we recommend two (very different) farm homestays in West Bengal. Both need to be booked in advance.

Perched on an idyllic mountainside three hours' bumpy jeep ride from Darjeeling (p153) or two hours' drive from Rimbik, at the end of the Singalila Ridge Trek (p166; it's a great place to kick back if you've just finished the trek), **Karmi Farm** (☎ UK 0208-903 3411; www.karmifarm.com; karmifarm@yahoo.co.uk; per person incl full board Rs1500) overlooks Sikkim in one direction and Nepal in another. It's managed by Andrew Pulger, whose Sikkimese grandparents once ran an estate from the main house here, where delicious home-cooked (and often home-grown) meals are now served up to visitors on the old kitchen table. The simple but very comfortable double and family rooms are attractively decorated with colourful local fabrics, and bathrooms have 24-hour hot water. A small clinic for villagers is run from the farm, providing a volunteer opportunity for medical students and doctors. Treks and other activities can be organised, but you may not be able to drag yourself from the rooftop deck; it would be easy to sit here for a week with a book and a pot of tea, overlooking the bird- and flower-filled gardens in the foreground and towering peaks in the distance. Highly recommended.

Back down on the plains and halfway across the state, endless miles of brilliant-green paddy fields stretch out from the simple adobe farmhouse at **Basudha Farm** (☎ Kolkata 033-25928109, 9434062891; www.cintdis.org/basudha.html; per person incl full board Rs300), less than an hour's drive from Bishnupur (above). Basudha was founded by ecologist Dr Debal Deb, who operates a seed bank of indigenous rice strains. At Basudha he grows and experiments with rice, using organic methods, and teaches these methods to other farmers as an alternative to using genetically modified rice varieties. Visitors to the farm are assumed to be interested in the work and the local culture; members of WWOOF (Willing Workers on Organic Farms) get free board in exchange for farm work. Accommodation is basic, with limited (solar) power, and all water needs to be pumped from the well (men are encouraged to piss on the garden to add nitrates to the soil). The all-veg food is mostly grown on the farm, and is cooked in the local style. The strictly vegetarian Dr Deb assured us that the snakes in jars (decorating the guest room) died of natural causes.

styles. Intricately detailed façades of numerous temples play out scenes of the Hindu epics Ramayana and Mahabharata. The most striking temples are the Jor Bangla, Madan Mohan, the multiarched Ras Mancha and the elaborate Shyam Rai. You need to pay for your ticket at Ras Mancha, and show it at the other temples. Cycle-rickshaw-wallahs offer tours (the best way to negotiate the labyrinth of lanes) for Rs150.

There's a small **museum** (Rs10; 11am-7pm Tue-Sun) that's worth a look for its painted manuscript covers, stone friezes, musical instruments and folk-art gallery.

Bishnupur is in Bankura district, famous for its pottery, particularly the stylised Bankura horse, and Baluchari silk saris. Reproductions of detailed terracotta tiles from the temples are sold everywhere.

Bishnupur Tourist Lodge (252013; College Rd; d from Rs300, with AC from Rs600;) is a typically sleepy government-run hotel with adequate, unremarkable rooms and a restaurant. It's close to the museum, and a Rs40 rickshaw ride from the train station. It's often full – book ahead.

Almost next door is **Udayan Lodge** (252243; off College Rd; s/d from Rs150/200) The basic rooms are small and the walls need a paint, but it's otherwise clean. The staff (especially the owner, Mr Chandra) are very friendly and can set you up for sightseeing. There's a basic restaurant.

Regular buses run to Kolkata (Rs70, five hours). For Shantiniketan (Rs65, five hours) you may have to change in Durgapur (see p144). Two trains run daily to Howrah (2nd class/chair Rs81/285, four hours); the *Rupashi Bangla Express* 2884 departs at 5.23pm and the *Howrah Express* 2828 departs at 7.33am.

SHANTINIKETAN
 03463

Shantiniketan is the epitome of its Bengali name, which connotes 'peaceful' *(shanti)* 'abode' *(niketan)*. The mystic, poet and artist Rabindranath Tagore (1861–1941) founded a school here in 1901, which later developed into the Visva-Bharati University, with an emphasis on humanity's relationship with nature. It's a relaxed place with students from all over India and overseas.

The **post office** (Santiniketan Rd; 9am-5pm Mon-Sat) is on the main road, opposite the turn-off to the university entrance. The **State Bank of India** (Santiniketan Rd; 10am-3pm Mon-Fri), on the same road, has an ATM and changes foreign currency and Amex travellers cheques.

Spread throughout the leafy university grounds are eclectic **statues**, the celebrated **Shantiniketan Murals** and the **Tagore Prayer Hall**. The **museum and art gallery** (adult/student Rs5/3; 10.30am-1pm & 2-4.30pm Thu-Mon, 10.30am-1pm Tue) within the Uttarayan complex (Tagore's former home) are worth a peek if you are an aficionado of Tagore. Reproductions of his sketches and paintings are sold here. The bookshop at the main gate has plenty of Tagore's titles (Rs80 to Rs250) in English.

The **Women's Handicraft Centre** (253963; 9.30am-1pm & 5-7pm) is opposite the tourist lodge, and many other shops and stalls sell embroidered bags and batik work on the road between here and the university.

Sleeping & Eating
Bolpur Lodge (252737, 252662; Bhubandanga; d from Rs200) Quiet, friendly and cheap, but rooms are threadbare and only passably clean.

Hotel Santiniketan (254434; Bhubandanga; s/d from Rs250/300, d with AC Rs700;) This salmon-coloured (inside and out) balconied hotel provides good value, with clean rooms (though the sheets and towels have seen much better days). The ground-floor rooms are cool and there's a pleasant garden. The restaurant (mains Rs35 to Rs80) dishes up a limited range of Indian standards.

Hotel Rangamati (252305; Hwy 31, Bhubandanga; s/d from Rs550/700, with AC from Rs650/850) A fun 'jungle hut' theme with faux branches, wooden fittings and lots of fish tanks at the entrance. Rooms are clean with big bathrooms and dark-wood furniture. There's a basic restaurant.

Camellia Hotel & Resort (262042; Prantik; d Rs1150, with AC from Rs1450;) The Camellia has a pleasant country setting about 1km from the university, with leafy gardens and green lawns. Tasteful art and furniture make the rooms especially comfortable; the suites have fridge and bathtub. Pick-up from the train station is available.

Green Chilli (9832277095; Bhubandanga; mains Rs20-55, thalis Rs30) This place provides good Indian breakfasts and a range of tasty curries and Chinese food. Stylishly done up with bright colours, it's a pleasant spot to grab a bite. It's just off the highway on the way to Hotel Santiniketan.

WEST BENGAL

Getting There & Away

Several trains ply between Bolpur station, 2km south of the university, and Kolkata daily. The best is *Shantiniketan Express* 2337/8 (2nd class/chair Rs69/235, 2½ hours) departing at 10.10am from Howrah and 1.10pm from Bolpur. To New Jalpaiguri choose between *Kanchenjunga Express* 5657 (sleeper/3AC Rs190/505, eight hours) departing at 9.40am or *Kolkata Haldibari Superfast Express* 2563 (2nd class/chair Rs126/425) departing at 11.31am on Tuesday, Thursday and Saturday. There's a **train booking office** (Santiniketan Rd; ⊗ 8am-noon & 12.30-2pm Thu-Tue) near the post office.

The Jambuni bus stand is in Bolpur. Buses go to Berhampore/Murshidabad (Rs55, four hours) and Bishnupur (Rs65, five hours) but direct buses can be hard to find: you may need to change in Durgapur for Bishnupur and Suri for Berhampore.

NABADWIP & MAYAPUR

☎ 03472 / pop 115,036

Nabadwip, 114km northwest of Kolkata, is an important Krishna pilgrimage centre, attracting throngs of devotees, and is an ancient centre of Sanskrit culture. The last Hindu king of Bengal, Lakshman Sen, moved his capital here from Gaur.

Across the river from Nabadwip, Mayapur is a centre for the Iskcon (Hare Krishna) movement. There's a large, colourful temple and the basic but clean **Iskcon Guest Houses** (☎ 245620; mghb@pamho.net; d/tr/q from Rs300/350/450, d without bathroom from Rs100). Iskcon runs a private bus to Kolkata (Rs200, five hours) early on Friday, Saturday and Sunday mornings, returning in the evening; for details or to make a booking call **Iskcon Kolkata** (☎ 033-30289258, 30280865).

MURSHIDABAD & BERHAMPORE

☎ 03482 / pop 36,894

In Murshidabad, rural Bengali life and 18th-century architecture meld on the verdant shores of the Bhagirathi River. When Siraj-ud-daula was nawab of Bengal, Murshidabad was his capital, and he was assassinated here after the defeat at Plassey (now Palashi).

The main draw here is the **Hazarduari** (Indian/foreigner Rs5/100; ⊗ 10am-4.30pm Sat-Thu), a palace famous for its 1000 doors (real and false), built here for the nawabs in 1837. It houses an astonishing collection of antiquities from the 18th and 19th centuries. The Great Imambara on the palace grounds is being renovated and may be closed; have a peek through the gates.

Murshid Quli Khan, who moved the capital here in 1705, is buried beneath the stairs at the impressive ruins of the **Katra Mosque**. Siraj-ud-daula was assassinated at the **Nimak Haram Deohri** (Traitor's Gate). Within the **Kathgola Gardens** (admission Rs7; ⊗ 6.30am-5.30pm) is an interesting Jain Parswanath Temple and a museum.

Berhampore is 11km south of Murshidabad and acts as its bus and railway hub.

Sleeping & Eating

Hotel Samrat (☎ 251147; fax 253091; NH34 Panchanantala; s/d from Rs175/250, with AC from Rs600/700; ⊗) We'd recommend Samrat even if it wasn't pretty much the only hotel in Berhampore: it's excellent value, with fresh, brightly painted rooms with new furnishings, and helpful staff who can organise sightseeing for you. The fancy-pants new restaurant (mains Rs30 to Rs80), all faux marble and low lighting, has a bar and a big range of dishes, mainly Indian.

Hotel Manjusha (☎ 270321; Murshidabad; d Rs300-400) A wonderful setting on the bank of the Bhagirathi, behind the Great Imambara. Downstairs rooms are cheapest, while rooms 201 to 203 have both river and Hazarduari views. It's all about the location and period charm – the rooms themselves are threadbare and fading, and some are slightly whiffy.

Getting There & Around

There's a daily express train *Bhagirati Express* 3103/4 to/from Kolkata (2nd class/chair Rs67/236, four hours), departing Sealdah Station, Kolkata at 6.25pm and Berhampore at 6.34am. Regular buses leave for Kolkata (Rs65, six hours) and Malda (Rs55, four hours). To Shantiniketan/Bolpur (Rs55, four hours) there are occasional direct buses but you may need to change in Suri.

Shared autorickshaws (Rs10) whizz between Murshidabad and Berhampore. Cycle-rickshaws/taxis offer guided half-day tours to see the spread-out sites for Rs150/400.

MALDA

☎ 03512 / pop 161,448

Malda, 347km north of Kolkata, is a convenient base for visiting the ruins of Bengal's former capitals in nearby Gaur and Pandua. Malda is also famed for its Fajli mangoes ripening in spring; even if it's not mango season, you'll probably get mango pickle on the side with any food you order here.

State Bank of India and ICICI ATMs are on the highway, near the turn-off to the bus station. **i-Zone** (per hr Rs20; 8am-7pm), behind the bus station on the way to the museum, has fast internet connections. **Malda Museum** (admission Rs2; 10.30am-5pm Thu-Tue) is next to the library and has a small collection of sculpture and coins from Gaur and Pandua.

Continental Lodge (252388; fax 251505; 22 KJ Sanyal Rd; s/d from Rs150/250, d with AC from Rs650;) is a friendly lodge almost directly opposite the bus station; it offers fairly clean, oddly furnished rooms for every budget.

Hotel Pratapaditya (268104; Station Rd; s/d from Rs200/250, d with AC from Rs650-800;) is the quietest option and is just off the highway, only 500m from the train station. It offers a wide variety of rooms and a good Indian and continental restaurant (mains Rs35 to Rs75).

Hotel Kalinga (284503; www.hotelkalingamalda .com; NH34, Ram Krishna Pally; d with/without AC from Rs800/425;) is a big place on the highway, about halfway between the bus and train stations. The AC rooms are fine, but the cheaper ones are grubby and bare. The restaurant on the top floor has an Indian/Chinese/ continental menu (mains Rs40 to Rs90) and great views over the town.

The best train from Kolkata (Sealdah station) is *Kolkata Haldibari Superfast Express* 2563 (2nd class/chair Rs111/372, six hours), departing 9.05am Tuesday, Thursday and Sunday. It continues to New Jalpaiguri (Rs91/301, four hours), departing at 3.20pm. If returning to Kolkata take the *Intercity Express* 3466 to Howrah (2nd class/chair Rs96/342, seven hours), departing 6.10am Monday to Saturday. Buses depart regularly for Siliguri (Rs120, six hours), Berhampore/Murshidabad (Rs55, four hours) and Kolkata (from Rs140, 10 hours).

GAUR & PANDUA

Rising from the flooded paddy fields of Gaur (16km south of Malda) are mosques and other vestiges of the 13th- to 16th-century capital of the Muslim nawabs. Little remains from the 7th- to 12th-century pre-Muslim period, when Gaur was the capital of the successive Buddhist Pala and Hindu Sena dynasties.

Wander through the ruins of the impressive **Baradwari Mosque** and the intact arcaded aisle of its corridor, or beneath the fortresslike gateway of **Dakhil Darwaza** (1425). The **Qadam Rasul Mosque** enshrines the flat footprint of the Prophet Mohammed. The adjacent **tomb of Fath Khan** (1707) startlingly informs you that he 'vomited blood and died on this spot'. Lotus-flower motifs grace the terracotta facade of the **Tantipara Mosque** (1480), while remnants of colourful enamel cling to the **Lattan** and **Chamkati Mosques**.

North of Pandua (18km north of Malda) are the vast ruins of the 14th-century **Adina Masjid**, once India's largest mosque. Within an intact section of arched and domed bays sits the tomb of Sikander Shah (1364–79), the builder of this mosque. About 2km away is the **Eklakhi mausoleum**, so-called because it cost Rs1 lakh (Rs100,000) to build.

The monuments are spread throughout Gaur and Pandua along some of the worst roads in India; it's worth hiring a taxi from Malda for half a day (Rs600).

WEST BENGAL HILLS

SILIGURI & NEW JALPAIGURI
 0353 / pop 655,935 / elev 119m

The crowded trading hub encompassing the twin towns of Siliguri and New Jalpaiguri (NJP) is the jumping-off point for Darjeeling, Kalimpong, Sikkim, the Northeast States, eastern Nepal and Bhutan. There's not a lot to see here: for most travellers, Siliguri is an overnight transit point where you can catch a glimpse of snowy peaks.

Orientation
Most of Siliguri's hotels, restaurants and services are spread along Tenzing Norgay Rd, better known as Hill Cart Rd. NJP Station Rd leads southward to NJP station, while branching eastward off Hill Cart Rd are Siliguri's other main streets, Sevoke and Bidhan Rds.

Information
INTERNET ACCESS
Cyber Space (Hotel Vinayak, Hill Cart Rd; 10am-8pm) Internet (Rs30), USB connection and CD burning (Rs25).
iWay (Hill Cart Rd; per hr Rs30; 9am-9pm) A tangerine dream, with bright-orange walls and cubicles. Down behind a shop.
Netcafe (9434020017; Hospital Rd; per hr Rs15; 10am-10pm) Small, hot, crowded and half the price of anywhere else.

WEST BENGAL

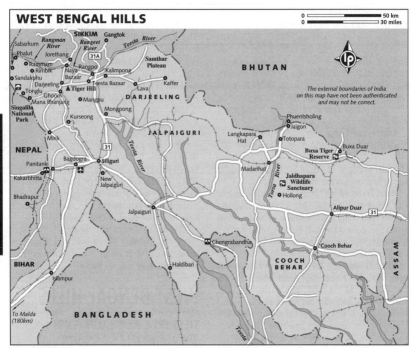

WEST BENGAL HILLS

The external boundaries of India on this map have not been authenticated and may not be correct.

MEDICAL SERVICES
Sadar Hospital (☎ 2436526, 2585224; Hospital Rd)

MONEY
There are ATMs for Standard Chartered Bank, State Bank of India and UBI Bank on Hill Cart Rd.

Delhi Hotel (☎ 2516918; Hill Cart Rd; ☉ 9am-8pm) Currency and travellers cheques exchanged.

Multi Money (☎ 2535321; 143 Hill Cart Rd; ☉ 9.30am-7pm Mon-Sat) Exchanges currency and Amex travellers cheques. Western Union agent.

POST
General post office (☎ 2538850; Hospital Rd; ☉ 7am-7pm Mon-Sat, 10am-3pm Sun) No parcel service late afternoon or Sunday.

TOURIST INFORMATION
Darjeeling Gorkha Hill Council tourist office (DGHC; ☎ 2518680; Hill Cart Rd; ☉ 8am-5pm Mon-Fri, 8am-1pm Sat & Sun) A friendly office with brochures on Darjeeling, Kalimpong, Kurseong and Mirik.

Government of Assam tourist office (Pradhan Nagar Rd; ☉ 10am-4pm Mon-Fri) No phone, six pamphlets, and you have to sign in triplicate to confirm you took a pamphlet.

Sikkim tourist office (☎ 2512646; SNT Terminal, Hill Cart Rd; ☉ 10am-4pm Mon-Sat) Issues permits for Sikkim. If you apply in the morning, your permit should be ready by the afternoon; bring your passport and one passport-sized photo.

West Bengal tourist office (☎ 2511979; Hill Cart Rd; ☉ 10am-5pm Mon-Fri) Can also book accommodation for the Jaldhapara Wildlife Sanctuary. Less helpful information desks are also at the airport and NJP train station.

TRAVEL AGENCIES
Private transport booking agencies line Hill Cart Rd.

Help Tourism (☎ 2433683; www.helptourism.com; 143 Hill Cart Rd) A recommended agency with a strong environmental and community-development focus. It has links to homestays and lodges around the hills, and can organise tour and trekking packages that get rave reviews.

Sleeping
BUDGET
Conclave Lodge (☎ 2514102; Hill Cart Rd; s/d from Rs200/350) Tucked away behind the more visible Hotel Conclave, this lodge is the best budget option, with clean, quiet whitewashed rooms with TV.

Hotel Hill View (☎ 2519951; Hill Cart Rd; d 400, s/tr without bathroom Rs200/350) This vintage 1951 place has some tiny vestiges of colonial charm (mainly on the exterior), but rooms are basic and run down. The friendly manager doesn't try to oversell his 'very simple rooms'.

Hotel Chancellor (☎ 2432372; cnr Sevoke & Hill Cart Rds; d Rs285, with TV Rs335) A no-frills, friendly Tibetan-run place that gets some traffic noise. Rooms are clean, but ongoing renovations mean you might have to navigate past exposed concrete and piles of junk to get there.

Hotel Mount View (☎ 2512919; Hill Cart Rd; d from Rs500) Rooms contain an odd mix of cheap and quality furniture. Take a look at a few rooms as some (mainly upstairs) are much nicer than others.

MIDRANGE & TOP END

Hotel Conclave (☎ 2516144; www.hotelconclave.com; Hill Cart Rd; s/d from Rs500/600, with AC from Rs750/900; 🖳) A recommended contemporary hotel with fine woodwork and artwork, quality mattresses and an unexpected external glass elevator. The rooms are spotless and downstairs is the excellent Eminent Restaurant.

Hotel Central Plaza (☎ 2516119; Hill Cart Rd; s/d from Rs500/650; 🖳) Hotels in this price range often feature a sparkling lobby and grotty rooms, but here you'll find the opposite: walk past the nondescript lobby to find surprisingly modern and very clean rooms with blond-wood beds and newly painted feature walls.

Hotel Vinayak (☎ 2431130; fax 2531067; Hill Cart Rd; d Rs500-800, with AC Rs1000-3200; 🖳) Small, unremarkable rooms with cheap furniture; the non-AC rooms are better value. There's a pretty good restaurant here.

Hotel Himalayan Regency (☎ 650 2955; Hill Cart Rd; s/d from Rs500/600, with AC from Rs1100/1200; 🖳) Comfortable rooms with big, clean bathrooms. A lot of thought has obviously gone into the design and colour scheme here (not necessarily by someone with good taste).

Hotel Sinclairs (☎ 2517674; www.sinclairshotels.com; off NH31; d from Rs2900; 🖳 🖳) This comfortable three-star hotel escapes the noise of Hill Cart Rd, about 2km north of the bus terminal. The rooms are spacious, if a little tired, but there's an excellent restaurant-cum-bar and the chance to dive into a cool, clean pool.

SILIGURI

Approximate Scale 0 — 500 m 0 — 0.3 miles

INFORMATION	
Cyber Space	(see 20)
Darjeeling Gorkha Hill Council (DGHC) Tourist Office	1 A1
Delhi Hotel	2 A1
General Post Office	3 B3
Government of Assam Tourist Office	4 B1
Help Tourism	(see 6)
iWay	5 B2
Multi Money	6 B3
Netcafe	7 B3
Sadar Hospital	8 B3
SBI ATM	9 B2
Sikkim Tourist Office	(see 28)
Standard Chartered Bank ATM	(see 6)
UBI ATM	10 B3
West Bengal Tourist Office	11 B2

SLEEPING 🏠	
Conclave Lodge	12 A2
Hotel Central Plaza	13 A1
Hotel Chancellor	14 B2
Hotel Conclave	15 A2
Hotel Hill View	16 A2
Hotel Himalayan Regency	17 A1
Hotel Mount View	18 A1
Hotel Sinclairs	19 A1
Hotel Vinayak	20 B2

EATING 🍴	
Khana Khazana	21 A1
Madira	22 B2
Mapasand	(see 9)
New Ranjit Hotel	23 B3
Sartaj	(see 23)

SHOPPING 🛍	
Hong Kong Market	24 B2

TRANSPORT	
Darjeeling & Kurseong Jeep Stand	25 A1
Indian Airlines	26 A1
Jet Airways	(see 20)
Kalimpong Jeep Stand	27 A1
SNT Terminal	28 A2
Tenzing Norgay Central Bus Terminal	(see 25)
Tourist Service Agency	29 A1
Train Booking Office	30 B3

Cindrella Hotel (☎ 2544130; www.cindrellahotels .com; 3rd Mile, Sevoke Rd; s/d from Rs3300/3500; 🅿 🖳 🛜 🅿) The top place in town is very luxurious; rooms have polished floorboards, comfy couches, huge beds, minibar and stylish lighting. There's a small pool and gym.

Eating

Mapasand (☎ 2778704; Mangaldeep Blg, Hill Cart Rd; sweets from Rs5; 🕑 8am-9pm) While other bakeries embrace the trend towards lurid Westernstyle cakes, this clean shop presents enticing trays of classic Indian sweets such as *barfi* (a fudgelike sweet; complete with real silver) and *ladoo* (sweetmeat balls made with gram flour).

New Ranjit Hotel (☎ 2431785; Hill Cart Rd; mains Rs25-70) Beneath Sartaj, this busy vegetarian restaurant is the place to find wonderful dosas and other South Indian snacks. North Indian and Chinese veg dishes are also available.

Madira (☎ 2435980; Hill Cart Rd; mains Rs25-150) A small bar-restaurant, reached via a tunnel beside Airview Lodge. Decorated in cute bright colours it serves a range of north Indian dishes and snacks, along with some Chinese of the 'American Chopsuey' variety.

Khana Khazana (☎ 2517516; Hill Cart Rd; mains Rs40-90) The secluded outdoor area here makes a nice lunch spot. The extensive menu ranges from pizzas and Chinese and South Indian specials to Mumbai (Bombay) street snacks, and includes plenty of vegetarian options.

Sartaj (☎ 2431759; Hill Cart Rd, mains Rs45-180; 🅿) A sophisticated and cool (literally – it's heaven when the AC hits you) restaurant with a huge range: first-rate North Indian tandooris and curries, good Chinese and top service. There's a bar, and alcohol is served to your table.

Shopping

There are numerous markets here, from the bright and traditional hawkers' market near NJP station to Siliguri's high-rise Hong Kong Market. Siliguri is also known for its caneware, and you will find everything from letter racks to lounge suites spread along Hill Cart Rd. If you didn't pick up enough tea in the hills, there are plenty of shops selling nicely packaged leaves.

Getting There & Away

AIR

Bagdogra airport is 12km west of Siliguri. **Indian Airlines** (☎ 2511495; www.indianairlines.in; Hill Cart Rd; 🕑 10am-1pm & 1.45-4.30pm Mon-Sat) has three flights a week to Kolkata (one hour), five to Delhi (four hours), and two to Guwahati (50 minutes). **Jet Airways** (☎ 2538001; www.jetairways .com; Hill Cart Rd; 🕑 9am-5.30pm Mon-Sat) flies to Kolkata (daily), Delhi (daily; some flights via Guwahati) and Guwahati (four per week). **Kingfisher Airlines** (☎ 39008888; www.flykingfisher .com) has daily flights to Kolkata and Delhi, and three flights a week to Guwahati. Check websites for fares, which can vary widely.

Daily helicopter flights (Rs3000, 30 minutes, 10kg luggage limit) go from Bagdogra to Gangtok at 2pm daily. You can buy tickets from **Tourist Service Agency** (TSA; ☎ 2531959; tsaslg@sancharnet.in; Pradhan Nagar Rd), close to the Delhi Hotel.

BUS

Most of the North Bengal State Transport Corporation (NBSTC) buses leave from **Tenzing Norgay central bus terminal** (Hill Cart Rd), as do many private buses plying the same routes.

Sikkim Nationalised Transport (SNT) buses to Gangtok (Rs96, 4½ hours) leave at 9.30am, 11.30am, 12.30pm and 1.30pm from the **SNT terminal** (Hill Cart Rd). There is also a deluxe bus (Rs110) departing here at 12.30pm. If travelling to Sikkim, you'll require a permit available in Siliguri at the adjacent Sikkim tourist office (p146).

PRODUCING THE PERFECT CUPPA

Live-in training courses for aspiring tea experts are popular in the West Bengal Hills. The following estates have good reputations and use organic methods.

Lochan Tea Limited (www.lochantea.com, www.doketea.com; Siliguri) Offers a three-month course in international tea trading that includes tea tasting and practical experience in buying tea at auction. Students live at the company guest house in Siliguri.

Makaibari Tea Estate (www.makaibari.com; Kurseong) Courses include five-day intensives (Rs10,000) in tea manufacturing and biodynamics; accommodation is available on the estate or at nearby Cochrane Place (p152). For more about Makaibari see the boxed text, p152.

NBSTC BUSES FROM SILIGURI

Destination	Fare (Rs)	Duration (hr)	Frequency
Darjeeling	80	3½	every 30min
Guwahati	280	12	5pm only
Kalimpong	50	3	every 2hr
Kolkata	266	12-16	5 daily
Kurseong	42	2	every 30min
Madarihat	65	3	hourly
Malda	115	6½	every 30min
Mirik	50	2½	every 2hr

JEEP

A faster and more comfortable way of getting around the hills is by share jeep. There are a number of jeep stands: for Darjeeling (Rs120, 2½ hours) and Kurseong (Rs60, 1½ hours), look around and opposite the bus terminal; for Kalimpong (Rs80, 2½ hours) there's a stand on Sevoke Rd; and for Gangtok (Rs140, four hours) jeeps leave from next to the SNT terminal. Share and charter jeeps for all these destinations also leave straight from the NJP train station.

Chartering a jeep privately costs roughly 10 times that of a shared ticket. An option for XL-sized Westerners is to pay for and occupy all the front three seats next to the driver.

TRAIN

The fastest of the four daily services to Kolkata is the *Darjeeling Mail* 2344 (sleeper/3AC Rs263/684, 13 hours, departs 5.25pm), which stops in Malda. A better option for Malda is the *New Jalpaiguri Sealdah Express* 2504 (2nd class/chair Rs111/372, four hours, departing 9.45am Monday, Wednesday and Saturday). The *North East Express* 2505 is the fastest to Delhi (sleeper/3AC Rs437/1174, 27 hours, departs 5.05pm), travelling via Patna (Rs229/587, 11 hours). Eastward, train 2506 reaches Guwahati (sleeper/3AC Rs207/527, eight hours, departs 8.40am).

There's a **train booking office** (☎ 2537333; cnr Hospital & Bidhan Rds; ☼ 8-11.30am & noon-8pm Mon-Sat, to 2pm Sun) in Siliguri.

Toy Train

The diesel toy train climbs the 88km from New Jalpaiguri to Darjeeling in eight long hours (2nd/1st class Rs42/247, departs 9am). It's wise to make reservations (booking fee Rs15/30) two to three days in advance at NJP station or the train booking office. If steam is your passion, you can catch the steam version to Darjeeling from Kurseong (p152).

Getting Around

From the bus terminal to NJP train station a taxi/autorickshaw costs Rs200/90, while cycle-rickshaws charge Rs50 for the 35-minute trip. Taxis between Bagdogra airport and Siliguri cost Rs300.

JALDHAPARA WILDLIFE SANCTUARY

☎ 03563 / elev 61m

This rarely visited **sanctuary** (☎ 262239; Indian/foreigner Rs25/100, camera/video Rs5/2500; ☼ mid-Sep–mid-Jul) protects 114 sq km of lush forests and grasslands along the Torsa River and is a refuge for more than 50 Indian one-horned rhinoceros (*Rhinoceros unicornis*).

The best time to visit is mid-October to May, particularly March and April when wild elephants, deer and tigers (rarely seen) are attracted by new grass growth. Your best chance of spotting a rhino is aboard an elephant (Indian/foreigner Rs120/200 per hour); these lumbering safaris are booked by the tourist lodges, and if staying elsewhere, you'll be last in line. You can't book ahead for elephant rides, so if an elephant falls sick or a VIP wants a ride, you might miss out.

The West Bengal tourist offices in Kolkata (p107) and Siliguri (p146) organise overnight **tours** (per person Rs2050; ☼ departs 10am Sat, returns 5pm Sun) from Siliguri to Jaldhapara, which include an elephant ride, transport, accommodation at the Hollong Tourist Lodge and all meals.

Sleeping & Eating

The two lodges should be booked well in advance through the West Bengal Tourist Office in Siliguri, Darjeeling or Kolkata; they won't take direct bookings.

CROSSING INTO BANGLADESH, BHUTAN & NEPAL

To/From Bangladesh

A number of private agencies in Siliguri, including **Shyamoli** (☎ 9932627647; Hotel Central Plaza complex, Hill Cart Rd) run regular AC buses direct to Dhaka (Rs650) – you'll need to get on and off at the border at Chengrabandha.

Regular buses go from the Tenzing Norgay central bus terminal to Chengrabandha (Rs42) starting from 7.30am. The border post is open from 8am to 6pm daily. From near the border post you can catch buses on to Rangpur, Bogra and Dhaka. Visas for Bangladesh can be obtained in Kolkata (Calcutta) and New Delhi. For more information, see p330.

To/From Bhutan

Bhutan Transport Services have a counter inside Tenzing Norgay central bus terminal in Siliguri. Two buses leave daily for Phuentsholling (Rs75, departs 7am and 2pm). Indian immigration is in Jaigon, between the police station and Hotel Kasturi. Non-Indian nationals need a valid visa authority from a Bhutanese tour operator to enter Bhutan. See www.tourism.gov.bt and Lonely Planet's *Bhutan* for details.

To/From Nepal

For Nepal, local buses pass the Tenzing Norgay central bus terminal in Siliguri every 15 minutes for the border town of Panitanki (Rs20, one hour). Share jeeps to Kakarbhitta (Rs70) are readily available in Siliguri. The Indian border post in Panitanki is officially open 24 hours and the Nepal post in Kakarbhitta is open from 7am to 7pm. See p165 for information on buses from Darjeeling to Kathmandu. Onward from Kakarbhitta there are numerous buses to Kathmandu (17 hours) and other destinations. Bhadrapur airport, 23km southwest of Kakarbhitta, has regular flights to Kathmandu. Visas for Nepal can be obtained at the border, or in Kolkata or New Delhi. For more information, see p331.

Jaldhapara Tourist Lodge (☎ 262230; dm Rs300, cottage Rs650, d Rs1000) This WBTDC hotel is outside the park precincts near Madarihat. All meals are included in the room rates. Check out rooms in both blocks.

Hotel Relax (☎ 262304; Madarihat; d Rs350) A very basic option opposite the Jaldhapara Tourist Lodge, with OK beds, cement floors and squat toilets. Expect some odd smells.

Hollong Tourist Lodge (☎ 262228; d Rs1000, plus compulsory Rs175 per person for breakfast & dinner) This is a smaller and more comfortable option within the park itself. Lunch is available for an additional Rs75.

Getting There & Away

Jaldhapara is 124km east of Siliguri. Buses frequent the route from Siliguri to Madarihat (Rs65, three hours, hourly 6am to 4pm), 9km from Jaldhapara. A taxi from Madarihat to Hollong inside the park is Rs150.

MIRIK

☎ 0354 / pop 9179 / elev 1767m

Nestled near the Nepal border, halfway be-tween Siliguri and Darjeeling, is this low-profile hill station. Mirik is surrounded by an undulating carpet of tea estates, orange orchards, cardamom plantations and forests of tall, dark Japanese cedars. It has a quiet charm and relaxed vibe that make it quite different from Darjeeling or Kalimpong. Some of Mirik's higher hilltops offer won-derful views of morning's first light striking Khangchendzonga (8598m).

Information

Krishnanagar Cyber Cafe (Main Rd, Krishnanagar; per hr Rs30), opposite Hotel Jagjeet, has a slow dial-up connection. There are no money-changing facilities but there's a reliable State Bank of India ATM next to Hotel Jagjeet.

Foreigners should register (just show your passport) at the **Frontier Check Post** (Main Rd, Krishnanagar) if staying overnight. The check post is on your right on the way down to the lake, near the bottom of the hill; staff are relaxed and keen to chat.

Sights & Activities

Mirik is centred on the artificial murky-coloured **Sumendu Lake** and there's a walk around its 3.5km circumference. On the west side of the lake, climb the steps to the diminutive Hindu **Devi Sthan temple complex**. Perched high above Mirik, the richly painted **Bokar Gompa** has bright murals; take a bracing walk up Monastery Rd if you don't want to be gouged Rs80 for a taxi.

Pedal boats (per 30min Rs60) can be hired near the bridge and **pony rides** (half/full round-the-lake trips Rs80/160) are offered for various trips around Mirik.

Sleeping & Eating

Prices can drop by up to 50% from December to February and June to September.

Hotel Mhelung (☎ 9932282875; dm Rs100, d Rs600, q Rs800) A clean, quiet and simple place with attractive wooden furniture, TV and geyser.

Lodge Ashirvad (☎ 2243272; s Rs180, d Rs250-350) A friendly family-run budget hotel down a lane just off the main road. The rooms are clean and there's a rooftop terrace with a great view across the monastery. Hot-water buckets cost Rs10. Home-cooked food is served in a slightly dank basement from October to November and March to May.

Buddha Lodge (☎ 2243515; d Rs300-400) Spotless, charming rooms with TV and nice furniture; upstairs rooms have especially appealing wood panelling.

Hotel Ratnagiri (☎ 2243243; www.hotelratnagiri .com; d Rs600-800) This hotel has warm, wood-panelled doubles upstairs (with cute sloping ceilings) plus larger family suites. Some rooms have balconies and views of Sumendu Lake; all have TV and geyser. There's a good garden restaurant out back (mains Rs30 to Rs90).

Hotel Jagjeet (☎ 2243231; www.jagjeethotel.com; d from Rs1000) The best hotel in town, with a variety of clean and comfy rooms, most with balconies, and attentive service. The restaurant (mains Rs30 to Rs115) is deservedly popular, serving excellent Indian, Chinese and continental dishes. Toothsome sweets, including *barfi*, are sold at a separate counter here.

Mirik Orange County Retreat (Swiss Cottages; ☎ 9733331510; cottages Rs1300-1800) These two-storey cottages afford glorious views of the township (the lake is much prettier from this distance) and surrounding countryside, including Khangchendzonga. The stone cottages are very cute from outside, but inside things are a bit bare and run-down for the price, and the staff is indifferent; you're really only paying for the view. It has recently been taken over by the West Bengal Tourism Corporation, which might explain things.

Samden Restaurant (☎ 2243295; mains Rs10-20; ☉ 5.30am-9pm) A great 'local', next to Hotel Jagjeet, drawing monks and those in love with *momos* and noodle soups (*thukpas* and *thankthuks*).

Sukh Sagar Restaurant (mains Rs15-60) At the bottom of the hill near the lake, a pure-veg cafeteria-type place catering to lakeside day trippers with good snacks and South Indian favourites. A thali with the works is Rs70.

Getting There & Away

Buses leave for Darjeeling and Siliguri (both Rs50, three hours). Share jeeps depart regularly to Darjeeling and Siliguri (both Rs55, 2½ hours) and Kurseong (Rs60, three hours).

Mirik Out Agency (Main Rd, Krishnanagar; ☉ 9am-noon & 1-4pm), opposite Hotel Ratnagiri, sells a quota of tickets for trains from NJP.

KURSEONG

☎ 0354 / pop 40,067 / elev 1458m

Kurseong, 32km south of Darjeeling, is the little sister of (and quiet alternative to) the Queen of the Hills further up the track. Its name derives from the Lepcha word *kurson-rip*, a reference to the small white orchid prolific in this area. Surrounded by tea estates, it is the southern terminus for the steam-powered toy trains of the Darjeeling Himalayan Railway.

Hill Cart Rd (Tenzing Norgay Rd) – the shop-lined main thoroughfare from Siliguri to Darjeeling – and its remarkably close shadow, the railway line, wind through town.

There are numerous good walks in the area, including one to Eagle's Crag (2km return) that affords splendid views down the Teesta and the plains to the south. Along Pankhabari Rd, the lushly overgrown **old graveyard** at St Andrews has poignant reminders of the tea-planter era, while the organic **Makaibari Tea Estate** (boxed text, p152) and **Amboitia Tea Estate** (☎ 9434045602) welcome visitors to their aromatic factories. The **Kunsamnamdoling Gompa** is a lovely monastery run by Red Hat *ani* (Tibetan Buddhist nuns).

Check email at **Kashyup Computers & Systems** (Hill Cart Rd; per hr Rs30) and **Kay Deez** (per hr Rs25), off Hill Cart Rd on your left as you walk into town from the train station.

Sleeping & Eating

A number of hotels near the station have grotty, overpriced rooms; it's well worth going the extra few steps to the following places.

Hotel Delhi Darbar (☎ 2345862; delhidarbarinn @yahoo.com; Hill Cart Rd; d/tr Rs300/400) A budget option a few blocks from the train station. It's friendly but only just clean (go for the rooms with new lino rather than icky old carpet), hot water comes by the bucket and there's TV. You can order in good cheap food from the restaurant below (mains Rs20 to Rs45) – we had the world's best *aloo paratha* (potato-filled bread) here.

Kurseong Tourist Lodge (☎ 2344409; Hill Cart Rd; d Rs800-900) The staff don't care a whole lot but the building is very inviting, with warm, wood-lined rooms that feature stunning views. The toy train whistles past the cafe where you can snack on *momos*, or you can enjoy an Indian, Chinese or continental meal at its scenic restaurant (mains Rs30 to Rs80).

Cochrane Place (☎ 2330703; www.imperial chai.com; 132 Pankhabari Rd; s/d from Rs2250/2650) With 360-degree views around tea plantations, the Himalaya and the lights of Siliguri, this quirky, charming boutique hotel is a destination in its own right. Rooms are individually decorated with antiques and have either a garden or a balcony. Delicious meals and a range of teas are available. The hotel is wheelchair-friendly, provides airport (Siliguri's Bagdogra airport) and train station pick-up, and staff can point you towards trails and sights in the region. Also on offer are tea tastings and spa treatments. Significant discounts available June to September and December to February.

Zimba's (Hill Cart Rd; dishes Rs10-20) This outdoor place in a bus and jeep depot at the Darjeeling end of town is the unlikely setting for shockingly cheap, fresh and tasty Indian and Tibetan snack foods – try the *momos* (Rs10).

Gorkha Bhansa Ghar (Hill Cart Rd; mains Rs20-45; ☯ 8am-7.30pm) Real Gurkha food is served at low communal tables opposite the train station; the ever-changing, meat-heavy chalkboard menu is in Nepali only, so ask. You're likely to encounter bright-red *alu dum* (potato curry), buffalo curry, and a menu option described to us as 'buffalo abdominals'; each dish is accompanied by chewy, deep-fried bread. The owner says his hot curries will help with hangovers caused by traditional rice and ginger wines (also available). He also explained that the interesting Gurkha clothes, weapons, musical instruments and crafts on display are not so much aimed at tourists as at young Gurkhas who may have lost touch with traditional culture.

Getting There & Away

Numerous share jeeps run to Darjeeling (Rs40, 1½ hours), Siliguri (Rs60, 1½ hours), Kalimpong (Rs100, 3½ to four hours) and Mirik (Rs60, 2½ hours). Buses leave from near the train station for Darjeeling (Rs25, two hours) and Siliguri (Rs40, 2½ hours).

THUNDERBOLT RAJAH

One of the most recognisable figures in the Darjeeling region and a guru in the tea industry, Rajah Banerjee is the fourth generation of the Banerjee family to own and manage the **Makaibari Tea Estate** (Pankhabari Rd; www.makaibari.com) near Kurseong. A patrician man in a self-designed safari suit, he's usually found astride a horse that takes him through the winding forest paths of the estate. The first person to bring organic and biodynamic tea farming to the region, he's also one of the very few estate owners to actually live and work in the hills.

Banerjee came to visit his father at the estate more than 30 years ago, after studying in the UK. 'I had no intention of living in Makaibari, I came for a holiday, but man proposes, God disposes', he says. Riding through the estate one day, he was thrown from his horse; as he fell, he says, he had a vision of the trees calling out to be saved. 'I knew then that I had to spend the rest of my life at Makaibari.'

Permaculture, the taste of tea, the welfare of estate workers, biodiversity and the biodynamics philosophy of Rudolf Steiner are just some of the passions that drive the 'Thunderbolt Rajah' (the nickname comes from the Tibetan meaning of Darjeeling, 'land of the thunderbolt'). The factory at Makaibari is open to visitors (as well as to volunteers and students), and in between the huge sorting and drying machines and the fields of green bushes, you may just run into the tea guru himself.

Darjeeling Himalayan Railway's steam toy train for Darjeeling (2nd/1st class Rs18/159, four hours) leaves at 3pm, weather permitting, while the diesel version (originating at New Jalpaiguri) departs around 1.35pm. A diesel train (originating in Darjeeling) to Siliguri (2nd/1st class Rs27/182, four hours) departs at 12.05pm.

Kurseong station has a limited quota of tickets for major departures from NJP that can be booked between 9am and 11am. The available services are on display at the station.

DARJEELING

☎ 0354 / pop 109,160 / elev 2134m

Spread over a steep mountain ridge, surrounded by tea plantations, with a backdrop of jagged white Himalayan peaks floating over distant clouds, the archetypal hill station of Darjeeling is rightly West Bengal's premier attraction. When you aren't gazing at Khangchendzonga (8598m), you can explore colonial buildings, Buddhist and Hindu temples, botanical gardens and a zoo for Himalayan fauna. The steep narrow streets are crowded with colourful souvenir and handicraft shops, and a good steaming brew and excellent Indian and Tibetan fare are never far away. Walkers can enjoy superb treks that trace ancient trade routes and provide magnificent viewpoints.

Most tourists visit after the monsoon (October and November) and during spring (mid-March to the end of May) when skies are dry, panoramas are clear and temperatures are pleasant. Tourist attractions and other establishments will often extend their hours during these periods (specified as 'high season' in the following reviews), although they are not set in stone, so it is worth checking ahead rather than relying on those extended hours.

History

This area belonged to the Buddhist chogyals (kings) of Sikkim until 1780, when it was annexed by the invading Gurkhas from Nepal. The East India Company gained control of the region in 1816 then returned most of the lands back to Sikkim in exchange for British control over any future border disputes.

During one such dispute in 1828, two British officers stumbled across the Dorje Ling monastery, on a tranquil forested ridge, and passed word to Calcutta that it would be a perfect site for a sanatorium; they were sure to have also mentioned its strategic military importance in the region. The Chogyal of Sikkim (still grateful for the return of his kingdom) happily leased the uninhabited land to the East India Company in 1835 and a hill station was born.

Forest gradually made way for colonial houses and tea plantations, and by 1857 the population of Darjeeling reached 10,000, mainly because of a massive influx of Gurkha labourers from Nepal.

After Independence, the Gurkhas became the main political force in Darjeeling and friction with the state government led to calls for a separate state of Gorkhaland in the 1980s. In 1986, violence and riots orchestrated by the Gurkha National Liberation Front (GNLF) brought Darjeeling to a standstill, leading to the Darjeeling Gorkha Hill Council (DGHC) being given a large measure of autonomy from the state government.

Calls for full secession have continued, and in 2007 the political party Gorkha Janmukti Morcha (GJM), headed by Bimal Gurung, was formed out of the GNLF. It has encouraged people to agitate for a separate state of Gorkhaland by 2010 by using tactics ranging from strikes (see p157) and nonpayment of bills and taxes to active support for the Gurkha contestant on *Indian Idol* (who eventually won season three).

Orientation

Darjeeling sprawls over a west-facing slope in a web of interconnecting roads and steep flights of steps. Near the top of town is the square known as Chowrasta. Further north is the forested Observatory Hill and skirting the hill is Bhanu Bhakta Sarani. The zoo lies to the northwest.

Hill Cart Rd (aka Tenzing Norgay Rd), which runs the length of town, is Darjeeling's major vehicle thoroughfare. From Chowk Bazaar it leads north towards the zoo and Himalayan Mountaineering Institute, and heads south past the train station en route to Ghoom. Nehru Rd (aka the Mall), the main shopping street, heads south from Chowrasta, meeting Laden La Rd (which leads to Hill Cart Rd) and Gandhi Rd at a junction called Clubside.

Information

BOOKSHOPS

Oxford Book & Stationery Company (Map p156; ☎ 2254325; Chowrasta; ☼ 9.30am-7.30pm Mon-Sat,

WEST BENGAL

daily high season) The best bookshop in Darjeeling, selling a vast selection of books and maps on Tibet, Nepal, Sikkim, Bhutan and the Himalaya. It will mail worldwide.

Photo Sale & Service (Map p156; Nehru Rd; ☒ 9am-7pm) A small range of English-language books including Lonely Planet titles, attractive postcards, a limited range of maps, stationery, film, and some nice photos and prints of the Darjeeling area.

EMERGENCY

Police assistance booth (Map p156; Chowrasta)
Sadar Police Station (Map p156; ☎ 2254422; Market Rd)

INTERNET ACCESS

There are dozens of internet cafes around the town, all charging about Rs30 per hour with a minimum of Rs10 to Rs15. The outlet at Glenary's (p163) is the most convenient to the Mall.

Compuset Centre (Map p156; Gandhi Rd; per hr Rs30; ☒ 8am-8pm) Digital-camera friendly. Does printing and photocopying.

Loyang Cyber Zone (Map p156; Gandhi Rd; per 30min Rs10; ☒ 9am-7.30pm) Does scanning and colour printing, and has Skype set up.

Pineridge Cybercafe (Map p156; Dr Zakir Hussain Rd; per 30min Rs15; ☒ 9.30am-8pm) Small, friendly place up on the ridge near the budget accommodation.

MEDICAL SERVICES

Planter's Hospital (D&DMA Nursing Home; Map p156; ☎ 2254327; Nehru Rd) The best private hospital.
Yuma Nursing Home (Map p156; ☎ 2257651; Ballen Villa Rd)

MONEY

A number of shops and hotels around Darjeeling can change cash and travellers cheques at fairly good rates; shop around.

ICICI Bank ATM (Map p156; Laden La Rd) Accepts most international bank and credit cards. There's another ATM on HD Lama Rd.

Poddar's (Map p156; Laden La Rd; ☒ 8.30am-9pm, later high season) Inside a clothing store next to the State Bank. Better rates than the State Bank, and changes most currencies and travellers cheques. It accepts credit cards and is a Western Union agent.

State Bank of India (Map p156; Laden La Rd; ☒ 10am-4pm Mon-Fri, to 1pm Sat) Changes US dollars, euros and pounds sterling, and travellers cheques issued by Amex (in US dollars) and Thomas Cook (in US dollars, euros and pounds sterling). The commission rate is Rs100 per transaction. It has an adjacent ATM, another in the bazaar and another in Chowrasta; all accept Visa cards.

PHOTOGRAPHY

Compuset Centre (left) Memory-card reader and CD burning.

Das Studios (Map p156; ☎ 2254004; Nehru Rd; ☒ 9.30am-6.30pm Mon-Fri, to 2.30pm Sat, daily in high season) Film and printing, lots of camera gear, passport pics (six for Rs50), burns two CDs for Rs75.

Joshi Studio (Map p156; ☎ 9832346413; HD Lama Rd; ☒ 9am-7pm Mon-Sat) Passport photos, film developing and processing, CD burning (Rs50) and DVD burning (Rs100).

POST

Main post office (Map p156; ☎ 2252076; Laden La Rd; ☒ 9am-5pm) Reliable parcel service and poste restante.

TOURIST INFORMATION

Darjeeling Gorkha Hill Council Tourist Reception Centre (DGHC; Map p156; ☎ 2255351; Jawahar Rd West; ☒ 9am-6pm Mon-Fri, 9am-1pm every 2nd Sat, 9am-1pm Sun high season) The staff are friendly, well-organised and the best source of information in Darjeeling. The centre also has counters at the train station and on Laden La Rd.

West Bengal Tourist Bureau (Map p156; ☎ 2254102; Chowrasta; ☒ 10am-5pm Mon-Fri) Little useful information but sells a basic map of the town (Rs3) and can book accommodation at government lodges, including those at Jaldhapara Wildlife Sanctuary (p149).

TRAVEL AGENCIES

Most of the travel agencies here can arrange local tours and some can also arrange treks, rafting trips and other activities. Agencies that take you to Sikkim usually help with permits. The DGHC (above) and Darjeeling Transport Corporation (p165) also do local tours. Reliable agencies and their specialities include the following:

Clubside Tours & Travels (Map p156; ☎ 2254646; www.clubside.in; JP Sharma Rd; ☒ 9.30am-6pm) Arranges treks and tours in West Bengal and Sikkim, and wildlife tours in Kaziringa and Manas National Parks and Jaldhapara Wildlife Sanctuary. It can also do domestic airline reservations. Bookings in advance through the website are preferred – walk-ins aren't encouraged.

Diamond Tours & Travels (Map p156; ☎ 9832094275; Old Super Market Complex; ☒ 8am-7pm) Books buses to various destinations from Siliguri. Can organise airport transfers.

Himalayan Travels (Map p156; ☎ 2252254; kkgurung@ cal.vsnl.net.in; 18 Gandhi Rd; ☒ 8.30am-7pm) Experienced company arranging treks and mountaineering expeditions in Darjeeling and Sikkim. Can supply tents and equipment.

Kasturi Tours & Travels (Map p156; ☎ 2254430; Old Super Market Complex; ☒ 8am-7pm) Sells bus tickets to various destinations from Siliguri.

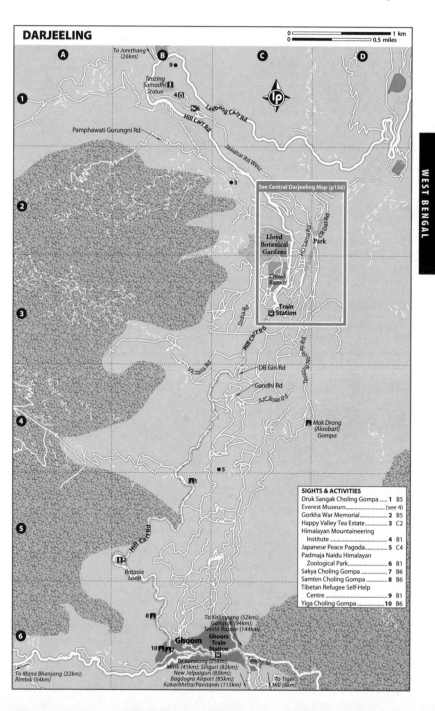

DARJEELING

0 _____ 1 km
0 _____ 0.5 miles

To Jorethang (26km)

Tenzing Samadhi Statue

Pamphawati Gurungni Rd

Lebong Cart Rd

Hill Cart Rd

Jawahar Rd West

See Central Darjeeling Map (p156)

Lloyd Botanical Gardens

Park

CR Das Rd

HD Lama Rd

Chowk Bazaar

Train Station

Sidrap Rd

Hill Cart Rd

Victoria Rd

DB Giri Rd

Gandhi Rd

AJC Bose Rd

Tenzing Rd

Chandi Rd

Mak Drong (Aloobari) Gompa

Hill Cart Rd

Batasia Loop

To Kalimpong (52km); Gangtok (94km); Teesta Bazaar (144km)

Ghoom

Ghoom Train Station

Senchal Rd

To Mana Bhanjang (22km); Rimbik (54km)

To Kurseong (25km); Mirik (45km); Siliguri (82km); New Jalpaiguri (85km); Bagdogra Airport (85km); Kakarbhitta/Panitanki (115km)

To Tiger Hill (8km)

SIGHTS & ACTIVITIES

Druk Sangak Choling Gompa	1	B5
Everest Museum	(see 4)	
Gorkha War Memorial	2	B5
Happy Valley Tea Estate	3	C2
Himalayan Mountaineering Institute	4	B1
Japanese Peace Pagoda	5	C4
Padmaja Naidu Himalayan Zoological Park	6	B1
Sakya Choling Gompa	7	B6
Samten Choling Gompa	8	B6
Tibetan Refugee Self-Help Centre	9	B1
Yiga Choling Gompa	10	B6

WEST BENGAL

WEST BENGAL

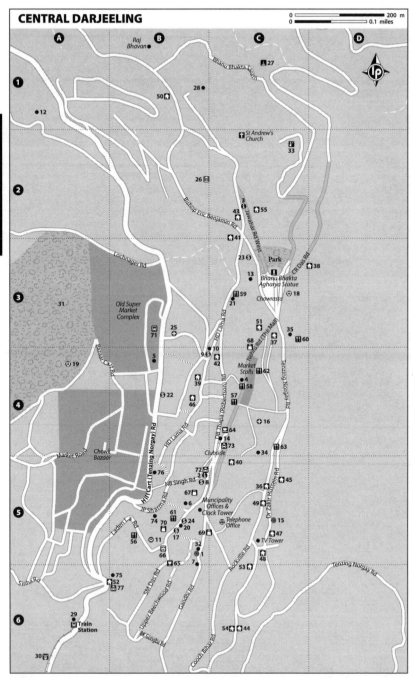

INFORMATION		
Compuset Centre	1	B5
Darjeeling Gorkha Hill		
Council Booth	2	B5
Darjeeling Gorkha Hill		
Council Tourist		
Reception Centre	3	C2
Das Studios	4	C4
Diamond Tours &		
Travels	5	B4
Foreigners' Regional		
Registration Office	6	B5
Himalayan Travels	7	B5
ICICI Bank ATM	8	B5
ICICI Bank ATM	9	B4
Joshi Studio	10	C4
Kasturi Tours & Travels	(see 5)	
Loyang Cyber Zone	(see 69)	
Main Post Office	11	B5
Office of the District		
Magistrate (ODM)	12	A1
Oxford Book &		
Stationery Company	13	C3
Photo Sale & Service	14	C4
Pineridge Cybercafe	15	C5
Planter's Hospital	16	C4
Poddar's	17	B5
Police Assistance Booth	18	C3
Sadar Police Station	19	A4
Samsara Tours, Travels		
& Treks	20	B5
Somewhere Over the		
Rainbow Treks & Tours	21	C3
State Bank of India ATM	22	B4
State Bank of India ATM	23	C3
State Bank of India	24	B5
West Bengal Tourist		
Bureau	(see 37)	
Yuma Nursing Home	25	B3

SIGHTS & ACTIVITIES		
Bengal Natural History		
Museum	26	B2
Bhutia Busty Gompa	27	C1
Darjeeling Gymkhana		
Club	28	B1
Darjeeling Himalayan		
Railway (Toy Train)	29	A6
Dhirdham Mandir	30	A6
Lloyd Botanical Gardens	31	A3
Manjushree Centre of		
Tibetan Culture	32	B5
Observatory Hill	33	C2
Planters' Club		
Darjeeling	34	C4
Pony Stables	35	C3
Trek Mate	(see 64)	

SLEEPING		
Andy's Guesthouse	36	C5
Bellevue Hotel	37	C3
Classic Guesthouse	38	D3
Crystal Palace Hotel	39	B4
Dekeling Hotel	40	C5
Elgin	41	C2
Fortune Resort Central	42	C4
Hotel Alice Villa	43	C2
Hotel Aliment	44	C6
Hotel New Galaxy	45	C5
Hotel Seven Seventeen	46	B4
Hotel Tower View	47	C5
Hotel Tranquility	48	C5
Hotel Valentino	49	C5
Mayfair Darjeeling	50	C2
Pineridge Hotel	51	C3
Red Rose	52	B6
Travellers Inn	53	C6
Triveni Guesthouse	54	C6
Windamere Hotel	55	C2

EATING		
Big Bite	56	B5
Danfay Munal	(see 2)	
Dekevas Restaurant	(see 40)	
Frank Ross Café	57	C4
Frank Ross Pharmacy	(see 57)	
Glenary's	58	C4
Hot Pizza Place	59	C3
Hotel Sonali	60	C3
Park Restaurant	61	B5
Shangrila	62	C4
Sonam's Kitchen	63	C4

DRINKING		
Buzz	(see 58)	
Goodricke, the House of Tea	64	C4
Joey's Pub	65	B5

ENTERTAINMENT		
Inox Theatre	66	B5

SHOPPING		
Hayden Hall	67	B5
Life & Leaf Fair Trade Shop	68	C3
Mandala	69	B5
Nathmull's Tea Room	70	B5
Trekking Shop	(see 64)	

TRANSPORT		
Chowk Bazaar Bus/Jeep Station	71	B3
Clubside Taxi Stand	72	B5
Clubside Taxi Stand	73	C4
Clubside Tours & Travels	74	B5
Darjeeling Transport		
Corporation	75	B6
Hill Cart Rd Jeep Stand	76	B5
Indian Airlines Office	(see 37)	
Pineridge Travels	(see 51)	
Taxi Stand	77	B6

WEST BENGAL

Samsara Tours, Travels & Treks (Map p156;

☎ 2252874; samsara1@sancharnet.in; 7 Laden La Rd)
Helpful and knowledgeable agency offering good-value
rafting and trekking trips. Recommended.

Somewhere Over the Rainbow Treks & Tours (Map

p156; ☎ 9832025739, 9775955105; kanadhi@yahoo
.com; HD Lama Rd; ⏰ 8am-6pm, later in high season)
Organises some off-the-beaten-track walks around Darjeeling, as well as rafting, climbing and trekking in Sikkim,
with a particular interest in West Sikkim.

Dangers & Annoyances

General strikes in support of the GJM's
call for a separate Gurkha state were sem-
iregular at the time of research. While there
has been little violence and tourists have
not been targeted, everything simply shuts
down during the strikes, including all banks
and transport.

Sights & Activities

See p166 for information on trekking around
Darjeeling.

MOUNTAIN VIEWS

Himalayan views are a big attraction in
Darjeeling. The skyline is dominated by
Khangchendzonga, India's highest peak
and the world's third-highest mountain. The
name 'Khangchendzonga' is derived from
the Tibetan words for 'big five-peaked snow
fortress'. Views from lookouts along Bhanu
Bhakta Sarani, which runs from Chowrasta
around the north side of Observatory Hill,
can be stunning in clear weather.

Many hotels have rooftop or balcony areas
that are perfect for early-morning photo opportunities, and staff may even knock on your
door to let you know when the sun's hitting
the mountain in just the right way.

TIGER HILL

To set your eyes on a spectacular 250km
stretch of Himalayan horizon, including
Everest (8848m), Lhotse (8501m), Makalu
(8475m), Khangchendzonga, Kabru (6691m)
and Janu (7710m), rise early and get to **Tiger**

Hill (off Map p155; 2590m), 11km south of Darjeeling, above Ghoom.

The sunrise over the Himalaya from here can be spectacular if the weather is clear, and has become a major tourist attraction, with convoys of jeeps leaving Darjeeling for Tiger Hill every morning around 4.30am. At the summit, you can either pay Rs10 to stand in the pavilion grounds, or buy a ticket for one of the heated lounges in the pavilion (Rs20 to Rs40). It can be a real bunfight, even outside of the high season, with crowds jostling for the best viewing spots.

Organised sunrise trips (usually with a detour to Batasia Loop on the way back) can be booked through a travel agency (see p154) or directly with jeep drivers at the Clubside taxi stand. It's also possible to jump on a jeep going to Tiger Hill from along Gandhi or Laden La Rds between 4am and 4.30am, allowing you to check whether skies are clear before you go. Return trips cost around Rs70/600 per person/jeep.

Some people take the jeep one way to Tiger Hill and then spend their day wandering back to Darjeeling, visiting the gompas (Tibetan Buddhist monasteries) in Ghoom along the way.

TOY TRAIN
The **Darjeeling Himalayan Railway** (Map p156), known affectionately as the toy train, made its first journey along its precipice-topping, 61cm-wide tracks in September 1881 and is one of the few hill railways still operating in India. Besides its regular diesel service to/from New Jalpaiguri and steam service to/from Kurseong (see p165), there are joy rides (Rs250) during the high season that leave Darjeeling at 10.40am and 1.20pm for a two-hour steam-powered return trip to Ghoom. It's wise to book at least a day ahead at the **train station** (Map p156; Hill Cart Rd).

TEA PLANTATIONS
Happy Valley Tea Estate (Map p155; Pamphawati Gurungni Rd; ☉ 8am-4pm Mon-Sat), below Hill Cart Rd, is worth visiting when the plucking and processing are in progress. March to May is the busiest time, but occasional plucking also occurs from June to November. Outside of high season there's no plucking on Sunday, which means most of the machinery isn't working on Monday. An employee will whisk you through the aromatic factory and its various processes before politely demanding a tip – Rs20 from each visitor is appropriate. Take the turn-off 500m northwest of the Office of the District Magistrate, or take Lochnager Rd from Chowk Bazaar.

OBSERVATORY HILL
Sacred to both Buddhists and Hindus, this **hill** (Map p156) was the site of the Dorje Ling monastery, the gompa that gave the city its name. Today, devotees come to a temple in a small cave, below the crest of the hill, to honour Mahakala, a Buddhist deity and an angry form of the Hindu god Shiva. The summit is marked by several shrines, a flurry of colourful prayer flags and the notes from numerous devotional bells. A path leading up to the hill through giant Japanese cedars starts about 300m along Bhanu Bhakta Sarani from Chowrasta. Be careful of the marauding monkeys.

GOMPAS & PAGODAS
Darjeeling and Ghoom are home to a number of fascinating Buddhist monasteries. The most scenic is **Bhutia Busty Gompa** (Map p156), with Khangchendzonga providing a spectacular backdrop. Originally on Observatory Hill, it was rebuilt in its present location by the chogyals of Sikkim in the 19th century. It houses a fine gold-accented mural and the original copy of the Tibetan Book of the Dead, but permission is required to see it. To get here, follow CR Das Rd downhill for 400m from Chowrasta and take the right fork where the road branches.

Yiga Choling Gompa (Old Monastery; Map p155; camera per photo Rs10), the region's most famous monastery, has wonderful old murals and is home to monks of the yellow-hat sect. Built in 1850, it enshrines a 5m-high statue of the Maitreya Buddha (Future Buddha) and 300 beautifully bound Tibetan texts. It's just west of Ghoom, about a 10-minute walk off Hill Cart Rd. Other gompas of interest in this area include the fortresslike **Sakya Choling Gompa** (Map p155) and the **Samten Choling Gompa** (New Monastery; Map p155), with the protector Garuda atop the ornate backdrop to the Buddha; it has a festive air, with tour groups and souvenir stalls. These gompas are on Hill Cart Rd and can be reached by share jeep from Darjeeling (Rs12); some people organise to visit on the way back from Tiger Hill (p157).

About halfway between Ghoom and Darjeeling is the vast **Druk Sangak Choling Gompa** (Map p155), inaugurated by the Dalai Lama in 1993. Known for its vibrant frescoes, it houses 300 Himalayan monks who study philosophy, literature, astronomy, meditation, dance and music.

On the opposite side of the ridge is the welcoming **Mak Drong Gompa** (Map p155). It's also known as Aloobari Gompa and is a pleasant walk (45 minutes) from town.

Perched on a hillside at the end of AJC Bose Rd is the gleaming white **Japanese Peace Pagoda** (Map p155; ☺ pujas 4.30-6am & 4.30-6.30pm), one of more than 70 pagodas built by the Japanese Buddhist Nipponzan Myohoji organisation around the world. Drumming resonates through the forested grounds during the daily *pujas* (offerings or prayers). It's about a 35-minute walk from Clubside along Gandhi and AJC Bose Rds.

PADMAJA NAIDU HIMALAYAN ZOOLOGICAL PARK

This Himalayan **zoo** (Map p155; admission incl Himalayan Mountaineering Institute Indian/foreigner Rs30/100; ☺ 8.30am-4.30pm Fri-Wed, ticket counter closes 4pm), one of India's best, was established in 1958 to study, conserve and preserve local fauna. Housed within the rocky and forested environment is India's only collection of Siberian tigers, as well as Himalayan black bears, red pandas, snow leopards and Tibetan wolves.

The zoo is a pleasant 30-minute walk down from Chowrasta along Jawahar Rd West; alternatively, take a share jeep from the Chowk Bazaar bus/jeep station (Rs10, about 10 minutes) or a private taxi (Rs70).

HIMALAYAN MOUNTAINEERING INSTITUTE

Tucked away within the grounds of the zoological park, this prestigious **mountaineering institute** (HMI; Map p155; ☎ 2254087; www.explore darjeeling.com/hmidarj.htm; admission incl zoo Indian/ foreigner Rs30/100; ☺ 8.30am-4.30pm Fri-Wed) was founded in 1954 and has provided training for some of India's leading mountaineers. Within the complex is the fascinating **Everest Museum**, which traces the history of attempts on the world's highest peak. Next door is the **Mountaineering Museum**, with a relief model of the Himalaya, dusty specimens of Himalayan fauna and more historic mountaineering

equipment. The **souvenir shop** (☺ 9am-4.30pm) has a small, hodge-podge collection of vaguely mountaineering-related items such as vacuum mugs for sale.

On a nearby hilltop, where Tenzing Norgay was cremated, stands the **Tenzing Samadhi statue**. The intrepid mountaineer lived in Darjeeling for most of his life and was the director of the institute for many years.

Various mountaineering courses are offered here. See p160 for more information.

TIBETAN REFUGEE SELF-HELP CENTRE

Established in 1959, this **refugee centre** (Map p155; Lebong Cart Rd; ☺ dawn-dusk Mon-Sat) comprises a home for the aged, school, orphanage, clinic, **gompa** and **craft workshops** that produce carpets, woodcarvings, leatherwork and woollen items. There's also an interesting, politically charged **photographic exhibition** (you might have to ask for the hall to be opened) portraying the establishment and workings of the centre.

The refugees are welcoming, so wander through the workshops. The handicrafts are for sale in the **showroom** (☎ 2252552; ☺ 8am-4.30pm), which doesn't have as many knickknacks as the souvenir shops in town, but the proceeds go straight back into the Tibetan community. See p164 for details regarding Tibetan carpets.

Share jeeps from the Chowk Bazaar bus/jeep station run along Lebong Cart Rd and pass the turn-off to the centre (Rs20, about 20 minutes). A chartered taxi costs around Rs300 return.

LLOYD BOTANICAL GARDENS

These pleasant **gardens** (Map p156; ☎ 2252358; admission free; ☺ 8am-4.30pm) contain an impressive collection of Himalayan plants, most famously orchids and rhododendrons, as well as temperate trees from around the world. Follow the signs along Lochnager Rd from the Chowk Bazaar bus/jeep station. A map and guide is available from the park office.

OTHER ATTRACTIONS

The most conspicuous Hindu temple in Darjeeling, **Dhirdham Mandir** (Map p156), is a replica of the famous Pashupatinath Temple in Kathmandu. It's easy to find – just below the Darjeeling train station. There's a great view over Darjeeling from its grounds.

If you're travelling on the toy train, or walking back from Tiger Hill, look out for the

WEST BENGAL

scenic and sobering **Gorkha war memorial** (Map p155; admission Rs5; ☼ dawn-dusk) where the train makes its famous **Batasia Loop**. Some tours come here after the sunrise trip at Tiger Hill; the views are almost as good, and the atmosphere much more serene.

The **Bengal Natural History Museum** (Map p156; Bishop Eric Benjamin Rd; adult/child Rs5/2; ☼ 9am-5pm), established in 1903, houses a mildewed and moth-eaten collection of Himalayan and Bengali species. Hidden away in a compound just off Bishop Eric Benjamin Rd, it's well signed, and remarkably popular. The enormous leeches in jars will provoke a shudder.

WHITE-WATER RAFTING
Darjeeling is the easiest place to organise white-water rafting trips along the Rangeet and Teesta Rivers. Rafting trips leave from Teesta Bazaar (p172), along the road to Kalimpong. The rapids are graded from Grade II to Grade IV, and the best times for rafting are September to November and March to June.

The DGHC (p154) runs trips for minimums of four to six people (moderate rapids 11/18/25km trip Rs350/450/700, challenging rapids Rs500/600/800) and can also arrange transport to Teesta Bazaar (Rs350) and accommodation at its Chitrey Wayside Inn (p172). Private companies, such as Samsara Tours, Travels & Treks (p157), offer similar routes for a minimum of four people, and prices include lunch and transport.

OTHER ACTIVITIES
The **Darjeeling Gymkhana Club** (Map p156; ☎ 2254341; Jawahar Rd West; membership per day/week/month Rs50/250/600) offers tennis, squash, badminton, roller skating and table tennis; call to check the schedules.

Be an aristocrat for the day and join the **Planters' Club Darjeeling** (Map p156; ☎ 2254348; per day Rs100). Lounge in style or rack them up in the billiards room (Rs100 per person per hour).

From Chowrasta, children can take a **pony ride** around Observatory Hill for Rs50, or through tea estates to visit a monastery for Rs90 per hour.

Courses
LANGUAGE
Beginner and advanced lessons in written and spoken Tibetan are offered at the **Manjushree Centre of Tibetan Culture** (Map p156; ☎ 2256714; www.manjushree-culture.org; 12 Ghandi Rd; 3-/6-/9-month courses

Rs9030/13,760/18,490 plus Rs1350 registration; ☼ Mar-Dec). It also supplies discounted guest-house accommodation for students.

MOUNTAINEERING
The Himalayan Mountaineering Institute (p159) puts on 15-day adventure courses (Indian/foreigner Rs2000/US$325), including climbing, jungle survival and canoeing, and 28-day basic and advanced mountaineering courses (Indian/foreigner Rs4000/US$650), between March and December. Some courses are women-only. Foreigners should apply directly to the centre at least three months in advance.

YOGA
Krishna Milan Pradhan (☎ 9434131468; krimilan93@yahoo.com), one of the proprietors of the Hotel Tower View (below), is an experienced yoga teacher who regularly runs six-day intensive yoga and meditation courses (Rs750) in a number of venues around town.

Tours
During the high season the DGHC and other travel agencies offer a variety of tours around Darjeeling, usually including the zoo, Himalayan Mountaineering Institute, Tibetan Refugee Self-Help Centre and several viewpoints. See p157 for Tiger Hill sunrise-tour information.

Taxis can be hired for custom tours for around Rs750 per half-day.

Sleeping
Darjeeling has some excellent-value accommodation; only a small selection is mentioned here. Prices given are for the high season (October to early December and mid-March to June), when it's wise to book ahead. In the low season prices can drop by 50%.

BUDGET
Hotel Tower View (Map p156; ☎ 2254452; Dr Zakir Hussain Rd; dm Rs70, d with/without shower Rs350/250) Rooms are basic but clean (go for one upstairs; downstairs can be cold and damp), but the real draw at this friendly, Tibetan-run place is the cosy restaurant area that doubles as the family kitchen and lounge, complete with books and games. The food (mains Rs20 to Rs40) is wholesome and delicious (try the veg soup if you're feeling a bit off – instant wellness) and there are fab mountain views.

Triveni Guest House (Map p156; ☎ 2253878; Dr Zakir Hussain Rd; s without bathroom Rs100, d/tr Rs200/250) This is a simple lodge and rooms are only passably clean, but it's friendly and prices are low. Some rooms have nice views, as does the inexpensive restaurant. Bucket hot water is Rs10.

Hotel New Galaxy (Hotel Kanika; Map p156; ☎ 5520771; Dr Zakir Hussain Rd; s Rs150, d Rs250-400, tr Rs500) A clean, acceptable budget option almost opposite Andy's, with wood-panelled walls, smallish rooms and hot-water buckets for Rs10. Try for room 104, with the best views across to the mountains.

Andy's Guesthouse (Map p156; ☎ 2253125; Dr Zakir Hussain Rd; s/d from Rs250/300) This simple, spotless, stone-walled place has airy, carpeted rooms, a comfy common area and a rooftop terrace with a great view. Andy's has especially friendly owners, and we think it's the best value for money in town.

Hotel Aliment (Map p156; ☎ 2255068; alimentwe @sify.com; 40 Dr Zakir Hussain Rd; d Rs250-400; 🖳) A travellers' favourite with good food (and cold beer), books, rooftop patio, helpful owners and cosy wood-lined rooms. The upstairs rooms have a TV and valley views. All rooms have geysers, but they only operate for an hour in the evening.

Hotel Tranquility (Map p156; ☎ 2257678; hotel tranquility@yahoo.co.in; Dr Zakir Hussain Rd; s Rs300, d from Rs400) This good-value new place is sparkling clean, with 24-hour hot water and uniformly duck-egg-blue walls and fittings. A rooftop garden restaurant was being built at the time of research, which should make it even homier. The helpful owners are local school-teachers, and can provide all kinds of info about the area; ask about the tragic story of the burned-out mansion you can see from the roof.

MIDRANGE

our pick **Dekeling Hotel** (Map p156; ☎ 2254159; www .dekeling.com; 51 Gandhi Rd; d Rs650-1400; 🖳 🛜) Dekeling is spotless and full of charming touches such as coloured diamond-pane windows, a traditional *bukhari* (wood-burning heater) in the lounge, wood panelling and sloping ceilings. Then there's the cosy common areas, very comfy rooms and possibly the best views in town. Good deals are available in the low season, and the whole place is a perfect combination of clean and homey, right down to the well-bathed and adorable dog.

Pineridge Hotel (Map p156; ☎ 2254074; pineridge hotel@yahoo.com; Nehru Rd; s/d/tr from Rs700/850/950) The location is great and the Raj-era building has renovation potential to make a decorator weep, but for now the reality is echoing corridors and draughty, dilapidated rooms. There are still some touches of period charm, and with a bucket of coal (Rs200) glowing in the fireplace maybe you can forget the broken window.

Hotel Alice Villa (Map p156; ☎ 2254181; hotel alicevilla@yahoo.com; 41 HD Lama Rd; d/tr from Rs750/850) This well-cared-for old bungalow close to Chowrasta provides inexpensive heritage accommodation. The rooms are spacious and the high ceilings in the older rooms can make them a bit chilly. A mezzanine floor has been built into one, making it a cosy and good-value option for families.

Red Rose (Map p156; ☎ 2256062; 37 Laden La Rd; s Rs800, d from Rs1000, tr Rs2200) Rooms are eclectically decorated, even by Darjeeling standards, and overpriced for what you get, but it's nonetheless superconvenient for the train station, the bathrooms are shimmeringly clean and some rooms have views.

Hotel Valentino (Map p156; ☎ 2252228; 6 Rockville Rd; d Rs800-1500, q Rs1200) Everything except the name is Chinese – the decor in the comfortable rooms tends toward Chinese fans, vases and paintings, and the menu at the restaurant-bar has a big range of regional Chinese dishes (mains Rs60 to Rs80).

Bellevue Hotel (Map p156; ☎ 2254075; pulger@redi ffmail.com; Chowrasta; d Rs800-1600) This rambling Tibetan-run complex has a variety of wood-panelled rooms. Most are spacious with grass-mat floors and a *bukhari*. The affable staff, communal breakfast/lounge area and location, not to mention the outlook over Chowrasta towards Khangchendzonga, all make this a popular choice. Don't confuse it with the Olde Bellevue Hotel up the road.

Travellers Inn (Map p156; ☎ 2258497; travellersinn2000@ gmail.com; Dr Zakir Hussain Rd; s/d/ste Rs1100/1500/2600) A beautifully decorated boutique hotel with stone fireplace, polished wood panelling, framed old photos of Darjeeling, and a terrace restaurant with stunning views (mains Rs40 to Rs80). Mountain-lodge-style rooms are stylish and comfy. On Sunday there's loud gospel music from the church next door.

Hotel Seven Seventeen (Map p156; ☎ 2252017; www.hotel717.com; 26 HD Lama Rd; s/d/ste from Rs1300/1500/2000) An inviting Tibetan-themed place with friendly service and clean rooms. Don't confuse it with the older Hotel Heritage Seven Seventeen, which is up the street. The colourful restaurant and bar (mains Rs50 to Rs90) has a big range of Indian, Chinese, Tibetan and continental dishes.

Classic Guesthouse (Map p156; ☎ 2257025; rajn _classic@hotmail.com; CR Das Rd; d from Rs1500, tr Rs1800) This small, welcoming hotel, just below Chowrasta, has just five rooms, all with valley views and vertigo-inducing balconies. The hosts are friendly and an electric heater (in winter) makes for a cosy stay. Breakfast is an extra Rs150.

Crystal Palace Hotel (Map p156; ☎ 2253317; www .crystalpalacedarjeeling.com; 29-30 HD Lama Rd; s/d from Rs1500/1800) Clean, attractively decorated and convenient to the bus/jeep station, the Crystal has nonetheless increased its rates much more dramatically than it has improved its facilities, to the point where it's not great value for money.

TOP END

These hotels offer rooms on the so-called 'American Plan', with breakfast, lunch and dinner included; taxes and service charges usually add 15% to 20% to the bill.

Fortune Resort Central (Map p156; ☎ 2258721; www.fortuneparkhotels.com; 12/1 DB Thapa Rd; d from Rs5000) In a beautiful old building that has been very thoroughly renovated, this central hotel features century-old polished wood, thick rugs and open fires, and spacious, luxurious rooms. There's a bar and restaurant, and a beauty parlour is on the way.

Windamere Hotel (Map p156; ☎ 2254041; www.win damerehotel.com; Jawahar Rd West; s/d from Rs6650/7750) The liveried staff at this quaint, old-fashioned place really look after you, and won't leave you hungry. This hotel on Observatory Hill is a rambling relic of the Raj, and while some rooms are getting a little tired they are comfortable, clean and spacious. High tea will be a joy for aficionados of things colonial.

Elgin (Map p156; ☎ 2257226; elgin@elginhotels.com; HD Lama Rd; s/d/ste Rs6800/5800/6800) A grand yet friendly heritage hotel full of colonial ambience. Most of the elegantly furnished rooms have separate sitting areas, open fireplaces and marble bathrooms with old clawfoot baths; the cosy 'attic room' is especially charming. The restaurant is pukka (proper) and the lovely gardens are the perfect place to relax and enjoy high tea.

Mayfair Darjeeling (Map p156; ☎ 2256376; www .mayfairhotels.com; Jawahar Rd West; d from Rs9000) Originally a maharaja's summer palace but renovated within an inch of its life, this plush choice sits among lovingly manicured gardens and a bizarre collection of kitschy sculptures. Soft carpets and coal fires add to the warm welcome; there's a choice of DVDs and a comfortable bar. The outside and common areas don't have quite the cosy charm of the Elgin, but inside the rooms are beautifully decorated in warm colours with fine art.

Eating

Most restaurants close their doors by 8pm or 9pm.

Danfay Munal (Map p156; ☎ 9434380444; Clubside Motor Stand; mains Rs20-70) A classic Darjeeling restaurant – simple set-up, great views, a range of cheap and tasty Indian, Chinese and Tibetan food (great *momos*), and it's right in the centre. They do takeaway picnic packs.

Frank Ross Café (Map p156; ☎ 2258194; 14 Nehru Rd, mains Rs20-105, full breakfast Rs85) Strictly vegetarian with a global menu, including pizzas, burgers, South Indian snacks and even enchiladas, tacos and nachos. The attached Frank Ross Pharmacy has groceries for self-caterers.

Big Bite (Map p156; Laden La Rd; mains Rs30-80, thalis Rs80) We don't know who copied whom, but Darjeeling has a few good 'pure veg' places that offer South Indian classics such as dosa (lentil-flour pancake) and *idli* (rice cake), alongside vegie burgers, pizza and other fast food. You'll know this one by the hot-pink entrance.

Hotel Sonali (Map p156; Dr Zakir Hussain Rd; thalis Rs35) Way off the tourist radar, this hole in the wall serves a few cheap Bengali basics. There's no menu, and no adjustment for the traveller's palate – even the 'plain omelette' is loaded with chilli. The back-room views are the real highlight: there's the valley and mountains outside, and the amazing murals on the wall (words can't really describe them, but suffice to say sexy ladies and animals are involved).

Hot Pizza Place (La Casse Croute; Map p156; ☎ 2257594; HD Lama Rd, mains Rs35-120) A one-table pizza joint with excellent pizza, pasta, panini, salads and sandwiches. Come here also for breakfast, pancakes and good coffee, as well as that hard-to-find bacon fix. Service is friendly but slow.

Dekevas Restaurant (Map p156; ☎ 2254159; mains Rs40-80) Cosy Dekevas is known for great Tibetan fare of *momos* and *thukpas* (noodle soups), but not legroom. Try the Tibetan butter tea (per flask Rs45).

Glenary's (Map p156; Nehru Rd; starters Rs35-120, mains Rs50-155; ⏰ 11.30am-9pm, later high season) This elegant restaurant situated atop the famous bakery and cafe receives mainly rave reviews: of note are the continental sizzlers, Chinese dishes, tandoori specials and the highly recommended veg gratin (especially if you're off spicy food). We've heard a few grumbles that it's coasting on its reputation, but most people love it.

ourpick Sonam's Kitchen (Map p156; Dr Zakir Hussain Rd; mains Rs40-90; ⏰ from 7.30am) Providing an island of real brewed coffee in a sea of tea, Sonam and her Nepali family serve up lovely breakfasts, pancakes, soups and pasta; the deliciously chunky wholemeal sandwiches can be packed to go for picnics. Mains need to be pre-ordered at least an hour and a half early, so someone can dash up the street to the nearby fruit and veg stalls to get just what you want. If you miss your mama's cooking, Sonam offers the next best thing.

Park Restaurant (Map p156; ☎ 2255270; Laden La Rd; mains Rs40-140) The Park is very popular with local tourists and fills up quickly. It has tasty North Indian curries or there's a good range of mainly fish and chicken Thai dishes from the Lemon Grass menu. The new bar has been a real hit, with snacks, cocktails (Rs90 to Rs100) and impressive mocktails (Rs25 to Rs80).

Shangrila (Map p156; ☎ 2254149; Nehru Rd; mains Rs45-145) This comfy bar-restaurant near the top of the Mall offers an upmarket version of the usual Indian/Chinese/continental food mix in appealing surrounds, with wooden floors, clean tablecloths and friendly service. Take a closer look at that painting of the Last Supper on the wall – yes, those apostles are Buddhist monks.

Drinking

Where in the world is a better place to sip a cup of Darjeeling tea? If a cool pint is your idea of drinking, there are a couple of good choices.

TEA

Glenary's (Map p156; Nehru Rd; small pot Rs25, cakes & biscuits Rs10-20; ⏰ 7.30am-8pm, to 9pm in high season) Below the restaurant, this cafe has massive windows and good views – order your tea, select a cake, grab your book and sink into

some wicker. Internet is available too (Rs30 per hour). There's a takeaway branch in the bazaar.

Goodricke, the House of Tea (Map p156; Nehru Rd) Sit and sip a range of brewed teas from local estates before purchasing packaged tea.

Classic high teas with local brews are served at Elgin (opposite) and Windamere Hotel (opposite).

BARS

Joey's Pub (Map p156; ☎ 2258216; SM Das Rd; beer Rs80; ⏰ noon-10pm) This classic pub, near the post office, is a great place to meet other travellers. It has sport on TV, warm rum and cold beer, and was expanding its premises at the time of research. Generally very friendly, though lone women have experienced some not entirely good-natured teasing from staff.

Buzz (Map p156; ⏰ 11am-9pm) A Hollywood-themed kitsch bar in the Glenary's basement.

The top-end hotels all have bars; the Windamere is the most atmospheric place to kick back with an early-evening G&T.

Entertainment

Inox Theatre (Map p156; ☎ 2257226; www.inoxmovies.com; Rink Mall, cnr Laden La & SM Das Rds; tickets Rs80-180) Three cinemas and several classes of seating. Shows Hindi blockbusters and fairly recent Hollywood fare.

Shopping
DARJEELING TEA

This is some of the very finest tea in the world and is a highly popular and portable souvenir.

Nathmull's Tea Room (Map p156; ☎ 2256437; www.nathmulltea.com; Laden La Rd; ⏰ 9am-7.30pm Mon-Sat, daily high season) is the best supplier, with more than 50 varieties. Expect to pay Rs80 to Rs150 per 100g for a decent tea and up to Rs1400 per 100g for the finest brews. You can ask for a tasting, which will be expertly brewed, and you can also buy attractive teapots and cosies. The family has run the business for 80 years, and is very knowledgeable. (The Nathmull's in the Rink Mall is a recent start-up, and no connection to this long-established business.)

Try before you buy at Goodricke, the House of Tea (above).

Cheaper tea is available in Chowk Bazaar, but the packaging isn't particularly sturdy. Avoid the tea in fancy boxes, because it's usually blended and packaged in Kolkata.

WEST BENGAL

ANYONE FOR TEA?

The tea bush was first brought to Darjeeling from Assam by British planters looking for a way to break China's monopoly over the tea trade. Credit for the discovery of tea as it's drunk in the Western world should really go to the Khamti and Singpho indigenous groups of Assam, who first introduced British explorers to the healing powers of fermented tea leaves brewed in hot water.

Darjeeling produces around 25% of India's tea, including some of the world's finest brews, but there's more to tea than just plucking and drying. After picking, the leaves are placed in a 'withering trough', where high-speed fans reduce the moisture content to around 30%, before they're rolled with heavy rollers to force the remaining water onto the surface. The rolled leaves are then fermented in a high-humidity chamber to produce their distinctive flavour; this is a fine art and too little or too much fermentation can spoil the entire batch. Fermentation is stopped by passing the leaves through a dry air chamber, which reduces the moisture to just 3%. With all this hot air flowing around, the smell of tea permeates every corner of the tea factory.

The finished tea is sorted into grades – unbroken leaves are set aside for Golden Flowery Orange Pekoe teas, while broken leaves end up as Golden Broken Orange Pekoe, Orange Fannings and Dust – and then graded by expert tasters, who march up and down long lines of teacups, sampling every crop and grading it according to colour, taste and fragrance. Low-grade leaves are blended into household teas, while the best leaves are sold to international tea traders. Teas from estates around Darjeeling and Kurseong (also marketed as Darjeeling tea) regularly and justifiably achieve the world's highest prices. To buy a brew, see p163.

TIBETAN CARPETS
Hayden Hall (Map p156; ☎ 2253228; Laden La Rd; ⏰ 9am-6pm Mon-Sat) Sells carpets as part of its charitable work (Rs5000 for a 90cm by 1.8m carpet).

The Tibetan Refugee Self-Help Centre (p159) makes gorgeous carpets to order and can ship the finished carpet to your home address (US$370/200 with/without shipping).

There are carpets in most souvenir shops, but they're not likely to be locally made.

TREKKING GEAR
Trekking Shop (Map p156; Singalila Market, Nehru Rd; ⏰ 10.30am-6pm) Sells waterproofs and jackets and Chinese- and Russian-made boots (larger sizes are rare), as well as some counterfeit clothing.

OTHER SOUVENIRS
There are numerous souvenir shops at Chowrasta and along Gandhi and Nehru Rds selling Nepali woodcarvings (including masks), *thangkas* (Tibetan cloth paintings), religious objects and jewellery.

You'll be spoiled for choice if you're feeling the cold – quality woollens, particularly shawls, are available everywhere, so you can afford to bargain. Woollens stalls stretch down Nehru Rd in high season.

Life & Leaf Fair Trade Shop (Map p156; ☎ 93333551831; 19 Nehru Rd) Supports local artisans and environmental projects, and sells stylish and cute bags, scarves, toys and organic tea.

Mandala (Map p156; ☎ 9800130872; 4 Gandhi Rd; ⏰ 9.30am-7.30pm) Has quality Tibetan jewellery, Buddhas and *thangkas*.

Das Studios (p154) sells photographic prints of Khangchendzonga and other places around Darjeeling from Rs125.

There are a couple of good fair-trade shops selling locally made clothes and handicrafts. Hayden Hall (left) has good knitwear and bags made by local women.

Getting There & Away
AIR
The nearest airport is 90km away at Bagdogra, about 12km from Siliguri. See p148 for details about flights to/from Bagdogra.

Indian Airlines (Map p156; ☎ 2254230; ⏰ 10am-5.30pm Mon-Sat) is at Chowrasta. **Clubside Tours & Travels** (Map p156; ☎ 2254646; www.clubside.in; JP Sharma Rd; ⏰ 9.30am-6pm) does domestic airline bookings. **Pineridge Travels** (Map p156; ☎ 2253912, 2253036; pineridge@mail.com; ⏰ 10am-5pm Mon-Sat) is an agent for a number of domestic airlines, and is the only agency in Darjeeling licensed for international-flight booking.

BUS

From the Chowk Bazaar bus/jeep station (Map p156), regular buses depart for Mirik (Rs40, three hours) and Siliguri (Rs60, three hours). Tickets can be bought from the ground-floor counter at the Old Super Market Complex that backs on to the station.

Kasturi Tours & Travels (p154) and Diamond Treks, Tours & Travels (p154) can book 'luxury' buses from Siliguri to destinations such as Kolkata (Rs900, 12 hours). Samsara Tours, Travels & Treks (p157) offers similar services. These tickets don't include transfers to Siliguri.

JEEP & TAXI

Numerous share jeeps and taxis leave the crowded south end of the Chowk Bazaar bus/ jeep station for Siliguri (Rs80, three hours) and Kurseong (Rs40, 1½ hours). Jeeps leave for Mirik (Rs50, 2½ hours) about every 1½ hours. Ticket offices on the ground floor of the Old Super Market Complex sell advance tickets for the frequent jeeps to Kalimpong (Rs90, two hours) and Gangtok (Rs130, four hours).

At the northern end of the station, three to four jeeps a day leave for Jorenthang (Rs80, two hours). You must already have a permit to enter Sikkim (see boxed text, below) via this route.

Darjeeling Transport Corporation (Map p156; ☎ 9832081338; Laden La Rd) has jeeps to Gangtok (share/charter Rs130/1300, four hours, share jeeps depart hourly) and to Siliguri (share/ charter Rs90/900, three hours, hourly).

To New Jalpaiguri or Bagdogra, get a connection in Siliguri, or charter a jeep or taxi from Darjeeling (Rs1000 to NJP, Rs1200 to Bagdogra).

TRAIN

The nearest major train station is at New Jalpaiguri, close to Siliguri. Tickets can be bought for major services out of NJP at the **Darjeeling train station** (Map p156; ☎ 2252555; ⏰ 8am-2pm).

Darjeeling Himalayan Railway

The diesel toy train (Map p156) leaves Darjeeling at 9.15am for NJP (2nd/1st class Rs42/247, seven hours), stopping at Ghoom (Rs21/96, 50 minutes), Kurseong (Rs37/159, three hours) and Siliguri (Rs48/232, 6½ hours). It's an exhausting haul to NJP, so if you simply want to experience the train, take the steam train to/from Kurseong or the joy ride (p158).

TO/FROM NEPAL

Foreigners are only permitted to cross the border into Nepal at Kakarbhitta/Panitanki (not at Pasupati).

Kasturi Tours & Travels (p154) and Diamond Treks, Tours & Travels (p154) sell tickets for buses from Darjeeling to Kathmandu (Rs800). Note that these are not direct buses and involve transfers in Siliguri and at the border – leaving room for problems. However, it's not difficult to do this yourself and you'll save some money. See the boxed text, p150, for Siliguri-to-Panitanki transport, as well as border and Nepali bus details.

Getting Around

There are several taxi stands around town, but the rates are absurd for short hops. You can hire a porter to carry your bags up to Chowrasta from Chowk Bazaar for around Rs60.

Share jeeps to anywhere north of the city centre (eg North Point for Rs7) leave from the northern end of the Chowk Bazaar bus/jeep station. To Ghoom, get a share jeep (Rs15) from the Hill Cart Rd jeep stand at Chowk Bazaar (Map p156).

PERMITS FOR SIKKIM

Forms for Sikkim permits (p175) are available at the **Foreigners' Regional Registration Office** (Map p156; ☎ 2254203; Laden La Rd; ⏰ 10am-7pm), and must then be taken to the **Office of the District Magistrate** (ODM; Map p156; ☎ 2254233; Hill Cart Rd; ⏰ 11am-1pm & 2.30-4pm Mon-Fri), downhill from the Chowk Bazaar bus/jeep station. The whole process takes about 1½ hours and there's no fee – bring your passport. Note that if you're crossing at Rangpo you don't have to go through this process – you can get a free 15-day permit on the spot at the border, though you'll need three passport photos. These rules looked likely to change again at the time of research, so you had best check with the Foreigners' Regional Registration Office.

WEST BENGAL

TREKKING AROUND DARJEELING

A number of rewarding and picturesque treks are accessible from Darjeeling. October and November's clear skies and warm temperatures make it an ideal time to trek, as do the long days and rhododendron blooms of May and early June. The Darjeeling Gorkha Hill Council (DGHC; p154) produces the excellent *Himalayan Treks* leaflet (Rs25), which includes a map and descriptions of major trekking routes.

Most popular is the **Singalila Ridge Trek** from Sandakphu to Phalut, which passes through the scenic **Singalila National Park** (admission Rs100, camera/video Rs25/250) and offers fantastic views of the Himalaya. Guides (about Rs350 per day) are mandatory within the park (the park entrance is near Tumling) and can be hired privately through the DGHC, travel agencies or at the trek's starting point in Mana Bhanjang, 26km from Darjeeling; you're more likely to get a good guide if you line it up beforehand. Mana Bhanjang is served by regular shared jeeps as well as a 7am bus from Darjeeling's Chowk Bazaar bus/jeep station (Rs30, three hours). The usual trekking itinerary is described in the boxed text, opposite. Some travellers have enjoyed doing just the first stage; the route is easy to follow and a guide isn't required (although you may be strongly encouraged to hire one anyway).

From Rimbik, there are two connecting morning buses to Darjeeling (Rs80, five hours, 6am and 12.30pm) and regular jeeps. If you don't have five days, there are short cuts available at Sandakphu and Sabarkum. At the time of research the basic trekkers' huts along the route were closed for renovation; check with the DGHC (p154). Better private accommodation options in small family 'guest houses' are available; Shikhara Lodge in Tumling has been especially recommended by trekkers. All-inclusive guided treks on this route, including porters, meals and accommodation, are offered by Darjeeling travel agencies (p154) for Rs1200 to Rs2000 per day depending on the level of service and number of people.

Nearer to Kalimpong is the **Rochela Trek**, which gives you a taste of the stunning Samthar Plateau. You can trek for four to eight days through dense forests, visiting remote villages and crossing a pass at 3000m. Note

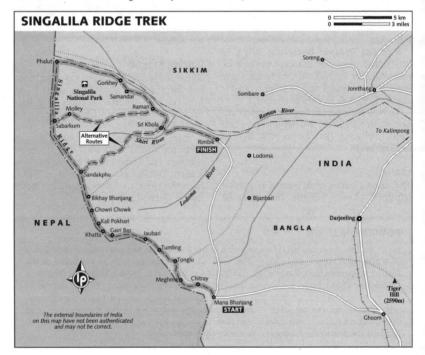

SINGALILA RIDGE TREK

0   5 km
0   3 miles

SIKKIM

INDIA

NEPAL

BANGLA

To Kalimpong

Phalut

Gorkhey

Singalila National Park

Samandar

Molley

Sabarkum

Raman

Sri Khola

Alternative Routes

Shiri River

Sandakphu

Bikhay Bhanjang

Chowri Chowk

Kali Pokhari

Khatta

Gairi Bas

Jaubari

Tumling

Tonglu

Meghma

Chitray

Mana Bhanjang
START

Rimbik
FINISH

Lodoma

Lodoma River

Bijanbari

Soreng

Sombare

Jorethang

Raman River

Darjeeling

Tiger Hill (2590m)

Ghoom

The external boundaries of India on this map have not been authenticated and may not be correct.

SINGALILA RIDGE TREK		
Day	Route	Distance (km)
1	Mana Bhanjang (2130m) to Tonglu (3100m) via Meghma Gompa	14
2	Tonglu to Sandakphu (3636m) via Kalipokhri & Garibas	17
3	Sandakphu to Phalut (3600m) via Sabarkum	17
4	Phalut to Rammam (2530m) via Gorkey	16
5	Rammam to Rimbik (2290m) via Srikhola	19

that it takes four days, with camping, to reach the highpoint of Rochela from Kalimpong.

Recommended trekking agencies include the following:

Darjeeling Gorkha Hill Council Tourist Reception Centre (Darjeeling p154; Kalimpong right) Charges about Rs2000 per day (all-inclusive) for Singalila Ridge, and organises guides/porters (Rs350 per day) for Rochela.

Gurudongma Tours & Travels (p168) Offering customised all-inclusive treks in this region, with knowledgeable guides and accommodation.

Samsara Tours, Travels & Treks (p157) Experienced agency offering reasonably priced rafting and trekking trips.

Trek Mate (Map p156; ☎ 2256611, 9832083241; chagpori@satyam.net.in; Nehru Rd) Recommended treks: all-inclusive guided treks run from Rs950 to Rs1450 per person per day depending on group size. The hire gear is clean and well maintained.

If you need clothing or gear (and you should carry your own sleeping bag even if relying on huts), it can be hired from Trek Mate (sleeping bag Rs30, down jacket Rs20, boots Rs30, rain gear Rs15 per day). The Trekking Shop (p164) stocks clothing and boots. The DGHC in Kalimpong has a few tents for rent.

KALIMPONG
☎ 03552 / pop 42,980 / elev 1250m

This bustling bazaar town sprawls along a ridge overlooking the roaring Teesta River and within sight of Khangchendzonga. It boasts Himalayan views, tranquil retreats, Buddha shops, temples and churches, and a fascinating nursery industry.

Kalimpong's early development as a trading centre focused on the wool trade with Tibet, across the Jelepla Pass. Like Darjeeling, Kalimpong once belonged to the chogyals of Sikkim, but it fell into the hands of the Bhutanese in the 18th century and later passed to the British, before becoming part of India at Independence. Scottish missionaries, particularly the Jesuits, made great efforts to win over the local Buddhists in the late 19th century and Dr Graham's famous orphanage and school is still running today.

The Gorkhaland movement is active in Kalimpong. The Gurkha leader CK Pradhan was assassinated here in October 2002, and is commemorated by a small shrine on the spot where he was gunned down.

Orientation & Information
Kalimpong is centred on its chaotic Motor Stand. Nearby are restaurants, cheap hotels and shopping, while most sights and quality accommodation are a few kilometres from town, accessed via DB Giri and Rinkingpong Rds.

The staff at the **Darjeeling Gorkha Hill Council Tourist Reception Centre** (DGHC; ☎ 257992; DB Giri Rd; ⏱ 9.30am-5pm) can help organise tours of the area. The private website www.kalimpong.org is a good resource.

The **post office** (☎ 255990; Rinkingpong Rd; ⏱ 9am-5pm Mon-Fri, to 4pm Sat) is behind the **police station** (Rinkingpong Rd).

There are State Bank of India and ICICI ATMs side by side on DB Giri Rd. Souvenir shops further up the hill offer to exchange various currencies and travellers cheques for a small commission. Internet options include **Net Hut** (per hr Rs30; ⏱ 9.30am-8pm), near the Motor Stand, and an unnamed place in an arcade known locally as 'the supermarket' at the post-office end of DB Giri Rd. In the same arcade, **Studio Foto Max** (☎ 260113; ⏱ 7.30am-7.30pm) does film developing and processing, and will burn pictures to a CD for Rs50.

Two small adjoining bookshops – **Kashi Nath & Sons** (DB Giri Rd) and **Blessings** (DB Giri Rd; ⏱ 10am-6.30pm) – have a good range on Buddhism, and books about Nepal and Tibet.

There is nowhere in Kalimpong to obtain permits for Sikkim, but free 15-day permits are available at the border at Rangpo (see boxed text, p165). You need to present three passport photos.

Sights

GOMPAS

Built in 1926, the **Tharpa Choling Gompa**, off KD Pradhan Rd, contains statues of the Bhaisajya, Sakyamuni and Maitreya Buddhas (past, present and future, respectively). Garuda protects each Buddha from above, his mouth devouring hatred and anger (the snake), while his feet hold down symbols of ignorance and worldly attachment. It's a 30-minute walk (uphill) from town, past the top of Tripai Rd.

Near the top of RC Mintri Rd, past JP Lodge, is the ancient **Thongsa Gompa** (Bhutanese Monastery). The monastery was founded in 1692, but the present building, surrounded by 219 small prayer wheels, was built in the 19th century after the Gurkhas rampaged across Sikkim.

Kalimpong's largest monastery, Zong Dog Palri Fo-Brang Gompa, aka **Durpin Gompa**, sits atop spectacular Durpin Hill (1372m) and was consecrated after its opening by the Dalai Lama in 1976. There are impressive wall and ceiling paintings in the main prayer room downstairs (photography is permitted), and interesting 3-D mandalas (circles symbolising the universe) on the 2nd floor. The monastery is located about 5km south of the town centre, and is best reached by chartered jeep (Rs80 return). The **Jelepla Viewpoint**, about 300m below the gompa, looks out to the Himalaya and over the Relli and Teesta Rivers.

ST TERESA'S CHURCH

A fascinating missionary **church** built in 1929 by Swiss Jesuits and designed to gain acceptance from the locals, St Teresa was constructed to mimic a Bhutanese gompa. The carved apostles look like Buddhist monks, and the carvings on the doors resemble *tashi tagye*, the eight auspicious symbols of Himalayan Buddhism. The church is found off 9th Mile, about 2km from town. Take a taxi or walk and ask for directions.

DR GRAHAM'S HOME

This working orphanage and school was built in 1900 by Dr JA Graham, a Scottish missionary, to educate the children of tea-estate workers, and now has more than 1300 students. There's a small **museum** (admission free; 9am-3.30pm Mon-Fri) that commemorates the founder and his wife, Katherine. The 1925 chapel above the school looks like it's straight out of Scotland, with its grey slate, spire and bell. It features fine stained-glass windows. The gate is 4km up the steep KD Pradhan Rd. Many people charter a taxi to get here (Rs90) and then walk back to town.

NURSERIES

Kalimpong is a major flower exporter and produces about 80% of India's gladioli as well as many orchid varieties. Visit **Nurseryman's Haven** (256936; 9th Mile) and the Orchid Retreat (p170) to have a look at orchids; **Santi Kunj** (BL Dixit Rd; 8.30am-noon & 1.30-4pm Sun-Fri) to see anthuriums and the bird of paradise flower (bulbs are also sold here); and **Pine View Nursery** (255843; www.pineviewcactus.com; Atisha Rd; admission Rs5) to gaze at its eminently photographable cactus collection. Pine View has a few rooms; see p170.

MANGAL DHAM

This ungainly modern **temple** (Relli Rd; 6am-7pm) is sacred to Krishna. In its ballroomlike prayer hall there are eight vibrant, life-sized dioramas from the Krishna Leela. The temple is dedicated to Guruji Shri Mangaldasji, who's commemorated in a shrine below the prayer hall. The temple is about 500m downhill from Thongsa Gompa, or you can walk from the centre of town along Relli Rd and turn left by the Roman Catholic church.

Activities

The DGHC Tourist Reception Centre (p167) can arrange treks (see p166 for trekking in this region) and the same rafting trips as the Darjeeling DGHC.

Gurudongma Tours & Travels (255204; www.gurudongma.com; Hilltop, Rinkingpong Rd) organises trekking, rafting, mountain-biking, bird-watching and fishing, around Kalimpong, Darjeeling and Sikkim.

Kalimpong-based Swede Roger Lenngren from **Himalayan Bike Tours** (9635156911; www.himalayanbiketours.se) offers extreme sports in the area, including paragliding tandem flights (Rs2000 including transport from landing place back to Kalimpong).

Sleeping

The better places to stay are well outside Kalimpong's busy core. The hotels closest to the Motor Stand are mainly grotty and overpriced; it's well worth going a few extra steps

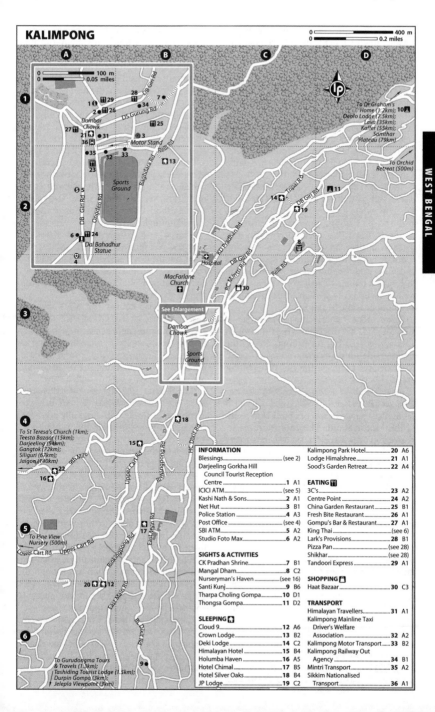

KALIMPONG

WEST BENGAL

INFORMATION	
Blessings	(see 2)
Darjeeling Gorkha Hill Council Tourist Reception Centre	**1** A1
ICICI ATM	(see 5)
Kashi Nath & Sons	**2** A1
Net Hut	**3** B1
Police Station	**4** A3
Post Office	(see 4)
SBI ATM	**5** A2
Studio Foto Max	**6** A2

SIGHTS & ACTIVITIES	
CK Pradhan Shrine	**7** B1
Mangal Dham	**8** C2
Nurseryman's Haven	(see 16)
Santi Kunj	**9** B6
Tharpa Choling Gompa	**10** D1
Thongsa Gompa	**11** D2

SLEEPING	
Cloud 9	**12** A6
Crown Lodge	**13** B2
Deki Lodge	**14** C2
Himalayan Hotel	**15** B4
Holumba Haven	**16** A5
Hotel Chimal	**17** B5
Hotel Silver Oaks	**18** B4
JP Lodge	**19** C2

Kalimpong Park Hotel	**20** A6
Lodge Himalshree	**21** A1
Sood's Garden Retreat	**22** A4

EATING	
3C's	**23** A2
Centre Point	**24** A2
China Garden Restaurant	**25** B1
Fresh Bite Restaurant	**26** A1
Gompu's Bar & Restaurant	**27** A1
King Thai	(see 6)
Lark's Provisions	**28** B1
Pizza Pan	(see 28)
Shikhar	(see 28)
Tandoori Express	**29** A1

SHOPPING	
Haat Bazaar	**30** C3

TRANSPORT	
Himalayan Travellers	**31** A1
Kalimpong Mainline Taxi Driver's Welfare Association	**32** A2
Kalimpong Motor Transport	**33** B2
Kalimpong Railway Out Agency	**34** B1
Mintri Transport	**35** A2
Sikkim Nationalised Transport	**36** A1

for a significant increase in quality. High-season rates (October to early December and mid-March to early June) are given here.

BUDGET

Lodge Himalshree (☎ 255070; Ongden Rd; dm/d without bathroom Rs100/200, tr Rs250) This extremely basic little place with an affable owner is on the top floor of a tall building right in the busiest part of town. The stairs are steep and the rooms are plain and passably clean. The dorm is pretty much the hotel lobby. Bathrooms are dank, and hot-water buckets cost Rs10.

Deki Lodge (☎ 255095; www.geocities.com/dekilodge; Tripai Rd; s/d/tr Rs250/550/900, deluxe d Rs950) This lovely Tibetan-owned lodge is close to the Thongsa and Tharpa Choling monasteries and still handy to town. It's a friendly, family-run place set in a garden with a pleasant cafe and rooftop viewing area. Rooms are spotless and appealing and the fluffy dogs will make you feel right at home. It's well worth the steepish walk to get up here – it's light years better than anything near the Motor Stand.

Crown Lodge (☎ 255846; off Baghdara Rd; s/d Rs350/600) This big place has large rooms with TVs and geyser, but furnishings are on the shabby side, and it's very noisy at night. Nonetheless it's probably the best of the Motor Stand–adjacent hotels.

Hotel Chimal (☎ 9832644124; nirranjit@yahoo.com; Rinkingpong Rd; s/d from Rs400/500) Hotel Chimal is set in nice terraced gardens about 1km south of the Motor Stand. The rooms are basic, sparse and only just clean (and there's a very scary clown painting in the lobby), but the hosts are friendly.

Pine View Nursery (☎ 255843; pineviewnursery @yahoo.co.in; Atisha Rd; d/tr 550/750) A few passably clean, simple and spacious rooms for those who have always wanted to sleep in a cactus nursery (not recommended for sleepwalkers).

MIDRANGE & TOP END

Tashiding Tourist Lodge (☎ 255929; Rinkingpong Rd; s/d from Rs600/800) This rustic stone lodge looks charming from the outside and has lovely views, but it's very neglected inside in spite of patches of colonial charm. Furnishings are threadbare and the big, peeling-wall bathrooms are of questionable functionality. For this price it is advised you check your room first.

our pick Holumba Haven (☎ 256936; www.holum ba.com; 9th Mile; s/d Rs700/1600, cottage from Rs4500) Described by its welcoming owners as 'more of a homestay than a hotel', this family-run guest house is situated in a splendid orchid nursery just 1km out of town. The spotless, comfy rooms are arranged in beautifully decorated cottages spread around the lush garden, and springwater is piped directly into the rooms. Good home-style meals (guests only) are available in the dining room. You'll want to be keen on animals – dogs, ducks and rabbits are just some of the beasts you'll bump into.

Cloud 9 (☎ 259554; cloud9kpg@yahoo.com; Rinkingpong Rd; d Rs800-1000) A very friendly place with wood-panelled rooms, a cosy TV lounge and a good restaurant, serving Bhutanese, Tibetan and Chinese food. Guitars in the lounge attest to many late-night jams.

JP Lodge (☎ 257457; www.jplodge.com; RC Mintri Rd; d Rs850-1250) Not quite the excellent value it used to be, but the hosts are friendly and the small rooms are clean and most have views. There's an interesting wood-lined attic with views to lounge about in.

Sood's Garden Retreat (☎ 260321; www.soods gardenretreat.com; 9th Mile; s/d from Rs900/1200) The eager-to-help owners at this new hotel can organise tours and trips, including rafting expeditions. The clean, inviting rooms are decorated with wood panelling and warm colours, but make sure you get one with a view.

Orchid Retreat (☎ 274489; www.theorchidretreat.com; Ganesh Villa; s/d from Rs1400/2000; 🖥) An attractive family-run getaway, with tastefully decorated cottages scattered through the grounds of a large orchid nursery that's heaven for birders. In line with the 'getting away from it all' theme there are no phones or TVs in rooms. Home-cooked, fixed-menu food is available in the airy dining room. Prior bookings are preferred.

Deolo Lodge (☎ 274452; Deolo Hill; d Rs1500) Commanding outstanding views (when not lost in the cloud) down to the town, this hotel sits atop Deolo Hill, several kilometres from town. The spacious rooms are clean and the staff friendly; there's a multicuisine restaurant and ample clean mountain air, though the hotel's grounds haven't been so well cared for. There's a Rs5 entrance fee for nonguests to enter the property and enjoy the views.

Kalimpong Park Hotel (☎ 255304; www.kalim pongparkhotel.com; s/d from Rs1500/2000) This former maharaja's home has oodles of Raj-era charm. Wicker chairs and flowers line the verandah and there's a supercute bar and restaurant. Rooms in the new wing lack some of the period charm of the old house but are still very appealing (and the big new slate-floor bathrooms are by far the best in town).

Himalayan Hotel (☎ 254043; www.himalayan hotel.co.in; Upper Cart Rd; s/d Rs1700/2700, with full board Rs2600/4500) This hotel was opened by the revered David MacDonald, an interpreter from Francis Younghusband's mission to Lhasa in 1904 and one of those who helped the 13th Dalai Lama escape Tibet in 1910. The original rooms have loads of Raj-era appeal beneath sloping Himalayan-oak ceiling, while new suites mesh old-world charm with modern comfort; their terraces gaze upon Khangchendzonga. It's a triumph of sympathetic renovation; comfortable but full of lovely original fittings.

Hotel Silver Oaks (☎ 255296; silveroaks@sancher net.in; Rinkingpong Rd; s/d Rs4800/5100) This centrally located Raj-era homestead has been renovated into a modern and very comfortable hotel. The rooms are plushly furnished (love the puffy satin bedheads) and offer grand views down the valley. The tariff includes all meals in the excellent restaurant and there's a sociable bar.

Eating
RESTAURANTS
Shikhar (☎ 255966; DB Giri Rd; dishes Rs10-20) A popular vegetarian restaurant with Tibetan and Indian snacks and meals, including good cheap *momos*. It's located under the Pizza Pan restaurant.

Fresh Bite Restaurant (☎ 274042; DB Giri Rd; mains Rs30-140) Upstairs, across the road from the DGHC, this place has a huge range of almost uniformly good food including some hard-to-find dishes that you might just have been craving, such as miso soup and bacon sandwiches.

Centre Point (DB Giri Rd; mains Rs35-60) A centrally located upstairs place, overlooking the Dal Bahadhr statue, with a tasty and well-priced selection of the usual Chinese and Indian standards.

China Garden Restaurant (☎ 257456; Lal Gulli, mains Rs35-90) In the China Garden Hotel near the Motor Stand, this is Kalimpong's best Chinese restaurant. The authentic soups, noodles and the spicy ginger chicken attract aficionados, though several Indian curries have snuck onto the menu.

Tandoori Express (DB Giri Rd; mains Rs40-90) A clean new place filling a gap in Kalimpong's food market by offering a good range of North Indian curries and tandoori dishes.

Gompu's Bar & Restaurant (☎ 257456; off DB Giri Rd; mains Rs45-90) Gompu's is famous for its massive *momos* (pork, chicken and veg), and has been pleasing locals and travellers with Tibetan, Bhutanese, Indian, Chinese and continental fare for ages. It's found within the hotel of the same name.

our pick King Thai (3rd fl 'supermarket', DB Giri Rd; mains Rs50-170) A multicultural hangout with a Thai name, Chinese food, Bob Marley posters and British soccer banners for decoration, and Hindi/Nepali live music for entertainment. The excellent food is mainly Chinese with some Thai and Indian dishes: four different versions of chop suey are offered, along with wantons as a change from *momos*. There's a bar with comfy chairs and a disco ball, and a regular crowd that mixes expats, monks, businessmen and Tibetan cool kids.

Pizza Pan (☎ 258650; DB Giri Rd; medium pizza Rs99-150, large Rs145-190) You can get a good coffee here, in addition of course to the perfectly satisfactory pizza, which comes in two sizes with a variety of veg and nonveg toppings, some more traditional than others.

QUICK EATS
Kalimpong cheese has been produced in Kalimpong since the Jesuits established a dairy here in the 19th century, and Kalimpong lollipops are made at the dairy from milk, sugar and butter.

3C's (DB Giri Rd; cakes & snacks Rs10-30) A popular bakery and restaurant offering a variety of mouth-watering pastries and cakes.

Lark's Provisions (DB Giri Rd) The best place to pick up Kalimpong cheese (Rs180 per kilogram) and a packet of Kalimpong lollipops (Rs25). Also sells groceries and yummy homemade pickles.

Shopping
Along RC Mintri Rd a profusion of fabric shops sell Tibetan cloth and Indian or Chinese silk brocade – both better quality and lower cost than those seen in Darjeeling.

Haat Bazaar (btwn Relli & RC Mintri Rds) On Wednesday and Saturday, this normally quiet bazaar roars to life.

Getting There & Away
All the bus and jeep options, and their offices mentioned here, are found at the chaotic Motor Stand.

BUS & JEEP

Bengal government buses run regularly to Siliguri (Rs55, 2½ hours), and there's also a single Sikkim Nationalised Transport (SNT) bus to Gangtok (Rs70, 3½ hours) at 1pm.

Himalayan Travellers (☎ 9434166498) runs minibuses or share jeeps to Gangtok (Rs90, three hours, four daily) and Lava (Rs50, 1½ hours, regular departures).

Kalimpong Mainline Taxi Driver's Welfare Association (KMTDWA; ☎ 257979) has regular share jeeps to Siliguri (Rs70, 2½ hours), Gangtok (Rs80, 2½ hours), Lava (Rs50, 1½ hours) and Kaffer (Rs60, 2½ hours), and one daily to Jorenthang (Rs60, two hours, departs 7.15am). **KS & AH Taxi Driver's Welfare Association** (☎ 259544) has regular jeeps to Ravangla in Sikkim (Rs100, 3½ hours). **Kalimpong Motor Transport** (☎ 255719) has a regular share-jeep service to Darjeeling (Rs80, 2½ hours).

Jeeps can also be chartered for Darjeeling (Rs900), Siliguri (Rs800) and for Gangtok (Rs850).

TRAIN

The **Kalimpong Railway Out Agency** (☎ 259954; Mani Rd; 🕙 10am-4pm Mon-Sat, to 1pm Sun) and **Mintri Transport** (☎ 2556997; DB Giri Rd; 🕙 10.30am-6pm) sell a small quota of tickets from New Jalpaiguri train station.

TO/FROM BHUTAN & NEPAL

A government bus makes the trip to the Bhutan border, Jaigon (Rs95, 5½ hours) at 8.40am, and KMTDWA has a 7.30am shared jeep (Rs130, five hours). The KMTDWA has regular jeeps to the Nepal border at Panitanki (Rs90, three hours), and Himalayan Travellers has a 7.30am jeep for Pashupati (Rs100, 3½ hours).

Border information can be found in the boxed text, p150.

Getting Around

Taxis can be chartered for local trips from along DB Giri Rd. A half-day rental to see most of the sights should cost Rs700.

AROUND KALIMPONG
Teesta Bazaar
☎ 03552

About 16km west of Kalimpong, Teesta Bazaar is an important centre for white-water rafting. Most people book at travel agencies in Darjeeling (see p154) or at the DGHC office in Kalimpong, but you can also book here with the **DGHC** (☎ 268261; Chitrey Wayside Inn, NH-31A), about 1.5km from Teesta Bazaar along the road to Kalimpong.

The friendly **Chitrey Wayside Inn** (☎ 213520; dm Rs100, d/ste with geyser Rs450/600) has a bar, restaurant and balcony over the banks of the Teesta River. The spacious rooms have hot water and are clean, if spartan, and meals are good.

Teesta Bazaar is about 30 minutes by road from Kalimpong; take any bus or share jeep (Rs25) in the direction of Darjeeling.

Lava & Kaffer

About 35km east of Kalimpong, Lava (2353m) is a small village with a Kagyupa **gompa** and a bustling **market** on Tuesday. The summit of Khangchendzonga can be seen from **Kaffer** (1555m), also known as Lolaygaon, about 30km further east. Both villages see few tourists and make peaceful and scenic getaways. The picturesque drive from Kalimpong passes through mist and moss-laden old-growth forests.

Daffey Munal Tourist Lodge (☎ 03552-277218; Kaffer; dm Rs100, d/tr Rs600/700) has huge, clean rooms with hot water and fireplaces. It's a rambling old DGHC place.

Jeeps and a daily bus serve Kalimpong from both Lava (Rs50, 1½ hours) and Kaffer (Rs60, 2½ hours).

Samthar Plateau

This remote plateau offers awesome views of Bhutan's Himalaya range and a chance to visit traditional villages. **Gurudongma Tours & Travels** (☎ 255204; www.gurudongma.com; Hilltop, Rinkingpong Rd, Kalimpong; s/d full board from Rs3800/4800) runs the cosy Farm House at Samthar. It'll arrange transport for its customers from Kalimpong.

Sikkim

If you're suffering from too much heat, city dust and dirt, or just crowd overload, then a spell in the little, former kingdom of Sikkim is the perfect antidote. Clean fresh mountain air sweeps the state; there's room to move and even feel alone, but the people are among India's most friendly, with a charming manner that's unobtrusive and slightly shy. To really savour some true Sikkimese atmosphere, visit a village tongba bar for some local millet beer.

Plunging mountain valleys are lushly forested, interspersed occasionally with rice terraces and groves of flowering rhododendrons. Tibetan-style Buddhist monasteries (gompas) add splashes of white, gold and vermilion to the green ridges and are approached through atmospheric avenues of colourful prayer flags on long bamboo flag poles.

Sikkim's big-ticket item is the majesty of Khangchendzonga (Kanchenjunga, 8598m), the world's third-highest mountain straddling the border between Sikkim and Nepal. Khangchendzonga's guardian spirit is worshipped in a series of spectacular autumn festivals and its magnificent white peaks and ridges can be spied from many points around the state. Dawn is its best show, when the sun lights up the eastern face.

An independent kingdom until 1975, Sikkim has long been considered one of the last Himalayan Shangri Las. But hurry. In the last few years a tourist boom has seen ever-multiplying numbers of domestic visitors escaping the lowlands' heat. Every year more concrete hotels protrude from once-idyllic villagescapes, and most towns are already architecturally lacklustre huddles of multistorey box-homes. However, old-style Sikkim can still be found by hiking away from metalled roads and getting into the forest. Just watch out for the leeches.

Sikkim is tiny, only approximately 80km from east to west and 100km north to south but, due to the terrain, it is slow to traverse. Your next destination, over the valley, looks so close but it may be three or four hours away.

HIGHLIGHTS

- Wonder at the might of nature carving out different landscapes on a trip from **Lachung** to **Yumthang Valley** (p196)
- Be enthralled by a *chaam* dance at **Rumtek Gompa** (p183)
- Wake up in **Pelling** (p187) to watch the dawn Khangchendzonga show from the comfort of your hotel
- Join the locals in some tongba (Himalayan millet beer) drinking, in mountain-edge villages like **Thanggu** (p197)
- Wander through the prayer-flag-bannered chorten compound of ancient **Tashiding Gompa** (p193) and have your sins washed away by gazing on the chorten of Thong-Wa-Rang-Dol

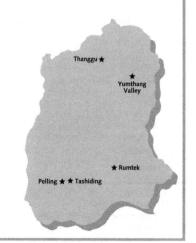

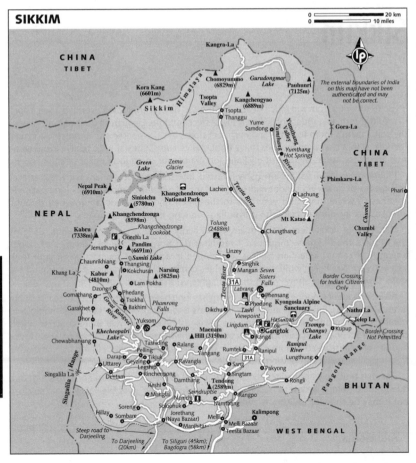

History

Lepchas, the 'original' Sikkimese people, migrated here from Assam or Myanmar (Burma) in the 13th century, followed by Bhutias (Khambas) who fled from religious strife in Tibet during the 15th century. The Nyingmapa form of Mahayana Buddhism

arrived with three refugee Tibetan lamas who encountered each other at the site of modern-day Yuksom. Here in 1641 they crowned Phuntsog Namgyal as first chogyal (king) of Sikkim. The capital was later moved to Rabdentse (near Pelling), and then to Tumlong (now hidden ruins behind Phodong) before finally settling in Gangtok.

At their most powerful the chogyals' rule encompassed eastern Nepal, upper Bengal and Darjeeling. However, much territory was later lost during wars with Bhutan and Nepal, and throughout the 19th century large numbers of Hindu Nepali migrants arrived, eventually coming to form a majority of Sikkim's population.

FAST FACTS

Population 540,490
Area 7096 sq km
Capital Gangtok
Main language Nepali
When to go late September to mid-November; April and May

In 1835 the British bribed Sikkim's chogyal to cede Darjeeling to the East India Company. Tibet, which regarded Sikkim as a vassal state, raised strong objections. In 1849, amid rising tensions, the British annexed the entire area between the present Sikkim border and the Ganges plains, repulsing a counterinvasion by Tibet in 1886. In 1903–04, Britain's real-life James Bond character Francis Younghusband twice trekked up to the Sikkim–Tibet border. There, with a small contingent of soldiers, he set about inciting a fracas that would 'justify' an invasion of Tibet.

Sikkim's last chogyal ruled from 1963 to 1975, when the Indian government deposed him after a revolt by Sikkim's Nepali population. China never recognised India's claim to Sikkim until 2005 so prior to this, in order to bolster pro-Delhi sentiment, the Indian government made Sikkim a tax-free zone, pouring crores (tens of millions) of rupees into road building, electricity, water supplies and local industry. As a result of this, Sikkim is surprisingly affluent by Himalayan standards.

Climate

Timing is crucial when visiting Sikkim. Summer's monsoonal rains hide the main attraction, those soaring mountains. The Yumthang and Tsopta Valleys are very cold by October and become really fingertip-numbing between December and February.

Information

The best times of year to visit Sikkim are from late September to mid-November and from March to May. These are the high seasons for domestic tourists: prices shoot up and normally serene monasteries are overrun. Crowd pressure is highest for Durga Puja celebrations (early October) and just afterwards, but immediately before the celebrations Sikkim is contrastingly very quiet.

PERMITS
Standard Permits

Foreigners require a permit to enter Sikkim. Happily, these are free and a mere formality, although you need photos and passport photocopies to apply. Permits are most easily obtainable at the following places:

- Indian Embassies abroad when getting your Indian visa (the best solution)
- Rangpo border post on arrival
- Sikkim House (☎ 1126883026; 12-14 Panchsheel Marg, Chankyapuri) in Delhi
- Sikkim House in Kolkata (p106)
- Sikkim Tourist Office in Siliguri, West Bengal (p146)
- major Foreigners' Regional Registration Offices (FRROs), including those in Kolkata (p103), Delhi (p322) or Darjeeling (p165)

Extensions

Permits are valid for 15 days from the date of entry. One or two days before expiry they

---

FESTIVALS IN SIKKIM

Sikkim has dozens of festivals; see www.sikkiminfo.net/fairs&festivals.htm. The most distinctive events feature colourful masked dances known as *chaams*, retelling stories from Buddhist mythology. Dates generally follow the Tibetan lunar calendar, which is handily listed under 'Government Holiday' on www.sikkim.gov.in.

Bumchu (Jan/Feb; Tashiding Gompa, p193) 'Bum' means pot or vase and 'chu' means water. The lamas open a pot of holy water to foretell the year's fortunes.

Losar (Feb/Mar; Pemayangtse, p189, Rumtek, p182) Sikkim's biggest *chaam* dances take place just before Tibetan New Year.

Khachoedpalri Mela (Mar/Apr; Khecheopalri Lake, p190) Butter candles float across the lake.

Drupchen (May/Jun; Rumtek, p183) *Chaam* dances form part of the annual group-meditation ceremony, with dances every second year honouring Padmasambhava.

Saga Dawa (May/Jun; all monastery towns) Buddhist scriptures paraded through the streets.

Diwali (Oct/Nov; widespread) Festival of lights and lots of fireworks.

Mahakala Dance (Nov; Ralang, p186)

Losoong (Dec/Jan; widespread incl Old Rumtek, p183, Lingdum, p183, Phodong, p194) Sikkimese New Year, preceded by *chaam* dances in many locations.

can be extended for a further 15 days and then twice again, giving a maximum of 60 days. For the extension:

- Gangtok Foreigners' Registration Office (p178)
- Tikjuk District Administration Centre, Superintendent of Police (p187), 5km from Pelling

Once you leave Sikkim, you must wait three months before applying for another permit. However, if you're on Sikkim-to-Sikkim public transport cutting through a corner of West Bengal (between Rangpo and Melli), your permit remains valid.

Permit Validity

The standard permit is valid for visits to the following areas:

- Gangtok, Rumtek and Lingdum
- South Sikkim
- anywhere on the Gangtok–Singhik road
- most of West Sikkim to which paved roads extend

Foreigners need additional permits beyond Singhik up to Yumthang north of Lachung, and the Tsopta Valley north of Lachen. Areas nearest to the Chinese border are out of bounds entirely. Indian citizens do not need a permit except north of Singhik, where they are subject to the same restrictions as foreigners. Indian citizens can also travel further, to Yume Samdong north of Yumthang, and Gurudongmar north of Thangu. They can also travel east past Tsomgo Lake to the Tibetan border at Nathu La.

NO BAGS PLEASE

The Sikkim Democratic Front (SDF) state government has earned a reputation as the most environmentally aware in India, banning plastic bags and fining people who pollute streams. But, as so many commodities – such as snacks and *paan* (betel nut and leaf mixture for chewing) – now come in plastic sachets, the banning of plastic bags only solves one part of the problem. Getting manufacturers to change their packaging, proper rubbish disposal and changing public attitudes to littering are the real answers.

Special Permits

High-altitude treks, including the main Goecha La and Singalila Ridge routes, require trekking permits valid for up to 15 days and organised by trekking agents.

Restricted-area permits for Tsomgo (Changu) Lake (day trips) and visits anywhere north of Singhik are issued locally through approved tour agencies. You'll have to join the agent's 'tour', but this simply means a rental jeep, guide and agreed itinerary. Virtually any Gangtok agency can arrange this within 24 hours. You'll need a minimum group of two; so single travellers have every excuse to make friends. You'll need a passport photo and copies of your existing permit, visa and passport details page.

Dangers & Annoyances

Sikkim is generally a very safe place; the only annoyance is the famous little leeches. They aren't dangerous, just a nuisance. They're ubiquitous in damp grass so stick to dry, wide paths.

Activities

Sikkim offers considerable **trekking** potential. Day hikes between villages follow age-old footpaths and normally don't require extra permits: the best-known options are along the Monastery Loop, notably between Yuksam and Tashiding (p193). Nepal-style multiday group treks head into the really high mountains to Goecha La at the base of Khangchendzonga. For this, permits and guides are required and, although there are variants, most groups tend to follow pretty much the same route (p192).

Tour agencies (p179) are striving to open new trekking areas, notably the fabulous route across Zemu Glacier to Green Lake in Khangchendzonga National Park. However, these permits still remain very expensive and take months to arrange, while other tempting routes close to the Tibetan border remain off limits.

EAST SIKKIM

GANGTOK

☎ 03592 / pop 31,100 / elev 1400-1700m

Sikkim's capital is mostly a functional sprawl of multistorey concrete boxes. But, true to its name (meaning 'hill top'), these are steeply

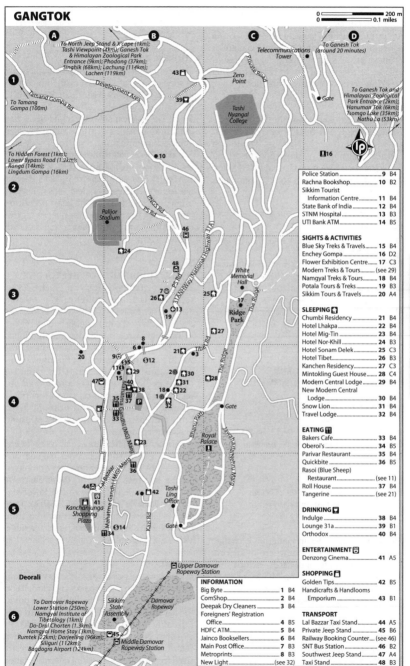

GANGTOK

0	200 m
0	0.1 miles

To North Jeep Stand & X'cape (1km);
Tashi Viewpoint (4km); Ganesh Tok
& Himalayan Zoological Park
Entrance (9km); Phodong (37km);
Singhik (68km); Lachung (114km);
Lachen (119km)

Development Area

Tamand Gompa Rd

To Tamang
Gompa (100m)

Zero Point

Private Road

Telecommunications
Tower

To Ganesh Tok
(around 20 minutes)

Gate

To Ganesh Tok and
Himalayan Zoological
Park Entrance (2km);
Hanuman Tok (6km);
Tsomgo Lake (35km);
Nathu La (53km)

To Hidden Forest (1km);
Lower Bypass Road (1.2km);
Ranga (14km);
Lingdum Gompa (16km)

Tashi
Nyangal
College

Paljor
Stadium

PS Rd

PNGS Rd

31 NH Way National Highway 31A

White
Memorial
Hall

Ridge
Park

The Ridge

Tibet Rd

The Ridge

Mahatma Gandhi (MG) Marg

Bhanu Path

Jawaharlal Nehru Marg

Royal
Palace

Gate

Lal Bazaar

Mahatma Gandhi (MG) Marg

PS Rd

Tashi
Ling
Office

Gate

Kanchanjunga
Shopping
Plaza

Deorali

To Damovar Ropeway
Lower Station (250m);
Namgyal Institute of
Tibetology (1km);
Do-Drul Chorten (1.3km);
Namgyal Home Stay (3km);
Rumtek (22km); Darjeeling (96km);
Siliguri (112km);
Bagdogra Airport (124km)

Sikkim
State
Assembly

Damovar
Ropeway

Upper Damovar
Ropeway Station

Middle Damovar
Ropeway Station

SIKKIM

Police Station **9** B4
Rachna Bookshop **10** B2
Sikkim Tourist
  Information Centre **11** B4
State Bank of India **12** B4
STNM Hospital **13** B3
UTI Bank ATM **14** B5

SIGHTS & ACTIVITIES
Blue Sky Treks & Travels **15** B4
Enchey Gompa **16** D2
Flower Exhibition Centre **17** C3
Modern Treks & Tours .... (see 29)
Namgyal Treks & Tours **18** B4
Potala Tours & Treks **19** B3
Sikkim Tours & Travels **20** A4

SLEEPING 🛏
Chumbi Residency **21** B4
Hotel Lhakpa **22** B4
Hotel Mig-Tin **23** B4
Hotel Nor-Khill **24** B3
Hotel Sonam Delek **25** C3
Hotel Tibet **26** B3
Kanchen Residency **27** C3
Mintokling Guest House **28** C4
Modern Central Lodge **29** B4
New Modern Central
  Lodge **30** B4
Snow Lion **31** B4
Travel Lodge **32** B4

EATING 🍴
Bakers Cafe **33** B4
Oberoi's **34** B5
Parivar Restaurant **35** B4
Quickbite **36** B5
Rasoi (Blue Sheep)
  Restaurant .... (see 11)
Roll House **37** B4
Tangerine .... (see 21)

DRINKING 🍷
Indulge **38** B4
Lounge 31a **39** B1
Orthodox **40** B4

ENTERTAINMENT 🎭
Denzong Cinema **41** A5

SHOPPING 🛍
Golden Tips **42** B5
Handicrafts & Handlooms
  Emporium **43** B1

TRANSPORT
Lal Bazzar Taxi Stand **44** A5
Private Jeep Stand **45** B6
Railway Booking Counter ..... (see 46)
SNT Bus Station **46** B2
Southwest Jeep Stand **47** A4
Taxi Stand **48** B3

INFORMATION
Big Byte **1** B4
ComShop **2** B4
Deepak Dry Cleaners **3** B4
Foreigners' Registration
  Office **4** B5
HDFC ATM **5** B4
Jainco Booksellers **6** B4
Main Post Office **7** B3
Metroprints **8** B3
New Light .... (see 32)

tiered along a precipitous mountain ridge. When clouds clear, (typically at dawn), views are inspiring with Khangchendzonga soaring above the western horizon. While Gangtok's artificial attractions are minor, it's a reasonable place to spend a day or two organising trekking permits or trips to the north.

Orientation

Gangtok's crooked spine is the Rangpo–Mangan road, National Hwy 31A, cryptically referred to as 31ANHWay. The tourist office, banks and many shops line the central pedestrianised Mahatma Gandhi (MG) Marg. Nearby Tibet Rd is the nearest Gangtok gets to a travellers' enclave.

Information
BOOKSHOPS
Jainco Booksellers (☎ 203774; 31ANHWay; 🕑 9am-8pm Mon-Sat) Small but central.
Rachna Bookshop (☎ 204336; www.rachnabooks.com; Development Area) Gangtok's best-stocked and most convivial bookshop. Occasional film (Small Town Film Club) and music events are held on the upstairs terrace.
Metroprints (31ANHWay) A little photocopy stall selling the excellent artist's-view map-guide, *Gangtok, in a Nutshell* (Rs60).

EMERGENCY
Police station (☎ 202033; 31ANHWay)
STNM hospital (☎ 222059; 31ANHWay)

INTERNET ACCESS
Connections are slow and erratic.
Big Byte (Tibet Rd; per hr Rs30; 🕑 8.30am-8pm)
ComShop (Tibet Rd; per hr Rs30; 🕑 9am-8pm)
New Light (Tibet Rd; per hr Rs30; 🕑 9am-7pm)

LAUNDRY
Deepak Dry Cleaners (☎ 227073; Tibet Rd; 🕑 7am-8pm Fri-Tue) Next-day laundry service.

MONEY
Stock up with rupees in Gangtok: exchange is virtually impossible elsewhere in Sikkim. ATMs accepting foreign cards include SBI, UTI Bank and HDFC all on MG Marg.
State Bank of India (SBI; ☎ 202666; MG Marg) Changes cash and major travellers cheques.

PERMIT EXTENSION
Foreigners' Registration Office (☎ 223041; Kazi Rd; 🕑 10am-4pm, 10am-noon public holidays) In the lane beside Indian Overseas Bank.

POST
Main post office (☎ 203085; PS Rd, Gangtok 737101) Poste restante service.

TOURIST INFORMATION
There are plenty of basic pamphlets and books available. One of the best is the lavishly illustrated *Sikkim* by Arundhati Ray (not to be confused with the author of *The God of Small Things*) available at Rachna Bookshop (left) and Golden Tips (p181). Maps, however, approach pure fiction.
Sikkim Tourist Information Centre (☎ 221634, toll free 204408; www.sikkimtourism.travel; MG Marg; 🕑 8am-4pm Dec-Feb & Jun-Aug, 10am-8pm Sep-Nov & Mar-May) has some useful free booklets, sells helicopter tours and can advise on the latest permit requirements. For more specific queries regarding trekking and permit-area travel, deal with a travel agent.

Sights
NAMGYAL INSTITUTE OF TIBETOLOGY
Housed in traditionally styled Tibetan architecture, this unique **institute** (☎ 281642; www.tibetology.net; admission Rs10; 🕑 10am-4pm Mon-Sat, closed 2nd Sat of month) was established in 1958 to promote research into Mahayana Buddhism and Tibetan culture. It contains one of the world's largest collections of Buddhist books and manuscripts, plus statuettes, *thangkas* (Tibetan cloth paintings) and sacred objects, such as a *kapali* (sacred bowl made from a human skull) and human thighbone trumpets. There are plenty of useful explanatory captions.

Further along the same road is the **Do-Drul Chorten**, a large white Tibetan pagoda surrounded by dormitories for young monks.

The institute sits in an **Orchid Sanctuary** and is conveniently close to the lower station of **Damovar Ropeway** (☎ 280587; per person Rs60; 🕑 9.30am-4.30pm), a cable car running from just below the Tashi Ling offices on the ridge. Views are stupendous.

THE RIDGE
With views east and west, it's very pleasant to stroll through shady parks and gardens on the city's central ridge. Sadly its focal point, the **Raj Bhawan (Royal Palace)**, is closed to visitors. When the orchids bloom (March) it's worth peeping inside the **Flower Exhibition Centre** (admission Rs10; 🕑 9am-5pm), a modestly sized tropical greenhouse full of exotic plants.

The once-grand 1932 **White Memorial Hall** (Nehru Marg) opposite is now a dilapidated children's sports hall.

ENCHEY GOMPA & VIEWPOINTS

Approached through gently rustling conifers high above Gangtok, this **monastery** (☼ 6am-4pm Mon-Sat), dating back to 1909, is Gangtok's most attractive, with some decent murals and statues of Tantric deities. It comes alive for the colourful **Detor Chaam** (December/January) masked dances.

From the gompa, follow the access road northeast around the base of an unmissable telecommunications tower. An initially obvious path scrambles up in around 15 minutes to **Ganesh Tok viewpoint**. Festooned in colourful prayer flags, Ganesh Tok offers superb city views and its minicafe serves hot teas. Across the road, a lane leads into the **Himalayan Zoological Park** (☎ 223191; admission Rs10, vehicles Rs25, video Rs500; ☼ 9am-4pm). Red pandas, Himalayan bears and snow leopards roam around in extensive wooded enclosures so large that you'll really value a car to shuttle between them.

Hanuman Tok, another impressive viewpoint, sits on a hilltop around 4km drive beyond Ganesh Tok, though there are shortcuts for walkers.

Perhaps Gangtok's best view of Khangchendzonga is from the **Tashi viewpoint** at the northwest edge of town beside the main route to Phodong.

Tours

Classic 'three-point tours' show you Ganesh Tok, Hanuman Tok and Tashi viewpoints (Rs500). Almost any travel agent, hotel or taxi driver offers variants, including a 'five-point tour' adding Enchey Gompa and Namgyal Institute (Rs700), or 'seven-point tours' tacking on old-and-new Rumtek (Rs900) or Rumtek plus Lingdum (Rs1200). Prices are per vehicle holding three or four passengers.

TOUR AGENCIES

For high-altitude treks, visits to Tsomgo Lake or tours to Northern Sikkim you'll need a tour agency. There are more than 180 agencies but only 10% of those work with foreigners; check with fellow travellers for the latest recommendations. Choose a government-registered agency, as it has to conform to certain guidelines including ecologically and culturally

responsible travel. Look for a company that belongs to TAAS (Travel Agents Association of Sikkim) as all their members are registered. Try these:

Blue Sky Treks & Travels (☎ 205113; bluesky tourism@yahoo.com; Tourism Bldg, MG Marg) Trekking and trips to Tsomgo Lake (Rs1600 per person).
Modern Treks & Tours (☎ 204670; www.modernresi dency.com; Modern Central Lodge, MG Marg) For trekking.
Namgyal Treks & Tours (☎ 203701; www.namgyal treks.net; Tibet Rd) Trekking, tours to northern Sikkim.
Potala Tours & Treks (☎ 200043; www.sikkimhima layas.com; PS Rd)
Sikkim Tours & Travels (☎ 202188; www.sikkim tours.com; Church Rd) Specialises in trekking, birdwatching and botanical tours.

SCENIC FLIGHTS

For eagle-eye mountain views, **Sikkim Tourist Information Centre** (☎ 281372; stdcsikkim@yahoo.co.in) arranges scenic helicopter flights. Book at least three days ahead. Prices are for up to five passengers (four for Khangchendzonga ridge): buzz over Gangtok (Rs7590, 15 minutes); circuit of West Sikkim (Rs82,500, 55 minutes); circuit of North Sikkim (Rs97,500, 65 minutes); Khangchendzonga ridge (Rs112,500, 75 minutes).

Sleeping

Rates typically drop by 15% to 30% in the low season (November to February and June to August), much more if demand is very low and you're good at bargaining. The high seasons, which influence accommodation prices, are March to May and September to November.

BUDGET

Many cheaper hotels quote walk-in rates of around Rs500. Some are worth it. Others are just waiting for you to bargain them down to Rs200. Check rooms carefully as standards can vary widely even within the same hotel. Foreigners generally flock around central Tibet Rd, the only area where a Rs200 room is likely to be habitable.

New Modern Central Lodge (☎ 201361; Tibet Rd; d Rs300, without bathroom s Rs100, d Rs150-250) A travellers' favourite for so long that people still come here despite somewhat ill-kept rooms and reports of falling standards. With plenty of cheap rooms and a useful meeting-point cafe-bar, it will probably remain a backpacker standby.

SIKKIM

Modern Central Lodge (☎ 221081; info@modern hospitality.com; 31ANHWay; dm Rs100, d Rs250-500) More rupees buy you a larger room at the top of the building away from the traffic noise below. All doubles have private bathrooms; the dorms share separate facilities. Great home-cooked food on the roof garden.

Hotel Mig-Tin (☎ 204101; Tibet Rd; d Rs300-600) Above a lobby with naive Tibetan-style murals and a great little meet-up cafe. Most rooms are worn but become good value out of high season with some bargaining. The cheapest rooms are damp and airless.

MIDRANGE & TOP END

All places listed here have cable TV and private bathroom with hot showers. Most add 10% tax and some a 10% service charge.

Kanchen Residency (☎ 9732072614; kanchen residency@indiatimes.com; Tibet Rd; d back/side/front Rs450/600/700) Above the dismal (unrelated) Hotel Prince, this sparklingly airy discovery is spacious, light and well run. Front rooms have great views.

Namgyal Home Stay (☎ 203701; www.namgyaltreks .net; s/d Rs800/1200) Parading space, simplicity and friendliness this homestay is 3km south on the 31ANHWay. Full board is available. Book through Namgyal Treks & Tours (p179).

Mintokling Guest House (☎ 204226; www.minto kling.com; Bhanu Path; s/d from Rs950/1250) Set within secluded gardens, this expanded family home is a real oasis with Bhutanese fabrics, timber ceilings and local design features. Very friendly.

Travel Lodge (☎ 203858; Tibet Rd; d Rs1000-1200) Popularity has caused high-season prices to shoot up but discounts of 50% to 60% are available at other times. Unusually good-value rooms have BBC World TV and well-heated showers with towels and soap provided, though the ground-floor cheapies have thin walls and upstairs a few smell musty.

Hotel Tibet (☎ 202523; htltibet@yahoo.com; PS Rd; s/d Rs1100/1475) A doorman in Tibetan dress greets you at this older hotel decorated in a Tibetan style. The rooms are well furnished, beds comfortable and the better rooms boast a bath and wooden parquet flooring.

Hotel Sonam Delek (☎ 202566; www.hotelsonam delek.com; Tibet Rd; d Rs1100-1500) A longstanding favourite with good service and reliable food; the best-value deluxe rooms come with soft mattresses and decent views. Bigger super-deluxe rooms have better views and balconies,

but the standard rooms are a very noticeable step down – in the basement.

Snow Lion (☎ 201024; www.snowlionhotel.com; Tibet Rd; d Rs1200-1800) You can't miss this sumptuously decorated hotel with its sculptural facade of lions and mythical Tibetan creatures. Discounts of 50% can be bargained out of season. Rooms are pleasant, well decorated and well furnished. There is an occasionally working lift to whisk you to the top floors.

our pick Hidden Forest(☎ 205197; www.hidden forestretreat.org; Middle Sichey; s/d Rs1500/1700) A wonderful, friendly family-run hideaway on the edge of town secluded on more than a hectare of orchid, fruit tree and flower nursery that's also home to birds and butterflies. The self-contained cottages are marvellously furnished with Tibetan motifs, polished wood floors and a real orchid adding a little touch of colour. Hidden Forest does its bit to help the environment: superb food comes from the solar-powered kitchen, a resident cow provides dairy produce and all vegetable matter is composted.

Chumbi Residency (☎ 226618; www.thechumbi residency.com; Tibet Rd; s/d from Rs2250/2950) This wonderfully central three-star hotel has comfortable but smallish rooms with fresh white walls, good furniture and equipment for making tea and coffee. There's little difference between the two grades of rooms but go for one with a view. The relaxed Tangerine bar-restaurant is firmly recommended.

Hotel Nor-Khill (☎ 205637; norkhill@elginhotels .com; PS Rd; s/d full board Rs5600/5900) Oozing 1930s elegance, this sumptuous 'house of jewels' was originally the king of Sikkim's royal guesthouse. Historical photos and artwork feature throughout, and the lobby has antique furniture and imperial-sized mirrors. The spaciously luxurious old-building rooms attract film stars and Dalai Lamas.

Eating

RESTAURANTS & CAFES

Most of the budget hotels have cheap cafe-restaurants that serve the standard Chinese/ Tibetan dishes, basic Indian meals and Western breakfasts.

Parivar Restaurant (MG Marg; dishes Rs25-70) Eat here for good-value South Indian vegetarian food; try the various *masala dosas* for breakfast or the all-inclusive thali for Rs70. The restaurant is downstairs from the HDFC Bank.

SIKKIM SHERBETS

In much of India, drinking alcohol seems such a shameful activity that boozers secrete themselves away in darkened bars as though they were too embarrassed to be seen. Not so in Sikkim where almost every cafe serves beer. Hit and Dansberg are superb thirst-quenching local brews superior to imported foreign products that sell on the cachet of being foreign rather than being good. The state is also famous for its liquors, but although quality is pretty good, telling the difference between Sikkimese rum, whisky and brandy isn't always easy on a blind tasting.

In Sikkimese villages, don't miss a chance to try tongba. Your host will offer you a hollowed bamboo tub of fermented millet seeds onto which you pour boiling water. You poke your bamboo straw down into the morass and suck mightily. It tastes a like a cross between English cider and Japanese sake. Regular topping up gradually dilutes the drink until it's time to ask for a fresh brew.

Bakers Cafe (MG Marg; mains Rs50-125; 8am-8pm) The perfect breakfast escape, this cosy Western-style cafe has great coffee (Rs35), scrunchy pastries and squidgy cakes.

our pick Tangerine (Ground fl, Chumbi Residency, Tibet Rd; mains Rs50-150) Descend five floors for sublime cuisine, tasty Western snacks or cocktails in the brilliant Japanese-style floor-cushioned bar area. Try the stuffed-tomato curry or sample Sikkimese specialities like *sochhya* (nettle stew). Stylishly relaxed decor with a waiter/origami-ist who turns napkins into birds.

Rasoi (Blue Sheep) Restaurant (MG Marg; mains Rs50-110; 8.30am-9.30pm) Still looking brand new, this well-patronised family restaurant serves good food, hot and fast. No booze.

QUICK EATS

Roll House (MG Marg; rolls Rs15-30; 8am-8pm) In an alley just off MG Marg this hole-in-the-wall serves delicious *kati* rolls (see p128) that upstage even the Kolkata originals.

Quickbite (MG Marg; snacks Rs20-40; 8am-8pm) Takeaway snacks from dosas to pizzas to Indian sweets.

Oberoi's (MG Marg; snacks Rs25-60; 7.30am-8.30pm) *Momos* (Tibetan dumplings), chow mein, sandwiches, Indian snacks and pizzas.

Drinking

Lounge 31a (Zero Point; beers Rs70; 10am-9.30pm) Swooping glass architecture offers Zen aesthetics and light-suffused sunset views from four storeys high, above the Sikkim State Bank.

Indulge (Tibet Rd; beers Rs70; 11am-11pm) Big windows overlooking MG Rd add to the airiness of this bar-cafe (snacks Rs40 to Rs120) with its white decor and curvy designs.

Orthodox (MG Marg; beers Rs55; 7am-10pm) Tables are squished together as tightly as lovers in this cosy bar. An intrusive ultra-violet light annoys at night but it's a bar for companionable beers with friends (or lovers). Solve the picture puzzles on the wall before too many beers. Meals Rs60 to Rs170, early-morning breakfasts until 10am.

Entertainment

Denzong Cinema (202692; Lal Bazaar; tickets from Rs25) Screens the latest Bollywood blockbusters in Hindi.

X'cape (228636; Vagra Cinema Hall; entry Rs400; 7.30pm-11.30pm Thu-Sun) Gangtok's leading nightclub.

Shopping

Several souvenir shops on MG Marg and PS Rd sell pricier Tibetan and Sikkimese handicrafts. Bustling Lal Bazaar has several stalls selling wooden tongba (Himalayan millet beer) pots, prayer flags and Nepali-style knives.

A few Sikkimese liquors come in novelty souvenir containers. Opening a 1L monk-shaped bottle of Old Monk Rum (Rs220) means screwing off the monk's head! Fireball comes in a bowling-ball-style red sphere.

Handicrafts & Handloom Emporium (9434137131; Zero Point; 10am-4pm Mon-Sat, daily Jul-Mar) Teaches traditional crafts to local students and sells their produce, which make good gifts – including purses (Rs75), handwoven carpets (from Rs4200), *thangkas* (Rs125 to Rs6800) and traditional women's dresses (Rs2000).

Golden Tips (www.goldentipstea.com; Kazi Rd; teas from Rs25; 12.30-9.30pm) An inviting tea show-room with a wide selection of blends to buy and taste.

SIKKIM

Getting There & Away

Landslides and route changes mean road journeys can take vastly longer than expected. If flying out of Bagdogra, play safe by making the Gangtok–Siliguri trip a full day ahead.

AIR

The nearest airport to Sikkim is Bagdogra (p148), 124km from Gangtok, near Siliguri in West Bengal, which has flights to Kolkata, Delhi and Guwahati. **TSA Helicopters** (☎ 0353-2531959; www.mountainflightindia.com) shuttles from Gangtok to Bagdogra (Rs3000, 35 minutes), departing at 11am and returning at 2.30pm, but services can be cancelled in adverse weather and if bookings are insufficient. In Gangtok, **Sikkim Tourist Information Centre** (☎ 221634) sells the tickets.

Fixed-price Maruti vans/Sumos (jeeps) go from Bagdogra direct to Gangtok (Rs1500/1700, 4½ hours). You might get slightly better prices from jeeps in the car park: look for Sikkim (SK) number plates.

BUS

Buses listed in the table below leave from the government **SNT bus station** (☎ 202016; PS Rd).

SHARED JEEPS & MINIBUSES

By regulation there are fixed departures for various destinations; in practice these are augmented by as many jeeps as passenger numbers require. Departures usually start at 6.30am for the more distant destinations and continue up to about 3pm.

From the hectic but well-organised **private jeep stand** (31ANHWay), shared jeeps/minibuses depart to Darjeeling (Rs125, five hours), Kalimpong (Rs90, three hours) and Siliguri (Rs125, four hours), some continuing to New Jalpaiguri train station (Rs135, 4½ hours). There are one-off jeeps to Kakarbhitta (Rs140, 4½ hours, 6.30am) on the Nepali border and Phuentsholing (Bhutan border, Rs220, six hours, 8.30am). Buy tickets in advance.

West Sikkim vehicles depart from **Southwest jeep stand** (☎ 203862; Church Rd) for Geyzing (Rs120, 4½ hours), Ravangla (Rs80, three hours), Namchi (Rs90, three hours) and Jorethang (Rs100, three hours). Jeeps for Yuksom, Tashiding and Pelling (Rs120 to Rs150, five hours) depart around 7am and again around 12.30pm. For independent travel, small groups can charter a vehicle.

Sumos to North Sikkim use the **North jeep stand** (31ANHWay), about 3km north of the centre. From here vehicles go to Mangan (Rs80), Singhik (Rs100) and Phodong (Rs50).

TRAIN

The nearest major train station is over 120km away at New Jalpaiguri (NJP). There's a computerised **railway booking counter** (☎ 220201; ☼ 8am-2pm Mon-Sat, 8-11am Sun & public holidays) at the SNT Bus Stand.

Getting Around

Hail a taxi on the street or pick one up at the various taxi stands around the city. There's a taxi stand in Lal Bazaar opposite the Denzong Cinema, and another in PS Rd just north of the post office.

AROUND GANGTOK

Rumtek and Lingdum Gompa are most easily visited on a 'seven-point tour' (see p179). Viewing the temples takes perhaps half an hour each, but the infinitely winding country lane that links them is a big part of the attraction, curving through mossy forests high above river valleys and artistically terraced rice-slopes.

Rumtek

☎ 03592 / elev 1690m

Facing Gangtok distantly across a vast green valley, Rumtek village is entirely dominated by its very extensive gompa complex. Spiritually the monastery is hugely significant as the surrogate home of Buddhism's

SIKKIM

BUSES FROM GANGTOK			
Destination	Cost (Rs)	Duration (hr)	Departures
Jorethang	70	4	7am
Kalimpong	70	4	7.15am
Namchi	68	3	7.30am
Pelling	90	5½	7am
Siliguri (via Rangpo)	85-110	5	hourly 6.30am-1.30pm

FLYING BLACK HATS

The Black Hat sect is so named because of the priceless ruby-topped headgear used to crown the Karmapa (spiritual leader) during key ceremonies. Being woven from the hair of angels, the hat must be kept locked in a box to prevent it from flying back to heaven. But maybe that's just what it has done. Nobody has seen it since 1993 when the 16th Karmapa died. Only when the 17th Karmapa is finally crowned will anyone dare to unlock the box and check.

Kagyu (Black Hat) sect. Visually it is not Sikkim's most spectacular and by day it can get annoyingly crowded in the high season. To experience Rumtek at its most serene, stay the night and hike around the delightful nearby hilltops at dawn.

SIGHTS
Rumtek Gompa Complex
This rambling and walled **complex** (☎ 252329; www.rumtek.org) is a village within a village containing religious buildings, schools and several small lodge-hotels. To enter, foreigners must show both passport and Sikkim permit. Unusually for a monastery, this place is guarded by armed police, as there have been violent altercations, and an invasion, by monks who dispute the Karmapa's accession.

The main **monastery building** (admission Rs5; ⏰ 6am-5pm) was constructed between 1961 and 1966 to replace the Tsurphu Monastery in Tibet, which had been destroyed during China's Cultural Revolution. The giant throne within awaits the crowning of Kagyu's current spiritual leader, the (disputed) **17th Karmapa** (Ogyen Trinley Dorje; www .kagyuoffice.org). This young lama fled from Tibet in 2000 but currently remains based at Dharamsala: Indian authorities are believed to have prevented him from officially taking up his Rumtek seat for fear of upsetting Chinese government sensibilities. Those who want to learn more about the 17th Karmapa might wish to read *Dance of 17 Lives* by Mick Brown.

Rear stairs lead up to the **Golden Stupa**. It's not really a stupa at all, just a smallish concrete room, but it holds the ashes of the 16th Karmapa in a jewel-studded reliquary to which pilgrims pay their deepest respects. If locked, someone from the colourful **Karma Shri Naland Institute of Buddhist Studies** opposite can usually open it for you.

Rumtek holds impressive masked *chaam* dances during the annual **Drupchen** (group meditation) in May/June, and two days be-

fore Losar (Tibetan New Year) when you might also catch traditional *lhamo* (Tibetan opera) performances.

Old Rumtek Gompa
About 1.5km beyond the gompa towards Sang, a long avenue of white prayer flags leads attractively down to the powder-blue **Old Rumtek Gompa**. Despite the name, the main prayer hall has been so thoroughly renovated that it looks virtually new. However, the interior is a riotous festival of colour and the lonely location is idyllic with some wonderful west-facing views. Two days before Losoong (Sikkimese New Year), Old Rumtek holds the celebrated **Kagyed Chaam** dance.

SLEEPING & EATING
Currently the **Sungay Guesthouse** (☎ 252221; dechenb@dte.vsnl.net.in; d/tr Rs400/250) is the only one open. The comfortable if rather Spartan rooms have faux wood–veneer walls and private bathrooms with geyser. Doubles have great balcony views, hence the higher price.

Further up, where the monastery access road bends, is the Sangay Hotel, which was being rebuilt when we visited. Outside the gompa walls and 300m back towards Gangtok, the **Shambhala Mountain Resort** (☎ 252240; resort_shambhala@sify.com) is also being renovated and may be open again by the time you read this.

Lingdum Gompa
Only completed in 1998, peaceful Lingdum Gompa is visually more exciting than Rumtek. Its structure grows out of the forest in grand layers with photogenic side buildings, though the exterior paintings are not especially accomplished. The extensively muralled main prayer hall enshrines a large Sakyamuni (historic) Buddha wreathed in an expansive gilded aura. Sonorous chanting at the 7.30am and 3.30pm *puja* (prayers or offerings) adds to the magical atmosphere. The isolated gompa complex has a

cafe and its **Zurmang Tara Hotel** (☎ 9933008818; s Rs600, d Rs1000) offers full board and lodging in reasonable rooms with parquet floors and private bathrooms.

Getting There & Away

Rumtek is 26km from Gangtok by a very winding road. Lingdum Gompa is a 2km walk from Ranga or Ranka village, reached by rough back lanes from Gangtok. Shared jeeps are too sporadic to rely on for a day out here so linking the two sites requires private transport or a tour.

TOWARDS TIBET
Tsomgo (Changu, Tsangu) Lake
elev 3780m

Pronounced Changu, this scenic lake is an established tour stop for Indian visitors, but permits are necessary. To get one, sign up for a 'tour' by 2pm and most Gangtok agents can get the permit for next-day departure (two photos required). Tours (ie guided shared taxis) typically cost Rs700/450 per person for groups of two/three. Individual travellers usually can't get the permit.

At the lakeside, food stalls sell hot chai, chow mein and *momos,* while short **yak rides** (about Rs100) potter along the shore. If you can muster the puff, the main attraction is clambering up a nearby hilltop for inspiring views.

Nathu La

Indian citizens are permitted to continue 18km along the spectacular road from Tsomgo Lake to the 4130m **Nathu La** (Listening Ears Pass). Here the border post to southeastern Tibet 'opened' with much fanfare in 2006. Only local villagers are eligible to cross, and only to travel 8km to the first Tibetan market. Maybe one day it will be possible to reach Yatung (52km) in Tibet's fabled **Chumbi Valley**, where the Sikkimese kings once had their summer palace. From there, the road towards Lhasa (525km) winds up onto the Tibetan plateau via the old fortress town of **Phari**, one of the world's highest settlements (4350m).

A few kilometres southeast of Nathu La, **Jelep La** was the pass used by Francis Younghusband in the British Great Game-era attack on Tibet (1904). Until 1962 Jelep La was the main trade route between Kalimpong and Lhasa, but it shows no signs whatsoever of reopening.

SOUTH SIKKIM

The main sights in South Sikkim are Namchi's gigantic statues. The region has plenty of other great viewpoints, too, but visitors generally hurry to Pelling leaving much of the region comparatively unvisited. Ravangla (p186) falls administratively within South Sikkim, but we cover it in the Gangtok to Pelling section (p186), where it fits more logically.

NAMCHI
☎ 03595 / elev 1524m

When Shiva on Solophuk Hill is completed two utterly vast statues will be facing each other from opposite hillsides across this quietly prosperous market town. The Buddhist one at Samdruptse is already finished. **Super Computer Point** (Main Bazaar; internet per hr Rs30; ☯ 8am-8pm) has internet on the 1st floor of the block containing the well-signed Anapurna Restaurant. An Axis Bank ATM is opposite the entrance to Main Bazaar.

Sights
SAMDRUPTSE

Painted in shimmering copper and bronze, the impressively vast 45m-high **Padmasambhava statue** (Indian/foreigner Rs10/100; ☯ 7am-5pm) dominates its hilltop. Completed in 2004 on a foundation stone laid by the Dalai Lama, it's visible from miles around, shining like a golden cone amid the forests of Samdruptse hill. Reputedly it can be seen from Darjeeling and most certainly by its rival, Shiva, on Solophuk Hill opposite. The site is 7km from Namchi, 2km off the Damthang road.

Taxis want around Rs300 return. Alternatively you could walk back to Namchi, shortcutting via steps down to and through a **rock garden** (admission Rs10). Or, more interestingly, follow the nose of the Samdruptse hill down to **Ngadak Gompa**. Ngadak's ruined **old dzong**, dating back to 1717, is delightfully 'real' despite the unsightly steel buttressing that stops it from falling down. Its unpainted stone exterior incorporates ancient carved door pillars and upstairs intriguing but very decrepit fragments of painting remain on the peeling old cloth wallpaper.

SOLOPHUK

A massive 33m **Shiva statue** is being raised on the memorably named Solophuk hilltop surrounded by a complex of temples representing many of India's Hindu temple styles. This will become a huge pilgrimage complex and the Namchi authorities are joining in by building a shopping mall and remodelling the Main Bazaar down in the town. Intended completion dates have come and gone and the latest we were given at the time of research was mid-2009. So by the time you read this it may be open; ask down in Namchi town.

Sleeping & Eating

Hotel Samdruptse (☎ 264708; Jorethang Rd; d Rs100-1000) Scuffed paint and damp patches shouldn't deter you from staying here except in the cheap dingy downstairs rooms. The higher the room rate the better the view from the Khangchendzonga-facing rooms. The hotel, including Namchi's finest restaurant, is 300m west of the centre facing the Solophuk-bound road junction.

Dungmali Guest House (☎ 263272, 9434126992; Solophuk Rd, Km4; d Rs500, without bathroom Rs350-400) For now, this family homestay offers just three rooms, the best having a private bathroom and a fabulous view window. The inspired owner Bimuka Dungmali will be adding three cottages, one each in Nepali, Lepcha and Bhutia style, plus another storey onto the house. The family already grows its own organic vegetables, offers birdwatching walks in 2.4 hectares of private jungle and can take you to meet a traditional healer.

Hotel Mayel (☎ 9434127322; Jorethang Rd; d Rs500-1500) Opposite the Samdruptse, it lacks the views but is an option if the latter is full.

There are several hotels within the Main Bazaar that was under massive reconstruction in association with the Solophuk Hill development. Consequently many of the hotels and businesses were closed when we visited. **Hotel Zimkhang** (☎ 263625) could be a good option once they put the bazaar back together.

Getting There & Around

Around 200m east in descending layers off the Rangpo road are the main market, the jeep stand and the **SNT bus stand** (☎ 263847). Buses go to Jorethang (Rs26, one hour, 7am, 11.30am and 1pm), Ravangla (Rs26, two hours, 11.30am and 2pm).

Shared jeeps leave when full to Jorethang (Rs25, one hour) and Ravangla (Rs30, one hour) plus to Gangtok (Rs90, 3½ hours, 6.30am, 7am, 7.30am, 8.30am and 3pm), Darjeeling (Rs110, four hours, 7.30am) and Siliguri (Rs100, four hours, 6.30am, 7am, 7.30am, 8am and 3pm). For Geyzing there are frequent jeeps (Rs70, three hours).

JORETHANG (NAYA BAZAAR)
☎ 03595 / elev 518m

This useful transport hub between West Sikkim, Namchi and Darjeeling/Siliguri could make a launching point for visits to interesting but lesser-known Sikkimese villages like **Rinchenpong** (country getaways) or **Reishi** (hot springs and holy cave).

At its westernmost edge, Jorethang's most striking feature is the **Akar Suspension Bridge**, 400m north of which are the passingly photogenic roadside Shiva niches of **Sisne Mandir** (Legship Rd).

The brightest, friendliest accommodation option remains **Hotel Namgyal** (☎ 276852; d Rs450), on the main drag 70m east of the bridge just before the SNT bus station. Rooms are clean, the ones at the back overlook the river and room 101's toilet has a commanding view. Across the road beside the Darjeeling jeep stand there's a particularly helpful **tourist office** (◷ 8am-4pm Mon-Sat Dec-Feb & Jun-Aug, 10am-8pm Sep-Nov & Mar-May) and several other back-up hotels.

Useful services from the SNT bus station are listed in the table, below.

From the main jeep stand, Sumos leave regularly for Darjeeling (Rs90, two hours), Gangtok jeeps (Rs100 via Melli, Rs112 via

BUSES FROM JORETHANG			
Destination	**Cost (Rs)**	**Duration (hr)**	**Departure**
Gangtok	72	4	12.30pm
Namchi	20	1	8.30am, noon, 4.30pm
Pelling (via Geyzing)	50	3	3pm
Ravangla (via Namchi)	45	2½	noon
Siliguri	71	3½	9.30am

SIKKIM

Namchi), Geyzing (Rs55, two hours), Namchi (Rs30, one hour) Siliguri (Rs100, three hours), Tashiding (Rs100, 1½ hours) and Yuksom (Rs150, three hours). For Nepal there's a 7am jeep to Kakarbhitta (Rs150, four hours). Buy tickets before boarding.

WEST SIKKIM

Sikkim's greatest tourist draw is simply staring at Khangchendzonga's white-peaked magnificence from Pelling. Most visitors then add excursions to nearby waterfalls and monasteries, plus perhaps a spot of walking. Some lovely one-day hikes start from the charming village of Yuksom. That's also the trailhead for serious multiday group-trek expeditions to Dzongri (group trekking permits required).

GANGTOK TO PELLING

There are three main routes from the capital to Sikkim's main tourist hub. The longest and least interesting loops a long way south to Rangpo, then back via Melli, Jorethang and Legship. Fortunately this is normally only used by public Sumos when landslides block the two possible routes via Singtam and Ravangla. Both of these are highly attractive, especially the longer, little-used route via Yangyang (hired jeep only), which approaches Ravangla along an extremely dramatic cliff-edge drive around the precipitous base of Maenam Hill.

Ravangla (Rabongla)

☎ 03595 / elev 2009m

Rapidly expanding Ravangla is spectacularly perched overlooking a wide sweep of western Sikkim, the gompas of Old Ralang, Tashiding, Pemayangtse and Sangachoeling all distantly visible against a horizon that's sawtoothed with snow-capped peaks.

The town is a modern creation with little aesthetic distinction, but useful as a hub to visit Ralang. Joining the main highway is the Main Bazaar, a concentration of shops, small eateries, plentiful hotels, the jeep stand and **Cyber Cafe** (☎ 9933003225; per hr Rs30; ☺ 8.15am-7pm).

At the junction is **Hotel 10-Zing** (☎ 260705; d Rs150-500), open all year. All rooms have private bathrooms and those in the Rs300 to Rs500 range have geysers; otherwise it's free bucket hot water. Good English is spoken here.

Hotel Snow White (☎ 9434864915; d Rs600-800) has small but clean rooms with private bathrooms and geysers. Some of the cheaper rooms have smelly carpets. There are good, if partially obscured, views from the rear. The restaurant (mains Rs20 to Rs60) is quite cheery with curtained alcoves for private liaisons.

Several more hotels, many with views, line the main road for about a kilometre.

Lonely **Mt Narsing Resort** (☎ 226822; www .yuksom-tours.com; bungalows s/d Rs600/700, cottages from Rs1400/1600) is a rustic bungalow place 5km out of Ravangla with fabulous tree-framed views towards the mountains.

The bus booking office is part of Hotel 10-Zing. Buses run to Namchi (Rs25, one hour, 9am and 2pm) and Siliguri (Rs89, five hours, 6.30am). From 8am to noon shared jeeps run to Gangtok (Rs80, three hours), Namchi (Rs40, one hour), Pelling (Rs80, three hours) and Legship (Rs30, one hour); for Yuksom, change at Legship.

Around Ravangla

RALANG

At Ralang, 13km below Ravangla, the splendid 1995 **Palchen Choeling Monastic Institute** (New Ralang Gompa) is home to about 200 Kagyu-order monks. Arrive early morning or around 3pm to hear them chanting in mesmerising unison. There's a 9m-high golden statue of the historical Buddha in the main hall, and locally the gompa is famous for elaborate butter sculptures. At November's very impressive **Mahakala dance** the dancers wear masks representing the Great Protector and chase away negative energy. Ask to peek inside the room where the amazing costumes are stored.

About 1.5km downhill on the same road is peaceful **Old Ralang Gompa**, established in 1768.

A chartered taxi to Ralang costs around Rs350 from Ravangla (return with two hours' wait).

BON MONASTERY

Beside the main Legship road, 5.5km from central Ravangla, small but fascinating **Yung Drung Kundrak Lingbon** is the only Bon monastery in Sikkim. The Bon faith preceded Buddhism in Tibet. Unusually for Sikkim, non-flash photography is allowed inside, but check first. Daily *pujas* are 5am and 4pm.

MAENAM HILL

A steep three- to four-hour hiking trail leads from the Ravangla–Ralang road to the top of **Maenam Hill** (3150m) through the rhododendrons and magnolia blooms of the **Maenam Wildlife Sanctuary**. The views are wonderful and you just might see rare red pandas and monal pheasants (Sikkim's state bird). A guide is useful to avoid getting lost in the forest on your return. Longer treks continue to **Borong** village.

GEYZING, TIKJUK & LEGSHIP
☎ 03595

The following three towns have little to offer a visitor apart from a permit extension at Tikjuk and transport changes at Geyzing. Geyzing is West Sikkim's capital, but for permit extensions you need Tikjuk, half way to Pelling.

Tikjuk

This is the District Administrative Centre for West Sikkim. Permits can be extended here at the **Superintendent of Police office** (☎ 250763; side wing 3rd fl; ⏲ 10am-4pm Mon-Sat, closed 2nd Sat of month).

Geyzing (Gyashaling)
elev 1552m

Apart from its vaguely interesting Sunday market, Geyzing is most useful as West Sikkim's transport hub.

For a pleasantly peaceful accommodation alternative, go 2.3km towards Sakyong for the **Tashigang Resort** (☎ 250340; www.tashigang resort.com; s Rs2700-3700, d Rs2900-3900), which offers magnificently wide views from a secluded ridgetop. Rooms are wood-panelled, giving off a pleasant pine-fresh aroma, some have balconies and there's no extra cost for those with a view. Go for room Nos 201, 301 or 302.

SNT buses go to Jorethang (Rs50, two hours, 8am) and Siliguri (Rs105, five hours, 8am). Frequent shared jeeps go to Jorethang

(Rs55, 1½ hours), Legship (Rs25, 30 minutes), Pelling (Rs20, 20 minutes), Tashiding (Rs55, 1½ hours) and Yuksom (Rs60, 2½ hours). Several serve Gangtok (Rs120, seven to nine hours, 6.15am), Ravangla (Rs60, one hour, 11.30am) and Siliguri (Rs135, four hours, 7am and 12.30pm).

Legship

When no other transport is available, especially to or from Tashiding, try connecting here. Should you get stranded, **Hotel Trishna** (☎ 250887; d/tr Rs200/300) is simple, with private bathrooms but bucket hot water, plenty of greenery and a rooftop terrace.

PELLING
☎ 03595 / elev 2083m

Pelling's raison d'être is its stride-stopping view of Khangchendzonga at dawn. It's not so much a town as a 2km string of tourist hotels, but don't be put off. The view *is* worth it. Despite hordes of visitors, locals remain surprisingly unjaded, and the best budget hotels

INFORMATION		
ATM	1	B2
Internet Cafe	2	B2
Tourist Office	3	B2
SIGHTS & ACTIVITIES		
Dolphin Tours	(see 7)	
SLEEPING 🛏		
Hotel Garuda	4	B2
Hotel Haven	5	A2
Hotel Kabur	6	B2
Hotel Parodzong	7	A2
Hotel Rabdentse Residency	8	A1
Hotel Simvo	9	A2
Hotel Sonamchen	10	A2
Newa Regency	11	A1
Norbu Ghang Resort	12	A2
Touristo Hotel	13	A1
EATING 🍴		
Taatopani Bar and Restaurant	14	B2
SHOPPING 🛍		
Rural Artisan Marketing Centre	15	B2
TRANSPORT		
Father Tours	16	B2
Shared Jeeps to Geyzing	17	B2
Simvo Tours & Travels	18	B2
SNT Counter	19	A1

SIKKIM

are great for meeting fellow travellers. The **helipad** gives magnificent panoramic views.

Orientation & Information

Pelling is nominally divided into Upper, Middle and Lower areas, though these effectively merge. A focal point of Upper Pelling is a small roundabout where the main road from Geyzing turns 180 degrees in front of Hotel Garuda. At the same point, minor roads branch south to Dentam and southwest to the helipad and **tourist office** (☎ 9434630876; 🕑 9am-5pm Dec-Feb & Jun-Aug, 8am-8pm Sep-Nov & Mar-May). A useful website is www.gopelling. com. Opposite the Hotel Garuda is an ATM and a few doors down an **internet cafe** (per hr Rs30; 🕑 7am-7pm).

Tours

Hotel Garuda (below; tours per day per 8-10 person jeep Rs1500-1600), **Simvo Tours & Travels** (☎ 258549; day tour per person/jeep Rs175/1600), **Dolphin Tours** (☎ 250621; Hotel Parodzong; jeep trips Dec-Feb & Jun-Aug/Sep-Nov & Mar-May Rs1200/2000) and many hotels plus several other agencies offer one-day tours. A popular choice visits Yuksom via Khecheopalri Lake and three waterfalls.

Sleeping

Budget

The Garuda and Kabur are backpacker specialists. Others are just cheap local hotels.

Hotel Garuda (☎ 258319; dm Rs60, d Rs250-350) A backpacker favourite with clean, unsophisticated rooms, unbeatable Khangchendzonga views from the roof and a cosy Tibetan-style bar-restaurant ideal for meeting other travellers. Tours (above) are good value and guests receive a handy schematic guide map.

ourpick **Hotel Kabur** (☎ 9735945598, 258504; r Rs150-600) Entry is via the top floor, which is a delightful restaurant fronted by a wooden balcony crowded with potted plants while, several floors down, a veranda and sun beds look out onto the mountains. Great-value rooms have cute wicker lamps, towels, soap, toilet paper and heaters in winter – all usually absent in rooms of this price. Rooms have TV with CNN, BBC and Star Movies. If you need to know something, do something or go somewhere, the owner, Deepen, is the person to ask. Local tours for up to six people cost Rs1800 per vehicle.

Hotel Haven (☎ 258238; d Rs400-700) Choose view rooms 501 or 502, which are big, very clean

and not cursed with carpets. Other rooms costing the same aren't nearly as good.

Hotel Parodzong (☎ 258239; r Rs400-1000) No-nonsense good-value rooms have clean squat toilets and water heaters. From those facing north you can see Khangchendzonga from your bed, albeit across a communal walkway terrace. Out of season prices drop by 50%.

Midrange & Top End

Most of Pelling's hotels are midrangers catering primarily to domestic tourists. Rates typically drop 30% in low season and are highly negotiable during low occupancy. Midrange hotels charge a 10% service charge.

Hotel Simvo (☎ 258347; d Rs500-1400) Down steps beside the Hotel Sonamchen and with similar fine views. The Simvo's upper, and more expensive, rooms are its best; the acceptable cheapies on the bottom floors aren't as dingy as the corridors might suggest.

Hotel Sonamchen (☎ 258606; www.sikkiminfo .net/sonamchen; s/d from Rs750/1000) A magnificently decorated lobby greets you but that's the best you get. Nonetheless, most rooms – even on the cheapest bottom floor – have truly superb Khangchendzonga views, but the upstairs rooms are overpriced.

Newa Regency (☎ 258596; www.hotelnewaregency .com; s/d from Rs2000/2150) Pelling's most stylish choice is a triangular slice of modern architecture decorated with Sikkimese touches, notably in the charming 1st-floor sitting room. The bar has an outside terrace. Front rooms like 201 have balconies and the best views.

Norbu Ghang Resort (☎ 258272; www.norbughang resort.com; s/d from Rs2500/2700; 🔀) A spread of pretty, self-contained cottages dots the hillside of this resort. All have Khangchendzonga views; lie in bed at dawn with a cup of tea and watch the sun wash the mountain in gold.

Elgin Mount Pandim (☎ 250756; mtpandim@elgin hotels.com; s/d from Rs4800/5100; 🔀 🖳) Pelling's most aristocratic hotel is a 10-minute stroll from Pemayangtse gompa, with arguably the best mountainscape viewpoint in all of Sikkim. The fairy godmother of renovation has waved her wand over the property and this former state-owned hotel now twinkles. Be prepared for serious cosseting.

Other options:

Touristo Hotel (☎ 258206; s Rs350-700, d Rs475-900) The best rooms have good Khangchendzonga views.

Hotel Rabdentse Residency (☎ 258612; rabdentse .pelling@yahoo.co.in; s/d from Rs750/850) Downstairs

PADMASAMBHAVA

Known as Guru Rinpoche in Tibetan, Sibaji in Nepali/Hindi or Padmasambhava in Sanskrit, this 8th-century 'second Buddha' is credited with introducing Tantric Buddhism to Tibet. Padmasambhava statues and murals are common throughout Sikkim. In his most classic form, he's usually shown sitting cross-legged with wild, staring eyes and a *tirsul* (a trident-headed staff) tucked into the folds of his left sleeve. This spears a trio of heads in progressive stages of decomposition representing the three *kayas* (aspects of enlightenment). Meanwhile Padmasambhava's right hand surreptitiously gives a two-fingered salute from behind a *dorje* (mini sceptre).

Padmasambhava has seven other manifestations. The most striking of these, Dorje Bhurpa Vajrakila, shows him with three frightful heads and a lusty wench gyrating on his groin.

behind the Touristo. Obliging staff and a great attention to detail.

Eating & Drinking

Pelling's best dining is in the hotels. The Norbu Ghang, Kabur and Rabdentse Residency serve particularly good food, while the Garuda's a great place for a beer and a travel chat.

Taatopani Bar & Restaurant (Middle Pelling; mains Rs50-90; ⏰ 10am-10pm Dec-Feb & Jun-Aug, to 12.30am Sep-Nov & Mar-May) has a long thin terrace bar tacked onto its restaurant. Mocktails are Rs90, cocktails Rs165 and beer Rs70 to Rs80; a band entertains during the high season.

Shopping

Rural Artisan Marketing Centre (⏰ 8am-7pm), just downhill from the tourist office, sells local crafts, traditional costumes and organic produce such as tea, cardamom and walnuts.

Getting There & Away

SNT buses run to Gangtok (Rs85, 5½ hours, 7am and 12.30pm) via Ravangla (Rs70, two hours) and Siliguri (Rs150, 4½ hours, 7am) via Jorethang (Rs40, 2½ hours). Booking ahead is advised at the **SNT counter** (☎ 250707; Hotel Pelling; ⏰ 7am-6pm Dec-Feb & Jun-Aug, 7am-9pm Sep-Nov & Mar-May) in Lower Pelling from where the buses depart.

The frequency of shared jeeps increases as the season progresses but year-round rides depart early morning and around noon to Gangtok (Rs160, five hours) and at 8am to Siliguri (Rs155, 4½ hours). Simvo Tours & Travels (opposite) also offers high-season Sumos to Darjeeling (Rs175, five hours, 8am). **Father Tours** (☎ 258219) has jeeps to Kalimpong (Rs135, four hours, 6.15am).

If nothing is available ex-Pelling, change in Geyzing. Shared jeeps to Geyzing (Rs20,

20 minutes) leave when full (around twice an hour) from near Hotel Garuda. They pass close to Pemayangtse, Rabdentse and Tikjuk District Administrative Centre.

For Khecheopalri Lake (Rs60) or Yuksom (Rs60) jeeps start from Geyzing and, although booking ex-Pelling is sometimes possible, it's often easier simply to join a day-trip tour and throw away the return ticket. A taxi for a day trip to Khecheopalri Lake, Pemayangtse Gompa and Rabdentse will cost Rs1200.

AROUND PELLING
Pemayangtse Gompa
elev 2105m

Literally translated as 'Perfect Sublime Lotus', the 1705 **Pemayangtse** (Indian/foreigner Rs10/20; ⏰ 7am-4pm Dec-Feb & Jun-Aug, 7am-6pm Sep-Nov & Mar-May) is one of Sikkim's oldest and most significant Nyingmapa gompas. Magnificently set on a hilltop overlooking the Rabdentse ruins, the atmospheric compound is ringed by gardens and traditional monks' cottages walled in stone. The contrastingly colourful prayer hall is beautifully proportioned, its doors and windows painted with Tibetan motifs. The statue is of Padmasambhava in his awful form as Dorje Bhurpa Vajrakila with multiple heads and arms. Upstairs, fierce-looking statues depict all eight of Padmasambhava's incarnations. On the top floor, **Zandog Palri** is an astounding seven-tiered model of Padmasambhava's heavenly abode, handmade over five laborious years by a single dedicated lama.

In February/March impressive *chaam* dances celebrating Losar culminate with the unfurling of a giant embroidered scroll and the zapping of evil demons with a great fireball.

Pemayangtse is 25 minutes' walk (1.3km) from Upper Pelling. The signposted turnoff from the Pelling–Geyzing road is near an obvious stupa.

SIKKIM

Rabdentse

The royal capital of Sikkim from 1670 to 1814, the now-ruined **Rabdentse** (admission free; ☻ dawn-dusk) consists of chunky wall-stubs with a few inset inscription stones. These would look fairly unremarkable were they not situated on such an utterly fabulous viewpoint ridge. The entrance to the site is around 3km from Upper Pelling. From the site's ornate yellow gateway, the ruins are a further 15 minutes' hike around a pond then across a forested hill.

Sangachoeling Gompa

The second-oldest gompa in Sikkim, Sangachoeling has some beautiful murals and a magnificent ridgetop setting. It's a steep 3km walk from Pelling starting along the track that veers left where the asphalted road rises to Pelling's new helipad.

A jungle trek continues 10km beyond Sangachoeling to **Rani Dhunga** (Queen's Rock), supposedly the scene of an epic Ramayana battle between Rama and 10-headed demon king Ravana. Take a guide.

Darap

For a relaxing day trip from Pelling, walk down to gently pleasant Darap village using the web of village footpaths through small rural hamlets. Khangchendzonga should be visible to your right most of the way, at least if the clouds are magnanimous. Hotel Garuda (p188) offers guided walks with a ride home afterwards.

THE MONASTERY LOOP
☎ 03595

The three-day 'Monastic Trek' from Pelling to Tashiding via Khecheopalri Lake remains possible; however, improvements to the Pelling–Yuksom road means dust clouds get stirred up by ever-more frequent tourist jeeps, diminishing the appeal of hiking the trek's on-road sections. Consider catching a ride to wonderful Yuksom (via Khecheopalri Lake using tour jeeps) and hiking from there to Tashiding (one day, no permit required). Even if you don't trek further than the Yak Restaurant, Yuksom is a delightful place to unwind.

Pelling to Yuksom

Tourist jeeps tend to stop at several relatively lacklustre time-filler sites. **Rimbi** and **Khangchendzonga Falls** are best after rains while **Phamrong Falls** are impressive any time. Although it's several kilometres up a dead-end spur road, virtually all Yuksom-bound tours visit Khecheopalri, dropping you for about half an hour at a car park that's a five-minute stroll from the little lake.

KHECHEOPALRI LAKE
elev 1951m

Pronounced catch-a-perry, this holy lake is highly revered by Sikkimese Buddhists who believe that birds assiduously remove any leaves from its surface. During **Khachoedpalri Mela** (March/April), butter lamps are floated out across the lake. Prayer wheels line the lake's jetty, which is backed by fluttering prayer flags and Tibetan inscriptions, but the setting, ringed with forested hills, is serene rather than dramatic. To appreciate this you could stay overnight and visit once the tourists have left. If you trek up to the **Dupok** viewpoint (ask at the Trekkers Hut) you'll see the outline of the lake as a footprint.

Trekkers Hut Guest House (☎ 9733076995; dm/tw without bathroom Rs50/150) is an isolated pale-green building about 300m back down the access road from the car park. The government owns the Hut and doesn't invest enough in its upkeep, but the tenant, the helpful Mr Teng, does what he can. So the rooms are basic but clean and share several bathrooms. You can get tongba (Rs30), filling meals (Rs50), trekking information and sometimes birdwatching or culturally themed guided hikes. If sleeping over, you'll have time to trek up to **Khecheopalri Gompa** above the lake.

Around the car park is a Buddhist nunnery (behind a shrine-style gateway), a small shop, and the very basic Jigme Restaurant serving tea, *momos* and chow mein. There's no village. We've heard, subsequent to our research, that the gompa operates the **Palas Guest House** (☎ 9832471253) where meditation is also taught. Facing the end of the car park take the small path wending upwards from the left-hand side.

Shared jeeps to Geyzing (Rs70, two hours) leave the lake at about 6am travelling via Pelling (23km).

The trail to Yuksom (9km, three to five hours) descends to the main road, emerging near the Khangchendzonga Falls. After a suspension bridge, follow the shortcut trail uphill to meet the Yuksom road, about 2km below Yuksom village. Ask at the Trekkers Hut for detailed directions.

Yuksom

☎ 03595 / elev 1780m

Loveable little Yuksom is historic, charming and unspoilt. Domestic tourists avoid it as it lacks the mountain views and it hasn't become a travellers' ghetto like Hampi or Manali. The town is the main trailhead for the Khangchendzonga Trek (p192); otherwise it's an ideal place for day walks. The **Community Information Centre** (internet per hr Rs50; ☺ 10am-1pm & 3-5pm) offers internet connections in an unlikely hut near Kathok Lake. Opposite is a small shop selling souvenirs and Tibetan-style woolly socks.

A number of trekking agencies in Yuksom, such as **Mountain Tours & Treks** (☎ 241248; www .sherpatreks.in), operate on the Khangchendzonga trek. Prices are around US$40 per person per day assuming a group of four.

SIGHTS

Yuksom means 'meeting place of the three lamas', referring to the trio of Tibetan holy men who crowned the first chogyal of Sikkim here in 1641. The site is now **Norbugang Park**, which contains a prayer house, big prayer wheel, chorten (stupa) and the supposedly original **Coronation Throne** (Norbugang). Standing beneath a vast cryptomeria pine, it looks something like an ancient Olympic medal podium made of whitewashed stone. Just in front is a spooky footprint fused into the stone, believed to be that of one of the crowning lamas: lift the little wooden guard-plank and you can see a distinct impression of sole and toes.

Walking to Norbugang Park past Hotel Tashi Gang you'll pass the murky **Kathok Lake**, from which anointing waters were taken for the original coronation.

When Yuksom was Sikkim's capital, a royal palace complex known as **Tashi Tenka** sat on a slight ridge to the south with superb almost 360-degree views. Today barely a stone remains but the views are still superb. To find the site take the small path marked by two crumbling little whitewashed stupas near the village school. The site is less than five minutes' walk away through tiny

SIKKIM

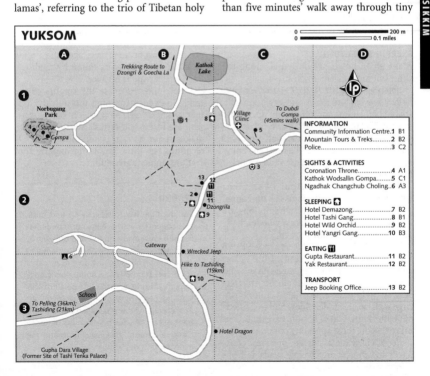

YUKSOM

0 ———— 200 m
0 ———— 0.1 miles

INFORMATION
Community Information Centre.**1** B1
Mountain Tours & Treks..........**2** B2
Police....................................**3** C2

SIGHTS & ACTIVITIES
Coronation Throne....................**4** A1
Kathok Wodsallin Gompa........**5** C1
Ngadhak Changchub Choling..**6** A3

SLEEPING
Hotel Demazong.....................**7** B2
Hotel Tashi Gang....................**8** B1
Hotel Wild Orchid...................**9** B2
Hotel Yangri Gang.................**10** B3

EATING
Gupta Restaurant...................**11** B2
Yak Restaurant......................**12** B2

TRANSPORT
Jeep Booking Office...............**13** B2

Gupha Dara, a subhamlet of around a dozen semitraditional houses.

High on the ridge above Yuksom, **Dubdi Gompa** is set in beautifully tended gardens behind three coarsely hewn stupas. Established in 1701, it's likely to be Sikkim's oldest monastery but the prayer house looks vastly newer. There's no resident monk but there should be a caretaker on site during the daytime. Start the steep 45-minute climb from Yuksom's village clinic; the way rises through thickets of trumpet lilies and some lovely mature forest. Beware of leeches.

Yuksom has two photogenic new gompas. **Kathok Wodsallin Gompa** near Hotel Tashi Gang has an impressively stern statue of Guru Padmasambhava surrounded by a collection of yogis, gurus and lamas in glass-fronted compartments. Similarly colourful is **Ngadhak Changchub Choling**, accessed through an ornate gateway opposite Hotel Yangri Gang. A many-handed and -headed Buddha gazes benignly at the monks, who perform *puja* here at 6am and 7pm.

The trail to Dzongri and Goecha La passes the police post where trekking permits are carefully checked and then continues uphill past the driveway to the Hotel Tashi Gang

SLEEPING & EATING
Many small hotels are dotted all along the short but meandering main street.

Hotel Demazong (☎ 241215, 9775473687; dm Rs100, r without bathroom Rs200-500) A budget option with shared bathrooms and off-season discounts.

Hotel Wild Orchid (☎ 241212; tw/tr without bathroom Rs150/225) This neat, clean half-timbered house is rather ragged but the most charming budget option. Bathrooms are shared, bucket hot water Rs10.

Hotel Yangri Gang (☎ 241217; d Rs350-800, without bathroom Rs200) Basement rooms are functional concrete cubes, but the upstairs options are airy with clean wooden floors, wooden half-panelling and good hot showers.

Hotel Tashi Gang (☎ 241202; s/d from Rs850/1100) The colours of the bedspreads, frilly yellow and red ceiling curtains in the restaurant, and *thangkas* in some bedrooms all show a reference to Sikkimese monastic art. Rooms are large with clean wooden floors and well fitted-out bathrooms. Out of season, bargaining can make this the most appealing option in town.

Beers, chow mein, curries, breakfast cornflakes and *thukpa* are cheaply available from a pair of atmospheric restaurants, Yak and Gupta, side by side at the bus/jeep stand. Both have an outside get-around-and-be-friendly table with thatched roof, but Gupta has the more pleasant interior. Mains are Rs35 to Rs70. Eat early as doors close by 8pm.

GETTING THERE & AWAY
Around 6.30am, several shared jeeps leave for Jorethang (Rs90, four hours) via Tashiding (Rs40, 1½ hours), Gangtok (Rs150, six hours) and Geyzing via Pelling (Rs60, approximately 2½ hours). Best to book at the hut opposite the Yak restaurant the day before.

Dzongri & Goecha La – The Khangchendzonga Trek
For guided groups with permits, Yuksom is the starting point of Sikkim's classic trek to Goecha La, a 4940m pass with quite fabulous views of Khangchendzonga.

Taking seven to 10 days, trek costs start at US$40 to US$55 per person per day (assuming a group of four), including food, guides, porters and yaks. For more information, see the route notes and boxed text on opposite.

Trekking agencies will sort out the permits. Paperwork must be done in Gangtok, but given two or three days, agents in Pelling or Yuksom can organise things by sending a fixer to the capital for you.

Don't underestimate the rigours of the trek. Don't hike too high too quickly: altitude sickness (see p349) usually strikes those who are fittest and fastest. Starting at dawn makes sense, as rain is common in the afternoons, spoiling views and making trail sections annoyingly muddy.

WARNING

For the final leg to Goecha La and back, some agencies will have their groups depart from Thangsing at 1am to avoid camping at Lamuni because they do not carry camping equipment. This is unadvisable as it makes for a very long day (12 hours plus stops), at high altitude, and the first part involves walking over rocky ground by torchlight in the dark, where a sprained ankle might be the least of your troubles. Far better to camp at Lamuni, take your time and see everything in daylight.

KHANGCHENDZONGA TREK SCHEDULE		
Stage/Day	Route	Duration (hr)
1	Yuksom to Tsokha, via Bakhim	6-7
2	Acclimatisation day at Tsokha	1 day
3	Tsokha to Dzongri	4-5
4	Acclimatisation day at Dzongri, or continue to Kokchuran	1 day
5	Dzongri (or Kokchuran) to Lamuni, via Thangsing	6-7
6	Lamuni to Goecha La, then down to Thangsing	8-9
7	Thangsing to Tsokha	6-7
8	Tsokha to Yuksom	5-6

ROUTE NOTES

The route initially follows the Rathong Valley through unspoilt forests then ascends steeply to **Bakhim** (2740m) and the rustic village of **Tsokha** (3050m), where spending two nights helps with acclimatisation.

The next stage climbs to pleasant meadows around **Dzongri** (4025m). Consider another acclimatisation day here and stroll up to **Dablakang** or **Dzongri La** (4550m, four-hour round trip) for fabulous views of Mt Pandim (6691m).

From Dzongri, the trail drops steeply to **Kokchuran** then follows the river to **Thangsing** (3840m). Next day takes you to camping at **Lamuni** 15 minutes before **Samiti Lake** (4200m) from where a next-morning assault takes you to head-spinning **Goecha La** (4940m) for those incredible views of Khangchendzonga. Readers have recommended an alternative viewpoint reached by climbing an hour up from the left side of Samiti Lake.

The return is by essentially the same route but with shortcuts that are sometimes a little overgrown. Alternatively at Dzongri you could cut south for about a week following the **Singalila Ridge** along the Nepal–Sikkim border to emerge at **Uttarey**, from where public transport runs to Jorethang.

SLEEPING

There are trekkers' huts at Bakhim, Tsokha, Dzongri, Kokchuran and Thangsing. Most have neither furniture nor mattresses; you just cuddle up with fellow trekkers on the floor. Bring a mat and a good sleeping bag. Huts sometimes get booked out during high trekking season, so some camping might be involved.

EATING

You (or your porter) will need to carry supplies, but limited food (and tongba) is available at Dzongri.

Yuksom to Tashiding Trek

Starting in Yuksom is easier than coming the other way for this long but highly rewarding one-day trek. No trekking permits are required.

Start down the pathway between hotels Yangri Gang and Penathang. The most attractive but longest route leads around behind the **Phamrong Falls** (heard but not seen) then rises to **Tsong**, where the trail divides. The upper route leads up fairly steeply to lonely **Hongri Gompa**, a small, unusually unpainted ancient monastery building with a superlative ridge-top location. Local folklore claims the gompa was moved here from a higher spot where monks kept being ravaged by yeti.

To this point the route is relatively easy to follow, with stone grips. But descending from Hongri there are slippery patches with lurking leeches. At **Nessa** hamlet, finding the way can be mildly confusing. A few minutes beyond in attractive **Pokhari Dara** the trail divides again beside the village shop. Descending takes you the more direct way to Tashiding. Continuing along the ridge brings you to **Sinon Gompa** very high above Tashiding. The final approach to that monastery has some fascinating, ancient **mani walls** (stone walls with sacred inscriptions) but the descent to Tashiding is long and steep by the shortcut paths or almost 10km of long switchbacks by road.

Tashiding
elev 1490m

Little Tashiding is just a single, sloping spur-street forking north off the Yuksom–Legship road, but its south-facing views are wide and impressive. Walking 400m south from the junction towards Legship takes you down past a series of **mani walls** with bright Tibetan inscriptions to a colourful **gateway**. A 2.4km uphill driveable track leads to a car park from

SIKKIM

where a sometimes-slippery footpath leads up steeply between an avenue of prayer flags to the ancient **Tashiding Gompa**, about 15 minutes' walk away.

Founded in 1641 by one of the three Yuksom lamas (see p191), the monastery's five colourful religious buildings are strung out between more functional monks' quarters. Notice the giant-sized prayer wheel with Tibetan script picked out in gilt. Beautifully proportioned, the four-storey **main prayer hall** has a delicate filigree topknot and looks noble from a distance. On closer inspection most of the exterior decor is rather coarse, but wonderfully wide views from here across a semiwild flower garden encompass the whole valley towards Ravangla.

Beyond the last monastic building, a curious compound contains dozens of white chortens, including the **Thong-Wa-Rang-Dol**, said to wash away the sins of anyone who gazes upon it. Smaller but more visually exciting is the golden **Kench Chorgi Lorde** stupa. Propped all around are engraved stones bearing Buddhist prayers; at the back of the compound is the engraver's lean-to.

In January or February, the monastery celebrates the **Bumchu** festival during which lamas gingerly open a sacred pot. Then, judging from the level of holy water within, they make all-important predictions about the coming year.

Tashiding village's three basic, friendly hotels all have shared bathrooms. **Hotel Blue Bird** (☎ 243248; r without bathroom Rs100), at the bottom of the street, is the cheapest but more decrepit. The neater **Mt Siniolchu Guest House** (☎ 243211, 9733092480; r without bathroom Rs100-200) is a better option. **New Tashiding Lodge** (☎ 243249; Legship Rd; tr without bathroom Rs200), 300m south of the market, has fine views from Rooms 3, 4 and 5 and even better ones from the shared bathroom.

Shared jeeps to Gangtok (Rs120, four hours) via Legship (Rs30, one hour) pass the main junction, mostly between 6.30am and 8am. A few jeeps to Yuksom pass through during early afternoon but if you want an early start it's better to go via Legship or Geyzing.

NORTH SIKKIM

☎ 03592

The biggest attractions in North Sikkim are the idyllic Yumthang and Tsopta Valleys. Reaching them and anywhere north of

Singhik requires a special permit but that's easy to obtain (see p175), although foreign visitors are only allowed to travel in North Sikkim in groups of two or more. It's perfectly possible to visit Phodong and Mangan/Singhik independently using public jeeps but they can also be conveniently seen during brief stops on any Yumthang tour and at no extra cost.

GANGTOK TO SINGHIK
The narrow but mostly well-paved 31ANHWay clings to steep wooded slopes high above the Teesta River, occasionally descending in long coils of hairpins to a bridge photogenically draped in prayer flags, only to coil right back up again on the other side. If driving, consider brief stops at Tashi Viewpoint (p179), Kabi Lunchok, Phensang and the Seven Sisters waterfall

Kabi Lunchok
This atmospheric glade, 17km north of Gangtok, decorated with memorial stones is the site of a 13th-century peace treaty between the chiefs of the Lepcha and Bhutia peoples. They swore a blood brotherhood until the River Rangit ran dry and Khangchendzonga ceased to exist.

Phensang
This small 240-year-old monastery belonging to the Nyingmapa sect has lower- and upper-floor prayer halls that are beautifully decorated. It's all recent, though, as the monastery was rebuilt after a 1957 fire. The Chaam festival is celebrated here on the 28th and 29th days of the Tibetan 10th month, usually December.

Seven Sisters Waterfall
A multistage cascade cuts a chasm here above a roadside cardamom grove and plummets into a rocky pool and then a ravine. An ancient girder bridge spans the ravine, 30km north of Gangtok, while on the south side there's a welcome chai shop.

Phodong
elev 1814m
The little strip of roadside restaurants at Phodong make it a popular lunch stop. Simple rooms are available at the **Hotel Yak & Yeti** (☎ 9434357905; dm Rs100; d without bathroom Rs200-250), where English is spoken.

NORTH SIKKIM TOUR TIPS

■ A group size of four or five people is ideal for sharing costs while not overfilling the jeep.

■ To find jeep-share partners, try hanging out in the cafe at New Modern Central Lodge (Gangtok; p179) around 6pm a few days before you plan to travel. There's no fixed system, just ask other travellers.

■ Less than four days is too rushed to comfortably visit both Yumthang/Lachung and Lachen. Three-night/four-day tours start at Rs2500 per person for groups of five, depending on accommodation standards.

■ Leave Gangtok early on the first day: it's a shame to arrive in the dark.

■ Your (obligatory) 'guide' is actually more of a translator. Don't assume he'll stop at all potential points of interest without prodding.

■ Bring a torch for inevitable power cuts.

■ Don't miss tasting tongba (tiny extra cost).

About 1km southeast near the Km39 post, a 15-minute walk along a very degraded former road leads to the **Phodong Gompa** (established in 1740) belonging to the Kagupa sect. The beautiful two-storey prayer hall contains extensive murals and a large statue of the 9th Karmapa. A rear room contains a hidden statue of Mahakla, a protective deity of the monastery.

Walk on another 30 minutes to the much more atmospheric and peaceful **Labrang Gompa** (established in 1884). Its prayer-hall murals repeat the same Padmasambhava pose 1022 times. Upstairs a fearsome depiction of Guru Padmasambhava sports a necklace of severed heads. *Chaam* dances take place in early December.

Phodong to Singhik

North Sikkim's district headquarters, **Mangan** (Km67 post) proudly declares itself to be the 'Large Cardamom Capital of the World'. On a sharp bend some 1.5km beyond, stupas, blackened by weather, mark a small footpath; a three-minute descent leads to a panoramic **viewpoint**.

Apart from the stunningly magnificent scenery there's nothing specific to stop for between Mangan and Lachen or Lachung, which are the places where visitors stop for the night.

Singhik

This small town has two decent accommodation choices, both with more great views. Set in a roadside flower garden, **Friendship Guest House** (☎ 234278; s/d Rs250/420) has rooms

with shared bathrooms within the home of an adorable Sikkimese family (who speak no English).

Singhik Tourist Lodge (☎ 234287; Km 71; d Rs580) is a clean if slightly musty hotel where rooms have heaters and private bathrooms with geysers. There's a restaurant, too, but it's usually only open when groups are prebooked (through the tourist office in Gangtok).

Singhik is a Rs62 taxi ride from Mangan, which is served by regular jeeps from Gangtok.

BEYOND SINGHIK

With relevant permits and an organised tour you can continue north beyond Singhik. At Chungthang, the next settlement, the Teesta divides into the Lachung Chu (valley) and the Lachen Chu.

Accommodation is available in Lachung and Lachen, with two more basic options in Thanggu. We have listed a few favourites but normally your tour agencies will preselect for you. Some family places stay open on the off chance of passing Indian tourists, but most lodges close up when there's no prebooked group due.

Cheaper hotels tend to have a mixed bag of rooms whose prices are the same whether or not the room has geyser, shower, heating, window or balcony. It's pot luck, so try to see a few different rooms even if you can't choose your hotel.

Lachen and Lachung are both Lepcha villages with a unique form of local democracy in which the *pipon* (headman) is elected every year.

Lachung Chu

LACHUNG

elev 3000m

Soaring rock-pinnacled valley walls embroidered with long ribbons of waterfall surround the scattered village of Lachung. To appreciate the full drama of its setting, take the metal cantilever bridge across the wild Yumthang River to the Sanchok side then climb 1.5km along the Katao road for great views from the **Lachung Gompa** (established 1880). The gompa's refined murals include one section of original paintings (inner left wall as you enter) and its twin giant prayer wheels chime periodically. Two large dragons keep guard above the entrance. **Internet** (per hr Rs30; ⏰ 10am-4pm Mon-Sat) is available in a room across the other side of the football field of the local secondary school.

Mt Katao, nearly 30km beyond, is popular with Indian tourists, who drive up to the top to play in the snow. However, it remains off-limits to foreign tourists.

Many hotels are dotted around Lachung, with the most convenient concentration around Faka Bazaar just over the bridge. Rates start at Rs300 for the most basic, but will double in high season. Many outwardly modern places maintain traditional Tibetan-style wood-fire stoves and can churn salt-butter tea for you in a traditional churn plunger device.

Open year-round, the family-run and friendly **Sila Inn Lodge** (☎ 214808; r without bathroom Rs300-500) has a typically mixed bag of rooms above a friendly hostelry-restaurant. Best rooms are on the top floor.

Nearby hotels **Le Coxy** (www.nivalink.com/lecoxy resort) and Sonam Palgey are more upmarket.

In a side lane around 3km south of Lachung, a brilliantly colourful flight of fancy rises like a fairy-tale Tibetan monastery. Staying at the **Modern Residency** (Tagsing Retreat; ☎ 214888; Singring Village; d Rs2500) is one great advantage of taking a tour with Modern Treks & Tours (p179). Rooms have local design features and are comfortable, though walk-in prices are very steep. Even if you don't stay, the building is well worth visiting. One upper floor has a veritable mini-museum and the top-floor roof, above the prayer room, offers magnificent views across the valley.

YUMTHANG VALLEY

The main point of coming to Lachung is continuing 23km further north to admire the majestic Yumthang Valley, which starts some 10km after leaving Lachung. This point is also the entry to the Singba Rhododendron Sanctuary where both vegetation and landscape change from the preceding steep-sided Lachung Chu. The valley widens and flattens, and is spotted with stands of conifers festooned with woollen strands of lichen. Stumps of trees from indiscriminate felling flank the roadway and mosses cover the bare rocks in green, while everywhere rhododendron bushes flourish. From March to early May this valley lives up to its other name, the Valley of Flowers, as primulas, rhododendrons and a host of other plants burst into flower and carpet the valley floor.

At the 23km point there are a number of snack shacks that open up in the high season and where the Sikkim tourism authority is building a guesthouse. On the other side of the river a grimy, unlit, two-sq-metre pool in a rubbish-ringed hut presents itself as **hot springs**. The real drama starts about 1km north of here down by the riverbank. Weather permitting, you should have 360-degree views of an utterly magnificent Himalayan scene: glaciers, spiky peaks and a veritable candelabra of white jagged mountains rising towards Tibet. Lucky Indian tourists are allowed to venture a further 23km to Yume Samdong.

Lachen Chu

LACHEN

elev 2750m

Until recently Lachen was an untouched, traditional Lepcha village. That's changing fast with pretty roadside houses being progressively replaced by concrete house-hotels. Nonetheless, alleyways remain sprinkled with old wooden homes on sturdy stone bases, and Tibetan-style constructions with colourful, faceted window frames. Logs are stacked everywhere for winter fuel.

Lachen Gompa is about 15 minutes' walk above the town. While the grey brick exterior is unappealing no interior surface has been left uncovered. All display different manifestations of Guru Padmasambhava.

Lachen is the trailhead for expeditionary treks to **Green Lake** along the Yeti-infested **Zemu Glacier** towards Khangchendzonga's northeast face. These require long advance planning and very expensive permits.

If you can choose your accommodation, a great budget option is super-friendly **Bayul Lodge** (tw without bathroom Rs250), whose upper facade is colourfully carved with Tibetan motifs. It's above the tiny video-cinema, beside the post office.

Sinolchu Lodge (☎ 9434356189; d Rs300-400) has the advantage of being open all year. Rooms are small but cosy and the beds piled with thick blankets. It's here that you relish bringing along a sleeping sheet, as there are no bed sheets. Rooms have attached bathrooms but only the dearer rooms have geysers. Otherwise it's bucket hot water.

The **Hotel Sonam Palgey** (www.sonampalgey.com; d Rs3000) is considered the most comfortable place in town.

THANGGU & TSOPTA
elev 4267m

Beyond a sprawling army camp 32km north of Lachen, **Thanggu** has an appealing end-of-the-world feel. It's too high for leeches, there are no phones (mobile or otherwise), the Chinese are only 15km away and the only electricity is solar-generated.

Misleadingly named **Thanggu Resort** (d or tr without bathroom Rs500) is outwardly an ordinary family house incorporating a traditional-styled kitchen, dining area and tongba-drinking den (tongba Rs10). Rooms are simple but two have attached squat toilet and views of the river. Open May to November.

A boulder-strewn moorland stream leads on 2km to tiny **Tsopta**. Just above the tree line, the scenery feels rather like Glencoe (Scotland) but the valley's western horizon has the added drama of a glacier-toothed mountain wall. Yak, dzho (cattle-yak crossbreed) and donkey convoys wander through on missions to supply some of the Indian military's more far-flung outposts way beyond. Indian visitors can continue 30km north to **Gurudongmar Lake** up the Tsopta Valley, but for foreigners the only option is to park by the army post at the bend leading into the valley. Still there's plenty to appreciate. Below is a verdant dried lakebed and to its left a long ridge of high land forested with rhododendrons and conifers. This moraine, left by a glacier, is responsible for damming the Tsopte River and creating the lake. As you return towards Thanggu you'll notice that at one place the dammed river has broken through and descends the moraine in a series of scintillating cascades.

SIKKIM

Northeast States

India's 1947 partition left the Northeast States dangling like a fragile appendage to the main body of the country, way out on the edge of the map and national perception.

The Northeast States only figure in the national consciousness when something dramatic happens. Likewise the region is off the tourist map for most foreign visitors, perhaps because of its lack of a Taj Mahal–style, 'must-see' place. Despite this, the region has many attractions worth seeking out.

The great, flat Brahmaputra valley and its wide muddy river is a traditional Hindu heartland, and is the backdrop to several Krishna tales. Lying mostly within Assam, the valley is home to beautiful tea plantations and national parks with rhinoceroses, elephants and tigers.

In contrast, the mountainous surrounding states are home to Adivasi peoples whose varied cultures and faces have more in common with Burma, China and Tibet than with mainstream India.

Despite the region's attractions, infuriating permits (not required for Assam, Meghalaya or Tripura) and safety worries deter most travellers from visiting the northeast. This makes it a place for adventurers who want something different from their India experience. You'll meet very few foreigners in the region's magnificent national parks. And you'll get vast tracts of fabulous rice fields, tea plantations and mountain scenery all to yourself. A few insurgency campaigns do rumble on, but generally the people here are among the friendliest in the whole subcontinent.

NORTHEAST STATES

HIGHLIGHTS

- Ride through boggy grassland visiting rhinos atop a lumbering elephant in **Kaziranga National Park** (p213)

- Touch the clouds at the 4176m pass of Se La before descending to **Tawang Valley** (p224), Arunachal Pradesh's 'little Tibet'

- Visit intriguing Adivasi villages around **Ziro** (p220) and meet the last of the bizarrely adorned Apatani women

- Gaze down on the plains of Bangladesh from the lofty escarpment around **Cherrapunjee** (Sohra; p243), incised by waterfalls and burrowed into by caves

- Feel as if you've stepped out of India into a different culture and country in Nagaland's **Mon** (p229)

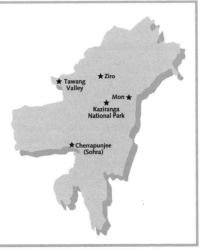

Information

Tourist season is October to April. However, most national parks only open from November and you'll see many more of the big animals if you wait till February.

PERMITS

Permits remain a perennial pain in the arse, being too bureaucratically involved for many foreign visitors. However those who take the trouble will be richly rewarded. Permits are mandatory for Nagaland, Arunachal Pradesh, Mizoram and Manipur, and entry without one is a serious matter. You might just be able to travel independently into Arunachal and Mizoram, but much depends on the officials at each border point. Indian citizens just need an inner line permit, issued with little fuss in Guwahati or Kolkata (p106). The rest of this section applies to foreigners who'll require a Restricted Area Permit (RAP).

Minimum Group Size

Permit applications need a four-person minimum group. Exceptions are Nagaland, for a legally married couple with marriage certificate; and Arunachal Pradesh for a minimum of two people.

In Nagaland and Manipur, authorities may refuse you entry if some people listed on your permit are 'missing', Mizoram doesn't seem to bother and Arunachal Pradesh is now much more relaxed.

Validity & Registration

Permits are valid for 10 days from a specified starting date, but Arunachal now allows 30 days.

You *might* be able to extend your permit, but only in state capitals at the Secretariat, Home Department. Be aware that permits only allow you to visit specified districts, so plan carefully as changing routes might be problematic.

Be sure to make multiple photocopies of your permit to hand in at each checkpoint, police station and hotel.

Registration is compulsory on arrival in the state and for each night in a new location, although your hotel might do that for you. If you're on a tour then your guide will look after this.

Where to Apply

Applications through the **Ministry of Home Affairs** (☎ 011-23385748; Jaisalmer House, 26 Man Singh Rd, Delhi; ✆ inquiries 9-11am Mon-Fri) or the appropriate State House in Delhi can take weeks and end in frustration. Kolkata's **Foreigners' Regional Registration Office** (FRRO; Map p108; ☎ 22837034; 237 AJC Bose Rd; ✆ 11am-5pm Mon-Fri) can issue permits but it seems to want to exclude Tawang from Arunachal, restrict access to Nagaland and not allow you into Mizoram.

The easiest and most reliable way to get permits is through a reputable agency; see the boxed text, p200. Start the application process at least six weeks ahead.

TOURS

Visiting the permit states by tour smooths the bureaucracy but travel is still comparatively slow and rugged. Agencies simply supply a Sumo jeep, guide and driver-cum-mechanic, plus a tent for emergencies. Accommodation and meals in some places can be basic and

---

TRAVELLING SAFELY IN THE NORTHEAST STATES

In recent decades many ethnolinguistic groups have jostled – often violently – to assert themselves in the face of illegal Bangladeshi immigration, governmental neglect and a heavy-handed defence policy. Some want independence from India, others autonomy, yet more are effectively fighting clan or turf wars. Although many Western governments currently advise against travel in Manipur, Tripura, Nagaland and Assam (it might affect your travel insurance), it's worth noting that not all of these states are equally affected. At the time of writing Arunachal Pradesh, most of Assam, Meghalaya, Mizoram, and the tourist areas of Nagaland and Tripura seem the most peaceful.

The problem is that trouble can flare up suddenly and unpredictably. Bombings have hit the normally safe cities of Guwahati (2008), Agartala (2008) and Dimapur (2004) just as they have struck London and Madrid, so the level of danger to travellers is hard to quantify. Communal violence surged in 2008 in northern Assam between the Bodo people and Bangladeshi immigrants, but as most of the tourist sites are south of the Brahmaputra, visitors were not affected.

Still it's wise to keep abreast of latest news with the *Assam Tribune* (www.assamtribune.com) and if you're with a tour group, ensure it is up to date with the latest situation.

TRAVEL AGENCIES ARRANGING PERMITS & TOURS

Agency	Based in	Best for
Himalayan Holidays (p223)	Bomdila	all areas, notably Arunachal
Network Travels (p206)	Guwahati	all areas
Jungle Travels India (p206)	Guwahati	all areas
Serow Travels (p233)	Aizawl	Mizoram
Omega (p233)	Aizawl	Mizoram
Purvi Discovery (p217)	Dibrugarh	Arunachal, Nagaland
Rhino Travels (p206)	Guwahati	all areas
Abor Country Travels (p219)	Itanagar	Arunachal
Tribal Discovery (p227)	Kohima	Nagaland
Alder Tours & Travels (p227)	Kohima	Nagaland

delays are a probability. It's all part of the experience and still vastly more comfortable and adaptable than travelling by packed-full, over-fast local transport.

Climate

You will find decent AC rooms preferable when you're staying anywhere not well up a mountain until early October. But by December even sweaty Guwahati can feel chilly at night. Warm clothes will be useful at any time in Tawang, which can be cut off by snowdrifts from December (they are usually cleared within a day or two), and where temperatures can dip as low as -15°C in January.

National Parks

Assam's top attractions are its national parks, with the bigger ones subdivided into autonomous 'ranges'. Undoubtedly the most popular is Kaziranga (p213), where your chance of seeing wild rhinos (albeit often at a considerable distance) is very high, at least in the central range. However, the hordes of tourists during peak season can be off-putting. For peace and scenery it's hard to beat Nameri (p213), but you won't see bigger animals there. The great attraction at

both Manas (p210) and the less interesting Orang (p211) is sleeping within the parks' lodges to watch the jungle awakening at dawn. Pobitora (p210) has the advantage of being very near to Guwahati and having the highest concentration of rhinos. You'll need to book well ahead for Manas (via Barpeta Road, p211).

All of the parks have similar pricing structures. To your **entrance fees** (Indian/foreigner per day Rs20/250) add Rs50/500 for a still camera or Rs500/1000 for a video camera. Whether you bring your own jeep or rent locally, there's also a **vehicle toll fee** (Rs150), including the services of an armed escort (who is customarily tipped an additional Rs50). Visiting by jeep is not like going on safari in east Africa, as routes here are confined to set tracks to avoid the many marshy areas. This can cause frustrating traffic jams in peak season. Parks are only opened once the tracks have been hand-cleared of overgrowth (usually in late October).

Many park ranges offer dawn **elephant rides** (Indian/foreigner Rs280/750) before opening to jeep traffic (book the night before). These are typically better than jeeps for getting close to bigger animals, but only last an hour so you don't travel very far. Even an hour seems quite

NATIONAL PARK OVERVIEW

National Park	Elephant rides	Open jeeps	Season	Main appeal
Kaziranga (p213)	yes	easy to rent	Nov-Apr	rhinos, elephants, easy access
Manas (p210)	some	limited rental	Oct-Mar	park lodges, Bengal floricans, Bodo community involvement
Nameri (p213)	no	no (walk)	Nov-Apr	hikes, scenery, birds, rafting
Orang (p211)	yes	bring your own	Nov-Apr	peace, park lodge
Pobitora (p210)	yes	no	Nov-Apr	highest concentration of rhinos

NORTHEAST STATES

NORTHEAST STATES

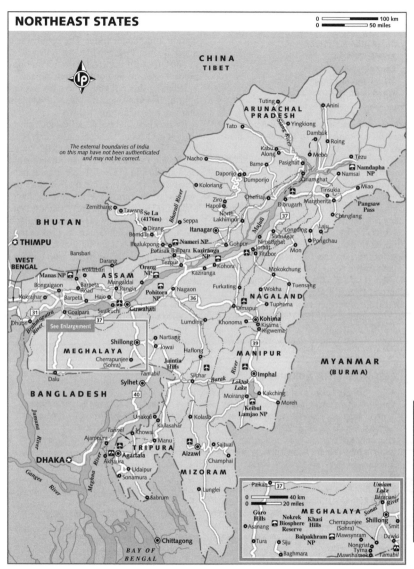

long if there are four people crushed onto one elephant.

A bonus attraction is the unusually delightful places to stay close to Kaziranga (Wild Grass, p214), Nameri (Eco-Camp, p213) and Manas (Bansbari Lodge, p211), all managed by enthralling, larger-than-life characters.

ASSAM

Fascinating Assam (Asom, Axom) straddles the fertile Brahmaputra valley, making it the most accessible of India's Northeast States. The archetypal Assamese landscape offers golden-green vistas over seemingly endless rice fields patched with palm and bamboo

ASSAM FAST FACTS

Population 26.6 million
Area 78,438 sq km
Capital Guwahati
Main languages Assamese, Bengali, Bodo
When to go October to March

groves, and distantly framed by Arunachal's hazy-blue mountains. In between lie manicured tea estates.

Assamese people might look Indian, but Assamese culture is proudly distinct: their Vishnu-worshipping faith is virtually a regional religion (see boxed text, p216) and the *gamosa* (a red-and-white scarf worn by most men) is a subtle mark of regional costume.

However, by no means is all of Assam ethnically Assamese. Before the Ahom invasions of the 13th and 15th centuries much of today's Assam was ruled from Dimapur (now Nagaland) by a Kachari-Dimasa dynasty. The Chutiaya (Deori-Bodo) kingdom was an important force further west. The Dimasa and Bodo peoples didn't just disappear; during the 20th century increasing ethnic consciousness led their descendents to resent the Assamese in much the same way as the Assamese have resented Bangladeshi immigration and greater India. The result was a major Bodo insurgency that was only settled in 2004–05 with the creation of an autonomous 'Bodoland' in northwestern Assam.

Don't let this put you off. Assam is a delightful, hospitable and deeply civilised place that you can easily grow to love.

Assam's beautiful rice fields look their emerald best in October. National parks rarely open before November and, even then, the state's iconic rhinoceroses remain hard to spot amid elephant-height grasses. These grasses have burnt off by February, but by that stage the plains will have turned a relatively drab brown. Make sure you try the delicious Assamese food: fruity, mild and finely pH-balanced using a unique banana-alkaline extract called *khar*.

Rongali Bihu is a spring festival marking the beginning of the sowing season happening around the spring equinox or mid-April. Assamese wear new and colourful clothes, visit neighbours, friends and family and distribute sweets. Grand feasts may also be held to celebrate the occasion.

For more information, visit www.assamtourism.org.

FESTIVALS IN THE NORTHEAST

Adivasi dances linked to the crop cycle take place year-round.

Torgya (Jan) and **Losar** (Jan/Feb) Tibetan-Buddhist *chaam* (ritual masked dances performed by some Buddhist monks in gompas to celebrate the victory of good over evil and of Buddhism over pre-existing religions) held most spectacularly at Tawang Gompa (p224).

Chapchar Kut (Mar; Mizoram statewide; http://mizotourism.nic.in/festival.htm) Spring festival, song and dance.

Rongali Bihu (late Apr; Assam statewide) Springtime celebrated with song and dance.

Ambubachi Mela (Jun; Kamakhya Mandir, Guwahati; p204) Tantric rituals and even more animal sacrifices than usual.

Kang (Rath Yatra; Jul; Manipur & Assam statewide) Chariot fest for Krishna's birthday.

Durga Puja (Oct; all Hindu areas) The region's biggest festival.

Buddha Mahotsava (variable; Tawang; http://tawang.nic.in/tawangbm/main.html) Government-sponsored Buddhist cultural festival.

Diwali (Oct/Nov; all Hindu areas) Lamps lit on banana-stem posts outside homes, Kali images dunked in rivers, general good humour.

Kwak Tenba (Oct/Nov; Imphal; p230) Fourth day of Durga Puja, religious ceremonies and re-enactments of past battles.

Wangala (Oct/Nov; Meghalaya statewide) Four-day Garo harvest festival with impressive dancing.

Nongkrem (Nov; Smit, p243) Five-day Khasi royal festival.

Ras Mahotsav Festival (3rd week of Nov; Majuli Island, p215) Major Vishnu festival with plenty of Krishna-epic recitations and dance-theatre.

Pawl Kut (Nov/Dec; Mizoram statewide) Mizoram's harvest festival.

Hornbill Festival (Dec; Kohima, p228) Nagaland's biggest event with wildly costumed dance performances by all main Naga peoples.

NORTHEAST STATES

BRAHMAPUTRA EXPERIENCES

The Brahmaputra is one of India's greatest rivers. It rises as the Tsangpo near Mt Kailash in Tibet and flows eastwards along the northern side of the Himalaya before breaking through in a 250km-long canyon. Within this canyon the river drops from 3000m to 300m and becomes the Siang once in its gushing Arunachal reaches, where powerful rapids around Tuting (p222) and Karko will one day surely be regarded as among the world's top rafting challenges. By the time it reaches Assam the river, now called the Brahmaputra or son of Brahma, is truly vast, cutting the state in two with kilometre upon kilometre of sandbanks and flood plains. You might even spot blind, Gangetic dolphins (January is the best time to see them). Cheap ways to experience this entrancing, flat enormity include public ferry rides to the world's biggest river island (Majuli, p215) or along the longer Pasighat to Dibrugarh route (p222). Rhino Travels' Mou Chapori (p215) lets you sleep on an otherwise uninhabited Brahmaputra sandbank-islet, Wild Grass (p214) can organise four-person, three-day boat-and-camp trips around Dibrugarh or Kaziranga, while **Assam-Bengal Navigation** (www.assambengalnavigation.com) runs a variety of comparatively luxurious cruises in restored former mail steamers, which are bookable through Jungle Travels India (p206) in Guwahati.

History

The Brahmaputra Valley had a dazzling golden era as the Kamarupa kingdom in the 4th to 9th centuries; its dynasties founded splendid cities and its Asura 'demon' kings fought epic battles with Krishna and sons. By the 12th century a Kachari kingdom controlled the east, and Chutiyas the west, all to be eventually subjugated by the Ahoms who invaded from Southeast Asia and fought ongoing battles with Mughal India for centuries. Ahom (locally spelt Asom, hence Assam) rule was fatally undermined by fearsome Burmese attacks in 1817, which decimated the population and carted off many of the survivors as slaves, leaving Assam's fertile valleys sparsely populated. This proved a windfall to the colonial Brits who arrived to fill the power vacuum. They nabbed much of the best land to experiment with a newfangled Chinese shrub they called tea. With few local labourers available to work the new plantations, the Brits imported Adivasi workers from Jharkhand and beyond. These workers never intermarried with local people and their 'tea-tribe' descendants, remarkably, still form the vast majority of estate tea pickers (while Assamese have taken over the desk jobs of the colonial planters).

During the colonial era, Assam was much larger, covering most of the Northeast. It was here that India's first commercial oil wells were developed, making Assam among the richest areas in British India. But Independence proved an economic disaster. Assam was initially slated to join East Bengal

in East Pakistan (which would eventually become Bangladesh). However, frantic last-minute negotiations reversed the decision. Assam finally joined India, albeit without Muslim Sylhet, which decided by referendum to go to East Pakistan. Partition meant that Assam's oil and tea exports could no longer take the sensible, direct rail line to the nearest port (Chittagong) but now had to wind right through northern Bengal. Like Kolkata, Assam was suddenly flooded with millions of Hindu Bengalis preferring not to live in Pakistan. This created enormous and ever-growing ethnic tensions, made all the worse after 1970 when a second wave of Muslim Bengalis started fleeing the war in proto-Bangladesh. A third wave of Bangladeshi immigrants has moved to Assam in recent years for economic advantage.

Providing the bulk of India's oil, but gaining few of the benefits, Assam felt economically cheated by India. This sentiment bubbled over into widespread rebellion after India's meek response to the brief 1962 Chinese invasion (which approached close to Tezpur at one stage). Assamese student groups turned militant and the United Liberation Front of Asom (ULFA) started its violent demands for Assamese independence. At the same time tensions were simmering in the hill areas where local Adivasi people were in turn offended by the condescendingly 'colonial' attitude of their Assamese overlords. Greater Assam was eventually split into today's seven sister states, but not before decades of separatist conflicts.

GUWAHATI
☎ 0361 / pop 964,000
A casual glance might place Guwahati alongside any other Indian city but wander the back alleys around Jorpulkuri Ponds, away from the central business district concrete jungle, and you might think yourself in a village made up of ponds, palm trees, small single-storey traditional houses and old colonial-era mansions. Come here to arrange tours to the Northeast States.

History
Guwahati is considered the site of Pragjyotishpura, a semimythical town founded by Asura king Naraka who was later killed by Lord Krishna for a pair of magical earrings. The Kamakhya temple (right) has long been one of tantric Hinduism's great shrines. Scores of beautiful carvings found beneath the dowdy 1970s Reserve Bank of India (Station Rd, Ambari) show that the city had reached an artistic peak in the 14th century. In the 17th century, Guwahati was the theatre of intense Ahom–Mughal fighting, the city changing hands eight times in 50 years before the Ahoms' final victory in 1681. Guwahati became the last capital of the Ahoms in their declining years after King Rudra Singh's conversion to Hinduism and the loss of their former capital Rangpur (now in Bangladesh). A huge earthquake in 1897 wiped out the 19th-century British administrative outpost located here, along with most of the old city. The earthquake was followed by a series of devastating floods. The city became capital of Assam in 1972 and the Asom State Government is now ensconced in a Disneyesque new secretariat complex, 6km south of the train station in the Dispur district.

Orientation
Hectic commercial bustle animates the central Fancy and Panbazaar areas, and stretches 10km southeast down Guwahati Shillong (GS) Rd from Paltan Bazaar (the bus station area).

Information
EMERGENCY
Police station (☎ 2540126) On Hem Barua (HB) Rd.

INTERNET ACCESS
CyberWeb (HB Rd, Panbazaar; per hr Rs20; ⏱ 9am-10pm)
i-way (Lamb Rd; per hr Rs25; ⏱ 9am-last customer)

MEDICAL SERVICES
Downtown Hospital (☎ 2331003; GS Rd, Dispur) The area's best.

MONEY
ATMs are everywhere. Change foreign currency and travellers cheques here as facilities are very limited elsewhere.
HDFC (Durgeswari Shopping Complex, MC Rd) ATM.
State Bank of India (SBI; ☎ 2544264; 3rd fl, MG Rd) ATM, changes major currencies and travellers cheques.
Thomas Cook (☎ 2664450; J Borooah Rd; ⏱ 9.30am-6pm Mon-Sat) Shop behind Jet Airways. Changes 26 currencies and travellers cheques, no Bangladeshi taka though.

PERMITS
Indian citizens can obtain inner line permits below but foreigners shouldn't expect any assistance (for permits for foreigners, see p199).
Arunachal House (☎ 2229506; Rukmini Gao, GS Rd)
Manipur Bhawan (☎ 2540707; Rajgarh Rd)
Mizoram House (☎ 2529411; GS Rd, Christian Basti)
Nagaland House (☎ 2332158; Sachel Rd, Sixth Mile, Khanapara)

POST
Main post office Chaotic. On Ananda Ram Barua (ARB) Rd.

TOURIST INFORMATION
Assam Tourism (☎ 2547102; www.assamtourism.org; Station Rd) Informal help desk within the Tourist Lodge and a tour booth just outside.

Sights
KAMAKHYA MANDIR
While Sati's disintegrated body parts rained toes on Kolkata (see p101), her yoni (genitalia) fell on Kamakhya Hill. This makes Kamakhya Mandir (admission for queue/short queue/no queue free/Rs100/500; ⏱ 8am-1pm, 3pm-dusk) important for sensual tantric worship of female spiritual power (shakti). Goats, pigeons and the occasional buffalo are ritually beheaded in a gory pavilion and the hot, dark inner womblike sanctum is painted red to signify sacrificial blood. The huge June/July Ambubachi Mela festival celebrates the end of the mother goddess' menstrual cycle with even more blood. Nine nearby mandirs represent incarnations of Shakti.

Kamakhya is 7km west of central Guwahati and 3km up a spiralling side road. Occasional buses from Guwahati's Kachari bus stand run all the way up (Rs5, 20 min-

NORTHEAST STATES

utes). Continue 1km further for sweeping Brahmaputra views.

RIVERSIDE GUWAHATI

Umananda Mandir complex sits on a pretty forested river island, accessed by a 15-minute ride on a ferry (Rs10 return, half-hourly 8am to 4.30pm) from **Kachari Ghat**, which itself offers attractive afternoon river views.

Sukreswar Devalaya comprises three modern-looking temples, including one where holy water dribbles continuously over a Shiva lingam from a suspended bell-metal amphora. Almost adjacent, little **Sukreswar Ghat Park** (MG Rd; adult/child/camera Rs5/2/5; 9am-9pm) contains a playful, multi-arched **ornamental gateway** built by the British. Two of its eight missile-

shaped spires are leaning precariously, perhaps due to the devastating 1897 earthquake that destroyed virtually every other building in Guwahati.

FANCY BAZAAR

Guwahati's commercial centre around Fancy Bazaar is chaotically fascinating with minarets, a silver-spired church and a Sikh temple dome all rising like lighthouses above the stacked signboards and shop fronts. At night Guwahati's homeless curl up here in front of the shuttered shops.

ASSAM STATE MUSEUM

This worthwhile **museum** (2540651; adult/camera/video Rs5/10/100; 10am-4pm Tue-Sun), on

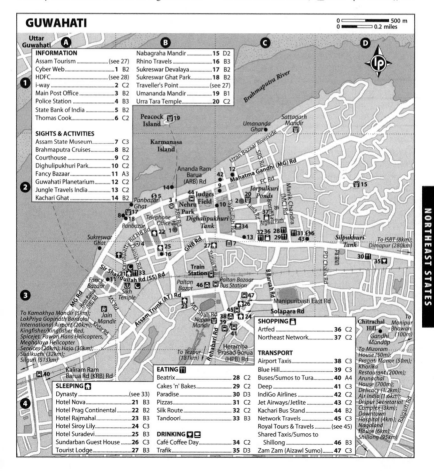

GUWAHATI

0 —————— 500 m
0 —————— 0.2 miles

INFORMATION
Assam Tourism	(see 27)
Cyber Web	1 B2
HDFC	(see 28)
i-way	2 C2
Main Post Office	3 B2
Police Station	4 B3
State Bank of India	5 B2
Thomas Cook	6 C2

SIGHTS & ACTIVITIES
Assam State Museum	7 C3
Brahmaputra Cruises	8 B2
Courthouse	9 C2
Dighulipukhuri Park	10 C2
Fancy Bazaar	11 A3
Guwahati Planetarium	12 C2
Jungle Travels India	13 C2
Kachari Ghat	14 B2

Nabagraha Mandir	15 D2
Rhino Travels	16 B3
Sukreswar Devalaya	17 B2
Sukreswar Ghat Park	18 B2
Traveller's Point	(see 27)
Umananda Mandir	19 B1
Urra Tara Temple	20 C2

EATING
Beatrix	28 C3
Cakes 'n' Bakes	29 C2
Paradise	30 D3
Pizzas	31 C2
Silk Route	32 C3
Tandoori	33 B3

DRINKING
Café Coffee Day	34 C2
Trafik	35 D3

SLEEPING
Dynasty	(see 33)
Hotel Nova	21 B3
Hotel Prag Continental	22 B2
Hotel Rajmahal	23 B3
Hotel Siroy Lily	24 C3
Hotel Suradevi	25 B3
Sundarban Guest House	26 C3
Tourist Lodge	27 B3

SHOPPING
Artfed	36 C2
Northeast Network	37 C2

TRANSPORT
Airport Taxis	38 C3
Blue Hill	39 C3
Buses/Sumos to Tura	40 A4
Deep	41 C2
IndiGo Airlines	42 C2
Jet Airways/Jetlite	43 C2
Kachari Bus Stand	44 B2
Network Travels	45 C3
Royal Tours & Travels	(see 45)
Shared Taxis/Sumos to Shillong	46 B3
Zam Zam (Aizawl Sumo)	47 C3

Peacock Island 19
Karmanasa Island

Uttar Guwahati

Brahmaputra River

Umananda Ghat
Sattagarh Mandir

Uzan Bazaar Riverside

Ananda Ram Barua (ARB) Rd

Mahatma Gandhi (MG) Rd

Panbazar Ghat
Nehru Park
Judges Field
Jorpukhuri Ponds

Telephone Office
Dighalipukhuri Tank
Argwali Path

Sukreswar Ghat

Panbazar

Silpukhuri Tank

To ISBT (8km); Dimapur (280km)

GNB Rd

Sir Shadullah Rd (SS) Rd

Fancy Bazaar
Sikh Temple

Train Station

Palton Bazaar Bus Station

Assam Trunk (AT) Rd

Manipuribasti East Rd

Solapara Rd

MG Rd
Jain Mandir
Nepali Mandir
Shah Rd
Heramba Prasad Borua (HPB) Rd

Kaliram Barua Rd (KRB) Rd

To Kamakhya Mandir (5km); LokPriya Gopinath Bordoloi International Airport (20km); Kingfisher/Kingfisher Red, Spicejet, Pawan Hans Helicopters, Meghalaya Helicopter Services (20km); Hajo (30km); Sualkuchi (32km); Siliguri (513km)

To Tezpur (181km)

Chitrachal Hill
Manipur Bhawon
Gandhi Mandap (100m)

To Mizoram House (50m); Pragati Manor (50m); Khorika Restaurant (200m); Arunachal House (700m); Delicacy (1.2km); Air India (1.6km); Dispur Secretariat Complex (3km); Downtown Hospital (4km); Nagaland House (6km); Shillong (95km)

NORTHEAST STATES

GN Bordoloi (GNB) Rd, has a large sculpture collection, while the upper floors are devoted to informative Adivasi culture displays. You get to walk through reconstructed Adivasi homes.

OLD GUWAHATI

The distinctive beehive dome of the **Courthouse** (MG Rd) rises above mildly attractive **Dighulipukhuri Park** (HB Rd; admission Rs5, boats per adult/child Rs25/15; ⏱ 9.30am-8pm) tank. The nearby **Guwahati Planetarium** (☎ 2548962; MG Rd; shows Rs15; ⏱ noon & 4pm, closed 1st & 15th of the month) looks somewhere between a mosque and a landed UFO.

The half-hidden **Urra Tara Temple** (Lamb Lane) is Guwahati's second holiest, backed by the gently attractive **Jorpulkuri ponds**.

NABAGRAHA MANDIR

Several hilltops are crowned by minor curiosities. One such is **Nabagraha Mandir** (Temple of the Nine Planets; admission Rs80-100), northeast of Central Guwahati by autorickshaw, famed as a centre of astrology. Beyond its aggressive monkey guardians, a darkly atmospheric inner sanctum holds nine ancient stone Shiva lingams.

Tours

Traveller's Point (☎ 2604018; www.assamtourism.org; Tourist Lodge, Station Rd) is Assam Tourism's commercial booth. It runs day excursions to Hajo via the silk-weaving centre of Sualkuchi (adult/child Rs450/375, minimum five people). It also offers two-day all-inclusive packages to Kaziranga National Park (Indian/foreigner from Rs1280/2280).

Network Travels (☎ 2605335; www.networktravels india.net; GS Rd; ⏱ 5am-9pm) is a highly experienced agency whose operations cover the whole of the northeast with tailor-made and fixed itinerary tours. It operates the Eco-Camp (p213) in Nameri National Park. Organising permits is a speciality.

Jungle Travels India (☎ 2660890; www.jungletravels india.com; 1st fl, Mandovi Apt, GNB Rd) is another experienced agency covering the entire northeast with tailor-made tours and fixed-date departures for Nagaland and Arunachal Pradesh. It organises all the permits. With two boats, it runs Brahmaputra cruises (see www.assambengalnavigation.com) for four to 10 nights at US$320 per person per night and also runs the Bansbari Lodge in Manas National Park (p211).

Rhino Travels (☎ 2540666), on M Nehru (MN) Rd, offers tours in Assam and Arunachal Pradesh, from Rs52,000 for two for seven days/six nights. It also runs Mou Chapori River Resort (p215).

Forerunning what one day could be commonplace on the river, **Brahmaputra Cruises** (☎ 2600244; www.brahmaputrarivercruises.com; packages US$780-910) run six- to seven-day cruises, sleeping on board and visiting Adivasi villages, Kaziranga National Park, Majuli Island and Tezpur.

Travel the Unknown (www.traveltheunknown.com) is an England-based company running specialised tours to the northeastern states.

Sleeping

BUDGET

Hotel Suradevi (☎ 2545050; MN Rd; s/d Rs250/350, without bathroom Rs100/250) Well-organised warren of spartan rooms but check in early to get a room.

Sundarban Guest House (☎ 2730722; s/d from Rs200/300, d with AC Rs700-800; ⚡) A cheery, colourful hotel that's the best budget option in town. Rooms are atypically clean and tidy, and management is helpful. Non-AC Rs500 rooms are the best value. It's off Manipuribasti East (ME) Rd, in the first side lane. Many nastier, cheap hotels line the surrounding lanes.

Tourist Lodge (☎ 2544475; Station Rd; s/d from Rs330/440; ⚡) Convenient for the train station, the rooms are OK but the staff could do with a brush up in hospitality management. It's a genuine bargain, though, but be prepared for some train noise and up to five-storeys of stairs.

MIDRANGE & TOP END

All the hotels listed here offer cable TV and private bathrooms with hot water. Many add a 15% tax and 10% service charge.

Hotel Siroy Lily (☎ 2608492; Solapara Rd; s/d Rs700/900, with AC Rs1100/1300; ⚡) Professionally run, well-maintained hotel with a lift, a pleasantly air-conditioned foyer, complimentary breakfast and free newspapers delivered to your door.

Hotel Nova (☎ 2511464; SS Rd; s/d from Rs750/1300, with AC Rs1350/1650; ⚡) In the buzzing Fancy Bazaar area, this 15-room hotel is clean, functional and unglamorous. It's just a place to lay a weary head.

Hotel Prag Continental (☎ 2540850; MN Rd; s Rs850-1600, d Rs1200-2000; ⚡) A pleasantly run popular hotel in a quiet central street. Accommodating its mainly business clientele, it has a gents' beauty parlour and a good restaurant.

Hotel Rajmahal (☎ 2549141; www.rajmahalhotel .com; s/d with fan from Rs1200/1800, with AC from Rs1900/2500; ✺ ☐ ☎ ☒) On Assam Trunk (AT) Rd. A long lobby with an appealing cakes stand leads you into this 10-storey semi-international tower-hotel. There's a cool and enticing rooftop swimming pool with a poolside cafe.

Pragati Manor (☎ 2341261; pragatimanor@lycos .com; GS Rd; s/d from Rs1800/2100; ✺ ☎) Were it nearer the centre, Pragati Manor would be Guwahati's undisputed upmarket pick. A costumed doorman ushers you into this 47-room oasis where modern architecture is softened with Indian art. Back rooms look out over palm-swathed hillocks and there's a glass-pod external elevator. Added attractions are wi-fi, bar and restaurant.

Dynasty (☎ 2516021; www.hoteldynastyindia .com; s/d from Rs3400/3800, ste Rs6000-15,000; ✺ ☐) Guwahati's top hotel with all the luxury and services that you'd expect although from its location in crowded Fancy Bazaar and unappealing exterior you'd think otherwise. On Sir Shahdullah (SS) Rd.

Eating

Delicacy (cnr GS & RGB Rds, Ganeshguri; dishes Rs20-100; ✹ 9am-4pm & 8-11pm; ✺) Tucked beneath a repulsive overpass junction, the odd location is far from central but worth the trek for another of Guwahati's selection of northeastern cuisine styles.

Beatrix (dishes Rs30-70) Upbeat and cartoon-walled, Beatrix is just a peg above a student-style hangout. Its eclectic menu offers fish and chips, *momos* (Tibetan dumplings), Hakka Chow and a mysterious 'con est soir'. It's on Manik Chandra (MC) Rd.

Silk Route (GNB Rd; mains Rs30-80; ✹ 11am-9pm) Good-value Indian, Chinese and Thai food served in a cosy, two-storey place. Its cold fruit beer (nonalcoholic) is an absolute thirst-killer.

Khorika Restaurant (GS Rd; dishes Rs50-120; ✹ 10.30am-4pm & 6pm-10.30pm) Named after the Assamese *khorika* (barbecued dishes), this restaurant may be canteen-style but it has authentic Assamese cuisine. For the whole hog share the sample-everything *khorika* (Rs500) with friends.

Tandoori (☎ 2516021; Dynasty, SS Rd; mains Rs100-300; ✹ noon-3pm & 7pm-11pm) Majestic North Indian cuisine served at stylish low tables by waiters in Mughal uniforms accompanied by gentle live tabla music. The prawn dishes, yes a little expensive, are delightful.

Paradise (1st fl, GNB Rd; mains Rs110-280) Well known for its authentic Assamese cuisine, its thali is the best way to get a lot of small tasters. Assamese food is not a lip tingler like typical Indian food and for some this cuisine can seem rather bland, but it's the subtleties you're after rather than the heat.

QUICK EATS
MC Rd offers **Pizzas** (pizzas Rs40-285) for tasty pizzas and **Cakes'n'Bakes** (mains Rs15-25) for delicious fresh pastries (from Rs6).

Drinking
Café Coffee Day (Taybullah Rd; espresso Rs23; 10am-10pm) Guwahati's central coffee shop, pumping out contemporary music, attracts the city's student and nouveau-riche youth with perfect (if very slow) macchiatos. It also has a branch at the airport.

Trafik (GNB Rd; beers Rs60; ✹ 10am-10pm) This under-lit bar has a vast screen for cricket matches or *filmi* (slang term describing anything to do with Indian movies; in this case, Bollywood music) clips.

Shopping
Northeast Network (☎ 2631582; www.northeastnet work.org; JN Borooah Lane; ✹ 11am-4pm Mon-Fri) This NGO seeds self-help projects in rural villages including several handloom-weaving cooperatives. Buying beautiful (and good-value) cottons here supports this fine work.

Artfed (GNB Rd; ✹ 10am-8pm) Well stocked with bargain bamboo crafts, wickerwork and many a carved rhino. Several nearby shops specialise in Assam's famous golden-toned silks.

Getting There & Away
AIR
Guwahati's orderly Lok-Priya Gopinath Bordoloi International Airport is occasionally international when Air India schedules Bangkok flights. Getting into town costs Rs450/100/70 for taxi/shared taxi/airport bus. The following fly from Guwahati.
Air India (Indian Airlines; IC; ☎ 2264425, Ganeshguri)
IndiGo Airlines (SG; ☎ 9954890345; Brahmaputra Ashok Hotel, MG Rd)

FLIGHTS FROM GUWAHATI

	Air India (frequency/week, fare from)	IndiGo	Jet & JetLite	Kingfisher Red	spiceJet
Agartala	d, Rs3432		4x, Rs3603	d, Rs2828	
Aizawl	d, Rs3663				
Bagdogra	2x, Rs3432		3x, Rs3764	3x, Rs2828	d, Rs2828
Delhi	d, Rs6798	d, Rs5691	d, Rs5691	d, Rs5691	d, Rs5891
Dibrugarh	4x, Rs2828			4x, Rs2828	
Dimapur	4x, Rs3356			3x, Rs2853	
Imphal	5x, Rs3432	d, Rs2828	5x, Rs2828	3x, Rs2828	
Jorhat	2x, Rs2828			4x, Rs2828	
Kolkata	d, Rs3432	d, Rs2828	d, Rs2828	d, Rs2828	d, Rs2828
Lilabari	2x, Rs2828				
Silchar	d, Rs2828				

d = daily, 4x = four services per week

Jet Airways/Jetlite (9W; ☎ 2668255; GNB Rd)
Kingfisher/Kingfisher Red (IT; ☎ toll free 18001800101; airport)
spiceJet (SG; ☎ toll free 18001803333; airport)

Helicopter
Pawan Hans Helicopters (☎ 2229501; www.pawahans .nic.in; airport) shuttles to Shillong (Rs945, 45 minutes, twice daily), Tura (Garo Hills, Rs1750, 50 minutes, thrice weekly), Naharlagun near Itanagar (Rs3400, 1¼ hours, six times weekly) and Lumla (Rs3400, twice weekly) for Tawang. Phone your booking then pay at the airport if the service flies (weather and passenger numbers permitting). **Meghalaya Helicopter Service** (☎ 09435145033; airport) has two daily flights to Shillong (Rs945, 20 minutes, 9am and 12.30pm); return trips are at 9.40am and 1.10pm.

Helicopter travel in India has a poor safety record.

BUS & SUMO
Distance buses leave from the new Interstate Bus Terminal (ISBT) 8km east of Guwahati. Private bus operators run shuttle services from their offices to the ISBT. With extensive networks are **Network Travels** (☎ 2739634; GS Rd), **Royal**

NORTHEASTERN TRAINS

Trains from Guwahati

Departure/arrival	Train 5929	Train 2067	Train 5665	Train 4056
Guwahati	5.25am	6.30am	2.00pm	2.15pm
Lumding	9.15am	9.15am	5.35pm	6.25pm
Dimapur	10.50am	10.31am	7.25pm	7.55pm
Jorhat	1.10pm			
Dibrugarh	8.55pm			4.00am

Trains to Guwahati

Departure/arrival	Train 5666	Train 5960	Train 2423	Train 5604
Dibrugarh		6.00pm	8.15pm	
Jorhat				
Dimapur	9.45pm	1.55am	1.25am	11.30pm
Lumding	11.55pm	3.45am	2.57am	1.15am
Guwahati	3.45am	7.45am	7.05am	4.45am

Train number & name: 5929 – Chennai Dibrugarh Express; 2067 – Guwahati Jorhat Jan Shatabdi; 5665 – Guwahati Dimapur Express; 4056 – Delhi Dibrugarh Express; 5959 – Howrah Dibrugarh Express; 5603 – Guwahati Ledo Expressp; 5666 – Dimapur Guwahati Express; 5960 – Dibrugarh Howrah

NORTHEAST STATES

Tours & Travels (☎ 2739768; GS Rd), **Deep** (☎ 2152937) on Heramba Prasad Borua (HPB) Rd and **Blue Hill** (☎ 2607145; HPB Rd). Buses run to Agartala (Rs480 to Rs500, 24 to 26 hours), Dibrugarh (Rs300 to Rs350, 12 hours), Dimapur via Numaligarh (Rs250, 10 hours), Imphal via Mao (Rs600, 18 to 20 hours), Jorhat (Rs210 to Rs250, eight hours), Kaziranga (Rs150 to Rs210, six hours), Kohima (Rs330, 13 hours), Shillong (Rs100, 3½ hours), Silchar (Rs310, 12 to 15 hours), Siliguri (Rs350, 13 hours), Sivasagar (Rs250, 9½ hours), and Tezpur (Rs110, five hours). All companies charge the same regulated fares.

For Shillong shared taxis and Sumos (jeeps; known after the Tata Sumo, a popular 4WD) leave from outside Hotel Tibet (taxi/Sumo Rs110/150). For Aizawl (Mizoram), **Zam Zam** (☎ 2639617; ME Rd, 2nd side lane) runs several daily Sumos (Rs650, 16 hours) via Silchar (Rs350, 11 hours). Buses/Sumos to Tura (Rs175/230, six/10 hours) in western Meghalaya depart from Kaliram Ram Barua (KRB) Rd.

TRAIN
Of the four daily trains to Delhi, the *Guwahati New Delhi Rajdhani* (Nos 2423/35; 3AC/2AC Rs1481/2079, 31 hours, 7.05am) is the fastest; others take up to 43 hours. The best daily train to Kolkata (Sealdah) is the *Kanchenjunga Express* (No 5658; sleeper/3AC/2AC Rs301/845/1174, 21 hours, 10.30pm). The

same train is also best for New Jalpaiguri (for Darjeeling and Sikkim; sleeper/3AC/2AC Rs164/459/638, nine hours).

For trains to and from Lumding, Dimapur, Jorhat and Dibrugarh, see the table, opposite. Transfer at Lumding for Silchar (Train 5692, sleeper/2A Rs96/376, 13 hours, 5.30am). The overnight to Silchar leaves at 8.45pm (train 5694, sleeper Rs96, 12 hours).

Trains to Jorhat and Dibrugarh cut through Nagaland, but you don't need a Nagaland permit as long as you stay on the train (the same rule doesn't apply for buses however).

Getting Around
Shared taxis to the airport (per person/car Rs100/500, 23km) leave from outside the poorly run Hotel Mahalaxmi on GS Rd. From the Kachari bus stand city buses run to Kamakhya Mandir, Hajo (bus 25; Rs20, one hour) and Sualkuchi (bus 22; Rs18, one hour). Autorickshaws charge Rs25 to Rs50 for shorter hops.

AROUND GUWAHATI
Hajo
Some 30km northwest of Guwahati, the pleasant little town of Hajo attracts Hindu and Buddhist pilgrims to its five ancient temples topping assorted hillocks. Haigriv Madhav temple is the main one accessed by a long flight of steps through an ornate

Train 5959	Train 5603	Fare (Rs) Sleeper	Fare (Rs) 3AC	Fare (Rs) AC
4.00pm	10.30pm			
7.55pm	2.00am	86	241	335
9.30pm	3.45am	109	305	425
6.30am	9.00am	148	416	578
		203	569	791

Train 4055	Train 5606	Fare (Rs) Sleeper	Fare (Rs) 3AC	Fare (Rs) 2AC
10.45pm		203	569	791
	7.05pm	74	206	287
5.40am	11.30pm	127	356	495
7.30am	1.15am	148	416	578
12.15pm	4.45am			

Express; 2423 – Dibrugarh Delhi Rajdhani; 5604 – Ledo Guwahati Express; 4055 – Dibrugarh Delhi Mail; 5606 – Jorhat Guwahati Express

LITTLE MECCA

Hazarat Shah Sultan Giasuddin Aulia Rahmatullah Alike was a sultan of Baghdad and, like the Buddha, gave up his temporal powers and wealth, but in his case to spread the word of Islam in India. He brought with him 250gm (one poa) of soil from Mecca, which was buried with him when he died. Poa Mecca can be literally translated as 'quarter Mecca' and many believe, although imams don't accept it, that four visits to Poa Mecca are equivalent to one haj visit to Mecca.

quasi-Mughal gateway. The images inside of Madhav, an avatar of Krishna, are alleged to be 6000 years old.

Poa Mecca

Two kilometres east of Hajo is a **mosque** (☾ 24hr) sheltering the tomb of the multi-named Hazarat Shah Sultan Giasuddin Aulia Rahmatullah Alike who died some 800 years ago. Muslims need to walk (the less pious may drive) 4km up a spiral road to reach the mosque, which is architecturally unremarkable.

Madan Kamdev & Baihata Chariali

From this busy NH31 crossroads at **Baihata Chariali** (30km north of Guwahati) it's easy to find bus connections to virtually anywhere in northern Assam. Just 2km east then 3.5km south by asphalted road (Rs150 return by autorickshaw) are the **Madan Kamdev**

ruins. Here on a gentle hill behind what is possibly the world's cheapest **museum** (admission Rs1; ☾ 10am-4pm Tue-Sun) lies a curiously haphazard jumble of 11th-century carved fragments, including Khajuraho-style scenes with lions mounting cows and horses humping young maidens. Madan Kamdev probably isn't worth a special trip but makes a pleasant tea stop if you're driving by.

Pobitora National Park

Only 40km from Guwahati, this small national park has the highest concentration of rhinoceroses in the world. Entrance fees are the same as Kaziranga National Park, p213. Getting into the park involves a boat ride over the river boundary to the elephant-mounting station. From there it's a one-hour trip atop an elephant lumbering through boggy grassland and stirring up petulant rhinos. An armed guard rides with you in case a rhino gets too close up and personal although a trumpeting, head-shaking elephant seems to do the job just as well.

Kunki's Resort (☎ 0361-2637644, 9854612196; purbanchalvikash@gmail.com; dm Rs250, r old building Rs800, new building Rs1200; ☒) Quiet countryside retreat with an open-air restaurant just a few minutes from the park. The upper rooms at the rear of the new building (all AC) give the best possible views of the odd rhino wandering by.

NORTHWESTERN ASSAM (BODOLAND)
Manas National Park
☎ 03666

Bodoland's Unesco-listed **Manas National Park** (www.manas100.com; ☾ Oct-Mar) has two 'ranges' – Bansbari and Koklabari – with different

BODOLAND

Linguistically related to the Garos of Meghalaya, the Bodo (pronounced Boro) plains people comprise around 16% of Assam's population. Their often-violent two-decade struggle for a Bodo homeland was initially led by the All Bodo Students Union (ABSU). In 1993 the ABSU legitimised themselves and created an autonomous council whose decrees included a demand that all Bodo women should wear *dokhona* (bright-coloured traditional Bodo costume). However, splits in the leadership caused a resumption of hostilities by the breakaway Bodoland Liberation Tigers Force (BLTF) faction. Peace was finally achieved after the BLTF signed up to a territorial council (BTC, www.bodolandcouncil.org) in 2004 and was rewarded with partial authority over a large Bodo autonomous district (BTAD), nicknamed 'Bodoland'. With a 'capital' at Kokrajhar, Bodoland consists of a long, narrow strip of northwestern Assam stretching as far as Orang. A rival Bodo group, the pro-independence National Democratic Front of Bodoland (NDFB) still seeks to gain its own piece of the pie, but its power was undercut in late 2004 when it was ejected from its guerrilla bases in southeastern Bhutan in an attack by over half of Bhutan's entire armed forces.

In Bodo language, 'thank you' is *gwjwnthwng* (pronounced 'g'jn-tng').

access points. National park fees are as for
Kaziranga (p213).

KOKLABARI RANGE
This, the eastern range, is *the* place to spot
an ultrarare Bengal florican (a type of bus-
tard). Inspiring community-based **MMES** (Manas
Maozigendri; ☎ 268052; mahammes4_U@yahoo.com) im-
aginatively employs former Bodo insurgents
to protect the forest from poachers. The gateway village of **Koklabari** has a fascinating little
museum (admission Rs30) displaying impounded
poaching weapons, and a **handicraft workshop**
that sells traditional Bodo *aronai* scarves,
which are usually delicate and handwoven
and often given as gifts.

BANSBARI RANGE
Famous for tigers (though you'll probably
only see their pug marks), this range is
comparatively accessible and can be appreciated in delightful comfort from **Bansbari
Lodge** (☎ 3612602223 www.assambengalnavigation.com
/bansbari.htm; d Rs1250, jungle package Rs6000). Jungle
packages cover full board, early morning elephant safari, jeep safari, guide and park entry
fee. Ask about river rafting. For guests staying two or more days the lodge runs trips
to Koklabari range. Contact Jungle Travels
India in Guwahati (p206) for bookings.
Access is from Barpeta Road.

Manas Ever Welfare Society (MEWS; ☎ 9435759488;
mewssociety@yahoo.com) is a conservation and
ecotourism society that will be providing accommodation and tours within the
national park.

Barpeta Road has the useful and good-
value **Manas Guest House** (☎ 260935; Choudhury
Shopping Complex; dm Rs60, s without bathroom Rs100, d
Rs250-300, with AC Rs700; 🗷) with a restaurant
and an internet place next door.

MOTHANGURI LODGE
Staying at Mothanguri is Manas' top highlight. Two simple, lonely **lodges** (per person Rs200)
are 20km north of Bansbari beside an un-
guarded Bhutan border crossing. Choose the
seven-room upper lodge with its enchanting views across the Beki River and a lounge
with a man-eating tiger (stuffed). Bring food
for the *chowkidar* (caretaker) to cook for you
and diesel fuel for the generator. Book weeks
ahead through the **Manas Field Director's Office**
(☎ 260289, 9435080508; abhijitrabha@hotmail.com; Main
Rd, Barpeta Road).

ROADSIDE EATING
Some of the best food in India can be found
in the roadside *dhabas* (snack bars) along
the main highways. They have a limited
menu, know how to cook it just right and
have the throughput to ensure that the
ingredients are fresh and the food newly
cooked. How do you find one? Look for Tata
trucks outside; the more you see the better
the *dhaba* is likely to be. These long distance drivers crawl out of their cabs, plonk
themselves on a charpoy (string bed), eat
their stacked-high plates of food off a board
across the bed and then fall sound asleep.
If you're travelling between Manas and
Tezpur, stop off at the NRL Dhaba 3km east
of Siphajhai on the way to Mangaldai.

GETTING THERE & AWAY
Guwahati–Kokrajhar buses serve Pathsala
junction and pass within 3km of Barpeta Rd.
Two buses run Pathsala to Koklabari (Rs15,
two hours, 1.30pm and 2.30pm). Barpeta
Rd–Bansbari buses (Rs15, 1½ hours) leave
twice hourly until 5pm just north of the
railway line.

The *Kamrup Express* (No 5960, sleeper
Rs121, 2¼ hours, 7.45am) and *Brahmaputra
Mail* (No 4055, sleeper Rs121, 2¼
hours, 12.15pm) connect Guwahati and
Barpeta Rd.

Jeep rental is available at Koklabari,
Barpeta Rd and (for guests) at Bansbari
Lodge to reach Mothanguri.

Orang National Park
The main attraction within this recently de-
creed **national park** (☎ 9954177677; Indian/foreigner
Rs50/250; ☼ Nov-Apr) is the chance to sleep at
the relatively basic two-room **Satsimolo Lodge** (r
Rs400). Unfortunately, the lodge doesn't have a
phone, so it's a case of turning up on spec and
hoping for a bed. On the plus side, it overlooks
a waterhole where Orang's comparatively limited population of big animals often come
for a dawn wallow. Elephant-back excursions
are available but for a jeep tour (and even to
reach Satsimolo) you'll need your own vehicle.
There's much less chance of seeing rhinos here
than at Kaziranga, but with very few other
visitors, the experience is altogether calmer.
There's a **Tourist Lodge** (☎ 9854165351; Indian/
foreigner Rs300/500) just outside the park gate.

The park is 125km from Guwahati, 70km from Tezpur and 15km off the NH52 by a smooth but unasphalted road that turns south at Dhansirghat. Dhansirghat is 7km west of Orang village, where informally renting a jeep to the park gates costs from Rs800 (or Rs1200 return with park excursion, vehicle entry fee is Rs200). Guwahati–Tezpur buses pass regularly through Orang village.

TEZPUR

☎ 03712 / pop 59,000

Tezpur is probably Assam's most attractive city thanks to beautifully kept parks, attractive lakes and the enchanting views of the mighty Brahmaputra River as it laps the town's edge. **Cinex Computers** (Santa Plaza; per hr Rs20; ☉ 10am-9pm) on Shyama Charan (SC) Rd, 250m north of the Baliram Building restaurants has internet.

Sights

Chitralekha Udyan (Cole Park; Jenkins Rd; adult/child/camera/video Rs10/5/10/100; ☉ 9am-7pm) has a U-shaped pond wrapped around pretty manicured lawns, dotted with fine **ancient sculptures**. The bearded chap in Mesopotamian-style costume is Banasura. A block east, then south, stands **Ganeshgarh temple** backing onto a ghat overlooking the surging river, a good place for Brahmaputra sunsets. Nearly 1km east along the narrow, winding riverside lane is **Agnigarh Hill** (Padma Park; adult/child/camera/video Rs10/5/20/100; ☉ 8.30am-7.30pm) that might have been Banasura's fire fortress site. River views are lovely from the top and there's a snack bar; statues-in-action all around it vividly illustrate the Usha legend.

Across town is a boulder-strewn **Bhamuni Hill**, location for a set of demolished Vishnu temples that were only revealed after the 1889 earthquake.

Some 5km west of the city, the ruined 6th-century **Da-Parbatia Mandir** (pronounced do-par-*bu*tiya) has a celebrated Gupta-style carved door frame but is otherwise simply a stone platform in a field that nonspecialists might find underwhelming.

East of Tezpur, **Bharali Mukh**, the junction of the Bharali (Kameng) and Brahmaputra Rivers, is reputedly the best place in Assam to spot rare, blind **Gangetic dolphins** (☉ Nov-Jan), but finding a boatman to see them is hit and miss.

Sleeping & Eating

Hotel Luit (☎ 222083; luit@rediffmail.com; Ranu Singh Rd; s/d old wing Rs200/300, new wing Rs600/700, with AC Rs1000/1200; 🖳) Close to the bus station, the Luit is on a small lane linking Jenkins Rd with Main Rd. Reception is professional and budget rooms are remarkably reasonable, while a lift whisks you up to the 5th-floor AC offerings. The very tired 'old wing' rooms are to be renovated in 2009.

Indralay Hotel (☎ 232918; s Rs250, d Rs450-800) On Naren Chandra (NC) Rd. The wonders of fresh white paint make this an airy and pleasant hotel. Cheap rooms are a little small but good, consider room 102.

Hotel Durba (☎ 224276; KK Rd; s/d Rs300/500, d with AC Rs1000-1200; 🖳) There's no room for catswinging in these hospital-green rooms but they are clean and cheap.

Tourist Lodge (☎ 221016; Jenkins Rd; dm Rs100, r with/without AC Rs550/330; 🖳) Facing Chitralekha Udyan, two blocks south of the bus station, the Tourist Lodge offers good-value spacious rooms with bathrooms (some squat toilets) and mosquito nets. The dorm is for the desperate.

The modern glass tower Baliram Building, on the corner of Naren Bose (NB) and NC/SC Rds, contains several floors of good dining. The ground-floor stand-up-and-eat **dosa house** (snacks from Rs25; ☉ 6am-9pm) serves South Indian fare and cheap breakfasts. Semismart **China Villa** (meals from Rs275; ☉ 10am-10.30pm) of-

---

BLOODY TEZPUR

Banasura, the thousand-armed demon-king was so overprotective of his beautiful daughter Usha that he locked her into an impregnable 'fire fortress' (Agnigarh) to keep away unwanted suitors. The ploy failed. A dashing prince, Aniruddha, magically found his way in and secretly married her. Banasura was not a happy demon. He considered feeding Aniruddha to his pet snakes, but the lad turned out to be Lord Krishna's grandson. Krishna sent in his troops and an almighty battle ensued. The resulting carnage was so appalling that the site has been known ever since as Tezpur (or Sonitpur), the City of Blood.

SOME LIKE IT HOT

How hot is a chilli pepper? Incredibly, there's a whole science that assesses peppers in Scoville units of pungency. Pimento scores 500, Tabasco sauce tops 2500 and jalapeño peppers go up to 8000. But that's nothing compared to Tezpur's *bih-jolokia* (literally 'poison-chilli'; see p71) which has been recorded at a phenomenal 1,041,427. That made it the world's hottest pepper – at least, until March 2006, when it was out-hotted by a Dorset Naga chilli grown in unexotic rural England.

fers Indian and Chinese food in AC comfort, while the rooftop **Chat House** (snacks from Rs20; 8am-9.30pm) has an open-sided, but roofed, terrace for cooling breezes, good views, Indian snacks, noodles, pizzas and *momos*.

Getting There & Away

Air India's agent is **Anand Travels** (220083; Jenkins Rd) near the Tourist Lodge. Tezpur airport was being rebuilt at the time of research.

Sumos have their booking counters in Jenkins Rd. Bargain for a taxi in the same street for Guwahati (Rs1700), Eco-Camp at Potasali (Rs400) and Kaziranga (Rs1300). A little further on is the **bus station** (225140; Jenkins Rd) with frequent services to Guwahati (Rs115, five hours), Jorhat (Rs115, four hours) and Kohora for Kaziranga (Rs80, two hours).

Tezpur's delightfully parochial train station has a computerised **booking office** (2737155; 8am-2pm & 2.30pm-8pm). Only one train serves this branch line terminus. Railway buffs might want to get up early for the 6am metre-gauge service to Rangapara and rattle through some pretty landscapes for an hour. You can return by shared jeep.

AROUND TEZPUR

Picturesque **Nameri National Park** (Indian/foreigner Rs20/250; Nov-Apr) specialises in low-key, walk-in birdwatching treks. Access is from **Potasali**, 2km off the Tezpur–Bhalukpong road (turn east at one-house hamlet Gamani, 12km north of Balipara).

Potasali's delightful **Eco-Camp** (9435250052; dm/d Rs100/1250, plus membership per person Rs60) organises all Nameri visits, including two-hour ornithological rafting trips (Rs1305

per boat). Accommodation is in 'tents', but colourful fabrics, private bathrooms, sturdy beds and thatched-roof shelters make the experience relatively luxurious. A bigger 'tent' offers great-value dorm beds and there's an atmospheric open-sided restaurant. At dawn, walk 1.3km to the idyllic Bharali riverbank, above which rise horizons of forested foothills crowned by a line of white-topped horizon peaks.

If the Eco-Camp is full, continue to **Bhalukpong** where the **Tourist Lodge** (03782-234037; r/cottage Rs260/633) has appealing cottages around a grassy area above a sweep of the Bharali River. Despite a desperate need for an overhaul by a gang of painters and spring cleaners, it's good value. Turn right shortly before the Arunachal border for the lodge.

KAZIRANGA NATIONAL PARK
 03776

Assam's must-do attraction is a rhinoceros-spotting safari through the expansive flat grasslands of this **national park** (1 Nov-30 Apr, elephant rides 5.30am-8.30am, jeep access 7.30am-noon & 2.30pm-dusk). Kaziranga's population of around 1900 Indian one-horned rhinos (just 200 in 1904) represents two-thirds of the world's total. There is a western, central and an eastern range. The central is the most accessible giving the best viewing chances for rhinos, elephants and swamp deer plus plenty of bird life (take binoculars). One-hour elephant-back rides, central range only for foreign visitors, are especially satisfying when a 'team' of elephants makes pincer movements, surrounding rhinos without frightening them off.

Elephant rides start from November, but at that time grass is elephant-high so the ride can feel like sailing mysteriously on a green sea. The grass burns off in December, improving visibility, and by February new sprouts tempt more big game into the open. In dry years the park opens for jeep safaris from mid-October.

Information

Kohora village is closest for Kaziranga's central range with an obvious Rhino Gate leading to the Kaziranga Tourist complex 800m south. Here you'll find the **range office** (262428; 24 hr), **elephant-ride booking office** (6-7pm, book the previous night) and **jeep rental stand** (rental from Rs600, ride hotel–elephant ride–hotel

NORTHEAST STATES

Rs250). Pay your fees at the range office before entering the park, 2km north.

Better hotels in the Tourist Complex organise everything.

Fees for Indians/foreigners are: entry fees Rs20/250 per day; cameras Rs50/500; videos Rs500/1000; Elephant rides Rs280/750; and vehicle toll fee Rs150/150 (including an armed escort – a Rs50 tip is customary).

Sleeping & Eating

Prices drop at least 30% when Kaziranga National Park closes.

TOURIST COMPLEX

All of the following are within a five-minute walk of the range office. Booking ahead is wise and advance payment is often required.

Aranya Lodge (☎ 262429; r Rs690, AC Rs863, AC cottages Rs863; ⊠) This is a could-be-anywhere concrete but garden-fronted lodge with a bar and decent restaurant.

Prashanti Cottage (d Rs863) This fine place has six modern split-level units overlooking a small river, the workplace of women dhobis and net fishermen. It's run by the Aranya Lodge.

Jupuri Ghar (☎ 9435196377, 9435843681; per cottage Rs1600; ⊠) A new resort with traditional-style cabins around a grassy area and an open-air restaurant. Visits to the park can easily be organised through their staff.

The two-room **Network Travels Motel** (☎ 262699; d Rs600) has a ground floor **cafeteria** (Rs30-50; ⌚ 11.30am-3pm & 8-11.30pm).

The following are run by and booked through **Bonani Lodge** (☎ 262423). **Kunjaban Lodge** (dm Rs50, r Rs150) has passable three- and 12-bed dorms, and double rooms. **Bonoshree Lodge** (r Rs260) offers ageing but acceptable rooms fronting onto a long shady verandah. **Bonani Lodge** (r ground/upper fl Rs380/410) has cool and airy rooms in a two-storey building with wicker furniture.

BEYOND THE COMPLEX

Uninspiring lodgings dot the road around Rhino Gate. None compare with those in the Tourist Complex. However, there are a few good options outside the complex.

Wild Grass Resort (☎ 262085; www.oldassam.com; s May-Oct/Nov-Apr negotiable/Rs900, d May-Oct/Nov-Apr Rs1250/1850; ⊠) This delightful, ecofriendly resort is so justifiably popular that it doesn't bother with a sign but carefully labels all the trees instead. Raj-inspired decor makes you feel that the clock has slowed for you. The atmospheric dining room serves tasty Assamese food and there's a jungle-edged summer-only swimming pool. Wild Grass entrance is opposite the Km373 marker on the National Highway (NH) 37. In season, bookings are essential.

Iora (☎ 262410; www.kazirangasafari.com; s Rs3300-5000, d Rs3900-5000; ⊠ ⊡ ⊠) This brand-new rambling modernist resort has Assamese design flourishes and is fronted by a lofty open entrance hall. Rooms are all you'd require for the price and maybe once the gardens have grown there'll be more of a resort atmosphere.

Camp Rhino (☎ 9435052608; www.kazirangaonline .com; cottages Rs950 & Rs1450) Provides access to the western range with its highest concentration of all animals. For rhino tracking by elephant guests are taken to the central range. Accommodation is in fan-cooled cottages spread around the site with a central restaurant providing three meals a day. The camp takes care of all paperwork and payments.

Getting There & Away

Network Travel buses travel to Guwahati (Rs230 to Rs300, five hours, hourly 7.30am to 4.30pm), Dibrugarh (Rs230 to Rs300, five hours, 11.30am, 12.30pm and 2pm), Tezpur (Rs60, two hours, hourly 7.30am to 3pm) and Shillong (Rs400, nine hours, 9pm). Many Network buses divert the 800m up to the Tourist Complex for a lunch stop. A small **public call office** (PCO; ☎ 09864779028) west of Rhino Gate books bus seats.

If stranded you could increase your chances of a ride by taking the twice-hourly local bus to Bokakhat (Rs10), 20km east. Overnight tours to Kaziranga run regularly from Guwahati.

UPPER ASSAM

Jorhat

☎ 0376 / pop 70,000

Bustling Jorhat is the junction for Majuli Island. Jorhat's commercial street (Gar-Ali) meets the main east–west thoroughfare – Assam Trunk (AT) Rd or NH37 – in front of a lively **central market** area. Head 200m west for a tall shopping complex Unnayan Bhawan with an **internet cafe** (per hr Rs20; ⌚ 9am-10pm). Opposite is the SBI Bank with an ATM.

Journey another 200m west along AT Rd, then south to find a small **museum** (☎ 9435247058;

admission free; Postgraduate Training College, MG Rd; (🕙 10am-4.30pm Tue-Sun) with Ahom artefacts and nearby **Assam Tourism** (🕙 10am-5pm Mon-Sat, closed 2nd & 4th Sat) in the good-value **Tourist Lodge** (☎ 2321579; MG Rd; s/d Rs210/330), which has tiled floors and mosquito nets.

Opposite the train station approach, **Hotel GK Palace** (☎ 2309972; Gar-Ali; s/d Rs500/700, with AC from Rs750/950; 🖳) is a smart new business hotel with obliging staff, a 'Chill Bar' and a reluctance to let cheaper rooms.

Tucked conveniently behind the Assam State Transport Corporation (ASTC) Bus Station (AT Rd), Solicitor Rd has half-a-dozen hotels. **Hotel Janata Paradise** (☎ 2320610; Solicitor Rd; d Rs280-450) has budget fan rooms. Maybe it's the chintzy rugs and paintings in the rooms plus the corridor-housed chair collections but this quirky place has a soul. Its **lobby-restaurant** (🕙 11am-4pm & 8-9pm) serves excellent-value 10-dish Assamese thalis (Rs40).

The wedding-cake-exterior **Hotel Heritage** (☎ 2327393; Solicitor Rd; s/d from Rs250/425, d with AC Rs800; 🖳), with lift, is a friendly midrange choice with the non-AC rooms the best value.

Next door in the faded Hotel Paradise you'll find both **Air India** (☎ 2320011), offering Kolkata (thrice weekly, from Rs3432) and Guwahati (twice weekly, from Rs2828) flights, and **Jet Airways** (☎ 2325652) flying to Kolkata (thrice weekly, from Rs4820).

ASTC bus station (☎ 2301896; AT Rd) has very frequent services to Sivasagar (Rs30, 1½ hours) and Tezpur (Rs70 to Rs115, four hours). Guwahati buses (Rs210, eight hours, eight buses 6am to noon) pass Kaziranga en route.

The *Jorhat Guwahati Jan Shatabdi* (No 2068, CC Rs209, 6¾ hours, 1.55pm Monday to Saturday) goes to Guwahati.

For east-bound trains see the Northeastern trains table, p208.

Around Jorhat
TEA ESTATE GETAWAYS
Colonial-era heritage bungalows offer relaxing, do-nothing stately getaways. Bookings are essential.

Sangsua (☎ 2385075, bookings 9954451548; www.heritagetourismindia.com/sangsua.html; s/d Rs2400/2700) dates from the 1870s and has wonderful lawns and verandahs overlooking a tea estate. There's antique furniture including two Bombay fornicators – chairs with reclining backs and extending arms for putting your legs up on…get the picture? The site is 7km down rural tracks from Km442 on NH37 (Jorhat–Deragaon road).

With a classical portico and wide, immaculate lawns, **Thengal Manor** (☎ 2339519, bookings 2304267; Jalukanburi; s/d Rs2700/3300) oozes grandeur. Old photos, four-post beds and medal certificates from King George VI add atmosphere to this stately mansion. Thengal is 15km south of Jorhat down MG Rd towards Titabor.

DHEKIAKHOWA
This major neo-Vaishnavite **pilgrimage site** was the home-temple of Madhavdev (Mahavadeva), Sankardeva's major disciple and convert. There's plenty of *kirtan* (chanting and singing), especially between 10am and noon, and at any time during **Bhadra** (17 Aug-18 Sep). You're likely to be given a very generous welcome, but the temple complex itself isn't really photogenic. It's 12km east of Jorhat, then 3km north off the NH37 at Km471 passing some typical Assamese houses of mud-plastered bamboo en route.

NIMATIGHAT
This windswept sandbank pockmarked with chai shacks is the departure point for photogenically overcrowded ferries to Majuli Island.

An otherwise deserted river-island reached by private launch (Rs50) accommodates the **Mou Chapori River Resort** (☎ 9435357171; camprhino@gmail.com; 2 days/1 night ex-Guwahati per person Rs5500) with traditionally styled hut accommodation. The one-day group tours (Rs800 per person) from here are a particularly convivial way to visit Majuli Island. Book with Rhino Travels (p206).

Nimatighat is a jarring 12km-ride from Jorhat by shared autorickshaw (Rs70, 40 minutes). With your own transport, stop 2km before the ferry at Green View Resort restaurant for fish freshly caught through a hole in the floor.

Majuli Island
☎ 03775 / 54,000
The great muddy-brown Brahmaputra River's ever-shifting puzzle of sandbanks includes **Majuli**, the world's largest river island. Contemplate landscapes of rice fields and water meadows with fish traps, and meet the local Mising people; or learn about the neo-Vaishnavite philosophy at one of Majuli's 22

SATRAS

A *satra* is a monastery for worshipping Vishnu, Assam's distinctive form of every-man-Hinduism. Formulated by 15th-century Assamese philosopher Sankardev, the faith eschews the caste system and idol worship, focussing on Vishnu as God, especially in his Krishna incarnation. Much worship is based around dance and the melodramatic play-acting of scenes from the holy Bhagavad Gita. The heart of any *satra* is its *namghar,* a large, simple, prayer hall usually open-sided and shaped like an upside down oil tanker. Beneath the eastern end, an inner sanctum hosts an eternal flame, the Gita and possibly a horde of instructive (but not divine) images. *Satras* are highly spiritual, but don't expect anything especially photogenic.

---

ancient *satras* (Hindu Vaishnavite monasteries and centres for art; see above).

Ferries arrive 3km south of **Kamalabari**; the main village **Garamur** is 5km further north. The most interesting, accessible *satras* are the large, beautifully peaceful **Uttar Kamalabari** (1km north, then 600m east of Kamalabari) and **Auniati** (5km west of Kamalabari), where monks are keen to show you their little **museum** of Ahom royal artefacts. The best chances of observing chanting, dances or drama recitations are around dawn and dusk or during the big **Ras Mahotsav Festival** (third week of November).

Contact **Jyoti Naryan Sarma** (☎ 9435657282; jyoti24365@gmail.com, majulitourism@rediffmail.com; per day Rs500) for local guiding, accommodation or bicycle hire. **Danny Gam** (☎ 9435205539) provides similar services.

SLEEPING & EATING

Accommodation is very basic: bring a sleeping sheet or bag.

Donipolo (☎ 9435205539; dm Rs120) In the same lane as La Maison de Ananda is this similar house, with four beds.

Hotel Island (☎ 274712; s/d/tr without bathroom Rs120/240/350) At the crossroads in Garamur. A less-than-exciting dive with shared bathrooms, squat toilets and no hot water; mosquito nets though are a plus.

La Maison de Ananda (☎ 9435205539; dm Rs200) On a green Garamur back lane, this is a traditionally styled thatched house on bamboo

stilts with three bamboo beds and locally made fabrics. It's run by local guide/fixer Danny Gam.

Seuj Bilas (☎ 27345; r Rs600-750) Opposite the police station, this is Kamalabari's only option. Rooms are utilitarian and the more expensive comes with a sitting room. The basic restaurant is also the only eating place in the village.

Those actively interested in neo-Vaishnavite philosophy can usually arrange space at a *satra* guesthouse.

GETTING THERE & AWAY

Packed-full little passenger ferries (adult/jeep Rs15/550, 2½ hours) depart from Nimatighat at 10.30am, 1.15pm and 3pm; return journeys are at 7.15am, 10am and 2pm. The ferry schedule makes day trips pointless unless you charter your own boat (Rs5000); ask the **harbour manager** (☎ 9854022724).

GETTING AROUND

Jam-packed buses meet arriving ferries then drive to Garamur (Rs10) via Kamalabari where three-wheelers are easier to rent. For a few days consider arranging a bicycle through Jyoti, Danny or by asking around. For a few months at flood water an additional **ferry** (free; ☾ dawn-dusk) operates over a flooded section of road between Kamalabari and Garamur.

Sivasagar
☎ 03772 / pop 64,000

Despite being an oil-service town Sivasagar exudes a residual elegance from its time as the capital of the Ahom dynasty that ruled Assam for more than 600 years. The name comes from 'waters of Shiva', the graceful central feature of a rectangular reservoir dug in 1734 by Ahom queen Ambika. Three typical Ahom **temple towers** rise proudly above the tank's partly wooded southern banks – to the west **Devidol**, to the east **Vishnudol** and in the centre, the 33m-high **Shivadol Mandir**, India's tallest Shiva temple. Its uppermost trident balances upon an egg-shaped feature whose golden covering the British reputedly tried (but failed) to pilfer in 1823. Sadhus line the temple approach path; the interior is eerie and the floor slippery. Unusually the lingam is inverted being just a hole in the ground rather than proud-standing stone.

Dominating the tank's western side is the almost-perpetually under-renovation red-painted **Assam Tai Museum**. At the tank's southwest corner, Assam Tourism is within the great-value, garden-sited **Tourist Lodge** (☎ 222394; s/d Rs210/260), whose six large rooms have clean tiled floors and tidy beds.

Around 500m from Shivadol a gaggle of hotels line AT Rd, the most appealing of which is the surprisingly swish **Hotel Shiva Palace** (☎ 222629; hotelshivapalace@rediffmail.com; economy s/d Rs450/550, with AC Rs850/950; ⚡), incorporating a decent **restaurant** (mains Rs50-180).

Hotel Siddhartha (☎ 222276; e7safari@rediffmail .com; s/d from Rs174/200, AC r from Rs620; ⚡) is a worthy midrange option with rooms better than the corridors suggest. The owner is a talented multi-instrumentalist who composes and plays his own Indian fusion music.

The **ASTC bus station** (☎ 222944; cnr AT & Temple Rds) has frequent services to Jorhat (Rs30, one hour) and Dibrugarh (Rs40, two hours) plus buses to Tezpur (Rs150, five hours, 9.30am and 10.30am) and Guwahati (Rs249, eight hours, frequent 7am to 9.30am). Many private buses have ticket counters on nearby AT Rd. For Kareng Ghar, use Gargaon buses (Rs12, 45 minutes), which depart from an unmarked stop on Bhuban Gogoi (BG) Rd, 300m north up AT Rd then 50m right.

Around Sivasagar

Dotted around Sivasagar are many lemon-squeezer-shaped temples and ochre-brick ruins built by the Ahom monarchs during their 17th- and 18th-century heyday.

TALATALGHAR

This famous (but not spectacular) Ahom ruin is 4km down AT Rd from central Sivasagar. Some 2km beyond a WWII-era metal **lift-bridge**, look right to see the rather beautiful **Rang Ghar** (Indian/foreigner Rs5/100; ☽ dawn-dusk). From this two-storey, oval-shaped 'pavilion', Ahom monarchs once watched buffalo and elephant fights.

Just beyond, a left turning passes the **Golaghar** or Ahom ammunition store, the stonework of which is held together with a mix of dhal, lime and egg. Beyond are the two-storey ruins of **Talatalghar** (Indian/foreigner Rs5/100; ☽ dawn-dusk), the extensive, two-storey Ahom palace built by Ahom king Rajeswar Singha in the mid-18th century. Like Rang Garh, the lumpy brick structure and its beautifully tended gardens are arguably more attractive viewed at a distance from the entrance gate.

KARENGHAR

Dramatic if largely unadorned, this 1752 brick **palace** (Indian/foreigner Rs5/100; ☽ dawn-dusk) is the last remnant of the Ahom's pre-Sivasagar capital. The unique four-storey structure rises like a sharpened, stepped pyramid above an attractive forest-and-paddy setting spoilt by nearby electricity substations. It's 900m north of the Sivasagar–Sonari road: turn just before Gargaon (14km) from Sonari.

GAURISAGAR

Like a practice run for Sivasagar, Gaurisagar has an attractive tank and a trio of distinctive 1720s temples – **Vishnudol**, **Shivadol** and **Devidol** – built by 'dancing girl queen' Phuleswari. The more impressive is Vishnudol, not as tall as Sivasagar's Shivadol but sporting finer, but eroded carvings. Gaurisagar is on the main NH37 at Km501.5.

Dibrugarh
☎ 0373 / pop 122,000
Travelling to Dibrugarh ('Tea City') usefully closes a loop between Kaziranga and the Ziro–Along–Pasighat route. It's a rapidly growing city with a new road-and-rail bridge being built at Bogibeel Ghat (opening 2010) that will extend the railway system to north of the Brahmaputra.

From Dibrugarh Town train station, Radha Kanta Borgohain (RKB) Path follows the rail tracks northeast passing Hanuman Singhania Road (HS) Rd that leads to market area. After 800m RKB Path intersects Mancotta Rd at Thana Charali. Around this junction are places to eat, hotels and internet cafes such as **Ajmera** (Sachit Studio, Mancotta Rd; per hr Rs20; ☽ 9am-9pm), and **Internet Cafe** (HS Rd; ☽ 9am-7.30pm Mon-Sat, 9am-2pm Sun) down an alley next to the Grand Hotel. **SBI Bank** (☎ 2321999; RKB Path) changes travellers cheques and foreign currency. Its ATM (on RKB Path) is next to the City Regency hotel.

Purvi Discovery (☎ 2301120; www.purviweb.com; Medical College Rd, Jalan Nagar) organises regional tours, **kayaking days** (Rs3000) and **horse-riding trips** (per day incl meals Rs7800). Given three days' notice it can organise two-hour **tea estate visits** (admission Rs400; ☽ Tue-Sat Apr-Nov). Purvi also handles bookings for two colonial-era tea bungalow retreats: the delightful 1849 **Mancotta Chang Bungalow** (Mancotta Rd, Mancotta; s/d main bldg Rs2600/5200; ⚡), 4km from town, and **Jalannagar South Bungalow** (Convoy Rd; s/d Rs1500/2600, with AC Rs3200/3700; ⚡), 700m from the bus station.

NORTHEAST STATES

In both cases choose the upper rooms that have polished hardwood floorboards and a wonderful heritage feel.

The conveniently central **Hotel East End** (☎ 2322698; New Market; s/d from Rs375/550, with AC Rs625/780; 🕃), just off HS Rd, has basic but clean budget rooms and attached cold showers. The standard deluxe specials are worth the extra Rs75 to Rs100.

City Regency (☎ 2326805; city_regency@sify.com; RKB Path; s/d from Rs1350/1600; 🕃) is a good-priced mid-range hotel, well (but not lavishly) furnished, and with a lift. A few rooms have no view. El Dorado is suave, under-lit lounge bar.

Another expanding hotel is **Hotel Natraj** (☎ 2327275; natrajhotel@gmail.com; HS Rd; s/d from Rs560/900; 🕃) Its cheapest rooms are also its cleanest and best value.

H2O (Mancotta Rd; mains Rs50-110, beers Rs65) is an upstairs bar-restaurant with elements of spaceship decor. Upbeat little **Flavours** (Mancotta Rd; mains Rs30-70; 🕒 10am-10pm) before the railway bridge serves snacks and the most refreshing Soda Sikanji (Rs20) – just the thing for a sultry day.

GETTING THERE & AWAY

JetLite (☎ 0361-39893333; airport) flies to Kolkata (daily except Sunday, from Rs4081), **Kingfisher Red** (☎ toll free 18002093030; airport) flies to Guwahati (four times a week, from Rs2828) and **Air India** (☎ 2300658; Paltan Bazaar Circuit House Rd) flies four times a week to Guwahati (from Rs2828) and Imphal (from Rs6110), and Kolkata daily (Rs4836). Mohanbari airport is 16km northeast of Dibrugarh, 4km off the Tinsukia road.

From the main **bus station** (Mancotta Rd) ASTC buses depart for Sivasagar (Rs60, two hours, frequent 6am to 9am), Jorhat (Rs90, three hours, frequent 6am to 9am), Tezpur (Rs207, six hours, 7.45am and 8.15am) and Guwahati (Rs355, 10 hours, 9am). Various private overnight services to Guwahati (Rs310 to Rs355, 12 hours, 6pm to 10pm) leave from Mancotta Rd or from outside the train station.

The *Kamrup Express* is the best-timed overnight train for Guwahati (No 5960; sleeper/3AC/2AC Rs203/569/791, 14 hours, 6pm).

Kusum Hotel (☎ 2320143; Talkiehouse Rd) sells a jeep-ferry-jeep combination ticket to Pasighat (Rs280) in Arunachal Pradesh. Hotel departure is 7.30am, boat departure 8.15am, boat arrival at Majibari Ghat 10.30am and Pasighat arrival 1.30pm.

The rough-and-ready **DKO Ferry** (passenger Rs67, vehicle Rs2500-3100) cruises daily to Oriamghat where it's met by a bus to Pasighat. It can carry just two jeeps. There's little shelter and the journey takes around eight hours (5½ hours downstream), so bring an umbrella, water and sunscreen. Brief stops en route give scenic glimpses of isolated riverside hamlets. Exact departure points depend on the Brahmaputra's water level.

SOUTH ASSAM

The attractive **Cachar Hills** are suffering serious insurgency from DHD Dimasa separatists whose poetically named subfactions (like 'Black Widow', led by Jewel Gorlosa) are also embroiled in a bloody 'turf war'. Visiting **Haflong**, once a popular hill station, is not advised, but further south, the predominantly Bengali city of Silchar is safe.

Silchar
☎ 03842 / pop 155,000
With great value hotels, flat, sprawling Silchar is a good night stop between Shillong and Mizoram or Tripura. Club, Central and Park Rds converge at a small roundabout near the main bus station.

Three-year-old **Hotel Kanishka** (☎ 260316; Narshingtola; s/d from Rs350/600, with AC Rs530/770; 🕃), with art deco designs on its doors and a repro grandfather clock in the little lobby still maintains its freshness to make it Silchar's best bet. Take the dirt lane down the side off Narshingtola.

Hotel Sudakshina (☎ 230156; Sillong Patty; s/d from Rs350/650, d with AC Rs650; 🕃) has a lift and care has been taken to make it well presented. Beds don't have top sheets so ask for one plus bucket hot water (free).

The all-AC **Hotel Borail View** (☎ 248561; borailview@gmail.com; Park Rd; s/d from Rs750/900; 🕃) claims it has been refurbished but any such attention is not apparent. Rooms and private bathrooms are good but the shower plumbing takes some working out. There's a dimly lit bar with good Indian beers on offer.

Silchar's **Kumbeergram airport** (☎ 282311) is 30km northeast. Shared taxis (per person/car Rs100/500) depart from outside. **Air India** (☎ 245649; Club Rd; 🕒 10am-5pm), flies daily to Kolkata, Guwahati and Imphal, and thrice weekly to Agartala. **Kingfisher Red** (☎ toll free 18002093030; airport) has daily flights to Guwahati and Kolkata, and thrice-weekly to Imphal.

Capital Travels (☎ 262396; Club Rd) has bus services to Guwahati (Rs360, 12 hours, 6.30am, 5pm, 5.30pm and 6pm) calling in along the way at Shillong (Rs360, eight hours), Aizawl (Rs250, 10 hours, 7.30pm) and Agartala (Rs200, 11 hours, 6.30am). Agartala-bound transport has to join guarded military convoys, making progress dreadfully slow: consider breaking the trip via Kailasahar (for Unakoti, p239).

ARUNACHAL PRADESH

The 'Land of Dawn-Lit Mountains' abruptly rises from the Assam plains as a mass of densely forested hills. These in turn rise to fabulous snow-capped peaks along the China border. At least 25 Adivasi groups with traditional settlements live in Arunachal's valleys, and high in the dramatic Tawang Valley there are several splendid Monpa monastery villages.

The region was known as Northeast Frontier Agency (NEFA) under the British, who mostly left it to fend for itself, as China was then not a power to question a largely British-imposed border. After Independence, Arunachal Pradesh was administered by Assam until 1972 and it only became a fully fledged state in 1987.

China has never formally recognised Indian sovereignty here and it took their surprise invasion of 1962 before Delhi really started funding significant infrastructure. The Chinese voluntarily withdrew. Now border passes are heavily guarded by the Indian military and the atmosphere is extremely calm.

Arunachal Tourism (www.arunachaltourism.com) has additional information.

ITANAGAR

☎ 0360 / pop 38,000

Built since 1972, Arunachal's pleasantly green, tailor-made c3apital is named for the mysterious **Ita Fort** whose residual brick ruins crown a hilltop above town. Itanagar is useful for onward transport to central Arunachal. There's a stack of ATMs in Mahatma Gandhi Marg along with several internet cafes. **Abor Country Travels** (☎ 2211722; B Sector) runs trekking, rafting, Adivasi visits and angling in western and central Arunachal. They also visit Pemako, a

holy Buddhist site, which is north of Along near the Chinese border.

With an oversized foyer better suited as a car showroom, **Hotel Arun Subansiri** (☎ 2212806; Zero Point; s/d Rs900/1000) has comfortably large rooms with soft beds. It's within walking distance of the decent **State Museum** (☎ 2222518; Indian/foreigner Rs10/75; ✦ 9.30am-4pm Sun-Thu) and the gorgeously decorated **Centre for Buddhist Culture** gompa set in gardens on the hill above. The **Poong Nest** (VIP Rd, mains Rs30-100; ✦ 8am-9pm; ✿) is a friendly place for refreshing beers and meals; it serves local Adivasi dishes – boiled chicken or pork, with bamboo shoots and vegies.

Some 3km west on Mahatma Gandhi Marg is **Ganga Market** landmarked by a red, triple-spired temple and nearby clock tower. The especially good-value **Hotel Blue Pine** (☎ 2211118; dm Rs100, s Rs200-300, d Rs300-450, r with AC d Rs750; ✿) is here with well-maintained rooms and private bathrooms with squat toilets. Don't mind the caged receptionist, he's quite tame and helpful.

The **APST bus station** (☎ 2212338; Ganga Market) has services to Along (Rs230, eight hours, 5.30am Tuesday to Sunday), Tezpur (Rs110, four hours, 5.30am), Pasighat (Rs170, eight hours, 6.30am Thursday to Tuesday), Lilabari, for airport, (Rs80, 1½ hours, 7.15am Monday to Saturday) and Guwahati (Rs190, 11 hours, 6am).

Over the road **Royal Sumo Counter** (☎ 2290455) has daily services to Ziro (Rs250, four hours, 5.30am and 2.50pm), Daporijo (Rs480, 14 hours, 5.30am), Along (Rs400, 12 hours, 5.30am), Pasighat (Rs300, eight hours, 5.30am), Lilabari (Rs250, 3½ hours, 6.30am) and Bhalukpong (Rs250, four hours, 6.30am).

Helicopter tickets are only sold at **Naharlagun Helipad** (☎ 2243262; ✦ 7.30am-4pm Mon-Sat), 16km east of Itanagar's Zero-Point. Flights run daily (except Sunday) to Guwahati (Rs3400) and weekly to many destinations, including Along (Rs3400), Ziro (Rs1500), Daporijo (Rs1700) and Pasighat (Rs2700).

ARUNACHAL PRADESH FAST FACTS

Population 1.1 million
Area 83,743 sq km
Capital Itanagar
Main languages Hindi and Assamese
When to go October to March

AROUND ITANAGAR
North Lakhimpur
☎ 03752

Although it's actually in Assam, North Lakhimpur can make a useful stop in transit to central Arunachal. In some seasons it's possible, if adventurous and unreliable, to take muddy back roads from here towards Majuli Island (p215) using multiple river crossings.

Passably intriguing are two amusingly kitschy **temples** on the NH52. One (6km west)

is shaped like a boat rowed by mice. The other, at the western local bus stand (2km west), sports a Mexican-hat tower, around which is coiled a vast concrete cobra.

CENTRAL ARUNACHAL PRADESH
Ziro Valley
☎ 03788

More vale than valley, the district's rice fields and fenced bamboo groves are attractively cupped by pine-clad hills. Tall *babo* (poles)

CENTRAL ARUNACHAL'S ADIVASI GROUPS

The various peoples of central Arunachal Pradesh consider themselves very different from one another but in reality most are related. Virtually all come from Tibeto-Burman stock and before the very recent arrival of Christianity, most practised Donyi-Polo (sun and moon) worship (see the boxed text, opposite). A few traditional-minded old men still wear their hair long, tied around to form a topknot above their foreheads. For ceremonial occasions, village chiefs typically wear scarlet shawls and a bamboo-wicker hat spiked with a porcupine quill or hornbill feather. Women favour hand-woven wraparounds like Southeast Asian sarongs.

Following are the major groups you're likely to encounter.

Adi
Divided into five major subgroups, notably Gallong and Minyong, the Adi peoples live mostly between Pasighat and Daporijo. Historically they were often called 'Abor', meaning nonsubmissive. Much more than the Nagas of Nagaland, Adi villages (but not towns) still retain a high proportion of beautifully built traditional homes, many still luxuriantly roofed with thick palmyra-leaf thatch. Some men still wear bright green or purple waistcoats with a line or two of embroidery and in the rainy season some still wear boat-shaped basketware hats, known as a *bolup*.

Nishi, Tagin & Hill Miri
To an outsider these three groups are somewhat hard to differentiate, all living in bamboo stilt houses that are much simpler and less picturesque than those of the Adi. The Nishi have traditionally been known as a warlike people.

Apatani
Although famous as local traders, the Apatani homeland is confined to the comparatively tiny Ziro Valley plateau (see below). Historically Apatani women were considered the region's most beautiful and were prone to kidnapping by Nishi men whose territory surrounds Ziro. As a 'defence', Apatani women received facial tattoos and extraordinary nose plugs known as *dat*: blue-black disks sometimes the size of Rs5 coins inserted into holes made in their upper nostrils. Peace with the Nishis in the 1960s meant an end to that brutal practice, so only women in their 50s and older are now show the evidence of it. Meeting these women is undoubtedly a fascinating glimpse of Adivasi history, but photography is a sensitive issue, so even more than usual it should be with the consent of the subject. Some Apatani women have had cosmetic surgery to remove their tattoos.

The landscape around Apatani villages is very different than that of their neighbours. They are not slash-and-burners inhabiting ridge tops, but rather cultivators of wet rice in fields near water sources. These fields are systematically weeded between planting and harvesting and the flooded fields support fish farming. All this is done without machinery or animal assistance.

The Apitani are well known for their ecologically sustainable approach to agriculture. Rather than depleting forests for firewood they systematically lock up patches of woodland and allow them to mature before harvesting the wood. Once the trees are lopped, the land is replanted to provide a future crop.

DONYI-POLO

Followers of the Donyi-Polo religion believe that the sun and moon are the eyes of God and that nothing can escape the deity's notice. The religion, increasingly under attack from Christian and Hindu conversionists, is the major belief system of around 30 different Adivasi groups in Arunachal Pradesh. As an oral tradition it's passed from one generation to another and has four main tenets, which will seem quite familiar: speak no evil, hear no evil, see no evil and do no evil. Followers believe in the interconnectedness of all living things and that every organism, no matter how insignificant, has a part to play in the life of humankind. This no doubt partly explains the Apatani sustainable approach to agriculture.

---

and traditional *lapang* (meeting platforms) add interest to the tight-packed villages of the utterly intriguing **Apatani people**.

The voyeuristic main attraction here is meeting older Apatani women who sport alarming **facial tattoos** and bizarre **nose plugs** (see opposite). Most people work in the fields so a good time to see village activity is late afternoon. The most authentic Apatani villages are **Hong** (the biggest and best known), **Hijo** (more atmospheric), **Hari**, **Bamin** and **Dutta**. None are more than 10km apart.

Sprawling **Hapoli** (New Ziro), starting 7km further south than **Ziro**, has hotels and road transport. Just below the commissioner's office on a bend in MG Rd, is an SBI ATM. In an alley under **Hotel Pine Ridge** is **Mom & Dot's Cyber Cafe** (Hapoli; per hr Rs50; ☼ 9am-9pm). The **Emporium Crafts Centre**, a government organisation teaching the indigenous crafts of weaving, carpet making and bell-metal casting, sells its work in its **shop** (☎ 225327; Hapoli; ☼ 9.30am-1pm & 2.30-4pm, Mon-Fri).

The warrenlike **Hotel Pine Ridge** (☎ 224725; MG Rd; s Rs350, d Rs500-700), in a courtyard off the main road, is a good option with the Rs500 rooms the best value. The helpful receptionist speaks good English.

Hotel Blue Pine (☎ 224812; s/d Rs300/450), is its best lodging, albeit a slightly long walk from town (unlit at night). The restaurant is worthy of a visit but service can be slow; if staying order your meals in advance.

Hotel Valley View (☎ 225398; JN Complex, MG Rd) will be a possible alternative once their reconstruction is complete.

Sumos depart from MG Rd, Hapoli (near SBI ATM), for Itanagar (Rs250, five hours, 5.30am, 6am, 10.30am, 11am and 11.30am) and Lakhimpur (Rs170, four hours); prebook. The journey has some particularly beautiful forest sections. A jeep from Itanagar continues to Daporijo (Rs250,

around 9.30am) leaving from outside the Nefa Hotel, opposite the high school on the Hapoli–Ziro road.

Ziro to Pasighat

A peaceful lane winding on and on through forested hills and Adivasi settlements links Ziro to Pasighat via Along. Highlights are dizzying suspension footbridges and thatched Adi villages around Along.

DAPORIJO
☎ 03792 / pop 14,000 / elev 699m

Probably the dirtiest and most unsophisticated town in Arunachal Pradesh but it is a necessary stopover. You have little choice in places to sleep. The four-room **Circuit House** (☎ 223250; d Rs320) is scenically plonked on a hilltop overlooking the town but requires a visit to the *babus* (clerks) in the district commissioner's office to get the required *chit* (permission to stay). The other option is **Hotel Santanu** (☎ 223531; New Market; s/d from Rs300/400) setting new standards of basicness but serving good local delicacies in its cheerless restaurant.

Sumos leave New Market at 6am for Itanagar (Rs480, 12 hours) and Ziro (Rs300, six hours). The **bus station** (☎ 223107) has a lackadaisical 6am service to Along (Rs110, six hours) on alternate days – depending on when the bus returns from Along.

Dumporijo, 10km towards Along, has an **Inspection Bungalow** (☎ 255014; r Rs320), requiring a *chit* from the nearby EAC's (extra assistant commissioner) office. It's atop another hill and has pleasant rooms, beds with mosquito nets and cloth-covered sofas. Food is available.

AROUND DAPORIJO

The wooded mountain scenery is attractive if not world beating. While several Nishi and Hill Miri villages around Daporijo are made of traditional bamboo and thatch, few have anything like the grace of Adi equivalents near Along or Pasighat. Nonetheless, it's worth watching out for curious bamboo **totem poles** erected at the roadside to commemorate the recently deceased. They are strung with cane and bamboo-thread loops and often topped, surreally, with an umbrella. Notice the basket near the top of such constructions, which, for a few days after the pole's erection, would have held a chicken. The bird is later set free symbolising the release of the commemorated person's spirit.

If travelling on to Along during October look out for the stalls selling local pineapples. They're the sweetest and juiciest pineapples you will ever taste. We got through three in one go.

ALONG

☎ 03783 / pop 20,000 / elev 302m

This friendly, nondescript market town has an **internet cafe** (☎ 9436632430; Abu-Tani Centre, Nehru Chowk; per hr Rs40; ☼ 7am-7pm) opposite the APST bus station, and an SBI ATM in Main Rd just below the Circuit House that's adjacent to an informative little **district museum** (☎ 222214; admission free; ☼ 9am-4pm Mon-Fri), 300m east selling Adi-related books. The **Crafts Centre** (☎ 222145; ☼ 9am-4.30pm), 1km south on Main Rd teaches weaving, carpet making, blacksmithing and bamboo work. Buy your Adi-style hat here.

The best accommodation choice is **Hotel Holiday Cottage** (☎ 222463; Hospital Hill; r Rs400-500) southwest of the helipad. Pay the extra Rs100 for a deluxe room and preferably take room 104.

There are Sumos to Itanagar (Rs370, 12 hours, 5.30am and 5pm) and Pasighat (Rs200, five hours, 5.30am and 11pm) but not to Daporijo.

AROUND ALONG

The whole point of coming this far is to visit the area's attractive Gallong-Adi villages. **Paia** is a great choice for a balance between accessibility and a relatively unspoilt vibe. To get there drive 8km west of Along and 1km beyond **Podbi**, then walk across the metal-plate suspension foot bridge. Paia climbs the hill above and, apart from the school, most buildings are made of bamboo and thatch. Some village youths speak English.

When returning you can stroll 3km along the riverbank then cross back over an alternative bridge to **Kabu**. This bridge is a lot more picturesque, being mostly formed of cane with narrow bamboo slat-planks. As many bamboo planks are missing, crossing can be a little too 'exciting' for some tastes. Kabu village is interesting if less photogenic than Paia. Both Kabu and Podbi are on the road from Along towards Tato in the fabled Mechuka valley, home of the Tibetan-Buddhist Memba people.

Readers have recommended a more strenuous hike (with steep sections) starting and finishing at Patum Bridge, 6km east of Along and climbing to the ridge villages of Jomlo Mobuk and Mori. A guide is required.

There are many picturesque Adi villages en route to Pasighat, notably **Lokpeng** (17km) and **Koreng** (88km, 2km before Pangin town). Just 2km before Koreng the road divides, the left fork heading north via **Boleng** to **Yingkiong** and (eventually) **Tuting**. In this region the Siang River canyon offers some phenomenal Class V+ **rafting** challenges, but special permits are required and no local facilities are available, so it's expeditions only.

Pareng is a truly idyllic, little-visited Minyong-Adi village 14km from Boleng up a dead-end country lane.

Pasighat

☎ 0368 / pop 22,000

Nestled before a curtain of luxuriantly forested foothills, Pasighat holds the Minyong-Adi people's **Solung Festival** (1 to 5 September). The **internet cafe** (per hr Rs60; ☼ 7.30am-8pm) is 50m from the Hotel Aane and there's an SBI ATM just along from the Sumo stand in the central market area.

Sleep at friendly, central **Hotel Oman** (☎ 2224464; Main Market; s Rs250-300, d Rs400-500) or plusher **Hotel Aane** (☎ 2223333; d Rs1000, d AC Rs1500; ❄), which has hot showers and an appealing rooftop terrace.

GETTING THERE & AWAY

Helicopters from **Pasighat Aerodrome** (☎ 2222088; ☼ 8am-noon Mon-Sat), 3km northeast, serve Naharlagun (Itanagar) via Mohanbari (Dibrugarh) on Monday, Wednesday and Friday; Guwahati via Naharlagun on Tuesday; and Along on Friday.

The inconveniently located APST bus station (take an autorickshaw) has services to Along (Rs100, 5½ hours, 7am Wednesday to Monday) and Itanagar (Rs170, 10 hours,

---

FLORAL CARNIVORES

Pitcher plants (Nepenthes khasiana) are only found in the Khasi and Jaintia Hills of Meghalaya. The business portion of the plant is shaped like a pitcher or jug with the topmost lip shaped like a pourer and the inside lined with downward-pointing hairs to prevent the victim's escape. Insects such as flies, bees or even ants are attracted by the plant's scent, climb in and drown in the toxic liquid at the bottom of the pitcher. Their corpses are then digested at the plant's leisure.

6am Tuesday to Sunday). Sumos run to Along (Rs220, five hours, 6am and noon) and Itanagar (Rs300, six hours, 6am). **Hotel Siang** (☎ 2224559; central market area) sells jeep-boat-jeep combination tickets (Rs250, 5½ hours, 5.30am) to Dibrugarh (Assam) via Majerbari Ghat.

The ferry departs from Oriamghat (Assam), a lonely sandbank 30km from Pasighat (7km off the NH52). En route notice picturesque **Sille** village set in wide rice fields 20km from Pasighat (NH52, Km 523).

WESTERN ARUNACHAL PRADESH

Culturally magical and scenically spectacular, a mountain-hopping journey to Tawang through lands inhabited by Monpa (a people of Tibetan-Buddhist origin) is one of the northeast's greatest attractions. Ideally budget at least five days return from Guwahati (or Tezpur) breaking the journey each way at Dirang or less interesting Bomdila. Be prepared for intense cold in winter.

Come cashed up as there are no ATMs on this route, bar an occasionally dysfunctional SBI ATM at Tenga Haat, a military shopping centre just north of Tenga, some 40km north of Bhalukpong.

Bhalukpong to Dirang

After permit checks in Bhalukpong, the Tawang road passes an **orchidarium** (☎ 03782-23444718; admission free; 9am-noon & 2-4pm Mon-Sat) at **Tipi**. This place is important for its collection of carnivorous pitcher plants (see the boxed text, above).

After 6km, the road starts winding steadily upwards through lush stands of mature forest for around 60km. The trees start thinning after the big roadside **Nag Mandir** temple, but what was once a charming glade has now been transformed into a long strip of army camps that mar the scenery for the next 30km. Most transport takes a break

at Nag Mandir between Bhalukpong and Bomdila, in which case try the best *momos* around at Hotel Mount View.

Around 16km before Bomdila, a 2km detour takes you into **Rupa**. Above this otherwise scrappy village, there's an ancient Sherdukpen **gompa** with *mani* (stone carved with the Tibetan-Buddhist mantra) wall and a few obviously old houses.

BOMDILA
☎ 03782 / elev 2682m

The town is an alternative sleeping place to Dirang with the traditionally decorated, newly furnished Tibetan-style **Doe-Gu-Khill guest house** (☎ 223643; sonchuki@yahoo.com; r/ste Rs700/1500) just below the monastery and providing fabulous views. Alternatively there's the plusher fortress-style **Hotel Siphiyang Phong** (☎ 222286; hotelsiphiyangphong@rediffmail.com; s Rs650, d Rs1200-1500) on the Bomdila–Dirang road. The reliable tour-agency **Himalayan Holidays** (☎ 222017; www .himalayan-holidays.com; ABC Bldg, Main Market; 8am-6pm) organises tours and treks in Arunachal, arranges permits, sells Sumo tickets and has **internet** (per hr Rs50).

Dirang
☎ 03780 / elev 1621m

Fabulous **Old Dirang**, 5km south of Dirang, is a picture-perfect Monpa stone village. The main road separates its rocky **minicitadel** from a huddle of picturesque streamside houses above which rises a steep ridge topped with a timeless **gompa**.

All Dirang's commercial services are in **New Dirang** with a strip of cheap hotels, eateries and Sumo counters around the central crossroads. Look out in the main street for the local gambling obsession, *jhandi dasmunda*, which involves betting on large tumbled dice hidden under an upturned bucket.

You could decide to while away a few days here and take time wandering through Old Dirang, visiting the hot springs 2km north of Dirang, saying hello to a few yaks at the yak breeding farm at Nyukmadung (28km from Dirang) or taking a 50km round-trip to Mandala top, a journey with some fine mountain vistas, rhododendrons and birdwatching opportunities.

Dirang Resort (☎ 242352; d Rs750), on Inspection Bungalow (IB) Rd, is a basic, rather over-priced, but friendly family hotel in an old-style hill house with a wooden wraparound balcony crowded with colourful potted plants. Nicest is the homely **Hotel Pemaling** (☎ 242615; s/ste Rs750/3000, d Rs1000-2000), 1km south over-looking New Dirang. The food is superb, try the *paneer masala* (cottage cheese in a creamy spicy saucy); the front garden and suites have sit-down-and-watch views towards the some-times snowbound Se La.

Consider a homestay in **Thembang** village, 13 km from Munna just before Old Dirang. Funded by the WWF, the village is involved in conservation projects, one of which is re-sponsible tourism. **Homestays** (☎ 09436635835; tbccamc@rediffmail.com; s/d Rs300/400) are available in five houses; facilities are comfortable but pretty basic. Thembang is a fortified village like Old Dirang with gates and walls from its days as the base of a powerful regional king. The village also offers guided treks lasting from one to five days. Get off at New Dirang and arrange a taxi.

Dirang to Tawang Valley

The road zigzags sharply upward eventually leaving the forest behind. **Se La**, a 4176m pass, breaches the mountains and provides access to Tawang Valley. There can be snow on the pass as early as October and one tiny little shack at the top serves tea. The bare rocky peaks and tundra-fringed lakes here are an enormous contrast to the forested foothills below. Beyond would be a Scottish glen were it not for the yaks. A totally out-of-place tour-ist lodge is under construction here. Twenty kilometres on is **Jaswantgarh**, a memorial to an Indian soldier who died heroically tak-ing out a Chinese machine gun post in the 1962 Indo–Chinese conflict. The army pro-vides free chai. From here the road plum-mets down the mountainside into the belly of Tawang Valley.

Tawang Valley

☎ 03794 / elev 3048m
Calling the Tawang Valley a valley just doesn't do justice to its incredible scale; it's more a mighty gash in the earth ringed by immense mountains. Patchworking the slop-ing ridges of the lower hills is a vast sweep of fields dotted with Buddhist monasteries and Monpa villages.

Yet it's all brushed green with a most un-Tibetan fertility. Above the valley rises an enormous bowl of soaring, sharpened peaks, several reaching over 5000m. Way beneath, the Tawang River cuts a very deep 'V' as it froths its way towards Bhutan. Crossing this or other rivers often means an interminable descent: two villages that appear close on a map might be hours apart in reality.

Indeed, just descending from Jaswantgarh to partially attractive **Jang** takes nearly an hour. Another 5km below are the impressive **Jang Falls** (1km detour), where the Narangan River tumbles almost 80m into the Tawang River. Once across the river, the road wiggles back up for the last 30km to Tawang town. Of all the attractive villages en route, the most inspiring is **Rhou**, 18km before Tawang. Rhou's road-side section is photogenic enough, but hidden away above the road, the old village core has a series of brilliantly timeless tower-houses scat-tered up narrow stone stairways and paths. Access is up some initially unpromising con-crete steps 200m east of Km297.

The biggest attraction is magical **Tawang Gompa** (☎ 222243; admission free, camera/video Rs20/100; ☽ dawn-dusk) backdropped by snow-speckled peaks. Founded in 1681, this medieval cita-del is reputedly the world's second-largest Buddhist monastery complex and famed in Buddhist circles for its library. Within its fortified walls, narrow alleys lead up to the majestic and magnificently decorated **prayer hall** containing an 8m-high statue of **Buddha Shakyamuni**. Across the central square is a small but interesting **museum** (Rs20; ☽ 8am-5pm) containing images, robes, telescopic trumpets and some personal items of the sixth Dalai Lama. Spectacular *chaam* (ritual masked dances performed by some Buddhist monks in gompas to celebrate the victory of good over evil and of Buddhism over pre-existing religions) are held during the **Torgya**, **Losar** and **Buddha Mahotsava festivals**.

Other enchanting **gompas** and **anigom-pas** (nunneries) offer great day hikes from Tawang, including ancient if modest **Urgelling Gompa** where the sixth Dalai Lama was born. By road, it's 6km from Tawang town but closer on foot downhill from Tawang Gompa.

TAWANG TOWN
☎ 03794 / elev 3048m

Tawang town is a transport hub and service centre for the valley's villages; its setting is more beautiful than the town itself. Many enchanting **gompas** ring the town (see opposite) and the area's Buddhist pedigree is impeccable. The sixth Dalai Lama was from Tawang, the 13th holed up here in 1911 avoiding Chinese attacks on Lhasa and the present (14th) Dalai Lama fled this way in April 1959. At that time there were no roads to the outside world and it took him four days to walk to Bomdila. China launched a surprise invasion in 1962 and although they withdrew almost as quickly as they had arrived, the status of Tawang remains a stumbling block in Sino–Indian rapprochement. Above Tawang town the hillside is dominated by Indian military camps designed to deter any future attack.

Colourful **prayer wheels** add interest to the central old-market area. These are turned by apple-cheeked Monpa pilgrims, many of whom sport traditional black yak-wool *gurdam* (skullcaps that look like giant Rastafarian spiders). Just 50m east is **Monyul Cyber Café** (Rs50; ◷ 8.30am-8pm). **PL Traders** (☎ 222987; Old Market; ◷ 7am-7.30pm) opposite the Tourist Lodge, sells handicrafts and traditional clothing (including *gurdam*).

Tawang has a number of small hotels. **Tourist Lodge** (☎ 222359; tw Rs300-1050) is exceedingly tatty, the only good-value reasonable-quality rooms happen to be the cheapest. It's 150m above the main drag. The **tourist office** (☎ 222359; ◷ 5am-8pm) is also here with a rather fine illustrated brochure on Tawang.

Outwardly smart, pseudo-Tibetan, **Hotel Gorichen** (☎ 224151; hotelgorichen@indiatimes.com; s Rs600, d Rs500-1800) in the upper old-market area has traditional wood-lined rooms. The cheaper rooms are perfectly acceptable if you like to be cosy. Prices drop June to September.

Tawang Inn (☎ 224096; d from Rs1000-1200, ste Rs1500), which you enter from a back lane 400m southeast of the market, is central Tawang's most polished choice.

The nearby **Hotel Buddha** (☎ 222954; r Rs1000-1500) is another upmarket option, similarly decorated with lots of wood and with a bit more character than the Gorichen.

While each of these hotels have good restaurants the cosy 14-seater **Chinese Restaurant** (Old Market; mains Rs35-80) is the town's best eatery with freshly made food (Indian as well as Chinese) that you may have to wait a while for.

TIBETAN COMMUNITIES OF WESTERN ARUNACHAL

In western Arunachal much of the population is Tibetan in appearance and Buddhist in religion. Older village houses are sturdy, stone constructions with colourfully faceted and carved window frames and every horizontal ledge filled with flower pots. The Sherdukpen and relatively isolated Bugun peoples inhabit valleys around Rupa and Tenga, while the better-known Monpas constitute over 95% of the (nonmilitary) population of the Tawang Valley. Some Monpa women still daily wear a traditional dress with heavy silver and turquoise jewellery and even more don this costume for special days like festivals. Some older men and women sport a curious black yak-felt skullcap called a *gurdam*.

Getting There & Away

From Lumla, 42km towards Zemithang, helicopters (Rs3400, two hours) fly Monday and Wednesday to Guwahati. APST buses leave Tawang 5.30am Monday and Friday for Tezpur (Rs290, 12 hours) calling at Dirang (Rs130 six hours), Bomdila (Rs170, seven hours) and Bhalukpong (Rs240, 10 hours) and return the next day. More frequent public Sumos to Tezpur depart at dawn from Tawang for Dirang, Bomdila and Bhalukpong.

NAGALAND

The Naga people originated in Southeast Asia and are distributed all along the India–Myanmar border. However, in Nagaland they form a majority everywhere except in Dimapur, which is historically a Kachari-Bodo city and now Nagaland's dull but useful main transport hub. Historically Nagas were great warriors. For centuries the 20-plus Naga groups valiantly fought off any intruders and, in between, kept themselves busy by fighting each other. The antagonistic groups developed mutually unintelligible languages, so today to communicate with each other Nagas speak a 'neutral' lingua franca called Nagamese (a sort of market Assamese), or use English. Major Naga groups include the developed Angami and Rengma of Kohima district, the Lotha of Wokha district (famed for their cooking) and the Konyak of Mon district, who have the most exotic traditional costumes and architecture. For festivals, Naga women wear a handwoven shawl that's distinctive for each subtribe, while the men dust off their old warrior-wear, loincloth and all.

It's festival Nagaland that most tourists imagine when booking a Nagaland tour. And Kohima's December Hornbill Festival easily justifies the trip. At other times some visitors may find the lack of spectacle disappointing. But if you lower your *National Geographic* image expectations, there's still lots of interest in meeting peoples whose cultures, in the words of one Indian journalist, have been through '1000 years in a lifetime'.

History

The Nagas were once feared headhunters. Never fully conquered, the various Naga peoples finally came to an uneasy coexistence with British India after the second battle of Khonoma (p229) in 1879. The British decided the Naga Hills were too much trouble to colonise, so they largely left them alone. However, they encouraged Christian missionaries, whose religion proved more effective than force at subduing the Naga temperament. Christianity started to give rise to a pan-Naga identity. After fierce WWII battles that devastated many Naga settlements, this Naga sentiment was fanned by charismatic separatist leader AZ Phizo. When India declared independence in 1947, Phizo's Naga National Congress (NNC) declared Independence for Nagaland too. India didn't agree, considering the Naga Hills to be part of Assam. Brutal military actions in the mid-1950s strengthened public support for the NNC, stoking what was to become one of the most brutal and long-lasting insurgencies in the whole northeast. Tensions were eased somewhat when Nagaland achieved statehood in 1963 and with the 1980 signing of the Shillong

Accords. However, since then the NNC has been superseded by the Maoist National Socialist Council of Nagaland (NSCN), which has fought on, though split into two mutually antagonistic factions. Both effectively control and tax the rural areas, leading to continued instability, especially around the Burmese and Manipur borders. In late 2008 a third splinter faction arose, further complicating the issues and presenting the state with the distinct possibility of turf wars.

Dangers & Annoyances

Since 1947 Naga insurgents have battled for an independent Nagaland and some remote areas are partially under rebel control. A truce exists, most major Nagaland towns are stable, though can't be considered totally safe. Always check the current security situation before visiting anywhere in the region. Even in Kohima virtually everything closes by 7pm and travel by night is highly discouraged.

DIMAPUR

☎ 03862 / pop 308,000 / elev 260m

Nagaland's flat, uninspiring commercial centre was the capital of a big Kachari kingdom that ruled much of Assam before the Ahoms showed up. All that remains are some curious, strangely phallic pillars of a former palace complex dotted about scraggy **Rajbari Park** (admission free) near an interesting **market**. The only reason tourists visit Dimapur is to transfer to Kohima. Right beside the NST bus station, the **Tourist Lodge** (☎ 226355; Kohima Rd; s/d Rs250/300) is a basic but acceptable budget option.

de Oriental dream (☎ 231211; deorientaldream @yahoo.com; Bank Colony; s/d from Rs300/600, with AC Rs750/950; ✕) is a surprisingly different hotel with a European exterior and clean rooms with new and soft mattresses, but a notice in the foyer states it doesn't accept 'illegal or unmarried couples'.

Hotel Saramati (☎ 234761; Naga Shopping Arcade; hotelsaramati@yahoo.co.in; s/d from Rs1000/1200; ✕) is somewhat past its prime and with little to look forward to, but it's a safe option for a night's sleep.

Air India (☎ 229366, 242441) flies to Kolkata, Guwahati and Imphal. The airport is 400m off the Kohima road, 3km out of town. The **NST bus station** (☎ 227579; Kohima Rd) runs services to Kohima (Rs65, three hours, hourly) and Imphal (Rs190, seven hours, 6am).

For trains consult the tables, p208.

NORTHEAST STATES

NAGALAND FAST FACTS

Population Two million
Area 16,579 sq km
Capital Kohima
Main languages Nagamese, various Naga languages, Hindi, English
When to go October to March

NAGA CULTURE

Naga villages are perched defensively on top of impregnable ridgetops. Many are still subdivided into *khel*s (neighbourhoods) guarded by ceremonial *kharu* (gates) with some still retaining their massively heavy, strikingly carved, wooden or stone doors. Although exact designs vary considerably, the central motif is usually a Naga warrior between the horns of a *mithun* (distinctive local bovine), with sun, moon, breasts (for fertility) and weaponry all depicted. *Kharu* also provide an ornamental entranceway into villages and usually behind them is a dedicated head-hanging tree where once the tribe's collection of heads would have been displayed.

As a sign of wealth, *mithun* skulls also adorn traditional Naga houses, especially around Mon, whose designs typically have rounded prow-fronts. Conversion to Christianity has meant a loss of Naga tradition. Fortunately headhunting has ended, but Christian villages no longer retain *morungs* (bachelor dormitories) where young men lived communally while learning traditional skills.

Headhunting was officially outlawed in 1935, with the last recorded occurrence in 1963. Nonetheless, severed heads are still an archetypal artistic motif found notably on *yanra* (pendants) that originally denoted the number of human heads a warrior had taken. Some villages, such as Shingha Changyuo in Mon district, still retain their 'hidden' collection. Some intervillage wars continued into the 1980s, and a curious feature of many outwardly modern settlements is their 'treaty stones' recording peace settlements between neighbouring communities.

Visiting a Naga village without a local guide is unproductive, there will be language difficulties and you'll be unaware of local cultural expectations. The guide will also know the local security situation.

KOHIMA

☎ 0370 / pop 96,000 / elev 1444m

Nagaland's agreeable capital is scattered across a series of forested ridges and hilltops. Avoid Kohima on Sunday as apart from hotels, places are closed; for security reasons, the town shuts down by 5pm.

Orientation

The central commercial area's one-way system means that only northbound traffic passes the NST bus station (and nearby hotels), while southbound traffic passes Stadium Approach for the market. To the south three roads rejoin at the State Legislature building near the Hotel Pine. About 300m further south the Dimapur road branches west, above which is the War Cemetery. Continue 1km towards Imphal and there's a secondary hub around the roundabout facing a grandiose new police headquarters.

Some 400m north of the NST bus station the traffic-clogged Mokokchung road leads north from Chinatown Restaurant, passing the access lane to T-Khel shortly after then continuing 1km to the museum turn-off.

Information

Alder Tours & Travels (☎ 9436011266; kevi_alder toursntravels@rediffmail.com; AG Colony) Nagaland cultural tours, birdwatching trips and permits.

Amizone (cnr Dimapur & Imphal Rds; per hr Rs30; ⏰ 10am-5.30pm Mon-Sat) Internet downstairs from Dream Café.

Axis Bank (Stadium Approach, Razhu Point) One of several ATMs.

Kohima Computer Centre (NTS Rd; ⏰ 9am-7pm; per hour Rs30) Internet.

Secretariat, Home Department (☎ 2221406; Secretariat Bldg) Permit extensions.

Tribal Discovery (☎ 9436000759, 9856474767; yiese _neitho@rediffmail.com; Science College Rd) Neithonuo Yeise ('Nitono') is an eloquent guide to local sites and can arrange permits.

Sights & Activities

An immaculate **War Cemetery** (⏰ dawn-dusk, Mon-Sat) contains graves of 1200 British, Commonwealth and Indian soldiers. It stands at the crucially strategic junction of the Dimapur and Imphal roads, the site of intense fighting against the Japanese during a 64-day WWII battle. This reached its climax on the deputy commissioner's tennis court (marked out) with seven days of incredibly short-range grenade-lobbing across the net. Deuce!

The superbly presented exhibits of the **State Museum** (☎ 2220749; admission Rs5; ⏰ 9.30am-3.30pm Tue-Sun), 3km north, includes plenty of mannequin-in-action scenes depicting different traditional Naga lifestyles plus everyday tools.

The original site of Kohima is **T-Khel** (aka Tsütuonuomia Khel, Kohima Village or Bara Basti). Although practically all the older homes here have been demolished and redeveloped, the village *karu* (gate) remains impressive with two old door panels visible beside and behind it. Eight **monoliths** are obvious on your right as you climb the stairway beside ancient-looking mossy stone walls.

At the fascinating if tiny **central market** (Stadium Approach; ☉ 6am-4pm), Adivasi people sell such 'edible' delicacies as *borol* (wriggling hornet grubs).

Sleeping & Eating

Accommodation becomes extremely scarce for kilometres around during the Hornbill Festival, book well in advance.

Capital Hotel (☎ 2224365; Main Rd; s/d from Rs150/250) One of several cheapies across from the NST bus station and it would be last-resort lodging but for the cleanish rooms, cheap price and fabulous views from the rear balcony.

Hotel Pine (☎ 2243129; d Rs400-800) Down a side lane off Phool Bari this small hotel is suitable for a night's stay being centrally located, well kept and in reasonable condition. Top sheets only come with the more expensive rooms, but you could ask for one.

Viewpoint Lodge (☎ 2241826, 9436002096; 3rd fl, Keditsu Bldg, PR Hill; s/d Rs700/1000) Perched above two handy internet cafes at Police Station Junction (1km south of the bus station), Viewpoint Lodge offers sparklingly clean rooms with neatly tiled floors. Singles are at the front so choose a double for the good rearside views.

Hotel Japfü (☎ 2240211; hoteljapfu@yahoo.co.in; PR Hill; s/d from Rs1000/1400) This high-service hotel on a small hill directly above Police Station Junction has glassed-in balconies, hot showers and only slightly worn decor. The restaurant food is superb but service is woeful – best to order meals well in advance.

Razhü Pru Guesthouse (☎ 2290291; razhupru@yahoo .co.in; Rs2000-4000) Offering old colonial opulence this overpriced place is on the hill on the way up to Kohima Village, with lots of wickerwork furniture, colourful rugs and polished wooden floors.

Popular Bakery (PR Hill; from Rs5; ☉ 5.30am-8.30pm) Stroll two minutes down the hill from Viewpoint Lodge for delicious breakfast pastries or Indian sweets.

Dream Café (☎ 2290756; cnr Dimapur & Imphal Rds; instant coffee Rs10; ☉ 10am-6pm) Beneath UCO Bank is Kohima's youth meeting point, with twice-monthly live minigigs and CDs of Naga music for sale. Great views from the back windows, a bunch of magazines to read and homemade cakes make this is a good lingering place.

Rendezvous (Main Rd; dishes Rs40-80; ☉ 10am-8pm) Mostly a college-student hangout offering soft drinks, snacks and meals. It's closed on Sunday.

Flaming Wok (Rs40-90; ☉ 10am-7pm Mon-Sat) On Nagaland State Transport (NST) Rd; upstairs overlooking the taxi stand. The fare is mainly Chinese but with some Indian dishes. A guitar is available if you wish to serenade your fellow diners.

Shopping

Nagaland Handicrafts (☎ 2291371; NST Rd) has colourful Naga-design waistcoats (Rs1500), shawls (from Rs550), bamboo mugs (Rs50) and a sharp *dao* (machete; Rs200) used for headhunting.

Getting There & Away

The **NST bus station** (☎ 2291018; Main Rd) has services to Dimapur (Rs65, three hours, hourly Monday to Saturday, 7am Sun), Mokokchung (Rs132, seven hours, 6.30am Monday to Saturday) and Imphal (Rs123, six hours, 7.30am Monday, Wednesday and Friday). The taxi stand opposite has share taxis to Dimapur (Rs150, 2½ hours). A car for a day out to Kisama and Khonoma costs Rs600 to Rs1000. A railway line is being built from Dimapur to Kohima.

AROUND KOHIMA

Kisama Heritage Village

This **open-air museum** (Rs10; ☉ 8am-6pm May-Sep, 8am-4.30pm Oct-Apr) has a representative selection of traditional Naga houses and *morungs* (bachelor dormitories) with full-size log drums. Nagaland's biggest annual festival, the **Hornbill Festival** (1–7 Dec) is celebrated here with various Naga groups converging for a weeklong cultural, dance and sporting bash, much of it in full warrior costume. Simultaneously Kohima also hosts a **rock festival** (www.hornbillmusic.com). Kisama is 10km from central Kohima along the well-surfaced Imphal road.

Kigwema village, 3km south of Kisama, has Angami-Naga homes with traditional-style *kikeh* (crossed-horn gables). There's a sign on a building in the main square announcing that Japanese troops arrived in Kigwema on '4-4-44 at 3pm'. Some houses are still roofed with corrugated metal sheets donated by the British army after the village was burnt out in a battle to take it back from the Japanese. Down a narrow stone lane lined with the winter's wood is an old *kharu* (gate) – two, in fact, as the previous one is stored behind its replacement.

A roadside sign 3km north of Kisama points to a hiking trail and invites you to trek to the world's tallest rhododendron bush (supposedly 20m) somewhere in the floral **Dhüku Valley**.

There's a small restaurant on site and 1km on the road towards Kigwema is **Dimori Cove restaurant** (mains Rs60-120) with a mainly Chinese menu.

Khonoma

The road from Kohima down to Khonoma battles some rugged forested terrain, but about 5km before the village the route breaks out to reveal a magnificent **viewpoint** with a large monolith declaiming that Nagaland will never be part of India.

This historic **Angami-Naga village** was the site of two major British-Angami siege battles in 1847 and 1879. Built on an easily defended ridge (very necessary back in headhunting days), Khonoma looks beautifully traditional. Amid flowers and pomelo trees, squash gourd vines and megaliths, the houses range from corrugated shacks to sturdy concrete homes still decorated with *mithun* (distinctive local bovine) skulls. Basket weavers work quietly at their open doors, public rubbish bins are regularly emptied and graves are dotted everywhere along the neatly laid stone stairways that form the main thoroughfares. Notice the *dahu* circles or wide circular stone pedestals. These are a show-off symbol of family wealth as building one requires the preamble of funding a feast for the whole village.

There are several *karu* stone gateways with stylised pictogram doors. Through one of these, steps lead up past a *morung* to the remains of a **fort** with an out-of-place modern building atop. From the fort there are splendid panoramic views of rice terraces nestled within an arc of forested mountains. Steps from here lead down to another, more interesting reconstructed **fort**. A heritage museum is being built on the lower slopes of the village below this fort and will open in 2010.

A small sanctuary near Khonoma is one of the few places where ornithologists have a good chance of spotting a wild **Blyth's tragopan** (a rare type of pheasant).

Of three simple homestay-guesthouses the best option is **Via Meru's House** (☎ 943619378, 9436011266; s/d Rs400/700, meals extra). The three wooden-floored twin rooms are well kept and one room has a delightful balcony from where the top section of the village is perfectly framed. The place exudes character and the aroma of polished wood pervades the house.

KOHIMA TO MON

Road conditions require you to travel some of the way through Assam and the journey is usually broken with a night's stay at the friendly and well-run **Tourist Lodge** (☎ 0369-2229343; touristlodgemkg@yahoo.com; dm Rs200, r Rs600-1000; 🖳) in unexceptional **Mokokchung**. An alternative is **Tuophema Tourist Village** (☎ 0370-2270786; s/d/tr Rs800/1200/1200), where you sleep in comfortable but traditionally styled Naga thatched bungalows set in a delightful flower garden giving great sunset views.

The main problem for Tuophema, as with so much of Nagaland, is that there's not a lot to see or do within easy reach. Typical excursions show you Rengma-Naga villages but though these sport photogenic rice barns, they're not enormously atmospheric. Around 9km beyond Tseminyu (the Rengma 'capital', 14km from Tuophema), **Tesophenyu** is marginally the best of the bunch with a 24-head wooden totem pole and one last remaining thatched, round-ended traditional house.

NORTHERN NAGALAND

This is the most unspoiled part of the state with many Adivasi groups living in villages of thatched longhouses. However, it's rugged country and only a few villages are easily accessible by road.

The most accessible villages are the Konyak settlements around Mon. Traditional houses abound, and some villages have *morungs* and religious relics from pre-Christian times. Village elders may wear traditional costume and Konyak of all ages carry the fearsome-looking *dao* – a crude machete used for headhunting right up until the mid-20th century.

The impoverished hill town of **Mon** is in a gorgeous setting but feels like a frontier town. Reporting to the incredibly dilapidated police station on arrival is essential.

While welcoming, they're twitchy about the very few foreigners who come here; we even had a 'courtesy visit' next day from a Central Intelligence Bureau agent (India's MI5/FBI) who did a passport and permit check and asked a lot of questions.

Accommodation is at the delightful **Helsa Cottage** (☎ 9436433782, 9436657434; r Rs800) run by Aunty who can organise transport and local guides. The cottage has an impressive log drum and stored in the courtyard are some examples of traditional Naga beds. The occupants of these 100-year-old wooden-slab beds were kept warm in winter by the live coals stacked up underneath. Talk to Aunty and she'll tell you how much Mon and Nagaland have changed. She relates the time she came to Mon in the early 1960s when there were no roads and she was carried up from the plains, aged seven, on the back of a porter to be greeted by a population that wore no clothes.

Shingha Chingyuo village (20km; population 5900) has a huge longhouse decorated with *mithun* and deer skulls, three stuffed tiger carcases, and a store of old human skulls. There used to be 10 *morungs* in this village. **Longwoa** (35km) is on the India–Burma border with one longhouse actually straddling the border. **Chui** (8km) includes an elephant skull in its longhouse collection. **Shangnyu** village has a shrine full of fertility references such as tumescent warriors, a crowing cock, a large snake, a man and woman enjoying sex, and to complete the picture a double rainbow.

MANIPUR

This 'Jewelled Land' is home to Thadou, Tangkhul, Kabul, Mao Naga and many other Adivasi peoples, but the main grouping is the predominantly neo-Vaishnavite Meitei who are battling to have Meitei script used in local schools. Manipuris are famed for traditional dances, spicy multidish thalis and the sport of polo that they claim to have invented. Manipur's forested hills provide cover for rare birds, drug traffickers and guerrilla armies making it by far the Northeast's most dangerous state.

Permit conditions usually restrict foreigners to Greater Imphal although this represents more a zone of safety rather than a geographical area. Most foreigners fly into Imphal; however, with a guide, driving in from Kohima (Nagaland) or Silchar (Assam) to Imphal is possible. Travelling east of Kakching towards the Burma border is not permitted.

MANIPUR FAST FACTS

Population 2.4 million
Area 22,327 sq km
Capital Imphal
Main languages Manipuri (Meitei), Assamese, Bengali
When to go October to March

IMPHAL
Orientation

Major highways, including Airport Rd, intersect at Kanglapat, which skirts Kangla, the former fortified centre of Imphal. MG Ave runs off Kanglapat north of NC Rd. The airport is 9km to the southwest.

Information

Click Communication (☎ 9862241707; MG Ave; per hr Rs20; ⊗ 8am-7pm Mon-Sat, 11am-2pm Sun) Internet.
SBI ATM (MG Ave) About 100m from Hotel Nirmala.
Tourist office (☎ 224603; Jail Rd; http://manipur.nic.in /tourism.htm) For brochures.

Sights

Fortified **Kangla** (admission free; ⊗ 9am-4pm Nov-Feb, 9am-5pm Mar-Oct) was the off-and-on-again regal capital of Manipur until the Anglo–Manipuri War of 1891 saw the defeat of the Manipuri maharaja and a British takeover. A previous 1869 earthquake destroyed many of the earlier buildings that were replaced and strengthened by Chandrakriti, the last-but-one reigning maharaja. It was once a well-fortified citadel of defensive walls and moats, some of which remain today, although much is now grassland, including a polo field and an army encampment.

Entrance is by way of an exceedingly tall gate on Kanglapat. The interesting, older, buildings are at the rear of the citadel guarded by three recently restored large white *kangla sha* (dragons). During the Anglo–Manipuri War the chief commissioner of Assam and several captured British soldiers were executed in front of these dragons. Although the citadel buildings are shells of what they once were, they're worth a look as indeed is the gruesome Luphou

Nung. This large stone slab is where the skulls of kings were placed to dry off after exhumation from their initial burial place.

In the northern section of the fort are three very English bungalows built by the British, one is now the headquarters of the ASI (Archaeology Survey of India) with a small collection of antiquities, while another was the WWII HQ of Field Marshall Slim, who commanded the local Allied Forces.

Manipur State Museum (☎ 2450709; off Kangla Rd; Indian/foreigner Rs3/20; ۞ 10am-4pm Tue-Sun) has a marvellous collection of historical, cultural and natural history ephemera. Given that Manipur is a landlocked state, some curator must have a considerable interest in sea life to have amassed several display cases worth of pickled crustaceans, sea fish and seashells. Adivasi costumes, royal clothing, historical polo equipment, stuffed carnivores in action and pickled snakes compete with a two-headed calf for the visitor's attention.

The 1776-built **Shri Govindajee Mandir**, with two rather suggestive domes, is a neo-Vaishnavite temple with Radha and Govinda the presiding deities. Guarding the outside of the temple are Garuda (the vehicle of Vishnu) and the monkey god Hanuman. Afternoon *puja* (offerings, prayers) is for one hour at 4pm in winter and 5pm in summer.

Adjacent to the Mandir is the **Royal Palace**, closed to visitors except for the annual **Kwak Tenba festival**. Then a colourful procession in traditional costume and headed by the titular maharaja walk to the polo ground for religious ceremonies and cultural festivities. The festival takes place on the fourth day of Durga Puja.

Khwairamband Bazaar (Ima Market; ۞ 7am-5pm) is a photogenic all-women's market run by some 3000 *ima* (mothers). Divided by a road, one side sells vegetables, fruit, fish and groceries while the other deals in household items, fabrics and pottery.

Imphal War Cemetery (Imphal Rd; ۞ 8am-5pm) contains the graves of more than 1600 British and Commonwealth soldiers killed in the battles that raged around Imphal in 1944. It's a peaceful and well-kept memorial. Off Hapta Minuthong Rd is a separate **Indian War Cemetery** (۞ 8am-5pm).

Paona Bazaar is the place where smuggled goods are sold, mostly Chinese, brought in through Burma as part of a thriving drug and contraband trade.

Sleeping & Eating

State tax, disappointingly, adds 20% to your bill.

Hotel White Palace (☎ 2452322; 113 MG Ave; s/d Rs160/280, VIP s/d Rs200/310, ste Rs450-700) A fairly standard hotel that despite its abuse of the terms 'VIP' and 'suite' has some good budget rooms, although a few have no external windows. They all come with mosquito nets and some sort of TV, and we felt that room 14 was the best.

Hotel Bheigo (☎ 2400796; Keishampat Wahengbam Leikai; s/d from Rs250/350, with AC Rs1000/1500; ☒) Some of the suites have room for a dinner dance but the doubles are less ambitious and come smallish and clean. You'll need to pester for top sheets.

Hotel Nirmala (☎ 2459014; MG Ave; s/d from Rs250/400, AC from Rs600/800; ☒) A friendly place with an ultra quick-service restaurant although it doesn't open until 10am so breakfast has to be by room service. The rooms are nothing special but you do feel a sense of belonging staying here.

Anand Continental (☎ 2449422; Khoyathong Rd; hotel_anand@rediff.com; s/d from Rs425/800, with AC Rs675/1000; ☒) Smallish rooms, a little too much furniture, friendly management and possession of a vacuum cleaner characterise this acceptable hotel. Hot water flows 6am to 11am, thereafter by a free bucket-load.

The state tourism's Imphal Hotel is under-going reconstruction.

Getting There & Away

Private buses to Guwahati (Rs600, 20 hours, 10am) and Dimapur (Rs330, 10 hours, frequent between 6am and 10.30am) via Kohima (Rs240, six hours) are run by **Manipur Golden Travels** (☎ 9856247872; MG Ave; ۞ 5.30am-7pm). Next door, Royal Tours has buses to Shillong (Rs660, 20 hours, 10am). A train line to Imphal is being planned.

Air India (☎ 2450999; airport) flies to Aizawl (thrice weekly, from Rs3663), Delhi (twice weekly, from Rs7831), Dimapur (four times weekly, from Rs2828), Guwahati (five times weekly, from Rs3432), Kolkata (daily, from Rs3613) and Silchar (daily, from Rs2828). **IndiGo** (☎ 18001803838 toll free; airport) flies to Agartala (four times weekly, from Rs2526), Kolkata (daily, from Rs2828) and Delhi (daily, from Rs5841). **Jetlite** (☎ 2455054; airport) flies to Guwahati (five times a week, from Rs2675) and Kolkata (five times a week, from Rs2675). **Kingfisher Red** (☎ 18002093030, toll free; airport) flies to Dimapur (thrice weekly, from Rs2675), Guwahati (thrice weekly, from Rs2828), Kolkata (daily, from Rs2828) and Silchar (four times weekly, from Rs2577).

AROUND IMPHAL

One area allowed on a foreigner's permit is along 48km of NH150, south to Loktak Lake. If you're part of a guided tour there are several tourist sites that you'll be taken to. **Lokpaching Battlefield** (Red Hill), 16km south of Imphal, has a rather uninspiring Japanese war memorial on a site that marks the last battle on Indian soil.

Conjure up an image of a shimmering blue lake broken up into small lakelets by floating 'islands' of thick matted weeds. Add bamboo bridges, Adivasi people in dugout canoes and thatched hut-villages anchored on to the floating islands, and you have **Loktak Lake**. This, apart from being India's largest freshwater lake, is a beautiful spot and well worth the drive from Imphal. More peculiar than floating villages are the large perfectly circular fishing ponds created out of floating rings of weeds. The best view is atop Sendra Island, more a promontory than island. Access is through a military checkpoint where you have to relinquish your mobile phone.

Moirang's **INA Museum** (Indian National Army; ☎ 0385-262186; admission Rs2; ☺ 10am-4pm Tue-Sun) celebrates the town's small but symbolic role in the Indian Independence movement. It was here on 14 April 1944 that the anticolonial INA first unfurled the Azad Hind (Free India) flag while advancing with Japanese WWII forces against British-held Imphal. The INA Museum is mostly dedicated to Netaji (dear leader) Subhas Chandra Bose, the head of the INA. Although revered by Indian freedom fighters, he had different socialist ideas to the likes of Jarwahal Nehru and the Congress party, with plans for wholesale takeover and nationalisation of industry and agriculture.

MIZORAM

Mizoram is slashed by deep north–south-running valleys, the remainder of the Himalaya foothills flung to the side as the Indian subcontinent collided with Asia all those millions of years ago. Mizoram is tidy and almost entirely Christian, and you'll see very few Indian faces among the local Thai-and Chinese-style features.

Mizoram runs to its own rhythm. Most businesses open early and shut by 6pm; virtually everything closes tight on Sunday. Mizos traditionally have two main meals, *zingchaw* (morning meal, 9am to 10am) and *tlaichaw* (afternoon meal, 4pm to 6pm). Both feature rice, boiled leaves and vegetables and boiled fatty smoked pork alongside. Flavour is added using *rawt,* a salsa of diced chillies, ginger and onion. On paper Mizoram is a dry state but an expensive beer can always be found if you make discreet enquiries.

Mizo culture has no caste distinctions and women appear liberated; in Aizawl girls smoke openly, wear jeans and hang out in unchaperoned posses meeting up with their beaus at rock concerts on the central field.

Two main Mizo festivals, Chapchar Kut (Kut is Mizo for festival) and Pawl Kut celebrate elements in the agricultural cycle. Chapchar Kut takes place towards the end of February and signals the start of the spring sowing season. Participants don national costume and celebrate in folk dancing and singing traditional songs as they do also for Pawl Kut held at the end of November. This time though it is to celebrate the harvest.

History

About every 50 years Mizoram's endless bamboo forests flower for three seasons, producing millions of egg-shaped fruit. Although inedible to humans, these fruit are adored by rats, which multiply rapidly to enjoy the free feast. But after the third year the bamboo stops fruiting. Suddenly hungry, the rats swarm onto anything else edible, notably human crops. This last happened in 1959 causing a serious famine. The Indian government's inept response left Mizos feeling entirely abandoned. The Mizo Famine Front (MFF) later spawned

---

MIZORAM FAST FACTS

Population 895,000
Area 21,081 sq km
Capital Aizawl
Main languages Mizo, English
When to go October to March

AW DEAR

Traditionally each Mizo clan has its own language, but there's a widely used Mizo lingua franca that's now taught in schools along with English or Hindi. It's written in Latin script using a system devised by Welsh missionaries that, confusingly for English speakers, spells the long, soft 'oh' sound as 'aw'. A typical Mizo greeting is *chibai*. Thank you is *kalawmeh* (kal-oh may).

the Mizo National Front (MNF) insurgents. In 1966 they launched a stunning surprise raid, briefly capturing Mizoram's then-tiny capital Aizawl. India's heavy-handed response was the infamous 'grouping' policy. The entire rural population was corralled into virtual concentration camps. The old *jhumming* (a traditional form of slash-and-burn agriculture) hamlets were then destroyed to deprive insurgents of resources (so don't look for ancient traditional homes in Mizoram). Obviously such tactics backfired massively, creating a huge wave of support for the rebels. However, after two decades of fighting, the 1986 ceasefire led to a lasting peace settlement. Today the MNF holds a majority in the democratically elected state government and Mizoram is proud of being the safest state in the northeast. Many Mizos remain bemused as to how their 'country' ever got attached to India, but everyone's relieved that at least they didn't end up within Myanmar.

Information
PERMITS
Agencies, notably Serow Travels and Omega Travels (right), can arrange and fax you a 10-day permit. Mizoram permit restrictions are perhaps the most lax of the Northeast States. If you are travelling on your own there'll be three ghost travellers who'll be attached to your permit, as the minimum group size is still four, but their absence will not be remarked upon. Be sure that all places you wish to visit are on your permit and you should be allowed to go anywhere in the state. Visit the Superintendent of Police, Criminal Investigation Department (SP-CID) (right) for 10-day permit extensions. Note though that the Kolkata FRO doesn't grant Mizoram permits.

AIZAWL
☎ 0389 / pop 275,000
From a distance Aizawl (pronounced eye-zole) seems a painted backdrop to an Italian opera, such is the steepness of the ridge on which it's perched. Backs of homes at road

level might be held there with stilts three times higher than their roofs.

Addresses refer to areas and junctions ('points' or 'squares'). The unnamed spaghetti of roads and steep linking stairways is confusing, but the central ridge road is reasonably flat joining Zodin Sq (old bus station), Upper Bazaar (shops), Zarkawt (hotels and long-distance Sumos) and Chandmari (east Mizoram Sumos).

Information
Directorate of Tourism (☎ 2333475; www.mizo tourism.nic.in; PA-AW Bldg, Bungkawn)
Omega Travels (☎ 2322283; Zodin Sq; ☺ 9am-5pm Mon-Fri, 9am-3pm Sat) Arranges tourist permits and tours. Staff member Zova (☎ 9436142938) speaks good English.
SBI ATM (Raj Bhawan Junction)
Serow Travels (☎ 2301509, 9436150484; D/74 Millennium Centre, Dawrpui; www.serowtours.com; ☺ 9.30am-6pm Mon-Sat) Arranges permits, Mizoram tours and village homestays. Helpful Ruati speaks excellent English.
Serps Connection (Zarkawt; per hr Rs30; ☺ 9am-10.30pm)
SP-CID (☎ 2333980, Maubawk Bungkawn; ☺ 10am-4pm Mon-Fri) Permit extensions.

Sights
Mizoram State Museum (☎ 2340936; Macdonald Hill, Zarkawt; admission Rs5; ☺ 9.30am-5pm Mon-Fri) has interesting exhibits on Mizo culture. It's up a steep lane from Sumkuma Point past Aizawl's most distinctive **church**, whose modernist bell-tower spire is pierced by arched 'windows'.

The **Salvation Army Temple** (Zodin Sq) has bell chimes that are endearingly complex and can be heard throughout the city especially on a bible-quiet Sunday morning.

The **KV Paradise** (Durtlang; admission Rs5; ☺ 10am-9pm Mon-Sat) site is 8km from Zarkawt, 1km off the Aizawl–Silchar road via an improbably narrow dirt lane. V is for Varte who died in a 2001 motor accident. K is for her husband Khawlhring who has since lavished his entire savings and energy creating a three-storey mausoleum to her memory. The marble fountain-patio has wonderful panoramic views.

Inside and downstairs is Varte's grave and upstairs an odd collection displays her wardrobe and shoe collection including the clothes (neatly laundered) she died in.

A Saturday **street market** (Mission Veng St) sprawls along the street with village women offering fruit, vegetables, maybe a dead pig, fish and live hens in individualised wickerwork carry-away baskets.

Sleeping

ZARKAWT

There's a convenient concentration of lower-midrange hotels around Zarkawt's Sumkuma Point. Hotels typically add a 10% service charge.

Imperial Hotel (☎ 2348168; s with shared bathroom Rs180, d with shared bathroom Rs250-300, d Rs260-600) Some 200m south of Sumkuma Point this large block of a hotel is a basic you-get-what-you-pay-for concrete box of rooms, but it's cheap.

Hotel Tropicana (☎ 2346156; hotel_tropicana@rediff mail.com; s Rs200-400, d Rs550-650) Resplendently green but with its name painted over, Hotel Tropicana is right at Sumkuma Point roundabout. The better double rooms are quite cosy but look at a few before deciding as some have no views and smell musty.

Hotel Chief (☎ 2341097; s/d from Rs380/540) The midrange rooms (the Delux) are the best value and still have the good views, the fridge and colourful bedspreads of the more expensive ones. Room 27 is pleasant.

Hotel Clover (☎ 2305736; G-16 Chanmari; www .davids-hotel-clover.com; s/d from Rs750/1500; ☎) The accommodation side of David's Kitchen with impressively decorated and furnished rooms but without external windows. Bonus is free wi-fi and a 30% discount at David's Kitchen.

UPPER KHATLA

Hotel Arini (☎ 2301557; Upper Khatla; s/d from Rs460/720) Only a small red sign announces the new semiboutique Hotel Arini, named after the owner's precocious three-year-old daughter. The rooms are cheerily bright and fresh-looking, and the staff pleasant and obliging. Choose a backside room with a stupendous down-valley view.

ZEMABAWK

Tourist Home (☎ 2352067; Berawtlang; d Rs350-500) High above Zemabawk, some 11km from Zarkawt, the peaceful Tourist Home has great new rooms and older, mustier cottages. However the hilltop setting is idyllic and Aizawl's best viewpoint is just a 10-minute stroll away. It's worth the Rs250 taxi ride for the views and a snack at the cafeteria.

Eating

David's Kitchen (☎ 2305736; Zarkawt; mains Rs65-210; 🕑 10am-9.30pm Mon-Sat, noon-9.30pm Sun) David's fine Mizo, Thai, Indian, Chinese and continental food, mocktails, friendly staff and pleasant decor will please everyone. It's 200m south of Hotel Chief.

Curry Pot (Upper Khatla; meals Rs50-120; 🕑 10am-9pm Mon-Sat) Next door to Hotel Arini, this place has tasty Indian and Chinese dishes on the menu with a rather good, well-portioned biryani on offer.

On Sunday only hotels and David's Kitchen will save you from starving.

Getting There & Away

Taxis charge Rs500 and shared Sumos charge Rs45 to efficient little Lengpui airport, 35km west of Aizawl. **Air India** (☎ 344733) flies to Guwahati (from Rs3432) and Kolkata (from Rs3432) daily, and Imphal (from Rs3130) four times a week. **Kingfisher Red** flies daily to Kolkata (from Rs2577).

Counters for long-distance Sumos are clustered around Zarkawt's Sumkuma Point. For Saitual the most central are **RKV** (☎ 2305452) and Nazareth in Chandmari. For details, see the boxed table, opposite.

NORTHEAST STATES

YMA NOT YMCA

Wherever you look in Mizoram you'll see red, white and black tricolours. No, that's not the Egyptian flag, but the colours of the ubiquitous Young Mizo Association (YMA). This is a community-based volunteer charity to which virtually every local under 45 years of age belongs. It helps the poor at times of need but also runs many day-to-day local services, including rubbish collection. The YMA notably organises free Christian burials: the idea of paying commercial undertakers for coffins and funerals seems a shocking commercialisation of death to most Mizos.

SERVICES FROM AIZAWL

Destination	Cost (Rs)	Duration (hr)	Departure
Guwahati	550	14-18	4pm
Saitual	75	3	1pm, 3pm
Shillong	435	15	4pm
Silchar	265	5½	6.30am, 10am, 1pm

Getting Around

Frequent city buses run Zodin Sq–Upper Bazaar–Zarkawt–Chandmari–Lower Chatlang–Zasanga Point, then either climb to Durtlang or curl right round past the new Chunga Bus Station (6km) to Zemabawk. Maruti-Suzuki taxis are ubiquitous and reasonably priced.

RURAL MIZORAM

Foresty **Reiek Tlang** with a lookout peak is one hour from Aizawl by winding road. It's a popular Mizo day-out place and the site of the June Anthurium Flower Festival, that is an occasion for song and dance. **Reiek Tourist Resort** (☎ 0389-2567344; s/d Rs150/250) has adequate rooms and self-contained cottages surrounding a restaurant on the edge of the woodland. An adjacent **'model' village** (admission Rs10; ☼ 9.30am-4pm) displays a number of typical Mizo rural huts.

Mizoram's pretty, green hills get higher as you head east. **Champhai** is widely considered the most attractive district. But for a more accessible taste of small-town Mizo life, visit **Saitual**. An incredibly good-value **Tourist Lodge** (☎ 2562395; d Rs250) in a hilltop garden, 700m north of Saitual market, offers extensive views. There's little to do but meet the locals and find some biscuits for dinner. However, a very bumpy 10km side trip to **Tamdil Lake** is mildly memorable. This local beauty spot is ringed by lush mountains, patches of poinsettia and a few musty if pleasantly situated **cottages** (☎ 94361449479; d Rs400). There are paddleboats to rent (Rs10), but there's no cafe.

TRIPURA

Tripura is culturally and politically fascinating, and the state's royal palaces and temples draw a growing flow of domestic tourists. However, if you're expecting the exotic grandeur of Rajasthani castles, Tripura might seem a long detour for relatively little.

History

Before joining India in 1949, Tripura (Twipra) was ruled for centuries by its own Hindu royal family (the Manikyas), based first at Udaipur, then Old Agartala (Kayerpur) and finally Agartala. In the 1880s Tripura's maharaja became a benefactor of Bengal Renaissance poet and philosopher Rabindranath Tagore. Indian partition flooded Tripura with Bengali refugees leaving the local Borok-Tripuri people a minority in their own state.

Dangers & Annoyances

The Agartala, Udaipur and Kailasahar areas are generally safe. However, there is serious instability in north-central Tripura. All vehicles must travel in armed convoys through two sections of the Agartala–Kailasahar road. While attacks are rare, they do happen.

Compared to the shy greetings and glances elsewhere in the northeast, Tripura's more forthright stares and slightly forced hospitality can seem a little invasive.

AGARTALA

☎ 0381 / pop 189,330

Tripura's low-key capital is centred on the imposing Ujjayanta Palace. If you've come from early-closing Manipur, Nagaland or Mizoram, it's delightful to find that life continues after 6pm. If you've arrived from Bangladesh, whose border is just 3km east, the town feels refreshingly organised and manageable. **Durga puja** is enthusiastically celebrated with huge imaginative *pandals* (marquee-like

TRIPURA FAST FACTS

Population 3.2 million
Area 10,486 sq km
Capital Agartala
Main languages Bengali, Kokborok
When to go November to February

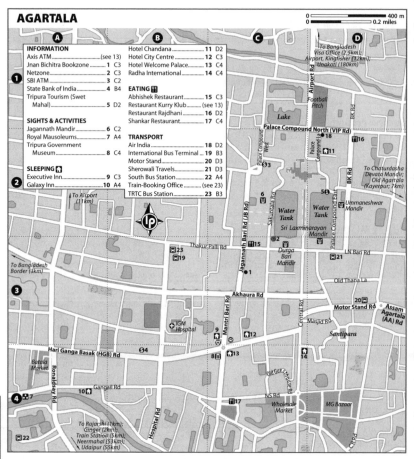

AGARTALA

0 ———————— 400 m
0 ———————— 0.2 miles

INFORMATION
Axis ATM.........................(see 13)
Jnan Bichitra Bookzone.......**1** C3
Netzone...............................**2** C3
SBI ATM...............................**3** C2
State Bank of India.............**4** B4
Tripura Tourism (Swet
Mahal).............................**5** D2

SIGHTS & ACTIVITIES
Jagannath Mandir................**6** C2
Royal Mausoleums..............**7** A4
Tripura Government
Museum..........................**8** C4

SLEEPING
Executive Inn......................**9** C3
Galaxy Inn.........................**10** A4

Hotel Chandana..................**11** D2
Hotel City Centre...............**12** C3
Hotel Welcome Palace........**13** C4
Radha International............**14** C4

EATING
Abhishek Restaurant..........**15** C3
Restaurant Kurry Klub.....(see 13)
Restaurant Rajdhani..........**16** D2
Shankar Restaurant...........**17** C4

TRANSPORT
Air India............................**18** D2
International Bus Terminal ..**19** B3
Motor Stand.......................**20** D3
Sherowali Travels...............**21** D3
South Bus Station..............**22** A4
Train-Booking Office.......(see 23)
TRTC Bus Station...............**23** B3

temporary temples built from wood and cloth). We came across one built as a human head and another as a European castle.

Information

BOOKSHOP
Jnan Bichitra Bookzone (11 JB Rd; 9am-9pm;) Welcoming, well-stocked bookshop selling postcards and music.

INTERNET ACCESS
Netzone (6 Sakuntala Rd; per hr Rs20; 8am-10pm) Best of several closely grouped options.

MONEY
Axis ATM (Hotel Welcome Palace, HGB Rd)

SBI (2311364; top fl, SBI Bldg, HGB Rd) Changes cash and travellers cheques, but allow at least an hour. Also has an ATM.
SBI ATM (Palace Compound West)

TOURIST INFORMATION
Tripura Tourism (2225930; http://tripura.nic.in /ttourism1.htm; Swet Mahal, Palace Complex; 10am-5pm Mon-Sat, 3-5pm Sun) Helpful and enthusiastic with many great-value tours.
TripuraInfo (2380566; www.tripurainfo.com) Useful news and tourism website.

Sights
Agartala's indisputable centrepiece is the striking, dome-capped **Ujjayanta Palace**. Flanked by two large reflecting ponds,

the whitewashed 1901 edifice was built by Tripura's 182nd maharaja. It looks particularly impressive floodlit at night, but for security reasons the grounds and interior are not open to the public.

Of four Hindu temples around the palace compound, much the most fanciful is **Jagannath Mandir** (✆ 4am-2pm & 4pm-9pm). Its massive sculptured portico leads into a complex with wedding cake architecture painted in ice-cream sundae colours. Sculptures of deities appear all over the place, including the upper balcony of the ashram, as though they've just popped out of their rooms for a look-see.

The small **Tripura Government Museum** (☎ 2326444; http://tripura.nic.in/museum/welcome.html; Post Office Circle; admission Rs2; ✆ 10am-1.30pm & 2pm-5pm Mon-Fri) has a variety of Adivasi displays plus some interesting musical instruments made from bamboo. The upstairs gallery has several portraits of the various maharajahs, including one with Tagore.

Several **royal mausoleums** are decaying quietly on the riverbank behind Batala market. Be discreet as it's also the burning ghats (crematorium).

OLD AGARTALA

Chaturdasha Devata Mandir (Temple of Fourteen Deities) hosts a big seven-day July **Kharchi Puja festival** in Old Agartala, 7km east down Assam Agartala (AA) Rd (NH44) at Kayerpur.

Sleeping

State taxes add 10% to your bill.

Hotel Chandana (☎ 2311216; Palace Compound Lane; s/d/tr Rs95/210/285) Lacklustre but cheap and bearable, the Chandana's simple rooms have mosquito nets and cold showers. Peaceful yet central.

Radha International (☎ 2384530; 54 Central Rd; s/d from Rs180/500, with AC from Rs500/750; ✷) The good-value AC rooms are neatly tiled and doubles have a little sitting area but private bathrooms are cupboard size.

Hotel City Centre (☎ 2385092; www.hotelcitycentre .co.in; 39 HGB Rd; s/d from Rs350/450, AC from Rs650/1000; ✷ ▯) Choose from a variety of different rooms depending on your requirements for features such as fridges, fancy carpets or plush sofas. The midpriced rooms are the better value. There's internet at the friendly reception.

Rajarshi (☎ 2201030; Circuit House Rd; r Rs350, AC Rs450-1500; ✷) A sprawling nipple-pink affair

fronted by a long verandah keeping the heat off the clean largish rooms behind.

Galaxy Inn (☎ 2310342; Gangail Rd; s/d Rs385/495; ✷) In a quiet neighbourhood near the south bus station, Galaxy has budget rooms with a mix of bed types and sit-down and squat toilets.

Executive Inn (☎ 2325047; hotelexecutiveinn@yahoo .com; 9 Mantri Bari Rd; old bldg r Rs450-800, new bldg s from Rs800, d from Rs1000-1500; ✷) Go for the better value Rs1000 modern AC doubles in the new building; with no hot water or bed top-sheets the old building's fan-cooled rooms are overpriced.

Hotel Welcome Palace (☎ 2384940; HGB Rd; s from Rs500, d Rs700-1800; ✷) This hard-to-beat option has helpful English-speaking staff, eager room service and superb food. Rooms are neat if not huge; some may not have external windows.

Ginger (☎ toll free 18002093333, 2303333; www .gingerhotels.com; Airport Rd; s/d Rs1499/1999; ✷ ▯ ▯ 🛜) Part of the new Tata-owned Ginger chain of hotels this brand-spanking place has superb rooms with wi-fi, real coffee and a small gym. There's also a room for someone with disabilities.

Eating

Eating out in Tripura is disappointing and despite the state not being dry no restaurant serves alcohol. Better restaurants include the following.

Shankar Restaurant (mains Rs30-70) Provides some of Agartala's best food; nothing fancy just straightforward rice and veg in an AC street cafe. On Netaji Subhash (NS) Rd.

Restaurant Kurry Klub (Hotel Welcome Palace, HGB Rd; mains Rs40-150; ✆ 10am-10pm) Very tasty food served in a small dining room whose decor would be rather striking if only the lighting was improved. If you're staying in the hotel, room service is faster and beers can be acquired.

Restaurant Rajdhani (Hotel Rajdhani, BK Rd; mains Rs35-120; ✷) A top-floor restaurant with a faux-forest setting, burbling waterfall and bird's-eye city views, it's OK for a snack but the main meals are disappointing.

Abhishek Restaurant (LN Bari Rd; mains Rs60-100) Reliable food served either on an inviting outdoor terrace or in a marine-themed dining room with good AC. A prawn curry comes with one large prawn. 'Very expensive, sah', the waiter explained.

NORTHEAST STATES

CROSSING INTO BANGLADESH AT AGARTALA

Border Hours

The border at Agartala is open from 7am to 6pm.

Foreign Exchange

There's no exchange booth and Agartala banks don't sell Bangladeshi taka, so changing money is hit and miss; ask local traders or border officials.

Onward Transport

From central Agartala the border is just 3km along Akhaura Rd (Rs25 by rickshaw). On the Bangladesh side the nearest town is Akhaura, 5km beyond reached by 'baby taxi' (autorickshaw). Akhaura train station is on the Dacca–Comilla line. However for Dacca–Sylhet trains, continue 3km further north to Ajampur train station. Coming eastbound be sure to pay your Bangladeshi departure tax at a Sonali bank before heading for the border.

Visas

Unhelpful, but the northeast's only **Bangladesh visa office** (☎ 2324807; Airport Rd, Kunjaban; ◷ application 9am-1pm Mon-Thu, 9am-noon Fri, collection same day 4pm) hides down a small lane in Agartala, about 2km north of the Ujjayanta Palace.

Getting There & Around

Air India (☎ 2325470; VIP Rd), flies daily to Kolkata (from Rs3432) and Guwahati (from Rs3432), and three times a week to Silchar (from Rs2743). **IndiGo** (☎ 2325602; TRTC bus station) flies daily to Kolkata (from Rs3028), and three times a week to Imphal (from Rs2675). **Jet Airways** (☎ 2325602; TRTC bus station) flies to Guwahati (four times a week, from Rs3603) and Kolkata (daily, from Rs3603). **Kingfisher** (☎ 18002093030; airport) flies daily to Kolkata (from Rs3703) and Guwahati (from Rs2828). Agartala's airport is 12km north, Rs70/90/100 by bus/autorickshaw/share taxi and Rs400 to Rs500 by taxi. Arrive early and before entering get your tickets endorsed at the airline counters outside the terminal, then visit the immigration desk across the arrivals hall (yes, for domestic departures).

Private bus operators clustered on LN Bari Rd include **Sherowali Travels** (☎ 2216608); others leave from the **TRTC bus station** (☎ 2325685; Thakur Palli Rd). Sumos use the **Motor Stand** (Motor Stand Rd) and **South Bus Station** (SBS; ☎ 2376717; Ronaldsay Rd). Destinations for bus and Sumo trips are as follows:

Guwahati bus (Rs530, 20 hours, 6am and noon); Sumo (Rs500, 24 hours, 11.30am)

Kailasahar bus (Rs73, eight hours, 6am); Sumo (Rs120, seven hours, 7am, 10am and noon)

Melaghar (for Neermahal) bus (Rs24, 1½ hours)

Shillong bus (Rs530, 18 hours, 6am and noon); Sumo (Rs410, 20 hours, 11.30am)

Silchar bus (Rs250, 12 hours, 6am); Sumo (Rs136, 12 hours, 6am)

Udaipur bus (Rs25, 1¾ hours)

Opposite the TRTC is the **International Bus Terminal** (☎ 9863045083) where Bangladesh Road Transport Corporation's daily bus departs for Dhaka (Rs232, six hours, 1pm).

Agartala's brand-new, palace-style train station is 5km south on the Udaipur road. Currently there are only two trains a day, to Silchar (No 863; Rs67, eight hours, 2pm) and Lumding (No 5696; Rs95, 18 hours, 1.15pm). At the time of research trains were still such a novelty that people were turning up at the station to see the two daily departures.

There's a computerised **train-booking office** (◷ 8am-7.30pm Mon-Fri, 8am-11.30am Sun) at Agartala's TRTC bus station.

AROUND AGARTALA

Southern Tripura's best known sights can be combined into a long day trip from Agartala, though sleeping at Neermahal is worthwhile. Any of Agartala's hotels can arrange a taxi or engage **Banti Bhattacharjee** (☎ 9856877883) for about Rs1800 per day trip for three people in an AC car. All transport passes the gates of **Sepahijala Wildlife Sanctuary** (☎ 2361225; Km23, NH44 extension; admission/camera/video Rs5/10/500; ◷ 8am-4pm Sat-Thu), a local picnic and boating spot famous for its **spectacled monkeys**.

Udaipur
☎ 03821

Udaipur was Tripura's historic capital and remains dotted with ancient temples and a patchwork of tanks. Ruined but still massive, **Jagannath Mandir** is a most curious temple, overgrown with creepers Angkor Wat–style. It sits at the southwest corner of the huge **Jagannath Digthi tank**, around 1km from Udaipur bus stand, behind a more modern temple. The famous Jagannath statue of Puri once resided here, but has been replaced by another idol that, like the original, still takes an annual chariot ride to its holiday home.

You'll pass two 17th-century temple complexes en route to the Gomati River. They're most distinctive in having solid and stubby bases, capped by Bengali-styled arched roofs and then topped with a mini stupa. None are 'in service'. From the river turn left and walk 10 minutes uphill to find the **Bhuveneswari Temple** (small but celebrated in Tagore's writings) just beyond the lumpy brick ruins of the **Rajbari**, hardly recognisable as a 17th-century palace.

MATABARI

When Sati's toes fell on Kolkata (see p101), her divine right leg dropped on Matabari, a village 4km south of Udaipur. This gruesome legend is piously celebrated at the **Tripura Sundari Mandir** (☉ 4.30am-1.30pm & 3.30pm-9.30pm), a 1501 Kali temple where a steady stream of pilgrims make almost endless animal sacrifices that leave the grounds as bloody-red as the temple's vivid *shikhara* (Buddhist monastery). Even more people come here at the big **Diwali festival** (Oct/Nov) to bathe in the fish-filled tank. The temple is 100m east of the NH44.

SLEEPING

Gonabati Guest House (☎ 267939; dm/d Rs66/165) Overlooking the tank at the mandir, this place has simple rooms and beds with mosquito nets. There's no restaurant here so eat out or bring your own food.

Gouri Hotel (☎ 222419; Central Rd; s/d from Rs175/300, with AC Rs500/700; ✄) In central Udaipur, with good fan-cooled rooms (free bucket hot water), plus two smarter AC rooms with bathroom geysers.

GETTING THERE & AROUND

Udaipur's bus stand has quarter-hourly departures to Agartala (Rs23, 1¼ hours)

and Melagarh (Rs13, 45 minutes). An auto-rickshaw for an around-Udaipur tour will cost Rs300.

Neermahal & Melagarh
☎ 0381 / pop 21,750

Tripura's most iconic building, the 1930 Neermahal, is a long, red-and-white **water palace** (admission Rs3; ☉ 9am-4pm), empty, but shimmering on its own boggy island in the lake of Rudra Sagar. Like its counterpart in Rajasthan's Udaipur, this was a princely exercise in aesthetics; the finest craftsmen building a summer palace of luxury in a blend of Hindu and Islamic architectural styles. The palace is now an empty echo of its past and desperately needs a lick of paint. The delightful waterborne approach by **speed boat** (motorboat; passenger/boat Rs15/300) or **fancy boat** (rowboat; passenger/boat Rs15/75) is the most enjoyable part of visiting.

Boats leave from near the remarkably decent **Sagarmahal Tourist Lodge** (☎ 2524418; dm Rs60, d from Rs160, d with AC Rs300-400; ✄) where most rooms have lake-facing balconies and a good restaurant presides downstairs. Non-AC rooms take the ground floor while the advantages of AC also bring upstairs lakeside views. The lodge is 1km off the Agartala–Sonamura road, 1.3km from Melagarh bus stand.

NORTH TRIPURA
☎ 03824

Around 180km from Agartala, North Tripura's regional centre is **Kailasahar**, where the excellent **Unakoti Tourist Lodge** (☎ 223635; d with/without AC Rs330/165) is a real bargain. **Unakoti** itself, around 10km away, is an ancient pilgrimage centre famous for 8th-century bas-relief rock carvings, including a 10m-high Shiva. Reaching Kailasahar from Agartala requires transiting Tripura's most sensitive areas. Foreign tourists are very rare and will turn heads.

MEGHALAYA

Carved out of Assam in 1972, hilly Meghalaya (The Abode of Clouds) is a cool, pine-fresh contrast to the sweaty Assam plains. Set on dramatic horseshoes of rocky cliff above the Bengal plains, Cherrapunjee and Mawsynram are statistically the wettest places on earth. Most rain falls April to

---

MEGHALAYA FAST FACTS

Population 2.3 million
Area 22,429 sq km
Capital Shillong
Main languages Khasi, Garo, Assamese, Bengali
When to go October to March

September creating very impressive waterfalls and carving out some of Asia's longest caves. Important in Garo culture are the Wangala dances held at harvest time to honour Saljong, the sun-god of fertility. These have been formalised into the 100-drum festival held at Asanang 18km north of Tura

Eastern and central Meghalaya are mainly populated by the closely related Jaintia, Pnar and Khasi peoples (see p242), originally migrants from Southeast Asia. Western Meghalaya is home to the unrelated Garo people. Despite their different ethnic backgrounds, these two groups still use a matrilineal system of inheritance with children taking the mother's family name.

SHILLONG
☎ 0364 / pop 268,000
This sprawling hill station was the capital of British-created Assam from 1874 until 1972. Since becoming the state capital it has rapidly developed into a typical modern Indian town and in doing so some of its older building have been demolished. In parts it still retains its charm, the air is refreshingly cool and it has become a favourite holiday destination for domestic tourists.

Information
BOOKSHOPS
National Book Agency (OB Shopping Mall, Jail Rd) Stocks Lonely Planet guides, Indian and English-language fiction.

INTERNET ACCESS
None are fast, all charge Rs20 per hour.
Sids Cyber (1st fl, MUDA Complex, Police Bazaar; ☽ 9am-8pm) Central but very cramped.
Techweb (basement Zara's Arcade, Keating Rd; per hr Rs20; ☽ 9am-8.30pm) Bright and relatively comfy.

MONEY
Purchase of Bangladeshi taka is not possible. There are many ATMs.
SBI (☎ 2211439; Kacheri Rd) Exchange of foreign currency and travellers cheques; ATM outside.

POST
Post office (Kacheri Rd; ☽ 10am-5pm Mon-Sat)

TOURIST INFORMATION
Cultural Pursuits Adventures (☎ 9436303978; Hotel Alpine Continental, Thana Rd; www.culturalpursuits.com) Experienced agency for caving, trekking, village stays and off-the-beaten-track stuff.
Government of India tourist office (☎ 2225632; Tirat Singh Syiem Rd; ☽ 9.30am-5.30pm Mon-Fri, 10am-2pm Sat) Free basic maps and brochures.
Meghalaya Tourism (☎ 2226220; Jail Rd; ☽ 7am-8.30pm Sep-Nov, 7am-7.30pm Dec-Aug) Sells good-value tours.

Sights & Activities
COLONIAL SHILLONG
Colonial-era Shillong was planned around the ever-attractive **Ward's Lake** (admission/camera Rs5/10; ☽ 8.30am-5.30pm Nov-Feb, 8.30am-7pm Mar-Oct) with its pretty **ornamental bridge**. The city's half-timbered architecture has been rather swamped by drab Indian concrete, but areas such as Oakland retain many older houses and even a few gems remain in the centre. The **Pinewood Hotel** (Rita Rd), a 1920s tea-growers' retreat, is particularly representative and looks great at night. The 1902 **All Saints' Cathedral** (Kacheri Rd) would look perfect on a biscuit tin. Nearby the turreted **Das-Roy House** (closed to the public) lurks behind a traffic circle that harbours five forgotten **Khasi monoliths** and a mini Soviet-style **globe monument**.

MUSEUMS
The very professional **Don Bosco Museum of Indigenous Cultures** (www.dbcic.org; Sacred Heart Theological College; Indian/foreigner Rs50/150, student Rs30/90; ☽ 9.30am-4.30pm Mon-Sat, 1.30pm-4.30pm Sun) displays a truly vast, very well laid-out collection of Adivasi artefacts interspersed just occasionally with gratuitous galleries on Christian missionary work. The hexagonal museum building is an impressive, symbolic tower, seven storeys high for the seven states of the northeast. Tours (compulsory) last over an hour departing on the half-hour. For an extra Rs50, a video explains the Nongkrem festival (p243) or you could choose from various film alternatives.

The memorably named **Wankhar Entomology Museum** (☎ 2544473; Riatsamthiah; admission Rs25; ☽ 11am-4pm Mon-Fri or by arrangement) is a remarkable one-room display of pinned butterflies, gruesome rhinoceros beetles and incredible stick-insects in the home of the original collector.

IEW DUH

This vast **market** (Bara Bazaar; ☷ Mon-Sat) is one of the most animated in the northeast. Thousands of Khasi people flock in from their villages, selling everything from Adivasi baskets to fish traps and edible frogs.

SIAT KHNAM

All around Shillong gambling booths offer 'Forecast' odds on Siat Khnam. This is a unique 'sport'. A semicircle of weather-beaten Khasi men fire hundreds of arrows at a drum-shaped straw target for a set time before a canvas curtain is raised to keep fur-

ther arrows off the target. Those that stick in are counted and bets predict the last two digits of this total. It's effectively a lottery but the shooting is a gently fascinating spectacle. Shoots are usually at 4pm and 5pm daily, timings can vary somewhat by season. The easy-to-miss Siat Khnam site is a small grassy area approximately opposite the big Nehru Stadium on the south river bank. To drive there head east past the Mizo Church, fork left up Bampfyled Rd, then after crossing the hill and descending to the river, turn left: the ground is almost immediately on your right. If walking, take the footpath down to Ginger Restaurant/Polo Towers Hotel. Continue just beyond to Polo Market, then turn right. Walk in front of the Matri

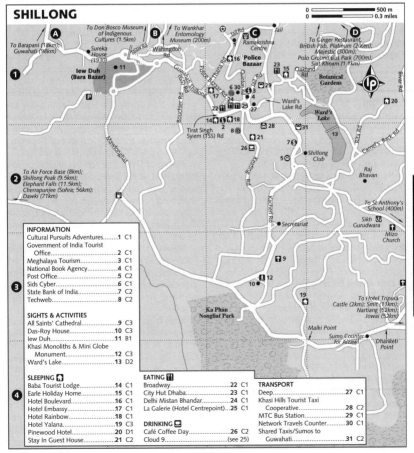

KHASI CULTURE

Meghalaya is dotted with timeless stone monoliths erected as memorials for Adivasi chieftains. Local Khasi 'monarchies' are still nominally ruled by a *syiem* (traditional ruler). Although they might lack political power, the Syiem of Mylliem remains a considerable economic force effectively controlling Shillong's vast Iew Duh market, while the Syiem of Khrim is elaborately feted at Smit's annual Nongkrem festival (opposite).

Many Khasi women wear a *jaiñkyrsha* (pinafore) in gingham-checked cotton, fastened on one shoulder and overlaid with a tartan shawl. Most Khasis consider *kwai* (betel) chewing a semi-religious habit. Khasi markets work on an eight-day rotation and some village fairs feature *yaturmasi* (bull versus bull fights). 'Thank you' in Khasi is *'kublei'*.

Mandir (north side) and along the riverside road for about 1km. The ground is almost opposite the entrance to an army officers' housing area.

Tours

Meghalaya Tourism's city tours (Rs120) lure domestic tourists to a viewpoint at **Shillong Peak** (1960m) and the picnic spot at **Elephant Falls** (adult/car/camera Rs5/3/10; ☉ 8.30am-5pm). While pretty enough, neither are exactly mind-blowing.

Sleeping

Tariffs are seasonal and highly negotiable in the low season. During peak periods hotels fill fast, but there are dozens of choices around the Police Bazaar area so just keep looking. Taxes are a discouraging 20%.

Hotel Embassy (☎ 2223164; AC Lane; s/d from Rs220/375) Central yet quiet, bright and very clean compared to the many other cheapies nearby. Rooms 105 and 207 are good ones. Beware of hefty taxes, 30%.

Hotel Yalana (☎ 2211240; Laitumkhrah; s/d from Rs325/435) Good-value rooms make this a useful sleeping option although it's 2 to 3km away from the centre. Taxes are included.

Earle Holiday Home (☎ 2228614; Oakland Rd; r from Rs350-1500) The cheapest rooms are original half-timbered affairs within a classic 1920 Shillong hill house adorned with little turrets. Pricier rooms in the concrete annexe are less atmospheric but more comfortable. The Rs750 rooms are the best. There's also a good, inexpensive restaurant (City Hut Dhaba, see opposite).

Baba Tourist Lodge (☎ 2211285; GS Rd; d/tr Rs500/700) Ageing but clean and popular with backpackers, Baba hides behind a deceptively small PCO shop. The best rooms have windows and views out onto greenery. Bucket showers and bucket hot water.

Hotel Rainbow (☎ 2222534; TSS Rd; s/d/tr Rs500/875/975) Nine pleasantly styled rooms with wood panelling decor (but no geyser) are managed by a friendly man called Vicky. The best is room 103 with a little balcony.

Stay In Guest House (☎ 2223965; Keating Rd; s/d from Rs600/800) The sauna-style wood panelling gives these rooms a cosy feeling without being claustrophobic, as their big windows front onto Keating Rd. Cold water only, so hot water comes free by the bucket load.

ourpick Hotel Boulevard (☎ 2229823; Thana Rd; s/d from Rs890/1190) Among dozens of similarly priced hotels, the Boulevard stands out for its modernist chic and unusually luxurious standards even in the cheapest rooms. Don't miss the view from the stylish top-floor bar-cafe where you'll take your free breakfast.

Pinewood Hotel (☎ 2223116; Rita Rd; s/d from Rs1200/1400) British-era heritage and elegance almost make up for over-large, slightly damp and cold rooms in the garden-located cottages. You'd stay here for the history and not the luxury, and certainly cool rooms would be a plus in the height of summer.

Majestic (☎ 2506597; info@majesticmonsoon shillong.com; Polo Market; s/d from Rs1350/1650; 🖳 🛜) A 2007-built hotel with rooms floored with rush matting and rustic-coloured paintwork giving a warm country feel. All rooms are AC and have wi-fi.

Hotel Tripura Castle (☎ 2501111; Cleve Colony; s/d from Rs1680/2160) Tucked away on a wooded hillside is the distinctively turreted summer villa of the former Tripura maharajas. It's this private 'castle' that features in hotel brochures, but accommodation is actually in a mostly new, if pseudo-heritage building behind. Pine-framed rooms have a gently stylish, slightly Balinese vibe with some period furniture and a level of service that's hard to beat.

Eating & Drinking

City Hut Dhaba (Oakland Rd; mains Rs50-140) Tucked behind Earle Holiday Home, modestly priced City Hut serves a variety of Indian, Chinese and barbecue food, and ice creams in four different eating rooms, including a family-only room and an attractive, flower-decked straw pavilion.

Broadway (GS Rd; mains Rs60-130) A no-nonsense restaurant serving the usual mix of Indian and Chinese meals although staff here have taken that literally with bicultural offerings such as Szechwan paneer (unfermented cheese in a chilly Chinese sauce).

La Galerie (☎ 2220480; Hotel Centrepoint, TSS Rd; mains Rs60-170) A suave restaurant compartmentalised into booths by photographs of local scenes offers excellent Indian food. Booking is advisable. Cloud 9 is the top-floor bar and restaurant serving dainty Thai dishes, cold beers and cocktails.

Sink into cream-leather seating and enjoy a break from Indian fare with pasta, crêpes, cannelloni, stroganoff or just a fruit sundae at **Ginger Restaurant** (☎ 2222341; Hotel Polo Towers, Polo Bazaar; mains Rs65-200; 🕙 11am-10pm). Attached is the futuristic, metal-panelled bar **Platinum** (beers Rs120; 🕙 1pm-9pm), and a faux-**British pub** (🕙 1pm-9pm). PS: Early closing is a government restriction.

Cheap street stalls abound around Police Bazaar with many dreary but inexpensive eateries along Thana Rd. There's real coffee and good cakes at **Café Coffee Day** (Keating Rd; from Rs5; 🕙 9am-10pm). **Delhi Mistan Bhandar** (Police Bazaar Rd; from Rs5) is a popular sit-down sweet shop with lassies, snacks and gorgeous *gulab jamun* (deep-fried balls of dough soaked in rose-flavoured syrup).

Getting There & Away

From an air force base 8km towards Cherrapunjee, **Meghalaya Transport Corporation** (☎ 2223129) offers helicopter flights to Guwahati (Rs725, 30 minutes, twice daily except Sunday) and Tura (Rs1525, 1½ hours, thrice weekly). Book at the MTC bus station.

The **MTC bus station** (☎ 2540330; Jail Rd) also has a computerised railway-reservation counter (nearest station is Guwahati), frequent minibuses to Guwahati (Rs85, 3½ hours), Tura (Rs268, 12 hours via Guwahati, 7.15am and 4pm), and overnight buses to Silchar (Rs199, 10 hours, 7pm) and Siliguri (Rs393, 16 hours, 3pm).

More comfortable private buses for Agartala (Rs480, 20 hours, 5pm), Silchar (Rs280, 10 hours, 9pm), Dimapur (Rs350, 14 hours, 3.30pm), Siliguri (Rs390, 14 hours, 3pm) and Aizawl (Rs460, 15 hours, 7.30pm) depart from Dhanketi Point; book tickets from counters around Police Bazaar, including **Network Travels** (☎ 9863060458; Shop 44, MUDA Complex, Police Bazaar) and **Deep** (☎ 9836047198; Ward's Lake Rd).

From a Kacheri Rd parking area, shared taxis/Sumos leave frequently to Guwahati (Rs190/140, 3½ hours). Some shared taxis continue to Guwahati airport (Rs220).

The **Khasi Hills Tourist Taxi Cooperative** (☎ 2223895; Kacheri Rd) charges Rs190/300 for a shared taxi to Guwahati/Guwahati airport for Rs760/1200 for the whole vehicle. For a day trip to Cherrapunjee the cost is Rs1600, to drop at the Bangladesh border near Dawki it's Rs1500 and a day about town is Rs1000.

AROUND SHILLONG
Smit

Framing itself as the Khasi cultural centre, Smit hosts the major five-day **Nongkrem Festival** (October). This features animal sacrifices and a slow-motion shuffling dance performed in full costume in front of the thatched bamboo '**palace**' of the local *syiem* (traditional ruler). Smit is 11km from Shillong, 4km off the Jowai road.

Umiam Lake

Accessed from **Barapani**, 17km north of Shillong, Umiam Lake is a hydroelectric reservoir that's popular for water sports and picnics and has a couple of expensive resort hotels.

Cherrapunjee (Sohra)
☎ 03637 / pop 11,000

Once you leave the outskirts of Shillong the road to Cherrapunjee passes through pretty scenery that becomes dramatic at **Dympep viewpoint** where a photogenic V-shape valley slit deeply into the plateau attracts numerous domestic tourists and their cameras. There are several chai and snacks shops here.

Although straggling for several kilometres, Cherrapunjee (known locally as Sohra) has a compact centre. Huddling beside the marketplace are the Sumo stand and a one-computer internet place.

SIGHTS & ACTIVITIES

In sunny weather, the landscape is glorious: in cloudy weather it's misty-atmospheric, but

NORTHEAST STATES

LIVING BRIDGES *Laurence Mitchell*

The people of Meghalaya's east Khasi Hills have developed an ingenious means of crossing the fast-flowing streams that separate their villages by taking advantage of the natural growth habits of the rubber trees indigenous to the region. The trees have strong secondary roots that always grow towards the light, and this characteristic is cunningly exploited by the Khasis, who train them across streams using hollowed-out betel palm trunks. Several roots are woven together for strength to provide a floor and handrails, and stones are used to fill gaps in the floor. Given time, the roots anchor in the soil of the opposite bank and a living bridge is created.

These fascinating Tolkienesque structures take about 20 years to become fully functional but, once mature, will last for several hundred years and actually grow stronger with age. The resultant bridges – superb examples of grassroots bioengineering – are perfectly suited to the tough local conditions, being able of withstanding high soil erosion and attack by termites. They are also undeniably beautiful.

The root bridges were first documented in 19th-century colonial records but awareness of them has waned until recently when there has been a minor renewal of interest. Denis P Rayen, a retired Tamil banker and amateur meteorologist, who runs the Cherrapunjee Holiday Resort in Laitkynsew, a ridge-top village 20km south of Cherrapunjee, is one such enthusiast.

Several root bridges may be reached on day treks from Laitkynsew, although all entail a steep descent through dense forest to reach them. The closest is the bridge at Ummonoi, which at several hundred years old is one of the oldest examples to be found in the area. More bridges can be seen by turning off the main Cherrapunjee–Laitkynsew road at Mawshamok, and descending down steep concrete steps past Tyrna to the valley-floor village of Nongriat, which has several bridges nearby. One of the longest, with a 30m span, is found just outside Nongthymmai, a settlement a couple of kilometres before Nongriat on the way down. Another may be found between Nongthymmai and Nongriat, although this is in poor repair and has since been replaced with a less exotic steel-cable structure. The most iconic of the bridges, the Umshiang 'double-decker'– a bridge built on two levels to allow two-way traffic – lies just beyond Nongriat, across the river.

when the monsoon starts the whole show arrives with drama. The rain may cascade down for up to 10 days continuously, all accompanied by an orchestra of thunder and vivid displays of lightning.

The surrounding grassy moors do justify Meghalaya's over-played 'Scotland of the East' tourist-office sobriquet, although they're dotted with Khasi monoliths and scarred by quarrying. Much more impressive is the series of 'grand canyon' valleys that plunge into deep lush chasms of tropical forest sprayed by a succession of seasonally inspiring waterfalls. The **Nohkalikai Falls**, fourth highest in the world, are particularly dramatic especially in the monsoon when their capacity increases 20-fold. You can see them easily enough without quite entering the official **viewpoint** (admission/camera Rs5/200; 8am-5pm), 4.4km southwest of Sohra market.

Cherrapunjee's **Ramakrishna Mission** (admission free; 9.30am-3.30pm) has an interesting one-room collection of everyday Adivasi artefacts plus a discordant display of 78rpm records.

Nothing could seem more incongruous than sari-clad women stooping through the low passages of the 150m-long **Mawsmai Cave** (admission/camera/video Rs5/15/50; 9.30am-5.30pm) but the cave is immensely popular with domestic tourists. Mawsmai's tall row of roadside **monoliths** is as impressive as the cave but doesn't receive the same attention.

Better than any of this is descending the narrow 14km-road to **Mawshamok** for views back up to the falls and an escarpment sliding down to the plains of Bangladesh. Few places in the northeast can better these views.

The most fascinating visit is to the incredible **root bridges**, living rubber fig-tree roots that ingenious Khasi villagers have trained across streams to form pathways (see the boxed text, above). Three of these root bridges (including a 'double-decker') are near **Nongriat**. It's a two-hour very steep trek down from **Tyrna**, a pretty, palm-clad village that's 2km from Mawshamok. This hike is strenuous and en route there's a truly hair-raising wire bridge to cross, but the scenery is magnificent and there's a natural swimming pool to enjoy. The Cherrapunjee Holiday Resort (below) provides maps.

SLEEPING & EATING

Sohra Plaza Hotel (☎ 235762; s/d Rs450/550) This convivially run two-room place is by the market. The hotel is basic but colourful and has an extension planned. Its restaurant (mains Rs35 to Rs100; open 8am to 9pm Monday to Saturday) has the best-ever *momos*.

Coniferous Resort (☎ 9436178164; d/tr Rs1000/1600) The road to Mawsmai passes this new place, with a big family room and tidy, comfortable rooms on the 1st floor. It also has a large restaurant that's popular with day-trip domestic tourists.

`our pick` **Cherrapunjee Holiday Resort** (☎ 244218; www.cherrapunjee.com; Laitkynsew village; d Rs1300-1400; ▢) Ecofriendly, with six eminently comfortable rooms, this resort is run by truly delightful hosts. They offer a selection of hikes, either self-orientated (using their hand-drawn maps) or with a local guide (Rs150 to Rs300). Built on a ridge, rooms either look down to Bangladesh or up to the escarpment. During peak times tent accommodation (Rs500) is available with shared bathrooms but no hot water. The resort encourages summer 'monsoon tourists' to experience first hand the rain, unforgettable thunder and the drama of its brewing storms rushing up from the Bangladesh plains. A taxi from Cherrapunjee costs Rs250 to Rs300.

Dawki

☎ 03653 / pop 5500
You'll probably only go to Dawki for the Bangladesh border crossing, but the journey from Shillong includes a dramatic 10km section along the lip of the vast green **Pamshutia Canyon**. It then descends through mildly picturesque Khasi villages amid waving betel-nut palms, finally crossing a suspension bridge over the surreally blue-green **Umngot Creek** where waters are dotted with flimsy local fishing boats.

If coming northbound from Bangladesh, sleep in Sylhet and start very early as Dawki's only accommodation, the Inspection Bungalow, usually refuses tourists. Shillong–Dawki–Sylhet is considerably easier southbound.

JAINTIA HILLS

☎ 03562
Situated in pretty, rolling countryside (think Sussex with rice), **Nartiang** is famous for its **forest of monoliths**, a Stonehenge wannabe tucked behind the village football pitch. Raised to honour the Jaintia kings, the highest stone is almost 8m tall. Around 1km away, the famous but heavily over-renovated **Durga temple** was once used for human sacrifices. Spot the 'endless hole' into which severed heads were once tipped.

Nartiang probably doesn't justify a special trip from Shillong (54km each way), but if you're travelling the Silchar–Shillong route, it offers blessed respite from the endless coal trucks. Nartiang's 12km off the main road: turn northeast at Ummulong. By public transport change in **Jowai**, the district centre of eastern Meghalaya's Jaintia Hills. Although architecturally drab, Jowai's vibrant market is full of *kwai* (betel) chewing, traditionally

NORTHEAST STATES

CROSSING INTO BANGLADESH

Border Hours
The border is open from 6am to 5pm.

Foreign Exchange
There's no official exchange booth but ask at the Bangladesh customs office.

Onward Transport
The border post is at Tamabil, 1.7km from Dawki market. That's Rs40 by taxi (southbound) but northbound expect to walk. Northbound beware that Tamabil has no Sonali bank, so prepay your Tk300 Bangladeshi departure tax in Sylhet or in Jaintiapura. Frequent Tamabil–Sylhet minibuses pick up from a triangular junction 350m from the checkpoint.

Visas
The nearest Bangladeshi visa offices are in Kolkata (Calcutta), or Agartala in Tripura.

dressed local women. The town gets particularly lively during the July **Behdienkhlam festival** when towers of cloth and wood are erected to the accompaniment of music, dancing and archery competitions.

GARO HILLS

Although they are part of Meghalaya, the lush green Garo Hills are easier to visit from Guwahati than from Shillong. The landscape's undulations vary from charming patchworks of rice fields, cassava-patches and orange orchards to sad slash-and-burn hillsides of depleted jungle. Towns here aren't visually distinctive, but most houses in the small hamlets remain traditionally fashioned from bamboo-weave matting and neatly cropped palm thatch.

Tura

☎ 03651 / pop 58,400

Sprawling Tura is the western Garo Hills' regional centre and an unhurried transport hub. Most key facilities are within two minutes' walk of the central market area around which Circular Rd makes a convoluted one-way loop. An SBI ATM can be found in Tura Bazaar opposite the Tura Dala (TD) Rd district branch of the bank. The **tourist office** (☎ 242394; 🕑 10am-5pm Mon-Fri) is 4km away towards Nazing Bazaar. Friendly staff offer brochures and sketchy maps, and arrange guides for anywhere in the Garo Hills including a three-day hike to **Nokrek Biosphere Reserve**. There it's possible to watch for Hoolock gibbons from a traditional-style *borang* (Garo

tree house). By road the reserve is around 50km from Tura.

SLEEPING & EATING

Rikman Continental (☎ 220744; Circular Rd; s/d from Rs455/546, AC Rs11364/1582; 😢 🖳) Just seconds from the central market and transport booths is this ultra-friendly place. Although some cheaper rooms are small and worn, the more expensive ones have huge windows, bathtubs with hot water and AC. Rikman's restaurant is probably the best place to taste Garo cuisine; breakfast is complimentary and there's a bar. Internet is available in the lobby (per hour Rs50).

One block from the Rikman, **Hotel Sundare** (☎ 224610; Circular Rd; dm Rs250, s/d from Rs450/600, AC Rs900; 😢) is a reasonable alternative with similar rooms.

The well-out-of-town **Orchid Lodge** (☎ 242394; Narging Bazaar Rd; dm Rs100, s/d from Rs546/655) is beside the tourist office; it has peaceful but spartan rooms.

GETTING THERE & AWAY

On Monday, Wednesday and Friday, triangular **helicopter flights** (☎ 0364-2223206) run to Guwahati.

Booths selling bus and Sumo tickets are dotted around the central market. For Guwahati, most Sumos (Rs250, six hours) depart at 6.30am and 2pm. They're faster than buses (Rs175, eight to 10 hours), which mostly leave at 6.30am and 7.30pm. Buses to Shillong (Rs230, nine hours, around 8pm) pass close to Guwahati airport. **Aashirwad**

THE GARO PEOPLE

Garo facial features range from Burmese to almost African. Traditionally animist *jhum* (slash-and-burn) farmers, the matrilineal Garo were among the first northeastern targets for Christian missionary work, possibly because the Garo language is so relatively simple. Now an estimated 80% of Garos are Christian. Nonetheless 'witch doctors' are still active and superstitious *jhum* villages still practise Wangala dances before the harvest. These dances have been formalised into a four-day '100-Drum' cultural festival, held at Asanang (Asananggri), 18km north of Tura, in early November. Check exact dates with Tura's tourist office.

Not surprisingly given the flora, a mainstay of Garo cuisine is *me'a* (bamboo-shoot), often fermented as *me'a mesing*. *Na'tok* (fish) is often cooked in fresh bamboo tubes giving a distinctive flavour. Like in Assam, *khar* (an alkaline banana-extract) and *na'kham* (dried fish) are almost ubiquitous ingredients in Garo recipes, the most classic of which is *kap'a*, a delicious ginger-chilli concoction usually incorporating *do'o* (boiled chicken) or *wak* (fatty pork). *Pura* adds rice flour for thickening.

The standard Garo greeting is '*Nameng-a ma?*' And reply '*Nameng-a*'. In Garo 'thank you' is *m'tela*, '(very) beautiful' is *(bilong'en) si'la*.

(☎ 9436322845) runs a handy but grindingly slow overnight bus to Siliguri (Rs280, 15 to 17 hours, 4pm).

A chartered/shared autorickshaw to the tourist office costs Rs60/20 from outside Dura Travels by the Hotel Sundare.

Baghmara & Siju
☎ 03639

Almost on the Bangladesh border, **Baghmara** is the southern Garo Hills' district centre. Sitting above the town is the pleasantly quiet **Tourist Lodge** (☎ 222141; dm Rs200, r Rs400-500) commanding outstanding views.

Included in that vista is the prominent Chitmang Hill, which features prominently in Indian folklore. In the Ramayan saga, Hanuman was tasked with bringing a medicinal herb from this hill to Sri Lanka to cure a critically injured Laxman. Not knowing his herbs he scooped up the whole hill and transported it to Sri Lanka. After the herb was found he returned the hill back to Meghalaya and dumped it in back in approximately the same place he took it from.

From Baghmara you can visit the **Balpakhram National Park** (admission Rs50, camera/video Rs50/500), 45km away, but jeep (from Rs1200) and guide (from Rs500) hire will have to be organised in Tura. Traditionally Balpakhram is considered by Garo people as the 'abode of souls' where people temporarily go after they die. The park is thick with wild flowers and butterflies in spring, and its little 'grand canyon' separates the Garo and Khasi Hills.

Speleologists can visit **Siju Cave** (34km from Baghmara), reputedly the third-longest cave in the Indian subcontinent with 5km explored and more to go. Bring your own equipment and follow the golden rules of caving, never go alone and don't touch the formations. Curious noncavers will be able to penetrate about 100m into the gaping entrance with natural light and further with a torch, but in monsoon time the cave is mostly flooded out.

NORTHEAST STATES

Orissa

A captivating state with diverse, vibrant cultures and an unrivalled architectural legacy, Orissa has nonetheless slipped under the radar of mass tourism and is refreshingly laid back.

Beautiful medieval temples are still dotted through the streets of the capital, Bhubaneswar, and serene stone carvings of exceptional beauty continue to be excavated from early Buddhist sites. The World Heritage–listed Sun Temple in Konark bursts with brilliantly worked scenes of Orissan life, while stone carving, painting, silverwork and textiles are produced by modern artists across the state.

Wonderful national parks and wildlife sanctuaries are another highlight: elephants and tigers crash and prowl through the mountainous Similipal National Park, a key tiger reserve. Chilika Lake, Asia's largest lagoon, hosts the rare Irrawaddy dolphin as well as millions of migratory birds, including pink flamingos. Bhitarkanika Wildlife Sanctuary has dolphins, a surfeit of birdlife and monster crocodiles. In January masses of olive ridley marine turtles pull themselves up onto Orissa's long beaches to lay their eggs.

Inexpensive seaside retreats are dotted along Orissa's coast, making it a draw for weary travellers ready to kick back at the beach. Inland there's a different India, where Adivasis (tribal people) live precariously on the edge of mainstream society, yet manage to retain their colourful, fascinating traditions.

Travellers are waking up to Orissa's charm, so it's worth seeing now. Tourist infrastructure is still unsophisticated, but the flip side of this is relaxed and genuine friendliness and an almost entire lack of tourist-industry touting and harassment.

HIGHLIGHTS

- Chill out in a beachside thatched restaurant in traveller favourite **Puri** (p258)

- Spy on the herons, cranes and flashy flamingos nesting around **Chilika Lake** (p266)

- Get away from it all in a hot bath or treetop cottage in the tiny hot-springs hamlet of **Taptapani** (p269)

- Barter in the colourful Adivasi marketplaces of **Onkadelli** (p272) and **Chatikona** (p270)

- Watch carved scenes of the everyday, the erotic and the exotic unfold at the stunning Sun Temple in **Konark** (p265)

- Hire a boat and explore the wildlife-rich mangroves of **Bhitarkanika Wildlife Sanctuary** (p275)

ORISSA

History

Orissa (formerly Kalinga) was once a formidable maritime empire, with trading routes down into Indonesia, but its history is hazy until the demise of the Kalinga dynasty in 260 BC at the hands of the great emperor Ashoka. Appalled at the carnage he had caused, Ashoka forswore violence and converted to Buddhism.

Around the 1st century BC Buddhism declined and Jainism was restored as the faith of the people. During this period the monastery caves of Udayagiri and Khandagiri (in Bhubaneswar) were excavated as important Jain centres.

By the 7th century AD, Hinduism had supplanted Jainism. Under the Kesari and Ganga kings, trade and commerce increased and Orissan culture flourished – countless temples from that classical period still stand. The Orissans defied the Muslim rulers in Delhi until finally falling to the Mughals during the 16th century, when many of Bhubaneswar's temples were destroyed.

Until Independence, Orissa was ruled by Afghans, Marathas and the British.

Since the 1990s a Hindu fundamentalist group, Bajrang Dal, has undertaken a violent campaign against Christians in Orissa in response to missionary activity. The often illiterate and dispossessed Adivasi people have suffered the most from the resulting communal violence, which has been as much about power, politics and land as religious belief.

Violence flared up again in 2008 after the killing of a Hindu leader in Kandhamal district, and thousands of Christians were moved to government relief camps outside the district after their homes were torched.

The creation of the neighbouring states of Jharkhand and Chhattisgarh has prompted calls for the formation of a separate, Adivasi-oriented state, Koshal, in the northwest of Orissa, with Sambalpur as the capital. A separatist political party, the Kosal Kranti Dal (KKD), fielded candidates in the 2009 state election.

The last few years have seen something of an industrial boom in Orissa, with an influx of big steel plants.

Climate

Monsoon time is July to October, when cyclones are likely. Cyclones and severe monsoonal rains can have a substantial impact on transport. A particularly devastating cyclone

FAST FACTS

Population 36.7 million
Area 155,707 sq km
Capital Bhubaneswar
Main language Oriya
When to go November to March

struck Orissa in 1999 causing significant damage and the loss of thousands of lives, and in 2008 serious flooding destroyed crops and villages and led to mass evacuations.

While the coastal regions of Orissa can reach soaring temperatures, much of the state's interior is forested plateau, which remains surprisingly temperate in the summer and can be very cool in the winter, especially in the Eastern Ghats region of the south.

National Parks

The admission fee for foreigners to visit any of Orissa's national parks and wildlife sanctuaries is Rs1000 per day, a hefty cost that Orissa's private tour operators have protested against.

Information

Orissa Tourism (www.orissatourism.gov.in) has a presence in most towns, with offices for information and tour/hotel booking. It also maintains a list of approved guides for Adivasi-area visits.
Orissa Tourism Development Corporation (OTDC; www.panthanivas.com), the commercial arm of Orissa Tourism, runs tours and hotels throughout the state. OTDC-run hotels, which often house an Orissa Tourism desk or office, are usually called Panthanivas.

Dangers & Annoyances

Mosquitoes here have a record of being dengue and malaria carriers. See p346 for advice, and consider bringing a mosquito net.

Getting There & Away

Air routes connect Bhubaneswar with Delhi, Mumbai (Bombay) and Kolkata (Calcutta). There were no flights to Chennai (Madras) at the time of research, but they may start up again. Major road and rail routes between Kolkata and Chennai pass through coastal Orissa and Bhubaneswar with spur connections to Puri. Road and rail connect Sambalpur with Kolkata, Chhattisgarh and Madhya Pradesh.

ORISSA

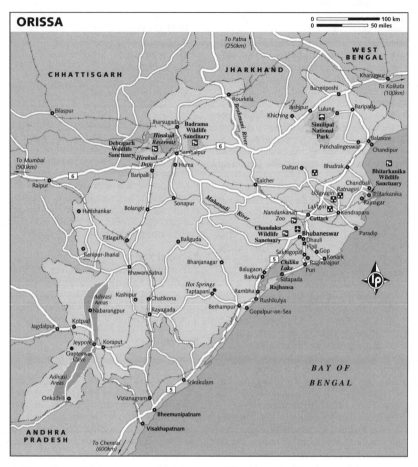

Getting Around

Public transport in the coastal region is good with ample long-distance buses and trains. For touring around the interior hiring a car is the best option, although buses and trains are available if you're not in a hurry.

BHUBANESWAR

☎ 0674 / pop 647,310

On its edges, Bhubaneswar has wide avenues, green belts and public artwork that reflects its temple-town heritage, but its centre is typically polluted and congested. The old city's spiritual centre is around Bindu Sagar where, from the thousands that once stood, 50-odd stone temples remain, survivors from the heyday of Orissan medieval temple architecture.

Orientation

Cheaper lodgings, restaurants, banks and transport are within an area bounded by Cuttack Rd, Rajpath, Sachivajaya Marg and the train station.

Information

BOOKSHOPS

Modern Book Depot (☎ 2502373; Station Sq; ⏱ 9.30am-2pm & 4.30-9pm) This place stocks maps, English-language novels, coffee-table books, postcards and books on Orissa. If you're interested in learning some Oriya, ask the owner about the well-regarded *Oriya in Small Bites*.

EMERGENCY

Police (☎ 2533732; Capitol Police Station, Rajpath)

INTERNET ACCESS

Cyber World (cnr Janpath & Rajpath; per hr Rs20; 🕑 9am-9.30pm Mon-Sat, 10am-6pm Sun)

Ganpati Travel & Communication (Kalpana Sq; per hr Rs30; 🕑 8.30am-9.30pm)

Sify Iway (cnr Janpath & Rajpath; per hr Rs17; 🕑 8.30am-9.30pm)

MEDICAL SERVICES

Capital Hospital (☎ 2401983; Sachivajaya Marg) Has a 24-hour pharmacy on site.

MONEY

Indian Overseas Bank (Station Sq; 🕑 10am-4pm Mon-Fri, 10am-1pm Sat) Currency exchange and travellers cheques.

State Bank of India (☎ 2533671; Rajpath; 🕑 10am-4pm Mon-Fri, 10am-2pm Sat, closed 2nd Sat of month) Cashes travellers cheques and exchanges foreign currency. ATMs around town, including Lewis Rd and Kalpana Sq.

Thomas Cook (☎ 2539892; 130 Ashok Nagar, Janpath; 🕑 10am-2pm Sat) Cashes travellers cheques, including Amex, and exchanges foreign currency.

POST

Post office (☎ 2402132; cnr Mahatma Gandhi & Sachivajaya Margs; 🕑 9am-7pm Mon-Sat)

TOURIST INFORMATION

Orissa Tourism (www.orissatourism.gov.in) airport (☎ 2534006); main office (☎ 2431299; Paryatan Bhavan, behind State Museum, Lewis Rd; 🕑 10am-5pm Mon-Sat,

closed 2nd Sat of month); train station (☎ 2530715; 🕑 24hr) Tourist information, maps and lists of recommended guides.

Orissa Tourism Development Corporation (OTDC; ☎ 2432382; behind Panthanivas Bhubaneswar, Lewis Rd; 🕑 8am-8pm Mon-Sat) Commercial arm of Orissa Tourism. Books sightseeing tours and hotels.

Sandpebbles Tour N Travels (☎ 2541452, 25545868; www.sandpebblestours.com; NH5) Bookings for forest rest houses in Dangmal (p276).

Sights

BINDU SAGAR

Also known as Ocean Drop Tank, Bindu Sagar reputedly contains water from every holy stream, pool and tank in India. During the Ashokastami festival (see boxed text, below), the Lingaraj Mandir's deity is brought here for ritual bathing.

TEMPLES

Bhubaneswar's medieval temples are a mix of 'live' (still in use as places of worship) and 'dead' (archaeological sites); a live temple will always have a red flag fluttering above it.

Unless you're on an organised tour, a priest will probably approach you and expect a donation; Rs20 is reasonable. Consider it a guiding fee as undoubtedly the priest will reveal something about his temple.

To see all the major temples, charter an autorickshaw for two to three hours (about Rs300).

FESTIVALS IN ORISSA

Makar Mela (2nd week of Jan; Kalijai Island, Chilika Lake, p266) Celebrates the sun entering the orbit of Capricorn. Surya, the sun god, is the attention of worship.

Adivasi Mela (26-31 Jan; Bhubaneswar, opposite) Features art, dance and handicrafts of Orissa's Adivasi groups.

Magha Mela (Jan/Feb; Konark, p264) Sun festival, with pilgrims bathing en masse at the beach before sunrise then worshipping at the temple.

Maha Shivaratri (Feb/Mar; Bhubaneswar, opposite) Devotees fast and perform *pujas* (prayers or offerings) throughout the night ready to witness the priest placing a sacred lamp on the top of Lingaraj Mandir.

Ashokastami (Apr/May; Bhubaneswar, opposite) The idol of Lord Lingaraj is taken by chariot to Bindu Sagar for ritual bathing and then to Rameswaram Temple for a four-day stay.

Rath Yatra (Jun/Jul; Puri, p258) Immense chariots containing Lord Jagannath, brother Balbhadra and sister Subhadra are hauled from Jagannath Temple to Gundicha Mandir.

Beach Festival (Nov; Puri, p258) Song, dance, food and cultural activities, including sand artists, on the beach.

Tribal Festival (16-18 Nov; location varies) An exposition of Orissan indigenous dances and music. Contact Orissa Tourism (above) as the location changes yearly.

Baliyatra (Nov/Dec; Cuttack, p275) Four days commemorating past trading links with Indonesia. A huge fair is held on the river bank.

Konark Festival (1-5 Dec; Konark, p264) Features traditional music and dance and a seductive temple ritual. Festivities are in the open-air auditorium with the Sun Temple as the backdrop.

BHUBANESWAR

0 ━━━━━━━━━ 3 km
0 ━━━━━━━━━ 2 miles

INFORMATION
Capital Hospital.......................1 B5
Cyber World...........................2 A6
Ganpati Travel & Communication......3 A6
Indian Overseas Bank................(see 34)
Modern Book Depot...................4 A5
Orissa Tourism.......................5 A6
Orissa Tourism Development Corporation
  (OTDC).............................(see 40)
Police Station........................6 C5
Post Office...........................7 C4
Sandpebbles Tour N Travels..........8 B3
SBI ATM..............................9 C5
SBI ATM.............................(see 35)
Sify Iway............................10 A6
State Bank of India..................11 C5
Thomas Cook.........................12 A5

SIGHTS & ACTIVITIES
Alternative Tours....................13 B5
Bindu Sagar.........................14 C6
Brahmeswar Mandir..................15 D6
Discover Tours.......................16 C5
Kedargauri Mandir.................(see 24)
Lingaraj Mandir......................17 C6
Mukteswar Mandir.................(see 24)
Museum of Tribal Arts & Artefacts...18 A4
Orissa Modern Art Gallery...........19 B5
Parsurameswar Mandir...............20 C6
Pathani Samanta Planetarium........21 C3
Raja Rani Mandir....................22 C6
Regional Science Centre.............23 C3
Siddheswar Mandir.................(see 24)

State Museum.........................25 A6
Swosti Travels.......................26 A5
Udayagiri & Khandagiri Caves.......27 A5
Vaital Mandir........................28 C5

SLEEPING
Bhubaneswar Hotel...................29 A5
Ginger..............................30 B3
Hotel Bhagwat Niwas...............(see 33)
Hotel Kalinga Ashok.................31 A6
Hotel Keshari........................32 A5
Hotel Padma.........................33 A6
Hotel Pushpak.....................(see 33)
Hotel Richi..........................34 A5
Hotel Shatabdi......................35 A6
Hotel Suryansh......................36 B2
Hotel Upasana.......................37 A5
Mayfair Lagoon......................38 B3
New Marrion.........................39 C4
Panthanivas Bhubaneswar...........40 C5
Trident Hotel........................41 B3

EATING
Cafe Coffee Day....................(see 39)
Cafe Coffee Day....................(see 30)
Hare Krishna Restaurant.............42 A5
Khana Khazana....................(see 33)
Maurya Gardens..................(see 34)
Mithai Shop and AC Restaurant......43 A6
Park Inn Bar & Restaurant...........44 A6
Reliance Fresh.......................(see 3)
Shanghai Express..................(see 39)
Tangerine 9.......................(see 42)
Truptee Restaurant................(see 33)
Zaika...............................45 C5

SHOPPING
Ekamra Haat.........................46 C4
Orissa State Handloom Cooperative
  (Utkalika).........................47 A5

TRANSPORT
Baramunda Bus Station..............48 A4
Bus Stop for Cuttack & Puri.........49 A6
City Bus Stand......................50 A5
Former Capital Bus Stand............51 C4
Indian Airlines......................52 C4

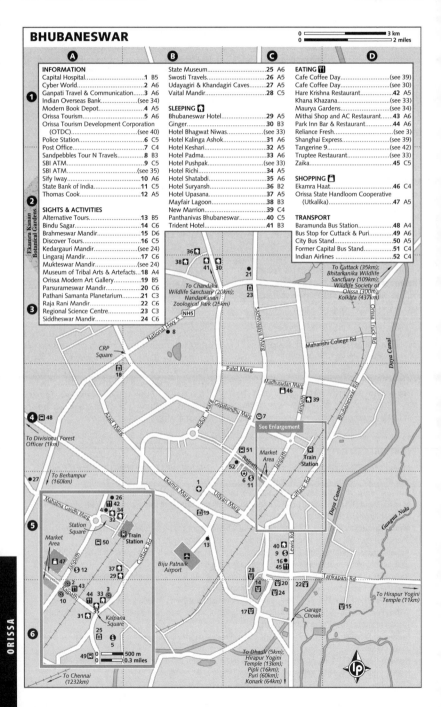

To Cuttack (35km);
Bhitarkanika Wildlife
Sanctuary (109km);
Wildlife Society of
Orissa (300m);
Kolkata (437km)

To Chandaka
Wildlife Sanctuary (20km);
Nandankanan
Zoological Park (25km)

NH5

CRP
Square

National Hwy 5

Patel Marg

Madhusudan Marg

Gopabandhu Marg

Maharishi College Rd

To Divisional Forest
Officer (1km)

See Enlargement

Market
Area

Train
Station

To Berhampur
(160km)

Ekamra Marg

Udyan Marg

Rajpath

Biju Patnaik
Airport

Lewis Rd

Garage
Chowk

Tankapani Rd

To Hirapur Yogini
Temple (11km)

Mahatma Gandhi Marg

Station
Square

Market
Area

Train
Station

Cuttack Rd

Kalpana
Square

500 m
0.3 miles

To Chennai
(1232km)

To Dhauli (5km);
Hirapur Yogini
Temple (13km);
Pipli (16km);
Puri (60km);
Konark (64km)

Gangua Nala

Daya Canal

Orissa Truck Rd

Bhubaneswar Rd

Sachivalaya Marg

Janpath

Lingaraj Mandir

The 54m-high Lingaraj Mandir is dedicated to Tribhuvaneswar (Lord of Three Worlds). The temple dates from 1090 to 1104 (although parts are over 1400 years old) and is surrounded by more than 50 smaller temples and shrines. The granite block, representing Tribhuvaneswar, is bathed daily with water, milk and bhang (marijuana). The main gate, guarded by two moustachioed yellow lions, is a spectacle in itself as lines of pilgrims approach, *prasad* (temple-blessed food offering) in hand.

Because the temple is surrounded by a wall, and closed to non-Hindus (Indira Gandhi wasn't allowed in, as her husband was a Parsi), foreigners can see it only from a viewing platform (this can also include foreign Hindus, as some Indian Hindus do not believe in conversion). Face the main entrance, walk around to the right and find the viewing platform down a short laneway to the left. There have been reports of aggressive hassling for 'donations' at the viewing platform; again, Rs20 is enough, and there's no fee to stand there.

Vaital Mandir

This 8th-century temple, with a double-storey 'wagon roof' influenced by Buddhist cave architecture, was a centre of Tantric worship, eroticism and bloody sacrifice. Look closely and you'll see some very early erotic carvings on the walls. Chamunda (a fearsome incarnation of Devi), representing old age and death, can be seen in the dingy interior, although her necklace of skulls and her bed of corpses are usually hidden beneath her temple robes.

Parsurameswar Mandir

Just west of Lewis Rd lies a cluster of about 20 smaller but important temples. Best preserved is Parsurameswar Mandir, an ornate Shiva temple built around AD 650. It has lively bas-reliefs of elephant and horse processions, and Shiva images.

Mukteswar, Siddheswar & Kedargauri Mandirs

Not far from Parsurameswar is the small but beautiful 10th-century **Mukteswar Mandir**, one of the most ornate temples in Bhubaneswar; you'll see representations of it on posters and brochures across Orissa. Intricate carvings show a mixture of Buddhist, Jain and Hindu styles – look for the Nagarani (snake queen), easily mistaken by Westerners for a mermaid, who you'll also see at the Raja Rani Mandir. The ceiling carvings and stone arch are particularly striking as is the arched *torana* (architrave) in front, clearly showing Buddhist influence.

Siddheswar Mandir, in the same compound, is a later but plainer temple with a fine red-painted Ganesh.

Over the road is **Kedargauri Mandir**, one of the oldest temples in Bhubaneswar, although it has been substantially rebuilt.

Raja Rani Mandir

This **temple** (Indian/foreigner Rs5/100, video Rs25; ☼ dawn-dusk), built around 1100 and surrounded by manicured gardens, is famous for its ornate *deul* (temple sanctuary) and tower. Around the compass points are pairs of statues representing eight *dik-palas* (guardians) who protect the temple. Between them, nymphs, embracing couples, elephants and lions peer from niches and decorate the pillars. The name of the temple isn't for a particular king and queen, but is the name of the stone used in the temple's construction.

Brahmeswar Mandir

Standing in well-kept gardens, flanked on its plinth by four smaller structures, this 9th-century temple is a smaller version of Lingaraj Mandir. It's notable for its finely detailed sculptures with erotic elements.

STATE MUSEUM

This **museum** (☎ 2431797; Lewis Rd; admission Indian/foreigner Rs5/50, camera Rs10/100; ☼ 10am-4.30pm Tue-Sun) boasts Orissa's best collection of rare palm-leaf manuscripts, traditional and folk musical instruments, Bronze Age tools, an armoury and a display of Orissan Adivasi anthropology. Don't miss the salvaged colonial gravestone on the front lawn. The magnificent collection of Buddhist and Jain sculptures, which is displayed in chronological order, holds the most important antiquities in the museum.

MUSEUM OF TRIBAL ARTS & ARTEFACTS

For anyone considering a visit to the Adivasi areas, this **museum** (☎ 2563649; admission free;

ORISSA

10am-5pm Mon-Sat), off National Hwy 5 (NH5), is recommended. Dress, ornaments, weapons, household implements and musical instruments are displayed.

ORISSA MODERN ART GALLERY

Housing a high standard of contemporary art by local artists, this small **gallery** (☎ 2595765; 132 Forest Park; admission free; 11am-1.30pm & 4-8pm Tue-Sat, 4-8pm Sun) also has prints and originals for sale.

UDAYAGIRI & KHANDAGIRI CAVES

Six kilometres west of the city centre are two hills riddled with **rock-cut shelters** (admission both sites Indian/foreigner Rs5/100, video Rs25; dawn-dusk). Many are ornately carved and thought to have been chiselled out for Jain ascetics in the 1st century BC.

Ascending the ramp at Udayagiri (Sunrise Hill), note **Swargapuri** (Cave 9) to the right with its devotional figures. **Hathi Gumpha** (Cave 14) at the top has a 117-line inscription relating the exploits of its builder, King Kharavela of Kalinga, who ruled from 168 to 153 BC.

Around to the left you'll see **Bagh Gumpha** (Tiger Cave; Cave 12), with its entrance carved as a tiger mouth. Nearby are **Pavana Gumpha** (Cave of Purification) and small **Sarpa Gumpha** (Serpent Cave), where the tiny door is surmounted by a three-headed cobra. On the summit are the remains of a defensive position. Around to the southeast is the single-storey elephant-guarded **Ganesh Gumpha** (Cave 10), almost directly above the two-storey **Rani ka Naur** (Queen's Palace Cave; Cave 1), carved with Jain symbols and battle scenes.

Continue back to the entrance via **Chota Hathi Gumpha** (Cave 3), with its carvings of elephants, and the double-storey **Jaya Vijaya Cave** (Cave 5) with a bodhi tree carved in the central compartment.

Across the road, Khandagiri offers fine views over Bhubaneswar from its summit. The steep path splits about one-third of the way up the hill. The right path goes to **Ananta Cave** (Cave 3), with its carved figures of athletes, women, elephants and geese carrying flowers. Further along is a series of **Jain temples**; at the top is another (18th-century) Jain temple.

Buses don't go to the caves, but plenty pass nearby on NH5, or take an autorickshaw (about Rs80 one way).

REGIONAL SCIENCE CENTRE

Kids will love this parkland **museum** (Prehistoric Life Park; ☎ 2542795; Sachivajaya Marg; admission Rs7; 10.30am-7pm Tue-Sun, 10am-5.30pm Mon) with its giant dinosaurs. Included in the admission is a 30-minute movie screened hourly. Other treats are hands-on demonstrations of the laws of physics and displays on astronomy and insects. You may have the whole place to yourself if a school group isn't there.

PATHANI SAMANTA PLANETARIUM

This interesting **planetarium** (☎ 2581613; JL Nehru Marg; child/adult Rs10/15; hourly 2-6pm Tue-Sun, show in English 4pm) features hour-long 'out-of-this-world' shows.

Tours

Orissa Tourism runs a hop-on, hop-off **bus service** (per day Rs250) starting at the OTDC (p251). The AC buses do a loop of the city's temples every hour.

The OTDC runs a **city tour** (non-AC/AC Rs150/200) every day except Monday, covering the Nandankanan Zoo, Dhauli, the Lingaraj and Mukteswar temples, the State Museum and Udayagiri and Khandagiri Caves. Another tour goes to Pipli, Konark and Puri (non-AC/AC Rs180/250, daily). Both tours leave from the Panthanivas Bhubaneswar hotel. These prices don't include entry fees, which can add up to more than Rs300 for foreigners.

Private tour operators organise customised tours into Orissa's Adivasi areas; these can also include visits to handicraft villages, and Similipal National Park and Bhitarkanika Wildlife Sanctuary. Prices will depend on number of people, transport and hotel standards, but expect to pay at least US$60 per person per day for tours that include transport, accommodation and a professional guide. Adivasi tours usually start on a Sunday or Monday to synchronise with village markets.

Alternative Tours (☎ 2593463; www.travelclubindia .com; Room 5 BDA Market Complex, Palaspalli) Operates Adivasi and wildlife tours.

Discover Tours (☎ 2430477; www.orissadiscover.com; 463 Lewis Rd) A helpful, recommended agency specialising in Adivasi and textile village tours as well as Bhitarkanika and Similipal.

Swosti Travels (☎ 2535773; www.swosti.com; Hotel Swosti, Janpath) Apart from hotel and airline bookings and car rental, it runs tours to the Adivasi areas and national parks. More of a focus on domestic tourists than Alternative and Discover.

Sleeping

Bhubaneswar has plenty of accommodation, but a real dearth of anything in the way of clean or appealing family-run places or traveller dens in the budget and lower mid ranges. Conversely, it has a great selection of top-end hotels and one excellent midrange place. Rates drop substantially during the monsoon season, June to September, and most places will negotiate.

BUDGET

Hotel Padma (☎ 2313330; Kalpana Sq; s without bathroom Rs70, d Rs200, with TV Rs250) Cheap and not very cheerful; the very cheap singles are like prison cells. Slightly more comfort comes with paying more.

Hotel Bhagwat Niwas (☎ 2313708; Kalpana Sq; s Rs180-250, d Rs300-450, d with AC Rs750-1000; 🆒) Behind the Hotel Padma and signed down a small lane, the friendly Bhagwat has simple, relatively clean rooms with TV, some with a balcony. Checkout is 24 hours, and it pays to book ahead.

Bhubaneswar Hotel (☎ 2313245; Cuttack Rd; s/d from Rs200/260, with AC Rs700/800; 🆒) A friendly enough hotel with rooms that are par for the course in their price range: just clean enough, a tad threadbare, with dank bathrooms. The hierarchy of room rates is determined by your TV choice.

Hotel Richi (☎ 2534619; fax 2539418; 122A Station Sq; s/d from Rs300/500, d with AC from Rs900; 🆒) Proximity to the train station and decent rooms make this place (very) popular. Booking ahead is advised. Rates include bed, tea and breakfast. Checkout and the coffee shop are open 24 hours.

Hotel Shatabdi (☎ 2314202; 71 Buddhanagar, Kalpana Sq; d Rs400-600) A cleanish, acceptable budget choice; rooms are small and fittings a bit shabby, but the more expensive rooms have been brightly painted, giving a cheerful feel.

MIDRANGE & TOP END

Hotel Upasana (☎ 2310044; off Cuttack Rd; upasana_bbsr@rediffmail.com; d from Rs700, with AC from Rs850; 🆒) Behind the Bhubaneswar Hotel. The rooms are not dissimilar to the pricier rooms at the Bhubaneswar, though it's marginally more clean and welcoming, plus it's off the main road so it's less noisy.

Hotel Pushpak (☎ 2310185; Kalpana Sq; s/d from Rs800/900, with AC Rs1400/1700; 🆒 🖳) A recent refit has seen this hotel go upmarket, with not-quite-justifiable price increases for cheerful renovated rooms with bright-coloured walls. The non-AC rooms are about as good as you'll get for this price, and the veg restaurant is popular.

Hotel Keshari (☎ 2535095; keshari@orissaindia.com; 113 Station Sq; s/d from Rs900/1000, with AC Rs2100/2300; 🆒) Five minutes' walk from the train station, Keshari has a decent restaurant and noon checkout. Inspection is essential as some rooms are definitely better than others, especially when it comes to bathroom cleanliness. The hotel asks you pay in foreign currency but you can argue to pay in rupees.

Panthanivas Bhubaneswar (☎ 2432314; Lewis Rd; d 1500; 🆒) Well located in pleasant grounds, Panthanivas is quiet and is the closest hotel to the temples. The rooms are tired for the price, though renovations were under way at research time, and the restaurant is decidedly ordinary. Staff are less than enthusiastic.

our pick Ginger (☎ 2303933; www.gingerhotels.com; Jayadev Vihar, Nayapalli; s/d Rs1799/2299; 🆒 🖳 🛜) Young friendly staff, clean modern lines, and a self-service philosophy that means you're not constantly surrounded by tip-demanding bag-carriers, laundry peons etc. The fresh, spotless rooms have LCD TVs, tea and coffee, minifridge and silent AC. Meals are served buffet style in the restaurant and there's a 24-hour branch of Cafe Coffee Day that will deliver to your room. Save Rs300 or more if you book online. It's a Rs60 auto ride out of town in an upmarket area, next to (and dwarfed by) the Swosti Plaza hotel.

Hotel Kalinga Ashok (☎ 2431055; www.hotelkalingaashok.com; Gautam Nagar; s/d/ste from Rs2995/3695/5995; 🆒 🖳) Rooms are on the small side (and you don't expect flaking paint in the bathrooms in this price range), but they're clean and stylish with tasteful artwork. Also appealing is the restaurant and bar, and friendly, helpful staff.

Suryansh Hotel (☎ 230 3300; fax 230 3680; www.suryanshhotels.com; s/d from Rs3000/4000; 🆒 🖳 🎦) Not quite as stylish as the top players in town, but it's spotless and very comfortable, with all the mod cons, and the bonus of a rooftop swimming pool with fabulous views over the city.

New Marrion (☎ 2380850; www.hotelnewmarrion.com; 6 Janpath; s/d from Rs6100/6500; 🆒 🖳 🎦) A centrally located hotel where rooms have contemporary, classy design – LCD TVs, dark-wood panelling and extraordinarily stylish bathroom sinks – and you can negotiate the price.

ORISSA

Great restaurants here include south Indian, Italian-Mexican combo and Chinese, and a cafe with real coffee.

Mayfair Lagoon (☎ 2360101; www.mayfairhotels .com; Jaydev Vihar; d cottages from Rs8000, d villas Rs24,000; ✆ 🖳 🏊) Quirky, colourful, even kitschy, but thoroughly luxurious at the same time. In the jungle-like grounds you'll find static tigers, an elephant, even a twin-prop 1942 aircraft. The cottages are scattered around a lagoon and facilities run to a complimentary breakfast, a British-style pub, and Chinese and Indian restaurants. There's a spa and gym, as well as a hairdresser.

Trident Hotel (☎ 2301010; www.tridenthotels .com; CB-1, Nayapalli; s/d/ste from Rs10,000/11,000/14,000; ✆ 🖳 🏊) The cool, high-ceilinged lobby of the Trident, inspired by Konark's temple architecture, will take your breath away. The restrained whitewash-and-sandstone colour scheme extends into the very comfortable rooms, which feature sketches of Konark temples and inset terracotta tiles replicated from local temples. As distinctive and charming an ambience as the Mayfair's, but very different.

Eating & Drinking

Cafe Coffee Day (drinks Rs22-80, snacks Rs10-65) Janpath (New Marrion Hotel); Nayapalli (Ginger, Jayadev Vihar) Yes it's a chain but you'll appreciate the real coffee beans, the refreshing iced drinks and the chilly AC on any typically sweltering day.

Khana Khazana (outside Hotel Padma, Kalpana Sq; snacks & mains Rs20-70; ✆ from 5.30pm) A popular street stall with a few chairs and tables scattered outside. Alfresco diners savour tandoori chicken, chicken biryani or large serves of delicious chow mein featuring chicken, vegetables and prawns. Traditional Bengali hot rolls (try the tandoori chicken) are the cheapest and tastiest snack in town for Rs20.

Truptee Restaurant (☎ 231565; under Hotel Padma; mains Rs30-60; ✆) This clean and cool basement restaurant has all the South Indian favourites (and it opens at 7.30am, so it's ideal for an *idli* – spongy, round, fermented rice cake – and *vada* breakfast) plus a range of northern curries, including a few good paneer (unfermented cheese) dishes.

Zaika (Lewis Rd; mains Rs30-70) A clean, modern oasis on busy, dusty Lewis Rd. As well as excellent curries and tandoori there is an extensive Chinese menu. Fresh prawns and fish are ritually tandooried on Wednesday and Sunday.

Mithai Shop & AC Restaurant (☎ 253003; Rajpath; mains Rs30-80) In addition to its range of North and South Indian breads and curries, this place is Jagannath's gift to thali lovers and connoisseurs of Indian sweets and ice cream; just don't expect too much from the menu to actually be available. Cyclone-force fans make it difficult to hold the menu but are most refreshing when the heat strikes.

Park Inn Bar & Restaurant (Rajpath; meals Rs40-120; ✆ 11.30am-midnight; ✆) A cinema-dark bar with attentive waiters always ready to suggest another cold beer, with a range of chicken, fish, mutton or prawn dishes. Put your mozzie repellent on before venturing in, and lone women should remember that as with most bars, the staff here are fine but the patrons might make you uncomfortable (they'll mostly just look astonished at your presence).

Maurya Gardens (☎ 2534619; Hotel Richi, Station Sq; mains Rs40-150) A darkened restaurant where you may have trouble reading the menu of Indian, Chinese and continental dishes. The curries are nice and hot, but if you want a beer to cool it down you'll have to eat (same menu) in the bar next door. Nearest to the train station, it's suitable for pre- or post-travel drinks.

Hare Krishna Restaurant (☎ 2534188; Station Sq; mains Rs60-120; ✆) The menu says 'Surrender to the pleasure of being vegetarian', and it's not difficult at this excellent veg restaurant. In dimly lit, upmarket surrounds you can enjoy mainly Indian dishes, including a wide range of tasty biryanis and pilaus, along with a good selection of soups and desserts. The lassi is outstanding. It's upstairs; enter though a shopping arcade.

ourpick Tangerine 9 (☎ 2533009; Station Sq; mains Rs69-249; ✆) If you're not ready to surrender to vegetarianism, step next door to Tangerine 9, also upstairs, where there's all the meat you can handle and all the dishes burst with the flavour of fresh herbs and spices. There's a big range of Indian (especially tandoori) and Chinese, plus some nicely executed Thai dishes. Pan-Asian starters include *momos* (Tibetan dumplings) and salt-and-pepper prawns. Decor is blonde wood and signature tangerine.

Shanghai Express (☎ 2380850; New Marrion, Janpath; mains Rs110-230; ✆) A wide variety of delicious, authentic Chinese food – vegetarian, fish, chicken, even lamb dishes – from different provinces. Starters include *wantons* and spring rolls (Rs70 to Rs100) and you can finish with

---

SHOPPING IN ORISSA

Ancient Orissa's diverse guilds of *shilpins* (artisans) grew rich on Puri's pilgrimage status and are still in business today. The appliqué work of Pipli (near Bhubaneswar) features brightly coloured patches of fabric, and Cuttack is known for its *tarakasi* (silver-filigree ornaments). Raghurajpur (near Puri) is famous for its *pattachitra* (paintings on specially prepared cloth) and *chitra pothi* (intricate images from the Kamasutra, painstakingly inscribed onto palm leaves).

Many Orissans work as handloom weavers, producing numerous types of unique silk and cotton fabrics. The Sambalpur region specialises in *ikat* fabrics, a technique involving tie-dyeing the thread before it's woven.

The best places to pick up these items are where they are produced, more specifically from the artists or workers themselves. Ekamra Haat (below) in Bhubaneswar is the best place to shop for all of Orissa's crafts.

---

classic Chinese-restaurant desserts – lychee and ice cream, and fried ice cream (both Rs75). While you wait, read about your Chinese zodiac sign on the placemats; apparently this author is honest and pennypinching – probably good traits for a guidebook writer.

Self-caterers can stock up in AC comfort at **Reliance Fresh** (☎ 6547004; Kalpana Sq; 9am-10pm;). In addition to bread and cake, packaged snacks and even refrigerated fruit, it's a good place to grab toiletries, batteries and so on.

Shopping

A wide-ranging exposition of Orissan handicrafts (and snack stalls) can be found at **Ekamra Haat** (☎ 2403169; Madhusudan Marg; 10am-10pm), a permanent market in a large garden space. While the gates open at 10am, many stalls don't get going until later.

Orissan textiles, including appliqué and *ikat* (a technique involving tie-dyeing the thread before it's woven) works, can be bought at the **Orissa State Handloom Cooperative** (Utkalika; Eastern Tower, Market Bldg; 10am-1.30pm & 4.30-9pm Mon-Sat) and a number of shops nearby on Rajpath.

Getting There & Away

AIR

Indian Airlines (☎ 2530544; www.indianairlines.in; Rajpath; 10am-1.15pm & 2-4.45pm Mon-Sat) flies daily to Delhi, Mumbai, Bengaluru (Bangalore) and Kolkata. **Jet Lite** (☎ 2596180; www.jetlite.com; airport) flies direct to Delhi and Kolkata daily, with connections on to Mumbai, Hyderabad and Bengaluru. Check the websites for schedules and latest fares.

BUS

Baramunda bus station (☎ 2400540; NH5) has frequent buses to Cuttack (Rs13, one hour),

Puri (Rs31, 1¼ hours) and Konark (Rs35, two hours). Less frequent services go to Berhampur (Rs98, five hours), Sambalpur (Rs200, nine hours) and Baripada (Rs200, seven hours). There are several daily services to Kolkata (Rs300 to Rs600, 12 hours) where price relates to comfort.

Cuttack buses also go from the city bus stand, just off Station Sq, and the bus stop at the top end of Lewis Rd, from where buses also go to Puri.

TRAIN

The *Coromandal Express* 2841 travels daily to Chennai (sleeper/3AC/2AC Rs377/1014/1450, 20 hours, 9.40pm). The *Purushotlam Express* 2801 goes to Delhi (Rs493/1331/1825, 31 hours, 11.25pm) and the *Konark Express* 1020 to Mumbai (Rs493/1358/1873, 37 hours, 3.15pm).

Howrah is connected to Bhubaneswar by the *Jan Shatabdi* 2074 (2nd class/chair Rs142/439, seven hours, 6.20am daily except Sunday) and the daily *Howrah Dhauli Express* 2822 (Rs123/439, seven hours, 1.15pm). To Sambalpur, the *Bhubaneswar-Sambalpur Express* 2893 (chair Rs339, five hours, 6.45am) is quick, comfortable and convenient.

Getting Around

No buses go to the airport; a taxi costs about Rs150 from the centre. An autorickshaw to the airport costs about Rs80, but you'll have to walk the last 500m from the airport entrance. Prepaid taxis from the airport to central Bhubaneswar cost Rs100, and to Puri or Konark Rs700. Another way to get to Puri or Konark in relative comfort is to go one-way on an OTDC tour (p254; let the guide know you won't be returning).

ORISSA

AROUND BHUBANESWAR

Nandankanan Zoological Park

Famous for its blue-eyed white tigers, the **zoo** (☎ 2466075; admission Indian/foreigner Rs10/100, camera/ video Rs5/500; ☽ 8am-5pm Tue-Sun) also boasts rare Asiatic lions, rhinoceroses, copious reptiles, monkeys and deer. Don't get food out of your bag in front of any of the monkeys that roam free around the zoo; trust us.

The highlight is the **lion and tiger safari** (Rs30) which leaves on the hour from 10am to noon and 2pm to 4pm. Other attractions include a toy train and boat rides. A **cable car** (Rs30; ☽ 8am-4pm) crosses a lake, allowing passengers to get off halfway and walk down (300m) to the State Botanical Garden. Early or late in the day you might catch the elephants having a bath in the lake.

OTDC tours stop here for an (insufficient) hour or so. From Bhubaneswar, frequent public buses (Rs6, one hour) leave from Kalpana Sq (near Hotel Padma) and outside the former Capital bus stand for Nandankanan village, about 400m from the entrance to the zoo. By taxi, a one-way trip costs about Rs350.

Dhauli

In about 260 BC one of Ashoka's famous edicts was carved onto a large rock at Dhauli, 8km south of Bhubaneswar. The rock is now protected by a grill-fronted building and above, on top of a hillock, is a carved elephant.

On a nearby hill is the huge, white **Shanti Stupa** (Peace Pagoda), which was built by the Japanese in 1972. Older Buddhist reliefs are set into the modern structure. You have to climb the hot stairs barefoot (ow! ow! ow!) but it's worth it for the four lovely images of the Buddha and great views of the surrounding countryside.

The turn-off to Dhauli is along the Bhubaneswar–Puri road, accessible by any Puri or Konark bus (Rs8). From the turn-off, it's a flat 3km walk to the rock, and then a short, steep walk to the stupa. By autorickshaw/taxi, a one-way trip costs about Rs100/250.

Chandaka

Chandaka Wildlife Sanctuary (City Sanctuary; admission Indian/foreigner Rs10/1000; ☽ 8am-5pm Tue-Sun) was declared primarily to preserve wild elephants and elephant habitat. If you're lucky you might also see leopards, deer, mugger crocodiles and over 100 species of birds.

Facilities include five watchtowers, two of which contain rest houses for overnight stays. Before you visit you must pay for and collect an entry permit, gain permission for photography and reserve a rest house, all at the office of the **divisional forest officer** (☎ 2472040; Chandaka Wildlife Division, SFTRI campus, Ghatika; ☽ 10am-5pm Mon-Fri) in Bhubaneswar. Chandaka is about 20km by road from Bhubaneswar, and visits and transport are best organised through a travel agent in Bhubaneswar.

Hirapur

Among iridescent-green paddies, 15km from Bhubaneswar, is a small village with an important **Yogini Temple**, one of only four in India. The low, circular structure, open to the sky, has 64 niches within, each with a black chlorite goddess. Getting here requires hired transport or coming on an OTDC tour (p254).

Pipli

This town, 16km southeast of Bhubaneswar, is notable for its brilliant appliqué craft, which incorporates small mirrors and is used for door and wall hangings and the more traditional canopies hung over Lord Jagannath and family during festival time. Lampshades and parasols hanging outside the shops turn the main road into an avenue of rainbow colours. The work is still done by local families in workshops behind the shops; you may be able to go back and have a look. Pipli is easily accessible by any bus between Bhubaneswar and Puri or Konark.

SOUTHEASTERN ORISSA

PURI

☎ 06752 / pop 157,610

Hindu pilgrims, Indian holidaymakers and foreign travellers all make their way to Puri, setting up camp in different parts of town. For Hindus, Puri is one of the holiest pilgrimage places in India, with religious life revolving around the great Jagannath Mandir and its famous Rath Yatra (Car Festival).

Puri's other attraction is its long, sandy beach and esplanade. Backing this, in Marine Pde, is a long ribbon of hotels, resorts and company holiday homes that become instantly full when Kolkata rejoices in a holiday.

In the 1970s Puri became a scene on the hippie trail through Southeast Asia, attracted here by the sea and bhang, legal in Shiva's Puri. There's little trace of that scene today; travellers come just to hang out, gorge on good food and recharge their backpacking spirit.

Orientation

The action is along a few kilometres of coast, with the backpacker village clustered around Chakra Tirtha (CT) Rd to the east, busy Marine Pde to the west and resorts in the middle. A few blocks inland is the holy quarter's chaotic jumble of streets. Buses arrive in the centre of town.

Information

BOOKSHOPS

Loknath Bookshop (☎ 9861332493; CT Rd; ☻ 9am-10pm) Sells and exchanges secondhand books.

Om Travels (CT Rd; ☻ 7am-9pm) Books on spirituality and a good range about Orissa, as well as meditation CDs and homeopathic medicines.

EMERGENCY

Seabeach police station (☎ 222025; CT Rd)

Town police station (☎ 222039; Grand Rd)

INTERNET ACCESS

Internet places have sprung up all along CT Rd; most charge Rs20 per hour.

Nanako.com (CT Rd; ☻ 8am-10.30pm) CD burning Rs30, DVDs Rs60.

Travel Fair (CT Rd; ☻ 7am-10pm)

MEDICAL SERVICES

Headquarters Hospital (☎ 223742; Grand Rd)

MONEY

The State Bank of India has a number of reliable MasterCard and Visa ATMs around town, including a convenient one in the main traveller-hotel stretch of CT Rd.

ICICI Bank (Grand Rd; ☻ 8am-8pm) MasterCard and Visa ATM; does foreign exchange but not travellers cheques.

Samikshya Forex (☎ 2225369; CT Rd; ☻ 6am-10pm) Cashes travellers cheques and foreign currencies and does credit-card advances. Thomas Cook agent.

POST

Post office (☎ 222051; cnr Kutchery & Temple Rd; ☻ 10am-5pm)

TOURIST INFORMATION

Orissa Tourism CT Rd (☎ 222664; CT Rd; ☻ 10am-5pm Mon-Sat); train station (☎ 223536; ☻ 7am-9pm) Tourist information, hotel, vehicle and tour booking.

OTDC (☎ 223526; Marine Pde; ☻ 6am-10pm) Booking office and start/finish point for day tours.

TRAVEL AGENCIES

There are numerous travel agencies within and around the hotels on CT Rd that can arrange air, bus and train tickets and car hire.

Gandhara International (☎ 2224623; www.hotel gandhara.com; Hotel Gandhara, CT Rd; ☻ 8am-7pm Mon-Fri, 8am-1pm Sun)

Love & Life Travels (☎ 224433; Hotel Love & Life, CT Rd; ☻ 7am-10pm)

Samikshya Forex (☎ 2225369; CT Rd; ☻ 6am-10pm)

Dangers & Annoyances

Ocean currents can be treacherous in Puri, and drownings are not uncommon, so don't venture out of your depth. Ask one of the *nolias* (fishermen/lifeguards), with their white-painted, cone-shaped wicker hats, for the best spots.

Muggings and attacks on women have been reported along isolated stretches of beach, even during the day, so take care. Foreign men may be approached by young boys on the beach; Puri has an ongoing problem with paedophiles giving gifts to, and abusing, local youngsters.

Hassle from persistent hotel touts, souvenir sellers and so on is low-key compared to most tourist hot spots in India, but it can be frustrating if you've been elsewhere in Orissa, where such hassle is nonexistent.

Sights

JAGANNATH MANDIR

This mighty temple belongs to Jagannath, Lord of the Universe and incarnation of Vishnu. The jet-black deity with large, round, white eyes is hugely popular across Orissa; figures of Jagannath are tended and regularly dressed in new clothes at shrines across the state. Built in its present form in 1198, the temple (closed to non-Hindus) is surrounded by two walls; its 58m-high *sikhara* (spire) is topped by the flag and wheel of Vishnu.

Guarded by two stone lions and a pillar crowned by the Garuda that once stood at the Sun Temple at Konark, the eastern entrance (Lion Gate) is the passageway for the chariot procession of Rath Yatra.

ORISSA

ORISSA

PURI

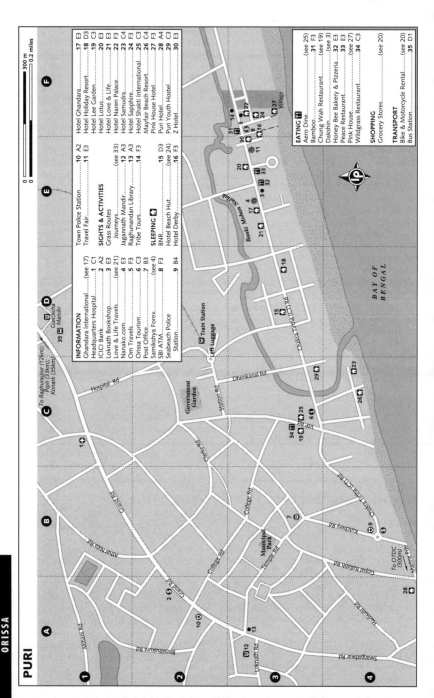

BAY OF BENGAL

0   300 m
0   0.2 miles

Jagannath, brother Balbhadra and sister Subhadra reside supreme in the central *jagamohan* (assembly hall). Priests continually garland and dress the three throughout the day for different ceremonies. Incredibly, the temple employs about 6000 men to perform the complicated rituals involved in caring for the gods. An estimated 20,000 people – divided into 36 orders and 97 classes – are dependent on Jagannath for their livelihood.

Non-Hindus can spy from the roof of **Raghunandan Library** (cnr Temple Rd & Swargadwar Rd; ❂ 9am-1pm & 4-7pm Mon-Sat) opposite; a 'donation', while not officially compulsory, is expected (Rs10 is fine). On Sunday a nearby hotel (whose touts will find you) takes over the scam and demands Rs50 – easily negotiated down to Rs20.

BEACH

Puri is no palm-fringed paradise – the beach is wide, shelves quickly with a nasty shore break and is shadeless; but it is the seaside. To the east it's a public toilet for the fishing village.

By Marine Pde the beach is healthier (although still not particularly pleasant for swimming) and often crowded with energetic holidaymakers, especially at night. Look out for artists constructing **sand sculptures**, a local art form.

It's worth getting up before sunrise to watch the fishermen head out through the surf.

Tours

OTDC (☎ 223526; Marine Pde; ❂ 6am-10pm) runs a series of day trips. Tour 1 (Rs170, departs 6.30am Tuesday to Sunday) skips through Konark, Dhauli, Bhubaneswar's temples, Udayagiri and Khandagiri Caves plus Nandankanan Zoo. Tour 2 (Rs130, departs 7am daily) goes for a boat jaunt on Chilika Lake. Tour 3 (Rs100, departs 7am daily) goes to Konark. Various fees are additional to the tour cost.

Several tour operators organise tours into Orissa's Adivasi areas that can include visits to handicraft villages plus Similipal National Park and Bhitarkanika Wildlife Sanctuary. Adivasi tours have to be approached cautiously as not all agencies have the necessary local contacts to conduct a responsible tour. For recommended options in Bhubaneswar see p254 and for more details see the boxed text, p271.

Grass Routes Journeys (Adventure Odyssey; ☎ 2226642, 9437022663; www.grassroutesjourneys.com; CT Rd) This recommended agency works from a philosophy of environmental and cultural sustainability, with contacts in the Adivasi communities and policies about appropriate ways to photograph people and contribute to the welfare of the community. It plans to offer filtered-water refills from the office, as Orissa has no plastic recycling facility. Its recently opened 'travellers lounge' offers a resource library of books and maps.

Tribe Tours (☎ 2224323; tribetours@hotmail.com; CT Rd; ❂ 7.30am-9pm) Organises Chilika Lake day tours

---

RATH YATRA – THE CAR FESTIVAL

One of India's greatest annual events, **Rath Yatra**, takes place each June or July (second day of the bright half of Asadha month) in Puri (and elsewhere across Orissa), when a fantastic procession spills forth from Jagannath Mandir. Rath Yatra commemorates Krishna's journey from Gokul to Mathura. Jagannath, brother Balbhadra and sister Subhadra are dragged along Grand Rd in three huge 'cars', known as *ratha,* to Gundicha Mandir.

The main car of Jagannath (origin of 'juggernaut') stands 14m high. It rides on 16 wheels, each more than 2m in diameter – in centuries past, devotees threw themselves beneath the wheels to die gloriously within the god's sight. Four thousand professional temple employees haul the cars, which take enormous effort to pull and are virtually impossible to turn or stop. In Baripada a woman-only team pulls Subhadra. Hundreds of thousands of pilgrims (and tourists) swarm to witness this stupendous scene, which can take place in temperatures over 40°C. Take real care if you're going to join the crowds; in 2008 a number of devotees were suffocated to death and trampled near the temple.

The gods take a week-long 'summer break' at Gundicha Mandir before being hauled back to Jagannath Mandir, in a repeat of the previous procession. After the festival, the cars are broken up and used for firewood in the temple's communal kitchens, or for funeral-pyre fuel. New cars are constructed each year.

Periodically, according to astrological dictates, the gods are disposed of and new images made. The old ones are buried in a graveyard inside the northern gate of Jagannath Mandir.

(Rs600 to Rs2100 per person depending on group size, stops, food and transport) and overnight camping trips (about Rs6000 for two people all-inclusive).

Festivals

A four-year calendar of festivals and events can be consulted at www.orissatourism.gov.in. Highlights of the festival-packed year include the celebrated festival of **Rath Yatra** (see the boxed text, p251) and the **Puri Beach Festival** (23 to 27 November; p251) featuring magnificent sand art, food stalls, traditional dance and other cultural programs.

Sleeping

For Rath Yatra, Durga Puja (Dussehra), Diwali or the end of December and New Year, book well in advance.

Prices given are for October to February. Significant discounts can be negotiated during the monsoon, while prices can triple during a festival. Many hotels have early checkout times – often 8am.

BUDGET

Puri Youth Hostel (☎ 222424; CT Rd; dm/d Rs50/200, d with AC Rs500; ✸) This is a cavernous, run-down, deserted-feeling old place where you might struggle to find someone at the front desk. But the non-AC doubles aren't bad value – they're basic but clean, with mosquito nets, and are right on the beach.

Hotel Love & Life (☎ 224433; loveandlife@hotmail .com; CT Rd; s/d from Rs150/250, d with AC Rs750; ✸) The dorms, rooms and cottages in the three-storey building are simple and drab, but adequate. The hosts are friendly and run a travel agency (p259).

Hotel Derby (☎ 223660; off CT Rd; r Rs150-350, with AC Rs650; ✸) This is an older-style hotel, with 10 small, dank rooms set around a garden close to the beach. Mozzie nets are provided, but it's pretty run down, with the charm mostly lying in the garden and beach setting; the AC rooms in particular are not worth the cost.

Hotel Gandhara (☎ 224117; www.hotelgandhara.com; CT Rd; dm Rs75, s/d without bathroom Rs175/250, s/d from Rs450/650, with AC Rs750/950; ✸ 🖳) A wide range of rooms for different budgets. The rear five-storey block has rooftop AC rooms catching breezes and views; other rooms are arrayed around a tree-shaded garden and have balconies. There's a rooftop restaurant and a travel agency that does foreign exchange.

ourpick **Z Hotel** (☎ 222554; www.zhotelindia.com; CT Rd; dm women only Rs100, r Rs700, s/d without bathroom Rs250/500) This former maharaja's home has huge, clean, airy rooms, many of them facing the sea. Great common areas include a TV room with movies screened nightly, and a 'restaurant' (table on a verandah) with a friendly cook who will chat with you, gauge your tastes and bring you something fantastic that isn't on the menu. Shared bathrooms are spotless.

Pink House Hotel (☎ 222253; off CT Rd; r without bathroom Rs150-200, r Rs250) Right on the beach with sand drifting to your front door, the Pink House is an almost-romantic remnant of 1970s Puri. The very basic rooms, either on the beach side with little verandas, or round at the back, are only just clean. Mozzie nets are provided and the toilets are all squat.

Hotel Lotus (☎ 227033; CT Rd; d Rs300-450, with AC Rs950; ✸) The Lotus has a range of inexpensive rooms that are clean and comfortable and even feature some tasteful artwork. The non-AC rooms are some of best value for money in Puri, though the front rooms may suffer a bit of street noise. The friendly owner, who also runs the vegetarian Harry's Cafe downstairs, will point out various landmark temples from the hotel roof.

Puri Hotel (☎ 222114; www.purihotel.in; Marine Pde; d from Rs400, with AC from Rs800; ✸) Saris and underwear adorn the balconies, while, inside, the place has the feel of crowded hospital ward. Nevertheless the Puri Hotel is a Bengali holiday institution and the place to bring the whole family; room sizes go all the way to sleeping 10. Children under eight stay free and checkout is 24 hours; the restaurant is surprisingly small and basic.

Also recommended:

Hotel Sapphire (☎ 226488; off CT Rd; d Rs200-600, with AC Rs850-1850; ✸) A wide range of clean rooms with sea views, bright-coloured walls and noisy AC.

Hotel Beach Hut (☎ 225704; hotel_beachhut2001 @yahoo.co.in; off CT Rd; d Rs350-650, with AC Rs950; ✸) Similar to the Sapphire; clean, with sea views, cool tiled floors and not much character.

MIDRANGE & TOP END

Hotel Lee Garden (☎ 223647, leegarden@rediffmail.com; VIP Rd; d from Rs650, with AC from Rs1100; ✸) This welcoming hotel has a range of spacious, spotless good-value rooms with balconies (but not particularly good views). The pricier rooms are quite stylish. A bonus of staying here is the excellent Chinese restaurant, Chung Wah (p264). Checkout is 7am!

Hotel Samudra (☎ 222705; www.samudrahotel .com; off CT Rd; d Rs650-800, with AC from Rs1200; ⬛) Backing onto the beach, the Samudra's clean and comfy rooms have a dark-wood-and-whitewash charm and in many ways it's one of the best places in town. But depending on the sensitivity of your nose, the heat of the sun and the direction of the wind, you might find the whole place stinks more than you can bear, not to mention attracting a trillion mosquitoes, because of the malodorous open-drain 'creek' nearby.

BNR (☎ 222063; CT Rd; incl breakfast s/d from Rs900/1000, with AC Rs1350/1500; ⬛) BNR stands for Bengal National Railways, which explains the steam locomotive parked out front. This huge remnant of the Raj has colonial charm up the wazoo and untapped renovation potential that will make you weep. The capacious rooms are rather threadbare, but the liveried staff, billiard room, dusty library and lethargic restaurant have a certain charm. Recent, massive price rises are completely unwarranted.

Hotel Naren Palace (☎ 220043; www.hotelnaren palace.com; off CT Rd; d Rs1200-2500; ⬛ ⬛) New, spotless and character-free hotel that offers good value any time and excellent discounts off season. There's very little difference between the standard and deluxe rooms, so unless you're really keen on having a mini-fridge, go with the standard.

Hotel Holiday Resort (☎ 222440; www.holidayresort puri.com; CT Rd; r Rs1330-4000, d cottages Rs1800; ⬛ ⬛) Yes it's blot on the landscape, a huge white edifice with a neon sign that probably guides the fishermen home at night. But inside are sea views from clean and welcoming rooms with warm colour schemes and Mughal reproductions on the walls. Cottages have pleasant lawn areas out front and there's a pool (nonguests Rs100 for two hours) full of roughhousing Bengali men.

Hotel Shakti International (☎ 222388; www.shakti international.in; VIP Rd; s/d incl breakfast from Rs2500/3000; ⬛) A sparkling new modern place with requisite conference hall, aimed mostly at business travellers. Rooms have comfy and stylish furniture, plasma TV and all the mod cons, plus two restaurants, one of which, Aero Dine, will blow your mind.

Mayfair Beach Resort (☎ 227800; www.mayfairhotels .com; r from Rs6000; ⬛ ⬛) The benchmark for Puri luxury features spacious units nestled into idyllic gardens dotted with carved statues.

The guests-only swimming pool comes with a swim-up bar, and there's a semiprivate beach, a gym and a spa. Some rave about the restaurants (mains Rs105 to Rs575), but we found the seafood a bit hit-and-miss and the staff somewhat snooty. The white-wicker charm of the Verandah deck restaurant makes it a lovely setting for a drink or two.

Eating

You can find excellent fresh seafood almost anywhere in Puri, and in CT Rd homesick travellers can find muesli, pancakes and puddings. Low-season opening times can be erratic.

Dakshin (☎ 9937552252; CT Rd; dosas Rs25-35, thali Rs50) Standing out in CT Rd's string of ageing sand-floor banana-pancake joints, this clean new place has a simple menu of well-prepared South Indian dishes. The excellent thali includes *puri* (flat dough that puffs up when deep fried) and desert. There are nice touches like lime-scented finger bowls.

Bamboo (CT Rd; mains Rs30-90) A traveller-oriented place with muesli, pancakes and other usual suspects, all in the open air with thatched umbrellas and friendly staff who'll give you a game of chess when things are quiet. Ask the price of off-menu seafood suggestions before you order; they can cost three times more than anything on the menu.

Pink House (☎ 222253; off CT Rd; mains Rs30-120) Right on the beach, the Pink House is another open-air restaurant that does all the things travellers seem to demand: pancakes for breakfast; and lots of fish and prawns for dinner. On a good day the chilled vibe is pleasantly 1970s Puri; when we were there a shirtless young hippy was kicking back playing *Stairway to Heaven* on his acoustic guitar.

Peace Restaurant (CT Rd; mains Rs30-150) 'Peace Restaurant world famous in Puri but never heard of anywhere else.' So reads the menu, which features curries, macaroni, the best muesli in town and tasty fish dishes; the fish *dopiaza* (cooked with onions and garnished with raw or fried onions) is fab. This simple row of tables with thatch canopies is deservedly popular. Your food might take a while to arrive but it will be worth it, and you can enjoy a cold beer while you wait.

Honey Bee Bakery & Pizzeria (☎ 320479; CT Rd; mains Rs40-140; ⌚ 8.30am-2pm & 6-10pm) The pizzas aren't bad, the pancakes are great, the real coffee, toasted sandwiches and fry-up brekkies (including bacon!) might be just

ORISSA

what you've been craving, and the lassis are excellent.

Wildgrass Restaurant (☎ 9437023656; VIP Rd; mains Rs45-140; ✗) With mismatched sculptures and precarious tree-huts scattered through its grounds, Wildgrass is a secret garden gone wild. The garden surrounds a small restaurant with an Indian and Continental menu enlivened with excellent seafood dishes and Orissan specialties.

our pick **Chung Wah Restaurant** (☎ 223647; VIP Rd; mains Rs55-135) The Chung Wah is a first-rate Chinese restaurant serving the real thing. Favourites on the menu include spring rolls, sweet-and-sours and a commendable Sichuan chicken.

Aero Dine (☎ 222388; Hotel Shakti International, VIP Rd; mains Rs70-250; ✗) Are you in Puri or are you in a 1960s movie set in a futuristic spaceship? This very surprising place has white modular furniture, random flashing lights and monitors, and there's even a 'cockpit' area for kids to play. The menu brings you back down to earth a little with Indian, Chinese and Continental standards, but there are a few wildcards thrown in: Waldorf salad, crêpes suzette or tom yam soup anyone?

Shopping

Shops along Marine Pde sell fabric, beads, shells and bamboo work, while shops on CT Rd sell Kashmiri and Tibetan souvenirs.

Near Jagannath Mandir, many places sell Jagannath images, palm-leaf paintings, handicrafts and Orissan hand-woven *ikat*, which you can buy in lengths or as ready-made garments.

A couple of general **grocery stores** on CT Rd (mainly around the Hotel Lotus) stock a good range of toiletries that might be hard to find elsewhere in Orissa, eg women's deodorant.

Getting There & Away

BUS

From the sprawling **bus station** (☎ 224461) near Gundicha Mandir, frequent buses serve Konark (Rs20, one hour), Satapada (Rs39, three hours) and Bhubaneswar (Rs25, two hours). For Pipli and Raghurajpur, take the Bhubaneswar bus. For other destinations change at Bhubaneswar.

TRAIN

Book well ahead if travelling during holiday and festival times. The booking counter at the train station can become incredibly crowded, but CT Rd agencies will book tickets for a small fee.

The *Purushottam Express* 2801 travels to Delhi (sleeper/3AC/2AC Rs501/1354/1856, 32 hours, 9.45pm), while Howrah can be reached on the *Puri-Howrah Express* 2838 (Rs236/641/866, nine hours, 8.05pm) and the *Sri Jagannath Express* 8410 (Rs227/611/836, 10 hours, 10.30pm). The *Neelachal Express* 2875 goes to Varanasi (Rs377/1005/1372, 21 hours, 10.55am), continuing to Delhi, on Tuesday, Friday and Sunday. To Sambalpur, the *Puri-Sambalpur Express* 8304 (2nd class/chair Rs100/356, six hours, 3.45pm), running every day except Sunday, is best.

Getting Around

Several places along CT Rd (mainly around the Hotel Lotus) rent bicycles from Rs20 per day and both mopeds and motorcycles from Rs250. From CT Rd, cycle-rickshaws charge about Rs10 to the train station and Rs20 to the bus station or Jagannath Mandir.

RAGHURAJPUR

The artists' village of **Raghurajpur**, 14km north of Puri, is two streets and 120 thatched brick houses adorned with murals of geometric patterns and mythological scenes – a traditional art form that has almost died out in Orissa.

The village is most famous for its *patachitra* – work made using a cotton cloth coated with a mixture of gum and chalk and then polished. With eye-aching attention and a very fine brush, artists mark out animals, flowers, gods and demons, which are then illuminated with bright colours.

Take the Bhubaneswar bus and look for the 'Raghurajpur The Craft Village' signpost 11km north of Puri, then walk or take an autorickshaw for the last 1km.

KONARK

☎ 06758 / pop 15,020

The majestic Sun Temple at Konark – a Unesco World Heritage Site – is one of India's signature buildings and Konark's raison d'être. Most of the visitors are daytrippers from Bhubaneswar or Puri, and accommodation is limited, but it's possible to stay overnight.

Originally nearer the coast (the sea has receded 3km), Konark was visible from far out at sea and known as the 'Black Pagoda'

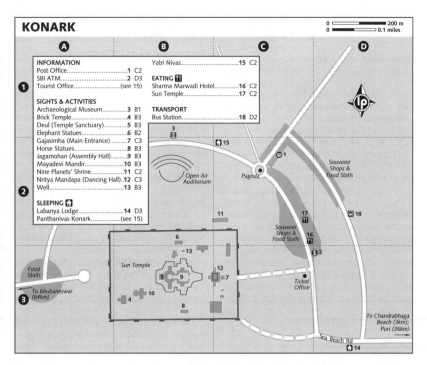

KONARK

0 _____ 200 m
0 _____ 0.1 miles

INFORMATION
Post Office.............................1 C2
SBI ATM...............................2 D3
Tourist Office......................(see 15)

SIGHTS & ACTIVITIES
Archaeological Museum.............3 B1
Brick Temple.........................4 B3
Deul (Temple Sanctuary)...........5 B3
Elephant Statues.....................6 B2
Gajasimha (Main Entrance)........7 C3
Horse Statues........................8 B3
Jagamohan (Assembly Hall)........9 B3
Mayadevi Mandir..................10 B3
Nine Planets' Shrine...............11 C2
Nritya Mandapa (Dancing Hall)..12 C3
Well...................................13 B3

SLEEPING
Labanya Lodge.......................14 D3
Panthanivas Konark...............(see 15)

Yatri Nivas..........................15 C2

EATING
Sharma Marwadi Hotel............16 C2
Sun Temple..........................17 C2

TRANSPORT
Bus Station..........................18 D2

Souvenir
Shops &
Food Stalls

Pagoda

Open Air
Auditorium

Souvenir
Shops &
Food Stalls

Food
Stalls

To Bhubaneswar
(64km)

Sun Temple

Ticket
Office

To Chandrabhaga
Beach (3km);
Puri (36km)

Sea Beach Rd

---

by sailors, in contrast to the whitewashed Jagannath of Puri.

Orientation & Information

The road from Bhubaneswar swings around the temple and past a couple of hotels and eateries before continuing to meet the coastal road to Puri. To the north and east of the temple is the **post office** (10am-5pm Mon-Sat), a State Bank of India ATM, the bus station and numerous souvenir shops. The **tourist office** (236821; Panthanivas Konark hotel; 10am-5pm Mon-Sat) can line up a registered guide to meet you at the temple.

Sights

SUN TEMPLE

The massive **Sun Temple** (Indian/foreigner Rs10/250, video Rs25, guides per hr Rs100; dawn-dusk) was constructed in the mid-13th century, probably by Orissan king Narashimhadev I to celebrate his military victory over the Muslims, and was in use for maybe only three centuries. In the late 16th century marauding Mughals removed the copper over the cupola; this may have led to the partial collapse of the 40m-

high *sikhara* (spire), and subsequent cyclones probably compounded the damage. As late as 1837 one half of the *sikhara* was still standing but it collapsed completely in 1869. Gradually, shifting sands covered the site, with only the *deul* and *jagamohan* rising proud of its burial mound. Excavation and restoration began in 1901; the *jagamohan* was closed off and filled with rocks and sand to prevent it from collapsing inwards.

The entire temple was conceived as the cosmic chariot of the sun god, Surya. Seven mighty prancing horses (representing the days of the week) rear at the strain of moving this leviathan of stone on 24 stone cartwheels (representing the hours of the day) that stand around the base. The temple was positioned so that dawn light would illuminate the *deul* interior and the presiding deity, which may have been moved to Jagannath Mandir in Puri in the 17th century.

The **gajasimha** (main entrance) is guarded by two stone lions crushing elephants and leads to the intricately carved **nritya mandapa** (dancing hall). Steps, flanked by straining horses, rise to the still-standing **jagamohan**.

Behind is the spireless **deul** with its three impressive chlorite images of Surya aligned to catch the sun at dawn, noon and sunset.

The base and walls present a chronicle in stone of Kalinga life; you'll see women cooking and men hunting. Many are in the erotic style for which Konark is famous and include entwined couples as well as solitary exhibitionists.

Around the grounds are a small shrine called **Mayadevi Mandir**; a deep, covered **well**; and the ruins of a **brick temple**. To the north are a couple of **elephant statues**, to the south a couple of **horse statues**, both trampling soldiers.

If there's anywhere worth hiring a guide, it's here. The temple's history is a complicated amalgam of fact and legend, and religious and secular imagery, and the guides' explanations are thought-provoking. They'll also show you features you might otherwise overlook – the woman with Japanese sandals, a giraffe (proving this area once traded with Africa) and even a man treating himself for venereal disease! Be sure your guide is registered. There are only 29 registered guides in Konark, listed on the name board by the entrance.

NINE PLANETS' SHRINE

This 6m-chlorite slab, once the architrave above the *jagamohan*, is now the centrepiece of a small shrine just outside the temple walls. Carved seated figures represent the Hindu nine planets – Surya (the sun), Chandra (moon), Mars, Mercury, Jupiter, Venus, Saturn, Rahu and Ketu.

ARCHAEOLOGICAL MUSEUM

This interesting (and refreshingly cool and quiet) **museum** (☎ 236822; admission Rs5; ☼ 10am-5pm Sat-Thu), just west of Yatri Nivas, contains many impressive sculptures and carvings found during excavations of the Sun Temple. Highlights include the full-bellied Agni (the fire god) and the larger-than-life, voluptuous Bina Badini. Check out the carved *Lady with a Bird* – it's pecking her in a place that can't be comfortable.

CHANDRABHAGA BEACH

The local beach at Chandrabhaga is 3km from the temple down the Puri road. Walk, cycle or take an autorickshaw (Rs60 return), or use the Konark–Puri bus. The beach is quieter and cleaner than Puri's, but beware of strong currents; there have also been reports of thefts on the beach. To the east is a fishing village with plenty of boating activity at sunrise.

Sleeping & Eating

Labanya Lodge (☎ 236824; Sea Beach Rd; s from Rs75, d Rs150-350; ☐) The best budget choice, this friendly place has a garden and a fresh coconut drink to welcome guests. The bright-coloured rooms come in different sizes, and there's a rooftop terrace. This is the only internet facility (per hour Rs60) in town and there's bike hire (per day Rs25). The roll-out of geysers to all rooms should be complete by now.

Panthanivas Konark (☎ 236831; d with/without AC Rs750/450; ❄) One of two adjoining OTDC properties; this one has tired rooms that can get mosquito-ridden. The restaurant (mains Rs30 to Rs80) has a small and lacklustre range, though the set breakfasts aren't bad and there are sometimes seafood specials.

Yatri Nivas (☎ 236830; d Rs1500; ❄) Set in a large garden next to the museum, the Yatri Nivas has new, clean, unremarkable rooms with silent AC systems. You may need to go through reception next door at the Panthanivas.

Sharma Marwadi Hotel (thalis Rs30-55) Reputedly the best of the *dhabas;* select from eight generous and delicious thalis or order south Indian snacks and more from the inexpensive menu.

Sun Temple (mains Rs30-180) A busy, friendly place with a big range of Indian veg and non-vegetarian dishes, including recommended seafood dishes. It also has a decent stab at traveller favourites like chips and banana pancakes.

Getting There & Away

Overcrowded minibuses regularly run along the coastal road between Puri and Konark (Rs20, one hour). There are also regular departures to Bhubaneswar (Rs40, two hours). Konark is included in OTDC tours from Bhubaneswar (p254) and Puri (p254). An autorickshaw will take you to Puri, with a beach stop along the way, for between Rs200 and Rs300, depending on the season and your bargaining skills. Because the Puri–Konark road is flat, some diehards even cycle the 36km from Puri.

CHILIKA LAKE

Chilika Lake is Asia's largest brackish lagoon. Swelling from 600 sq km in April/May to 1100 sq km in the monsoon, the shallow lake is separated from the Bay of Bengal by a 60km-long sand bar called Rajhansa.

The lake is noted for the million-plus migratory birds – including grey-legged geese, herons, cranes and pink flamingos – that flock here in winter (from November to mid-January) from as far away as Siberia and Iran and concentrate in a 3-sq-km area within the bird sanctuary on Nalabana Island. Changes in salinity have caused some birds to move to Mangaljodi near the northern shore. Other problems, such as silting and commercial prawn farming, are also threatening this important wetland area and the livelihood of local fisherpeople.

Other attractions are rare Irrawaddy dolphins near Satapada, the pristine beach along Rajhansa, and Kalijai Island temple where Hindu pilgrims flock for the Makar Mela festival (p251) in January.

Satapada
☎ 06752

This small village, on a headland jutting southwestwards into the lake, is the starting point for most boat trips. There's an **Orissa Tourism office** (☎ 262077; Yatri Nivas hotel) here.

Boat trips from Satapada usually cruise towards the new sea mouth for a paddle in the sea and some dolphin and bird spotting en route. Travellers have reported dolphins being (illegally) herded and otherwise harassed; make it clear you don't want this.

OTDC (☎ 262077; Yatri Nivas hotel) has boats for hire (for large groups) or a three-hour tour (per person Rs80) at 10.30am, with another at 2pm if there's enough interest.

Dolphin Motor Boat Association (☎ 262038; Satapada jetty; 1-8hr trips per boat Rs400-1300), a cooperative of local boat owners, has set-price trips mixing in dolphin sightseeing, Nalabana Bird Sanctuary and Kalijai Island temple.

Chilika Visitor Centre (☎ 262013; admission Rs10; ☼ 10am-5pm) is an exhibition on the lake, its wildlife and its human inhabitants. The centre has an upstairs observatory with a telescope and bird-identification charts.

A regular ferry (Rs30, four hours) plies between Satapada and Balugaon just north of Barkul, departing at 1pm and returning at 6.30am the next day. Tour operators and travel agents lining CT Rd in Puri can organise return trips on comfortable buses for around Rs100, including about four hours in Satapada where you can organise your own boat.

Yatri Nivas (☎ 262077; d Rs250, with AC Rs650; ▨) is a government-run hotel whose best rooms have balconies with lake views. The restaurant (mains Rs30 to Rs80) has a small selection of standard Indian fare and a couple of seafood dishes.

Hotel Avinandan (Satapada jetty; thalis Rs30-200) is opposite the Dolphin Motor Boat Association. This food hall has a thriving business in quick, tasty thalis, including the massive house special that includes fish, crab and tiger prawns.

Several shops and food stalls line the road to the jetty. Don't forget to take water on your boat trip.

Barkul
☎ 06756

On the northern shore of Chilika, Barkul is just a scatter of houses, basic 'lodges' and food stalls on a lane off NH5. From here boats go to Nalabana and Kalijai Island. Nalabana is best visited in early morning and late afternoon, November to late February.

With a minimum of seven people, the **OTDC** (Panthanivas Barkul) runs tours to Kalijia (Rs50), and Nalabana and Kalijia (Rs150). Otherwise, a boat with a quiet engine (that doesn't scare birds) can be hired from Rs450 to Rs1150 per hour. Private boat owners (with no insurance and often no safety gear) charge around Rs350 an hour; a recommended operator is fisherman **Babu Behera** (☎ 9937226378).

Panthanivas Barkul (☎ 220488, 211078; r Rs650, with AC Rs1500; ▨) has a great setting, with comfortable rooms overlooking the garden to the lake. The new cottages are clean and inviting, with lake views. The very air-conditioned restaurant (mains Rs30 to Rs100) is good, with seafood specials such as crab masala. We found this and the nearby hotel at Rambha (p268) to be the best of the government-run hotels in Orissa.

Frequent buses dash along NH5 between Bhubaneswar (Rs40) and Berhampur (Rs70). You can get off anywhere on route.

A ferry (Rs30) goes to Satapada at 6.30am from Balugaon, a couple of kilometres north of Barkul – autos and taxis whiz up and down the route.

Rambha
☎ 06810

The small town of Rambha is the nearest place to stay for turtle watching on Rushikulya beach. Not as commercial as

Barkul, Rambha is a very pleasant little backwater. Boat hire costs Rs500 for a three-hour trip around the lake.

Panthanivas Rambha (☎ 278346; dm Rs150, d Rs550, d/d cottage with AC Rs990/2000; ❄), about 200m off the main road, and 1km west of Rambha centre, looks a tad battered outside but has fine rooms (the AC rooms are better) with big clean bathrooms and balconies overlooking the lake. The new cottages with terracotta-tile ceilings have charm and views, and all beds have mozzie nets. The restaurant (mains Rs30 to 100) is very good, especially the seafood.

There are regular buses to/from Bhubaneswar (Rs70) and Berhampur (Rs60).

Rushikulya

The nesting beach for olive ridley marine turtles is on the northern side of Rushikulya River, near the villages of Purunabandh and Gokharkuda. The nearest accommodation is in Rambha, 20km away; taxis and autos run between the two towns.

During nesting and hatching there will be conservationists on the beaches and activity takes place throughout the night. Do not use lights during hatching as they distract the turtles away from the sea.

GOPALPUR-ON-SEA
☎ 0680 / pop 6660
Gopalpur-on-Sea is a seaside town the British left to slide into history until Bengali holidaymakers discovered its attractions in the 1980s. Prior to this, it had a noble history as a seaport with connections to Southeast Asia, the evidence of which is still scattered through the town in the form of romantically crumbling old buildings.

It's no paradise, but the peaceful and relatively clean beach is great for a stroll and a paddle, or you can just relax and watch the fishing boats come and go. A recent clean-up of the beachfront saw a series of tacky statues added: look for the mermaid about to snog a fish.

Orientation & Information
The approach road from NH5 runs straight through town and terminates in front of the sea, where you'll find most of the hotels and restaurants. There's a PCO (Public Call Office) by Krishna's restaurant; the bus stand is 500m before the beach.

A modern new **post office** (NH5; ⏰ 9am-5pm Mon-Sat; internet access per hr Rs20) is near the bus stand, on your left on the way down to the beach.

Dangers & Annoyances
Foreigners, especially women, are always an attraction for the curious; it can be incredibly annoying. Cover up, and if you go for a walk find a fellow traveller for company or just attach yourself to an obliging Indian family and bask under their general protection.

Swimming in the nasty shore break at Gopalpur, where there are undercurrents, is an untested activity; most visitors are content with a paddle.

Sights
Peering over the town is the **lighthouse** (Indian/foreigner/child Rs10/25/3, camera Rs20; ⏰ 3.30-5.30pm), with its immaculate gardens and petite staff cottages. It's a late-afternoon drawcard and after puffing up the spiral staircase you're rewarded with expansive views and welcome cooling breezes.

Sleeping & Eating
Gopalpur-on-Sea can be booked out during holiday and festival time. Prices here are for the high season (November to January); discounts are available at other times.

Hotel Holiday Home (☎ 2242049; d Rs250-400) A reasonably clean budget place with friendly owners and a range of rooms – take a look at a few, as some are more appealing (and you'll get to see all the different '80s posters). It's cater-corner to the Sea Pearl. Checkout is 9am.

Hotel Green Park (☎ 2242016; greenpark016@yahoo .com; d Rs350-500, d/tr with AC Rs700/900; ❄) One street back from the beach, Green Park is a clean, friendly and good-value option (with no bar or restaurant). Some rooms have front-facing balconies and there's a 24-hour checkout.

Holiday World Plaza (☎ 9338859489; s/d Rs350/650, d with AC Rs750; ❄) Clean, spacious and right on the beach, with big windows for views and breezes. The singles are small and simple, but be warned that all doubles have bright-coloured cartoon murals on the walls – kids will like it.

Hotel Sea Side Breeze (☎ 2242075; d from Rs450) A great location on the beach, with most rooms facing the sand and catching the sea breezes. The rooms are bare and a bit run down but passably clean. It claims on its card to be the

---

ORISSA'S OLIVE RIDLEY TURTLES

One of the smallest of the sea turtles and a threatened species, the olive ridley marine turtle swims up from deeper waters beyond Sri Lanka to mate and lay eggs en masse on Orissa's beaches. The main nesting sites are Gahirmatha within the Bhitarkanika National Park, Devi near Konark and Rushikulya.

Turtle deaths due to fishing practices are unfortunately common. Although there are regulations, such as requiring the use of turtle exclusion devices (TEDs) on nets and banning fishing from certain areas, these laws are routinely flouted in Orissa. Another threat has been afforestation of the Devi beach-nesting site with casuarina trees. While preserving the beaches, the trees occupy areas of soft sand that are necessary for a turtle hatchery. Other potential threats include oil exploration off Gahirmatha and seaport development near Rushikulya.

Turtles mass at sea between late October and early December. Then in January they congregate near nesting beaches and, if conditions are right, they come ashore over four to five days. If conditions aren't right, they reabsorb their eggs.

Hatching takes place 50 to 55 days later. Hatchlings are guided to the sea by the luminescence of the ocean and can be easily distracted by bright lights; unfortunately NH5 runs within 2km of Rushikulya beach, so many turtles crawl the wrong way. However, villagers in the Sea Turtle Protection Committee gather up errant turtles and take them to the sea.

The best place to see nesting and hatching is at Rushikulya (opposite). Ask at Panthanivas Rambha (opposite) – staff can tell you what conditions are like. Autos and taxis can take you between Rambha and Rushikulya.

---

only hotel on the beach, which is patently not true.

Hotel Sea Pearl (☎ 2242556; d Rs600-750, with AC Rs950-1200; ✷) Any nearer the sea and it'd be in it; the big and popular Sea Pearl has some great rooms, especially the upper-storey, beach-facing, non-AC rooms, and a little private entrance to the beach. Look at a few rooms; price doesn't necessarily reflect quality here. There are two restaurants, with standard multicuisine menus (mains Rs40 to Rs120; one is on the roof.

Swosti Palm Resort (☎ 2243718; www.swosti.com; Main Rd; s/d Rs2600/3200; ✷) Further back in town, and an unfortunate walk past a rubbish tip, the Swosti has the best accommodation in town with comfortable, well-appointed rooms. The excellent multicuisine restaurant, Chilika, serves good seafood including authentic local dishes (mains Rs50 to Rs260).

Sea Shell (mains Rs15-60) A collection of open-air tables on the beachfront, Sea Shell is an ideal place to while away the day with a good book, some snacks (Chinese, Indian) and a resuscitating ice cream.

Krishna's (mains Rs20-100) Mainly Indian and Chinese standards (nicely executed) and excellent *kati rolls* (see p128) in the quiet season but, if you ask, the kitchen can produce good pancakes, pasta and fried calamari or fish and chips. Expect to pay Rs100 and up, though,

for some of the seafood. Naz Cafe, next door, is similar.

Beach restaurants don't serve alcohol, but there's a liquor shop on the road between the beach and Hotel Green Park where you can pick up a Kingfisher or two to enjoy on your balcony.

Getting There & Away

Frequent, crowded minibuses travel to Berhampur (Rs8, one hour), where you can catch onward transport by rail or bus. Alternatively, an autorickshaw costs about Rs150.

WESTERN ORISSA

Although permits aren't usually needed, there are Adivasi areas in western and central Orissa where foreigners have to register their details with the police. This is all done for you if you are on a tour but independent visitors should check their plans with the police in the nearest city.

TAPTAPANI
☎ 06816

Apart from the small **hot springs** in this attractive and peaceful village in the Eastern Ghats, there's not much else to see. The public baths (free; and full of soapy scunge) next to the

ORISSA

springs are particularly popular with people with skin diseases and other disorders. It's a sacred place, considered a manifestation of the goddess, and as such has various temple trappings set up around it, including some truly gory statuary.

For a great winter treat (December nights plunge to zero) book one of the hot-springs rooms at **Panthanivas Taptapani** (☎ 255031; d from Rs750, with AC Rs2000, with hot bath Rs2500, tree house Rs2000; 🔀). Hot spring water is channelled directly to vast tubs in the Roman-style bathrooms; these hot-tub rooms can be rented for the day (up to 4pm) for Rs1500. Other options on the leafy property include an appealing 'tree house' with charming rattan furniture that puts you right up in the treetops (it's reportedly best avoided in windy weather, though it's noisily creaky rather than dangerous) and less interesting cabins (overpriced, though perfectly clean and comfortable). The cool, clean restaurant (mains Rs30 to Rs100) has the standard Panthanivas menu and fabulous views over the ghats.

Buses go regularly to Berhampur (Rs25, two hours). You can ask the driver to let you off the bus about halfway between Taptapani and Berhampore at Digapahandi, from where you can catch an autorickshaw to the textile village of **Padmanavpur**, 5km away. Here traditional weaving is done on old-fashioned looms, and brightly coloured saris are stretched out in the sun.

BALIGUDA
☎ 06846

This tiny one-street town is the base for visits to the Belghar region, home to fascinating and friendly Desia Kondh and Kutia Kondh villages. At the time of research it was closed to visitors following an outbreak of communal violence in the area; for the latest news, check with tour operators in Bhubaneswar or Puri.

The State Bank of India ATM accepts Visa, and you can check email at **Mahakali Communication** (Main Rd). The only place to stay in Baliguda is the **Hotel Santosh Bhavan** (☎ 243409; s Rs150-300, d Rs250-500), and food is confined to a few *dhaba*-style (cheap and basic) restaurants.

RAYAGADA
☎ 06856

Rayagada is the base for visiting the weekly Wednesday market at **Chatikona** (about 40km

north). Here, highly ornamented Dongria Kondh and Desia Kondh villagers from the surrounding Niayamgiri Hills bring their produce and wares to sell. Alongside piles of chillies and dried fish are bronze animal sculptures made locally using the lost wax method.

The friendly **Hotel Rajbhavan** (☎ 223777; Main Rd; d incl breakfast from Rs500, with AC from Rs950; 🔀) has bright and airy rooms and a good multicuisine restaurant (mains Rs40 to Rs80). Breakfast is an *idli*. It's just across the main road from the train station. **Hotel Vamsi Krishna** (☎ 224622; New Colony; incl breakfast s/d Rs500/600, with AC from Rs800/900; 🔀) is of a similar standard, with rather more gaudy furnishings and sparkling bathrooms, and a bigger Indian breakfast. The restaurant has Indian and Chinese standards (mains Rs40 to Rs140), along with South Indian snacks, and a couple of private booths where they'll hustle travellers who want to have an undisturbed beer. **Hotel Sai International** (☎ 225554; JK Rd; d Rs600-1500; 🔀) has spotless, comfortable rooms, hot water and a good restaurant (mains Rs50 to Rs200).

There's a regular local bus from Rayagada to Chatikona (Rs17, two hours), as well as shared jeeps (Rs20). The *Hirakhand Express* 8447 leaves Bhubaneswar daily at 8pm and reaches Rayagada at 5.10am on its way to Koraput.

JEYPORE
☎ 06854 / pop 77,000

Jeypore is the base for visiting the amazingly colourful Onkadelli market. The derelict palace, with heavy decorated gates, was built in 1936 and is off limits. There's a State Bank of India ATM on Main Rd and another near the bus stand. There's little in the way of budget accommodation for independent travellers; you're better off in temple accommodation in Koraput.

Hotel Mani Krishna (☎ 321139; MG Rd; www.hotel manikrishna.com; s/d Rs500/600, with AC from Rs800/900; 🔀) has spotless, tastefully decorated rooms, with interesting old photos of Adivasi people. The downstairs restaurant has a good selection of tasty Indian and Chinese food (mains Rs40 to Rs90, thalis from Rs35). The menu has tourist information and terrible jokes for you to read while you wait.

Next door, **Hotel Sai Krishna** (☎ 230253; www .hotelsaikrishna.com; MG Rd; s/d from Rs600/750, with AC from Rs800/900; 🔀) is very similar, with gaudier decor, super-clean bathrooms and two restaurants (mains Rs40 to Rs125), both of which serve local specialties alongside the usual Indian and Chinese fare.

Until recently, **Hello Jeypore** (☎ 231127; www.hoteljeypore.com; NH Rd; s/d from Rs795/995, with AC Rs995/1195; ✕ ▣) was pretty much the only

player in town and didn't have to try too hard. Happily, it has lifted its game and is still the best place to stay, with clean, comfortable rooms with contemporary design and an excellent restaurant (mains Rs35 to Rs120) serving fresh produce. There's an eerily lit bar and a pleasant garden.

ORISSA'S INDIGENOUS GROUPS

Sixty-two Adivasi (tribal) groups live an area that encompasses Orissa, Chhattisgarh and Andhra Pradesh. In Orissa they account for one-quarter of the state's population and mostly inhabit the jungles and hilly regions of the centre and southwest. Regardless of their economic poverty, they have highly developed social organisations and distinctive cultures expressed in music, dance and arts.

Adivasi influence on Indian culture is little recognised, but it is claimed that early Buddhist sanghas were modelled on Adivasi equality, lack of caste and respect for all life. Many of the Hindu gods, including Shiva and Kali, have roots in Adivasi deities. Many Adivasis have become integrated into Hindu society performing menial jobs, while others have remained in remote hilly or forested areas.

Most Adivasis were originally animists but over the last 30 years have been targeted (with varying degrees of success and cultural sensitivity) by both Christian missionaries and Hindu activists. Naxalites (members of an ultra-leftist political movement) have used Adivasis as foot soldiers while claiming to defend them.

The Adivasis have become something of a tourist attraction. Visits are possible to some villages and *haats* (village markets) that Adivasis attend on a weekly basis. There are arguments regarding the morality of visiting Adivasi areas. Usually you need to gain permission to visit the villages, whereas at the *haats* you are free to interact with and buy directly from the villagers. However, it remains the case that tourism still brings very little income to the Adivasis.

Of the more populous groups, the Kondh number about one million and are based around Koraput in the southwest and near Sambalpur in the northwest. The Santal, with a population above 500,000, live around Baripada and Khiching in the far north. The 300,000 Saura live near Bolangir in the west. The Bonda, known as the 'Naked People' for wearing minimal clothing, have a population of about 5000 and live in the hills near Koraput.

It is important to visit these areas on an organised tour for the following reasons:

▪ Some areas are prohibited and others require permits, which are much more easily obtained by a tour operator.

▪ Some Adivasi areas are hard to find and often not accessible by public transport.

▪ Adivasis often speak little Hindi or Oriya, and usually no English.

▪ Some Adivasi people can get angry, even violent, if foreigners visit their villages uninvited and without official permission.

Some operators are more sensitive to the issues than others; it's worth asking about the size of your group and attitudes to photography (some people do not allow themselves to be photographed), and trying to get a feel for how interactions will be handled. Communal violence involving Adivasi people can flare up (see p249) and, while tourists haven't been targeted, a good operator should be honest and careful about avoiding areas experiencing trouble. Try to meet the guide who will be travelling with you rather than just speaking with the boss in the office. See p261 and p254 for details of recommended agencies.

Most tours start from Bhubaneswar or Puri, take in the more accessible areas in the southwest and can then go on to visit Similipal National Park. Options can include jungle trekking, staying at a village (tents and cooking supplied by the tour operator) and visiting one or more of the *haats*.

The main bus station is 2km out of town but buses also stop in town to pick up passengers. An auto between the centre of town and the station will cost about Rs30. Frequent buses go to Koraput (Rs15, 45 minutes); others go to Berhampur (Rs200, 12 hours), Bhubaneswar (Rs300, 14 to 16 hours) and Rayagada (Rs70, three hours).

Slow passenger trains Nos 1VK and 2VK connect Jeypore with Visakhapatnam daily.

AROUND JEYPORE

Onkadelli and Kotpad are best accessed by hired car and Onkadelli should only be visited with a professional guide. You'll get much more out of the experience with a guide, who will usually be able to take you to visit craftspeople. This doesn't mean you have to come all the way from Bhubaneswar or Puri with a group or guide – it's feasible to come to Jeypore independently and organise a guide at your hotel.

Koraput
☎ 06852

Koraput is just a few kilometres from Jeypore and is an attractive town that's emerging as an alternative base for Adivasi visits. The temple is fascinating, especially for those non-Hindus who couldn't enter the Jagannath temple (p259) in Puri.

The **tourist office** (☎ 250318; Jeypore Rd; ☮ 10am-5pm Mon-Sat, closed 2nd Sat of month) has information and can arrange car hire. It's housed in the new, bright-blue Panthanivas Koraput, which had yet to open its rooms at the time of research; expect simple non-AC doubles for about Rs200.

The **Tribal Museum** (admission free; ☮ 10am-5pm) has an extensive exhibition of Adivasi culture including utensils, tools and clothes, as well as some paintings for sale. The museum will open out of hours if you can find the friendly caretaker. The open-air Jungle Restaurant here does Indian and Chinese dishes in a cool, leafy setting.

The **Jagannath temple** has an exhibition of gods of the different states of India. There's also a selection of local forms of *ossa* (also known as *rangoli*), traditional patterns made with white and coloured powders on doorsteps. At the back of the temple there is a series of apses containing statuettes of Jagannath in his various guises and costumes.

The temple operates two budget hotels just outside its grounds. **Atithi Bhaban** (☎ 250610; atithibhaban@hotmail.com; d without/with AC Rs200/400; ✵) is the older building, with 'pure veg' restaurant and simple, clean-enough rooms. **Yatri Nivas** (☎ 9337622637; d Rs150) was only two months old when we visited, and had simple but very clean rooms. It has become popular fast; don't count on the 'very clean' lasting for long. Food can be ordered in from Atithi Bhaban.

The *Hirakhand Express* 8447/8 plies daily between Bhubaneswar and Koraput, and there are regular buses to Jeypore (Rs15, 45 minutes).

Onkadelli

This small village, 65km from Jeypore, has a most remarkable and vibrant Thursday **market** (best time 10am to 1pm) that throngs with Bonda, Gadaba, Mali and Didai villagers.

The market is popular with tour groups; if you stand back and watch Westerners photographing Adivasi people, you may well see Indian tourists taking photos of the equally exotic Westerners. Photographs should only be taken with the consent of the subject and will often come with a request for Rs10 or more; carry small denomination notes. Souvenir shopping is pretty much limited to jewellery sold by Bonda women.

Alcohol is an important ingredient in this social event; combined with the hunting bows and arrows it's a further incentive to make use of a professional guide. Police may shoo you away from the designated drinking areas.

Kotpad

This town, 40km north of Jeypore on the road to Sambalpur, has a thriving home-based fabric-dyeing and weaving industry. Along the lanes you'll see ropes of thread in a rich range of colours from reds and burgundies to browns laid out to dry. You can buy scarves and shawls (Rs600 to Rs3000) in silk and cotton direct from artisans – the distinctive local animal designs are especially appealing.

Nabarangpur

Northeast of Kotpad, this town is the home of families who produce distinctive lacquer work on bamboo jewellery boxes traditionally given to women when they're married. In recent years the same decorative methods have been used on wood and clay to produce bright-coloured vases and images of Jagannath. Purchases can be made from a small shop in the main street, **Sarala Lac & Handicraft Centre** (☎ 9437374451; set of 5 boxes Rs400).

SAMBALPUR
☎ 0663 / pop 154,170
Sambalpur is the centre for the textile industry spread over western Orissa, and Gole Bazaar is the place to buy *ikat* or *sambalpuri* weaving. The town is a base for nearby Badrama National Park, and Debrigarh Wildlife Sanctuary on the edge of Hirakud Dam.

Orientation & Information
NH6 passes through Sambalpur to become VSS Marg. Laxmi Talkies Rd crosses VSS Marg and leads down to the government bus stand and Gole Bazaar.

Orissa Tourism (☎ 2411118; Panthanivas Sambalpur, Brooks Hill; ☺ 10am-5pm Mon-Sat, closed 2nd Sat of month)

Police station (☎ 403224; Laxmi Talkies Rd)

sify e-port (VSS Marg; per hr Rs20; ☺ 8.30am-10pm; ☒) Cool, clean, reliable internet access and friendly. Upstairs above a row of shops.

State Bank of India (VSS Marg; ☺ 10-30am-4.30pm Mon-Fri, 10.30am-1.30pm Sat) Next to Sheela Towers. Does currency exchange and has a MasterCard and Visa ATM. There's another ATM in the bazaar.

Sleeping & Eating
Hotel Uphar Palace (☎ 2400519; fax 2522668; VSS Marg; s/d from Rs450/500, with AC from Rs750/850; ☒) The sparkling cleanliness of the lobby doesn't quite carry into the bathrooms, though the rooms themselves are clean enough and it's the friendliest place in town. The Sharda restaurant has an Indian and Chinese menu (mains Rs45 to Rs130).

Panthanivas Sambalpur (☎ 2411282; www.panthanivas.com; Brooks Hill; d Rs550, with AC from Rs800; ☒) The usual uninterested staff, but rooms are clean and spacious, and it's a quiet and leafy setting you won't find anywhere else in town.

Sheela Towers (☎ 2403111; www.sheelatowers.com; VSS Marg; s/d from Rs995/1095; ☒) Staff can be unhelpful to the point of rudeness and the AC is arctic, but this is still Sambalpur's top hotel, with a range of comfortable rooms. The restaurant (mains Rs50 to Rs185)

has a good range of tasty food and erratic opening hours.

New Hong Kong Restaurant (☎ 2532429; VSS Marg; mains Rs40-180; ☺ closed Mon) For 18 years the Chen family has been providing authentic Chinese in Sambalpur; we met expats who'd driven 60km cross-country to eat here. The menu also includes several Thai dishes and some tasty Indian-Chinese fusion dishes like Sichuan paneer. Ultraviolet light and doof music at night give it a clubby feel.

Getting There & Away
The government bus stand has buses running to Jeypore (Rs215, 14 hours), Bhubaneswar (Rs190, eight hours) and Berhampur (Rs207, 12 hours). Travel agencies in the street between the government bus station and Laxmi Talkies Rd book (usually more comfortable) buses leaving from the private **Ainthapali bus stand** (☎ 2540601), 3km from city centre (Rs10 by cycle-rickshaw). Several buses go to Bhubaneswar (Rs195), Raipur (Rs180, eight hours) and Jashipur for Similipal (Rs200, 10 hours).

The *Tapaswini Express* 8451 goes to Puri (sleeper/3AC/2AC Rs178/471/643, nine hours, 10.50pm) via Bhubaneswar (Rs160/420/573, seven hours). The *Koraput-Howrah Express* 8006 goes to Howrah (Rs243/654/896, 10 hours, 6.15pm).

AROUND SAMBALPUR
Huma
The leaning **Vimaleswar temple** at Huma, 32km south of Sambalpur, is a small Shiva temple where the *deul* slants considerably in two directions. The puzzle is that the porch of the temple appears square and there are no apparent filled-in gaps between the porch and *deul*. Was it built that way?

Baripalli
The Costa Pada area in Baripalli, on the road to Jeypore, is where to discover how tie-dye *ikat* textiles are created. Skeins of threads separated into cords are wrapped around frames. Painstakingly, these cords are then tied in red cotton to mark out the dyeing pattern. Strips of rubber are then wound around to protect the undyed areas. Dyed and dried, the threads are then woven on the many looms you can see through open doorways. There's also a thriving terracotta industry here.

ORISSA

DEBRIGARH & BADRAMA WILDLIFE SANCTUARIES

The 347-sq-km **Debrigarh Wildlife Sanctuary** (☎ 0663-2402741; admission per day Indian/foreigner Rs20/1000; � 8am-5pm 15 Nov-1 Jun), 40km from Sambalpur, is an easy day out. Mainly dry deciduous forest blankets the Barapahad Hills down to the shores of the vast Hirakud reservoir, a home for migratory birds in winter. Wildlife here includes deer, antelopes, sloth bears, langur monkeys and the ever-elusive tigers and leopards. **Badrama Wildlife Sanctuary** (admission per day Indian/foreigner Rs20/1000), 37km from Sambalpur, shelters elephants, tigers, panthers and bears. It can be closed with no notice in the event of bad weather.

Access to the sanctuaries usually requires a 4WD, which can be arranged through Orissa Tourism, a private tour agency, or your hotel in Sambalpur for about Rs1000 for a half day.

NORTHEASTERN ORISSA

SIMILIPAL NATIONAL PARK
☎ 06792

The 2750-sq-km **Similipal National Park** (admission per day Indian/foreigner Rs40/1000, camera per 3 days Rs50/100; � 6am-noon day visitor, to 2pm 15 Nov-15 Jun with accommodation reservation) is Orissa's prime wildlife sanctuary.

The scenery is remarkable: a massif of prominent hills creased by valleys and gorges, and made dramatic by plunging waterfalls, including the spectacular 400m-high **Barheipani Waterfall** and the 150m-high **Joranda Waterfall**. The jungle is an atmospheric mix of dense sal forest and rolling open savannah. The core area is only 850 sq km and much of the southern part is closed to visitors.

There's a huge range of reptile, bird and mammal species. The tigers aren't tracked; the best chance to spot them will be at the **Joranda salt lick**. What you're more likely to see is your first wild elephant (there are over 400 in the park), most probably at the **Chahala salt lick**. The best time to visit is early in the season before high visitor numbers affect animal behaviour.

There are two entrances, **Tulsibani**, 15km from Jashipur, on the northwestern side, and **Pithabata**, near Lulung, 25km west of Baripada. Options are a day visit or an overnight stay within the park. Overnight accommodation

needs to be booked 30 days in advance, and remember you'll have to pay the Rs1000 entry fee for both days you're here.

Entry permits can be obtained in advance from the **assistant conservator of forests** (☎ 06797-232474; National Park, Jashipur, Mayurbhanj District, 757091), or the **field director, Similipal Tiger Reserve Project** (☎ 06792-252593; Bhanjpur, Baripada, Mayurbhanj District, 757002). Alternatively a day permit can be purchased from either gate.

Visitors either come on an organised tour or charter a vehicle (Rs1200 to Rs2000 per day for 4WD); hiring a guide (around Rs500) is advisable.

If you want to avoid the hassles of arranging permits, transport, food and accommodation, an organised tour from Bhubaneswar, Puri or Baripada is the answer.

Forest Department bungalows (d Indian/foreigner from Rs600/800) has seven sets of bungalows; Chahala, Joranda and Newana are best for animal spotting and Barheipani for views. The very basic accommodation has to be booked well in advance with the field director at Baripada – see above. You have to bring your own food (no meat or alcohol allowed) and water.

In March 2009 Maoist rebels blew up three forest offices inside the park and raided the Chahala bungalow, robbing tourists who were staying there. At the time of going to print the park had been completely shut off to tourists. The situation should be resolved by the time the park is due to re-open in November 2009, but check with tour operators or the field director.

JASHIPUR
☎ 06797

This is an entry point for Similipal Park and a place to collect an entry permit and organise a guide and transport. Accommodation is very limited.

Sairam Holiday Home (☎ 232827; NH6; s Rs80, d with/without AC from Rs550/250; ☒) has basic, clean rooms with mosquito nets. The owner can help arrange Similipal trips.

Ramatirtha Eco Resort (d Indian/foreigner Rs700/900) is outside Jashipur on the way to the Tulsibani park entrance. This place is run by the forestry department and needs to be booked well in advance through the field director at Baripada – see left. It has basic food, decent rooms with nets and clean bathrooms.

There are regular buses between Jashipur and Sambalpur (Rs200, 10 hours).

BARIPADA
☎ 06792 / pop 95,000

This town is the best place to organise a Similipal visit; if you're planning an independent trip, see **Orissa Tourism** (☎ 252710; Baghra Rd; ◷ 10am-5pm Mon-Sat, closed 2nd Sat of month). Recommended agency **Mayur Tours & Travels** (☎ 253567; mayur_tour@rediffmail.com; Lal Bazaar) can also organise tours and has capable guides.

Hotel Sibapriya (☎ 255138; Traffic Sq; s/d Rs130/250, d with AC from Rs600; ◈) has a restaurant and tackily decorated rooms. The cheaper ones are a bit grubby but the AC rooms are fine. The clean and comfortable **Hotel Ambika** (☎ 252557; hotel_ambika@yahoo.com; s/d from Rs300/350, with AC from Rs900/950; ◈) has a good bar and restaurant. It can organise Similipal trips.

Regular buses go to Kolkata (Rs140, three hours) and frequently to Bhubaneswar (Rs170, five hours) and Balasore (Rs35, one hour). The Bhubaneswar–Baripada Express (BBS–BPO Express) 2892 (Rs70, second-class seats only, five hours, 5.10pm) runs from Bhubaneswar every day except Saturday, and returns as the 2891 at 5.00am every day except Sunday.

CUTTACK
☎ 0671 / pop 535,140

Cuttack, one of Orissa's oldest cities, was the state capital until 1950; today it's a chaotic, crowded city. The **tourist office** (☎ 2309616; Panthanivas, Buxi Bazaar; ◷ 10am-5pm Mon-Sat) is a little way out of town on a congested road, and not very helpful.

The 14th-century **Barabati Fort**, about 3km north of the city centre, once boasted nine storeys, but only some foundations and moat remain. The 18th-century **Qadam-i-Rasool shrine**, in the city centre, is sacred to Hindus as well as Muslims (who believe it contains footprints of the Prophet Mohammed).

Shopping is great in Cuttack: handloom saris, horn and brassware are crafted here, along with the famed, lacelike, silver filigree work *(tarakasi)*. The best jewellers are on Naya Sarak and Chowdary Bazaar, while you can see pieces being crafted in Mohammedia Bazaar.

Bhubaneswar is less than an hour away and Cuttack can easily be covered in a day trip. If you get stuck, **Hotel Akbari Continental** (☎ 2423251; hotelakbari@yahoo.co.in; Dolmundai; s/d from Rs1250/1600; ◈) has comfortable rooms.

Express buses whiz back and forth between Cuttack and Bhubaneswar every 10 minutes (Rs13, one hour).

BALASORE
pop 106,000

Balasore, the first major town in northern Orissa, was once an important trading centre. Now it's a staging post for Chandipur or Similipal National Park.

The **Orissa Tourism** (☎ 262048; ◷ 10am-5pm Mon-Sat) is located in **Panthanivas Balasore** (☎ 240697; Police Line; d with/without AC Rs700/400; ◈), which has friendlier-than-average staff and worn but clean rooms; they're fine for a night.

Several buses leave from Remuna Golai at around 10pm for Kolkata (Rs200, seven to eight hours) and more frequently for Bhubaneswar (Rs100, five hours). The infrequent bus service to Chandipur makes an autorickshaw (Rs200) a better option.

CHANDIPUR
☎ 06782

This cute and laid-back seaside village ambles down to the ocean through a short avenue of casuarina and palm trees. It amounts to a couple of hotels, snack places and some souvenir shops. It has a huge beach at low tide when the sea is some 5km away; it's safe to swim here when there's enough water.

There's a bustling fishing village 2km further up the coast at a river mouth; in the early morning, walk up and watch the boats unloading fish and prawns.

Hotel Chandipur (☎ 270030; d without/with AC from Rs250/650; ◈) has basic, clean rooms overlooking a courtyard with a (dry) fountain and fragrant frangipani trees. **Panthanivas Chandipur** (☎ 270051; dm Rs150, d with/without AC from Rs990/650; ◈) has a great location overlooking the beach, but is otherwise not the best value. Best of the bunch is **Hotel Shubham** (☎ 270025; d with/without AC from Rs900/480; ◈), with spotless, comfortable rooms, a pleasant garden and a good restaurant. **Hotel Golden** (☎ 270021; mains Rs20-100), on the main drag, does a limited selection of mainly veg Indian food, plus recommended local seafood; crab masala (Rs100) is the house speciality.

Regular buses ply the NH5 between Bhubaneswar and Balasore. From Balasore, taxis and autorickshaws can take you the 15km to Chandipur.

BHITARKANIKA WILDLIFE SANCTUARY
Three rivers flow out to sea at Bhitarkanika forming a tidal maze of muddy creeks and mangroves. Most of this 672-sq-km delta forms **Bhitarkanika Wildlife Sanctuary** (☎ 272460;

Indian/foreigner per day Rs20/1000), a significant ecosystem containing hundreds of estuarine crocodiles that bask on mud flats waiting for the next meal to swim by. Dangmal Island contains a successful breeding and conservation program for these crocodiles. Pythons, water monitors, wild boars and timid spotted deer can also be seen. The best time to visit is from December to February.

Birdwatchers will find eight species of brilliantly coloured kingfishers, plus 190 other bird species. A large heronry on Bagagahan Island is home for herons that arrive in early June and nest until early December, when they move on to Chilika Lake. Raucous open-billed storks have set up a permanent rookery here.

The only way to get around the sanctuary is by boat. Many boats are a tad battered, with old tyres on ropes for life preservers: this definitely adds piquancy to the thrill of boating on waters where enormous crocodiles can suddenly surface rather close to you.

Orientation & Information
Permits, accommodation and boat transport can all be organised in the small port of **Chandbali**. Organise a boat (per day Rs2000, negotiable) with one of the private operators, such as the recommended **Sanjog Travels** (☎ 06786-220495; Chandbali Jetty), which can also help with obtaining the permit from the **divisional forest officer** (☎ 06729-272460; Rajnagar).

Sights
First stop is a permit check at Khola jetty before heading to **Dangmal Island** for the crocodile conservation program (and accommodation).

The heronry at **Bagagahan Island** is reached by a narrow pathway leading to a watchtower, where you can spy on a solid mass of herons and storks nesting in the treetops.

Back at Khola, a 2km walk leads to Rigagada with its interesting 18th-century **Jagannath temple**, built with some erotica in Kalinga style. While there, take an amble through this typical Orissan village.

Sleeping & Eating
Forest rest houses (r per person Indian/foreigner from Rs434/574) This comfortable accommodation at Dangmal has solar lights, mosquito nets and shared bathrooms. The restaurant has a limited menu of mainly veg food along with fresh seafood (thalis Rs50 to Rs80). At the time of research the only way of booking

was in advance through Sandpebbles Tour N Travels (p251) in Bhubaneswar.

Aranya Nivas (☎ 06786-220397; Chandbali; with/without AC d Rs1000/500;) Within 50m of the Chandbali jetty, it has somewhat threadbare and less-than-spotless rooms with lots of mozzies; the restaurant serves up a limited menu that has to be ordered from in advance (mains Rs30 to Rs80). Boats can be organised here.

Getting There & Away
Chandbali is 55km and two hours southeast of Bhadrak on NH5. Buses go from Chandbali bazaar to Bhadrak (Rs25), Bhubaneswar (Rs75) and Kolkata (Rs150). The *Howrah-Bhubaneswar Dhauli Express* 2821/2 stops in Bhadrak at 10.27am going south to Bhubaneswar (2nd class/chair Rs71/232, two hours); and at 3.30pm going north to Howrah (2nd class/chair Rs104/346, five hours).

RATNAGIRI, UDAYAGIRI & LALITGIRI
These Buddhist ruins are about 60km northeast of Cuttack. There's no accommodation and inadequate transport, so the only feasible way to visit is by hired car organised in Bhubaneswar or Puri. The OTDC is building a Panthanivas hotel opposite the museum in Ratnagiri.

Ratnagiri
Ratnagiri has the most interesting and extensive **ruins** (admission Indian/foreigner Rs5/100, video Rs25; dawn-dusk). Two large monasteries flourished here from the 6th to 12th centuries. Noteworthy are an exquisitely carved doorway and the remains of a 10m-high stupa. The excellent **museum** (admission Rs2; 10am-5pm Sat-Thu) contains beautiful sculptures from the three sites; look for the exquisite miniature bronze images of the Buddha and Tara in gallery 4.

Udayagiri
Another **monastery complex** is being excavated here. There's a large pyramidal brick stupa with a seated Buddha and some beautiful doorjamb carvings. There's no entry fee, but unhelpful guides may attach themselves to you then ask for a donation (not compulsory).

Lalitgiri
Several **monastery ruins** (Indian/foreigner Rs5/100, video Rs25; dawn-dusk) are scattered up a hill leading to a small museum and a hillock with a shallow stupa. Excavations of the stupa in the 1970s found a casket of gold and silver relics.

Excursions

Being out east has its advantages. With a few easy-to-obtain visas, travellers can relive the glory days of the overland trail by hopping across the border to Nepal or Bangladesh. Border crossings abound and buses and trains provide easy transit from country to country – with time to spare, you could head east from Kolkata (Calcutta) through Bangladesh and loop back through the Northeast States and the West Bengal Hills, before heading on to Nepal.

The Nepal border crossings at Kakarbhitta, Birganj and Sunauli open up all sorts of interesting return routes to Kolkata, passing through Lumbini, where the Buddha was born, and Bodhgaya, where he achieved enlightenment. Alternatively, why not cut across Bangladesh, visiting bustling bazaar towns and ancient mosques en route to Agartala in Tripura?

The possible permutations are endless, so we've picked a handful of classic overland routes: a walk in the footsteps of Buddha in Bihar, a steamy detour east through Dhaka to Agartala, and the scenic route through Nepal, with stops in Kathmandu, Chitwan National Park and Lumbini. And we've covered the backwater border crossings too, in case you'd rather forge your own trail.

HIGHLIGHTS

- Soak up the essence of Buddha at the serene Mahabodhi Temple, then take a meditation class at a Buddhist monastery in **Bodhgaya** (p283)

- View the ashes of the Buddha, then shop for Mithila paintings in **Patna** (p278), the Bihari capital

- Tie on your bandana and follow the hippy overland trail to **Kathmandu** (p286), Nepal's eclectic capital

- Take a break from the borders with a detour to **Lumbini** (p292), the Nepali birthplace of Siddhartha Gautama Buddha

- Experience the rush of river life at Sadarghat in **Dhaka** (p295), the frenetic capital of Bangladesh

- Escape the beaten trail between Kolkata and Dhaka amongst the ruins of **Bagerhat** (p299), a treasure trove of Muslim monuments

EXCURSIONS

EXCURSIONS IN INDIA

The following destinations are interesting places to break the journey between the northeast and the various border crossings into central Nepal.

PATNA

☎ 0612 / pop 1.29 million

Bihar's busy capital spreads out over a vast area on the south bank of the swollen and polluted Ganges, just east of the river's confluence with three major tributaries. Patna was once the capital of the Magadha kingdom and later the capital of Maurya emperors Chandragupta Maurya and Ashoka, of Buddhist pillar fame. The town stretches along the southern bank of the Ganges for about 15km. The main train station, airport and hotels are in the western half, known as Bankipur, while most of the historic sites are in the teeming older Chowk area to the east.

Information

Bihar State Tourism Development Corporation

(BSTDC) tourist office (☎ 2225411; bstdc@sancharnet .in; Hotel Kautilya Vihar, Birchand Patel Path; ☽ 10am-5pm Mon-Sat) Books government tours and accommodation and can arrange cars with drivers.

Cyber World (Rajendra Path; per hr Rs20; ☽ 9.30am-9pm)

India Tourism (☎ 2348558; Sundama Pl, Kankerbagh Rd; ☽ 9.30am-6pm Mon-Fri) Helpful and knowledgeable office on 3rd floor.

Ruban Memorial Hospital & Ratan Stone Clinic

(☎ 2320446; Gandhi Maidan; ☽ 24hr) Emergency room, clinic and pharmacy.

State Bank of India (☎ 2226134; Gandhi Maidan; ☽ 10.30am-4pm Mon-Fri, 10.30am-1.30pm Sat) Currency and travellers cheques exchanged; other ATMs nearby.

Dangers & Annoyances

Avoid walking alone at night and be sure to take care of your valuables, as robbery can be a real problem.

Sights & Activities

GANDHI MAIDAN AREA

For a dome with a view, head up to the landmark **Golghar** (Danapure Rd; admission free; ☽ 24hr), a short walk west of Gandhi Maidan. This massive and bulbous beehive of a granary was built by the British army in 1786, in the hope of avoiding a repeat performance of the vicious famine in 1770. Nearby is a diminutive **Gandhi Museum** (☎ 2225339; Danapure Rd; ad-

mission free; ☽ 10am-6pm Sun-Fri), devoted to the Mahatma (great soul).

PATNA MUSEUM

Behind a fading Mughal- and Rajput- inspired exterior, this **museum** (☎ 2235731; Buddha Marg; Indian/foreigner Rs10/250; ☽ 10.30am-4.30pm Tue-Sun) houses a splendid collection of stone sculptures dating from the Mauryan and Gupta periods, plus a motley collection of stuffed animals and ethnological displays. You must pay an additional Rs500 to see the 'Relic of the Buddha' – a glass box reputedly containing ashes from Buddha's cremation, retrieved from Vaishali.

OTHER SIGHTS

Around 1km from Gandhi Maidan, **Khuda Bakhsh Oriental Library** (☎ 2300209; Ashok Raj Path; admission free; ☽ 9.30am-5pm Sat-Thu) was founded in 1900 and contains a renowned collection of Arabic and Persian manuscripts, and Mughal and Rajput paintings.

Around 3.5km east from the station are the often-submerged ruins of **Pataliputra** (Kankerbagh Rd; Indian/foreigner Rs5/100; ☽ 9am-dusk), the old Mauryan capital, surrounded by lovely gardens and a **museum** that details the site's historic past.

Behind a grand gate about 11km east of the centre is one of the nation's four holiest Sikh shrines, **Har Mandir Takht** (☎ 2642000), marking the spot where Guru Gobind Singh, the last of the 10 Sikh gurus, was born in 1660.

Nearby is **Qila House** (Jalan Museum; ☎ 2641121; Jalan Ave; ☽ by appointment only), a stately home overflowing with culturally significant antiques, from elaborate Mughal-period silverware to the pint-sized bed of Napoleon Bonaparte. Call to book a tour; provide a copy of your passport identity and visa pages.

With a car and driver (easy to arrange through the tourist office), you can visit more historic ruins at **Vaishali**, where the earthly body of the Buddha was reportedly cremated, and **Kesariya**, where the dying Buddha donated his begging bowl.

Sleeping

Most accommodation choices are around Fraser and Station Rds. There's a 5% tax for rooms below Rs1000, and 10% for rooms above that.

Hotel Kautilya Vihar (☎ 2225411; bstdc@sanchar net.in; Birchand Patel Path; dm Rs100, d Rs600-1000, with AC

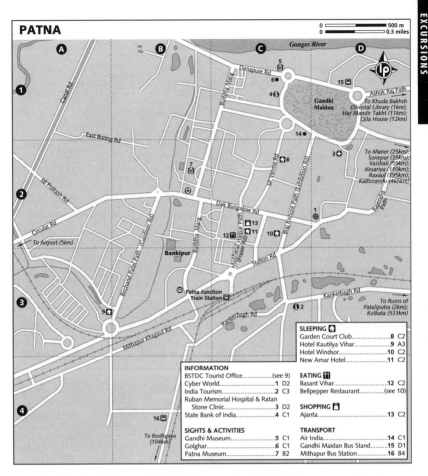

PATNA

Rs800-1200;) The state's sprawling hotel has clean and spacious rooms although it's well overdue for a paint job. It lacks atmosphere, but there's a restaurant, a bar and eager staff.

New Amar Hotel (2224157; s/d Rs260/400) The bright-green New Amar is the best of several budget hotels down a small lane off Fraser Rd. Rooms are simple, fan-cooled and come without hot water.

Garden Court Club (3202279; www.gardencourt club.com; SP Verma Rd; s/d Rs400/500, with AC from Rs700/900;) Take the lift within a small shopping complex to reach the intimate 13-room Garden Court Club. Rooms vary – we reckon the carpetless deluxe rooms are the best value. The lovely faux-forest open-air rooftop restaurant is a big attraction.

Hotel Windsor (2203250; www.hotelwindsorpatna .com; Exhibition Rd; s/d/ste Rs1000/1200/1500;) This is Patna's best midrange hotel, with well-designed rooms, spotless bathrooms, cheery and prompt service, a good restaurant and an internet centre.

Eating
Basant Vihar (Fraser Rd; mains Rs30-70) There's nothing like a delicious dosa (thin lentil-flour pancake) to tide you over. It's the 1st-floor restaurant you need, not the ground-floor one.

Bellpepper Restaurant (Hotel Windsor, Exhibition Rd; mains Rs55-220; noon-3.30pm & 7-11pm;) The Bellpepper is an intimate, contemporary restaurant popular for its tandoori treats and biryanis. No booze is available.

EXCURSIONS

EXCURSIONS

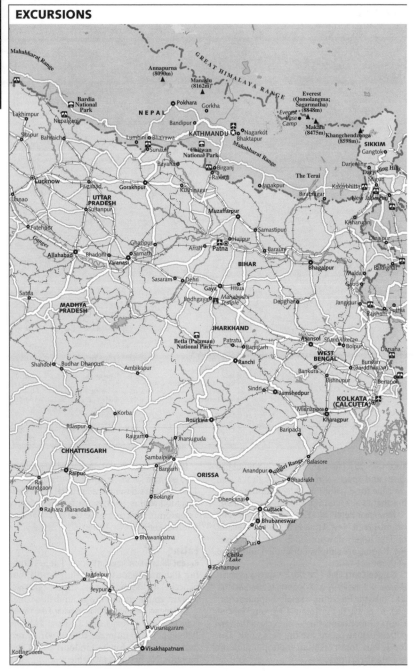

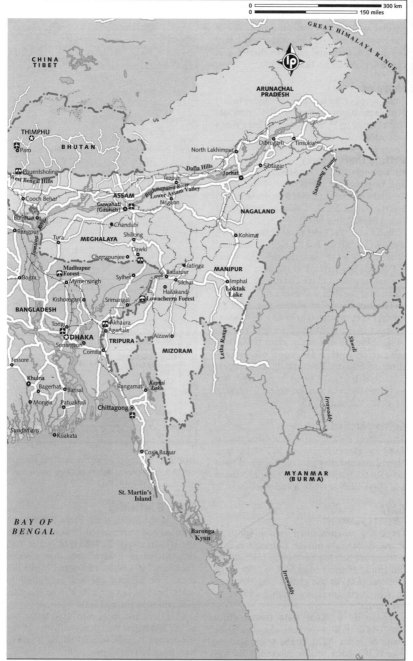

EXCURSIONS

Takshila (☎ 2220590; Birchand Patel Path; mains Rs125-375; ☺ noon-3.30pm & 7.30-11pm; ✸) Inside Hotel Chanakya, Takshila exudes the ambience of the North-West Frontier, with meat-heavy Mughlai, Afghan and tandoori dishes. You can order beers from the hotel bar.

Shopping
Patna is one of the best places in Bihar to buy Mithila paintings – **Ajanta** (☎ 2224432; Hotel Satka Arcade, Fraser Rd; ☺ 10.30am-8pm Mon-Sat) has Patna's best selection.

Getting There & Away
Air India (☎ 2222554), **Jet Airways** (☎ 3298224) and **Kingfisher Red** (☎ 18002093030; Patna airport) fly daily to Delhi (Rs4425 to Rs5496, 1½ hours); Kingfisher Red also serves Kolkata (from Rs4232, one hour).

Buses to Gaya (Rs50, three hours, hourly), Raxaul (for Nepal; Rs110, eight hours) and other towns leave from the new bus stand (Mithapur bus station), about 2km south of the train station, and the Gandhi Maidan bus stand near the river and museum.

The Patna Junction station has a **foreign-tourist ticket counter** (window No ; ☺ 8am-8pm) upstairs in the right-hand wing of the station. There are four daily trains to Kolkata (sleeper/3AC Rs173/485, eight to 13 hours), three to Siliguri/New Jalpaiguri (sleeper/3AC Rs203/569, 10 to 14 hours) and two to Gaya (sleeper/chair Rs54/122, 2½ hours, 11.40am, 9.25pm).

Getting Around
The airport is 7km west of the city centre – Rs80 by autorickshaw or Rs200 by taxi. Shared autorickshaws shuttle back and forth between the train station and Gandhi Maidan bus stand (Rs5), or take a cycle-rickshaw.

GAYA
☎ 0631 / pop 383,197
Gaya is a raucous town 100km south of Patna. Its primary interest to travellers is as a transport hub for Bodhgaya, 13km away, but Hindu pilgrims come here to offer pinda (funeral cake) at the ghats along the river to free their ancestors from bondage to the earth.

There is a **Bihar state tourist office** (☎ 2155420; ☺ 10am-8pm Mon-Sat) and a State Bank of India ATM at the train station. The ICICI Bank on Swarajayapur Rd has

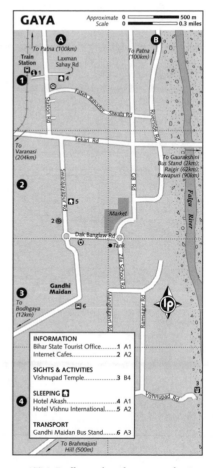

an ATM. Bodhgaya has the nearest foreign exchange. Several **internet cafes** (per hr Rs30) line Swarajayapur Rd.

Sights & Activities
Close to the banks of the Falgu River south of town and surrounded by funeral ghats, the *sikhara* (spired) **Vishnupad Temple** was constructed in 1787 to enshrine a 40cm 'footprint' of Vishnu imprinted into solid rock. Non-Hindus are not permitted to enter, but you can get a look from the pink platform near the entrance.

One thousand stone steps lead to the top of the **Brahmajuni Hill**, 1km southwest of the Vishnupad Temple, where Buddha is said to have preached the fire sermon.

Sleeping & Eating

Unless you arrive late or have an early departure, Bodhgaya is a better place to stay.

Hotel Akash (☎ 2222205; Laxman Sahay Rd; s/d Rs200/250) The pick of the budget places. The turquoise timber facade leads to an inner courtyard surrounded by clean, basic rooms with TV, and there's a relaxing open-air area upstairs. An air cooler costs an extra Rs150.

Hotel Vishnu International (☎ 2431146; Swarajayapur Rd; s Rs300, d Rs400-700, with AC Rs1000; ✵) While the attention lavished on the French-castle-like facade doesn't extend to the rooms, this is still the best value in town. It's clean and well kept, and most rooms have TV, but hot water comes by bucket (Rs10).

The hotel restaurants are the best places to eat.

Getting There & Away

The main Gandhi Maidan bus stand has regular buses to Patna (Rs50, three hours, hourly) and other towns.

Gaya has regular trains to major cities around India, including Kolkata (sleeper/3AC Rs176/493, eight hours) and Patna (sleeper/chair Rs54/122, 2½ hours).

Autorickshaw drivers can be bargained down to about Rs80 for the trip to Bodhgaya.

BODHGAYA

☎ 0631 / pop 30,883

This serene and spiritually important town attracts Buddhist pilgrims from around the world who journey here for prayer, study and meditation. It was here 2600 years ago that Prince Siddhartha Gautama attained enlightenment beneath a bodhi tree and became the Buddha. A beautiful temple marks the spot, beside a descendant of the original Bodhi Tree, and the surrounding countryside is dotted with monasteries and temples, built by foreign Buddhists in the national styles of home.

The best time to visit is October to March when Tibetan pilgrims come from McLeod Ganj in Dharamsala and Bodhgaya becomes a sea of maroon and orange robes. The Dalai Lama often visits in December and January.

Information

BSTDC Tourist Complex (☎ 2200672; cnr Bodhgaya Rd & Temple St; ✵ 10.30am-5pm Tue-Sat) Little more than dusty brochures.

State Bank of India (☎ 2200852; Bodhgaya Rd; ✵ 10.30am-4pm Mon-Fri, to 1pm Sat) Best rates for cash and travellers cheques; has an ATM.

Verma Health Care Centre (☎ 2201101; off Bodhgaya Rd; ✵ 24hr) Emergency room and clinic.

Vishnu Cyber Cafe (Bodhgaya Rd; per hr Rs30; ✵ 8am-9.30pm)

Sights & Activities

MAHABODHI TEMPLE

A tide of pilgrims in maroon and orange robes washes around the magnificent World Heritage–listed **Mahabodhi Temple** (admission free, camera/video Rs20/500; ✵ 5am-9pm). This place, where Buddha attained enlightenment and formulated his philosophy of life, forms the spiritual heart of Bodhgaya.

The Mahabodhi Temple was built in the 6th century AD atop the site of a temple erected by Emperor Ashoka almost 800 years earlier. Topped by a 50m-high pyramid-shaped spire, embossed with Buddha images, the ornate structure houses a 2m-high gilded image of a seated Buddha.

The broad-limbed **bodhi tree** beside the Vajrasana (Diamond Throne) is said to have been propagated from the original tree that shaded Siddhartha Gautama as he attained enlightenment.

MONASTERIES & TEMPLES

The monasteries offer a unique opportunity to peek into different Buddhist cultures and compare architectural styles. The **Indosan Nipponji Temple** (✵ 5am-noon & 2-6pm) is an exercise in quiet Japanese understatement compared with the ornate **Thai Monastery**, a gleaming *wat* (temple) covered with shimmering gold leaf and fringed by manicured gardens. Other noteworthy ones include those from **China**, **Myanmar (Burma)**, **Tibet**, **Bhutan**, **Vietnam** and **Nepal**. Monasteries are open dawn to dusk.

OTHER SIGHTS

A 25m-high **Great Buddha Statue** (✵ 7am-noon & 2-5pm) towers above a pleasant garden at the end of Temple St. Unveiled by the Dalai Lama in 1989, the statue is partially hollow and is said to contain some 20,000 bronze Buddhas.

The **archaeological museum** (☎ 2200739; Bodhgaya Rd; admission Rs2; ✵ 10am-5pm Sat-Thu) contains a small collection of local Buddha figures, but pride of place goes to part of the original granite railings and pillars from the Mahabodhi Temple.

EXCURSIONS

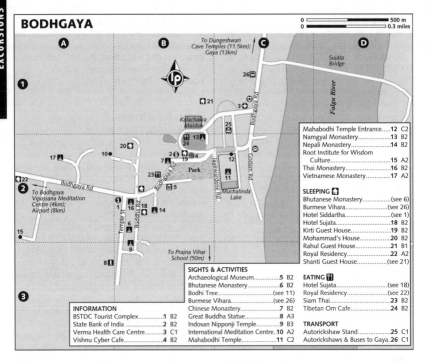

BODHGAYA

INFORMATION
BSTDC Tourist Complex	1 B2
State Bank of India	2 B2
Verma Health Care Centre	3 C1
Vishnu Cyber Cafe	4 B2

SIGHTS & ACTIVITIES
Archaeological Museum	5 B2
Bhutanese Monastery	6 B2
Bodhi Tree	(see 11)
Burmese Vihara	(see 26)
Chinese Monastery	7 B2
Great Buddha Statue	8 A3
Indosan Nipponji Temple	9 B3
International Meditation Centre	10 A2
Mahabodhi Temple	11 C2

Mahabodhi Temple Entrance	12 C2
Namgyal Monastery	13 B2
Nepali Monastery	14 B2
Root Institute for Wisdom Culture	15 A2
Thai Monastery	16 B2
Vietnamese Monastery	17 A2

SLEEPING
Bhutanese Monastery	(see 6)
Burmese Vihara	(see 26)
Hotel Siddartha	(see 1)
Hotel Sujata	18 B2
Kirti Guest House	19 B2
Mohammad's House	20 B2
Rahul Guest House	21 B1
Royal Residency	22 A2
Shanti Guest House	(see 21)

EATING
Hotel Sujata	(see 18)
Royal Residency	(see 22)
Siam Thai	23 B2
Tibetan Om Cafe	24 B2

TRANSPORT
Autorickshaw Stand	25 C1
Autorickshaws & Buses to Gaya	26 C1

Courses

South of Bodhgaya Rd, near the Royal Residency Hotel, the **Root Institute for Wisdom Culture** (☎ 2200714; www.rootinstitute.com; ☒ office 8.30-11.30am & 1.30-4.30pm) holds popular introductory 10-day meditation courses from late October to March (Rs7020 including accommodation and meals). Alternatively, anyone can come for the free 6.45am meditation sessions.

Bodhgaya Vipassana Meditation Centre (Dhamma Bodhi; ☎ 220437; www.dhamma.org) runs intensive 10-day *vipassana* courses twice each month throughout the year. The small compound is 4km west of town and runs on donations.

The courses at the **International Meditation Centre** (☎ 2200707; per day Rs100), north of the Hotel Embassy, are more informal and students can start and finish any time they choose, all year round.

Other courses are advertised at local restaurants and the Burmese Vihara.

Sleeping

Prices listed are for November through March and can fall by 50% outside these months, so negotiate.

BUDGET

Mohammad's House (☎ 9934022691, 9431085251; s/d Mar-Sep from Rs100/150, Oct-Feb from Rs200/300) This village homestay is popular with long-term stayers and Mohammad is a mine of useful information and advice. A rooftop terrace gives commanding views of rice paddies, sunsets and monasteries.

If you don't mind some simple rules, it's possible to stay at some of the monasteries – the **Burmese Vihara** (☎ 2200721, 06112-696464; Bodhgaya Rd; r Rs50) is popular with foreigners; there's a maximum stay of three days unless you're engaged in dharma studies.

Several guesthouses back onto Kalachakra Maidan. At **Rahul Guest House** (☎ 2200709; s/d Rs150/250) the upstairs rooms with whitewashed walls, breezes and simple furnishings are better than those on the ground floor. **Shanti Guest House** (☎ 2200129; www.shanti-guesthouse.com; s/d from Rs200/250, with AC Rs450/650; ☒ ☐) has similar rooms, the cheaper with shared bathrooms.

MIDRANGE & TOP END

Hotel Siddartha (☎ 2200127; Bodhgaya Rd; d Rs400, with AC Rs600) The best of the BSTDC accommodation though it's still a bit austere. Rooms are in an unusual circular building overlooking a quiet garden.

Kirti Guest House (☎ 2200744; kirtihouse744@yahoo .com; Bodhgaya Rd; s/d Rs800/1100) Run by the Tibetan Monastery, Kirti has clean, bright rooms behind a monastery-like facade – all rooms have TV and hot water and the best open onto the balcony.

Hotel Sujata (☎ 2200761; www.hotelsujata.com; Buddha Rd; s/d/ste Rs3200/3600/4800; 🍴 🖳) Swish, spacious rooms with soft beds, an excellent restaurant, and his and hers *ofuro* (communal Japanese baths) make this hotel opposite the Thai Monastery the most interesting in the top-end range.

Eating & Drinking

During the peak season, when Tibetan pilgrims pour into Bodhgaya, temporary tent restaurants are set up next to the Tibetan refugee market.

Tibetan Om Cafe (dishes Rs20-60; 🕑 7am-9pm) Inside the western courtyard of Namgyal Monastery, this relaxing place is run by friendly Tibetans who know all about traveller hunger for *momos* (dumplings), pancakes, brown bread, pies and cakes. For just Rs5 you can fill your water bottle with 'well-boiled filter water'.

Swagat Restaurant (Hotel Tathagat International, Bodhgaya Rd; mains Rs50-150) A really good choice with an innovative menu of veg and nonveg dishes, such as *mutton badam pasanda* (mutton stuffed with almonds and cooked in an almond gravy).

Siam Thai (Bodhgaya Rd; mains Rs80-400) A new restaurant serving some authentic Thai dishes. The walls are decorated with all the menu items you might consider, while an inscrutable and plump Buddha observes everything. Service is friendly and helpful.

The **Royal Residency** (Bodhgaya Rd; mains Rs70-150) and **Hotel Sujata** (Buddha Rd; mains Rs65-200) – two similar high-class restaurants in two of Bodhgaya's upmarket hotels – are the only places in town to serve alcohol (Rs240 for a beer).

Getting There & Away

Gaya airport is 8km west of town and **Air India** (☎ 2201155) flies once a week to Kolkata.

Overcrowded shared autorickshaws (Rs20) and occasional buses (Rs5) leave outside the Burmese Vihara for the 13km to Gaya. A private autorickshaw to Gaya should cost Rs80.

RAXAUL
☎ 06255 / pop 41,347

Grimy, overcrowded Raxaul (or Raxaul Bazaar) is the crossing point to Birganj in Nepal – see p331 for information on the crossing. There are private moneychangers on both sides of the border and the State Bank of India has an ATM. If you must spend the night here, head to **Hotel Kaveri** (☎ 221148; Main Rd; d from Rs300), which has the cleanest rooms.

From the Karai Tala bus stand (200m down a side road about 2km south of the border), there are night buses to Patna (Rs110, six hours, 9pm). The *Mithila Express* runs daily to Kolkata (No 3022, sleeper/3AC/ 2AC Rs210/591/821, 18 hours, 10am).

GORAKHPUR
☎ 0551 / pop 624,570

For most travellers Gorakhpur is merely a way station between India and Nepal. There are no major tourist attractions in the city, but you can visit a Buddhist museum near the lake on the southern outskirts, and the important Gorakhnath Temple, devoted to Guru Gorakhnath, situated 4km west of the station.

Information

Gorakhpur's train station is a convenient one-stop place for information. Inside is the helpful **Uttar Pradesh (UP) Tourism office** (☎ 2335450; 🕑 10am-5pm Mon-Sat) and just outside on the concourse is a State Bank of India ATM and the **Railtel Cyber Express** (per hr Rs23; 🕑 9am-9pm).

Sleeping & Eating

The street opposite the train station has a dozen or more cheap hotels.

Hotel Adarsh Palace (☎ 2201912; hotel.adarsh palace@rediffmail.com; Railway Station Rd; dm Rs150, s Rs300-400, d Rs500, with AC Rs700-800; 🍴) There's something for everyone at this smart place opposite the train station. The 10-bed dorm has lockers above each bed, cheap singles come with TV and bathroom and there are some decent-quality AC rooms too.

Hotel Sunrise (☎ 2209076; s Rs200, d Rs300-350, with AC Rs550; 🍴) If Adarsh is full, you'll find a host of slightly shabbier hotels directly opposite the train station. This is the least shabby, with clean rooms and a rooftop restaurant.

New Varden Restaurant (🕑 8am-10pm; mains Rs25-60) Next to Hotel Sunrise, this place is

EXCURSIONS

popular with travellers and will box-up your order for onward journeys.

Getting There & Away

Hourly buses run from the main bus stand, about 300m south of the train station, to Sunauli (Rs56, 2½ hours) on the Nepal border. Buses to Varanasi (Rs120, seven hours) leave from the separate Katchari bus stand, 3km south of the main bus stand, but the train is a better option.

Touts are dead keen to sell you 'direct' bus tickets to Kathmandu and other destinations in Nepal for around Rs400, but everyone has to change buses at the border.

Gorakhpur has direct train connections with Varanasi (sleeper/3A Rs134/345, 5½ hours, four daily) and also with Kolkata (Rs312/848, 24 hours, 1pm). Counter 811 serves foreign tourists.

NEPAL

Country code ☎ 977 / **pop 29.5 million**
With the elections in April 2008, Nepal became a federal republic, ending a decade of civil war. Trekkers are now flocking back to this fabled ex-kingdom, testing tendons and tenacity on the trails that snake through the Himalaya and recovering in Nepal's national parks and temple-filled medieval towns.

The overland trail from northeast India kicks off in Darjeeling and crosses into Nepal at Kakarbhitta, before running across the country to the atmospheric capital, Kathmandu. On the return leg to India, you can drop into Chitwan National Park to scour the *phanta* (grasslands) for rhinos, and pay your respects at the birthplace of the Buddha in Lumbini, before crossing the border at Sunauli or Birganj/Raxaul.

Information

At the time of writing, the political situation in Nepal was stable and the Maoist government was welcoming tourists (and their foreign currency) with open arms. However, it makes sense to check the political situation locally before you travel.

Travellers from countries in the South Asian Association for Regional Cooperation (Saarc; India, Nepal, Pakistan, Bangladesh, Bhutan, Maldives and Sri Lanka) are eligible for discounts at most attractions in Nepal.

FOREIGN EXCHANGE
The Nepali currency is the Nepali rupee (NRs), divided into 100 paisa. The Nepali rupee is pegged to the Indian rupee at a fixed exchange rate of INRs100 = NRs160. Note that you will have trouble changing Indian Rs500 and Rs1000 notes inside Nepal. Banks and exchange counters are everywhere in Nepal and there are ATMs in larger cities. Visas should be paid for in US dollars cash.

TOURIST INFORMATION
The Nepal tourism board offers extensive information through its website www .welcomenepal.com. Other useful websites include the following:
Nepal Tourism Department (www.tourism.gov.np)
Trek Info (www.trekinfo.com)
Visit Nepal (www.visitnepal.com)

VISAS
Indians can visit Nepal without a visa; for most other nationalities, multiple-entry tourist visas are available on arrival at Kathmandu's Tribhuvan international airport or at any of the border crossings into Nepal (two passport photos required) – see p331.

Getting There & Around
Kathmandu is well connected to India by air and by road. Air India (formerly Indian Airlines) flies between Kolkata and Kathmandu, or you can connect through Delhi. Travelling by land, the easiest option is to take the train to Siliguri in West Bengal, then a share jeep to the border crossing at Kakarbhitta. Alternative crossings are Raxaul in Bihar and Sunauli in Uttar Pradesh – see p331 for details. There's a NRs1695 departure tax if you leave Nepal by air (NRs1356 if travelling to India, Bhutan, Pakistan or Bangladesh), but no tax if you leave by land.

For travel within Nepal, the main options are domestic flights, buses, minivans, share-jeeps, taxis and rented motorcycles.

KATHMANDU
☎ 01 / pop 1 million
Despite the crowds, traffic and dust, the backstreets of Kathmandu offer a window onto Nepal's golden age, when the kings of the Kathmandu Valley embarked on a marathon of temple-building in a vain attempt to outshine each other with architectural brilliance. Modern Kathmandu, the capital city, stands

side by side with old Kathmandu, the medieval bazaar town with its wonky alleyways, hidden squares and tiered pagoda temples. Factor in a frenetic traveller scene and a pinch of Eastern mysticism and it's easy to see why Kathmandu became the grail at the end of the hippy overland trail.

Orientation

The old town of Kathmandu sprawls north and east of Durbar Sq. The main traveller district, Thamel, is at the north end of the old town, west of the junction of Tridevi Marg and Kantipath. Lazimpat is north from Thamel; Durbar Marg is due east.

Traffic circulates around the Tundikhel, an open parade ground jammed between Kantipath and the southern extension of Durbar Marg. The stand for local buses is on the west side of the Tundikhel, the long-distance bus stand is north of Thamel on the city ring road, which passes Tribhuvan airport.

Information

Internet cafes are everywhere in Thamel – expect to pay NRs50 per hour – and most also offer inexpensive international calls. Many restaurants have wi-fi access for laptop users. Thamel has hundreds of moneychangers and there are numerous ATMs, including one in the Kathmandu Guest House compound in Thamel.

Central Immigration Office (☎ 4223590, 4222453; www.immi.gov.np; Maitighar; 🕑 10am-4.30pm Sun-Thu, 10am-3pm Fri, 11am-1pm Sat) Southeast of the centre; issues visa extensions.

CIWEC Clinic Travel Medicine Center (☎ 4424111; www.ciwec-clinic.com; 🕑 9am-noon & 1-4pm Mon-Fri) Traveller-centric med centre northeast of Thamel.

Main post office (Sundhara; 🕑 7am-6pm Sun-Thu, 7am-3pm Fri) Close to the Bhimsen Tower, handles parcels up to 2kg.

Tourist Police (☎ 4247041; Bhrikuti Mandap)

Tourist Service Centre (☎ 24hr tourism hotline 4225709; www.welcomenepal.com; Bhrikuti Mandap; 🕑 10am-1pm, 2-5pm Sun-Fri) East of the Tundikhel; has free city maps.

Wayfarers (☎ 4266010; www.wayfarers.com.np; Thamel; 🕑 9am-7pm Mon-Fri, 9am-5pm Sat & Sun) Straight-talking travel agency for tours, flights etc.

Dangers & Annoyances

Kathmandu is occasionally subject to demonstrations and *bandhs* (strikes), which can turn violent. If you need to reach [illegible] during a *bandh*, travel at first light, o[illegible] your hotel about the government-operated bus. Kathmandu is plagued by power strikes lasting up to 16 hours a day – choose a hotel with a generator (and a room at the other end of the building).

Sights

Most of the interesting things to see in Kathmandu are clustered in the old part of town.

DURBAR SQUARE

Kathmandu's World Heritage–listed **Durbar Square** (admission Saarc/foreigner NRs25/200) was where the city's kings were once crowned, and where they ruled (*durbar* means 'palace'). Although most of the square dates from the 17th and 18th centuries, some structures were rebuilt after the great earthquake of 1934.

Arriving from the north along Mahkan Tole, the original bazaar in Kathmandu, you'll see the tiered roofs of the 16th-century **Taleju Temple**, which is only open to the public during the Dasain festival in September/October, when hundreds of sacrificial animals meet their maker on the temple steps. Around this part of the square are several other handsome pagoda temples dedicated to various incarnations of Shiva and Vishnu.

The next open area to the south contains more striking temples, including the **Jagannath Temple**, with risque erotic carvings on its roof struts. A nearby diabolical-looking statue is of **Kala (Black) Bhairab**, the 'fearsome' incarnation of Shiva. The handsome octagonal stone structure facing the Jagannath temple is the **Krishna Temple**, where dressed-up sadhus (spiritual men) pose for photographs in the hope of earning baksheesh (donations). Note the giant bell and drums in the pavilions to the north and south.

The next open area is dominated by the nine-stage ochre platform of the three-tiered **Maju Deval Temple**, a great vantage point for watching the constant hubbub in the square. Nearby, the five-tiered **Trailokya Mohan Narayan Temple** features finely carved windows and a handsome statue of Garuda, the man-bird vehicle of Vishnu. In the courtyard to the east of this temple is the **Kumari Bahal**, home to Kathmandu's living goddess, who can periodically be seen waving to devotees from the windows.

Mohan Narayan ... area, dominated ...oofed **Kasthamandap**, ...ter for pilgrims in the

H... ...OKA

The ... ...complex of **Hanuman Dhoka** (admission Saarc/foreigner NRs25/250; ✆ 10.30am-4pm Tue-Sat, Feb-Oct, 10.30am-3pm Tue-Sat Nov-Jan, 10.30am-2pm Sun) was founded during the Licchavi period (5th–8th centuries AD), but most of what you see today was constructed by King Pratap Malla in the 17th century. Inside are a series of *chowks* (town squares) full of statuary, temples and ceremonial structures.

NORTH OF DURBAR SQUARE

Between Thamel and Durbar Sq is a magical maze of winding lanes, hidden courtyards and bustling bazaars. Heading south from Thamel Chowk, you'll reach Thahity Tole and the grand **Kathesimbhu Stupa**, a focal point for Tibetan Buddhists. Go east at the next junction to reach the produce and spice market at **Asan Tole** and the three-storey **Annapurna Temple**.

Walk southwest from Asan Tole to reach the atmospheric **Seto Machhendranath Temple**, with its courtyard full of shrines and bronze statues. Just beyond is **Indra Chowk**, a market square full of blanket and cloth merchants. On the west side of the square is the facade of the imposing **Akash Bhairab Temple**, sacred to Bhairab, the wrathful incarnation of Shiva. West of Indra Chowk is **Itum Bahal**, the largest Buddhist *bahal* (courtyard) in the old town.

OTHER ATTRACTIONS

More highlights of Kathmandu are hidden away in the suburbs, either just inside or just outside the ring road, all easily accessible by taxi or rented bicycle.

Northeast of the centre, **Pashupatinath** (admission NRs250, under-10s free; ✆ 24 hr) is Nepal's most important Hindu temple, set among funeral ghats on the banks of the holy Bagmati River. Only Hindus can enter, but the site is surrounded by hundreds of tiny Shiva shrines, used as lodgings by sadhus.

Further northeast, the gigantic Buddhist stupa at **Bodhnath** (admission Saarc/foreigner NRs20/100) pulses with life as thousands of pilgrims perform a ritual circumnavigation of the dome.

The surrounding village is a vibrant centre for Tibetan Buddhist culture.

Northwest of the centre, and just inside the ring road, the hilltop stupa of **Swayambhunath** (admission Saarc/foreigner NRs50/100) is mobbed by troops of monkeys, giving rise to the nickname 'Monkey Temple'. The gold-topped stupa is reached via a steep stone stairway, and ringed by centuries-old statues and shrines.

Sleeping

There are literally hundreds of hotels in Kathmandu, particularly on the winding lanes of Thamel, west of Kantipath. Many travellers just rock up to Thamel and stroll up and down until they find somewhere that appeals. Prices are often quoted in dollars, but you can also pay in rupees. Remember that most places will add on 23% tax. The following places are the best in their class.

Kathmandu Guest House (✆ 4700800; www.ktmgh.com; r without bathroom US$2-14, r US$14-50, deluxe US$55-120; ✖ ✈) A former Rana palace, the KGH was the first hotel to open in Thamel and still serves as a central landmark. A huge range of rooms are available and the wi-fi-enabled front courtyard and rear garden provide a haven from the Thamel mayhem.

Hotel Ganesh Himal (✆ 4243819, 4263598; www.ganeshhimal.com; s/d US$11/14, deluxe US$16/19; ✖ ▣) In the south of Thamel at Chhetrapati, this well-run and friendly place is out of range of the tiger balm salesmen but close enough to restaurants for dinner. Rooms have endless hot water, satellite TV and lots of balcony and garden seating.

International Guest House (✆ 4252299; www.ighouse.com; s/d US$16/20, deluxe US$22/28, superior deluxe US$30/35, ste US$45; ▣) West of the main action in the Kaldhara district, this is a highly recommended and quite stylish place that boasts century-old carved woodwork, terrace sitting areas, a spacious garden and one of the best rooftop views in the city.

Kantipur Temple House (✆ 4250131; www.kantipurtemplehouse.com; s/d US$55/66, deluxe US$85/125) Hidden down an alley on the edge of the old town, this boutique-style hotel has been built in traditional Newari-temple style with meticulous attention to detail.

Dwarika's Hotel (✆ 4470770; www.dwarikas.com; s/d US$220/230, ste US$330-385; ✇) For stylish design and sheer romance, this outstanding hotel is unbeatable. Over 40 years the owners have rescued thousands of wood carvings from around the valley and incorporated them into the hotel design.

Eating

There are restaurants in Kathmandu serving every cuisine under the sun, particularly in Thamel. The following are some of the best. Most places add a 23% service charge and tax to the bill.

Yak Restaurant (mains NRs70-155) A bit of an institution, this cheap and cheerful Tibetan-run place south of Thamel Chowk feels a bit like a trekking lodge plonked in the middle of Thamel. The menu includes good *momos* (Tibetan dumplings) and tongba (hot millet beer).

Helena's (☎ 4266979; breakfast from NRs99, mains NRs150-295; ☽ 7am-10pm) Sprawling over eight floors, Helena's is deservedly popular for its set breakfasts, its cheap lunches and its rooftop views.

New Orleans Café (☎ 4700736; mains NRs270-425) Hidden down an alley near the Kathmandu Guest House, New Orleans offers a globe-trotting menu, live blues music and candlelit tables in a Newari courtyard.

Fire & Ice Restaurant (☎ 4250210; Tridevi Marg; pizzas NRs320-380; ☽ 8am-11pm) The finest pizzas in Thamel, and some would say all of Asia. This partly open-air place is justifiably popular, so come early or queue for a table.

Roadhouse Café (☎ 4267885; Arcadia Bldg; pizzas NRs320-400) A posttrek favourite, with a hearty international menu of pizzas, salads, soups, burgers and grills, served in classy surroundings.

Bhojan Griha (☎ 4416423; www.bhojangriha.com; Dilli Bazaar; set menu NRs997) A classy choice in a restored 150-year-old mansion just east of the city centre, serving traditional Newari food at traditional low Newari tables.

Drinking

Thamel has half a dozen bars with live music and cold beers, but few open later than 11pm. Top picks include Maya Cocktail Bar, with two-for-one cocktails between 4pm and 7pm, Tom & Jerry Pub, and Sam's Bar.

Tamas Lounge (☎ 4275658; www.tamaslounge .com; drinks NRs300) A grown-up cocktail bar for grown-up drinkers, in a converted Rana mansion down an alleyway south of Kathmandu Guest House, near the Ying Yang Restaurant.

Shopping

Everything and anything can be found in Kathmandu, from to hippy clothing and knock-off trekking gear to carpets and Hindu, Kashmiri, Tibetan and Buddhist curios. Stroll around the streets between Thamel and Durbar Sq and see what takes your fancy.

There are several stores in Lazimpat that stock high-quality handcrafts produced by charitable cooperatives, sold at fair prices. **Mahaguthi** (☎ 4438760; Lazimpat; ☽ 10am-6.30pm, 10am-5pm Sat) is highly recommended by local expats for its excellent stock and ethical policies.

Getting There & Away

Numerous airlines fly between Kathmandu and Delhi or Kolkata. The **airport** (☎ 4472256) is about 4km east of the centre. Prepaid taxis from the airport to the centre cost around NRs500; in the other direction, you can bargain down to NRs250 or less. Many hotels offer free pick-ups if you have a reservation.

Buses to destinations around the Kathmandu Valley run from the Ratna Park (City) bus station on the east side of the Tundikhel. Long-distance buses run from the Kathmandu bus station on the ring road (a NRs100 taxi ride from Thamel). There are regular buses to most towns in Nepal, including Birganj (Nrs375 to NRs400, 10 hours) and Sunauli (NRs425, eight hours). Overnight buses to Kakarbhitta (NRs1500, 24 hours) leave around 4pm.

Tourist buses to various destinations leave from the north end of Kantipath and can be booked at travel agencies and hotels in Thamel. Buses to Sauraha in Chitwan National Park (NRs250, five to seven hours) leave at around 7am.

Getting Around

Taxis provide an easy way to get around the city, but drivers are reluctant to use the meter so bargain for a fair price. Cycle-rickshaws are useful for exploring the old town, or you can rent bikes and motorcycles in Thamel. You can also get around by local bus and tempo.

EAST OF KATHMANDU

The Mahendra Hwy runs across eastern Nepal from the border post at Kakarbhitta to Kathmandu. For information on possible stops in eastern Nepal, pick up Lonely Planet's *Nepal* book.

EXCURSIONS

Kakarbhitta

☎ 023

The closest border crossing to northeast India, Kakarbhitta (Kakarvitta) is a short walk across the border from Panitanki in India. The crossing is staffed between 6am and 9pm; at other times, you'll need to go searching for the immigration officials.

ORIENTATION & INFORMATION

There's a **tourist information centre** (☎ 562035; ◷ 10am-4pm Sun-Fri) on the Nepal side of the border. Nearby, the **Nepal Bank** (◷ 7am-5pm) exchanges cash and cheques in major currencies. You can check your email at **Net Point Cyber Zone** (☎ 562040; per hr NRs30; ◷ 8am-8pm) near Hotel Mechi.

SLEEPING & EATING

Hotel Mechi (☎ 562040; dm NRs120, s NRs300-600, d NRs400-1200, s/d with AC US$10-20; ⊠) On the northern edge of the bus station, Mechi has rooms to suit all budgets. Rooms are large and comfortable, and excellent value. It also has a restaurant with tasty Indian dishes.

Hotel Rajat (☎ 562033; r NRs500-800, r with AC NRs1400; ⊠) The welcome is friendly here and there's a bistrolike restaurant with gingham tablecloths downstairs. The owner is a great source of advice for onward travel.

GETTING THERE & AWAY

The airport at Bhadrapur, 23km southwest of Kakarbhitta, has daily flights to Kathmandu (US$154, 50 minutes). A taxi to the airport costs NRs600.

Travel agents in Kathmandu and Darjeeling offer 'through-tickets' between India and Nepal, but everybody must change buses at Kakarbhitta, then again at Siliguri.

From the Nepali side, there are daily services to Kathmandu (NRs1500, 17 hours) and other towns. Note that this route was blocked in 2008 by floods – check the situation locally before you travel.

From Panitanki, there are regular bus services to Siliguri (NRs20, one hour), where you can pick up trains, buses and jeeps to Darjeeling (NRs80, 3½ hours) and other destinations in the northeast – see p148.

SOUTH OF KATHMANDU

On your way south to India, you can stop off at Chitwan National Park, or Lumbini, before crossing the border at Sunauli or Birganj.

Chitwan National Park

☎ 056

Created in 1973, the World Heritage–listed Chitwan National Park protects over 932-sq-km of sal forest, marshes and rippling elephant grassland along the Rapti River. Roaming through this lush landscape are rare one-horned rhinos, deer, monkeys, sloth bears, wild elephants, gharial crocodiles and 450 species of bird, as well as the biggest hitter of all, the Royal Bengal tiger. The park can be explored on elephant back or even on foot with a local guide. Depending on your budget, you can stay at one of the expensive lodges inside the park, or at one of the less formal lodges in Sauraha, a village on the northern fringes of the park.

The ideal time to visit Chitwan is from October to March – trails are normally impassable during the June-to-September monsoon. Wildlife is most easily spotted in January to March when the towering *phanta* grasses are cut back.

INFORMATION

Sauraha's **park office** (☎ 521932; admission per day foreigner/Saarc/children under 10 NRs500/200/free; ◷ ticket office 6-9am & noon-4.30pm) handles admission fees to the park (these are normally included if you organise a tour from Kathmandu).

Several private moneychangers in Sauraha accept foreign currency and travellers cheques at reasonable rates. The **Sauraha Cyber Café** (per hr NRs100; ◷ 7.30am-11pm) has slow connections.

SIGHTS

The main **National Park Headquarters** (☎ 521932) is inside the park, about 13km west of Sauraha. Most people visit as part of an organised jungle safari. At the **gharial breeding project** (admission NRs100) you can see both gharial and marsh mugger crocodiles up close.

About 3km west of Sauraha, the **elephant breeding centre** (☎ 580154; Saarc/foreigner NRs25/50; ◷ 6am-6pm) is the home for most of the elephants who ferry travellers around the park. Run by local volunteers, the nearby **bird education society** (☎ 580113, 9745003399; ◷ 7am-5.50pm) should be the first port of call for birders.

In Sauraha, the new **Wildlife Display & Information Centre** (admission NRs25; ◷ 7am-5pm) has educational displays on local wildlife, including a rather macabre collection of animal parts in jars.

ACTIVITIES

Elephants offer a fantastic vantage point over the tall grasses of the *phanta*. All the lodges inside the park arrange their own **elephant safaris**, or you can organise one- to two-hour safaris through the national park officials in Sauraha for NRs400/1000 (Saarc/foreigner). Less atmospheric half-day jeep safaris start at NRs1000 per person.

Guided walks can be arranged through **United Jungle Guide Service** (☎ 580034; half/full day NRs650/800). Canoe trips on the Rapti River, with a guided walk back to Sauraha, cost NRs350 to NRs1000 per person.

SLEEPING

Package tours arranged through travel agents in Kathmandu are the easiest way to visit Chitwan, or you can travel to Sauraha by tourist bus from Kathmandu. Three-day, two-night packages start from US$145, including accommodation, park fees and safaris, but not meals or transfers. Ask about discounts from May to September.

Inside the National Park

Island Jungle Resort (☎ in Kathmandu 01-4220162; www .islandjungleresort.com; 3-day/2-night package per person US$230, additional night per person US$90) A superb resort on a large island in the middle of the Narayani River at the western end of the park. The cottages at the main resort are simple but tasteful and decorated with animal paintings and there's a lovely riverside breakfast terrace.

Temple Tiger (☎ in Kathmandu 01-4221637; www .catmando.com/temple-tiger; packages per person per night US$250) Surrounded by dense jungle in the west of the park, Temple Tiger offers raised wooden cabins with thatched roofs, each with a private viewing platform looking over the *phanta*. Children under 12 are charged 50%.

Tiger Tops Jungle Lodge (☎ in Kathmandu 01-4361500; www.tigermountain.com; packages per person per night US$400) The original stilt-house jungle lodge, Tiger Tops offers some of the most characterful accommodation in Nepal. Set at the western end of the park, the spacious rooms have solar-powered lights and fans and there are always elephants wandering about the place. Tiger Tops also runs an extremely atmospheric tented camp about 3km east.

Sauraha

Chilax House (☎ 580260; chilaxhouse@yahoo.com; s/d without bathroom NRs100/150, s/d NRs200/300) Geared for travellers on the cheap, this family-run guesthouse is one of Chitwan's best budget options. Rooms in the small cottages are clean, and there's an organic restaurant serving veggies from the garden.

Hotel River Side (☎ 5800098; www.wildlifechitwan .com; r NRs500-1500) Take your choice between delightful thatched huts or the less atmospheric modern rooms with a balcony delivering unbeatable river views. There's a riverside restaurant and a garden full of hammocks.

Jungle Adventure World (☎ 580301, in Kathmandu 01-426 580064; r NRs700) This attractive lodge has a Tibetan Buddhist theme, and the cosy cabins are adorned with prayer flags and wall hangings.

Fewa Wildlife Resort (☎ 580150, in Kathmandu 01-4263185; www.fewawildliferesort.com; s/d US$20/25, s/d with AC US$30/35; ⚙ ☀) Tucked right on the border of the community forest, this is the closest place you'll get to the park without being inside. Rooms are fairly standard, but its gardens are a great place to read a book to the accompaniment of chirping birds.

Rhino Residency Resort (☎ 580095, in Kathmandu 01-420431; www.rhino-residency.com; r US$40; ⚙ ☀) Right by the entrance to the national park, this elegant resort's styling falls somewhere between English Regency and Malay Colonial. It has an inviting natural-style swimming pool, bar and restaurant.

EATING

Most lodges have restaurants and there are several independent places in the main bazaar at Sauraha. All serve cocktails and a familiar menu of travellers' fare. Most open from 6am and close at around 10pm to 11pm.

KC's Restaurant (mains NRs215-315) The most popular choice in Sauraha, KC's is set in a Spanish-style hacienda with an open terrace and a fire pit at the back. The menu runs from Nepali and Indian curries to pizzas and pasta.

There are several laid-back traveller eateries on the sandy banks of the Rapti River – **River Sunset Restaurant** (meals NRs95-450, BBQ NRs450-1350) is a popular spot for a sun-downer and evening barbecue.

GETTING THERE & AWAY

There are flights from Kathmandu to Bharatpur (US$86, 30 minutes), from where you can take a taxi to Sauraha for NRs700. Travel agents and hotels can make bookings.

EXCURSIONS

At around 7am every morning, tourist buses run from Kantipath in Kathmandu to Bachhauli (NRs250, five to seven hours), which is a 20-minute walk from Sauraha. Departures to Kathmandu from Bachhauli leave at 9.30am. Jeeps, and the dreaded hotel touts, await to transfer new arrivals to hotels for NRs50.

You can pick up public buses to Kathmandu (five to seven hours), and Sunauli (NRs300, five to six hours, 9.30am) at Tandi Bazaar (also known as Sauraha Chowk), on the Mahendra Hwy about 6km north of Sauraha. A jeep chartered in Sauraha will cost NRs400. In the opposite direction, a rickshaw will cost NRs70.

For local exploring, you can rent bicycles and motorcycles in Sauraha.

Sunauli & Bhairawa

Sunauli is easily the most popular tourist border crossing between Nepal and India. It's also a dusty hole that you won't want to hang around in for long. The border post is usually staffed from 6am to 10pm. If you need to stay the night, there are hotels on both sides of the border and in the more relaxed town of Bhairawa, 4km north into Nepal.

INFORMATION
There is a small **tourist information office** (☎ 520304; ☹ 10am-5pm Sun-Fri) on the Nepal side of the border, along with numerous moneychangers. The Nabil Bank in Bhairawa has an ATM. There are several net cafes around the junction of Bank Rd and New Rd in Bhairawa.

SLEEPING & EATING
There are hotels on both sides of the border, but wear mosquito repellent as the little buggers swarm round here. The following hotels are on the main road running through Sunauli to the border.

Nepal Guest House (☎ 071-520876; 4-bed dm NRs50, r NRs160) Travellers on a tight budget need look no further. Rooms here are pretty basic, but good for the money, and there's also a pretty decent restaurant.

Rahi Tourist Bungalow (☎ in India 05522-238201; ra hiniranjana@up-tourism.com; dm NRs75, s/d from NRs250/300, with AC NRs500/600; ⚙) On the Indian side, the least offensive option is this UP Tourism–run place located near the bus stand.

Hotel Aakash (☎ 071-524371; s/d NRs600/700, with AC NRs1200/1400; ⚙) Rather posh for this locale,

this business-class hotel has huge comfortable rooms with TV. It's popular with Indian travellers and has an excellent restaurant.

GETTING THERE & AROUND
Several airlines offer flights between Kathmandu and Bhairawa (US$114, 40 minutes). Bhairawa airport is about 1km west of town, easily accessible by rickshaw.

On the Nepali side, buses run regularly from both Sunauli and Bhairawa to Kathmandu (NRs425, eight hours). Minivans to Kathmandu cost about NRs460.

All travellers bound for India must change buses at the border. From the bus station on the Indian side there are regular buses to Gorakhpur (NRs56, three hours, until 9pm), where you can pick up trains to Varanasi, Kolkata and other cities – see p286 for more information. Early morning and afternoon buses run direct to Varanasi (NRs172, 11 hours).

Local buses for Lumbini (NRs35, one hour) leave from the junction of the Siddhartha Hwy and the road to Lumbini. Regular jeeps and local buses shuttle between the border and Bhairawa for NRs10, or hail a rickshaw.

Lumbini
☎ 071
Marking the site of the Buddha's birth, the Maya Devi temple at Lumbini is a pilgrimage site for Buddhists from all over the world, particularly during the Buddha Jayanti festival in April or May. Surrounding the temple is a huge compound of temples and monasteries – new structures are appearing here every year as Buddhists from around the world gather donations to honour the founder of Buddhism.

HISTORY
Archaeologists are now fairly certain that Siddhartha Gautama, the historical Buddha, was born at Lumbini in 563 BC. The Indian emperor Ashoka made a pilgrimage here in 249 BC, erecting one of his famous pillars, before the site was abandoned. Rediscovered in the 19th century, Lumbini is now creating a new archaeology for itself in the Lumbini Development Zone.

INFORMATION
There's a small **tourist information centre** (☹ 6am-6pm) at the ticket office that displays

the master plan of the complex. **64 Cyber-Zone** (per hr NRs60; ☉ 8am-8pm) in Lumbini Bazaar has slowish connections.

SIGHTS
The **Maya Devi Temple** (Saarc/foreigner NRs10/50, camera NRs70; ☉ 6am-6pm) sits on the exact site of the birth of the Buddha, according to Buddhist scholars. Excavations carried out in 1992 have revealed a succession of ruins on the site dating back at least 2200 years. For now, the ruins are protected by a plain brick pavilion – the focal point for pilgrims is a famous sandstone carving, left here by King Ripu Malla in the 14th-century.

The **sacred pond** beside the temple is believed to be where Maya Devi bathed before giving birth to the Buddha and dotted around the grounds are the ruined foundations of brick stupas and monasteries. Note the worn, sandstone pillar left by the emperor Ashoka in 249 BC.

Surrounding the Maya Devi temple is the vast **Lumbini Development Zone**, a fantasy garden of Buddhist monuments built using the donations from foreign Buddhists. There are monuments here from pretty much every Buddhist culture in Asia, with the monasteries of the Mahayana and Theravada sects divided by a long canal. Hire a bicycle in Lumbini Bazaar or rent one of the waiting rickshaws to explore the archaeological zone.

Tucked away at the back of the compound, the **Lumbini Museum** (☎ 580318; Saarc/foreigner NRs10/50; ☉ 10am-4pm Wed-Mon) is devoted to the life of the Buddha, with artefacts and photos from Buddhist sites around the world.

Outside the main compound, but easily accessible by bike, the gleaming-white **World Peace Pagoda** (☉ dawn-dusk) is surrounded by a sanctuary for rare sarus cranes.

TOURS
Holiday Tour & Travels (☎ 580432) attached to Lumbini Village Lodge, arranges tours that really get under the surface of life in the Terai. Guides are available for NRs500 per day, or you can get a map (NRs20) and make your own way by bike.

SLEEPING
Most of the budget options are in Lumbini Bazaar, opposite the entrance to the Lumbini Development Zone.

Lumbini Village Lodge (☎ 580432; lumbinivil lagelodge@yahoo.com; dm NRs100, s NRs250-450, d NRs350-750) This inviting lodge has a central courtyard shaded by a mango tree and big, clean rooms with fans and window nets.

Seven Angels Guest House (☎ 580338; tenzee sherpa@yahoo.com; r NRs800-1000) On the main road, this peaceful guesthouse has bright, sunny rooms looking out to mustard fields.

Buddha Maya Garden Hotel (☎ 580220, in Kathmandu 01-4700800; www.ktmgh.com/buddha; s/d from US$60/70; ⚡) Set in large grounds about 500m southeast of the site, this upmarket resort offers very comfortable rooms in calm surroundings. There's a good restaurant. Ask about discounts.

EATING
Lumbini Bazaar has several decent eateries. Try the lime-green **Peace Land Restaurant** (mains NRs60-220) or the **Fox Restaurant** (mains NRs110-200), with its colourful Buddhist curtains and murals.

GETTING THERE & AROUND
Local buses run regularly between Lumbini and the local bus stand in Bhairawa (NRs40, one hour); taxis charge NRs800. To get around, you can rent a bicycle for NRs100 per day, or a rickshaw for NRs150 per hour.

Birganj
☎ 051
As the main transit point for freight between India and Nepal, Birganj is mobbed by trucks, deafened by car horns and jostled by rickshaws. The border crossing to Raxaul is usually only staffed from 4am to 10pm. There's nothing much to see, but the fanciful **clock tower** in the centre of town is covered in Buddhist and Hindu iconography and just west is the popular **Gahawa Maysan Mandir**, sacred to Durga.

ORIENTATION & INFORMATION
Most hotels are on the streets running west of Main Rd, which runs down to the India border. The bus stand is at the end of Ghantaghar Rd (New Rd), which runs east from the clock tower.

Standard Chartered Bank (☉ 9.45am-3.30pm Sun-Thu, 9.45am-12.30pm Fri) changes money and Machhapuchchhre Bank has an ATM.

Fast internet access is available from **Shree Shyam Cyber Cafe** (per hr NRs30; ☉ 6.30am-8.30pm), around the corner from Hotel Kailas.

EXCURSIONS

SLEEPING & EATING

There are a number of noisy budget places near the main bus stand, and a handful of more upmarket choices in the centre.

Hotel Welcome Nepal (☎ 524057; Ghantaghar Rd; s/d without bathroom NRs150/250, d NRs350) The most salubrious choice near the bus stand, Hotel Welcome Nepal gets slightly less traffic noise than neighbouring hotels.

Hotel Makalu (☎ 523054; hmakalu@wlink.com.np; cnr Campus & Main Rds; r NRs800, with AC from NRs1200; 🔀) This recommended business-class hotel is very calm and relaxed – just what you need in hectic Birganj. Rooms have TVs, carpets and 24-hour hot showers and there's a very good restaurant.

GETTING THERE & AWAY

Several airlines fly daily between Kathmandu and Simara airport (US$79, 20 minutes), a 30-minute, NRs50-to-NRs100 rickshaw ride from Birganj.

From the bus stand on Ghantaghar Rd, there are many day and night buses to Kathmandu (NRs350 to NRs400, seven hours).

Rickshaws charge NRs50 to NRs100 to go from town to the Nepal border post and on to Raxaul Bazaar. For information on onward travel in India, see p285.

BANGLADESH

Country code ☎ 880 / pop 153.5 million

The world is full of last frontiers, but this term definitely fits Bangladesh, the steamy eastern half of Bengal that was snipped off from India at Independence. While travellers make a beeline for Kolkata and Kathmandu, the rice paddies of Bangladesh lie off the mainstream traveller circuit, which is good news if you want to escape the crowds and clichés of travel in South Asia.

Divided into a series of islands by the deltas of the Brahmaputra and Ganges Rivers, Bangladesh has history and culture to spare – the following excursion takes in some little-seen gems on the way from Kolkata through Dhaka to Agartala in Tripura. As well as being a fine scenic route, this is the most direct way to reach the Northeast States from Kolkata, next to taking the plane.

Information

The overland route from Kolkata to Dhaka and on to Agartala in Tripura provides a neat shortcut to the far northeast, and there are also less-used crossings to Meghalaya and the West Bengal Hills. However, you may need to get a special endorsement on your visa to leave Bangladesh by land – see visas, p330.

FOREIGN EXCHANGE

The currency of Bangladesh is the taka (Tk), which is divided into 100 paisa. When travelling around Bangladesh, the best currency to carry is US dollars, preferably in cash. Most moneychangers can change US dollars to taka, and taka back to US dollars when you leave (keep hold of enough taka to pay the departure tax). Standard Chartered and HSBC branches in major cities offer foreign exchange and have ATMs that accept international cards.

TOURIST INFORMATION

The **National Tourism Organisation of Bangladesh** (www.bangladeshtourism.gov.bd) provides information on planning a trip to Bangladesh. Other reliable sources of information include the following:

Bangladesh Online (www.bangladeshonline.com /tourism)

Bangladesh.com (www.bangladesh.com)

Discovery Bangladesh (www.discoverybangladesh.com)

VISAS

Visas for Bangladesh must be obtained in advance from Bangladeshi missions abroad – this is easily done in Kolkata (see p309) and Agartala (see the boxed text, p238). If you intend to enter Bangladesh overland, make sure the port of entry is marked on your visa. To exit Bangladesh overland, you will need an additional road permit, or 'change of route' permit, issued by the Directorate of Immigration and Passports in Dhaka – see p330 for more information.

Getting There & Around

Dhaka has good connections to Kolkata by plane, bus and train, and there are also buses from Siliguri. Alternatively you can do the journey in stages via the border crossings at Benapol (near Kolkata), Burimari (near Siliguri) and Dawki (near Shillong) – see p330 for details.

There's a Tk2500 departure tax if you leave Bangladesh by air (Tk1800 for travel to India, Bhutan, Pakistan or Nepal). Some border posts also charge a variable departure tax if you leave by land. Make sure your Bangladesh visa is stamped to allow entry and exit via your chosen border crossings – see opposite.

Local transport options include buses, trains, planes and boats, most famously the Bangladesh Rocket – an old-fashioned paddle-wheel ferry service that runs from Dhaka to Khulna. Autorickshaws are known locally as 'baby taxis'.

DHAKA
☎ 02 / pop 12.5 million

Dhaka is more than just a city, it is a giant whirlpool that sucks in anything and anyone who comes within its furious grasp. This is a city in perpetual motion and the glorious chaos is best viewed from the brilliantly painted cab of one of the city's 600,000 rickshaws. Everyone who comes to Bangladesh passes through at some stage, and some linger, captivated by this sometimes overwhelming but always mesmerising window onto Bangladeshi life.

History

Founded in the 4th century, Dhaka first rose to prominence in the 17th century under the Mughals, but its status as a centre for trade and commerce soon attracted the interest of the European traders. In 1666 the British East India Company established a trading post in Dhaka, and the city fell to the company's militias in 1765. In 1905 Bengal was divided into east and west, setting the ball rolling for the partition of Bengal at Indian Independence. However, Dhaka only became a recognised national capital in 1971 after separation from West Pakistan.

Orientation

The city can be divided into three areas. The bazaars of Old Dhaka are squeezed between the northern bank of the Buriganga River and Fulbaria Rd. The commercial heart of Dhaka is about 2km to the north, centred on Motijheel (moh-tee-*jeel*) and the Kamzz. Beyond are the cantonment (with the airport and international train station) and the upmarket districts of Banani, Gulshan and Baridhara.

Information
INTERNET ACCESS

There are numerous small business centres offering fax, telephone, photocopying and internet access for Tk40 to Tk50 per hour in the Banani Super Market on Kemal Ataturk Ave.

MEDICAL SERVICES
International Centre for Diarrhoeal Disease Research in Bangladesh Hospital (ICDDRB; ☎ 881 1751; 68 Shahid Tajuddein Ahmed Sharani, Mohakhali) Has a traveller's clinic.

MONEY
There are numerous banks with exchange facilities around Dilkusha II Circle in Motijheel. HSBC and Standard Chartered Bank have ATMs.

POST
Main Post Office (☎ 955 5533; cnr Abdul Ghani & North-South Rds; ◷ Sun-Thu) Near Baitul Mukarram Mosque; offers international parcel services.

TOURIST INFORMATION
Parjatan (☎ 811 7855/9; 233 Airport Rd) National tourism organisation, with brochures, car rentals and local tours.

Dangers & Annoyances

Petty theft is a minor risk, particularly after dark. Hartals (strikes) and accompanying violent demonstrations are common – stick to Gulshan at these times. The usual South Asian scams are common – see p307.

Sights
OLD DHAKA

Crowded, overwhelming and electrifying, the old town is centred on the Buriganga River, the muddy main artery of Dhaka. At Sadarghat, you can view a timeless panorama of river life, as triple-towered ferries and pint-sized canoes jostle for space with the hulks of cargo and fishing boats. The best way to view the action is to hire a water-boat at **Sadarghat boat terminal** (Ahsanullah Rd; admission Tk4) for around Tk100 per hour (bargaining required).

Ahsan Manzil

About 600m west of Sadarghat is the **Ahsan Manzil** (Pink Palace; Ahsanullah Rd; admission Tk2; ◷ 10.30am-5.30pm Sat-Wed, 3-7.30pm Fri Apr-Sep, 9.30am-4.30pm Sat-Wed, 3-7.30pm Fri Oct-Mar), built in 1872 to house Nawab Abdul Ghani, the city's wealthiest zamindar (landowner). The palace was saved from oblivion by massive restoration in the late 1980s and inside you can see family heirlooms and photos.

Sitara Mosque

About 1.5km northwest of Sadarghat, and north of Badam Tole, the **Sitara Mosque** (Star

Mosque; Armanitola Rd), was built in the 18th century. Its striking mosaic decoration makes it look like your granny's best tea-cups. Non-Muslims are normally welcome outside of prayer time, but you should dress appropriately; women should also cover their hair.

Lalbagh Fort
Visiting the **fort** (cnr Dhakeswari & Azimpur Rds; admission Tk10; ⊙ 10am-5pm Mon-Sat, 2.30-5.30pm Fri Nov-Mar, 10.30am-5.30pm Mon-Sat, 3-6pm Fri Apr-Oct, closed holidays) is like stepping into the misty past, when Bengal was ruled by emperors, nawabs and princesses. Inside, you can see former royal chambers, a small museum, a traditional *hammam* (Turkish bath), and the mausoleum of the Mughal princess Pari Bibi, who died in 1684.

CENTRAL DHAKA
North of Old Dhaka is the old European zone, now the modern part of town.

National Museum
A visit to the **museum** (Kazi Nazrul Islam Ave; admission Tk5; ⊙ 9.30am-4pm Sat-Wed, 3-7pm Fri) will whisk you through the nation's flora and fauna, its Buddhist and Hindu past, and the creation of the modern state. However, labels are poor and some exhibits are 90% dust and woodworm.

Liberation War Museum
This **war museum** (☎ 955 9091; 5 Segun Bagicha Rd; admission Tk3; ⊙ 10am-5pm Mon-Sat) chronicles the awful events of the 1971 War of Liberation, where perhaps as many as three million Bangladeshis died at the hands of their former allies from West Pakistan.

Activities
Tours of Dhaka by rickshaw cost about Tk80 per hour. **Guide Tours** (☎ 988 6983; www.guidetours .com; 1st fl, Darpan Complex, DIT II Circle, Gulshan) and **Bengal Tours** (☎ 883 4716; www.bengaltours.com; Block A, Banani) offer river and city tours – see the websites for details.

Sleeping
Discounts of up to 50% are usually available year-round. The highest concentration of budget and midrange hotels is in the area extending from Inner Circular Rd down to Old Dhaka.

OLD & CENTRAL DHAKA
Hotel Al-Razzaque International (☎ 956 6408; 29/1 North-South Rd; s/d Tk210/270) Al-Razzaque offers great value budget beds in rooms that are kept lovingly clean. For once the sheets aren't dis-turbingly stained and it has sit-down toilets. However, solo women will almost certainly not be allowed to stay.

Hotel Ramna (☎ 956 2279; 45 Bangabandhu Ave; s/d from Tk350/630) Don't get too excited by the glass-fronted reception area; the rooms are much more down-to-earth. However, they are kept clean and what you get for the price is excellent. It can be a little difficult to find in the maze of tailor shops.

Hotel Pacific (☎ 955 8148; www.hotelpacificdhaka .com; 120/B Motijheel; d with/without AC Tk1200/800, deluxe d Tk1600; ⚙) The Hotel Pacific continues to rule the roost as the best value cheapie in Central Dhaka. Rooms are spacious and homely with hot water in the bathrooms.

GULSHAN AREA
The greater Gulshan area, including Banani and Baridhara, is the heart of the diplomatic zone so prices are higher here than elsewhere in Dhaka.

Jame Prestige Abode (☎ 882 9474, jame@bijoy.net; House 97, Rd 4, Block B, Banani; economy/standard/deluxe r Tk1300/1700/2300, ste Tk3300) The closest Dhaka has to a travellers' centre, this place offers a warm welcome. The single rooms can be a little stuffy but the pastel-blue doubles are perfect for the discerning traveller couple. There's a 15% tax.

Laurel Hotel (☎ 883 4009; www.laurelhotelbd.com; House 54, Rd 18, Block J, Banani; s/d US$66/90; ⚙ ⚐) The Laurel has the look of a business-class hotel, without the formality. Its large, airy, and sunshine-bright rooms are kept spot-less, and prices include internet and break-fast. However, guests of Indian descent are not permitted.

Eating
OLD DHAKA
Decent Pastry Shop (Nawabpur Rd) A slightly incongruous sight in the den of the old town, the Decent Pastry Shop is a tower-ing pillar of calm, sanity, cleanliness and Western tastes.

Al-Razzaque (☎ 956 6408; 29/1 North-South Rd; meals Tk80) When locals tell you that this restau-rant (belonging to the Hotel Al-Razzaque International) is the king of old-town eateries, you'd better believe it. There are separate booths for women.

CENTRAL DHAKA

New Café Jheel (☎ 955 2255; 18/1 Topkhana Rd; mains Tk80; ☼ 6am-midnight) If you want to know what Bengali food is supposed to taste like, check out the thick, fiery curries at this bright and clean favourite.

Café Mango (☎ 913 6686; mains Tk100; ☼ 10am-10pm) To reach this little chestnut, turn onto Rd 13 (formerly Rd 32) from Mirpur Rd and take the first right. The superchilled atmosphere encourages you to linger and the menu runs to sandwiches, salads and creamy chocolate cake.

GULSHAN AREA

Gulshan area has the widest range of restaurants in the country and is the best place in which to indulge.

Gulshan Plaza Restaurant (Gulshan DIT II; mains Tk90; ☼ 7am-midnight) This place is a cheap and basic workman's restaurant that has all your Bangladeshi favourites, as well as kebabs and roast chickens – all of which are near enough to perfect.

Spitfire's Barbeque & Grill (☎ 885 1930; cnr Rd 55 & Gulshan Ave; mains Tk400-1000; ☼ 11.30am-3pm & 6-11pm) Located in the heart of the diplomatic quarter, Spitfire's offers lip-smacking steaks, and the atmosphere is far more relaxed than you'd expect.

Drinking

For a beer (Tk160 for a cold Heineken) try the Peacock Restaurant or Sukura Restaurant opposite the Sheraton Hotel on Minto Rd.

Shopping

For local souvenirs, head to **New Market** (Mirpur Rd; ☼ Wed-Sun, morning Mon). You can pick up a piece of lavishly decorated rickshaw trim as a souvenir from the Nazira Bazar on Bangsal Rd, near the Hotel Al-Razzaque International.

Getting There & Away

AIR

Air India (www.airindia.com), **Biman Bangladesh** (www.bimanair.com), **GMG Airlines** (www.gmgairlines.com) and many big carriers from Southeast Asia and the Gulf offer flights to/from Dhaka, and there are domestic services to many Bangladeshi cities. **Zia International Airport** (☎ 891 4870) is 19km north of Old Dhaka.

BOAT

The famous Rocket (paddle-wheel) boats to Khulna (Tk1010/610/150 for 1st/2nd/deck class, 27 to 30 hours) leave Sadarghat daily around 6pm. Buy tickets at **Bangladesh Inland Waterway Transport Corporation office** (BIWTC; ☎ 955 9779, 891 4771; Motijheel; ☼ Sun-Wed to 5pm, to 2pm Thu), a block east of Dilkusha Circle I. Smaller boats offer trips throughout the delta.

BUS

International buses to Kolkata via Benapol and Agartala – see p132 for details – leave from the Kamlapur Bus Station on DIT Ave in Motijheel.

On the northwestern side of town on Dhaka–Aricha Hwy (an 8km autorickshaw ride from the centre) Gabtali Bus Station has services to the west, including Jessore (Tk230 to Tk325, 6½ hours) and Khulna (Tk280, eight hours).

On the southeastern side of the town, Sayedabad Bus Station serves destinations in the south and west, including Sylhet (Tk200, five hours, between 5am and 11.30pm).

TRAIN

Dhaka's main train station is the modern Kamlapur station in Motijheel. There are daily express trains to Sylhet (seven hours) and Akhaura (for Agartala, 2½ hours), among other destinations. International trains to Kolkata (see p133) run from Dhaka Cantonment station, north of Gulshan.

Getting Around

Prepaid taxis from the airport to the centre cost around Tk750. In the other direction, you'll pay around Tk100 by baby taxi (autorickshaw) and Tk150 by taxi.

The easiest way get around town is by baby taxi or taxi. Metres are rarely used so bargain for a fare before you start your journey. Pedal rickshaws are the best way to get around Old Dhaka, though they form the most incredible rickshaw jams in the afternoon rush hour. To hire a car and driver, contact one of the big tour companies (opposite).

WEST OF DHAKA

Most people whistle through western Bangladesh en route to Dhaka, but Jessore, Kulna and Bagerhat are possible stops en route.

Jessore

☎ 0421

A hop and a skip from the border with India, Jessore is a perfect introduction to the Bangladeshi experience. There are no real sights but with a chartered baby taxi you could visit the 18th-century Sonabaria Shyam Sundar Temple, about 30km southwest of Jessore, or the pre-Mughal mosque at Baro Bazar, about 18km northeast of Jessore on the Magura highway.

SLEEPING

Grand Hotel (☎ 73038; grand@khulna.bangla.net; MK Rd; s/d Tk150/400) This budget hotel is managed like a midrange one and is the best budget base in Jessore. You enter the rooms through red theatre curtains and discover carefully looked-after rooms and the sort of boisterous welcome worthy of the theatre. Both men and women are welcome.

Banchte Shekha (☎ 66436/68885; Shaheed Mashiur Rahman Rd; r Tk300-800) Just off Airport Rd and east of the bypass road to Benapol, Banchte Shekha (*bach*-tah *shay*-kah) is surrounded only by the noise of leaves blowing in the breeze and chirping birds. The rooms are basic but more than adequate and come with hot showers, satellite TV and clean sheets smelling of mothballs, and your money will help fund a project aiding local women.

EATING

The K'Purti Rd area is a great place for street food, fresh produce and a carnival-like atmosphere.

New Nuru Hotel (MK Rd; mains Tk80) The unchallenged curry king of Jessore, but the fiery kebabs are also worthy of mention. Be prepared for some relentless staring.

Chun Beu Restaurant (4th fl, Hotel Magpie, MK Rd; soup Tk100, mains Tk250) A rare, authentic Chinese restaurant with a casual atmosphere helped along nicely by the equally casual blue-and-white checked tablecloths.

GETTING THERE & AWAY

There are daily flights to Dhaka (Tk2770, 40 minutes) from the airport, a 6km, Tk100 rickshaw ride west of the city centre.

Buses to Dhaka's Gabtali bus station (Tk230 to Tk475, seven to 10 hours) run throughout the day. Local buses run periodically to Khulna (Tk50, 1½ hours) and the border town of Benapol (Tk30, 1½ hours), with onward

connections to Kolkata on the far side. Kulna and Benopol are also served by train, but it's much easier to go by bus.

Benapol

Benapol (also spelt Benapole) is essentially a 2km-long road lined with trucks waiting to cross the border towards Kolkata. If you've arrived at a reasonable time, it's probably best to spend your first night in Jessore. Failing that, the **Parjatan Hotel** (r with/without AC Tk1000/600, ste Tk1500) has large, clean suites that for some reason have two bathrooms and two bedrooms.

Minibuses ply between Benapol and Jessore (Tk30, 1½ hours). Ask for both 'Benapol' and 'border' to avoid confusion. The word 'India' may also come in handy. See p132 for information on international bus services.

Khulna

☎ 041

Most people come to the capital of Khulna province to take the charmingly clunky Rocket paddle ships that cruise to Dhaka. The waterfront old town buzzes with activity that will stimulate and inspire the senses.

Khan A Sabar Rd, also known as Jessore Rd, is the main drag through the city, and KDA Ave is the major thoroughfare on the western side. There are net cafes in the New Market on Upper Jessore Rd. The Standard Chartered Bank on KDA Ave changes money and has an ATM.

At the riverside, you can rent small boats for a people-watching session along the river for Tk100 to Tk150. You can also visit the small **Divisional Museum** (admission Tk50).

Tours to the Bengali side of the Sunderbans can be arranged through **Bengal Tours** (☎ 724 355; 236 Khan Jahan Ali Rd), **Guide Tours** (☎ 731 384; www.guidetours.com; KDA Bldg, KDA Ave) and **Hotel Royal International** (☎ 721 638/9; 33 KDA Ave).

SLEEPING & EATING

Khulna's cheap hotels are about 1km south of the train station.

Hotel Arcadia (☎ 732 552; Khan A Sabar Rd; s/d Tk250/350) Excellent value budget rooms with – are you ready for this? – brand new, unsullied bedding! The rooms are small but well kept and the bathrooms have sit-down toilets, which is rare for this price range.

Hotel Royal International (☎ 721 638/9; royal @bttb.net.bd; 33 KDA Ave; s/d from Tk800/950) If '70s disco is your favourite music then the decor at the Royal will please. There's a travel agency in the lobby where you can make arrangements for car rental and guided trips to the Sundarbans.

Aloka Restaurant (☎ 733 342; 1 Khan A Sabar Rd; mains Tk60) We think this place is simply lovely and locals flock here to gorge on a feast of quality Bangladeshi fare.

Grillhouse (☎ 730 245; New Market; mains Tk150) Widely considered the best restaurant in Khulna, this place cooks up fine kebabs and Chinese dishes (which form the bulk of the menu).

GETTING THERE & AROUND

The office for the **Bangladesh Inland Waterway Transport Corporation** (BIWTC; ☎ 721 532) is just behind the train station. Rocket paddle ships sail up the delta to Dhaka (1st/2nd/deck class Tk1010/610/150) six times a week in each direction. Book a few days in advance for a 1st-class cabin.

About 2km northwest of the city centre, the KDA bus terminal has services to Dhaka (Tk280, 7½ hours) and Jessore (Tk50 to Tk60, one hour). To reach Bagerhat (Tk30, 45 minutes), head to the 'new bus station' on the southern edge of town.

Trains run daily to Jessore and Dhaka but most people prefer to take the bus.

Bagerhat

☎ 401

Hidden in green folds of countryside, this Unesco-protected complex of ancient mosques and mausoleums is one of Bangladesh's hidden gems. An ancient centre for the study of Islam, Bagerhat was founded by the Sufi mystic Khan Jahan Ali in the 15th century. Most people visit on a day trip from Khulna.

SIGHTS

The archaeological area is 5km west of Bagerhat. The most famous structure here is the 15th-century **Shait Gumbad Mosque** (admission Tk50) the largest and most magnificent pre-Mughal mosque in the country. There are three other historic mosques nearby, as well as a small museum, covered by the same entry ticket.

On the western bank of the Thakur Dighi Pond, the recently repaired **Nine-Domed**

Mosque features mihrabs (niches) embellished with terracotta floral scrolls and foliage motifs. About 2km east of Shait Gumbad is the splendid **Ronvijoypur Mosque**, with the largest dome in Bangladesh. Khan Jahan Ali died in 1459 and was interred in the **Mazhar Khan Jahan Ali**, set beside a pond with resident crocodiles.

About 11km from Bagerhat, near the village of Ayodhya, the weather-worn 17th-century **Khodla Math Temple** is one of the largest Hindu temples ever built in Bangladesh. To get here, take a rickshaw or baby taxi to the market town of Jatrapur, then ask directions to Ayodhya, 3km east along winding, paved paths.

SLEEPING & EATING

Hotel Momotaj (Rail Rd; r Tk200) Basic rooms are available at this basic Bangladeshi hotel, but they are grimy and overpriced.

There are some equally basic local restaurants and street stalls along the main road.

GETTING THERE & AROUND

Buses run regularly to/from Khulna (Tk30, 45 minutes), passing through the archaeological zone. Rickshaws and baby taxis can be hired by the hour for local sightseeing.

NORTHWEST OF DHAKA

Direct buses run from Dhaka and Siliguri in West Bengal to the border post between Burimari and Chengrabandha in India.

Burimari

Facing the Indian town of Chengrabandha, Burimari is a major border crossing into India, though it's hardly busy. The border is open 8am to 6pm – there is nowhere to change money on the Bangladeshi side of the border, so make sure that before you leave India you grab enough taka to get you to your next destination.

If you arrive late at night at Burimari, you can stay at **Mahoroma Hotel** (s/d Tk150/250), around the corner from the customs office. It has small but clean rooms with attached bathroom.

GETTING THERE & AWAY

Overnight buses run from Dhaka's Kamlapur Bus Station to Burimari (Tk250 to Tk400, 10 hours). See p150 for information about onwards transport to Siliguri.

EXCURSIONS

NORTHEAST OF DHAKA

Crossing the border from Dawki in Meghalaya, you'll have to make your way through Tamabil and Sylhet before heading south to Dhaka.

Sylhet

☎ 0821

Most Bangladeshis living in Britain hail from Sylhet, and the money they have sent home has created a surreal city of Western-style shopping malls with far too little stock inside. The whole place feels a little like a set for a Bangladeshi movie, but it's a cosmopolitan place and you'll hear plenty of people talking with thick Brummie or East London accents.

The town is divided by the Surma River, which is crossed by two bridges. Zinda Bazar Rd is littered with restaurants and shopping centres. There are a few internet cafes on Jaintiapur Rd, and the Standard Chartered Bank on Airport Rd has an ATM.

SIGHTS

In the north of the city, off Airport Rd, is the **Shrine of Hazrat Shah Jalal**, a 14th-century Sufi saint. The tomb is covered with rich brocade, and at night the space around it is illuminated with candles – the atmosphere is quite magical. Non-Muslim men (only, sadly) should be OK visiting the shrine but respectful dress and behaviour are essential.

In Nur Manzil, near the centre of town and east of Noya Sarok Rd, is the **Osmani Museum** (admission free; ☽ 10.30am-5.30pm Sat-Wed Apr-Sep, 9.30am-4.30pm Sat-Wed Oct-Mar, 3-8pm Fri year-round), dedicated to General Osmani, a key figure in the Liberation War.

SLEEPING

Most budget hotels are in the centre of town, along Taltala Rd, and in the adjoining Telihaor area.

Hotel Asia (☎ 711 278; Bandar Bazar; s/d Tk100/300, d with AC Tk800; ❄) Do yourself a favour and grab a bargain at this hotel in the heart of a colourful neighbourhood. The rooms are plain and honest budget treats that come without stains and mess.

Hotel Gulshan (☎ 717 263; Taltala Rd; s/d Tk300/500, d with AC Tk800; ❄) A long-time favourite with

visitors to Sylhet and easily the best in its class, this enormous hotel offers clean rooms, some with sit-down toilets and TV, but only the most expensive ones have hot water.

EATING

Cheap restaurants abound in the Telihaor area. Travellers rate the unmistakably turquoise **Jamania Restaurant** (meals Tk40-50).

There are more cheap Bengali eats on Zinba Bazar Rd – the lively and friendly **Agra Hotel & Restaurant** (meals around Tk60) is as full of character as it is full of characters.

GETTING THERE & AWAY

A 7km, Tk300 taxi ride north of town, Sylhet airport has frequent daily flights to Dhaka (Tk3720, 30 minutes).

Various luxury bus companies have offices on the road to the Shrine of Hazrat Shah Jalal, where you can buy tickets for Dhaka (Tk450, five hours). Buses to the India border at Tamabil (Tk75, 2½ hours) leave from the small Jaintiapur bus station, several kilometres east of the town centre.

On the south side of town, the train station has three daily express trains for Dhaka (1st/upper-2nd class Tk270/150, sleeping car AC/fan Tk610/425, seven to nine hours).

Tamabil

About 55km north from Sylhet, the Tamabil border crossing (open between 6am and 5pm) offers an interesting back route to Meghalaya in India. However, you must pay the Tk300 Bangladeshi departure tax at a branch of the Sonali Bank branch before you reach the border – closest is in Jaintiapur, 13km from Tamabil. There is nowhere to stay or change money, so carry some rupees and takas.

GETTING THERE & AWAY

The trip between Tamabil and Sylhet can be completed by bus (Tk75, 2½ hours) or taxi (Tk700). From the Tamabil bus stand, it's a 15-minute hike to the India border, then a 1.5km walk (or Rs30 taxi ride) on the far side to the town of Dawki, from where buses run to Shillong (Rs70, 2½ hours) till late morning. If you miss the bus, bargain for a taxi.

Directory

CONTENTS

ACCOMMODATION

The northeast has accommodation to suit all budgets, from grungy dives with cold showers and cockroaches to the former palaces of maharajas. Most towns have something for every pocketbook, but rates vary widely as you travel around the northeast and in some states you just have to make do with what you can get.

Accommodation listings in this book appear in price order under the Sleeping heading (sometimes divided into budget, midrange and top-end categories). Standout options are indicated with the Our Pick icon – **ourpick** – in this book. It is hard to pinpoint exact accom-

modation costs, but most hotels fall somewhere within the following ranges:

Budget Single rooms from Rs100 to Rs400, and doubles from Rs200 to Rs600.

Midrange Single rooms from Rs300 to Rs1300, and doubles from Rs450 to Rs1800.

Top end Single and double rooms from around Rs1900 to US$150 or more.

Unless otherwise stated, tariffs in this book are based on the cheapest room in each category. Rates listed don't include taxes unless otherwise indicated. State government taxes are added to the cost of rooms at all except the cheapest hotels. Taxes vary from state to state and are detailed in the regional chapters. Many upmarket hotels also levy an additional 'service charge' (usually around 10%).

As everywhere, hotels in tourist hangouts may double or triple their prices in the high season – normally summertime in the mountains (June to October), and the period before and after the monsoon in the plains (April to June and September to October). At other times, these hotels offer significant discounts. It's always worth asking for a discount if the hotel seems quiet. Many temple towns have additional peak seasons around major festivals and pilgrimages; advance bookings may be essential at these times – see p18 and the regional chapters for festival dates and details. Room rates in this book were collected outside the peak season unless otherwise stated.

Room quality can vary within hotels, so try to inspect a few rooms first. Avoid carpeted rooms at cheaper hotels unless you like the smell of mouldy socks. Always check the bathroom – leaky taps are a constant irritation. For the low-down on hotel bathrooms,

---

BOOK YOUR STAY ONLINE

For more accommodation reviews and recommendations by Lonely Planet authors, check out the online booking service at www.lonelyplanet.com/hotels. You'll find the true, insider low-down on the best places to stay. Reviews are thorough and independent. Best of all, you can book online.

see the boxed text, opposite. Noise pollution can be a real pain (especially in urban centres) – request a room that doesn't face onto a busy road. Light pollution is another problem, so keep the sleep-mask from your flight.

In winter, hotels in the mountains provide gas or electric heaters, or wood for the open fire, for an additional fee. Avoid charcoal-burning fires because of the risk of fatal carbon monoxide poisoning. Be aware that deforestation is often a problem in the areas that offer rooms with wood fires.

Credit cards are accepted at most top-end hotels and some midrange places; budget hotels require cash. Most hotels ask for deposit at check-in – ask for a receipt and be wary of any request to sign a blank impression of your credit card. Verify the checkout time when you check in – some hotels have a fixed checkout time (usually 10am or noon), while others give you 24 hours. Reservations are usually fine by phone without a deposit, but bookings often drop off the list, so call ahead to check the day before you arrive.

Be aware that in tourist hot spots, hotels often 'borrow' the name of a thriving competitor to confuse travellers, paying commissions to taxi and rickshaw drivers who bring them unsuspecting customers – see p308.

Budget & Midrange Hotels
At the cheapest hotels, rooms have a bed and not much else and the communal bathroom is normally down the hall. However, most budget places also offer rooms with private bathrooms of varying standards. Rooms generally have ceiling fans, except in hill areas where they are not needed. Better rooms have electric mosquito killers or window nets. Bringing your own sheets (or a sleeping bag liner) is a sound policy – some cheap places have sheets with more holes and stains than a string vest at an oyster-eating contest. Away from tourist areas, cheaper hotels may not take foreigners because they don't have the required foreigner-registration forms – if you get turned away, this is probably the reason

Midrange hotels offer comforts such as carpets (a mixed blessing as they can be musty and damp) and Indian cable TV, often with a few English-language channels. Some places offer noisy 'air-coolers' that cool air by blowing it over cold water, but it's worth paying more for real air-conditioning (AC). Note that some cheaper hotels lock their doors at night. Members of staff normally sleep in the lobby but waking them up can be a challenge. Let the hotel know in advance if you are arriving or returning to your room late in the evening.

Camping & Trekking Accommodation
Few people camp while travelling around the northeast, but larger hotels may let you camp in the grounds for a charge, and camping is often the only option if you go trekking. Sikkim has a network of rudimentary

---

PRACTICALITIES

- Electricity is 230V to 240V, 50 Hz AC and sockets are the three round-pin variety (two-pin sockets are also found). Blackouts are common – unplug your appliances to avoid a power surge when the power comes back on.
- Officially India is metric. Uniquely Indian terms you're likely to hear are: lakhs (one lakh = 100,000) and crores (one crore = 10 million).
- National English-language dailies are the *Hindustan Times, Times of India, Indian Express, Pioneer, Asian Age, Hindu* and *Economic Times*. The *Statesman* and *Telegraph* are published in Kolkata.
- Incisive current-affair reports are printed in *Frontline, India Today,* the *Week, Sunday* and *Outlook*. For India-related travel articles get *Outlook Traveller;* for the latest on the Indian movie scene, pick up *Stardust*.
- The national (government) TV broadcaster is Doordarshan. More people watch satellite and cable TV; English-language channels include BBC World, CNN, Star Movies, HBO and MTV (with local and international music). TV (and radio) program/frequency details appear in most major English-language newspapers.
- Numerous private channels and government-controlled All India Radio (AIR) transmit local and international news, music and more.

KNOW YOUR BATHROOM

Top-end and midrange hotels in India generally have sit-down flush toilets with toilet paper supplied. In cheaper hotels, squat toilets are the norm and the only wiping paraphernalia will be a jug of water and a tap. Squat toilets are variously described as 'Indian style', 'Indian' or 'floor' toilets, while the sit-down variety may be called 'Western' or 'commode' toilets. In a few places, you'll find the curious 'hybrid toilet', a sit-down toilet with footpads on the edge of the bowl.

Terminology for hotel bathrooms varies across India. 'Attached bath', 'private bath' or 'with bath' means that the room has its own en suite bathroom. 'Common bath', 'no bathroom' or 'shared bath' means communal bathroom facilities down the hall. 'Running', '24-hour' or 'constant' water means that hot water is theoretically available around the clock. 'Bucket hot water' is only available in buckets (sometimes for a small charge). Many places use small, wall-mounted electric geysers (water heaters) that need to be switched on an hour before use.

In this book, hotel rooms have their own private bathroom unless otherwise indicated.

---

trekkers' huts; most just offer floor space for travellers with sleeping bags and few offer meals, but they provide shelter from the elements. These places are often booked out by groups in peak season, so a tent is always a useful back up.

Dormitory Accommodation

Many hotels have cheap dormitories, though these are generally mixed and often used by intoxicated local drivers – not ideal conditions for single women. More salubrious dorms are found at the handful of hostels run by the YMCA, YWCA, and the Salvation Army– and (HI) Hostelling International–associate hostels (see www.yhaindia.org for listings). You may also end up sleeping in dormitory accommodation if you stay at any of the 'tourist bungalows' or 'circuit houses' run by state governments in the Northeast States – see below. Railway retiring rooms (right) also offer cheap dorm beds.

Government Accommodation & Tourist Bungalows

The Indian government maintains a network of guesthouses in remote areas for travelling officials and government workers, known variously as Rest Houses, Dak Bungalows, Circuit Houses, Public Works Department (PWD) Bungalows and Forest Rest Houses. These places may accept travellers if no government employees need the rooms, but you usually need permission to stay from local officials. If you arrange a tour to Adivasi areas of the northeast, your guide will make all the arrangements for you.

Many state tourism departments also run basic 'tourist bungalows' and more upmarket hotels; bookings can be arranged through tourist offices.

Homestays & Accommodation for Paying Guests

Staying with a local family is increasingly popular in India, and owners often provide delicious home-cooked meals. Local tourist offices can provide lists of families involved in homestay schemes, particularly in Kolkata (Calcutta), Gangtok and Darjeeling. Homestays can also be arranged in Mizoram and Nagaland.

Railway Retiring Rooms

Most large train stations have basic rooms for travellers in possession of an ongoing train ticket or Indrail Pass. Retiring rooms are noisy due to both passengers and trains, but they're useful for early morning train departures, and most stations offer dormitories as well as private rooms (24-hour checkout) for a bargain price. People come and go at all hours of the day and night so keep an eye on your belongings.

Resorts

Orissa has a handful of upmarket seaside resorts offering standard resort facilities, including swimming pools, though none are really luxurious. 'Resorts' in the mountains are normally just comfortable upmarket hotels, sometimes with adventure activities and cottages in the garden to add a bit of novelty to proceedings.

Assam and Meghalaya have some unusual nature-themed resorts and you can stay at some fabulous old Raj-era tea estates in Assam – see the entries for Jorhat (p215) and Dibrugarh (p217).

Temples & Pilgrims' Resthouses

Accommodation is available at some ashrams (spiritual communities), gurdwaras (Sikh temples) and *dharamsalas* (pilgrims' guesthouses), but check to make sure they are happy with foreign guests and always abide by any local protocols about smoking, drinking and making noise. A donation is always appropriate.

Top-End & Heritage Hotels

The northeast has plenty of comfortable top-end hotels, from five-star chain hotels to colonial-era palaces that don't even have a classification system (if they did, it would have to be five tiger-skin rugs). Most top-end hotels have rupee rates for Indian guests and US dollar rates for foreigners (including Non-Resident Indians, or NRIs). Officially, you are supposed to pay the dollar rates in foreign currency or by credit card, but many places will accept rupees adding up to the dollar rate.

BUSINESS HOURS

India still follows the same working schedule as the UK. Official business hours are 9.30am to 5.30pm Monday to Friday, but some offices open later and close earlier. Government offices may open on certain Saturdays (usually the first, second and fourth of the month), either for the whole day or just for the morning. Most offices have a lunch hour from around 1pm.

Shops generally open around 10am and stay open until 6pm or later; some close on Sunday. Note that night-time curfews apply in some areas – particularly in the Northeast States. Seek local advice and avoid walking around after curfew. Airline offices generally keep to standard weekday business hours, and some also open Saturday morning.

Banks are open from 10am to 2pm on weekdays (till 4pm in some areas), and from 10am to noon (or 1pm) on Saturday. Foreign-exchange offices open every day, for longer hours. Post offices are open from 10am to 5pm on weekdays, till noon on Saturday. Larger post offices in major cities may work a full day on Saturday and a half-day on Sunday – see regional chapters for details.

Restaurant opening hours vary regionally – you can rely on most places to be open from around 8am to 10pm, except in the Northeast States, where restaurants can close as early as 8.30pm. Exceptions are noted in the Eating sections of the regional chapters.

CHILDREN

Plenty of travellers bring their children to the northeast without problems, but remember that children are more vulnerable to illness, stress and exhaustion, particularly in a hot, noisy and unfamiliar environment. The normal risks are amplified in India, so pay close attention to hygiene and be *very* vigilant around traffic. Seek advice on appropriate vaccinations and medical treatments before you travel.

See Lonely Planet's *Travel with Children,* and the 'Kids to Go' section of the Thorn Tree forum on **LonelyPlanet.com** (thorntree.lonelyplanet.com) for more advice.

Practicalities
ACCOMMODATION

Many hotels have 'family rooms' and most will provide an extra bed for a small additional charge. Upmarket hotels may offer babysitting facilities and cable TV with English-language children's channels. Off the beaten track, you may all end up in one bed like in *Little House on the Prairie*.

FOOD & DRINK

Children are welcome in most restaurants, but only upmarket places and fast-food chains have high chairs and children's menus. Nappy-changing facilities are usually restricted to restaurant loos, which can be a) unhygienic and b) about the size of a shoebox. See p75 for hints on what to feed the kids while here.

HEALTH

Avoiding stomach upsets will be a daily battle – washing hands with soap or rubbing alcohol is your first line of defence (see p347). If your child takes special medication, bring along an adequate stock. Be warned that those cute-looking monkeys and street dogs can carry rabies – children may not report a bite so seek medical advice on vaccinations for rabies and other tropical diseases for your children before you travel.

TRANSPORT

On any long-distance road journeys, take plenty of food and toilet stops, particularly on rough roads. The slow pace of travel in India will bore children to tears – travel by train rather than bus to give children a change to lie flat and stretch their legs.

Children normally travel on adults' laps; child seats – or indeed any kind of seatbelts – are extremely rare. Travelling in the back seat may offer marginally more safety that sitting up front by the driver.

Discounts
On Indian trains, children under four years travel free and kids aged five to 12 pay half-price. Most airlines charge 10% of the adult fare for infants and 50% for under 12s. Many tourist attractions charge a reduced entry fee for children under 12 (under 15 in some states).

TRAVEL WITH INFANTS
Standard baby products such as nappies (diapers) and milk powder are available in most large cities. Essentials to bring from home include high-factor sunscreen, a snug-fitting wide-brimmed hat and a washable changing mat for covering dirty surfaces. Breastfeeding in public is frowned upon and bottle feeding with breast milk is complicated by the problem of sterilising bottles while travelling.

Sights & Activities
Some destinations are better for children than others – Kolkata has a number of child-friendly museums, as well as bowling alleys, a theme park, a popular planetarium and botanical gardens – see p107 and p119. There are also old-fashioned planetariums in Guwahati (p206) in Assam and Bhubaneswar (p254) in Orissa.

Kids will enjoy spotting India's exotic beasties. Wildlife safaris, particularly those offering elephant rides, are also worth considering (see p93). There are better-than-average zoos in (or near) Kolkata (p115), Darjeeling (p159) and Bhubaneswar (p258).

All children love the seaside, but you'll need to be careful of currents and tides. The northeast's best beaches are found in Orissa – the sands at Puri (p258), Konark (p264) and Gopalpur-on-Sea (p268) are OK for a paddle. Older kids may also enjoy rafting in Sikkim (p95).

Hill stations tend to be child-friendly, with lots of opportunities for peaceful forest picnics, paddle boating and pony rides. Kids will also appreciate the cooler weather. Top spots in the northeast include Darjeeling (p153), Mirik (p150) and Shillong (p240).

India's bounty of festivals may also capture your child's imagination, although some will be spooked by the crowds. For festival details, see p18. Read the regional chapters for more suggestions.

CLIMATE CHARTS
The northeast is a vast area and climatic conditions vary considerably with the changing topography. Generally speaking, the country

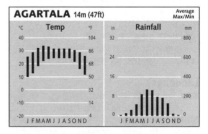

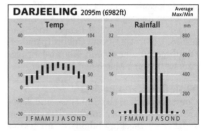

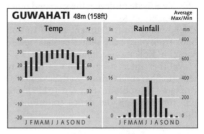

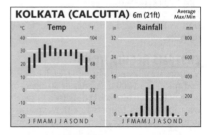

has a three-season year – the hot, the wet and the cool. For more details, see the charts, p305, and p14.

COURSES

Many travellers like to learn something new as they travel around India, and there are some interesting courses on offer in the northeast, from yoga and meditation to Indian cooking. To find out about local courses, inquire at tourist offices, ask fellow travellers, and browse local newspapers and noticeboards. See p95 for information on climbing courses and p76 for information on cooking courses.

Several centres in the northeast offer yoga courses – see p99 for more information.

Languages

You can't rush learning a language, so give yourself enough time for the lessons to sink in. Most language schools in Kolkata only cater to full-time students, but many volunteers take private lessons – contact the tourist office for advice on finding a teacher (p107).

In Darjeeling in West Bengal, the Manjushree Centre of Tibetan Culture (p160) offers three- to nine-month Tibetan-language courses between March and December.

Music & Performing Arts

Courses in Indian classical music and dance are offered in many traveller hangouts in India – try checking billboards for people offering private tuition in the sitar and other instruments in Kolkata. Alternatively, consider buying an instrument and a tuition book from one of the shops on Shakespeare Sarani in Kolkata – see Shopping (p317).

Another interesting option is to study Odissi, Bharatnatyam or Kathak dance at Kolkata's Aurobindo Bhawan (p119). See p57 for more on the dance traditions of the northeast.

Tea Appreciation

Details of courses in the art of tea appreciation in Siliguri and Kurseong can be found on p148.

CUSTOMS REGULATIONS

Visitors are allowed to bring 1L each of wine and spirits, and 200 cigarettes or 50 cigars or 250g of tobacco into India duty free. Officials occasionally ask tourists to enter expensive items such as video cameras and laptop computers on a 'Tourist Baggage Re-export' form to ensure they are taken out of India. There are no duty-free allowances when entering India from Nepal.

Technically you're supposed to declare any amount of cash or travellers cheques over US$10,000 on arrival, and rupees should not be taken out of India. However, this is rarely policed. Exporting antiques and products made from animals is prohibited – see the boxed text, p315.

DANGERS & ANNOYANCES

Few countries can match India when it comes to scams and dodgy deals. However, most problems can be avoided with a bit of common sense and a sensible level of caution. Above all else, follow the golden rule – if a deal sounds too good to be true, it is.

Scams change as dodgy characters find new ways to separate foreigners from their money, so chat with other travellers and tourism officials to stay abreast of the latest hazards. Also see the India branch of Lonely Planet's **Thorn Tree forum** (thorntree.lonelyplanet.com).

For region-specific scams and dangers, see the Dangers & Annoyances sections of the regional chapters. Women should also read the advice on p324.

Contaminated Food & Drink

Over the years there have been several cases of travellers being poisoned with bacteria in hotels or restaurants as part of scam by private medical clinics to defraud international insurance companies – if you become ill and need inpatient treatment, get a second opinion if possible.

Most bottled water is legit, but always ensure the lid seal is intact. Crush plastic bottles after use to prevent them being misused later, or better still, purify your own water with water-purification tablets or a filtration system (you'll also avoid contributing to India's rubbish problems).

Dangerous Animals

Venomous snakes are common, so be cautious when walking through vegetation. Crocodiles are found in some rivers and bull sharks are found in many estuaries, so be careful where you swim. Tigers, leopards and rhinos are probably in more danger from humans than the other way around, but it pays to observe these animals from a distance. The most serious risk to travellers comes from feral dogs and aggressive monkeys, both of which can carry rabies – see p347.

Drugs

A few towns – including Puri in Orissa – allow the legal sale of bhang (a derivative of marijuana) for religious reasons but elsewhere, courts treat possession of cannabis as severely as possession of heroin, with a penalty of at least 10 years in prison. If you do choose to take drugs, be *extremely* circumspect, and never try to transport drugs on domestic flights or across international borders.

Bhang is frequently administered in food and drinks, which can be incredibly potent, leaving intoxicated travellers vulnerable to robbery or accidents. The northeast also has problems with methamphetamine, imported from Myanmar (Burma) by drug cartels. For more on the drug situation, see p312.

Festivals

The sheer mass of humanity at India's festivals provides an incredible spectacle, but every year pilgrims are crushed or trampled to death on temple processions and train platforms. Be extra careful at these times, and avoid special pilgrim trains.

Care is also needed during the Holi festival (p18). As well as dousing passers-by with water and coloured dye, which can damage your clothes and camera and cause a skin reaction, some male revellers use the crowds as cover for groping women. It's wise to seek a companion before venturing onto the streets at festival time.

Noise

Shouting, traffic noise, dripping taps, slamming doors, wedding parties and loud music can all add up to a waking nightmare for light sleepers. Bring earplugs and request rooms that face away from busy roads. Indian holidaymakers travel in large groups and people often knock randomly on hotel room doors looking for members of their party – lock your door if you don't want people to walk in uninvited.

Rebel Violence

Most of the time, the northeast is no more dangerous than anywhere else in India, but certain areas are particularly prone to rebel

---

BEWARE BHANG LASSIS!

Many restaurants in tourist centres will clandestinely whip up a bhang lassi, a yoghurt and iced-water beverage laced with cannabis. Commonly dubbed 'special lassi', this potent concoction can cause a drawn-out high that verges on delirium and lasts for many hours. Many travellers have been badly hurt in accidents or been robbed of all their possessions after drinking this risky brew. Note that 'special lassi' should not be confused with 'special tea' – a popular pseudonym for beer in states that are officially 'dry'.

---

violence. There are estimated to be more than a hundred insurgent armies operating in the northeast, and bomb attacks on markets, trains, religious centres and tourist sights are an ongoing risk, particularly in Manipur, Nagaland and Assam. More than 80 people were killed in a string of bomb attacks in Assam in 2008, attributed to separatist rebels. In recent years, India has also been hit by a series of deadly bomb attacks by Islamic militants based in Pakistan and Kashmir.

People involved in tourism rarely admit the dangers, while embassies often exaggerate the risks – the best sources of information are international charities and local news sources. Useful resources are listed in the Northeast States chapter (p199).

Scams

India is notorious for tricks and scams designed to move money from your pockets into the pockets of con artists. Be highly suspicious of claims that you can purchase goods cheaply in India and sell them easily at a profit elsewhere. Precious stones and carpets are favourites for this con. If anyone asks you to carry goods home to sell on to their 'representatives' in your home country, you are being set up for a scam. The company may provide convincing-sounding testimonials from other satisfied customers, but without exception, the goods will be worthless.

It also pays to be cautious when sending goods home. Shops have been known to swap high-value items for junk, so send the package yourself from the post office to be safe. Be very careful when paying for souvenirs with

DIRECTORY

a credit card. Government shops are usually legitimate; private souvenir shops have a reputation for secretly running off extra copies of the credit-card imprint slip, which will be used for phoney transactions after you have left the shop. To play it safe, visit the nearest ATM and pay in cash.

While it's only a minority of traders who are involved in dishonest schemes, many souvenir vendors are involved in the commission racket – see right.

Swimming

Beaches can have dangerous rips and currents, and there are drowning deaths each year – the beaches at Puri, Konark and Gopalpur-on-Sea in Orissa are particularly prone to undercurrents. Swimming in rivers is also a gamble, not least because that innocent-looking floating log might turn out to be a hungry crocodile. Most locals prefer to stick to the safety of temple water tanks or swimming pools. Wherever you are, always check locally before swimming in unfamiliar waters.

Theft & Druggings

Theft is a small but significant risk in the northeast. On buses and trains, keep luggage securely locked (mini padlocks and chains are available at most train stations) and lock your bags to the metal baggage racks or the wire loops found under seats; padlocking your bags to the roof racks on buses is also a sensible policy (just don't lose the keys!).

Opportunistic thieves tend to target popular tourist train routes, such as Howrah to New Jalpaiguri. Armed bandits have also been known to rob train passengers in rural parts of Assam and Bihar. Be extra alert just before the train departs – this is prime time for the snatch-and-run routine. Airports are another place you should exercise caution – if someone offers to carry your bag, make sure you watch where it is going.

Occasionally tourists (especially those travelling solo) are drugged and robbed during train or bus journeys. Typically, a seemingly friendly stranger will strike up a conversation, offer you a spiked drink, then make off with your valuables. Politely decline drinks or food offered by strangers – stomach upsets are a convenient excuse.

Unfortunately some travellers make their money go further by helping themselves to other people's – take care in dormitories. For lost credit cards, immediately call the international lost/stolen number. For lost/stolen travellers cheques, contact the cheque-issuing company immediately – find out the local lost/stolen number before you travel and keep it somewhere separate.

A good travel-insurance policy is essential (see p310) – keep the emergency contact details handy and familiarise yourself with the claims procedure. Keep photocopies of your passport, including the visa page, separately from your passport along with a copy of your airline ticket, or otherwise email scans to yourself.

PERSONAL SECURITY

The safest place for your money and your passport is next to your skin, either in a moneybelt or a secure pouch under your shirt. If you carry your money in a wallet, keep it in your front trouser pocket, never the back pocket. In dodgy-looking hotels, put your moneybelt under your pillow when you sleep.

Never leave your valuable documents and travellers cheques in your hotel room when you go out. Better hotels will have a safe for valuables, and hostels normally provide a locker where you can use your own padlock. For peace of mind, use your own padlock in hotels where doors are locked with a padlock (common in cheaper hotels). If you cannot lock your hotel room securely from the inside at night, stay somewhere else.

It is usually wise to peel off at least US$100 and store it away separately from your main stash, just in case. Also, separate big notes from small bills so you don't display large wads of cash when paying for services or checking into hotels. Credit-card purchases are usually OK at businesses with electronic-point-of-sale machines, but avoid old-fashioned paper credit-card transactions.

Touts & Commission Agents

The best way to consider the commission system is as a kind of desperation-driven advertising. As a rule, good businesses don't need to pay someone a commission to bring punters through the door. If you are steered towards a hotel or shop by a tout, the price will be raised (by as much as 50%) to pay the fixer's commission. To get around this, ask taxis or rickshaws to drop you at a landmark rather than a hotel, so you can walk in alone and pay the normal price.

Train and bus stations are often swarming with touts. If anyone asks if this is your first trip to India, this is usually a ruse to gauge your vulnerability – say you've been here several times. You'll often hear stories about hotels that refuse to pay commissions being 'full', 'under renovation' or 'closed'. Check things out yourself. Be very sceptical of phrases such as 'my brother's shop' and 'special deal at my friend's place'.

On the flip side, touts can be beneficial if you arrive in a town without a hotel reservation during peak season – they'll know which places have beds.

Transport Scams
Many private travel agencies make extra money by scamming travellers for tours and travel tickets. Make sure you are clear about what is included in the price and the class of travel (get this in writing) to avoid charges for hidden 'extras' later on. Dodgy travel agents are often found in clusters around government tourist information offices, with signs claiming that they offer 'tourist information'.

When buying a bus, train or plane ticket anywhere other than the registered office of the transport company, make certain you are getting the ticket class you paid for. Be wary of travel agents selling 'through tickets' to Nepal – everyone changes buses at the border and the second bus may not be the class you were expecting.

Trekking
Trekking off the beaten track always carries risks and India is poorly set up for independent trekkers. We strongly recommend hiring local guides and porters or joining an organised trek before heading off into potentially dangerous terrain – see p95 for more information.

DISCOUNTS
Seniors
Air India (formerly Indian Airlines), Jet Airways and some other airlines offer discounts of up to 50% on domestic air travel for foreign travellers aged 65 or over. However, promotional fares and tickets on budget airlines are often cheaper than discounted full fares. If you're over 60, you're entitled to a 30% discount on the cost of train travel. Bring your passport as proof of age.

Student & Youth Travel
Hostels run by the **Indian Youth Hostels Association** (www.yhaindia.org) are part of the HI network; an HI card sometimes entitles you to discount rates. YMCA/YWCA members also receive discounts on accommodation.

Foreigners aged 30 or under receive a discount of up to 25% on some domestic air tickets, though standard budget airline fares may still be cheaper. Students studying in India (but not students studying elsewhere) get 50% off train fares.

EMBASSIES & HIGH COMMISSIONS
Most foreign diplomatic missions are based in Delhi, but the following nations operate consulates in Kolkata (area code ☎ 033). Most open from 9am to 5pm Monday to Friday with a lunch break between 1pm and 2pm.
Bangladesh (Map pp104-5; ☎ 22905208; www.bdhc kolkata.org; 9 Circus Ave)
Myanmar (Map pp104-5; ☎ 22178273; 4th fl, Block D, White House, 119 Park St)
Nepal (Map pp104-5; ☎ 24561224; 1 National Library Ave, Alipore)
Thailand (Map pp104-5; ☎ 24407836; www.thaiemb .org.in; 18B Mandeville Gardens, Ballygunge)
UK (Map p108; ☎ 2288 5172; http://ukinindia.fco.gov.uk; 1A Ho Chi Minh Sarani)
USA (Map p108; ☎ 3984 2400; http://kolkata.usconsulate .gov; 5/1, Ho Chi Minh Sarani)

For other countries, or for more complicated consular matters, contact the following missions in Delhi (area code ☎ 011).
Australia (☎ 41399900; www.ausgovindia.com; 1/50G Shantipath, Chanakyapuri)
Bangladesh (☎ 24121394; www.bhcdelhi.org; EP39 Dr Radakrishnan Marg, Chanakyapuri)
Bhutan (☎ 26889230; Chandragupta Marg, Chanakyapuri)
Canada (☎ 41782000; www.dfait-maeci.gc.ca/new-delhi; 7/8 Shantipath, Chanakyapuri)
France (☎ 24196100; www.france-in-india.org; 2/50E Shantipath, Chanakyapuri)
Germany (☎ 26871837; www.new-delhi.diplo.de; 6/50G Shantipath, Chanakyapuri)
Israel (☎ 30414500; http://delhi.mfa.gov.il; 3 Aurangzeb Rd)
Italy (☎ 26114355; www.ambnewdelhi.esteri.it; 50E Chandragupta Marg, Chanakyapuri)
Japan (☎ 26876564; www.in.emb-japan.go.jp; 50G Shantipath, Chanakyapuri)
Malaysia (☎ 26111291; www.kln.gov.my/perwakilan /newdelhi; 50M Satya Marg, Chanakyapuri)

Maldives (☎ 41435701; www.maldiveshighcom.in/; B2 Anand Niketan)

Myanmar (☎ 24678822; 3/50F Nyaya Marg)

Nepal (☎ 23327361; Barakhamba Rd)

Netherlands (☎ 24197600; http://india.nlembassy.org/; 6/50F Shantipath, Chanakyapuri)

New Zealand (☎ 26883170; www.nzembassy.com; 50N Nyaya Marg, Chanakyapuri)

Pakistan (☎ 24676004; 2/50G Shantipath, Chanakyapuri, Delhi)

Singapore (☎ 46000915; www.mfa.gov.sg/newdelhi; E6 Chandragupta Marg)

South Africa (☎ 26149411; www.dha.gov.za; B18 Vasant Marg, Vasant Vihar)

Sri Lanka (☎ 23010201; www.newdelhi.mission.gov.lk; 27 Kautilya Marg, Chanakyapuri)

Switzerland (☎ 26878372; www.eda.admin.ch; Nyaya Marg, Chanakyapuri)

Thailand (☎ 26118104; www.thaiemb.org.in; 56N Nyaya Marg, Chanakyapuri)

UK (☎ 26872161; www.ukinindia.com; Shantipath, Chanakyapuri)

USA (☎ 24198000; http://newdelhi.usembassy.gov/; Shantipath, Chanakyapuri)

FOOD

India has turned eating into an art form. To get a taste of what's on offer, see the Food & Drink chapter (p66) and the Eating sections of regional chapters. Restaurants are generally open from early morning (or lunchtime) to late at night – see p304 and the Eating sections for more information.

GAY & LESBIAN TRAVELLERS

Technically, homosexual relationships between men are illegal in India and the penalty for transgression can be anything up to life imprisonment. In practice, gays are more vulnerable to harassment than arrest by the authorities, though Kolkata manages to maintain a low-key gay scene, with a small Rainbow Pride march in June.

Physical contact and public displays of affection are generally frowned upon, for heterosexual couples as well as gay and lesbian couples. However, men holding hands in public is generally a sign of friendship rather than sexual orientation.

See p47 for information on the campaign to legalise homosexuality in India.

Publications & Websites

The gay and lesbian magazine *Bombay Dost* is available from bookshops in more progres-

sive Indian cities. Write to 105A Veena-Beena Shopping Centre, Bandra West, Mumbai – 400050, India, for more information.

For further information about India's gay scene, point your web browser towards the following sites:

Indian Dost (www.indiandost.com/gay.php)

Humrahi (www.geocities.com/WestHollywood/Heights /7258)

Humsafar (www.humsafar.org)

Support Groups

In Kolkata the **Counsel Club** (☎ 033-23598130; counselclub93@hotmail.com; c/o Ranjan, Post Bag No 794, Kolkata 700017) provides gay, lesbian, bisexual and transgender support and arranges meetings every other Sunday – contact the club for details. The associated **Palm Avenue Integration Society** (integration99@rediffmail.com; c/o Pawan Post Bag No 10237, Kolkata 700019) offers health advice and runs a gay library service – opening times and directions by request. **Sappho** (☎ 033-24419995; www.sapphokolkata.org; Kolkata) operates as a support group for lesbian, bisexual and transgender women.

HOLIDAYS

In India there are officially three national public holidays: Republic Day (26 January), Independence Day (15 August) and Gandhi Jayanti (2 October). Every state celebrates its own official holidays, which cover bank holidays for government workers as well as major religious festivals – usually Diwali, Durga Puja/Dussehra and Holi (Hindu), Nanak Jayanti (Sikh), Eid al-Fitr (Muslim), Mahavir Jayanti (Jain), Buddha Jayanti (Buddhist), and Easter and Christmas (Christian). For more on religious festivals, see the Events Calendar p18.

Most businesses (offices, shops etc) and tourist sights close on public holidays, but transport is usually unaffected. Make transport and hotel reservations well in advance if you intend visiting during major festivals.

INSURANCE

Every traveller should take out travel insurance – if you can't afford it, you definitely can't afford the consequences if something does go wrong. Make sure that your policy covers theft of property and medical treatment, as well as air evacuation and any adventure activities you might get involved in. When hiring a motorcycle in India, make sure the rental policy includes at least third-party insurance – see p337 and be aware that you may not be covered if you do not have a full motorcycle licence.

Always read the small print of your policy. Some policies pay doctors and hospitals directly; others expect you to pay upfront and claim the money back later (keep all documentation for your claim). It is crucial to get a police report in India if you've had anything stolen, or your claim will be rejected – this can take most of a day. Also see Insurance in the Health chapter (p342).

Worldwide coverage to travellers from over 44 countries is available online at www.lonely planet.com/travel_services.

INTERNET ACCESS

Internet cafes are widespread in the northeast, but away from the cities, connection speeds plummet. Internet costs vary regionally but most places charge between Rs20 and Rs65 per hour, usually with a 15-minute minimum.

It's a good idea to write and save your messages in a text application before pasting them into your browser in case of power cuts. Be wary of sending sensitive financial information from internet cafes because of the risk of identity theft. Using online banking on any nonsecure system is a definite no-no.

If you're travelling with a laptop, most internet cafes can supply you with internet access over a LAN Ethernet cable, and wi-fi access (🛜) is available in upscale hotels and chain coffeeshops. Alternatively, you can take out an account with a local ISP. Major ISPs in India include **Sify** (http://broadband.sify.com), **BSNL** (www.bsnl.co.in) and **VSNL/Tata Indicom** (www.vsnl .in). Make sure your modem is compatible with the telephone and dial-up system in India. For more information on travelling with a portable computer, see www.teleadapt.com.

Hotels offering internet access to guests are marked with the internet icon – 🖳 . See also p17 for useful India websites.

LAUNDRY

Almost all hotels offer a same- or next-day laundry service, and private laundries are plentiful in tourist areas. Most employ the services of dhobi-wallahs – washermen and women who will diligently bash your wet clothes against rocks and scrubbing boards, returning them slightly more worn but spotlessly clean and ironed. If you get a chance to observe the wallahs at work on the local dhobi ghat, it's quite a spectacle.

Most laundries and hotels charge per item (you'll be required to submit a list with your dirty clothes) or by dry weight. Hand clothes in before 9am if you want them back the same day. It can take longer to dry clothes during the humid monsoon. Note that many hotels ban washing clothes in their rooms.

LEGAL MATTERS

If you're in a sticky legal situation, immediately contact your embassy (see p309). However, be aware that all your embassy may be able to do is monitor your treatment in custody and arrange a lawyer.

You should carry your passport with you at all times – police are entitled to ask you for identification in all sorts of situations. Corruption is rife, so the less you have to do with local police the better (unless getting a written police report for your insurance in the event of theft).

If you are hauled up for an alleged offence and asked for a bribe, the prevailing wisdom is to pay it, as the alternative can be a trumped-up prosecution. The problem is knowing how much to pay – it's always better to avoid potentially risky situations in the first place.

YOUR OWN EMBASSY

It's important to realise what your own embassy – the embassy of the country of which you are a citizen – can and can't do to help you if you get into trouble.

Generally speaking, it won't be much help in emergencies if the trouble you're in is remotely your own fault. Remember that you are bound by the laws of India. Your embassy will not be sympathetic if you end up in jail after committing a crime locally, even if such actions are legal in your own country.

In genuine emergencies you might get some assistance, but only if other channels have been exhausted. Do not expect handouts. New passports can be issued, but a loan for travel home is exceedingly unlikely – the embassy would expect you to have insurance.

Anti-Social Behaviour

Smoking in public has been illegal in Sikkim since 1997 and smoking in public was banned across India in October 2008 – though you wouldn't know this from the number of people still smoking in public places, apart from venues with dedicated smoking rooms. A number of cities have also banned spitting and littering. The punishment for breaking these rules is a stiff (for locals) fine of at least Rs100. This is variably enforced, but the police do have the power, so heed the street signs.

Drugs

India was the focal point of the hippy overland trail for a reason – easily available recreational drugs – and these are just as prevalent today. We won't tell you not to take drugs, but be aware that possession of any illegal drug is treated as a serious criminal offence. If convicted, the *minimum* sentence is 10 years, with no chance of remission or parole, plus a hefty fine. The police have been getting particularly tough on foreigners who use drugs, so you should take this risk very seriously.

Marijuana grows wild throughout India, but picking and smoking it is still an offence. Bhang (cannabis) is sold by government-licensed shops in Puri for religious rituals, but foreigners are still liable to prosecution if caught carrying the drug. Be very cautious of pills sold in India – that tablet of 'ecstasy' could be anything from livestock tranquilliser to methamphetamine and baking soda.

MAPS

Maps available inside India are very variable, but you can find sheets published by TTK Discover India at bookshops all over the country. You can also find the following map series at good bookshops or online at the **India Map Store** (www.indiamapstore.com).

Eicher (maps.eicherworld.com) For street atlases and city maps.

Nelles (www.nelles-verlag.de) Produces a good map covering the northeast and Bangladesh (1:1.5 million).

Nest & Wings (www.nestwings.com) Publishes an extensive range of local maps and guidebooks.

Survey of India (www.surveyofindia.gov.in) Kolkata-based organisation publishing city, state and country maps, but some titles are restricted for security reasons.

MONEY

The Indian rupee (Rs) is divided into 100 paise (p), but the only time you'll see paise coins these days is at temples, where they are handed out as alms for the poor. Coins come in denominations of 5, 10, 20, 25 and 50 paise and Rs, 2 and 5 rupees; notes come in 10, 20, 50, 100, 500 and 1000 rupees (this last bill can be hard to change outside banks). Note that it can be impossible to exchange Indian Rs500 and Rs1000 notes in Nepal. The rupee is linked to a basket of currencies and its value is generally stable – see the inside front cover for the latest exchange rates.

Remember, you must present your passport whenever changing currency and travellers cheques. Commission for foreign exchange is becoming increasingly rare – if it is charged, the fee is nominal. For information about costs, read p15.

See the Theft & Druggings heading under Dangers & Annoyances (p308) for tips on keeping your money safe.

ATMs

Modern 24-hour ATMs linked to international networks are found in many large towns and cities. However, ATMs are often out of order or knocked off-line by power cuts, so always carry cash or travellers cheques as backup. The most commonly accepted cards are Visa, MasterCard, Cirrus, Maestro and Plus.

Banks impose higher charges on international ATM transactions, but this may be offset by the favourable exchange rates between banks. Always check in advance whether your card can access banking networks in India and let your bank know your travel dates or they may block your card (if this happens, you must call the bank and answer a series of security questions to unlock it). Indian ATMs take a long time to deliver the money and may snatch it back if you don't remove it quickly. If your card gets eaten by an ATM, contact bank staff immediately.

The ATMs listed in this book's regional chapters accept foreign cards (but not necessarily all types of cards). Always keep the emergency lost and stolen numbers for your credit cards in a safe place, and report any loss or theft immediately.

Black Market

Legal moneychangers are so common that there's no reason to use black-market moneychangers, except to change small amounts of cash at land border crossings. If someone comes up to you in the street and offers to change money, you're probably being set up for a scam.

Cash

The major currencies such as US dollars, UK pounds and euros are easy to change throughout the northeast, though some bank branches insist on travellers cheques only. A few banks also accept Australian, New Zealand and Canadian dollars and Swiss francs. Private moneychangers accept a wider range of currencies, but Pakistani, Nepali and Bangladeshi currency can be harder to change away from the border. When travelling off the beaten track, always carry a decent stock of rupees. Note that Indian rupees can be used as cash in many parts of Nepal at a fixed rate of 1.6 Nepali rupees (NRs) to one Indian rupee.

Some banks still staple bills together into bricks, which puts a lot of wear and tear on the currency. Do not accept any filthy, ripped or disintegrating notes, as these may not be accepted as payment. If you get lumbered with wrecked bills, you can change them to crisp new notes at branches of the Reserve Bank of India. Nobody in India ever seems to have change, so it's a good idea to maintain a constant stock of smaller currency – try to stockpile Rs10, Rs20 and Rs50 notes.

Officially, you cannot take rupees out of the country, but this is laxly enforced. However, you can change any leftover rupees back into foreign currency, most easily at the airport (some banks have a Rs1000 minimum). You may require encashment certificates (see below) or a credit card receipt and you may also have to show your passport and airline ticket.

Credit Cards

Credit cards are accepted at a growing number of shops, upmarket restaurants and mid-range and top-end hotels, and you can also use them to pay for flights and train tickets. However, be wary of credit-card fraud – see p308. MasterCard and Visa are the most widely accepted cards, and many banks offer cash advances on major credit cards over the counter. Tell the bank you are travelling to India before you leave home or your card may be 'locked'.

Encashment Certificates

For every foreign-exchange transaction, you will receive an encashment certificate, which will allow you to re-exchange anything up to this amount rupees into foreign currency when departing from India (see left). Printed receipts from ATMs may also be accepted as evidence.

Traditionally, money-exchange receipts have also been required when paying for tourist quota train tickets in rupees, but this requirement has been relaxed at most booking offices.

International Transfers

If you run out of money, someone at home can wire you money via moneychangers affiliated with **Moneygram** (www.moneygram.com) or **Western Union** (www.westernunion.com). To collect cash, bring your passport and the name and reference number of the person who sent the funds.

Moneychangers

Private moneychangers are open for longer hours than banks, and they are found almost everywhere. Many will exchange cash and cheques without a commission. Compare rates with those at the bank, and check you are given the correct amount. In a scrape, some upmarket hotels may also change money, usually at a diabolical rate.

Tipping, Baksheesh & Bargaining

Tipping is a way of life in India: as well as obligatory service charges at tourist-oriented restaurants and hotels, you may be asked for 'baksheesh' from anyone who does anything which might even vaguely be defined as a service, be it carrying your luggage or pointing out that the temple you were already walking towards is across the road!

Hotel bellboys expect around Rs20 to carry bags and bring up room service. It's not mandatory to tip taxi or rickshaw drivers, but we encourage tipping drivers who are honest about the fare to encourage good behaviour. Giving tips that haven't been earned will only ensure that future travellers are hit with the same requests.

Baksheesh is also the term for the alms given out to the poor and needy. India has a long history of giving alms to the needy and beggars deliberately target foreigners in many Indian cities. Whether you give or not is up to you, but try to treat people compassionately and consider what you might do if the positions were reversed.

DIRECTORY

Many Indians implore tourists not to hand out sweets, pens or money to children, as it is positive reinforcement to beg. To make a lasting difference, donate to a school or charitable organisation (see Volunteering, p323). Always make the donation to an adult, preferably someone in a position of authority, and think about what you are giving – toothbrushes and toothpaste are a lot more useful to children than caries-inducing sweets.

Apart from at fixed-price shops, bargaining is the norm – see the boxed text, p318.

Travellers Cheques

All major brands are accepted in India, but some banks may only accept cheques from American Express (Amex) and Thomas Cook. Pounds sterling and US dollars are the safest currencies. Charges for changing travellers cheques vary from town to town and bank to bank.

Always keep an emergency cash stash in case you lose your travellers cheques, and keep a record of the cheques' serial numbers separate from your cheques, along with the proof of purchase slips. If you are separated from your cheques, contact the emergency lost/stolen cheques number for the issuing company – see p308. Remember to get a police report as part of your claim.

PHOTOGRAPHY

For useful tips and techniques on travel photography, read Lonely Planet's *Guide to Travel Photography*, *Travel Photography: Landscapes* and *Travel Photography: People & Portraits*. Overexposure can be a problem in the mountains because of the bright light – a polarising filter can cut through the haze but it will darken the skies. Many pro snappers use a neutral density graduated filter to reduce the difference in exposure between the mountains and foreground and a warming filter to remove the blue cast created by the snow.

Digital

Memory cards for digital cameras are available from photographic shops in most large cities. However, memory cards sold in India are not always reliable. Cards can be purchased so cheaply online that it is worth stocking up before you leave home. To be safe, regularly back up your memory card to CD – internet cafes offer this service for Rs50 to Rs100 per disk. Some photographic

shops make prints from digital photographs for roughly the standard print and processing charge.

Print & Slide

Colour print film-processing facilities are available almost everywhere. Film is relatively cheap and the quality is usually good, but you'll only find colour slide film in major cities. Print and processing costs around Rs5 per 10cm by 15cm colour print plus Rs20 for processing. Passport photos are available from photo shops for around Rs100 to Rs125 (for four to 10 shots). Always check the expiry date on local film and slide stock, make sure you get a sealed packet. Avoid film that has been stored in direct sunlight – better shops will refrigerate their film.

Restrictions

The Indian authorities get twitchy about anyone taking photographs of strategically significant sites – including military posts, train stations, bridges, airports and border crossings. On flights to border regions, cameras may be banned from the cabin (or you may need to remove the batteries).

Many places of worship – monasteries, temples and mosques – also prohibit photography. Respect these proscriptions and always ask when in doubt to avoid causing offence. See p45 for etiquette about photographing people.

POST

India has the biggest postal network on earth, with more than 155,600 post offices, and amazingly almost every letter and parcel makes it to its intended destination. When sending things overseas, airmail is faster and more reliable than seamail, although it's best to use reputable international courier services (such as DHL) to send and receive items of value – expect to pay around Rs3000 per kilo to Europe, Australia or the USA.

Receiving Mail

To receive mail in India, ask senders to address letters to you with your surname in capital letters and underlined, followed by: poste restante, GPO (main post office) and the city or town in question. When picking up mail, check under both your names. Letters sent via poste restante are generally held for around one month before being returned. To claim mail, you'll need to show your passport. It's best to have any parcels sent to you by registered post so they don't vanish from the general pile.

Sending Mail

Mailing postcards/aerogrammes anywhere overseas costs Rs20/15 and airmail letters cost from Rs12 (1g to 20g). Sending a letter by registered post adds Rs15 to the stamp cost.

Posting parcels is quite straightforward; prices vary depending on weight and you have a choice of airmail (delivery in one to three weeks), seamail (two to four months) or Surface Air-Lifted (SAL; a curious hybrid system where parcels travel by air and sea; one month). Parcels must be packed up in white linen and the seams sealed with wax. Local tailors offer this service, or there may be a parcel service at the post office.

Carry a permanent marker to write the address and any information requested by the desk onto the package. Customs declaration forms must be filled out and stitched or pasted to the parcel. If the contents are a gift under the value of Rs1000, you won't have to pay duty at the delivery end. Never try to send drugs by post – the police will track the package to its destination with handcuffs at the ready.

Parcel post has a maximum of 20kg to 30kg depending on the destination, and charges vary depending on whether you go by air or sea. A small package costs Rs40 (up to 100g) to any country and Rs30 per additional 100g (up to a maximum of 2kg; different charges apply for higher weights). You also have the option of the express mail service (EMS; delivery within three days) for around 30% more than the normal airmail price.

Books or printed matter can go by inexpensive international book post for Rs350 (maximum 5kg), but the package must be wrapped with a hole that reveals the contents for inspection by customs – tailors are experienced in creating this viewing porthole. The website for **India Post** (www.indiapost.gov.in) has an online calculator for assorted domestic and international postal tariffs.

Be cautious with places that offer to mail things to your home address after you have bought them. Government emporia are usually fine, but for most other places it pays to do the posting yourself.

SHOPPING

Shopaholics beware – India is an Aladdin's cave of delights, with markets and shops dripping with precious metals, gemstones, silks, pearls, carpets and statues of Indian gods. Every region has its own special crafts – usually showcased in local state emporia and cottage-industry cooperatives. These shops normally charge very fair fixed prices; everywhere else, you'll have to bargain – see the boxed text, p318. Opening hours for shops vary – exceptions to standard hours are provided in the Shopping sections of the regional chapters.

Be suspicious of friendly seeming locals who offer to lead you to shops with 'special sales' – see the Dangers & Annoyances section (p308). Also see the warning on exporting antiques (p319).

Buddhist Paraphernalia

In Buddhist areas, including Sikkim, western Arunachal Pradesh and the West Bengal Hills, keep an eye out for 'Buddha shops', which sell all sorts of ceremonial objects used in

---

ETHICAL SHOPPING

Only a small proportion of the money brought to India by tourism reaches people in rural areas. You can make a greater contribution by shopping at community cooperatives, set up to protect and promote traditional cottage industries and provide education, training and a sustainable livelihood for rural families. Many of these projects focus on refugees, low-caste women, the disabled and other socially disadvantaged groups.

Prices are usually fixed and a share of the money goes directly into social projects, such as schools, health care and training. Shopping at the national network of emporia run by state governments or the **Khadi & Village Industries Commission** (www.kvic.org.in) will also contribute to rural communities. There are a number of community shops and cooperatives run by Tibetan refugees in Darjeeling (p164) and Sikkim (p181). Other recommended shops are listed in the Shopping sections throughout the regional chapters of this book.

DIRECTORY

CARPETS & CHILD LABOUR

There are thought to be at least 30,000 child carpet weavers in India, and 10% of these children are believed to have been trafficked from neighbouring countries. Unfortunately, the issue is more complicated than it first appears. In many areas, education is often not an option, for both economic and cultural reasons, and the alternative to child labour may not be school but hunger for the whole family.

The **Carpet Export Promotion Council of India** (www.india-carpets.com) is campaigning to eliminate child labour from the carpet industry by penalising factories that use children, and by founding schools to provide an alternative to carpet making. Ultimately, the only thing that will stop child labour completely is compulsory education, but the economic and social obstacles are significant.

We encourage travellers to buy from carpet-weaving cooperatives that employ adult weavers and provide education for their children, breaking the cycle of child labour. The carpets produced by Tibetan refugee organisations are almost always made by adults, while government emporia and charitable cooperatives are also reputable.

Buddhist rituals. Rolls of prayer flags, strings of prayer beads and small brass butter lamps make inexpensive and lightweight souvenirs. Also look out for pendants, rings and bangles embossed with the famous Buddhist mantra 'Om Mani Padme Hum' (Hail to the Jewel in the Lotus).

Many shops also sell drums, horns, cymbals, metal bells, *dorje* (celestial thunderbolts) and singing bowls, which emit a high-pitched ring when a wooden stick is stroked along the rim. Bronze statues of Buddha and the Tantric gods are made using the lost-wax technique and finished off with gilded and painted faces. The ancient art of repoussé work, where designs are hammered into a piece of metal from the inside, is used to make all sorts of Buddhist ceremonial objects. Also look out for prayer wheels, document cases and ceremonial horns made from brass or copper inlaid with silver and other metals.

Another unique Buddhist art form is the production of *thangkas* – ornate Tibetan cloth paintings of Tantric Buddhist deities and ceremonial mandalas. The selling of antique *thangkas* is illegal and you would be unlikely to find the real thing anyway. If you get caught with old *thangkas* at Indian customs, they will be confiscated. Tibetan refugees also produce handmade paper and woollen hats, gloves and scarves, sold in shops across West Bengal and Sikkim.

Carpets

Carpet making is a living craft in India, with workshops across the country producing fine wool and silk work in traditional and modern designs. In the northeast, Tibetan carpets predominate – most are produced by cooperative carpet workshops run by Tibetan refugees. You can also find shops selling Iranian-style carpets and rustic folk rugs from Kashmir and reproductions of tribal Turkmen and Afghan designs from Uttar Pradesh. Be warned – 'antique' carpets are rarely much older than last Friday.

The price of a carpet will be determined by the number and the size of the hand-tied knots, the range of dyes and colours, the intricacy of the design and the material. Silk carpets cost more and look more luxurious but wool carpets last longer. A 90cm by 1.5m Tibetan carpet in wool will cost around US$100; Kashmiri designs in silk can cost ten times as much.

Many people buy carpets under the mistaken belief that they can be sold for a profit back home. Unless you really know your carpets and the carpet market in your home country, buy a carpet because you love it. Many places can ship carpets home for a fee – though it may be safest to ship things independently to avoid scams.

If you can't stretch to a woven carpet, look out for coarse felt *numdas* (or *nandas*) embroidered with rustic designs in coloured wool, flat-weave *dhurries* (kilimlike cotton rugs) and striking *gabbas* (Kashmiri rugs) made from chain-stitched wool or silk.

Jewellery

Bangle shops abound in the northeast, selling an extraordinary variety of bangles at minimal prices (as little as Rs20 for a set of 12), made from plastic, glass, brass, bone, shell and wood. Traditionally, these are worn continuously until they break – Hindu widows break all their bangles as part of the mourning process. Most bangle shops also sell packs of stick-on bindi (the forehead mark worn by Hindu women).

Jewellery shops in big cities and tourist areas carry stock from all over India, including glittery Mughal-style necklaces and chunky Tibetan jewellery made from silver (or white metal) and semiprecious stones, which has a definite folksy appeal. Real antiques are rare, so buy something because you like it, not for its antique value.

Gemstones from Rajasthan and the western deserts are sold all over India, either set into jewellery or loose as cut stones and carvings. However, be wary of gem scams (see Scams, p307). Gold and silver jewellery is widely available, though the metal may not be the highest grade. Cuttack in Orissa (p275) is famed for its lacelike silver-filigree work known as *tarakasi*.

Pearls are produced by most seaside states and sold at bargain prices at government emporia in Kolkata and other state capitals. Prices vary depending on the colour and shape – you pay more for pure white pearls or rare colours such as black and red.

Leatherwork

As the cow is sacred in India, leatherwork is made from buffalo hide, camel, goat or some other substitute. Shops and markets in Kolkata and Guwahati are full of well-made, moderately priced leather handbags, belts and other leather accessories.

Chappals (leather sandals) are a particularly popular buy. Look out for jootis (traditional pointed shoes with curling toes) from Punjab and Rajasthan – buy a pair, if only as part of your genie costume for fancy-dress parties. Most big cities offer striking modern women's footwear and handbags at very competitive prices, often stitched with thousands of sequins.

Metalwork

In Sikkim, West Bengal and many other parts of India, small images of deities are created by the age-old lost-wax process. A model is sculpted from wax and covered in plaster to create a mould – when molten metal is poured in, the wax melts away. The plaster is then chipped off to reveal the metal sculpture inside. The West Bengalese employ the lost-wax process to make Dokra Adivasi bell sculptures.

You'll find copper and brassware throughout the northeast. No Assamese home would be complete without a *bota* – a brass platter on a stand with a dome-shaped cover known as a *xorai* – used to serve betel nut and paan to guests. These items are sold all over Assam; prices vary depending on the size and detail of the engraving.

In all Indian towns, you can find beaten brass pots, iron *kadai* (Indian woks, also known as *balti*) and shiny steel thali plates and other items of cookware for incredibly low prices.

Musical Instruments

Quality Indian musical instruments are available in larger cities in the northeast, especially along Rabindra Sarani in Kolkata (p131). Prices vary, but the higher the price the better the quality – and sound – of the instrument.

Decent quality tabla sets, with a wooden tabla (tuned treble drum) and metal *doogri* (bass tone drum), cost upwards of Rs3000. Sitars range from Rs4000 to Rs15,000 – a good starter sitar with quality-inlay work will cost upwards of Rs7000. Every sitar sounds different so try a few – make sure the strings ring clearly and check the gourd carefully for damage. Spare string sets, sitar plectrums and a second screw-in 'amplifier' gourd are useful additions.

Paintings

Reproductions of Indian Mughal miniature paintings, some featuring erotic scenes, are widely available, but quality varies – try the state emporia, particularly in Kolkata (p130). Beware of paintings purported to be antique – it's highly unlikely and export of antique paintings is banned.

The artists' community of Raghurajpur (p264) near Puri (Orissa) preserves the age-old art of *patachitra* painting. Cotton or *tassar* silk cloth is painted with images of deities and scenes from Hindu legends, using exceedingly fine brushes. Orissa also produces *chitra pothi*, where dried palm-leaf sections are etched with a fine stylus.

Throughout the country (especially in capital cities) look out for shops and galleries selling brilliant contemporary paintings by local artists. Cheaper options are the fabulously colourful posters of religious deities and folk heroes, sold in every street market. Also keep an eye out for vendors selling colourful religious stickers – kids love 'em.

Shawls, Silk & Saris

Warm and lightweight Indian shawls are sold everywhere. Cheaper shawls are made from lamb's wool, while more expensive shawls are made from sublimely soft *pashmina* goat and angora rabbit hair – expect to pay upwards of Rs200 for a wool shawl and Rs7000 for a genuine *pashmina*. Do not buy shahtoosh shawls as rare Tibetan antelopes are killed to provide the wool. Shawls from the Northeast States feature bold geometric designs that are specific to individual Adivasi groups. In Sikkim and West Bengal, you can also find intricately embroidered Bhutanese shawls.

Saris are a very popular souvenir, and they can be readily adapted to other purposes. Silk saris are the most expensive, and the silk usually needs to be washed before it becomes soft. Assam is renowned for its *muga, endi* and *pat* silks (produced by different species of silkworms), which are widely available in Guwahati (p207).

For sophisticated designer saris, your best bet is Kolkata – shops there sell extravagant silk and cotton saris from all over India, often embroidered with silver and gold thread and sequins. Look out for *baluchari* saris from Bishnapur in West Bengal, made using a traditional form of weaving with untwisted silk thread.

Statues & Stone-Carving

Kolkata produces some attractive terracotta work, including some fine images of deities and animal toys for children. At temple bazaars across the region you can buy small clay or plaster effigies of Kali, Durga and other deities, though these are tricky to transport. Stone carvings of gods are produced all over India and prices vary depending on the quality of carving and the material – easy-to-carve soapstone is cheaper than granite or marble.

Many souvenir shops sell ornaments made using pietra dura – the ancient Mughal art of inlaying marble with semiprecious stones. The reproduction models of the Taj Mahal are bit tacky but jewellery boxes, trays, vases and chess sets are more appealing.

Textiles

Textile production is India's major industry. Around 40% of textile output is *khadi* (homespun cloth) – hence the government-backed *khadi* emporia around the country. These inexpensive superstores sell all sorts of items made from village cloth, including the popular 'Nehru jackets' (a collarless jacket, modelled on the Indian sherwani) and kurta pyjamas (a long shirt with loose-fitting cotton trousers), and you'll have the satisfaction of knowing your purchases are supporting rural communities.

You will find a truly amazing variety of weaving and embroidery techniques in India. Indian textiles are stitched into handbags, wall hangings, cushion covers, bedspreads, clothes

---

THE ART OF HAGGLING

If you've seen Monty Python's *Life of Brian*, you'll have a pretty good idea of how to go about haggling in India. Prices are fixed at government emporia, department stores and modern shopping centres but everywhere else, you need to bargain. Foreigners are perceived to be wealthy, so souvenir shops are probably the least likely places of all to charge you a fair price.

The first 'rule' to haggling is never to show too much interest in the item you want to buy. Decide how much you would be happy paying and then express a casual interest. If you have absolutely no idea of what something should really cost, start by slashing the price by half. The vendor will make a show of being shocked at such a low offer, but the game is set and you can now work up and down respectively in small increments until you reach a mutually agreeable price. You'll find that many shopkeepers lower their so-called 'final price' if you head out of the shop saying you'll 'think about it'.

Haggling is a way of life in India, but it should never be an angry process. Locals treat it like a game and so should you. Keep in mind exactly how much a rupee is worth in your home currency to put things in perspective. If a vendor seems to be charging an unreasonably high price, simply look elsewhere or find something cheaper.

PROHIBITED EXPORTS

To protect India's cultural heritage, the export of many objects over 100 years old is prohibited. Reputable antique dealers know the laws and can make arrangements for an export clearance certificate for ancient items that you are permitted to export. If in doubt, contact the **Archaeological Survey of India** (☎ 011-23010822; www.asi.nic.in; Janpath; 🕑 9.30am-1pm & 2-6pm Mon-Fri) in Delhi. Quality reproductions of antiques are widely available, and buying these will help protect India's artistic legacy for future generations.

To protect endangered and threatened species, the Indian Wildlife Protection Act bans any form of wildlife trade. Resist the urge to buy anything made from horns, fur, shell or bone – the trade in animal parts is driving many species towards extinction.

---

and more. Every village in India has at least one tailor shop and most will take on bespoke tailoring projects, so you can buy fabric at the market and have a suit, shirt or dress made to measure.

Orissa is a major centre for the production of appliqué work and *ikat* (a Southeast Asian technique where thread is tie-dyed before weaving). You can see *ikat* being produced at Baripalli near Sambalpur (p273). The town of Pipli (p258) also produces eye-catching appliqué work. Women in West Bengal use the chain-stitching technique to make complex figurative designs called *kantha*.

Batik can be found throughout India. It is often used for saris and *salwar kameez* (a long dresslike tunic worn over trousers with a dupatta scarf). City boutiques produce trendy *salwar kameez* for women and the similar kurta Punjabi for men in a staggering array of fabrics and styles. Check out branches of **Fab India** (www.fabindia.com) for gorgeous designs made from traditional block-printed fabric.

Big Indian cities such as Kolkata are great places to pick up haute couture by talented Indian designers such as Narendra Kumar and Tarun Tahiliani. Western brand names at Indian prices are becoming increasingly common in the flashy shopping malls of Kolkata (p130).

Woodcarving

Woodcarving is a living art in India. Sandalwood carvings of Hindu deities are sold all over the country. You'll pay a king's ransom for the real thing – a 10cm-high Ganesh costs around Rs3000 in sandalwood, compared with Rs300 in *kadamb* wood – but it will release fragrance for years. Wood-inlay work from Bihar is also sold widely in the northeast, used in wooden wall hangings, tabletops, trays and boxes. Many shops also sell carved walnut-wood boxes from Kashmir.

The carved wooden massage wheels and rollers available at many Hindu pilgrimage sites are also good presents. In many towns, you can find printing blocks carved from teak wood – used to create traditional block-printed fabrics, but attractive in their own right. In Sikkim and other Buddhist areas, look out for traditional tongba pots (wooden tankards bound with metal, used to serve warm millet beer), carved wooden wall plaques featuring the Buddhist eight lucky signs, *choktse* (low Tibetan tables) and *chaam* masks, used for ritual dances.

Other Buys

Markets across the northeast sell all of the spices that go into garam masala (the 'hot mix' used to flavour Indian curries). Look out for vendors in the hills in Sikkim and Meghalaya selling big bags of black cardamoms and local cinnamon.

Attar (essential oil) shops can be found in many large cities, selling sandalwood oil and traditional fragrances prepared using aromatic oils from herbs, flowers and eucalyptus. Indian incense is exported worldwide and available across the northeast, though most brands are actually manufactured in south India.

Sikkim has a special license from the government to produce liquor and the Sikkimese spirits are highly respected. Many come in funky-shaped bottles – the 1L bottle of Old Monk rum comes in a monk-shaped bottle with a screw-off head.

Quality Indian tea is widely sold in Darjeeling and Kalimpong, Assam and Sikkim. The finest teas of all are the 'first flush' Golden Flowery Orange Pekoe teas from Darjeeling. You'll pay around Rs1000 for 100g of a top-quality brew.

In most traveller centres, you'll find traditional clay chillums and hookah pipes for smoking bhang. Drug paraphernalia is not illegal by itself but *used* paraphernalia can land you in a lot of trouble with customs when you get back home.

The Northeast States are noted for their lovely handwoven baskets and wickerware – each Adivasi group has its own unique basket shape. Basketware is also woven into furniture, lampshades, placemats and ornaments. Adivasi hats are a popular buy in the northeast – miniature *jaapi* (Assamese sun hats stitched with sequins) make great Christmas decorations.

The Adivasi of Meghalaya make bone-handled pocket knives and bamboo bows and arrows, easily purchased in Shillong (p240), but see the boxed text on p319 for ethical considerations.

Most souvenir shops and many state emporia sell lacquered papier-mâché from Kashmir in the form of bowls, boxes, letter holders, coasters, trays, lamps and Christmas decorations. Weight for weight, these are probably the most cost-effective souvenirs in India, but you need to transport them carefully.

You can find a phenomenal range of Indian books in Kolkata and other big cities – see the Bookshops sections of individual regional chapters. CDs by local musicians are good value.

SOLO TRAVELLERS

Traveller hubs such as Kolkata and Darjeeling in West Bengal and Gangtok and Pelling in Sikkim are good places for solo travellers to network. Traveller hotels and restaurants are good places to swap stories and find people to travel with. You might also try advertising for travel companions on the **Lonely Planet Thorn Tree** (www.thorntree.lonelyplanet.com). Throughout India, people tend to move in the same direction, so you'll probably see the same faces over and over again. Note that you need to be in a group of four or more to obtain permits for a number of the Northeast States.

Perhaps the most significant issue facing solo travellers is cost. Single-room rates at guesthouses and hotels are sometimes not much lower than double rates; some midrange and top-end places don't even offer a single tariff. However, it's always worth trying to negotiate a lower rate for single occupancy.

In terms of transport, you'll save money if you find others to share taxis and auto-rickshaws. This is also advisable if you intend

hiring a car with driver. For important information specific to women, see p324.

TELEPHONE

There are few payphones in the northeast, but private PCO/STD/ISD call centres do the same job, offering inexpensive local, interstate and international calls at much lower prices than calls made from hotel rooms. A digital meter displays how much the call is costing and provides a printed receipt when the call is finished. Faxes can be sent from some call centres or from the local telephone exchange or 'BSNL Customer Service Centre'.

Call centres charge the full rate from around 9am to 8pm. After 8pm the cost falls – the cheapest time to call is 11pm to 6am. Interstate calls are half-rate on Sunday. Direct international calls from call centres start from around Rs25 per minute depending on the country you are calling. Hotels charge much more all the time. Cheaper international calls can be made through internet cafes using Skype and other net-phone services.

Some places also offer a call-back service – you ring home, provide the phone number of the booth and wait for people at home to call you back – for a fee of around Rs10 on top of the cost of the preliminary call.

Note that getting a line can be difficult in remote country and mountain areas – an engaged signal may just mean that the exchange is overloaded, so keep trying. Be patient when making calls in India – phones are often answered by domestic staff, who may hang up if they do not understand what you are saying.

Useful online resources include the **Yellow Pages** (www.indiayellowpages.com), **Justdial** (www.justdial.com) and the **BSNL phone directory** (www.bsnl.co.in/onlinedirectory.htm).

Mobile Phones

Mobile-phone numbers in India usually have 10 digits, typically starting with '9'. There is roaming coverage for international GSM phones in Kolkata and other large towns and cities, but anywhere else, it makes sense to invest in a local phone (or a local SIM card).

Mobiles bought in Western countries are often locked to a particular network; you'll have to get the phone unlocked, or buy a local phone (available from Rs2300) to use an Indian SIM card. In most towns you simply buy a prepaid mobile-phone kit (SIM card and phone number, plus a starter allocation of calls) for around Rs150 from a phone shop or local PCO/STD/ISD booths. Thereafter, you must purchase new credits, sold as scratch cards in the same shops and call centres. Credit must usually be used within a set time limit.

Calls made within the state/city in which you bought the SIM card are cheap – less than Rs1 per minute – and you can call internationally for less than Rs25 per minute. SMS messaging is even cheaper. However, some travellers have reported unreliable signals and problems with international texting.

The most popular (and reliable) companies are Airtel, Hutch (Orange in some states), Idea and BSNL. Note that most SIM cards are state specific – they can be used in other states, but you pay for calls at roaming rates and you will be charged for incoming calls as well as outgoing calls.

Phone Codes

Regular phone numbers have an area code followed by up to eight digits. The government is slowly trying to bring all numbers in India onto the same system, so area codes can change and new digits may be added to numbers at short notice – check locally.

To make a call to India from overseas, dial the international access code of the country you're in, then ☎ 91 (international country code for India), then the area code (drop the initial zero when calling from abroad), then the local number. See this book's regional chapters for area codes.

To make an international call from India, dial ☎ 00 (international access code from India), then the country code (of the country you are calling), then the area code and the local number.

The Home Country Direct service gives you access to the international operator in your home country for the price of a local call. The number is typically constructed ☎ 000 plus the country code of your home country plus 17.

When making calls to local numbers, the person picking up may insist on knowing where you're calling from ('what is your station'). This dates back to operator-assisted dialling but the conversation will rarely proceed until this information has been imparted.

TIME

Indian Standard Time is 5½ hours ahead of GMT/UTC, 4½ hours behind Australian Eastern Standard Time (EST) and 10½ hours ahead of American EST. The floating half-hour was added to maximise daylight hours over such a vast country. Neighbouring countries have done the same thing, so India is 15 minutes behind Nepal and 30 minutes behind Bangladesh and Bhutan.

TOILETS

The cleanest toilets are at restaurants and fast-food chains, museums, upmarket shopping complexes and cinemas, but toilet paper is rarely provided – see the boxed text, p303, for more on Indian toilets. Many towns also have public urinals and squat toilets (an entry fee of Rs1 to Rs2 applies), but they can be unspeakable.

When it comes to effluent etiquette, locals prefer the 'hand and water' technique, which involves cleaning your bottom with a small jug of water and your left hand. It can feel a little intimate at first, but you get used to it (carry some soap or hand gel for hand washing). Alternatively, toilet paper is available from local grocery stores in cities and towns. Used paper (as well as sanitary napkins and tampons) goes in the rubbish bin beside the toilet, not into the easily-blocked drains.

TOURIST INFORMATION

In addition to the excellent national (Government of India) tourist offices, each state maintains its own network of tourist offices. Most have brochures and maps of varying quality, but some seem to exist solely to sell government-operated tours and excursions.

The first stop should be the tourism website of the **Government of India** (www.incredibleindia.org), with information in English, French, Hindi, Japanese and Chinese. For international and regional offices, click the 'Held Desk' bar; for details of state tourism offices, click on 'Links' at the bottom of the homepage.

You can also find useful information on the official state-government websites – there's a list at http://districts.nic.in. Local travel agents can be a useful source of information in the Northeast States – see the Information sections of this book's regional chapters.

TRAVEL PERMITS

Access to certain parts of India – particularly disputed border areas – is controlled by a complicated permit system that has been in place since British times. A permit known as an inner line permit (ILP) is required to visit northern parts of Sikkim along the disputed border with China/Tibet. Obtaining the ILP is a formality, but travel agents must apply on your behalf for certain areas, including many trekking routes. ILPs are issued by regional magistrates and district commissioners, either directly to travellers (for free) or through travel agents (for a fee). See the Sikkim chapter (p175) for more information.

Entering the Northeast States of Arunachal Pradesh, Nagaland, Manipur and Mizoram is much more complicated. Indians can visit with an ILP, but foreign tourists require a Restricted Area Permit (RAP), which must be arranged through approved Foreigners' Regional Registration Offices (FRRO) and the Ministry of Home Affairs in Delhi – without exception, your best chance of gaining a permit is to join an organised tour and let the travel agent make all the arrangements. See the Northeast States chapter for advice on applying for permits and the rules for each state (p199).

It's not a bad idea to double check with tourism officials to see if permit requirements have undergone any recent changes before you head out to these areas.

TRAVELLERS WITH DISABILITIES

If you have a physical disability or you are vision impaired, the crowded public transport, crush of humanity and variable infrastructure in India can be challenging. However, many travellers with disabilities rise above these obstacles.

The northeast has a limited number of wheelchair-friendly hotels (mostly top end) and ramps are found at some offices and top-end restaurants. Elsewhere, you will need to negotiate steps and stairs. Note that lifts frequently stop at mezzanines between floors – not the most useful solution for wheelchair users! Footpaths and pavements, where they exist at all, are potholed and packed with pedestrians, hindering movement. Try to book ground-floor hotel rooms and if you use crutches, bring along spare rubber caps for the tips.

If your mobility is considerably restricted, you may like to consider travelling with an able-bodied companion. Hiring a car with driver will make moving around a whole lot easier (see p334). However, note that LPG-powered taxis may not have space for a wheelchair in the boot because of the fuel tank.

Organisations that may offer further advice include the **Royal Association for Disability & Rehabilitation** (Radar; ☎ 020-7250 3222; www.radar .org.uk; 12 City Forum, 250 City Rd, London EC1V 8AF, UK) and **Mobility International USA** (Miusa; ☎ 541-343-1284; www.miusa.org; 132 E Broadway, Suite 343, Eugene, OR 97401, USA). There are also some good sites on the web, including www.access-able.com.

VISAS

You must get a visa before arriving in India but visas are easily available at Indian missions worldwide. Most people travel on the standard tourist visa, which is more than adequate for most needs. Student and business visas have strict conditions and also restrict your access to tourist services, such as tourist quotas on trains. An onward-travel ticket is a requirement for most visas, but the embassy rarely checks, unless you are applying for a 72-hour Transit Visa.

Six-month multiple-entry tourist visas are granted to nationals of most countries regardless of how long you intend to stay. You can enter and leave as often as you like, but you can only spend a total of 180 days in the country, starting from the date of issue. There are additional restrictions on travellers from Bangladesh and Pakistan, as well as certain Eastern European, African and Central Asian countries. Check any special conditions and the current visa prices for your nationality with the Indian embassy in your country.

For visas lasting more than six months, you need to register at the FRRO (see opposite) within 14 days of arriving in India – inquire about these special conditions when you apply for your visa.

Visa Extensions

Pay close attention to the expiry date of your visa – visa extensions are not granted lightly. You would be much better off leaving India and applying for a new tourist visa in a neighbouring country. This is easy to arrange in Kathmandu in Nepal, but the process can take up to a week.

If you intend to apply for an extension to an existing visa, Delhi's **Ministry of Home Affairs** (☎ 011-23385748; Jaisalmer House, 26 Man Singh Rd, Delhi; ☺ inquiries 9-11am Mon-Fri) has the power to grant 14-day visa extensions, but don't get your hopes up. The only circumstances where this might conceivably happen is if you were robbed of your passport just before you planned to leave the country at the end of your visa.

If you do need to apply for an extension, or if you need a replacement visa after losing your passport, contact the **FRRO** (Map p108; ☎ 033-22837034; 237 AJC Bose Rd; ☺ 11am-5pm Mon-Fri) in Kolkata. Although it has the authority to grant extensions, in all likelihood, you will be referred on to the **Delhi FRRO** (☎ 011-26195530; frrodelhi@hotmail.com; Level 2, East Block 8, Sector 1, Rama Krishna (RK) Puram, Delhi; ☺ 9.30am-5.30pm Mon-Fri).

If by some remote chance you meet the stringent criteria, the FRRO is permitted to grant an extension of 14 days (free for nationals of most countries; inquire on application). You must bring your confirmed air ticket, one passport photo and a photocopy of your passport (information and visa pages). Note that this system is designed to get you out of the country promptly with the correct exit stamps, not to give you two extra weeks of travel.

VOLUNTEERING

Volunteering is growing in popularity in India, but there is a growing international backlash against the kind of casual volunteering that exists mainly for the benefit of the volunteer. Better volunteer agencies work to make small, sustainable changes, letting the process be guided and informed by local people. Set aside enough time to make a difference – a month is a reasonable minimum time period to volunteer. It is possible to find a placement after you arrive in India, but most charities and NGOs prefer volunteers who apply in advance. Note that some religious charities have a proselytising agenda that may conflict with the interests of local people.

Agencies Overseas

There are hundreds of international volunteering agencies, and it can be bewildering trying to assess which ones have ethical policies. The organisation **Ethical Volunteering** (www .ethicalvolunteering.org) has some excellent guidelines for choosing an ethical sending agency.

Look for projects where you use your existing skills, rather than signing up for something that just sounds like a fun thing to do. Agencies that offer the chance to do whatever you like, whenever you like, for as long as you like, rarely have the best interests of local people at heart.

There are some tried and tested international projects, such as Britain's **Voluntary Service Overseas** (VSO; www.vso.org.uk), that place volunteers in serious professional roles, though the time commitment can be as much as two years. The international organisation **Indicorps** (www.indicorps.org) matches volunteers to projects across India in all sorts of fields, particularly social development. Many Indian NGOs also offer volunteer work – for listings click on www.indianngos.com.

To find sending agencies in your area, look at Lonely Planet's *Volunteering, Gap Year* and *Career Break* books, or search online:
Working Abroad (www.workingabroad.com)
World Volunteer Web (www.worldvolunteerweb.org)
Worldwide Volunteering (www.worldwidevolunteering .org.uk)

Aid Programs in India

The following programs in India may have opportunities for volunteers. Always contact them in advance, rather than turning up on the doorstep unannounced. Donations of money or clothing from travellers may also be welcome. Note that unless otherwise indicated, volunteers are expected to cover their own costs (accommodation, food, transport etc).

KOLKATA

Founded by Mother Teresa, the **Missionaries of Charity** (www.motherteresa.org) has opportunities at several care homes around Kolkata, including

---

TEACHING ENGLISH

Many of the volunteer placements available in India involve teaching basic English at local schools, but children will benefit massively if you study for a teaching qualification before you start volunteering. Consider enrolling on a four-week TEFL (Teaching English as a Foreign Language) and Tesol (Teachers of English to Speakers of Other Languages) certificate course, which will also enable you to find paid teaching work worldwide. Courses are available worldwide, including in Kolkata, for US$1200 to $1500 – contact **TEFL International** (http://teflindia .com) for details.

Nirmal Hriday (home for the dying), Prem Dan (for the sick and mentally ill) and Shishu Bhavan (for orphaned children). Enrolment sessions for volunteers take place at the **Shishu Bhavan** (Map pp104-5; 78 AJC Bose Rd; ☽ 3pm Mon, Wed & Fri). However, note that this organisation does not live up to all the guidelines suggested by the aforementioned organisation, Ethical Volunteering.

The **Situational Management & Inter-Learning Establishment** (Smile; ☎ 033-25376621; www.smilengo .org; Udayrajpur, Madhyamgram, No 9 Rail Gate) runs a residential home for destitute children and provides direct assistance to homeless children at Sealdah train station. Volunteers are accepted for two-week work camps and longer stays lasting up to a year (you pay a fee to participate, which covers meals and accommodation).

Started in 1979, **Calcutta Rescue** (Map p108; ☎ /fax 033-22175675; www.calcuttarescue.org; 4th fl, 85 Collins St) gives medical care and health education to the poor and disadvantaged of Kolkata and West Bengal. The organisation has six- to nine-month openings for experienced medical staff, teachers and administrators – contact them directly for current vacancies.

The **Calcutta Society for the Prevention of Cruelty to Animals** (CSPCA; Map p112; ☎ 033-22367738; http:// calcuttaspca.org/; 276 BB Ganguly St, Kolkata) has opportunities for qualified vets to help abused animals in Kolkata, but a minimum of one month is preferred.

Samaritans (☎ 033-22295920; http://thecalcutta samaritans.org; 48 Ripon Rd) welcomes caring listeners for their phone lines, and donations.

ORISSA
The **Wildlife Society of Orissa** (off Map p252; ☎ 0674- 2311513; www.wildlifeorissa.org; A320, Sahid Nagar, Bhubaneswar 751007) accepts volunteers to help with its work to save endangered species in Orissa, especially the olive ridley marine turtle (see the boxed text, p269).

SIKKIM
Placements for volunteer teachers at schools in Sikkim – including the Denjong Pedma Choling Academy near Pelling – can be arranged through the British-based charity **Himalayan Education Lifeline Programme** (HELP; ☎ 012-2726 3055; www.help-education.org; Mansard House, 30 Kingsdown Park, Whitstable, Kent CT5 2DF, UK). English speakers over 20 years old are preferred. See the website for comprehensive details.

Teaching placements in Sikkim can also be arranged through the **Muyal Liang Trust** (☎ 020- 7229 4774; 53 Blenheim Crescent, London W11 2EG UK).

WEST BENGAL
In Darjeeling, **Hayden Hall** (Map p156; ☎ 0354- 2253228; www.haydenhall.org; 42 Laden La Rd, Darjeeling) has volunteer opportunities (minimum six months) for people with health-care and pre-school-teaching backgrounds.

Northeast of Darjeeling near the border with Sikkim, the UK-run **Karmi Farm** (☎ in the UK 020-8903 3411; www.karmifarm.com, Kolbong) runs a clinic for villagers, providing a volunteer opportunity for medical students and doctors. Contact them for details.

Close to Bishnupur, **Basudha Farm** (☎ in Kolkata 033-25928109, 9434062891; www.cintdis.org/basudha.html) trains local farmers in organic farming techniques and offers volunteers on the **Willing Workers on Organic Farms** (WWOOF; www.wwoof.org) scheme the chance to work on the farm in exchange for free room and board.

The organic **Makaibari Tea Estate** (www.makai bari.com; Pankhabari Rd, Kurseong) has an established program that places volunteers in health, education and agriculture jobs that benefit plantation workers. It's popular with gap-year students.

Human Wave (☎ 033-26852823; http://humanwave -volunteer.org; 52 Tentultala Lane, Mankundu, Hooghly) runs community development and health schemes in West Bengal, including volunteer projects in the Sunderbans and youth projects in Kolkata.

WOMEN TRAVELLERS
Despite the number of female deities in the Hindu pantheon, emancipation for real women is making slow progress in India. Many people still hold rather old-fashioned notions about public morality and the role of women in society and India is still very much a patriarchal society.

Indian women always dress conservatively and rarely engage in small talk with men they do not know – female travellers can send the wrong signals by wearing revealing clothing and chatting to men in public places. To complicate matters, Indian men often have a somewhat confused perception of Western women as a result of imported Hollywood movies, where scantily clad heroines jump into bed with action heroes at the slightest provocation.

As an unfortunate consequence of this, many female travellers to India experience some form of sexual harassment – known locally as 'Eve-teasing'. This commonly takes the form of lewd comments, being stared at, being 'accidentally' bumped into in the street and invasion of personal space, though groping is not uncommon. Most cases are reported in urban centres and prominent tourist towns; the problem is much less prevalent in Adivasi and Buddhist areas in the hills.

While there's no need to be paranoid, you should be aware that that local men may be watching your behaviour and interpreting it in unintended ways. Getting constantly stared at is something you'll have to get used to – just be thick-skinned and try to rise above it. Refrain from returning male stares, as this may be considered a come-on – dark glasses can help.

Be particularly careful at festivals, where drunk men may be emboldened by crowds – see p307. Women travelling with a male partner are less likely to be harassed. However, mixed couples of Indian and non-Indian descent may get disapproving stares, even if both partners are from outside India.

One useful resource for female travellers is Louise Wates' *A Girls' Guide to India – a Survivor's Handbook*. Read the personal experiences of fellow women travellers on the India page at www.journeywoman.com.

Clothing

Avoiding culturally inappropriate clothing is a sure-fire way to reduce harassment – items to leave out of your rucksack include sleeveless tops, shorts, short skirts (ankle-length skirts are the safest choice) and any other skimpy, see-through or tight-fitting clothing.

Wearing Indian dress can help. The *salwar kameez* is regarded as respectable attire and wearing it will reflect your respect for local dress etiquette. The flowing outfit is also surprisingly cool in the hot weather, and the dupatta (long scarf) worn with it is very handy if you visit a shrine that requires your head to be covered.

Going into public wearing a choli (small tight blouse worn under a sari) or a sari petticoat (which many foreign women mistake for a skirt) is rather like strutting around half dressed – don't do it.

Although Orissa has beaches, take your cues from local women, who wear saris, *salwar kameez,* or long shorts and a T-shirt whenever

swimming in public view. When returning from the beach, use a sarong to avoid stares on the way back to your hotel.

Health

Sanitary pads and tampons are available from pharmacies in all large cities and most tourist centres. Carry additional stocks for travel off the beaten track. For other health issues affecting women, see p350.

Staying Safe

Women have reported being molested by masseurs and other therapists, especially in traveller centres. Check the reputation of any teacher or therapist and if you feel uneasy at any time, leave. For gynaecological health issues, seek out a female doctor.

Keep conversations with unknown men short, as idle chat may be interpreted as a come-on. Questions such as 'do you have a boyfriend?' or 'you are looking very beautiful' are indicators that the conversation may be taking a steamy tangent. Some women prepare in advance by wearing a pseudo wedding ring, or by announcing early on in the conversation that they are married or engaged (even if it isn't true).

If you still get the uncomfortable feeling that a man is encroaching on your space, he probably is. A firm request to keep away is usually enough, especially if your voice is loud enough to draw attention from passersby. Alternatively, the silent treatment (not responding to questions at all) can be remarkably effective.

When interacting with men on a day-to-day basis, adhere to the local practice of not shaking hands. Instead, say *'namaste'* – the traditional, respectful Hindu greeting – and bow slightly with the hands brought together at the chest or head level.

Female film goers will probably feel more comfortable (and decrease the chances of potential harassment) by going to the cinema with a companion. Lastly, it's wise to arrive in towns before dark and, of course, always avoid walking alone at night, especially in isolated areas.

Taxis & Public Transport

Officials recommend that solo women prearrange an airport pick-up with their hotel if their flight is scheduled to arrive late at night. If that's not possible, catch a prepaid taxi and

326 DIRECTORY ·· Work   lonelyplanet.com

make a point of (in front of the driver) writing down the car registration and driver's name and giving it to one of the airport police. Many female travellers prefer to wait until daybreak before leaving the airport. Avoid taking taxis alone late at night (when many roads are deserted) and never agree to having more than one man (the driver) in the car.

On trains and buses, being a woman has some advantages. Women are able to queue-jump without consequence and on trains there are special women-only carriages. Solo women have reported less hassle by opting for the more expensive classes on trains, especially for overnight trips. If you're travelling overnight in a three-tier carriage, try to get the uppermost berth, which will give you more privacy (and distance from wandering hands).

On public transport, don't hesitate to return any errant limbs, put some item of luggage in between you and, if all else fails, find a new spot.

WORK

Obtaining paid work in India is harder than you might expect, and the local wages rarely make this cost-effective for travellers. Visiting on a business trip is easy, but working for an Indian company requires visa sponsorship from an Indian employer and finding a job before you travel. Although not strictly legal, casual opportunities exist at some tourist resorts teaching adventure sports and holistic therapies. However, this may deprive locals of much-needed employment.

There may be opportunities with international package-holiday companies for tour reps in Goa and Kerala (though you normally need to complete seasons in Europe to qualify), and some language schools in large cities have opportunities for English teachers with a TEFL or Tesol certificate – see the boxed text, p323. Another thing to consider is applying for a job as a guide or driver with an overland tour company.

Transport

GETTING THERE & AWAY

The following sections contain information on transport to and around northeast India. Flights, tours and rail tickets can also be booked online at www.lonelyplanet.com/travel_services.

ENTERING THE COUNTRY

Although a visa must be obtained in advance, entering India by air or land is relatively straightforward, with standard immigration and customs procedures.

Passport

To enter India you need a valid passport and visa (see p322) and an onward/return ticket. If your passport is lost or stolen, immediately contact your country's representative (see p309) and also contact the Indian authorities to arrange a replacement visa. It's wise to keep photocopies of your airline ticket and the identity and visa pages from your passport in case of emergency.

AIR
Airports

The main gateway to the northeast is **Kolkata** (CCU; Netaji Subhas Chandra Basu International Airport;

☎ 033-25118787). The Indian government has plans to transform the airport at **Guwahati** (GAU; Lokpriya Gopinath Bordoloi International Airport; ☎ 0361-2840068) in Assam into a major international hub but, thus far, the airport has only received a few flights from Bangkok. It may be cheaper to fly into Delhi or Mumbai (Bombay) and pick up a domestic flight to the northeast.

Larger airports have free luggage trolleys; elsewhere, porters will eagerly lug your load for a negotiable fee. For flights originating in India, hold bags must be passed through the X-ray machine in the departures hall before you check in. Baggage tags are required for the security check for all cabin bags, including cameras.

Airlines

India's national carrier, **Air India** (airline code AI; www.airindia.com), has recently been merged with the state-owned domestic carrier **Indian Airlines** (airline code IC). Both airlines fly international routes but flights with an IC code tend to be less reliable and use older (sometimes much older) aircraft than flights with an AI code. Air India also has a budget subsidiary, **Air India Express** (airline code IX; www.airindiaexpress.in). The more dependable private airlines **Jet Airways** (airline code 9W; www.jetairways.com) and **Jetlite** (airline code S2; www.jetlite.com) offer domestic flights to cities across the northeast, connecting with international flights to Delhi and Mumbai.

Many international airlines no longer require reconfirmation of international tickets,

> **THINGS CHANGE...**
>
> The information in this chapter is particularly vulnerable to change. Check directly with the airline or a travel agent to make sure you understand how a fare (and the ticket you may buy) works and be aware of the security requirements for international travel. Shop carefully. The details given in this chapter should be regarded as pointers and are not a substitute for your own careful, up-to-date research.

TRANSPORT

CLIMATE CHANGE & TRAVEL

Climate change is a serious threat to the ecosystems that humans rely on, and air travel is one of the fastest-growing contributors to the problem. Lonely Planet regards travel, overall, as a global benefit, but we believe everyone has a responsibility to limit their personal impact on global warming.

Flying & Climate Change

Every form of motorised travel generates CO_2 but planes are far and away the worst offenders, not just because of the fuel they consume, but because they release greenhouse gases high into the atmosphere. Two people taking a return flight between Europe and the US will contribute as much to climate change as an average household's gas and electricity consumption over a whole year.

Carbon Offset Schemes

Climatecare.org and other websites use 'carbon calculators' that allow travellers to offset the level of greenhouse gases they are responsible for with financial contributions to sustainable travel schemes and tree-planting projects that offset the effects of global warming – including projects in India.

Lonely Planet, together with Rough Guides and other concerned partners in the travel industry, supports the carbon offset scheme run by climatecare.org. Lonely Planet offsets all of its staff and author travel. For more information check out our website: www.lonelyplanet.com.

---

but it is still a good idea to call to check that flight times haven't changed. The standard check-in time is about three hours before international departures, but remember to factor in the Indian traffic when planning your trip to the airport. Security regulations change all the time – contact your airline in advance for the latest requirements. For details of domestic flights, see p332.

AIRLINES FLYING TO/FROM NORTHEAST INDIA

Foreign airlines flying directly to Kolkata include (websites have contact details):

Biman Bangladesh Airlines (airline code BG; www.bimanair.com)
British Airways (airline code BA; www.britishairways.com)
China Eastern Airlines (airline code MU; www.ce-air.com)
Druk Air (airline code KB; www.drukair.com.bt)
Emirates (airline code EK; www.emirates.com)
GMG Airlines (airline code Z5; www.gmgairlines.com)
Gulf Air (airline code GF; www.gulfair.com)
Lufthansa Airlines (airline code LH; www.lufthansa.com)
Singapore Airlines (airline code SQ; www.singaporeair.com)
Thai Airways International (airline code TG; www.thaiair.com)
United Airways Bangladesh (airline code 4H; www.uabdl.com)

Tickets

An onward or return air ticket is a condition of the tourist visa, so few visitors buy international tickets inside India. It's best to book directly with airlines (see Transport Scams on p309). The departure tax of Rs500 (Rs150 for most subcontinent and Southeast Asian countries) and passenger service fee is included in the price of almost all tickets.

Fares and schedules fluctuate with availability and the current price of aviation fuel. Contact a travel agent or surf the web to get up-to-the-minute fares and flight schedules. Many of the big online booking sites offer good-value fares to India:

Ebookers (www.ebookers.com)
Expedia (www.expedia.com)
Flight Centre (www.flightcentre.com)
Flights.com (www.tiss.com)
STA Travel (www.statravel.com)
Travelocity (www.travelocity.com)
Yatra (www.yatra.com)

Africa

There are direct flights to India from South Africa (particularly Cape Town) and East Africa (particularly Nairobi), but you'll have to pick up a connecting flight to the northeast. **Rennies Travel** (www.renniestravel.com) and **STA Travel** (www.statravel.co.za) have offices throughout southern Africa. Check their websites for branch locations.

Asia

Kolkata has good connections to other parts of Asia, though you may have to connect through Delhi, Mumbai or another Asian hub. Competition has created some very reasonable fares to Bangkok, Singapore, Dhaka and Kathmandu. Periodically, there are also direct flights from Guwahati to Bangkok. For Tripura and the other Northeast States, you might consider taking a flight to Dhaka and travelling overland from there – see p330.

STA Travel has useful branches in **Bangkok** (☎ 0 2236 0262; www.statravel.co.th), **Hong Kong** (☎ 2736 1618; www.statravel.com.hk), **Malaysia** (☎ 2148 9800; www .statravel.com.my) and **Singapore** (☎ 6737 7188; www .statravel.com.sg). Other agencies include **No 1 Travel** (☎ 0332-056 073; www.no1-travel.com) in Japan and **Four Seas Tours** (☎ 2200 7760; www.fourseastravel .com/english) in Hong Kong.

Australia

Qantas has flights to Mumbai from Sydney and Brisbane, but the best way to reach the northeast is through Kolkata with a stop in Southeast Asia. Flights between Kolkata and New Zealand all go via Southeast Asia.

Flight Centre has branches all over **Australia** (☎ 13 31 33; www.flightcentre.com.au) and **New Zealand** (☎ 0800 243 544; www.flightcentre .co.nz). There are also STA Travel branches in most large cities in **Australia** (☎ 13 47 82; www .statravel.com.au) and **New Zealand** (☎ 0800 474 400; www.statravel.co.nz). For online bookings, try www.travel.com.au.

Canada

Canada has no direct flights to Kolkata, but you can connect through Delhi or Mumbai, or make a stop in Europe, Southeast Asia or the Gulf. From eastern and central Canada, most flights go via Europe; from Vancouver and the west coast, flights go via Asia. **Travel Cuts** (☎ 1-866-246-9762; www.travelcuts.com) is Canada's national student travel agency. For online bookings try www.expedia.ca and www.travelocity.ca.

Continental Europe

There are flights to Kolkata from most European capitals, either direct or with a stop in Delhi, Dubai or Bahrain. For discount fares, try the big online ticket agencies. **Ebookers** (www.ebookers.com) has regional flight-booking websites for countries across Europe, including France, Germany, Spain, the Netherlands, Denmark, Finland, Norway and Sweden. Other companies with branches around Europe include **STA Travel** (www.statravel.com) and

LastMinute (www.lastminute.com). Just click on the country links at the bottom of the websites.

Other agencies include **Anyway** (☎ 08 92 30 23 01; www.anyway.fr), **Nouvelles Frontières** (☎ 01 49 20 65 87; www.nouvelles-frontieres.fr) and **Voyageurs du Monde** (☎ 08 92 23 56 56; www.vdm .com) in France; **Just Travel** (☎ 089-747 33 30; www .justtravel.de) in Germany; **CTS Viaggi** (☎ 064 41 11 66; www.cts.it) in Italy; **Airfair** (☎ 0900-771 77 17; www .airfair.nl) in the Netherlands; and **Barcelo Viajes** (☎ 902 20 04 00; www.barceloviajes.com) in Spain.

UK & Ireland

There are easy connections to Kolkata from London and Dublin, either direct or with a change in a European hub or the Gulf. Alternatively, there are fast, easy and inexpensive connections through Delhi, Mumbai or other Indian hubs with Jet Airways and Air India.

Discount air travel is big business in London. Advertisements for many travel agencies appear in the travel pages of the weekend broadsheet newspapers, in *Time Out*, the *Evening Standard* and in the free magazine *TNT*.

Reliable travel agencies include the following:
Ebookers (☎ 020-3320 3320; www.ebookers.com)
Flight Centre (☎ 0870 499 0040; www.flightcentre .co.uk)
North-South Travel (☎ 012-456 08291; www.north southtravel.co.uk)
STA Travel (☎ 0871 2 300 040; www.statravel.co.uk)
Trailfinders (☎ 0845 058 5858; www.trailfinders.co.uk)
Travel Bag (☎ 0800 804 8911; www.travelbag.co.uk)

USA

Kolkata is halfway around the world from North America, so you can go east or west around the globe. Flying west involves a change in Asia; flying east normally involves a stop in Europe or the Gulf. It may be cheaper to fly to Delhi or Mumbai first, and pick up a cheap ticket on a budget airline.

San Francisco is the discount ticket agent capital of America, although some good deals can be found in Los Angeles, New York and other big cities. The *New York Times, Chicago Tribune, LA Times* and *San Francisco Examiner* all produce weekly travel sections in which you'll find any number of travel agency ads.

For reasonably priced fares, start with specialist travel agencies such as **Third Eye**

TRANSPORT

TRANSPORT

Travel (☎ 1-800 456 393; www.thirdeyetravel.com) and **USA Asia** (☎ 1-800 872 2742; www.usaasiatravel.com). Younger travellers and students can find good fares through **STA Travel** (☎ 1-800 781 4040; www.sta travel.com).

The online agencies www.cheaptickets .com, www.expedia.com, www.itn.net, www .lowestfare.com, www.orbitz.com and www .travelocity.com are also reliable.

LAND
Border Crossings
The northeast has land borders with Nepal, Bangladesh, Bhutan (only open to visitors on an organised tour), Tibet (China, only accessible as part of an organised tour) and Myanmar (closed to foreigners). If you enter India by bus or train, you'll be required to disembark at the border for immigration and customs checks. You must have a valid Indian visa in advance – see p322. Be aware that drug regulations are strictly enforced – this is not a part of the world to try your luck.

Drivers of cars and motorcycles will need the vehicle's registration papers, liability insurance and an international driving permit. You'll also need a *carnet de passage en douane,* which acts as a temporary waiver of import duty. To find out the latest requirements, contact your local automobile association.

See p334 and p337 for more on car and motorcycle travel.

BANGLADESH
Foreigners can use four of the land crossings between Bangladesh and India, all in West Bengal or the Northeast States. If you enter Bangladesh by air and intend to leave by land, you must obtain a road permit (or 'change of route' permit) from Dhaka's **Immigration & Passport Office** (☎ 02-889750; Agargaon Rd; ☽ Sat-Thu); allow two to three days to process the application. If you plan to enter Bangladesh by land, you may need to have the port of entry stamped on your visa. Some travellers have reported problems exiting Bangladesh overland with the visa issued on arrival at Dhaka airport.

Visas for Bangladesh can be obtained in advance from the Bangladeshi missions in Kolkata (see p309) and Agartala (see the boxed text, p238). Most offices issue visas in two working days with two passport photos; fees vary depending on nationality.

Heading from Bangladesh to India, you must prepay the exit tax at a designated branch of the Sonali Bank, which may be some distance from the border post.

Agartala to Dhaka
The Bangladesh border is 4km from Agartala and several daily trains run on to Dhaka from Akhaura on the Bangladesh side of the border. See the boxed text, p238, for more details.

Kolkata to Dhaka
There are daily bus services from Kolkata to Dhaka, crossing the India–Bangladesh border at Benapol – see p132 for more information. After years of delays, a train service has finally been created between Kolkata and Dhaka – the *Maitree Express* (Rs368 to Rs920, 12 hours) runs on Saturday and Sunday from Kolkata's Chitpur Station to Dhaka Cantonment station, via Darsana (Darshana). However, you must have this crossing marked on your Bangladesh visa. See p133 for more information.

Shillong to Sylhet
Share jeeps run every morning from Bara Bazaar in Shillong and drop over the edge of the plateau to the border post at Dawki, a short walk or taxi ride from Tamabil, which has regular buses to Sylhet – see the boxed text, p245, for more information.

Siliguri to Dhaka via Chengrabandha (Burimari)
This minor northern border crossing is accessible from Siliguri in West Bengal (accessible by train from Kolkata via New Jalpaiguri station). From Siliguri, you can take a direct private bus to Dhaka, disembarking for visa formalities at Chengrabandha (Burimari), or you can take a local bus to the border and change to a second bus on the other side. See p150 for more details.

BHUTAN
Opposite the town of Jaigon in West Bengal, Phuentsholing is the main land entry and exit point between India and Bhutan. You need a full Bhutanese visa to enter the country, which must be obtained at least 15 days before your trip from a registered travel agent listed under the **Bhutan Department of Tourism** (www.tourism.gov.bt).

Visitors to Bhutan pay an obligatory daily fee of US$200 per person per night (US$165 from July to August), which includes tours, meals, accommodation and local transport.

Bhutan Transport Services runs direct daily buses from several towns in West Bengal to the border post at Phuentsholing. See p132 for buses from Kolkata, p150 for buses from Siliguri and p172 for buses from Kalimpong.

There's also a rail route from Siliguri via Alipurduar (on the main train line between Siliguri and Guwahati) connecting with local buses to the border.

NEPAL

Things have been mostly peaceful in Nepal since the end of the Maoist uprising in 2008. However, it is still a good idea to check the political situation before you travel – news websites, for example www.kantipuronline .com, www.thehimalayantimes.com, www .nepalnews.com, www.nepalitimes.com.np and www.nepalnews.net, are good sources of information.

Political and weather conditions permitting, there are five land border crossings between India and Nepal: Raxaul in Bihar to Birganj in central Nepal, Panitanki in West Bengal to Kakarbhitta in eastern Nepal; Sunauli in Uttar Pradesh to Bhairawa in central Nepal; Jamunaha in Uttar Pradesh to Nepalganj in western Nepal; and Banbassa in Uttaranchal to Mahendranagar in western Nepal.

Only the Panitanki–Kakarbhitta crossing is really convenient for the northeast, but quite a few people enter Nepal using one crossing and leave via another. Be cautious of buying a through ticket from India to Kathmandu – all passengers must change buses at the border and there are numerous scams involving rundown local buses at deluxe bus prices. See the boxed text, above, for general information on crossing into Nepal.

Multiple-entry visas lasting up to three months are available at all the border crossings into Nepal (visas valid for 15/30/90 days cost US$25/40/100). Payment is in US dollars and you need two passport photos. Visas can be extended up to a maximum of 120 days once you reach Kathmandu. In Kolkata, the **Nepali consulate** (☎ 033-24561103/17; 1 National Library Ave, Alipore; ⊗ 9am-4pm Mon-Fri) issues visas while you wait.

Banbassa to Mahendranagar

The most westerly crossing in Nepal is a possible exit point towards Uttaranchal and Delhi, but transport links are poor on either side of the border. Check the roads are open before attempting this crossing.

Jamunaha to Nepalganj

This little-used crossing is too far west to be useful for travellers to the northeast. On the Indian side, access is by bus from Lucknow to Rupaidha Bazar (Rs160, seven hours).

Panitanki to Kakarbhitta

The handiest crossing for Darjeeling, Sikkim and the Northeast States. Buses and share jeeps run to the border from Siliguri and other towns in West Bengal, and there are regular buses on to Kathmandu. See the boxed text, p150, for details on crossing the border.

Raxaul to Birganj

This crossing in Bihar is reasonably convenient for Kolkata. The most comfortable way to reach Raxaul is the daily *Mithila Express* from Kolkata's Howrah train station (sleeper/3AC/2AC Rs276/748/1026, 16 hours). From the Indian border post at Raxaul, it's a Rs50 autorickshaw ride to Birganj, which has onward buses to Kathmandu (NRs350 to NRs400, seven hours) and Pokhara (NRs350 to NRs425, eight hours) and flights to Kathmandu (US$79, 20 minutes).

Sunauli

The easiest crossing for Varanasi or Delhi, with connections on to Kathmandu, Pokhara and Lumbini. Coming from Kolkata, the easiest option is to take a train from Howrah station to Gorakhpur in Uttar Pradesh (sleeper/3AC/2AC Rs312/848/1165, 20 hours), then a bus to Sunauli (Rs56, three hours). On the far side, crowded private buses run to Kathmandu and Pokhara (NRs300 to NRs425, eight hours).

PAKISTAN

All the border crossings between India and Pakistan are in the far west of the country – far from Kolkata and the northeast. Border crossings often close because of political tensions between India and Pakistan and trains and buses between the two countries have been repeatedly targeted by militant groups.

You must have a visa to enter Pakistan, and it is usually easiest to obtain this in

TRANSPORT

the Pakistan mission in your home country. There are three possible routes – the bus or train between Delhi and Lahore; the bus from Amritsar to Attari and Wagah; and the *Thar Express* train from Jodhpur in Rajasthan to Karachi via Munabao/Khokrapar. Check locally for details of all these routes.

SEA

There are several sea routes between India and surrounding islands but none leave Indian sovereign territory – see opposite. There has been talk of a passenger ferry service between southern India and Colombo in Sri Lanka but this has yet to materialise.

GETTING AROUND

AIR

Foreigners pay elevated US-dollar fares for flights run by Air India (and the rebranded Indian Airlines) and Jet Airways. Most budget airlines charge the same low rupee fares to everyone, particularly for seats booked online. Fares change daily, but you get a better deal the further you book in advance. Reconfirmation is normally only required if your ticket was bought outside India, but call a few days ahead to be safe. For details of discounts on airfares, see p309.

Check-in for domestic flights is an hour before departure, and hold luggage must be X-rayed and stamped before you check-in. Every item of cabin baggage needs a baggage label, which must be stamped as part of your security check. Note that batteries may need to be removed from all electronic items. The baggage allowance is 20kg (10kg for smaller aircraft) in economy class, 30kg in business.

Airlines in India

The largest network is operated by the state-owned Indian Airlines, which is in the process of being rebranded as part of **Air India** (www.airindia.com). This may lead to a much-needed overhaul of service standards and some newer, safer aircraft. Many travellers prefer to pay a little more for the superior services operated by **Jet Airways** (www.jetairways.com) and its budget subsidiary **JetLite** (www.jetlite.com).

For the cheapest fares, look to India's budget airlines, which offer discounted rupee fares over the internet. As a rough indication, fares for a one-hour flight range from US$150 on an established carrier to Rs1000 with a budget airline.

At the time of writing, the following airlines were serving destinations across India – the regional chapters and the airline websites have details of routes, fares and booking offices.

Air India (www.airindia.com) Operates the extensive domestic network of Indian Airlines, covering airports across the northeast.

IndiGo (www.goindigo.in) A growing budget carrier, with flights to Kolkata, Guwahati, Agartala, Imphal and Bhubaneshwar.

Jet Airways (www.jetairways.com) India's favourite private airline, serving Kolkata, Guwahati, Jorhat, Agartala and Bagdogra (for Sikkim).

JetLite (www.jetlite.com) Formerly Air Sahara, serving Kolkata, Guwahati, Imphal, Jorhat, Dibrugarh and Bhubaneshwar.

Kingfisher Airlines (www.flykingfisher.com) Yep, it's an airline owned by a beer company, serving Kolkata and airstrips across the northeast (some flights are operated by Kingfisher Red).

Spicejet (www.spicejet.com) Discount seats to hubs across India, including Kolkata, Guwahati and Bagdogra.

Air Passes

Air India offers the reasonably useful Discover India pass for Rs22,000/33,000/44,000 (or

---

STOP PRESS: DOMESTIC AIRLINE CHANGES

National carrier **Air India** (airline code AI) has merged with the state-owned domestic carrier **Indian Airlines** (airline code IC) and all flights have been rebranded as Air India flights. However, the airlines' offices may still list flights with an IC code as Indian Airlines flights. To further confuse matters, Air India also has its own budget airline, Air India Express.

Kingfisher Airlines and Air Deccan have also merged – flights are divided between Kingfisher Airlines and its budget carrier, Kingfisher Red. Meanwhile, Jet Airways has taken over Air Sahara, which has been rebranded as JetLite.

In this book, we've used airline names that were applicable on the ground at the time of research. Be aware that some dodgy travel agencies may try to confuse travellers with name changes.

HELICOPTER SERVICES

Several companies offer helicopter shuttle services around the northeast. The state-subsidised carrier **Pawan Hans Helicopters** (www.pawanhans.nic.in) connects Guwahati with several towns in Meghalaya and Arunachal Pradesh, and there are also flights from Bagdogra airport in West Bengal to Gangtok in Sikkim (see p182). However, helicopter travel in India has a shocking safety record, with four major accidents since 2002 and numerous minor crashes. We won't say don't use them, but be aware of the risks.

the US-dollar equivalent) for seven/15/21 days, plus the applicable passenger service fee and fuel surcharge for each flight sector. You can travel on any flight, except to the Lakshadweep Islands, but you can't visit the same place twice.

Air passes for foreigners and Non-Resident Indians are also available from Jet Airways and Kingfisher.

BICYCLE

The back roads of the northeast are a pleasure to cycle but the steep hills of Sikkim and West Bengal will test your calves to the max. Contact your airline for information about transporting your bike and customs formalities in your home country. Mountain bikes with off-road tyres give the best protection against India's potholed and puncture-prone roads.

Roadside cycle mechanics abound but bring spare tyres and brake cables, lubricating oil and a chain repair kit, and plenty of puncture repair patches. Bikes can often be carried for free on the roofs of public buses, or for a fee in the baggage car on trains.

Read up on bicycle touring before you travel – Rob van de Plas' *Bicycle Touring Manual*, Steve Butterman's *Bicycle Touring: How to Prepare for Long Rides* and Stephen Lord's *Adventure Cycle-Touring Handbook* are good places to start. The **Cycling Federation of India** (☎ in Delhi 011-23753528; www.cyclingfederation ofindia.org) can provide general advice on cycling in India.

Road rules are virtually nonexistent and national highways are hazardous places to cycle, so stick to quieter back roads wherever

possible. Stay off the roads after dark and be wary of cycling into rebel-held areas in the Northeast States (see p307). Always be conservative about the distances you expect to cover – an experienced cyclist can expect to cover 60km to 100km a day on the plains, 40km to 60km on sealed mountain roads and 40km or less on dirt roads.

See p94 for more on cycling in the northeast.

Hire

There are no specialist cycle-tour companies based in the northeast, but you can find bicycles for hire for local sightseeing. Expect to pay Rs30 to Rs100 per day for an Indian-made sit-up-and-beg bike. Hire places may require cash or an ID card as a security deposit.

Purchase

Kolkata is the best place to buy a sturdy, road-worthy bike – bicycle shops are concentrated along Bentinck St, just east of BBD Bagh. Mountain bikes from reputable brands such as Hero, Atlas, Hercules or Raleigh start at Rs3000. Reselling is quite easy – ask at local cycle shops or put up an advert on traveller noticeboards. You should be able to get 50% of what you originally paid, as long as the bike is in reasonably good condition.

BOAT

Regular scheduled ferries connect mainland India to Port Blair in the Andaman Islands. The journey takes around 56 hours from Kolkata's Kidderpore Docks (see p132).

There are also numerous ferry services across rivers, from chain pontoons to wicker coracles, and boat cruises along the Sunderbans delta in West Bengal and the Brahmaputra River in Assam – see the regional chapters and p94 for more information.

BUS

Although trains are much more comfortable, buses are the cheapest way to get around the northeast. State government–run bus companies are usually the safest and most reliable option, and seats can be booked up to a month in advance. Private buses tend to be cheaper, but drivers take insane risks and conductors cram as many passengers on as possible to maximise profits. Share jeeps supplement the bus service in mountainous areas – see p339.

334 GETTING AROUND •• Car

On any bus, sit between the axles to mini-mise the effect of bumps and potholes. Locals are extremely prone to travel sickness so be ready to give up your window seat to anyone who looks green. All buses make regular snack and toilet stops, providing a break from the rattle and shake but adding hours to journey times. Try to avoid travelling by bus out of Kolkata and other major cities – traffic jams will add hours to your journey.

Avoid night buses unless there is no al-ternative – drivers use the quieter roads as an excuse to take even more death-defying risks. Note that buses must travel in armed convoys through some parts of the north-east, particularly in northern Tripura – check the latest security situation before you travel (see p307).

Luggage is either stored in compartments underneath the bus (sometimes for a small fee) or it can be carried free of charge on the roof. You may prefer to carry your own bags up onto the roof to make sure they are locked shut and securely tied to the metal baggage rack.

Theft is a minor risk so keep an eye on your bags at snack and toilet stops and never leave your day pack unattended inside the bus. If you have a walkman or iPod, don't be surprised if an intrigued local grabs one of your earphones – it happens!

Riding on the roof on public buses used to be a thrilling way to see the Indian coun-tryside but the authorities have decided that it is a) dangerous and b) too much fun. It's now only possible on local buses between outlying villages.

Classes

Both state and private companies offer 'ordi-nary' buses – ageing rattletraps with wonky windows that blast in dust and cold air – or more expensive 'deluxe' buses with AC and reclining seating. The phrase to look for when booking a deluxe bus is 'two by two', meaning two seats, either side of the aisle. Try to book at least one day in advance. Be warned that travel agents have been known to book people onto ordinary buses at super-deluxe prices – try to book directly with the bus company.

Costs

On ordinary-class buses, expect to pay Rs40 to Rs80 for a three-hour daytime journey and Rs250 to Rs400 for an all-day or over-night trip. Add around 50% to the ordinary fare for deluxe services, double the fare for AC and triple or quadruple the fare for a two-by-two service.

Reservations

Deluxe buses can usually be booked in ad-vance – up to a month ahead for govern-ment buses – at the bus stand or through local travel agents. On ordinary-class buses you can secure a seat by sending a travel-ling companion ahead of you while you deal with the luggage, or pass a book or article of clothing through an open window and place it on an empty seat. If you board a bus midjourney, your luggage will probably end up on your lap.

At many bus stations there is a separate women's queue, although this isn't always obvious as signs are often in Hindi and men frequently join the melee. Local women will merrily push to the front and few people will object if female travellers do the same.

CAR

With the state of India's roads, few people bother with self-drive car rental, but hiring a car with a driver is surprisingly affordable, particularly if several people share the costs. Seatbelts are rarely working – if they are, use them, or hold on to handrails.

Hiring a Car & Driver

Hiring a car and driver is an excellent way to see several places in one day. However, many taxis can only operate in a designated area, dictated by their government permit. Taxi licences are issued on a state by state basis so expect an additional fee if you cross any state border. In larger towns, taxis usually operate from designated stands.

Try to find a driver who speaks some English and knows the region. For multiday trips, the fare should cover the driver's meals and accommodation, but confirm this when you book (preferably in writing). Drivers gen-erally make their own sleeping and eating arrangements in the evening.

Once you have agreed a fare, it is *essential* to set the ground rules from day one. Many travellers have complained of having their holiday completely dictated by their driver. Politely, but firmly, let the driver know from the outset that you're the boss.

ROAD DISTANCES (km)

	Agartala	Bhubaneswar	Bodhgaya	Darjeeling	Delhi	Guwahati	Kohima	Kolkata	Puri	Shillong	Varanasi
Agartala	---										
Bhubaneswar	2179	---									
Bodhgaya	1443	745	---								
Darjeeling	468	819	454	---							
Delhi	2584	1745	1015	1559	---						
Guwahati	599	1483	1044	550	1959	---					
Kohima	683	1822	1383	889	2298	339	---				
Kolkata	1680	441	456	681	1461	1081	1420	---			
Puri	1196	93	552	889	1538	2022	2361	1524	---		
Shillong	499	1583	781	650	2059	100	439	1181	2122	---	
Varanasi	1778	965	270	779	780	1179	1518	680	843	1279	---

TRANSPORT

COSTS

The cost of charter trips depends on the distance, the duration of the journey and the terrain. One-way trips often cost as much as return trips to cover petrol for the driver's return trip. Expect to pay around Rs800 for a day trip around a big city or Rs1500 to Rs2000 for a day trip around the countryside, including petrol and waiting time at sights along the way. Some taxi unions set a time limit or a maximum distance for day trips – if you go over, you'll have to pay extra. To avoid problems, confirm in advance that the fare covers petrol, sightseeing stops, all your chosen destinations and meals and accommodation for the driver.

You generally pay the fee at the end of the trip, though the driver may ask for an advance to cover petrol (ask for a written record of this at the time). A moderate tip is customary.

Self-Drive Hire

Self-drive car hire is possible in Kolkata, but given the hair-raising driving conditions most travellers don't take the gamble. To drive yourself, you'll need an international driving permit. International rental companies with representatives in India include **Budget** (www .budget.com) and **Hertz** (www.hertz.com). Kolkata has several local car-hire companies, including **Srisiddha Velocity** (www.srisiddha.com). For information on road rules and conditions, see p338.

HITCHING

Truck drivers supplement the bus service in some remote areas for a fee, but as drivers rarely speak English, you may have difficulty explaining where you want to go and working out how much is a fair price to pay. Don't be surprised if you end up in the back with the freight. As anywhere, women are strongly advised against hitching alone.

LOCAL TRANSPORT

Buses, cycle-rickshaws, autorickshaws, taxis, boats and urban trains provide transport around the cities of the northeast. On any form of transport without a fixed fare, agree on the fare *before* you start your journey and make sure it covers luggage and every passenger. If you don't, expect heated altercations over the fare when you get to your destination.

TRANSPORT

Even where local transport is metered, drivers may refuse to use the meter, demanding an elevated 'fixed' fare. If this happens, hail another taxi – moving taxis are more likely to charge a fair price than taxis parked at tourist sights. On some routes, particularly to airports, it may be impossible to get a metered fare.

Costs for public transport vary from town to town. Fares usually increase at night (by up to 100%) and some drivers charge a few rupees extra for luggage. Carry plenty of small bills for taxi and rickshaw fares as drivers rarely have change. In some areas, taxis may pick up additional passengers to earn extra from the ride.

Taxi and rickshaw drivers are often involved in the commission racket – for more information, see p308.

Autorickshaw, Tempo & Vikram

Also known as autos, scooters, tuk-tuks or Bajaj (after the company that makes them), Indian autorickshaws are three-wheeled motorcycles with a cab, providing room for two passengers and luggage. Autorickshaws tend to be cheaper than taxis and they are usually metered, though getting the driver to turn the meter on can be a challenge.

Tempos and vikrams are outsized autorickshaws with room for more passengers, running on fixed routes for a fixed fare. In country areas, you may also see the fearsome-looking 'three-wheeler' – a crude, tractorlike tempo with a front wheel on an articulated arm.

Boat

Various kinds of local ferries offer transport across and down rivers in the northeast, including the mighty Brahmaputra – see the regional chapters for details. Most boats will also carry bikes and motorcycles, even tiny canoes, for a fee.

Bus

Urban buses, particularly in the big cities, are fume-belching, human-stuffed, mechanical monsters that travel at breakneck speed (except during morning and evening rush hour, when they hardly move at all). Routes can be confusing and there is rarely any space for luggage – it's usually more convenient and comfortable to opt for an autorickshaw or taxi.

Cycle-Rickshaw

Based on a modified bicycle frame, cyclerickshaws have a bench seat for passengers over the two rear wheels and a lavishly decorated canopy that can be raised in wet weather, or lowered to provide extra space for luggage.

As with taxis and autorickshaws, fares must be agreed upon in advance. Locals invariably pay lower fares than foreigners, but considering the effort put in by the rickshaw-wallahs, it's hard to begrudge them a few extra rupees. Around Rs20 to Rs40 is a fair price to pay for a 1km to 2km journey in town and tips are always appreciated.

Kolkata is the last bastion of the humanpowered rickshaw, a handcart pulled directly by the rickshaw-wallah, though some people feel that being towed around by an impoverished local is a little too colonial for comfort. The government of West Bengal has plans to ban the rickshaws, but rickshaw-wallahs have so far resisted the ban.

Taxi

Most towns have metered taxis, but drivers routinely claim that the meter is broken and request an arbitrary fixed fare. Threatening to take another taxi will often miraculously fix the meter. It is usually less hassle to use a prepaid taxi (see the boxed text, below) from the airport or train station.

Getting a metered ride is only half the battle. Meters are almost always outdated, so fares are calculated using a combination of the meter reading and a complicated fare adjustment card. Predictably, this system is open to abuse. If you spend a few days in any town, you'll soon get a feel for the difference between a reasonable fare and a

---

PREPAID TAXIS

Most Indian airports and many train stations have a prepaid-taxi booth, normally just outside the terminal building. Here, you can book a taxi to town for a fixed price (which will include baggage) and hopefully avoid price hikes and commission scams. However, it makes sense to hold on to the payment coupon until your reach your chosen destination, in case the driver has any other ideas. Smaller airports and stations may have prepaid autorickshaw booths instead.

rip-off. Many taxi drivers supplement their earnings with commissions – refuse any unplanned diversions to shops, hotels or private travel agencies.

Other Local Transport

In some towns, tongas (two-wheeled horse or pony carriages) and victorias (horse-drawn carriages) still operate. Kolkata has a tram network and a fast and efficient underground train network. See regional chapters for further details.

MOTORCYCLE

With its quiet back roads, challenging terrain and spectacular scenery, the northeast is an amazing part of the country for long-distance motorcycle touring. However, riding in India can be quite an undertaking – there are some excellent motorcycle tours (see right) that will save you the rigmarole of going it alone.

The classic way to motorcycle around India is on an Enfield Bullet, still built to the original 1940s specifications. As well as making a satisfyingly throaty roar, these bikes are fully manual, making them easy to repair (parts can be found everywhere in India). On the other hand, Enfields are less reliable than many of the newer, Japanese-designed bikes.

Sikkim, West Bengal and Assam are popular destinations for motorcycle expeditions and a few groups make it into Arunachal Pradesh with help from local travel agencies. You may also be able to cross into Nepal, Bangladesh and Bhutan with the correct paperwork – contact the relevant diplomatic mission for details.

The most popular starting point for motorcycle tours is Delhi, partly because this is the easiest place to buy or rent a motorcycle. Even if your final destination is the northeast, it probably makes sense to fly into Delhi to rent or buy a bike before you travel across the country.

Driving Licence

Many rental places will accept the driving licence from your home country, but technically you are required to have a valid international driving permit endorsed for motorcycles to hire a bike in India. It is unlikely that you will be covered by insurance if you do not have the correct paperwork, and you are also opening yourself up to the risk of being hit for bribes by traffic cops.

Fuel & Spare Parts

Spare parts for Indian and Japanese machines are widely available in larger towns and cities, but it makes sense to carry spares (valves, fuel lines, piston rings etc). Seek local advice about fuel availability before setting off into remote regions – petrol stations can be few and far between.

For all machines, make sure you regularly check and tighten all nuts and bolts. Check the engine and gearbox oil level regularly (at least every 500km) and clean the oil filter every few thousand kilometres. Trips to puncturewallahs are par for the course – start your trip with new tyres (around Rs1500) and carry spanners to remove your own wheels.

Hire

Long-term motorcycle rental is not widely available in the northeast, so it's best to rent a bike in Delhi and get it to the northeast by train (see the boxed text, p338). Delhi's Karol Bagh is the best place to rent bikes. As a deposit, you'll need to leave your passport, air ticket or a big cash lump sum – the latter is preferable as you may have trouble checking into hotels without your passport and police can ask to see your papers at any time.

One consistently reliable company for long-term rentals is **Lalli Motorbike Exports** (☎ 011-28750869; www.lallisingh.com; basement 1740-A/55, Hari Singh Nalwa St, Abdul Aziz Rd, Karol Bagh, Delhi). For three weeks' hire, a standard 500cc Enfield costs Rs17,000 and a 350cc costs Rs15,000. The price includes excellent advice and an invaluable crash course in Enfield mechanics and repairs.

Insurance

Only rent a bike with third-party insurance: if you hit someone without insurance, the consequences can be severe. Reputable companies include third-party cover in their policies. Those that don't probably aren't reputable.

You must also arrange insurance if you buy a motorcycle. The minimum level of cover is third-party insurance – available for Rs400 to Rs500 per year. Comprehensive insurance (recommended) costs Rs500 to Rs2000 per year.

Organised Motorcycle Tours

A number of well-run motorcycle tour companies offer trips around Sikkim, Assam and West Bengal (usually combined with a trip through Bhutan), with a support vehicle,

TRANSPORT

mechanic and a guide, though these trips can be expensive. Below are some reputable companies (see websites for contact details, itineraries and prices):

Classic Bike Adventure (www.classic-bike-india.com)

Ferris Wheels (www.ferriswheels.com.au)

H-C Travel (www.hctravel.com)

Himalayan Roadrunners (www.ridehigh.com)

Lalli Singh Tours (www.lallisingh.com) For bespoke tours.

MotoDiscovery (www.motodiscovery.com)

Saffron Road Motorcycle Tours (www.saffronroad.com)

Shepherds Realms (www.asiasafari.com)

Purchase

If you are planning a longer tour, consider purchasing a motorcycle. Secondhand bikes are widely available from bike-repair shops and the paperwork is a lot easier than buying a new machine.

Again, Delhi's Karol Bagh is the best place to purchase a motorcycle. Hari Singh Nalwa St has dozens of motorcycle and parts shops, but we consistently receive good reports about Lalli Motorbike Exports (p337).

COSTS

A well-looked-after, secondhand 350cc Enfield will cost Rs18,000 to Rs40,000; the 500cc model will cost Rs45,000 to Rs75,000. Modern European-style bikes go for Rs40,000 to Rs50,000. You should be able to resell the bike for 50% to 60% of the original price if it's still in decent condition.

As well as the cost of the bike, you'll have to pay for insurance – see p337. An Enfield 500cc gives about 25km/L and the 350cc model gives slightly more. Shipping an Indian bike overseas is complicated and expensive – ask the shop from which you bought the bike to explain the process.

OWNERSHIP PAPERS

The registration papers are signed by the local registration authority when the bike is first sold and you'll need these papers when you buy a secondhand bike. You must make absolutely sure there are no outstanding debts or criminal proceedings associated with the bike, or else you will be liable. Foreign nationals cannot change the name on the registration. Instead, you must fill out the forms for a change of ownership and transfer of insurance. If you buy a new bike, the company selling it must register the machine for you, adding to the cost. The whole process is extremely complicated and it makes sense to seek advice from the company selling the bike. Allow around two weeks to get the paperwork finished and get on the road.

Road Conditions

Given the road conditions in India, this is not a country for novice riders. Hazards range from potholes and cows and chickens crossing the carriageway to unsteady pedal cyclists, broken-down trucks, jaywalking pedestrians, unmarked speed humps and children stopping traffic with a rope to collect money for local temples. Rural roads sometimes have crops strewn across them to be threshed by passing vehicles – a serious sliding hazard for bikers.

Try not to cover too much territory in one day and avoid travelling after dark. On busy national highways expect to average 50km/h without stops; on winding back roads and dirt tracks this can drop to 10km/h.

Road Rules

Traffic in India nominally drives on the left-hand side but, in reality, most people drive on the least-damaged stretch of tarmac in the middle of the road. Observe local speed limits (these vary from state to state) and give way to *all* larger vehicles. Locals tend to use the horn more than the brake, but travellers should heed the advice of the Border Roads Organisation – it is better to be Mr Late than the late Mr! Alcohol and riding never go together – it's illegal as well as insanely risky.

TRANSPORTING MOTORCYCLES BY RAIL

To transport your bicycle by train, first buy a standard train ticket for the journey, then take your bike to the station parcel office with your passport, registration papers, international driving permit and insurance documents. Packing-wallahs will wrap your bike in protective sacking for around Rs100 and you must fill out various forms and pay the shipping fee – around Rs1600 for a 350cc or smaller bike – plus an insurance fee of 1% of the declared value of the bike. You then bring the same paperwork to collect your bike from the goods office at the far end.

SHARE JEEPS

In mountain areas, jeeps supplement the bus service, charging similar fixed fares. In same areas, jeeps are known as 'Sumos' after the Tata Sumo. Although nominally designed for five to six passengers, most vehicles manage to squeeze in as many as 11. If you don't feel like playing squish the backpacker, pay extra for the more roomy seats beside and immediately behind the driver. Jeeps leave when full, but drivers will leave immediately if you pay for all the empty seats in the vehicle.

Jeeps run from jeep stands and 'passenger stations' at the junctions of major roads; ask locals to point you in the right direction. Be warned that many locals suffer from travel sickness – be prepared to give up your window seat to queasy fellow passengers.

TOURS

Tours are available all over India, run by tourist offices, local transport companies and travel agencies. However, it is often cheaper to organise your own bespoke tour by hiring a taxi and driver for the day. Be wary of touts claiming to be professional guides in tourist towns – ask the local tourist office for advice on reputable guides. Assess the experience of trekking guides by asking about routes, distances, equipment and the type of terrain involved – vague answers should set off alarm bells.

On any overnight tour or trek, ensure that all the necessary equipment is provided (eg first aid, camping gear) and inspect everything before you set off. Always confirm exactly what the quoted price includes (food, accommodation, petrol, trekking equipment, guide fees etc). Do not rely on being able to find reliable trekking gear for sale in the northeast – bring what you need from home.

See the Tours sections in the regional chapters for information on local tours. For more on treks and tours, read the Activities chapter (p92).

TRAIN

You don't have to be a trainspotter to get a thrill out of travelling by train in India. The rail network goes almost everywhere, prices are reasonable and the experience of travelling on an Indian train is a reason to travel all by itself. Around 14 million passengers travel by train in India every day so you'll have plenty of opportunities to interact with locals.

At first the process of booking a train seat can seem bewildering, but behind the scenes things are incredibly well organised – see p340 for tips on buying a ticket. Trains are far better than buses for long-distance and overnight trips – you can lie down, walk around and use the bathroom whenever you need to.

Train services to certain destinations are often increased during major festivals but the crowds make this a risky time to travel. Something else to be aware of is passenger drugging and theft – see p308.

We've listed useful trains throughout this book, but for more help planning journeys pick up the invaluable *Trains at a Glance* (Rs45), a list of every train service, available at train station bookstalls and city news-stands. Alternatively, you can use the train search engine on the **Indian Railways** (www.indianrail.gov.in) website. For a brilliant introduction to travelling on India's trains, point your browser towards www.seat61.com/India.htm.

Larger stations often employ English-speaking staff who can help with picking the best train. At smaller stations, midlevel officials such as the deputy station master usually speak English.

Classes

The key to travelling by train in India is learning the different classes. The cheapest and least-comfortable option on all trains is general class (2nd class) with unreserved seating in carriages that would make sardines feel claustrophobic (people even sit on the overhead baggage racks). Unless you have no other option, it's worth paying extra for a reserved seat. On day trains, there may be a 'chair car' with padded reclining seats and (usually) AC, or an executive chair car with better seats and more space.

For overnight trips, you have several choices. Sleeper berths are arranged in groups of six, with two roomier berths across the aisle, in fan-cooled carriages. Air-conditioned carriages have either three-tier air-con (3AC) berths, in the same configuration as sleepers, or two-tier air-con (2AC) berths in groups of four on either side of the aisle. Some trains also have flashier 1st-class air-con (1AC) berths, with a choice of two- or four-berth compartments with locking doors.

TRANSPORT

TRANSPORT

EXPRESS TRAIN FARES IN RUPEES						
Distance (km)	1AC	2AC	3AC	Chair car	Sleeper	2nd-class
100	542	322	158	122	56	35
200	794	430	256	199	91	57
300	1081	556	348	271	124	78
400	1347	693	433	337	154	97
500	1613	830	519	404	185	116
1000	2628	1352	845	657	301	188
1500	3328	1712	1070	832	381	238
2000	4028	2072	1295	1007	461	288

Bedding is provided in all AC sleeping compartments and there is usually a meal service, plus regular visits from the coffee- and chai-wallah. In sleeper class, bring your own bedding. Bring a padlock and a length of chain to secure your luggage to the baggage racks under or above the seats.

In sleeping compartments, the lower berths convert to seats for day-time use. If you'd rather sleep late, book the top berth. Note that there is usually a locked door between the reserved and unreserved carriages – if you get trapped on the wrong side, you'll have to wait till the next station to change.

There are also special train services connecting major cities. Shatabdi express trains are same-day services with seating only. Rajdhani express trains are long-distance, overnight, point-to-point services between Delhi and other state capitals – passengers travel in AC carriages and meals are included in the ticket price.

Costs

Fares are calculated by distance and class of travel, as shown in the table, above. Seniors, the disabled and other special categories of passenger (including war widows and freedom fighters who fought against the British) get discounted train tickets – see p309.

Rajdhani and Shatabdi express trains are slightly more expensive than ordinary mail and express trains, but the price includes meals. Most AC carriages have a catering service (meals are bought to your seat); in unreserved classes, carry snacks or jump out where the train stops to grab a snack from the platform (just don't get left behind!).

To find out fares, use the search engine on www.indianrail.gov.in. To find out which trains travel between any two destinations, go to www.trainenquiry.com and click on 'Find Your Train'.

Most major stations have 'retiring rooms' (see p303) and a left-luggage office (cloakroom). Locked bags (only) can be stored for a small daily fee if you have a valid train ticket. For peace of mind, chain your bag to the baggage rack and check the opening times to make sure you can get your bag when you need it. A locally made tin trunk closed with a padlock will keep your rucksack safe and secure.

Reservations

No reservations are required for general (2nd-class) compartments. You can reserve seats in all chair car, sleeper, 1AC, 2AC and 3AC carriages up to 60 days in advance – book ahead for all overnight journeys.

The reservation procedure is fairly simple – obtain a reservation slip from the information window and fill in the name of the station where you are starting your journey, the destination station, the class you want to travel in and the name and number of the train (this is where *Trains at a Glance* comes into its own). You then join the long queue leading to the ticket window to pay for and receive your ticket.

Almost all stations have a fast-track counter for female travellers and, in larger cities, there are dedicated ticket windows for foreigners (with English-speaking staff) and special counters for credit-card payments. Be prepared to fend off queue jumpers to keep your place in line.

If you'd rather avoid the melee of the general reservations hall, there are special reservation offices in Kolkata (see p133) and other major cities where you can book special 'tourist quota' seats, which are reserved exclusively for foreign tourists travelling between popular stations.

To book, you must show your passport and visa as ID. You can pay for tourist quota seats in rupees, UK pounds, US dollars or euros, in cash or Thomas Cook and Amex travellers cheques (change is given in rupees). However, some offices may ask to see foreign-exchange certificates before accepting payment in rupees.

A small number of tickets are reserved for sale within five days of travel under the *taktal* (immediate) system – these tickets are open to anyone but there is an additional service charge of Rs75 to Rs150 for seats and Rs200 to Rs300 for overnight berths.

Internet bookings are possible at www.irctc.co.in, and you can choose an e-ticket or have the tickets sent to you inside India by courier. See the 'How to buy tickets – from outside India' heading at www.seat61.com/India.htm.

Trains are frequently overbooked, but many passengers cancel. You can buy a ticket on the wait list and try your luck – there is usually a good chance of getting onto your chosen train, and you can obtain a full refund if you fail to get a seat. Refunds are available on any ticket, even after departure, with a penalty – the rules are complicated so check when you book.

If you don't want to go through the hassle of buying a ticket yourself, many travel agencies and hotels can arrange them for a small commission, though scams abound and you may not always end up in the class you paid for.

Reserved tickets show your seat/berth number (or wait-list number) and the carriage number. When the train pulls in, keep an eye out for your carriage number written on the side of the train. A list of names and berths is also posted on the side of each reserved carriage – a beacon of light for panicking travellers! Be aware that Indian trains can be dozens of carriages long – always give yourself plenty of time to find your seat.

It's wise to book well ahead if you plan on travelling during Indian holidays or festivals, when seats can fill up incredibly fast.

Train Passes

The Indrail pass permits unlimited rail travel for one to 90 days of travel, but it offers limited savings and you must still make reservations. You can book through overseas travel agents or station ticket offices in major Indian cities – click on the 'Information/International Tourist' link on www.indianrail.gov.in for prices and conditions.

TRANSPORT

Health Dr Trish Batchelor

CONTENTS

There is huge geographical variation in India, from tropical beaches to the Himalaya mountains. Consequently, environmental issues such as heat, cold and altitude can cause significant health problems. Hygiene is generally poor in most parts of India so food- and water-borne illnesses are common. Many insect-borne diseases are present, particularly in tropical regions. Medical care is basic in many areas (especially beyond larger cities) so it's essential to be prepared before travelling.

Travellers worry about contracting infectious diseases when in the tropics, but these rarely cause serious illness or death in travellers. Pre-existing medical conditions and accidental injury (eg in traffic) account for most life-threatening problems. Becoming ill in some way, however, is very common. Fortunately most travellers' illnesses can be prevented with common-sense behaviour or treated with a well-stocked traveller's medical kit – but never hesitate to consult a doctor while on the road, as self-diagnosis can be hazardous.

The following advice is a general guide only and certainly does not replace the advice of a doctor trained in travel medicine.

BEFORE YOU GO

Pack medications in their original, clearly labelled containers. A signed and dated letter from your physician describing your medical conditions and medications, including generic names, is very useful. If carrying syringes or needles, be sure to have a physician's letter documenting their medical necessity. If you have a heart condition, bring a copy of your ECG taken just prior to travelling.

If you take any regular medication, bring twice the amount you need ordinarily in case of loss or theft. You'll be able to buy quite a few medications over the counter in India without a doctor's prescription, but it can be difficult to find some of the newer drugs, particularly the latest antidepressant drugs, blood-pressure medications and contraceptive pills.

INSURANCE

Even if you are fit and healthy, don't travel without health insurance – accidents do happen. Declare any existing medical conditions you have – the insurance company will check if your problem is pre-existing and will not cover you if it is undeclared. You may require extra cover for adventure activities such as rock climbing and scuba diving. If your health insurance doesn't cover you for medical expenses abroad, consider getting extra insurance. If you're uninsured, emergency evacuation is expensive; bills of over US$100,000 are not uncommon.

It's a good idea to find out in advance if your insurance plan will make payments directly to providers or if it will reimburse you later for overseas health expenditures (in India, doctors usually expect payment in cash). Some policies offer lower and higher medical-expense options; the higher ones are chiefly for countries that have extremely high medical costs, such as the United States. You may prefer a policy that pays doctors or hospitals directly rather than you having to pay on the spot and claim from your insurance company later. However be aware that most medical facilities in India require immediate payment. If you do have to claim later, make sure you keep all relevant documentation. Some policies ask that you telephone back (reverse charges) to a centre in your home country where an immediate assessment of your problem will be made.

MEDICAL CHECKLIST

Recommended items for a personal medical kit:

- Antifungal cream, eg Clotrimazole
- Antibacterial cream, eg Muciprocin
- Antibiotic for skin infections, eg Amoxicillin/Clavulanate or Cephalexin
- Antihistamine – there are many options, eg Cetrizine for daytime and Promethazine for night
- Antiseptic, eg Betadine
- Antispasmodic for stomach cramps, eg Buscopan
- Contraceptive method
- Decongestant, eg Pseudoephedrine
- DEET-based insect repellent
- Diarrhoea medication – consider an oral rehydration solution (eg Gastrolyte), diarrhoea 'stopper' (eg Loperamide) and antinausea medication (eg Prochlorperazine). Antibiotics for diarrhoea include Norfloxacin or Ciprofloxacin; for bacterial diarrhoea Azithromycin; for giardia or amoebic dysentery Tinidazole.
- First-aid items such as scissors, sticking plasters, bandages, gauze, thermometer (but not mercury), sterile needles and syringes, safety pins and tweezers
- Ibuprofen or another anti-inflammatory
- Indigestion tablets, eg Quick Eze or Mylanta
- Iodine tablets (unless you are pregnant or have a thyroid problem) to purify water
- Laxative, eg Coloxyl
- Migraine medication if you suffer from them
- Paracetamol
- Pyrethrin to impregnate clothing and mosquito nets
- Steroid cream for allergic/itchy rashes, eg 1% to 2% hydrocortisone
- High-factor sunscreen and wide-brimmed hat
- Throat lozenges
- Thrush (vaginal yeast infection) treatment, eg Clotrimazole pessaries or Diflucan tablet
- Ural or equivalent if prone to urine infections

VACCINATIONS

Specialised travel-medicine clinics are your best source of up-to-date information; they stock all vaccines and will be able to give specific recommendations for you and your trip. The doctors take into account factors such as vaccination history, the length of your trip, activities you may be undertaking and underlying medical conditions such as pregnancy.

Most vaccines don't give immunity until *at least* two weeks after they're given, so visit a doctor four to eight weeks before departure. Ask your doctor for an International Certificate of Vaccination (otherwise known as the 'yellow booklet'), which will list all the vaccinations you've received.

Recommended Vaccinations

The World Health Organization (WHO) recommends these vaccinations for travellers to India (as well as being up to date with measles, mumps and rubella vaccinations):

Adult diphtheria and tetanus Single booster recommended if none in the previous 10 years. Side effects include sore arm and fever.

Hepatitis A Provides almost 100% protection for up to a year; a booster after 12 months provides at least another 20 years' protection. Mild side effects such as headache and sore arm occur in 5% to 10% of people.

Hepatitis B Now considered routine for most travellers. Given as three shots over six months. A rapid schedule is also available, as is a combined vaccination with Hepatitis A. Side effects are mild and uncommon: usually headache and sore arm. In 95% of people lifetime protection results.

Polio Only one booster is required as an adult for lifetime protection. Inactivated polio vaccine is safe during pregnancy.

Typhoid Recommended for all travellers to India, even those only visiting urban areas. The vaccine offers around 70% protection, lasts for two to three years and comes as a single shot. Tablets are also available; however, the injection is usually recommended as it has fewer side effects. Sore arm and fever may occur.

Varicella If you haven't had chickenpox, discuss this vaccination with your doctor.

These immunisations are recommended for long-term travellers (more than one month) or those at special risk (seek further advice from your doctor):

Japanese B Encephalitis Three injections in all. Booster recommended after two years. Sore arm and headache are the most common side effects. Rarely, an allergic reaction involving hives and swelling can occur up to 10 days after any of the three doses.

Meningitis Single injection. There are two types of vaccination: the quadravalent vaccine gives two to three years' protection; meningitis group C vaccine gives around 10 years' protection. Recommended for long-term backpackers aged under 25.

Rabies Three injections in all. A booster after one year will then provide 10 years' protection. Side effects are rare – occasionally headache and sore arm.

Tuberculosis (TB) A complex issue. Adult long-term travellers are usually recommended to have a TB skin test before and after travel, rather than vaccination. Only one vaccine given in a lifetime.

Required Vaccinations

The only vaccine required by international regulations is yellow fever. Proof of vaccination will only be required if you have visited a country in the yellow-fever zone within the six days prior to entering India. If you are travelling to India from Africa or South America, you should check to see if you require proof of vaccination.

INTERNET RESOURCES

There is a wealth of travel-health advice on the internet – www.lonelyplanet.com is a good place to start. Some other suggestions:

Centers for Disease Control and Prevention (CDC; www.cdc.gov) Good general information.

MD Travel Health (www.mdtravelhealth.com) Provides complete travel-health recommendations for every country, updated daily.

World Health Organization (WHO; www.who.int/ith/) Its helpful book *International Travel & Health* is revised annually and available online.

FURTHER READING

Lonely Planet's *Asia & India: Healthy Travel Guide* is a handy pocket size and packed with useful information, including pretrip planning, emergency first aid, immunisation and disease information, and what to do if you get sick on the road. Other recommended references include *Travellers' Health* by Dr Richard Dawood and *Travelling Well* by Dr Deborah Mills – check out the website of **Travelling Well** (www.travellingwell.com.au).

IN TRANSIT

DEEP VEIN THROMBOSIS (DVT)

Deep vein thrombosis (DVT) occurs when blood clots form in the legs during plane flights, chiefly because of prolonged immobility. The longer the flight, the greater the risk. Though most blood clots are reabsorbed uneventfully, some may break off and travel through the blood vessels to the lungs, where they may cause life-threatening complications.

The chief symptom of DVT is swelling or pain of the foot, ankle or calf, usually but not always on just one side. When a blood clot travels to the lungs, it may cause chest pain and difficulty in breathing. Travellers with any of these symptoms should immediately seek medical attention.

To prevent the development of DVT on long flights, walk about the cabin, perform isometric compressions of the leg muscles (ie contract the leg muscles while sitting), drink plenty of fluids, and avoid alcohol and tobacco.

JET LAG & MOTION SICKNESS

Jet lag is common when crossing more than five time zones; it results in insomnia, fatigue, malaise and/or nausea. To avoid jet lag try drinking plenty of fluids (nonalcoholic) and eating light meals. Upon arrival, seek exposure to natural sunlight and readjust your schedule (for meals, sleep etc) as soon as possible.

Antihistamines such as dimenhydrinate (Dramamine), promethazine (Phenergan) and meclizine (Antivert, Bonine) are usually the first choice for treating motion sickness. Their main side effect is drowsiness. One herbal alternative is ginger, which works wonders for some people.

IN INDIA

AVAILABILITY OF HEALTHCARE

Medical care is hugely variable in India, especially beyond the big cities. Some cities have clinics catering specifically to travellers and expatriates. These clinics are usually more expensive than local medical facilities, but are worth utilising, as they should offer a higher standard of care. Additionally, they understand the local system, and are aware of the most reputable local hospitals and specialists. They may also liaise with insurance companies should you need evacuation. Recommended clinics are listed under Information in the regional chapters of this book. It is usually difficult to find reliable medical care in rural areas.

Self-treatment may be appropriate if your problem is minor (eg traveller's diarrhoea), you are carrying the relevant medication and you cannot attend a recommended clinic. However, if you suspect you may have a serious disease, especially malaria, do not waste time; travel to the nearest quality facility to receive attention. It is always better to be assessed by a doctor than to rely on self-treatment.

Before buying medication over the counter, always check the use-by date and ensure the packet is sealed. Don't accept items that have been poorly stored (eg lying in a glass cabinet exposed to the sunshine).

INFECTIOUS DISEASES
Avian Flu

'Bird Flu' or Influenza A (H5N1) is a subtype of the type A influenza virus. This virus typically infects birds and not humans; however, in 1997 the first documented case of bird-to-human transmission was recorded in Hong Kong. Currently, very close contact with dead or sick birds is the principal source of infection and bird-to-human transmission does not easily occur.

Symptoms include high fever and typical influenza-like symptoms with rapid deterioration leading to respiratory failure and death in many cases. The early administration of antiviral drugs, such as Tamiflu, is recommended to improve the chances of survival. At this time it is not routinely recommended for travellers to carry Tamiflu with them – rather, immediate medical care should be sought if bird flu is suspected.

There is currently no vaccine available to prevent bird flu. For up-to-date information check these two websites:
■ www.who.int/en/
■ www.avianinfluenza.com.au

Coughs, Colds & Chest Infections

Around 25% of travellers to India will develop a respiratory infection. This usually starts as a virus and is exacerbated by environmental conditions, such as pollution in the cities, or cold and altitude in the mountains. Commonly a secondary bacterial infection will intervene – marked by fever, chest pain and coughing up discoloured or blood-tinged sputum. If you have the symptoms of an infection seek medical advice or consider commencing a general antibiotic.

Dengue Fever

This mosquito-borne disease is becoming increasingly problematic in the tropical world, especially in the cities. As there is no vaccine it can only be prevented by avoiding mosquito bites. The mosquito that carries dengue bites day and night, so use insect avoidance measures at all times. Symptoms include high fever, severe headache and body ache (dengue was previously known as 'breakbone fever'). Some people develop a rash and experience diarrhoea. There is no specific treatment, just rest and paracetamol – do not take aspirin as it increases the likelihood of haemorrhaging. See a doctor to be diagnosed and monitored.

Hepatitis A

A problem throughout the region, this food- and water-borne virus infects the liver, causing jaundice (yellow skin and eyes), nausea and lethargy. There is no specific treatment for hepatitis A, you just need to allow time for the liver to heal. All travellers to India should be vaccinated against hepatitis A.

Hepatitis B

The only sexually transmitted disease that can be prevented by vaccination, hepatitis B is spread by body fluids. The long-term consequences can include liver cancer and cirrhosis.

Hepatitis E

Transmitted through contaminated food and water, hepatitis E has similar symptoms to hepatitis A, but is far less common. It is a severe problem in pregnant women and can result in the death of both mother and baby. There is currently no vaccine, and prevention is by following safe eating and drinking guidelines.

HIV

HIV is spread via contaminated body fluids. Avoid unsafe sex, unsterile needles (including in medical facilities) and procedures such as tattoos. The growth rate of HIV in India is one of the highest in the world – also see p46.

Influenza

Present year-round in the tropics, influenza (flu) symptoms include fever, muscle aches, runny nose, cough and sore throat. It can be severe in people over the age of 65 or in those with medical conditions such as heart disease or diabetes – vaccination is recommended for these individuals. There is no specific treatment, just rest and paracetamol.

Japanese B Encephalitis

This viral disease is transmitted by mosquitoes and is rare in travellers. Like most mosquito-borne diseases it is becoming a more common problem in affected countries. Most cases occur in rural areas and vaccination is recommended for travellers spending more than one month outside of cities. There is no treatment, and a third of infected people will die while another third will suffer permanent brain damage. Ask your doctor for further details.

Malaria

For such a serious and potentially deadly disease, there is an enormous amount of mis-

information concerning malaria. You must get expert advice as to whether your trip actually puts you at risk. For most rural areas, especially, the risk of contracting malaria far outweighs the risk of any tablet side effects. Before you travel, seek medical advice on the right medication and dosage for you.

Malaria is caused by a parasite transmitted by the bite of an infected mosquito. The most important symptom of malaria is fever, but general symptoms, such as headache, diarrhoea, cough or chills, may also occur. Diagnosis can only be properly made by taking a blood sample.

Two strategies should be combined to prevent malaria – mosquito avoidance and antimalaria medications. Most people who catch malaria are taking inadequate or no antimalarial medication.

Travellers are advised to prevent mosquito bites by taking these steps:

- Use a DEET-containing insect repellent on exposed skin. Wash this off at night, as long as you are sleeping under a mosquito net. Natural repellents such as citronella can be effective, but must be applied more frequently than products containing DEET.
- Sleep under a mosquito net impregnated with pyrethrin
- Choose accommodation with proper screens and fans (if not air-conditioned)
- Impregnate clothing with pyrethrin in high-risk areas
- Wear long sleeves and trousers in light colours
- Use mosquito coils
- Spray your room with insect repellent before going out for your evening meal

There are a variety of medications available. The effectiveness of the chloroquine and Paludrine combination is now limited in many parts of South Asia. Common side effects include nausea (40% of people) and mouth ulcers.

The daily tablet doxycycline is a broad-spectrum antibiotic that has the added benefit of helping to prevent a variety of tropical diseases, including leptospirosis, tick-borne disease and typhus. The potential side effects include photosensitivity (a tendency to sunburn), thrush (in women), indigestion, heartburn, nausea and interference with the contraceptive pill. More serious side effects include ulceration of the oesophagus – you can help prevent this by taking your tablet with a meal and a large glass of water, and never lying down within half an hour of taking it. It must be taken for four weeks after leaving the risk area.

Lariam (mefloquine) has received much bad press, some of it justified, some not. This weekly tablet suits many people. Serious side effects are rare but include depression, anxiety, psychosis and having fits. Anyone with a history of depression, anxiety, other psychological disorders or epilepsy should not take Lariam. It is considered safe in the second and third trimesters of pregnancy. Tablets must be taken for four weeks after leaving the risk area.

The newer drug Malarone is a combination of atovaquone and proguanil. Side effects are uncommon and mild, most commonly nausea and headache. It is the best tablet for scuba divers and for those on short trips to high-risk areas. It must be taken for one week after leaving the risk area.

Rabies

This uniformly fatal disease is spread by the bite or possibly even the lick of an infected animal – most commonly a dog or monkey. You should seek medical advice immediately after any animal bite and commence postexposure treatment. Having pretravel vaccination means the postbite treatment is greatly simplified. If an animal bites you, gently wash the wound with soap and water, and apply iodine-based antiseptic. If you are not prevaccinated you will need to receive rabies immunoglobulin as soon as possible, and this is very difficult to obtain in much of India.

STDs

Sexually transmitted diseases most common in India include herpes, warts, syphilis, gonorrhoea and chlamydia. People carrying these diseases often have no signs of infection. Condoms will prevent gonorrhoea and chlamydia but not warts or herpes. If after a sexual encounter you develop any rash, lumps, discharge or pain when passing urine, seek immediate medical attention. If you have been sexually active during your travels, have an STD check on your return home.

Tuberculosis

While TB is rare in travellers, those who have significant contact with the local population (such as medical and aid workers and long-term travellers) should take precautions. Vaccination is usually only given to children under the age of five, but adults at risk are recommended to have pre- and post-travel TB testing. The main symptoms are fever, cough, weight loss, night sweats and fatigue.

Typhoid

This serious bacterial infection is spread via food and water. It gives a headache and a high and slowly progressive fever, and may be accompanied by a dry cough and stomach pain. It is diagnosed by blood tests and treated with antibiotics. Vaccination is recommended for all travellers who are spending more than a week in India. Be aware that vaccination is not 100% effective, so you must still be careful what you eat and drink.

TRAVELLERS' DIARRHOEA

This is by far the most common problem affecting travellers in India – between 30% and 70% of people will suffer from it within two weeks of starting their trip. In over 80% of cases, travellers' diarrhoea is caused by a bacteria (there are numerous potential culprits), and therefore responds promptly to treatment with antibiotics. Treatment with antibiotics will depend on your situation – how sick you are, how quickly you need to get better, where you are etc.

Travellers' diarrhoea is defined as the passage of more than three watery bowel actions within 24 hours, plus at least one other symptom, such as fever, cramps, nausea, vomiting or feeling generally unwell.

Treatment consists of staying well hydrated; rehydration solutions like Gastrolyte are the best for this. Antibiotics such as norfloxacin, ciprofloxacin or azithromycin should kill the bacteria quickly.

Loperamide is just a 'stopper' and doesn't get to the cause of the problem. It can be helpful, though (eg if you have to go on a long bus ride). Don't take loperamide if you have a fever, or blood in your stools. Seek medical attention quickly if you do not respond to an appropriate antibiotic.

Amoebic Dysentery

Amoebic dysentery is very rare in travellers but is often misdiagnosed by poor-quality labs. Symptoms are similar to bacterial diarrhoea: fever, bloody diarrhoea and generally

HEALTH

DRINKING WATER

- Never drink tap water

- Bottled water is generally safe – check the seal is intact at purchase

- Avoid ice unless you know it has been safely made

- Be careful of fresh juices served at street stalls in particular – they may have been watered down or may be served in unhygienic jugs/glasses

- Boiling water is usually the most efficient method of purifying it

- The best chemical purifier is iodine. It should not be used by pregnant women or those with thyroid problems.

- Water filters should also filter out viruses. Ensure your filter has a chemical barrier such as iodine and a small pore size (less than four microns).

---

feeling unwell. You should always seek reliable medical care if you have blood in your diarrhoea. Treatment involves two drugs: Tinidazole or Metronidazole to kill the parasite in your gut and then a second drug to kill the cysts. If left untreated complications such as liver or gut abscesses can occur.

Giardiasis

Giardia is a parasite that is relatively common in travellers. Symptoms include nausea, bloating, excess gas, fatigue and intermittent diarrhoea. The parasite will eventually go away if left untreated but this can take months; the best advice is to seek medical treatment. The treatment of choice is Tinidazole, with Metronidazole being a second-line option.

ENVIRONMENTAL HAZARDS
Air Pollution

Air pollution, particularly vehicle pollution, is an increasing problem in most of India's urban hubs. If you have severe respiratory problems, speak with your doctor before travelling to India. This pollution also causes minor respiratory problems, such as sinusitis, dry throat and irritated eyes. If troubled by the pollution, leave the city for a few days and get some fresh air.

Diving & Surfing

Divers and surfers should seek specialised advice before they travel, to ensure their medical kit contains treatment for coral cuts and tropical ear infections, as well as the standard problems. Divers should ensure their insurance covers them for decompression illness –

get specialised dive insurance through an organisation such as **Divers Alert Network** (DAN; www.danasiapacific.org). Have a dive medical before you leave your home country – there are certain medical conditions that are incompatible with diving.

Food

Eating in restaurants is generally the biggest risk factor for contracting travellers' diarrhoea. Ways to avoid problems include eating only freshly cooked food, and avoiding shellfish and food that has been sitting in buffets. Peel all fruit, cook vegetables and soak salads in iodine water for at least 20 minutes. Eat in busy restaurants with a high turnover of customers. See also p74.

Heat

Many parts of India, especially down south, are hot and humid throughout the year. For most people it takes at least two weeks to adapt to the hot climate. Swelling of the feet and ankles is common, as are muscle cramps caused by excessive sweating. Prevent these by avoiding dehydration and excessive activity in the heat. Take it easy when you first arrive. Don't eat salt tablets (they aggravate the gut); drinking rehydration solution or eating salty food helps. Treat cramps by stopping activity, resting, rehydrating with double-strength rehydration solution and gently stretching.

Dehydration is the main contributor to heat exhaustion. Symptoms include feeling weak, headache, irritability, nausea or vomiting, sweaty skin, a fast weak pulse and a normal or slightly elevated body temperature. Treatment involves getting out of the heat and/or sun, fanning the sufferer and applying cool wet cloths to the skin, laying the sufferer flat with their legs raised and re-hydrating with water containing one-quarter teaspoon of salt per litre. Recovery is usually rapid and it is common to feel weak for some days afterwards.

Heat stroke is a serious medical emergency. Symptoms come on suddenly and include weakness, nausea, a hot dry body with a body temperature of over 41°C, dizziness, confusion, loss of coordination, fits, and eventually collapse and loss of consciousness. Seek medical help and commence cooling by getting the person out of the heat, removing their clothes, fanning them and applying cool wet cloths or ice to their body, especially to the groin and armpits.

Prickly heat is a common skin rash in the tropics, caused by sweat being trapped under the skin. The result is an itchy rash of tiny lumps. Treat it by moving out of the heat and into an air-conditioned area for a few hours and by having cool showers. Creams and ointments clog the skin so they should be avoided. Locally bought prickly-heat powder can be helpful.

Tropical fatigue is common in long-term expatriates based in the tropics. It's rarely due to disease and is caused by the climate, inadequate mental rest, excessive alcohol intake and the demands of daily work in a different culture.

High Altitude

If you are going to altitudes above 3000m, you should get information on preventing, recognising and treating Acute Mountain Sickness (AMS). The biggest risk factor for developing altitude sickness is going too high too quickly – you should follow a conservative acclimatisation schedule such as can be found in all good trekking guides – and you should *never* go to a higher altitude when you have any symptoms that could be altitude related. There is no way to predict who will get altitude sickness and it is often the younger, fitter members of a group who succumb.

Symptoms usually develop during the first 24 hours at altitude but may be delayed up to three weeks. Mild symptoms include headache, lethargy, dizziness, difficulty sleeping and loss of appetite. AMS may become more severe without warning and can be fatal. Severe symptoms include breathlessness, a dry, irritative cough (which may progress to the production of pink, frothy sputum), severe headache, lack of coordination and balance, confusion, irrational behaviour, vomiting, drowsiness and unconsciousness.

Treat mild symptoms by resting at the same altitude until recovery, which usually takes a day or two. Paracetamol or aspirin can be taken for headaches. If symptoms persist or become worse, however, immediate descent is necessary; even 500m can help. Drug treatments should never be used to avoid descent or to enable further ascent.

The drugs acetazolamide and dexamethasone are recommended by some doctors for the prevention of AMS; however, their use is controversial. They can reduce the symptoms, but they may also mask warning signs; severe and fatal AMS has occurred in people taking these drugs.

To prevent acute mountain sickness:

- Ascend slowly – have frequent rest days, spending two to three nights at each rise of 1000m.
- It is always wise to sleep at a lower altitude than the greatest height reached during the day, if possible. Also, once above 3000m, care should be taken not to increase the sleeping altitude by more than 300m per day.
- Drink extra fluids. The mountain air is dry and cold, and moisture is lost as you breathe.
- Eat light, high-carbohydrate meals.
- Avoid alcohol and sedatives.

Insect Bites & Stings

Bedbugs don't carry disease but their bites can be very itchy. They live in the cracks of furniture and walls and then migrate to the bed at night to feed on you. You can treat the itch with an antihistamine. Lice inhabit various parts of your body but most commonly your head and pubic area. Transmission is via close contact with an infected person. Lice can be difficult to treat and you may need numerous applications of an antilice shampoo such as pyrethrin. Pubic lice are usually contracted from sexual contact.

Ticks are contracted while walking in rural areas. Ticks are commonly found behind the ears, on the belly and in armpits. If you have had a tick bite and experience symptoms such as a rash at the site of the bite or elsewhere, fever or muscle aches, you should see a doctor. Doxycycline prevents tick-borne diseases.

Leeches are found in humid rainforest areas. They do not transmit any disease but their bites are often intensely itchy for weeks afterwards and can easily become infected. Apply an iodine-based antiseptic to any leech bite to help prevent infection.

Bee and wasp stings mainly cause problems for people who are allergic to them. Anyone with a serious bee or wasp allergy should carry an injection of adrenalin (eg an Epipen) for emergency treatment. For others pain is the main problem – apply ice to the sting and take painkillers.

Skin Problems

Fungal rashes are common in humid climates. There are two common fungal rashes that affect travellers. The first occurs in moist areas, such as the groin, armpits and between the toes. It starts as a red patch that slowly spreads and is usually itchy. Treatment involves keeping the skin dry, avoiding chafing and using an antifungal cream such as clotrimazole or Lamisil. *Tinea versicolor* is also common – this fungus causes small, light-coloured patches, most commonly on the back, chest and shoulders. Consult a doctor.

Cuts and scratches become infected easily in humid climates. Take meticulous care of any cuts and scratches to prevent complications such as abscesses. Immediately wash all wounds in clean water and apply antiseptic. If you develop signs of infection (increasing pain and redness), see a doctor. Divers and surfers should be particularly careful with coral cuts, as they easily become infected.

Sunburn

Even on a cloudy day sunburn can occur rapidly. Always use a strong sunscreen (at least factor 30), making sure to reapply after a swim, and always wear a wide-brimmed hat and sunglasses outdoors. Avoid lying in the sun during the hottest part of the day (10am to 2pm). You can get burnt very easily when you are at high altitudes so be vigilant once above 3000m. If you become sunburnt,

stay out of the sun until you have recovered, apply cool compresses and, if necessary, take painkillers for the discomfort. One-percent hydrocortisone cream applied twice daily is also helpful.

WOMEN'S HEALTH

In most places in India, supplies of sanitary products (pads, rarely tampons) are readily available. Birth-control options may be limited, so bring adequate supplies of your own form of contraception. Heat, humidity and antibiotics can all contribute to thrush. Treatment is with antifungal creams and pessaries such as clotrimazole. A practical alternative is a single tablet of Fluconazole (Diflucan). Urinary-tract infections can be precipitated by dehydration or long bus journeys without toilet stops; bring suitable antibiotics. For gynaecological health issues, seek out a female doctor.

Pregnant women should receive specialised advice before travelling. The ideal time to travel is in the second trimester (between 16 and 28 weeks), when the risk of pregnancy-related problems is at its lowest and pregnant women generally feel at their best. Always carry a list of reputable medical facilities available at your destination and ensure you continue your standard antenatal care at these facilities. Avoid rural travel in areas with poor transport and substandard medical facilities. Most of all, ensure that your travel-insurance policy covers all pregnancy-related possibilities, including premature labour.

Malaria is a high-risk disease for pregnant women, and WHO recommends that pregnant women do *not* travel to areas with Chloroquine-resistant malaria. None of the more effective antimalarial drugs are completely safe in pregnancy.

Travellers' diarrhoea can quickly lead to dehydration and result in inadequate blood flow to the placenta. Many of the drugs used to treat various diarrhoea bugs are not recommended in pregnancy. Azithromycin is generally considered safe.

Language

CONTENTS

Northeast India's official languages are Assamese (state language of Assam), Bengali (state language of West Bengal), Hindi (the most predominant of India's languages, although only spoken as a mother tongue by about 20% of the population), Manipuri (spoken in the state of Manipur), and Nepali (the predominant language of Sikkim, where around 75% of the people are ethnic Nepalis).

While English is widely spoken throughout much of northern India, Bengali and Hindi will be the most useful indigenous languages for travel in the region.

For a far more comprehensive guide to Bengali and Hindi, get a copy of Lonely Planet's *Hindi, Urdu & Bengali Phrasebook*.

BENGALI

While Hindi is understood to some degree across most of Northeast India, Bengali is actually the most effective and widely spoken common language in the region; apart from anything else, a few words in Bengali will win you smiles from the locals you meet.

PRONUNCIATION

Pronunciation of Bengali is made difficult by the fact that the language includes a variety of subtle sounds with no equivalents in English. To make this language guide easier to use for basic communication we haven't tried to cover all the sounds, instead using nearest English equivalents – you're unlikely to have any trouble making yourself understood.

With regard to word stress, a good rule of thumb is to place the emphasis on the first and last syllables of words.

a	as in 'father'
b	as English 'b' or 'v'
ch	as in 'chant'
e	as in 'bet'
i	as in 'police'
j	as in 'jet'
o	similar to the 'o' in 'hold'
th	as in 'thing'
u	as in 'put'
v/w	a cross between English 'v' and 'w'
y	as in 'boy'

USEFUL VERBS

Two verbs that will undoubtedly come in very handy are *achhe* (there is, has), and *lagbe* (need). You can ask *khana a·che?* (Is there food?) or *bangti a·che?* (Do you have change?) The negative form of *a·che* is simply *nai*. Saying *baksheesh nai* means you don't have any baksheesh to give. You can say *pani lagbe* (lit: water is needed), or say *lagbe na* (lit: don't need) to turn down any unwanted offer.

ACCOMMODATION

Is there a hotel/ guesthouse nearby?	kache kono hotel/guesthouse a·che ki
Do you have a room?	rum a·che
May I see the room?	rum dekte pari
Is there a toilet?	paikana/toilet a·che
mosquito net	moshari
towel	toale

LANGUAGE

ACHA

Acha, the subcontinent's ambiguous 'OK/Yes/I see' is used widely, but the local slang equivalent is *tik assay* or just *tik*. The words *ji* or *ha* are more positive – if the rickshaw-wallah answers *acha* to your offered price, expect problems at the other end; if it's *tik* or *ji* he's unlikely to demand more money.

I'd like to book a room ...	*ami ekta rum buk ... korbo*
for one person	*ekjon thakbe*
for two people	*duijon thakbe*
How much is it ...?	*... thakte koto taka lagbe*
per person	*ek jon*
per night	*ek ra·te*
per week	*ek soptaho*

CONVERSATION & ESSENTIALS

If you travel to Bangladesh you should be aware that Bengali greetings vary according to religion and custom. The Muslim greeting is *asalam walekum* (peace be on you). The response is *walekum asalam* (unto you, also peace). In Northeastern India, however, you're unlikely to hear the Muslim greeting, and the Hindu *nomashkar* will be far more common (including when saying goodbye). This is accompanied by the gesture of joining the open palms of both hands and bringing them close to the chest.

'Please' and 'thank you' are rarely used in Bengali. Instead, these sentiments are expressed indirectly in polite conversation. The absence of these shouldn't be misread as rudeness. If you want to thank someone, you may use the Bengali equivalent for 'thank you (very much)', *(onek) donyobad*, or, alternatively, pay them a compliment.

Hello/Goodbye.	*nomashkar* (Hindu greeting and response)
See you later.	*po·re dakha ho·be*
See you again.	*abar deka ho·be*
Excuse/Forgive me.	*maf korun*
Thank you (very much).	*(onek) don·nobad*
Yes.	*ji* (polite)/*ha* (commonly used, with the 'a' given a very nasal pronunciation)
No.	*na*
How are you?	*(apni) kamon achen*

I'm well.	*bhalo achi*
friend	*bondhu* (often used in greetings)
What's your name?	*apnar nam ki*
My name is ...	*amar nam ...*
Where are you from?	*apnar desh ki*
My country is ...	*amar desh ...*
Not any/None.	*nai*
It's all right/ No problem.	*tik a·che*
Do you like ...?	*apnar ... bhalo lagge*
I like it (very much).	*amar eta (khub) bhalo lagge*
I don't like ...	*amar ... bhalo lagge na*
What do you want?	*ki lagbe*
It's available.	*pawa jai*
It's not available.	*pawa jai na*

DIRECTIONS

Where is ...?	*... kotai*
How far is ...?	*... koto dur*
I want to go to ...	*ami ... jabo*
Go straight ahead.	*shoja jan*
left	*ba·me*
right	*da·ne*
here	*ekha·ne*
there	*okhane*
north	*uttor*
south	*dokkin*
east	*purbodik*
west	*posh-chim*

HEALTH

I need a doctor.	*amar daktar lagbe*
antiseptic	*savlon*
nausea	*bomi-bhab*
sanitary napkins	*softex/modess* (brand names)
I'm a ...	*amar ... a·che*
diabetic	*diabetes*
epileptic	*mirghi rog*
I'm allergic to ...	*amar ... allergy a·che*
antibiotics	*antibiotikeh*
penicillin	*penisillineh*

LANGUAGE DIFFICULTIES

I understand.	*ami bujhi*
I don't understand.	*ami bujhi na*
Do you speak English?	*apni english/ingreji bolte paren*
I speak a little Bengali.	*ami ektu bangla bolte pari*
Please write it down.	*likhte paren*
How do you say ... in Bengali?	*banglai ... ki bo·le*

EMERGENCIES

Please help me!	amake shahajjo koren
Call a doctor!	daktar lagbe
Call the police!	pulish lagbe
I'm lost.	aami hariye gachi
Where is the toilet?	paikhana/toilet kotai
Go away!	jao

NUMBERS

Counting up to 20 is easy, but after that it becomes complicated, as the terms do not follow sequentially. In Bengali 21 isn't *bish-ek* or *ek-bish* as you might expect, but *ekush*; 45 is actually *poy-tal·lish*, but the simpler *pach-chollish* is understood.

0	shun·no
1	ek
2	dui
3	tin
4	char
5	pach
6	ch·hoy
7	shat
8	at
9	noy
10	dosh
11	egaro
12	baro
13	tero
14	chod·do
15	ponero
16	sholo
17	shotero
18	at·haro
19	unish
20	bish
30	tirish
40	chollish
50	ponchash
60	shatt
70	shottur
80	ashi
90	nob·boi
100	eksho
1000	ek hajar
100,000	ek lakh
10 million	ek koti
½	sha·re
1½	der
2½	arai

After two, the word *sha·re* is used before the number to indicate half, eg 3½ is *sha·re tin*.

SHOPPING & SERVICES

For many words, such as 'station', 'hotel' and 'post office', the English word will be understood.

Where is the ...?	... kotai
bank	bank
chemist/pharmacy	oshuder dokan
embassy	embassy
hospital	hashpatal
market	bajar
palace	rajbari
post office	post offish
town	taun
village	gram

What time does it open/close?	kokhon khole/bondo·hoy
How much is it?	dam koto
It's too expensive.	eta onek beshi dam
I'd like my change, please.	aami amar bhangti chai pleez
It's available.	pawa jai
It's not available.	pawa jai na

TIME & DATES

What is the time?	koto ba·je
When?	kokhon
2.45	po·ne tin ta (quarter to three)
1.30	der ta (one thirty)
4.15	shoa char ta (quarter past four)
hour	ghonta
day	din
week	shopta
month	mash
year	bochor
date (calendar)	tarikh
today	aj
tonight	aj ra·te
tomorrow	agamikal
yesterday	gotokal
in the morning	shokale
in the afternoon	bika·le
night	rat
every day	proti din
always	shob shomoy
now	ekhon
later	po·re
Monday	shombar
Tuesday	mongolbar
Wednesday	budhbar

LANGUAGE

Thursday	brihoshpotibar
Friday	shukrobar
Saturday	shonibar
Sunday	robibar

TRANSPORT

| I want to go to ... | ami ... jabo |
| Where is this bus going? | ey bas kotai ja·be |

When does the ... leave/arrive?	kokhon ... charbe/pochabe
boat	nouka/launch
bus	bas
car	gari
rickshaw	riksha
train	tren

HINDI

PRONUNCIATION

Most Hindi sounds are similar to their English counterparts, but there are a few tricky ones. The transliteration system we've used for Hindi in this language guide is designed to be as simple as possible, and for this reason it doesn't distinguish between all the sounds of spoken Hindi.

It's important to pay attention to the pronunciation of vowels and especially to their length, eg **a** compared to **aa**. The combination **ng** after a vowel indicates that it is nasalised (ie it's pronounced through the nose).

Vowels

a	as the 'u' in 'sun'
aa	as in 'father'
ai	as in 'hair' before a consonant; as in 'aisle' at the end of a word
au	as in 'haul' before a consonant; as the 'ou' in 'ouch' at the end of a word
e	as in 'they'
ee	as the 'ee' in 'feet'
i	as in 'sit'
o	as in 'shot'
oo	as the 'oo' in 'fool'
u	as in 'put'

Consonants

ch	as in 'cheese'
g	always as in 'gun', never as in 'age'
r	slightly trilled
y	as in 'yak'

EMERGENCIES

Help!	mada keejiye
Call a doctor!	daaktar ko bulaao
Call the police!	pulis ko bulaao
I'm lost.	maing raastaa bhool gayaa/ gayee hoong (m/f)
Where is the toilet?	gusalkaanaa kahaang hai
Go away!	jaao

ACCOMMODATION

Where is the (best/cheapest) hotel?
sab se (achaa/sastaa) hotal kahaang hai
Please write the address.
zaraa us kaa pataa lik deejiye
Do you have any rooms available?
kyaa koee kamraa kaalee hai

How much for ...?	... kaa kiraayaa kitnaa hai
one night	ek din
one week	ek hafte

I'd like a ...	mujhe ... chaahiye
double room	dabal kamraa
room with a bathroom	gusalkaanevaalaa kamraa
single room	singal kamraa

CONVERSATION & ESSENTIALS

Hello.	namaste/namskaar
Goodbye.	namaste/namskaar
Yes.	jee haang
No.	jee naheeng

'Please' is usually conveyed through the polite form of the imperative, or through other expressions. This book uses polite expressions and the polite forms of words.

Thank you.	shukriyaa/danyavaad
You're welcome.	koee baat naheeng
Excuse me/Sorry.	kshamaa keejiye
How are you?	aap kaise/kaisee haing (m/f)
Fine, and you?	maing teek hoong aap sunaaiye
What's your name?	aap kaa shubh naam kyaa hai
Where's a/the ...	... kahaang hai
Is it far from/near here?	kyaa voh yahaang se door/ nazdeek hai

HEALTH

I'm sick.	maing beemaar hoong
antiseptic	ainteeseptik
antibiotics	ainteebayotik
diarrhoea	dast

medicine	*davaa*
nausea	*gin*
tampons	*taimpon*

Where is a/the ...?	*... kahaang hai*
clinic	*davaakaanaa*
doctor	*daaktar*
hospital	*aspataal*

LANGUAGE DIFFICULTIES

Do you speak English?
kyaa aap ko angrezee aatee hai
Does anyone here speak English?
kyaa kisee ko angrezee aatee hai
I understand.
maing samjhaa-ee (m/f)
I don't understand.
maing naheeng samjhaa-ee (m/f)
Please write it down.
zaraa lik deejiye

NUMBERS

Rather than tens, hundreds, thousands, millions and billions, the Indian numbering system uses tens, hundreds, thousands, hundred thousands and ten millions. A hundred thousand is a lakh, and 10 million is a crore. These two words are almost always used in place of their English equivalents.

From one hundred thousand, written numbers have commas every two places, not three.

1	*ek*
2	*do*
3	*teen*
4	*chaar*
5	*paangch*
6	*chai*
7	*saat*
8	*aat*
9	*nau*
10	*das*
11	*gyaarah*
12	*bara*
13	*terah*
14	*chaudah*
15	*pandrah*
16	*solah*
17	*satrah*
18	*attaarah*
19	*unnees*
20	*bees*
21	*ikkees*
22	*baaees*
30	*tees*
40	*chaalees*
50	*pachaas*
60	*saat*
70	*sat·tar*
80	*as·see*
90	*nab·be/nav·ve*
100	*sau*
1000	*hazaar*
100,000	*ek laak* (written 1,00,000)
10,000,000	*ek krore* (written 1,00,00,000)

SHOPPING & SERVICES

Where's the nearest ...?
sab se karib ... kah hai

bank	*baink*
bookshop	*kitaab kee dukaan*
chemist/pharmacy	*davaaee kee dukaan*
general store	*dukaan*
market	*baazaar*
post office	*daakkaanaa*
public phone	*saarvajanik fon*
public toilet	*shauchaalay*

How much is this?
is kaa daam kyaa hai
I think it's too expensive.
yeh bahut mahegaa/i hai (m/f)
Can you lower the price?
is kaa daam kam keejiye
Do you accept credit cards?
kyaa aap vizaa kaard vagairah lete ha

TIME & DATES

What time is it?
kitne baje haing/taaim kyaa hai
It's (ten) o'clock.
(das) baje haing
Half past (ten).
saare (das)

When?	*kab*
now	*ab*
today	*aaj*
tomorrow/	*kal* (while *kal* is used for both, the
yesterday	meaning is made clear by context)
day	*din*
evening	*shaam*
month	*maheenaa*
morning	*saveraa/subhaa*
night	*raat*
week	*haftaa*
year	*saal/baras*

LANGUAGE

Monday	*somvaar*	**When is the ... bus?**	*... bas kab jaaegee*
Tuesday	*mangalvaar*	**first**	*pehlee*
Wednesday	*budvaar*	**next**	*aglee*
Thursday	*guruvaar/brihaspativaar*	**last**	*aakiree*
Friday	*shukravaar*		
Saturday	*shanivaar*	**What time does**	*... kitne baje jaayegee/*
Sunday	*itvaar/ravivaar*	**the ... leave/arrive?**	*pahungchegee*
		boat	*naav*

TRANSPORT

How do we get to ...?	*... kaise jaate haing*	**bus**	*bas*
A ticket to ...	*... keliye tikat deejiye*	**train**	*relgaaree*

LANGUAGE

Glossary

This glossary is a sample of the words and terms you may come across during your Indian wanderings. For definitions of food and drink, see p76.

abbi – waterfall
acha – 'OK' or 'I understand'
acharya – revered teacher; spiritual guide
Adivasi – tribal person
agarbathi – incense
Agni – major deity in the *Vedas*; mediator between men and the gods; also fire
ahimsa – discipline of nonviolence
AIR – All India Radio, the national broadcaster
air-cooler – big, noisy, water-filled fan
Amir – Muslim nobleman
amrita – immortality
Ananda – *Buddha's* cousin and personal attendant
Ananta – snake on which *Vishnu* reclined
angrezi – foreigner
ani – Tibetan Buddhist nuns; typically, nuns prefix their name with this syllable
anna – 16th of a rupee; no longer legal tender
Annapurna – form of *Durga*; worshipped for her power to provide food
apsara – heavenly nymph
Ardhanari – *Shiva's* half-male, half-female form
Arjuna – Hero of the *Bhagavad Gita* in the *Mahabharata*; a war leader who married Subhadra, took up arms and overcame many demons
Aryan – Sanskrit for 'noble'; term for the Central Asia tribes who settled in northern India
ashram – spiritual community or retreat
ashrama – the four stages of life for higher-caste Hindus: *brahmachari* (life of learning), *grihastha* (life of work), *vanaprastha* (transition to spiritual life) and *sanyasin* (withdrawal from the physical world in pursuit of *moksha*)
ASI – Archaeological Survey of India; an organisation involved in monument preservation
Atharva-Veda – one of the four main *Vedas*, or holy Sanskrit texts of Hinduism
atman – soul
attar – essential oil, used as a base for perfumes
autorickshaw – noisy, three-wheeled, motorised *rickshaw*, also known as bajaj and autos
Avalokiteshvara – in Mahayana Buddhism, the *bodhisattva* of compassion
avatar – incarnation, usually of a deity
ayah – children's nurse or nanny

ayurveda – the ancient and complex science of Indian herbal medicine and healing
azan – Muslim call to prayer

baba – religious master or father; term of respect
badmash – villain or hooligan; a recurring character in *Bollywood* action films
bagh – park or garden; also the local name for the Bengal tiger
bahadur – brave or chivalrous; an honorific title
baksheesh – tip, donation (alms) or bribe
Balarama – brother of *Krishna*
bandar – monkey
bandh – general strike
bandhani – tie-dye
banian – T-shirt or undervest
baniya – moneylender or trader
banyan – Indian fig tree; spiritual to many Indians
bearer – like a butler
begum – Muslim princess or woman of high rank
Bhagavad Gita – Hindu scripture telling the story of *Krishna* and *Arjuna* – part of the *Mahabharata*
Bhairava – the Terrible; refers to the eighth incarnation of *Shiva* in his demonic form
bhajan – devotional song
bhakti – surrendering to the gods; faith
bhang – dried leaves and flowering shoots of the marijuana plant
bhangra – rhythmic Punjabi music/dance
Bharat – Hindi for India
Bharata – half-brother of *Rama*; ruled while *Rama* was in exile
bhavan – house, building; also spelt bhawan
Bhima – *Mahabharata* hero; the brother of *Hanuman*, renowned for his great strength
bhisti – water carrier; also spelt bheesti
bhoga-mandapa – Orissan hall of offering
bhojanalya – see *dhaba*
bidi – small, hand-rolled cigarette
bindi – forehead mark (often dot-shaped) worn by women
BJP – Bharatiya Janata Party
Bodhi Tree – tree under which the *Buddha* sat when he attained enlightenment
bodhisattva – literally 'one whose essence is perfected wisdom' – a Buddhist saint who forgoes *nirvana* in order to help others attain it
Bollywood – India's answer to Hollywood; the booming film industry of Mumbai (Bombay)
Brahma – Hindu god; worshipped as the creator in the *Trimurti*

brahmachari – chaste student stage of the *ashrama* system

Brahmanism – early form of Hinduism that evolved from Vedism (see *Vedas*); named after *Brahmin* priests and *Brahma*

Brahmin – member of the priest/scholar caste, the highest Hindu caste

Buddha – Awakened One; the originator of Buddhism; also regarded by Hindus as the ninth incarnation of *Vishnu*

bugyal – high-altitude meadow

bund – embankment or dyke

burka – one-piece garment used by conservative Muslim women to cover themselves from head to toe

bustee – slum

cantonment – administrative and military area of a Raj-era town

caravanserai – traditional accommodation for camel caravans

Carnatic music – classical music of South India

caste – a Hindu's hereditary station (social standing) in life; there are four castes: *Brahmin*, *Kshatriya*, *Vaishya* and *Shudra*

cenotaph – a monument honouring a dead person whose body is somewhere else

chaam – ritual masked dance performed by Buddhist monks in *gompas* to celebrate the victory of good over evil and of Buddhism over pre-existing religions

chaitya – Sanskrit form of 'cetiya', meaning shrine or object of worship; often used to describe a Buddhist shrine centred on a *stupa*, or a small ornamental *stupa*

chakra – focus of one's spiritual power; disclike weapon of *Vishnu*

chalo, chalo, chalo – 'let's go, let's go, let's go'

Chamunda – form of *Durga*; a real terror, armed with a scimitar, noose and mace, and clothed in elephant hide, her mission was to kill the demons Chanda and Munda

chandra – moon, or the moon as a god

Chandragupta – Indian ruler, 3rd century BC

chappals – sandals or leather, thonglike footwear; flip-flops

charas – resin of the marijuana plant; also referred to as hashish

charbagh – formal Persian garden, divided into quarters (literally 'four gardens')

charpoy – simple bed made of ropes knotted together on a wooden frame

chedi – see *chaitya*

chela – pupil or follower, as George Harrison was to Ravi Shankar

chhatri – *cenotaph* (literally 'umbrella')

chillum – pipe of a hookah; commonly used to describe the pipes used for smoking *ganja*

chinkara – gazelle

chital – spotted deer

chogyal – Sikkimese king

choli – sari blouse

chorten – Tibetan for *stupa*

chowk – town square, intersection or marketplace

chowkidar – night watchman, caretaker, particularly of a government rest house

chuba – dress worn by Tibetan women

Cong (I) – Congress Party of India; also known as Congress (I)

coolie – labourer or porter, from the Hindi 'quli'

CPI – Communist Party of India

CPI (M) – Communist Party of India (Marxist)

crore – 10 million

dacoit – bandit (particularly armed bandit), outlaw

dada – paternal grandfather or elder brother

dagoba – see *stupa*

daitya – demon or giant who fought against the gods

dak – staging post, government-run accommodation

Dalit – preferred term for India's *Untouchable* caste; see also *Harijan*

Damodara – another name for *Krishna*

dargah – shrine or place of burial of a Muslim saint

darshan – auspicious viewing of a deity

darwaza – gateway or door

Dasaratha – father of *Rama* in the *Ramayana*

Dattatreya – Brahmin saint who embodied the *Trimurti*

desi – local, Indian

deul – temple sanctuary

devadasi – temple dancer

Devi – the mother goddess; the term is often used for incarnations of *Parvati*, the consort of *Shiva*

dhaba – basic restaurant or snack bar

dham – holiest pilgrimage places of India

dharamsala – pilgrim's rest house

dharma – for Hindus, the moral code of behaviour or social duty; for Buddhists, following the law of nature, or path, as taught by the *Buddha*

dharna – nonviolent protest

dhobi – person who washes clothes; commonly referred to as a dhobi-*wallah*

dhobi ghat – place where clothes are washed

dhol – traditional, large, two-headed drum

dholi – man-carried portable 'chairs' or palanquins; people are carried in them to hilltop temples etc

dhoti – like a *lungi*, but the ankle-length cloth is then pulled up between the legs; worn by men

dhurrie – rug

dikpala – temple guardian

Din-i-Ilahi – Akbar's philosophy asserting the common truth in all religions

diwan – principal officer in a princely state; royal court or council

dorje – the celestial thunderbolt, from Tibetan Buddhist mythology

dowry – money and/or goods given by a bride's parents to their son-in-law's family; illegal but common in arranged marriages

Dravidian – general term for the cultures and languages of the deep south of India

dukhang – Tibetan prayer hall

dun – valley

dupatta – long scarf for women often worn with the *salwar kameez*

durbar – royal court; also a government

Durga – the Inaccessible; a war-like form of *Shiva's* consort, *Parvati*; also revered as an incarnation of *Devi*, the mother goddess, or *shakti* (female spiritual power); her vehicle is the tiger

dwarpal – doorkeeper; sculpture beside the doorways to Hindu or Buddhist shrines

elatalam – small, hand-held cymbals

Emergency – period in the 1970s during which Indira Gandhi suspended many political rights

Eve-teasing – sexual harassment

fakir – Muslim who has taken a vow of poverty; may also apply to a *sadhu* and other Hindu ascetics

ferengi – the Hindi word for foreigner, later used as the name for a race of aliens in *Star Trek*!

filmi – slang term describing anything to do with Indian movies

firman – royal order or grant

gabba – appliquéd Kashmiri rug

gaddi – throne of a Hindu prince

gali – lane or alleyway

Ganesh – Hindu god of good fortune; popular elephant-headed son of *Shiva* and *Parvati*, he is also known as Ganpati and his vehicle is a ratlike creature

Ganga – Hindu goddess representing the sacred Ganges River; said to flow from the toe of *Vishnu*

ganga aarti – river worship ceremony, when leaf boats with candles are floated on the river at sunset

ganj – market

ganja – dried flowering tips of the marijuana plant

gaon – village

garh – fort

gari – vehicle; 'motor gari' is a car and 'rail gari' is a train

Garuda – man-bird vehicle of *Vishnu*

gaur – Indian bison

Gayatri – sacred verse of *Rig-Veda* repeated mentally by *Brahmins* twice a day

geyser – hot-water unit found in many bathrooms

ghat – riverside steps, range of hills, or road up hills

ghazal – Urdu song derived from poetry; poignant love theme

gherao – industrial action where the workers lock in their employers

giri – hill

Gita Govinda – erotic poem by Jayadeva relating the early life of *Krishna* as *Govinda*

godown – warehouse

gompa – Tibetan Buddhist monastery

Gonds – aboriginal Indian race, found in remote jungles of Orissa

goonda – ruffian or tough; political parties have been known to employ them in gangs

Gopala – see *Govinda*

gopi – milkmaid; *Krishna* was fond of them

gopuram – soaring pyramidal gateway tower of South Indian Dravidian temples

gora – white person, European

Govinda – *Krishna* as a cowherd; also just cowherd

grihastha – householder or working stage of the *ashrama* system; followers discharge their duty to ancestors by having sons and making sacrifices to the gods

gufa – cave

gumbad – dome on an Islamic tomb or mosque

gurdwara – Sikh temple

guru – holy teacher; in Sanskrit literally 'goe' (darkness) and 'roe' (to dispel)

Guru Granth Sahib – Sikh holy book

haat – village market

haj – Muslim pilgrimage to Mecca

haji – Muslim who has made the *haj*

halal – literally 'permissible'; foods that have been prepared in accordance with Islamic law

hammam – Turkish bath; public bathhouse

Hanuman – Hindu monkey god, prominent in the *Ramayana*, and a follower of *Rama*

Hara – one of *Shiva's* names

Hari – another name for *Vishnu*

Harijan – name (no longer considered acceptable) given by Gandhi to India's *Untouchables*, meaning 'children of god'

hartal – strike

hashish – see *charas*

hathi – elephant

hijab – headscarf used by Muslim women

hijra – eunuch, transvestite

Hind – an alternative name for India; part of the patriotic chant 'Jai Hind' (Victory to India)

hindola – swing

Hiranyakasipu – *daitya* king killed by *Narasimha*

hookah – water pipe used for smoking *ganja* or strong tobacco

howdah – seat for carrying people on an elephant's back

iftar – breaking of the *Ramadan* fast at sunset

ikat – fabric made with thread that is tie-dyed before weaving

imam – Muslim religious leader

imambara – tomb dedicated to a Shi'ia Muslim holy man

IMFL – Indian-made foreign liquor
Indo-Saracenic – style of colonial architecture that integrated Western designs with Islamic, Hindu and Jain influences
Indra – significant and prestigious Vedic god of rain, thunder, lightning and war

jagamohan – assembly hall
Jagannath – Lord of the Universe; a form of *Krishna*, famously worshipped at Puri in Orissa
jali – carved lattice (often marble) screen; also used to refer to the holes or spaces produced through carving timber or stone
Janaka – father of *Sita*
jataka – tale from the various lives of *Buddha*
jati – social communities often linked to specific occupations
jawan – policeman or soldier
jheel – swampy area
jhuggi – shanty settlement; also called *bustee*
jhula – bridge
ji – honorific that can be added to the end of almost anything as a form of respect; thus Babaji, Gandhiji
jihad – holy war (Islam); most commonly associated with Islamic militants
jooti – traditional, often pointy-toed, slip-in shoes; commonly found in north India
juggernaut – huge, extravagantly decorated temple chariots dragged through the streets during Vaishnavite festivals; named for *Jagannath*
jumkahs – earrings
jyoti linga – most important shrines to *Shiva*, of which there are 12

kabaddi – traditional game (similar to tag)
Kailasa – sacred Himalayan mountain; home of *Shiva*
Kali – the wrathful, evil-destroying form of *Devi*; commonly depicted with black skin, dripping with blood and wearing a necklace of skulls
Kalki – White Horse; future (10th) incarnation of *Vishnu* who will appear at the end of Kali-Yug, when the world ceases to be
Kama – Hindu god of love
kameez – woman's shirtlike tunic
kangling – sacred Tibetan flute made from a human thigh bone
Kanyakumari – Virgin Maiden; another name for *Durga*
kapali – sacred bowl made from a human skull, still used by followers of the extreme Hindu Aghori sect
karma – Hindu, Buddhist and Sikh principle of retributive justice for past deeds
karmachario – workers
Kartikiya – Hindu god of war, son of *Shiva*
kata – Tibetan prayer shawl, traditionally given to a *lama* when pilgrims come into his presence
Kedarnath – name of *Shiva* and one of the 12 *jyoti linga*

khadi – homespun cloth; Mahatma Gandhi encouraged people to spin this rather than buy English cloth
Khalsa – Sikh brotherhood
Khan – Muslim honorific title for a ruler
kirtan – Sikh devotional singing
kohl – black eyeliner
koil – Hindu temple
kolam – see *rangoli*
kompu – C-shaped, metal trumpet
kos minar – milestone
kot – fort
kothi – residence or mansion
kotwali – the eighth incarnation of *Vishnu*, revered as *Govinda*, the flute-playing herdsman who cavorted with the *gopis*; often depicted with blue skin
Kshatriya – Hindu caste of soldiers or administrators; second in the caste hierarchy
kund – lake or tank
kurta – long shirt with either short collar or no collar
Kusa – one of the twin sons of *Rama*

lakh – 100,000
Lakshmana – half-brother and aide of *Rama* in the *Ramayana*
Lakshmi – consort of Vishnu, Hindu goddess of wealth
lama – *dharma* teacher; Tibetan Buddhist priest or monk
lathi – heavy stick used by police, especially for crowd control
Laxmi – see *Lakshmi*
lhamo – Tibetan opera
lingam – phallic symbol; auspicious symbol of *Shiva*; plural is linga
LOC – Line of Control; the de facto border between India and Pakistan in Kashmir
lok – people
Lok Sabha – lower house in the Indian parliament (House of the People)
Losar – Tibetan New Year
lungi – a loose, skirt-like garment worn by men (similar to a sarong)

machaan – observation tower
madrasa – Islamic seminary
maha – prefix meaning 'great'
Mahabharata – Great Hindu Vedic epic poem of the Bharata dynasty, containing approximately 10,000 verses describing the battle between the Pandavas and the Kauravas
Mahabodhi Society – founded in 1891 to encourage Buddhist studies
Mahadeva – Great God; *Shiva*
Mahadevi – Great Goddess; *Devi*
Mahakala – Great Time; *Shiva* and one of the 12 *jyoti linga* (also one the Tibetan protector deities)
mahal – house or palace
maharaja – literally 'great king'; princely ruler

maharani – wife of a princely ruler or a ruler in her own right

mahatma – literally 'great soul'

Mahavir – last *tirthankar*

Mahayana – the 'greater-vehicle' of Buddhism, with emphasis on teaching the renunciation of *nirvana* (ultimate peace and cessation of rebirth) in order to help other beings to achieve enlightenment

Mahayogi – Great Ascetic; *Shiva*

Maheshwara – Great Lord; *Shiva*

Mahisa – Hindu demon

mahout – elephant rider or master

maidan – open (often grassed) area; parade ground

Maitreya – future *Buddha*; the successor to the historical *Buddha* who will appear on earth ushering in a new age of enlightenment

Makara – mythical sea creature and the vehicle of *Varuna*; crocodile

mala – garland or necklace

mali – gardener

mandal – shrine

mandala – circle; graphical representation of the universe in Hindu and Buddhist art

mandapa – pillared pavilion or temple forechamber

mandi – market

mandir – temple

mani stone – stone carved with the Tibetan-Buddhist mantra *'Om* mani padme hum' (Hail the jewel in the lotus)

mani walls – Tibetan stone walls with sacred inscriptions

mantra – sacred word, syllable or phrase used by Buddhists and Hindus to aid concentration

Mara – Buddhist personification of that which obstructs the cultivation of virtue; also the god of death

Maratha – central Indian people who fought the Mughals and British

marg – road

Maruts – Hindu storm gods

masala – spice mix; also a genre of *Bollywood* action films

masjid – mosque

masti – fun

mata – mother

math – monastery

maund – unit of weight now superseded (about 20kg)

maya – illusion

mehndi – henna; ornate henna designs on women's hands (and often feet)

mela – fair or festival

memsahib – Madam; respectful way of addressing women (literally 'Mrs Sir')

Meru – mythical mountain found in the centre of the earth; on it is *Swarga*

mihrab – mosque prayer niche that faces Mecca

misthan bhandar – South Indian sweet shop and vegetarian restaurant, found all over India

mithun – a kind of buffalo, found in the Northeast States

mithuna – pairs of men and women; often seen in temple sculptures

Moghul – see *Mughal*

Mohini – *Vishnu* in his female incarnation

moksha – liberation from *samsara*

monsoon – rainy season

morcha – mob march or protest

mudra – ritual hand movements used in Hindu religious dancing; gesture of *Buddha* figure

muezzin – one who calls Muslims to prayer, traditionally from the minaret of a mosque

Mughal – Muslim dynasty of emperors from Babur to Aurangzeb

mujtahid – divine

mullah – Muslim scholar or religious leader

mund – village

murti – statue, often of a deity

nadi – river

Naga – mythical serpent deities capable of changing into human form

namaskar – see *namaste*

namaste – traditional Hindu greeting (hello or goodbye); also *namaskar*

namaz – Muslim prayers

namkeen – savoury (often spicy) nibbles (also 'namkin')

Nanda – cowherd who raised *Krishna*

Nandi – bull, vehicle of *Shiva*

Narasimha – man-lion incarnation of *Vishnu*

Narayan – incarnation of *Vishnu* the creator

Narsingh – see *Narasimha*

natamandir – dancing hall

Nataraja – *Shiva* as the cosmic dancer

nautch – dance

nawab – Bengali Muslim ruling prince or powerful landowner (also 'nabob')

Naxalites – ultraleftist political movement characterised by violence in support of rural peasant farmers

Nilakantha – form of *Shiva*; his blue throat is a result of swallowing poison that would have destroyed the world

nilgai – antelope

nirvana – this is the ultimate aim of Buddhists and the final release from the cycle of existence

niwas – house, building

noth – the Lord (Jain)

NRI – Non-Resident Indian: Indians living abroad, who make a huge contribution to the Indian economy

nullah – ditch or small stream

Om – sacred invocation representing the essence of the divine principle; often used as a mantra (also spelt aum)

Osho – the late Bhagwan Shree Rajneesh, controversial leader of the Osho cult, which emphasises sexuality

padma – lotus; another name for the Hindu goddess *Lakshmi*

padyatra – 'foot journey' made by politicians to raise support at village level

pagal – insane, crazy; often said in jest

pagoda – see *stupa*

paise – the Indian rupee is divided into 100 paise

palanquin – boxlike enclosure carried on poles on four men's shoulders; the occupant sits inside on a seat

Pali – the language in which the Buddhist scriptures were recorded

palia – memorial stone

palli – village

Panchatantra – series of traditional Hindu stories about the natural world, human behaviour and survival

panchayat – village council

pandal – marquee for festivals and marriages

pandit – expert or wise person; sometimes used to mean a bookworm

Parasurama – *Rama* with the axe; sixth incarnation of *Vishnu*

Parsi – adherent of the Zoroastrian faith

Partition – formal division of British India into two separate countries, India and Pakistan, in 1947

Parvati – the consort of *Shiva*; another form of *Devi*

pashmina – fine woollen shawl

patachitra – Orissan cloth painting

PCO – Public Call Office from where you can make local, interstate and international phone calls

peepul – fig tree, especially a bo tree

peon – lowest grade clerical worker

pietra dura – marble inlay work characteristic of the Taj Mahal

pir – Muslim holy man; title of a *Sufi* saint

POK – Pakistan Occupied Kashmir

pradesh – state

pranayama – study of breath control; meditative practice

prasad – temple-blessed food offering

puja – literally 'respect'; offerings or prayers

pujari – temple priest

pukka – proper; a Raj-era term

pukka sahib – proper gentleman

punka – cloth fan, swung by pulling a cord

Puranas – a set of 18 sacred Hindu texts, written in Sanskrit verse, covering the creation of the universe, the genealogy of the Hindu gods and the rise of humanity

purdah – custom among some conservative Muslims (also adopted by some Hindus, especially the Rajputs) of keeping women in seclusion; veiled

Purnima – full moon; considered to be an auspicious time

putli-wallah – puppeteer; also known as 'kathputli'

qawwali – Islamic devotional singing

qila – fort

Quran – the holy book of Islam, also spelt Koran

Radha – favourite mistress of *Krishna* when he lived as a cowherd

raga – a formal pattern of melody and rhythm; forms the structure of traditional Indian music, around which musicians improvise

railhead – station or town at the end of a railway line; termination point

Raj – rule or sovereignty; commonly used to refer to British rule

raja – king; sometimes *rana*

rajkumar – prince

Rajput – Hindu warrior caste, former rulers of north-western India

Rajya Sabha – upper house in the Indian parliament (Council of States)

rakhi – amulet

Rama – seventh incarnation of *Vishnu*

Ramadan – the Islamic holy month of sunrise-to-sunset fasting (no eating, drinking or smoking); also Ramazan

Ramayana – epic sacred Hindu poem telling the story of *Rama* and *Sita* and their conflict with *Ravana*

rana – king; sometimes *raja*

rangoli – elaborate chalk, rice-paste or coloured-powder design; also known as *kolam*

rani – female ruler or wife of a king

ranns – deserts

rath – temple chariot or car used in religious festivals

rathas – rock-cut Dravidian temples

Ravana – demon king of Lanka who abducted *Sita* in the *Ramayana*

rawal – nobleman

rickshaw – three-wheeled passenger vehicle based on a bicycle; two-wheeled hand-pulled rickshaws are found in Kolkata

Rig-Veda – original and longest of the four main *Vedas*, or holy Sanskrit texts of Hinduism

rishi – any poet, philosopher, saint or sage; originally a sage to whom the hymns of the *Vedas* were revealed

rudraksh mala – strings of beads made from seeds of the rudraksha tree, used in *puja*

Rukmani – wife of *Krishna*; died on his funeral pyre

sadar – main

sadhu – ascetic, holy person; one who is trying to achieve enlightenment; often addressed as 'Swamiji' or 'Babaji'

safa – turban

sagar – lake, reservoir

sahib – respectful title applied to a gentleman, equivalent to 'sir'

salai – road

salwar – trousers usually worn with a *kameez*

salwar kameez – traditional dresslike tunic and trouser combination for women

Sama-Veda – one of the four main *Vedas*, or holy Sanskrit texts of Hinduism

samadhi – in Hinduism, ecstatic state, sometimes defined as 'ecstasy, trance, communion with God'; in Buddhism, concentration

sambalpuri – Orissan fabric

sambar – deer

samsara – the cyclical process of birth, death and rebirth that is a core belief of Hindus, Buddhists, Sikhs and Jains. The quality of each rebirth is dependent on the karma accrued in previous lives.

sangam – meeting of two rivers

sangeet – music

sangha – community of monks and nuns

Sankara – *Shiva* as the creator

sanyasin – the final stage of life in the *ashrama* system, where devotees abandon worldly things and give themselves over to the pursuit of *moksha*

Saraswati – wife of *Brahma*, goddess of learning; sits on a white swan, holding a *veena*

Sati – wife of *Shiva* who became a sati (honourable woman) by immolating herself; also used for the act of self-immolation

satra – Hindu *Vaishnavite* monastery and centre for art

satsang – discourse by a swami or guru

satyagraha – nonviolent protest involving a hunger strike, popularised by Mahatma Gandhi; from Sanskrit, literally meaning 'insistence on truth'

Scheduled Castes – official term used for the *Untouchables* or *Dalits*

sepoy – formerly an Indian solider in British service

serai – accommodation for travellers

seva – voluntary work, especially in a temple

shahadah – Muslim declaration of faith ('There is no God but Allah; Mohammed is his prophet')

Shaivism – worship of *Shiva*

Shaivite – follower of *Shiva*

shakti – female spiritual power; this power is worshipped by devotees of Shaktism

sharia – Islamic law

sher – the Hindi word for tiger, as in Sher Khan (tiger king) from *The Jungle Book*

Sheshnag – the supernatural snake on which *Vishnu* reclines (Ananta)

shikhar – hunting expedition

shirting – colloquially, material from which shirts are made

Shiva – Destroyer; also the Creator, in which form he is worshipped as a *lingam*

shola – virgin forest

shree – see *shri*

shri – honorific male prefix; Indian equivalent of 'respected sir'

Shudra – caste of labourers

sikhara – Hindu temple-spire or temple

Singh – literally 'lion'; a surname adopted by Sikhs

sirdar – leader or commander

Sita – the Hindu goddess of agriculture; more commonly associated with the *Ramayana*

sitar – Indian stringed instrument with sympathetic strings and a gourd soundbox

Siva – see *Shiva*

Skanda – another name for *Kartikiya*

sonam – karma accumulated in successive reincarnations

sree – see *shri*

sri – see *shri*

stupa – Buddhist religious monument composed of a solid hemisphere topped by a spire, sometimes known as a dagoba or pagoda

Subhadra – the incestuous sister of *Krishna*

Subrahmanya – another name for *Kartikiya*

Sufi – Muslim mystic

Sufism – Islamic mysticism

suiting – colloquial term for the material from which suits are made

Surya – the sun; a major deity in the *Vedas*

sutra – string; list of rules expressed in verse

swami – title of respect meaning 'lord of the self'; given to initiated Hindu monks

swaraj – independence

Swarga – heaven of *Indra*

sweeper – lowest caste servant, performs the most menial of tasks

tabla – twin drums

tal – lake

taluk – district

tandava – the cosmic victory dance of *Shiva*

tank – reservoir; pool or large receptacle of holy water found at temples

tantric Buddhism – Tibetan Buddhism with strong sexual and occult overtones

tatty – woven grass screen soaked in water and hung outside windows to cool the air

tempo – large three-wheelers used for public transport; bigger than an autorickshaw

thakur – nobleman

thangka – Tibetan cloth painting

theertham – temple tank

Theravada – orthodox form of Buddhism, characterised by its adherence to the Pali canon; literally, 'dwelling'

thiru – holy

tikka – a mark Hindus put on their foreheads

tilak – auspicious forehead mark of devout Hindu men

tirthankars – the 24 great Jain teachers

tonga – two-wheeled horse or pony carriage

topi – cap

torana – architrave over a temple entrance

toy train – narrow-gauge train; minitrain

Trimurti – triple form; the Hindu triad of *Brahma*, *Shiva* and *Vishnu*

Tripitaka – classic Buddhist scriptures, divided into three categories, hence the name 'Three Baskets'
tripolia – triple gateway

Uma – the consort (an avatar of *Kali*) of *Shiva*; light
Untouchable – lowest caste or 'casteless', for whom the most menial tasks are reserved; formerly known as *Harijan*, now *Dalit*
Upanishads – ancient texts forming part of the *Veda*, delving into weighty matters such as the nature of the universe and soul
urs – death anniversary of a revered Muslim; festival in memory of a Muslim saint

vaastu – creation of a cosmically favourable environment
Vaishnavite – one of the two main schools of Hinduism, with Vishnu as the supreme deity
Vaishya – member of the Hindu caste of merchants
Valmiki – author of the *Ramayana*
Vamana – fifth incarnation of *Vishnu*, as the dwarf
vanaprastha – the third stage of life in the Hindu *ashrama* system – preparation for the final pursuit of spirituality in old age
varku – sacred flute made from a human thigh bone; known as *kangling* in Tibetan Buddhism
varna – concept of caste
Varuna – supreme Vedic god
Vedas – collection of Hindu hymns composed in preclassical Sanskrit during the second millennium BC and divided into four sacred texts: *Rig-Veda, Yajur-Veda, Sama-Veda* and *Atharva-Veda*
veena – outsized, sitar-like, stringed instrument
vihara – Buddhist temple
vikram – *tempo* or a larger version of the standard *tempo*

vimana – principal part of Hindu temple
vipassana – the insight meditation technique of *Theravada* Buddhism in which mind and body are closely examined as changing phenomena
Vishnu – part of the *Trimurti*; Vishnu is the Preserver and Restorer who so far has nine *avatars*: the fish Matsya; the tortoise Kurma; the wild boar Naraha; Narasimha; Vamana; Parasurama; *Rama*; *Krishna*; and *Buddha*

wadi – hamlet
wallah – man; added onto almost anything, eg dhobi-wallah, chai-wallah, taxi-wallah
wazir – title of chief minister used in some former Muslim princely states

yagna – self-mortification
Yajur-Veda – one of the four main *Vedas*, or holy Sanskrit texts of Hinduism
yakshi – maiden
yali – mythical lion creature
yantra – geometric plan said to create energy
yatra – pilgrimage
yatri – pilgrim
yogi – follower of a spiritual life; an adherent of certain Hindu or Buddhist spiritual practices (eg yoga)
yogini – female *yogi*; attendant to a goddess
yoni – female fertility symbol

zakat – tax in the form of a charitable donation, one of the five Pillars of Islam
zamindar – Bengali landowner
zari – gold or silver thread used in weaving
zenana – area of a home where women are secluded; women's quarters

The Authors

JOE BINDLOSS   Coordinating Author

Joe first visited India in the early 1990s as a student backpacker and something clicked. Since then he has been back dozens of times, travelling and working all over the country, particularly in the northeast, Kashmir, Ladakh and Mumbai. When not roaming around India for Lonely Planet, Joe writes for various guidebooks, newspapers, magazines and websites in London and Asia. If he had a free plane ticket to anywhere in the world, he'd be torn between Myanmar and the hills of Arunachal Pradesh.

MARK ELLIOTT   Kolkata (Calcutta)

Mark has been making forays to the subcontinent since a 1984 trip that lined his stomach for all eventualities. He has visited all the northeastern states except Manipur, encountering a wide range of characters including Buddhist lamas in Arunachal, Bodo ex-guerrillas in Assam and heavy-metal Christian cricketers in Mizoram. For this edition he returned to Kolkata, India's most misunderstood and most underrated metropolis. When not researching travel guides Mark lives a blissfully quiet suburban life with his beloved Belgian bride, Danielle, who found him at a Turkmen camel market. The camel would have been cheaper!

PATRICK HORTON   Sikkim, Northeast States

Patrick, writer and photographer, was born with restless feet. He travelled extensively in his native Britain before hitting the around-the-world trail and ending up in Melbourne. His journeys lead him to the more arcane areas of the world such as North Korea, Eritrea, Kosovo, East Timor, Serbia, Tonga, Cuba, and the Himalaya by motorcycle. But he is forever returning to India, a place that he considers another home. This research trip to uncover the jewels of northeast India and Sikkim completes a long-held ambition to visit every state in India.

LONELY PLANET AUTHORS

Why is our travel information the best in the world? It's simple: our authors are passionate, dedicated travellers. They don't take freebies in exchange for positive coverage so you can be sure the advice you're given is impartial. They travel widely to all the popular spots, and off the beaten track. They don't research using just the internet or phone. They discover new places not included in any other guidebook. They personally visit thousands of hotels, restaurants, palaces, trails, galleries, temples and more. They speak with dozens of locals every day to make sure you get the kind of insider knowledge only a local could tell you. They take pride in getting all the details right, and in telling it how it is. Think you can do it? Find out how at **lonelyplanet.com**.

KATE JAMES
West Bengal, Orissa

Melbourne-born Kate grew up in Ooty, India, where her parents taught at an international school. Her family holidayed across the subcontinent for eight years, carrying the very first edition of Lonely Planet *India* and memorably spending Christmas 1980 in an Adivasi village on the border of Andhra Pradesh and Orissa. Country and suburban journalism in Australia led Kate to an in-house editing job at Lonely Planet and then into a freelance writing and editing career. She is the author of *Women of the Gobi*. This is her first book as an author for Lonely Planet.

CONTRIBUTING AUTHOR

Dr Trish Batchelor wrote the health chapter. Trish is a general practitioner and travel medicine specialist who works at the CIWEC Clinic in Kathmandu, Nepal, as well as being a Medical Advisor to the Travel Doctor New Zealand clinics. Trish teaches travel medicine through the University of Otago, and is interested in underwater and high-altitude medicine, and in the impact of tourism on host countries. She has travelled extensively through Southeast and East Asia and particularly loves high-altitude trekking in the Himalayas.

Behind the Scenes

THIS BOOK

This is the 2nd edition of *Northeast India*. Joe Bindloss coordinated the project and wrote the front and back chapters. The regional chapters were written by Mark Elliott (Kolkata), Patrick Horton (Sikkim and Northeast States) and Kate James (West Bengal and Orissa). Dr Trish Batchelor wrote the Health text. This guidebook was commissioned in Lonely Planet's Melbourne office, and produced by the following:

Commissioning Editors Will Gourlay, Shawn Low, Suzannah Shwer
Coordinating Editors Laura Gibb, Kate Whitfield
Coordinating Cartographers Hunor Csutoros, Peter Shields
Coordinating Layout Designer Jim Hsu
Managing Editor Brigitte Ellemor
Managing Cartographer David Connolly
Managing Layout Designer Sally Darmody
Assisting Editors Andrew Bain, Adrienne Costanzo, Kate Evans, Rowan McKinnon, Katie O'Connell
Cover Image research provided by lonelyplanetimages.com
Project Manager Chris Girdler
Thanks to Lucy Birchley, Melanie Dankel, Quentin Frayne, Mark Germanchis, Lisa Knights, John Mazzocchi, Adrian Persoglia, Martine Power, Juan Winata

THANKS
JOE BINDLOSS

I would like to dedicate my work on this title to the new arrival in the Bindloss household, Tyler James, and to his mum, Linda, who made it all possible. In the northeast, thanks to Ashish Phookan and all the travellers who wrote or emailed in with tips. Thanks also to my fellow authors and editors.

MARK ELLIOTT

Eternal thanks as ever to my beloved wife (Danielle Systermans) and to my unbeatable parents: constant sources of love, help and inspiration. Thanks too to all at LP, to Jai Chand and family for their hospitality and insights, and to many fellow travellers including Maud and Niamh.

PATRICK HORTON

My really big thanks go to Hermanta Dass of Network Travels. As driver, guide and friend, he got me around this special region, laughed at my jokes and was always ready to join me in a late-night Kingfisher after the day's work was done (usually after 9pm). As a person who knows everyone in tourism in the northeast, he was able to browbeat and persuade those responsible for granting permits so

THE LONELY PLANET STORY

Fresh from an epic journey across Europe, Asia and Australia in 1972, Tony and Maureen Wheeler sat at their kitchen table stapling together notes. The first Lonely Planet guidebook, *Across Asia on the Cheap*, was born.

Travellers snapped up the guides. Inspired by their success, the Wheelers began publishing books to Southeast Asia, India and beyond. Demand was prodigious, and the Wheelers expanded the business rapidly to keep up. Over the years, Lonely Planet extended its coverage to every country and into the virtual world via lonelyplanet.com and the Thorn Tree message board.

As Lonely Planet became a globally loved brand, Tony and Maureen received several offers for the company. But it wasn't until 2007 that they found a partner whom they trusted to remain true to the company's principles of travelling widely, treading lightly and giving sustainably. In October of that year, BBC Worldwide acquired a 75% share in the company, pledging to uphold Lonely Planet's commitment to independent travel, trustworthy advice and editorial independence.

Today, Lonely Planet has offices in Melbourne, London and Oakland, with over 500 staff members and 300 authors. Tony and Maureen are still actively involved with Lonely Planet. They're travelling more often than ever, and they're devoting their spare time to charitable projects. And the company is still driven by the philosophy of *Across Asia on the Cheap*: 'All you've got to do is decide to go and the hardest part is over. So go!'

that I could visit every state. In Sikkim I could have got nowhere without Tensing Namgyal of Namgyal Tours & Travels who likewise helped with permits and provided transport and guides.

KATE JAMES
Chris and Luffy kept the home fires smoking: thanks, boys. At LP, thanks to the rolling CE team. In Orissa, thanks to Bijaya and Tutu at Discover Tours, and Pulak and Claire at Grass Routes. In West Bengal, thanks go to Andrew Pulger, Debal Deb and especially to Martyn Brown at Kali Travel Home. Thanks to fellow travellers who shared jeeps, beers and useful information: especially to Jo, Sarah and Naomi, for instant friendship at just the right time; and to Gary, for showing me the Diwali fireworks over Puri.

OUR READERS
Many thanks to the travellers who used the last edition and wrote to us with helpful hints, useful advice and interesting anecdotes:

Jantina M Bloem, Hirsh Cashdan, Gun Nidhi Dalmia, Manfred Lang, Gary Naumann, René Olde Olthof, Dan Taylor, Deborah Warton.

ACKNOWLEDGMENTS
Many thanks to the following for the use of their content:

Globe on title page ©Mountain High Maps 1993 Digital Wisdom, Inc.

SEND US YOUR FEEDBACK
We love to hear from travellers – your comments keep us on our toes and help make our books better. Our well-travelled team reads every word on what you loved or loathed about this book. Although we cannot reply individually to postal submissions, we always guarantee that your feedback goes straight to the appropriate authors, in time for the next edition. Each person who sends us information is thanked in the next edition – and the most useful submissions are rewarded with a free book.

To send us your updates – and find out about Lonely Planet events, newsletters and travel news – visit our award-winning website: **lonelyplanet.com/contact**.

Note: we may edit, reproduce and incorporate your comments in Lonely Planet products such as guidebooks, websites and digital products, so let us know if you don't want your comments reproduced or your name acknowledged. For a copy of our privacy policy visit lonelyplanet.com/privacy.

Index

000 Map pages
000 Photograph pages

MAP LEGEND

ROUTES

Tollway	Mall/Steps
Freeway	Tunnel
Primary	Pedestrian Overpass
Secondary	
Tertiary	Walking Tour
Lane	Walking Tour Detour
Under Construction	Walking Trail
Unsealed Road	Walking Path
One-Way Street	

TRANSPORT

Ferry	Rail
Metro	Rail (Underground)
Bus Route	Tram

HYDROGRAPHY

River, Creek	Canal
Intermittent River	Water
Swamp	Lake (Dry)
Mangrove	Lake (Salt)
Reef	Mudflats

BOUNDARIES

International	Regional, Suburb
State, Provincial	Ancient Wall
Disputed	Cliff

AREA FEATURES

Airport	Land
Area of Interest	Mall
Beach, Desert	Market
Building	Park
Campus	Reservation
Cemetery, Christian	Rocks
Cemetery, Other	Sports
Forest	Urban

POPULATION

CAPITAL (NATIONAL)	CAPITAL (STATE)
Large City	Medium City
Small City	Town, Village

SYMBOLS

Sights/Activities
- Beach
- Buddhist
- Castle, Fortress
- Christian
- Hindu
- Islamic
- Jain
- Jewish
- Monument
- Museum, Gallery
- Point of Interest
- Pool
- Ruin
- Sikh
- Skiing
- Trail Head
- Zoo, Bird Sanctuary

Eating
- Eating

Drinking
- Drinking
- Café

Entertainment
- Entertainment

Shopping
- Shopping

Sleeping
- Sleeping
- Camping

Transport
- Airport, Airfield
- Border Crossing
- Bus Station
- General Transport
- Parking Area
- Petrol Station
- Taxi Rank

Information
- Bank, ATM
- Embassy/Consulate
- Hospital, Medical
- Information
- Internet Facilities
- Police Station
- Post Office, GPO
- Telephone
- Toilets

Geographic
- Lighthouse
- Lookout
- Mountain, Volcano
- National Park
- Pass, Canyon
- River Flow
- Waterfall

LONELY PLANET OFFICES

Australia
Head Office
Locked Bag 1, Footscray, Victoria 3011
☎ 03 8379 8000, fax 03 8379 8111
talk2us@lonelyplanet.com.au

USA
150 Linden St, Oakland, CA 94607
☎ 510 250 6400, toll free 800 275 8555
fax 510 893 8572
info@lonelyplanet.com

UK
2nd fl, 186 City Rd,
London EC1V 2NT
☎ 020 7106 2100, fax 020 7106 2101
go@lonelyplanet.co.uk

Published by Lonely Planet Publications Pty Ltd
ABN 36 005 607 983

Mixed Sources
Product group from well-managed forests and other controlled sources
www.fsc.org Cert no. SGS-COC-005002
© 1996 Forest Stewardship Council
FSC